# Arts-Based Research in Educa



Presenting readers with definitions and examples of arts-based educational research, this text identifies tensions, questions, and models in the field and provides guidance for both beginning and more experienced practices.

As arts-based research grows in prominence and popularity, the barriers between empirical, institutional, and artistic research diminish, leading to an ever-increasing, global need to understand and navigate this evolving domain of research. Featuring contributions from a diverse range of leading *scholartists* in the field, this text weaves together critical essays about arts-based research in the literary, visual, and performing arts with examples of excellence in theory and practice. These essays introduce the theory and practice of arts-based research taking place in sites of teaching and learning. The third edition draws together all contributors from the previous editions, with revised reflective essays, new examples, and updates that bring these ground-breaking works up to date with current developments over the past decade of increased arts-based educational research activity in this rapidly expanding field.

This book is ideal for pre-service and in-service art educators. It can be utilized in art education teacher certification courses that focus on methods, or as a component of a larger foundations course on qualitative inquiry.

**Melisa Cahnmann**, Meigs Professor of Language and Literacy Education at the University of Georgia, has authored many books on arts-based research and pedagogy, including *The Creative Ethnographer's Notebook*. Recipient of a Fulbright Scholar Ambassadorship, the Meigs Distinguished Teaching Professorship, and the Beckman for Professors Who Inspire, she lives in Athens, GA, with her husband and two children.

**Richard Siegesmund** is Professor Emeritus of Art and Design Education at Northern Illinois University. His recent books include *Visual methods of inquiry: Images as research*, and he has regularly presented workshops on visual methods at the annual conference of the International Congress for Qualitative Inquiry. A recipient of two Fulbright awards in visual methodology, he and his wife now live in Switzerland dividing time between Zürich and the Upper Engadin.

# Arts-Based Research in Education

## Foundations for Practice

Third Edition

Edited by Melisa Cahnmann and Richard Siegesmund

Routledge
Taylor & Francis Group
NEW YORK AND LONDON

Designed cover image: Erin McIntosh

Third edition published 2026
by Routledge
4 Park Square, Milton Park, Abingdon, Oxon, OX14 4RN

and by Routledge
605 Third Avenue, New York, NY 10158

*Routledge is an imprint of the Taylor & Francis Group, an informa business*



First edition published by Routledge 2008
Second edition published by Routledge 2018

*British Library Cataloguing-in-Publication Data*
A catalogue record for this book is available from the British Library

ISBN: 978-1-032-51308-9 (hbk)
ISBN: 978-1-032-51270-9 (pbk)
ISBN: 978-1-003-41289-2 (ebk)

DOI: 10.4324/9781003412892

Typeset in Sabon
by KnowledgeWorks Global Ltd.

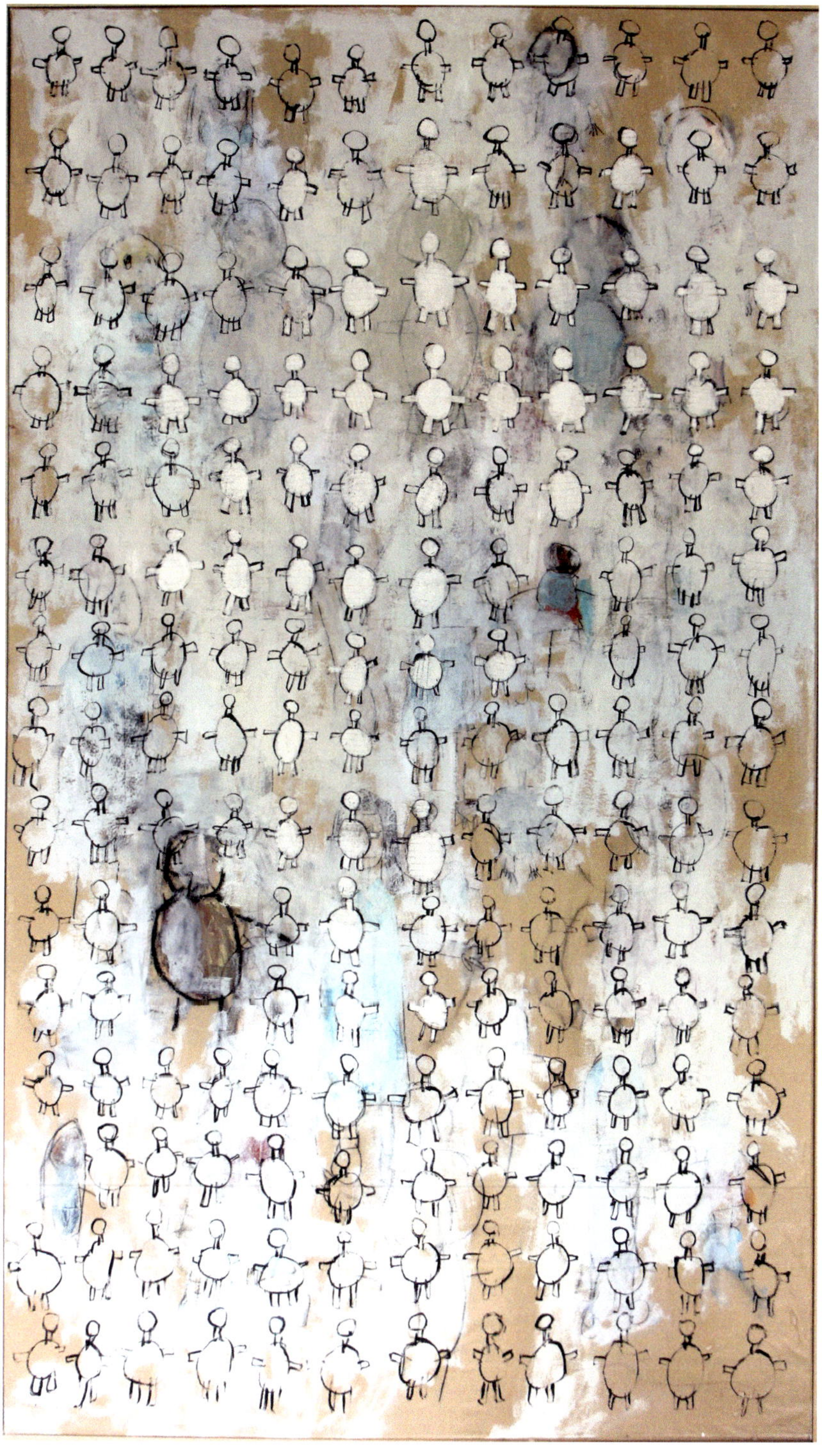

**Frontispiece**

Cover Image: "Ruled Paper People" (2002), Erin McIntosh, acrylic and paper on canvas, 43″ × 74″

# Contents

# About the Editors

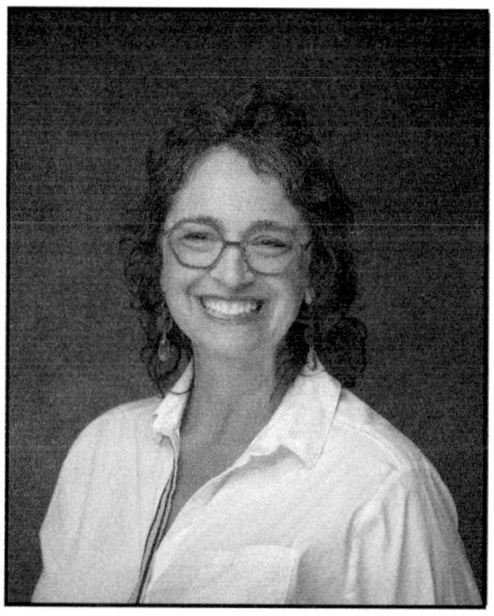

**Melisa Cahnmann**, Fulbright Scholar Ambassador, is Meigs Professor of Language and Literacy Education at the University of Georgia. She's authored books addressing intersections between language education and the literary, visual and performing arts including one book of poems, *Imperfect Tense*, and her newest titles, *The Creative Ethnographer's Notebook* and *Enlivening Instruction with Drama and Improv*. Supported by grants and prizes from the National Endowment for the Arts, Fulbright, and Beckman Award for Professors Who Inspire, her work narrates the heartache and joy of teaching and learning language. She lives in Athens, Georgia with her two children. Her website: www.melisacahnmanntaylor.com

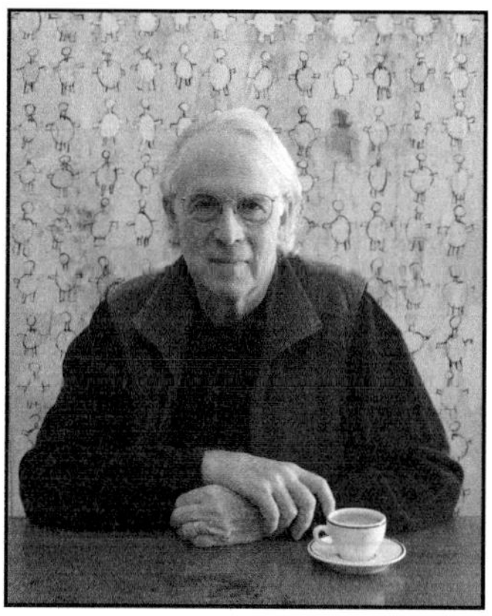

Photograph by Brigitta Hangartner.

**Richard Siegesmund** is Professor Emeritus of Art and Design Education at Northern Illinois University's School of Art and Design. He is the recipient of the Tom Barone Award for lifetime contributions from the Arts-Based Educational Research SIG of the American Educational Research Association. He co-authored *Visual methods of inquiry: Images as research* (2024, Routledge), and recently co-edited *Authentic secondary art assessment: Snapshots from art teacher practice* (2024, Routledge) and *Arts-based educational research trajectories: Career reflections by authors of outstanding dissertations* (2023, Springer). He and his wife, Brigitta Hangartner, now live in Switzerland dividing time between Zürich and the Upper Engadin.

# About the Contributors

**Tom Barone** is Professor Emeritus of Education at Arizona State University. With Elliot Eisner, he authored *Arts-Based Research*, published by SAGE (2012). He has individually authored *Touching Eternity: The Enduring Outcomes of Teaching*, published by Teachers College Press (2001) and *Aesthetics, Politics, and Educational Inquiry*, published by Peter Lang (2000).

**Ruth Behar's** work includes acclaimed ethnographies, *The Presence of the Past in a Spanish Village, The Vulnerable Observer, Translated Woman, An Island Called Home,* and *Traveling Heavy,* as well as prize-winning middle grade novels, *Across So Many Seas, Letters from Cuba,* and *Lucky Broken Girl,* and picture book, *Tía Fortuna's New Home.* She is the James W. Fernandez Distinguished University Professor of Anthropology at the University of Michigan.

**George Belliveau** is Professor of Theatre Education at the University of British Columbia, Canada, where he leads the UBC Research-based Theatre Lab. His latest co-edited book with G. W. Lea *Contact!Unload: Military Veterans, Trauma, and Research-based Theatre* (2020) explores a transdisciplinary project with military veterans, artists and counselors.

**Kakali Bhattacharya** is Professor of Qualitative Research at the University of Florida. Her scholarship explores transnational feminism, de/colonial methodologies, and contemplative arts-based inquiry. Through poetry, mixed-media art, and performative works, she examines the liminality of belonging while advocating for more just, healing-centered approaches to knowledge production in academia.

**Barbara Bickel**, PhD is an artist, writer, researcher, and educator. She is Associate Professor of Art Education Emerita at Southern Illinois University, Carbondale, Core Faculty at Southwestern College, Santa Fe, USA, and co-founder of Studio M*: Research Creation Lab Intersecting Arts, Culture and Healing based in Nanaimo, British Columbia, Canada. Her art and arts-based writing strives to embody and live matrixial, Earth-based feminist and Indigenous worldviews that celebrate and embrace the sacred. www.barbarabickel.ca www.StudioM.space

**Donald S. Blumenfeld-Jones** is Professor Emeritus of Education at Arizona State University. His research focuses on aesthetics-ethics-education-ABER. He has three books in these areas: *Curriculum and the Aesthetic Life* (Peter Lang), *Ethics, Aesthetics and Education* (Palgrave-Pivot), and *Teacher Education for the 21st Century* (IAP).

**John Borstel's** 30-year association with choreographer Liz Lerman includes a long tenure as Humanities Director for Liz Lerman Dance Exchange, co-authoring of multiple publications, and co-founding of the Critical Response Process Certification Program. His work as a visual artist has been seen in galleries in the United States and abroad; his writing has appeared in Youth Drama Ireland, Generations, Parterre Box, and multiple projects for Animating Democracy.

**Celeste Buckhalter** earned a B. Mus. Ed., from the University of Southern Mississippi and an MS in Human–Computer Interaction from Georgia Institute of Technology. She is a Senior Director of User Experience Research at Applause.

**Celia Hoi-Yan Chan** is Professor in the Department of Social Work at the University of Melbourne. She specializes in family and healthcare social work, pioneering psychosocial interventions through interdisciplinary research. Her work focuses on infertility counseling, perinatal bereavement, chronic illness, and trauma, strengthening family resilience and enhancing psychosocial support for individuals and families.

**Elliot Eisner** (1933–2014) was Professor of Art and Education at Stanford University, whose work spanned the fields of arts education, curriculum studies, program evaluation, and qualitative research methodology. He is considered one of the earliest champions of applying arts-based methods of inquiry to social science research as marked by his book *The Enlightened Eye*, first published in 1991. With Tom Barone, he wrote *Arts-Based Research* (2012).

**Joanne C. Elvy** retired from academia in 2015 and currently lives in Prague, Czech Republic. She now explores sites of memory in Europe, focusing on the rise of nationalism in the late 19th to mid-20th century, as well as the relationship between historical events and artistic representation.

**Charles R. Garoian** is Professor Emeritus of Art Education at the Pennsylvania State University. He is the author of *Performing Pedagogy: Toward an Art of Politics* (1999) and *The Prosthetic Pedagogy of Art: Embodied Research and Practice* (2013), both published by The State University of New York Press.

**Douglas Gosse,** PhD, is a tenured professor in the Faculty of Education and Professional Studies, Nipissing University. He served on the Ontario College of Teachers' Council and as Vice-Chair of the Selection and Nominating Subcommittee. Gosse hails from the storytelling island province of Newfoundland, Canada.

**Madeleine R. Grumet** has served as professor and dean of Education at the University of North Carolina at Chapel Hill, Hobart and William Smith Colleges, and Brooklyn College, City University of New York. Her field is curriculum theory with emphases on arts and humanities education, teacher education, and feminist theory. She is the author of *Bitter Milk: Women and Teaching* and co-author of *Toward a Poor Curriculum and Curriculum in Today's World.*

**Petula Sik-Ying Ho** is an honorary professor in the Department of Social Work & Social Administration at the University of Hong Kong. Recently joining the Ecumenical Hub Church, she applies her research and teaching experience to develop Little Three (The Other Woman) Theology.

**Brooke Anne Hofsess**, PhD, is a professor of art education at Appalachian State University. As a scholar in arts-based educational research (ABER), her work integrates curatorial methodologies to explore creative, ecological, and relational approaches in art teacher education. Her scholarship reimagines responsive and sustainable pedagogies, attuned to the evolving dynamics of community and place.

**Yohan Hwang** is an associate professor in the Department of English Language and Literature at Jeonbuk National University in South Korea. He holds a PhD in Language and Literacy Education with a specialization in TESOL and World Language Education from the University of Georgia. His articles have been published in Computers & Education, CALL, System, ETR&D, EAIT, RELC Journal, Language and Education, and Teaching and Teacher Education, among others.

**Rita L. Irwin** recently retired from The University of British Columbia where she was a Distinguished University Scholar, as well as a former Head of Department and Associate Dean of Teacher Education. She has a long-standing reputation as a leader of several national and international art education, curriculum studies, and educational research organizations, and is best known for employing a/r/tography in a range of contexts. rita.irwin@ubc.ca

**Kristina Jacobsen** is Assistant Professor of Music at the University of New Mexico in Albuquerque, where she also holds affiliations in Anthropology (Ethnology) and American Studies. A cultural anthropologist, Kristina is a touring singer/songwriter, co-facilitates the UNM honky Tonk Ensemble, and fronts the all-girl, Merle Haggard-inspired honky tonk band, Merlettes.

**Terry Jenoure** is dedicated to authenticity in creative expression. From her work with pioneers of the Black Arts Movement to her own multidisciplinary leadership, for five decades and throughout five continents, improvisation has remained her focus. Awards include Creative Capital; MAP Fund; South Arts Jazz Road; New England Foundation for the Arts; Massachusetts Cultural Council; and the National Endowment for the Arts.

**Omi Osun Joni L. Jones** employs Black Feminist principles and theatrical jazz aesthetics in all that she does. Her most recent book is Theatrical Jazz: Performance, Àṣẹ, and the Power of the Present Moment. She is Professor Emerita from the African and African Diaspora Studies Department at the University of Texas at Austin, a mother, a Queer wife, and a curious sojourner.

**Sui-Ting Kong** is an Associate Professor in the Department of Sociology at Durham University. She has developed multiple participatory methods/methodologies to support practice model building and theorization of personal lives and intimacy in a range of contexts. She is known for her work on social work practice research, participatory methods and violence against women in personal lives and social movements.

**Adrie Kusserow** is Chair of the Department of Sociology and Anthropology at St. Michael's College in Vermont. She incorporates local refugee work in Burlington, Vermont as part of her Community Engaged Learning classes and also teaches classes on ethnographic creative writing. She lives on the land she grew up on in Underhill, Vermont.

**Natalie LeBlanc** is an interdisciplinary artist who is currently an Associate Professor in Art Education at the University of Victoria, British Columbia, Canada, where she teaches studio art and digital art. She also teaches graduate level arts-based research methodologies courses and supervises master's and PhD students utilizing research-creation, visual inquiry, practice-led research, and a/r/tography.

**Roy Legette** is Professor of Music Education in the Hugh Hodgson School of Music at the University of Georgia in Athens, Georgia where he teaches courses in diversity and trends and issues in music education. His research interests include student motivation and teacher perceptions of teaching practice.

**Carl Leggo** (1953–2019) was a poet and professor in the Department of Language and Literacy Education at the University of British Columbia who promoted creative, interdisciplinary, cross-faculty approaches to teaching and research. His single authored books include *Teaching to Wonder: Responding to Poetry in the Secondary Classroom.*

**Jorge Lucero** is an artist from Chicago serving as Professor of Art Education in the School of Art & Design and as Associate Dean for Research in the College of Fine and Applied Arts at the University of Illinois, Urbana-Champaign. He has exhibited, published, and taught in lots of places.

**Kristina Lyons** is Associate Professor at the Department of Anthropology at the University of Pennsylvania. Since 2004, she has conducted participatory action and ethnographic research with rural and urban communities in the Colombian Amazon. Kristina is also the legal representative of the NGO Colectivo Ríos y Reconciliación and guardian of a civil society nature reserve, La Hojarasca, in the Andean-Amazonian foothills of Colombia.

**Kathleen McGovern** is an Assistant Professor of TESOL at the University of Southern Maine. Her theatrical work encompasses acting and directing and her research centers on the interconnections of language education and drama, with a particular focus on immigrant and refugee communities. She has also served as President of NNETESOL.

**Erin McIntosh** has created the cover art for each of the three editions of *Arts Based Research Foundations for Practice.* She has served as a credentialed public school elementary art teacher and is now Associate Professor of Painting at the University of North Georgia. Her work can be viewed at https://www.erinmcintosh.com.

**Monica Prendergast** is Professor of drama/theatre education in the Department of Curriculum and Instruction, University of Victoria. Her books include: *Applied Theatre and Applied Drama* (both with Juliana Saxton), *Staging the Not-Yet, Teaching Spectatorship, Drama, Theatre and Performance Education in Canada, Poetic Inquiry* (1&2), and *Applied Theatre: Ethics.*

**Jerry Rosiek** is Professor of Education Studies at the University of Oregon. His research documents patterns of racial and class inequality in schools by focusing on the broad effects of institutionalized racism on the minds and hearts of students. His work challenges narrow conceptions of educational outcomes, over-reliance on standardized testing, and increasingly prescriptive approaches to teacher education.

**Kathryn Roulston** is Professor in the Qualitative Research Program in the Mary Frances Early College of Education at the University of Georgia in Athens, Georgia, where she teaches qualitative research methods. Her research interests include qualitative research methods, qualitative interviewing, and analyses of talk-in-interaction.

**Johnny Saldaña,** MFA, is Professor Emeritus from Arizona State University's Herberger Institute for Design and the Arts. His 15 research methods books and editions have been cited and referenced in more than 42,000 qualitative studies conducted in over 135 countries.

**Nick Sousanis** is an Eisner-winning comics author and an associate professor of Humanities & Liberal Studies at San Francisco State University, where he started and runs a Comics Studies program. His dissertation, *Unflattening* (published by Harvard University Press) was written and drafted entirely in comic book form.

**Stephanie Springgay** is Director of the School of the Arts and Professor at McMaster University. She is a leading scholar of research-creation with a focus on walking, affect, queer theory, and contemporary art as pedagogy. She directs the SSHRC-funded research-creation project, The Pedagogical Impulse, which explores the intersections between contemporary art and pedagogy and directs WalkingLab—an international network of artists and scholars committed to critical approaches to walking methods.

**Mathangi Subramanian** is an award winning neurodiverse, South Asian American educator, author, and founder of Moon Rabbit Writing Studio, a boutique writing workshop supporting socially conscious authors with seriously busy lives. She's been a finalist for the Lambda Literary Award, and won the South Asia Book award.

**Monica Taylor** is an Adjunct Professor of Music at Liberty University. She holds a Bachelor of Music in Music Education, MMEd, and EdS degree in Music Education from the University of Georgia. Also, she holds the Doctor of Philosophy degree in Music Education from the University of South Carolina.

**Dana Mashoian Walrath** practices a border crossing blend of creative writing, comics, art, and anthropology. Her award-winning works include *Aliceheimer's*, a graphic memoir about her mother's dementia journey, *Like Water on Stone*, a verse novel about the Armenian genocide, and *The Book of Genocides*, an interactive art installation that uses artists books to counter dehumanization and genocide.

**Yen Yen Woo** leads the MA Arts Pedagogy and Practice Programme at LASALLE | University of the Arts Singapore. Beyond academia, she's a creative force, directing festivals, media and tech projects. Her work, from films to festivals and comics, has been showcased on global platforms like the App Store, Netflix, Amazon, and HBO.

**Kuo Zhang** is an Assistant Professor in Education at Siena College. Her research interests include arts-based research in education, teacher education, and intercultural discourse studies. Her poems and translated poetry have appeared in numerous literary magazines, including Rattle, Plume Magazine, Tupelo Quarterly, Mom Egg Review, Nine Mile, and The Roadrunner Review.

# Acknowledgments

During the time we spent generating the first edition of this book from idea to the present publication of the third, collected edition, many wonderful individuals and organizations influenced and inspired us. At the risk of omitting someone, we acknowledge some for their paramount contributions to this project.

First, we would like to acknowledge the love of our beloved family members who during these years have given us encouragement, sustenance and time to work together on these book projects. Richard is particularly thankful for the enduring support of his wife, Brigitta Hangartner, who has been with him for the entire journey that has led to the three editions of this book.

We extend appreciation to our home departments and institutions that support the hybrid spaces between the arts and educational inquiry. At the University of Georgia (UGA), we thank the departments of Language and Literacy Education in the Mary Frances Early College of Education, and Art Education in the Lamar Dodd School of Art, that provided opportunities to us to teach and learn across interdisciplinary boundaries. The Qualitative Interest Group (QUIG) at UGA was an early supporter of our work and in 2005 allowed us to co-chair its 18th annual conference on interdisciplinary qualitative studies. That conference, "Art as Research; Research as Art," provided the foundation for the first edition. At Northern Illinois University, we thank colleagues in the division of Art and Design Education, in the School of Art and Design for their encouragement, critical feedback, and support.

We have been fortunate to follow in the footsteps of scholars and scholartists who have come before us. Some of them graciously gave their voices to this book, but there are others who are equally important. There have been numerous *scholartists* who have been a part of our journey, many of whom are included here. Our gratitude to these contributors for their creative ideas. With this also comes our respect and deep felt appreciation for so many others: our numerous colleagues in arts-based research (ABR) whom we've met in intellectual spaces around the world and who have been so generous to us.

Finally, and most importantly, many students have contributed directly and indirectly to this book, helping us to articulate ideas in ABR. Some of these students we have encountered in our classes. Some we have taken on as formal advisees. Others have reached out to us from around the world, and we have responded as mentors, catching up with each other at international conferences, through email conversations, and video conferencing chats. Their fearless and undeterred courage to pursue ABR is humbling. In this span of time since the first edition, it is with admiration that we witness their growth as scholartists and leaders in their own right within the field of ABR. Our deepest gratitude to them all, as well as the students they themselves now nurture. This ever-expanding web continues to illustrate the power of ABR in education both by the examples they have already supplied and through the scholartistry yet to be explored in the future.

Chapter 1

# Introduction to the Third Edition

*Melisa Cahnmann and Richard Siegesmund*

Since the first edition of *Arts-Based Research in Education* (2008), the fields of Arts-Based Research (ABR) and Arts-Based Educational Research (ABER) have grown exponentially. Not only has there been continued and growing interest in pursuing alternative forms of data representation, including poetry, story, theatre, and visual image as means to increase attention to complexity, feeling, and new ways of seeing, but the empirical foundations of data themselves have been called into question. These trends were frequently prefigured in the chapters of the first and second editions. Thus, the third edition is a moment to take stock and see the paths that have both formed and been erased by doing ABR. Just as ABR has opened new ways of seeing, it also asks us to reconsider the ways we have previously framed the world.

Throughout academic inquiry and scholarship, particularly in social science fields, ABR has proliferated as a valid and valuable asset in the inquiry process. Numerous organizations and conferences have emerged since the publication of the first edition such as The Alliance for the Arts in Research Universities (a2ru), which began in 2013 and has continued annually, the Society for Artistic Research (SAR), which celebrated its 16th annual, global conference in May 2025 at the University of Porto, Portugal, and the Arts and Creativities Research Group (ACRG) at the University of Cambridge, which hosts an active list of events and activities in the United Kingdom. Conferences, blogs, performances, textbooks, and journal articles appear widely and in a variety of social science organizations. Today, there are two Special Interest Groups (SIGs) of the American Educational Research Association that specifically focus on ABR, with numerous other SIGs and divisions presenting ABR papers. The current sixth edition of the *SAGE Handbook of Qualitative Research* (Denzin et al., 2023), representing a range of disciplines from across the social sciences, is replete with chapters and examples of ABR. No longer restricted to arts departments and trained artists on campus, today creative practices and products are widespread across disciplines, campuses, and countries.

All of this is a dramatic change; Thomas Kuhn (1970) might even have called it a paradigm shift. A historian of science, Kuhn pointed out that major shifts in scientific thinking often occur suddenly, in relatively short periods of time. We feel that ABR marks such a moment. Twenty-five years ago, when we began writing the first edition of this series, scholars were concerned if ABR could be published, let alone taught in non-arts fields. In 2002, a report from the United States National Research Council dismissed ABR as unscientific and unworthy of research funding and specifically called out leading ABER scholar, Elliot Eisner, as a rogue social scientist (Shavelson & Towne, 2022). Since then, not much has changed within the United States in terms of federally funded research. As reflected in the

DOI: 10.4324/9781003412892-1

online "What Works Clearinghouse" (WWC) guidelines, federal funding agencies in the United States continue to strictly define "credible and reliable evidence" for educational decision-making (Institute of Education Sciences, n.d.). While arts-based rendering of learning, which may include narratives, poetry, or performance, has long been recognized by national governments outside the United States, it will not likely ever meet WWC criteria, and thus ABR will not be recognized by US government funding agencies or publications that adhere to their strict definitions of "evidence" in the social sciences. Despite these constraints, enterprising researchers in the United States have often found ways to fund ABR by emphasizing more conventional methodologies, diminishing or removing references to the arts in research proposals, and/or turning to alternative US funding agencies such as the US Fulbright commission and the National Endowment for the Arts for support (both organizations under threat of closure in 2025). However, at the time we publish this third edition, when all research funding in the United States is threatened, artistic inquiry practices (often low cost) may, ironically, have an even greater chance of thriving.

In several countries outside the United States, ABR has received explicit funding support (albeit sometimes begrudgingly). For example, Canada supports ABR through its Social Sciences and Humanities Research Council (SSHRC). Taking seriously the way ABR reconceptualized research, the SSHRC created the new funding category of *research-creation* to capture the distinctive opportunities afforded by ABR representation. A recent review of the SSHRC awards search engine showed over five million Canadian dollars of research funding for over 86 different ABR projects across Canada in FY 2024 alone. The Arts and Humanities Research Council in the United Kingdom, the Australian Research Council, the Dutch Creative Industries Fund, and the Royal Society of New Zealand all support research that integrates the arts, humanities, and sciences, including the use of artistic methodologies to address social, educational, and environmental challenges.

One way to account for rising social science interest in the arts is both creator and audience appeal: academics have permission to "feel" inquiry projects and audiences both inside and outside academic disciplines "get it." As reflected in numerous chapters in this book, the research resonates and wider and more diverse audiences, both academic and public, respond. Book publishers have taken note of this popularity and a number of noted houses such as Routledge, Springer, Palgrave, Peter Lang, and Brill have enthusiastically embraced ABR.

Another explanation for this explosive growth in ABR is the relentless improvement of digital technology accessible to a much wider range of users. Professional artistic equipment and software for photo capture and manipulation, video recording and editing, or sound mixing—that only a few years ago would have cost thousands of dollars and thus only be readily available to professionals—is now accessible through a standard cell phone and free, open-source applications. Additionally, "low-residency," online, and local creative arts-training programs provide greater access and flexibility to artistic study. Thus, arts-interested social science scholars have the power to explore and experiment in the arts on levels of sophistication never before possible. In addition, the social sciences have also seen an influx of scholars with substantial interdisciplinary training (including terminal degrees) in the fine arts. Graduate programs focused on the preparation of social science researchers have quickly adapted to this new demand for creative skills training, hiring more faculty with ABR training who identify both with the arts and social sciences.

Concurrent with the expansion of creative tools in the social sciences, there has been a growing acceptance of research teams to tackle problems. The romantic view in popular US cinema of an *Indiana Jones* scholar or a Jaime Escalante *Stand and Deliver* educator who is an inexorably independent polymath is giving way to the realization that no one person can or should do everything well. ABR demands interdisciplinary training and frequently requires collaborative efforts. As many of the contributors to this book attest, ABR often requires creative problem-solving in partnership. Acceptance of collaborative work has been crucial for ABR scholars to professionally advance in academia.

This third edition is a compilation of ABR scholars who have sought something fresh, creative, and new from expository language and numbers that can conflate and/or more often obscure the fulsomeness of lived human experience. Taking an expansive view of education, this edition freely draws on authors from a wide range of fields, including Education, Anthropology, Communications, and Health Sciences, working with multi-age populations of learners in educational settings. Each contributor shares their original contribution to the first or second editions and provides a postscript reflection looking back, present, and forward.

## Three Pathways of ABR

We trace three important trends in the evolution of ABR. The first is positioning ABR with the history of qualitative research within the social sciences. The second is considering ABR as an evolution in conceptualizing fine arts practice. The third looks at ABR as a paradigm shift that rethinks both the histories of "scientific" research and "artistic" research as separate rather than unified and/or becoming something wholly new.

### *Arts-Based Research Today as a Progression from What Has Come Before*

Methodologically, ABR can be viewed as the logical continuation of the shift to qualitative inquiry in the social sciences that began half a century ago. Furthermore, no longer are the social sciences the sole reserve of individuals who employ skills in quantitative analysis or those employing qualitative skills emulating hard science paradigms. New scholars entering the social sciences, many of whom now possess extensive training in the arts, accelerate this change.

In Chapter 3 of this book, Behar addresses how, previously, scholars who were artists felt the need to separate these two worlds, highlighting scholarly practice and hiding it from artistic engagement. The last ten years have seen this artificial wall collapse as young and veteran scholars fearlessly explore academic and artistic border crossing. Today, young scholars entering the field may not even be aware that such a wall once existed. As a result, new scholars with artistic leanings are less uninhibited to break old taboos, blending and juxtaposing these two realms of social science and art into new, fluctuating, contiguous relationships. In this collection, readers will find those who have created films, songs, poems, novels, comics, art installations, dances, and theatre, which illustrate the ways artistic tools allow scholars to inscribe ideas. In turn, these new inscriptions open fresh discussions and yet other forms of inscription that allow innovative possibilities to enter our ever-expanding conceptual and empirical frameworks. In short, ABR enriches our understanding and deepens our ability to productively, ethically, and holistically navigate the world.

Working this new ground, and with the widening popularity of methods, ABR goes by many names. Some labels emphasize "art" (e.g., *Arts-Based Research* (*ABR*), *Art-Based Educational Research* (*ABER*), and *Arts-Informed Research*) to include all creativity (e.g., dance, music, visual art, poetry). Others are more particular to the autonomous fields of arts production, e.g., *Artistic Research*, where *Socially Engaged Practice* is generating its own literature and methods. *Critical* and *Social Justice Arts-Based Research* emphasize a specific commitment to exposing and working to change social inequity. As with qualitative methods in general, some find inquiry to be a more appropriate word than research. In addition, social sciences like anthropology, sociology, and communications have opened their disciplines to specific art forms, such as *visual sociology*, *ethnographic performance*, *autoethnography*, or *poetic inquiry*. In these chapters, you will see authors describe what they are doing using varied terminology.

### *New Directions in the Fine Arts*

Significantly, as this field has expanded across the social sciences, there has been an important shift within the fine arts themselves. Parallel to the emergence of ABR within the social sciences, the fine arts have also increasingly sought to define their practice as research. This has produced a new—and often competitive—literature to social science-oriented ABR (jagodzinski & Wallin, 2013; O'Donoghue, 2009; Sullivan, 2010). While there is a long tradition of conceptualizing fine arts practice as research (e.g., the Renaissance anatomical drawings by Leonardo), a more insidious contemporary propulsion, currently driven by neoliberal efficiency forces within the European Union (EU) and the United States, has led to the consolidation of previously stand-alone national art schools into research universities. The EU Bologna Accords (a series of ministerial meetings seeking to facilitate the exchange of academic knowledge across Europe) had by 2008 called for the PhD in Studio Practice, rather than the MFA, as the terminal degree for artists who sought to hold positions in higher education. Replacing generative creativity at the Masters level exclusively with doctoral degrees requiring dissertations is likewise occurring in U.S. college degree programs in the arts. This has produced, by political necessity, the recasting of arts practice as research and brought fine arts practice directly into competition with the social sciences for research funding. In response, academic events such as the annual Iberian conferences (2013–2015) on Arts-Based and Artistic Research reflected a growing sense of urgency to define issues and sort these two competing paradigms in order to see where they are mutually inclusive and where they pursue different agendas.

However, this top-down approach to forcing the arts to reconceptualize themselves as research aroused, predictably, resistance. This resistance has sometimes taken a defensive posture by upholding previous modes of arts practice as inherently research-based and in no need of further change (Bishop, 2012). In these cases, art historian Claire Bishop has chided the artistic use of the term "research" as a merely decorative, meaningless word like putting "lipstick on the gorilla" (Bishop, 2014).

Not all of the changes in the fine arts have been top-down. Although the MFA was internationally recognized as a terminal degree that allowed the holder to teach in higher education, some within the arts disciplines argued that the PhD degree provided better professional training and a richer learning experience. Students in fine arts doctoral programs would be better qualified for competitive graduate teaching and research funding opportunities within their universities. The doctoral degree was also a clear edge for graduates as they entered competitive job markets. Just as the social sciences have seen an influx of doctoral students who have obtained the MFA degree, so too doctoral programs in studio practice have seen an influx of applicants who hold master's degrees in disciplines outside of the arts. The Ph.D. was an opportunity for a new kind of artist, one who was not reliant on a curator or cultural critic to interpret their work to the public, but artists who could theorize and speak for themselves.

Therefore, some programs located within schools of the fine arts have embraced a reconceptualization toward research. An example is Erin Manning, professor in the Faculty of Fine Arts at Concordia University (Montreal, Canada). A dancer, her SenseLab (founded in 2004) focuses on the body's movement and sense and explores the intersections of art practice and philosophy. Findings from SenseLab have taken the form of exhibitions at art biennales and museums around the world. Another example is the Studio for Creative Inquiry at Carnegie-Mellon University, which long predated the European Bologna Accords. The North American Alliance for the Arts in Research Universities is an organization that attempts to seize on the turn to research as opening new vistas of creative practice.

We see a positive outcome in this recasting of the arts as research. Artists always include empirical practices in their making—whether the close study of color and line as it appears in the natural world, or interviewing stakeholders to create a documentary performance such as the *Vagina Monologues* (Ensler, 1998). The move to research demands that artists read deeply into history, literature, psychology, philosophy and education to build the conceptual framework that sustains their creative work. As demonstrated by the methods discussed by many chapter contributors, the fine arts can provide important exemplars for criteria and methods through which the strength and resonance of ABR may be developed.

### *Scholartistry as Hybrid Inquiry*

These conflicting forces—the first coming from artistically trained and aesthetically engaged scholars from within the social sciences and the second coming from artists who have been drawn (or compelled by their institutions of higher learning) to philosophy and social theory—generate a confusing vortex of what ABR is and might be. In this collection we continue to use the term *scholartistry*, first offered by the poet and scholar Lorri Neilsen (1998), that has guided our concept of ABR.

Scholartistry, as we develop it, brings together a deep knowledge of scholarship in education as well as proficiency of a specific and/or multimodal art practice. This permits the scholartist to strive for both scholarly and artistic excellence. Additionally, our concept of scholartistry is profoundly rooted in the American Pragmatism of John Dewey and William James (Capps & Capps, 2005). American Pragmatism maintains that we live in an imperfect present and that we need to discover what we do not yet know to make our social life better. A key component of this better tomorrow is increasing the number of people who are allowed to participate and contribute to our social construct. Another essential element of American Pragmatism is its commitment to do no harm. If the policy results in people being hurt, change the policy and stop hurting people.

Such a concern and reflexivity toward the welfare of others can be in opposition to classical concepts of aesthetics and the artistic freedom of the artist. Since the 18th century, Western aesthetics has promoted the concept of artistic *autonomy* (Haskins, 1989), a philosophical position that the creative ideas of the artist could not be impinged. Artists were free to break rules and shock us with their disregard for convention. For example, to demonstrate his freedom from cultural constraint, contemporary Chinese artist Ai Weiwei recorded his intentional destruction of a financially valuable and culturally significant, 2000-year-old Han Dynasty urn (Guggenheim-Bilbao, 2018). The aesthetic justification for these provocations is that they generate new dialogue. Ethical concerns may simply limit authentic artistic expression.

This attitude permeates Lisa Erdman's (2021) arts practice doctoral dissertation research that included a public performance that was staged in the lobby of the Helsinki, Finland, main train station. To foster public dialogue about immigration experience and overmedicalization, Erdman installed a professionally designed information booth for *Finnexia*, a fictional medication that purported to facilitate the acquisition of the Finnish language. Erdman arranged for actors, dressed in medical attire, to engage with the public. Vulnerable populations, such as immigrants who struggled with language barriers, were deceived by Erdman's performance and believed Finnexia to be a real drug that could improve their lives. They went to pharmacies to obtain the medication, creating confusion as the pharmacies—and then the participants— discovered the drug was fictitious. When the national Finnish Medicines Agency learned of this, it notified Erdman to stop the performances and close her supporting website as it spread medical misinformation that instilled "false hope." Erdman refused, citing the autonomy of her artwork to catalyze public dialogue, essential for her ABR. Her sponsoring university supported this aesthetic rationale. In this view, the Finnish Medicines Agency's attempt to protect the vulnerable was merely confirming evidence of the "dialogue" provoked by Erdman's aesthetic intervention. For an American Pragmatist, there is no greater aesthetic good that makes deceit justifiable. People were being harmed. Stop it. Some of Erdman's Finnexia performers did exactly that. When they saw what the performance was doing by misleading its audience, they quit. A key question remains for arts-based researchers that resonates with all inquiry practices: Where should the line be drawn between pushing artistic and empirical boundaries and respecting the emotional and psychological well-being of the audience? Our positioning of scholartistry as adhering to the ethical concerns of American Pragmatism puts us potentially at odds with some forms of modern artistic practice and inquiry.

As the name scholartistry suggests, our view of ABR is deeply integrative. ABR that seeks to locate itself within the social sciences needs to adhere to the ethical principles for work with human subjects. In our view, to support the robust development of scholartistry, scholars would perhaps be better located within social science departments and working within these constraints rather than accepting the unfettered aesthetic independence within arts colleges. Artists and social scientists have much to learn from one another; collaboration and hybridity are key.

## Artistic Excellence in Scholartistry as Qualitative Reasoning

We define artistic excellence in scholartistry as demonstrating qualitative reasoning—a capacity of thought that Dewey (1934/1989) claimed was distinct from symbolic reasoning. Scholartists do more than invoke qualitative reasoning; they skillfully navigate it. Qualitative reasoning comes about through a direct encounter with the empirical world in which we are immersed. Scholartistry promotes a direct, embodied engagement with the sensory qualities of the world. The arts promote shedding our conventional categorical labeling and experiencing the smells, feelings, sounds, and sights of the world afresh. Scholartists working in educational fields feel researcher-teacher-student bodies moving through space. It is a full attentiveness to the movement that counts, not our efficiency in reaching a predetermined destination.

As Dewey (1934/1989) noted, these movements through space evoke resistance, throw us out of balance. It is precisely our struggles to regain balance—to make sense—that propel us into inquiry. Scholartists frame or recognize such moments in a deliberative, reflexive process. Although training in the arts prepares us for these moments with strategies and techniques for engagement, the application of these processes in the field and in the moment requires the exercise of judgment. There are no checklists to complete. There is instead a process of continuing judgments in the face of the new or previously unnoticed. Generative approaches coalesce to give shape to what had previously only been sensed. How the scholartist allows thinking to form, mutate, and evolve, and through experiential moments of direct materiality is an important criterion assessing a piece of research.

Creative encounters require us to step in and disrupt, distill, and reconfigure dynamic experience. They produced tacit knowledge (Polanyi, 1967): meanings and felt understandings that precede discursive or persuasive language. One has to find expressive means to discover what one is compelled to say. In response, an individual might reach for a metaphor. They might move with their body or create images that inscribe a sensed reality. For us, the melding of what can be said in words with the expressiveness of qualitative reasoning is the core of scholartistry.

In this book, we use ABR interchangeably with scholartistry, for both terms reflect the generative power of the arts to invigorate social science inquiry and social science to propel the arts. In their presentation of complexity, the scholartists presented in this edition suggest that the purpose of inquiry is to become more reflective on the magnitude of entanglements in which we operate. We believe scholartistry effectively captures this restless project of probing to ever-new discovery.

## Scholartistry as Critical Method

Scholartistry does not dictate a finding that the viewer must accept. Scholartistry opens conversations. This does not place scholartistry as outside social science critique. Rather, this creative work belongs within the parameters and conventions of social science where it serves to expand the field. Scholartistry can demand that we pay attention to aspects of the social and material world that we have ignored or neglected. Several contributors to this collection discuss the critical skills learned through the rigors of art-making that are necessary for deep engagement into uncertainty. However, along with many contributors to this volume, we caution readers about compromising art-making in pursuit of known social justice goals. The generative lessons in nuance, complexity, and contradiction that art has to teach us cannot be narrowed by a political agenda. Instead of political certainty, the arts reveal webs of human entanglement that lead to new perspectives into social justice. Many ABR scholars share an aim to make the invisible visible—telling stories, singing songs, devising theater, making poetry—humanizing those whose lives have come under their witness and watch.

## Making Theoretical Foundations, a Question of Diversity

Our focus on scholartistry separates us from other visual social science methodologies such as Photovoice (Latz, 2017) or Photo Elicitation (Harper, 2002), which, in our view, fall more within the conception that there is a world out there waiting to be recorded. We approach the arts as more procreant and searching. In particular, the arts are more than capturing and rearranging semiotic symbols and signs. Scholartists not *only* record data; they also *make it*. The concept of making data rejects the idea that the world is passive. The researcher, whether in conventional or creative social science, is in a dynamic give-and-take with the world at all stages of the research process. For scholartists, these processes can include keeping regular and reflexive notes, continuously reading deeply into literature while in "the field" for data collection/creation, composing, revising, recomposing, rethinking, rereading data and emergent/shape-shifting artistic form, all while creating moments to wait, test, share and listen. This interplay is not just marked by cool logic and procedure, but can also embrace wonderment, play, surprise, and unbridled aesthetic satisfaction. Formal analysis can include the awareness of joy, the disorientation of ambiguity, or the dissension of intentional rule-breaking. Scholartistry opens the possibility of making something new that allows us to see anew, an opening of perception.

## Further Questions in Art-Making: Craft and Skill

What aesthetic skills are recommended or required to engage in the process of qualitative reasoning? What technical skills should be considered as baseline to produce artful representations of research? Can those who identify as nonartists or not serious artists engage in ABR? Can they aspire to scholartistry? These questions are met with a range of answers from contributors with varying experience as artists—from the very novice to very experienced. Two contributors recently published *The Creative Ethnographer's Notebook* (Cahnmann-Taylor & Jacobsen, 2025) as a result of ABR conversations about the need to create a stand-alone pedagogical text that assists students and faculty trained in conventional ethnography to engage with creative practices in the arts. Contributors in this volume also address many different ways to think about the pedagogical applications of the arts to social science training and activity. In this book, co-editor Richard Siegesmund presents an exercise that he and his colleague Kerry Freedman have incorporated into their workshops for the International Congress of Qualitative Inquiry, to introduce researchers—both artists and nonartists—to one of Dewey's aesthetic criteria for qualitative reasoning. Other contributors to this edition argue for rigorous self-instruction, collaboration, and creativity as an urgent response for successful public work. Most argue implicitly or explicitly that scholartists should be risk-takers, learners, and bricoleurs who are attentive to assembling the skill sets needed. One takeaway from this book is that although a scholartist may not need extensive professional training in the arts, they do need to have more than a cursory exposure to an arts discipline. For graduate students, this would mean advanced coursework in the arts as part of a planned program of study. Scholartists have strategies for uncovering the knowledge embedded in the arts. This book contains strategies for exploiting the tacit levels of epistemology that can be accessed through different art disciplines. The arts are not an illustrative gloss to traditional qualitative research methods, rather they afford new skills and new ways of seeing.

## Benchmarks for ABR Excellence

In the first edition, we offered that only through practice would we eventually determine benchmarks of excellence. In the two decades that have followed, numerous models of high-quality work have helped guide ongoing discussions. For example, many of the scholars who have contributed to this edition have won prestigious national and international prizes and have already published their own ABR books. Others maintain their own professional art practice even as they produce academic scholarship at the highest levels.

"Excellence" is a high bar that is continually changing according to the context in which the scholartist chooses to participate. "Quality" can be a culturally loaded word that is wielded to exclude and silence some people while celebrating others. On the other hand, each arts discipline has its own skills that, when finely honed, allows the creative individual to push further into qualitative reasoning. In these places of discovery, there is the possibility to think of the world as it otherwise might be (Greene, 2001). Works of ABR strive to break silences and force us to see what has been pushed to the margins, while at the same time, they establish common ground that can bring people together and build consensus. Here, theory can play a critical role in reordering what may be considered to be settled. Theory shakes things up; it forces a reorientation of the world. Nevertheless, as important as theory may be, part of the required task for any arts-based researcher wishing to present findings as "art" is to pursue excellence in craft through serious and disciplined study and practice and/or to partner with talented artists to co-produce ABR. Scholartists in this book present many such strategies.

Always, when issues of quality are raised, it is important to recognize the cultural forces that preserve power by serving as self-appointed arbiters of excellence. It is important to recognize that "great art" is not culturally neutral. There are no culturally approved panels of experts that only award merit to the most deserving. As Dewey (1934/1989) observed in *Art as Experience*, our institutions, seemingly charged with cultural arbitration (our museums, theaters, movies, and symphony halls), are perhaps fatally compromised by societal values that turn the arts into commodities. Therefore, what is "good enough" art is a contextual issue not easily resolved, but what must remain a consideration under continuing deliberation and debate.

Expectations for "great art" become even less clear when education scholars practice art as a *process* to generate creativity in the data collection or empirical process, as a way to move away from what has traditionally been "done" and engage in discovery rather than pursue answers. Furthermore, scholartists often care deeply about communicating with audiences. They often explore alternatives to make research more accessible and satisfying to a larger public and/or more engaging to researchers and participants. Such works may embrace aesthetic pleasure as a means to increase engagement. Saldaña (2010) refers to this kind of work as "eduTainment"—that which educates while it entertains and engages. While reaching new audiences and finding new relevance for educational goals is at the heart of some ABR work, what makes it both aesthetic and educational is still a matter of debate, one this book addresses through explicit criteria as well as illuminating example.

ABR research, when done well, communicates educational findings in new, impactful, and more widely accessible ways. The arts have much to offer the educational researcher as a means to make our thinking robust, fresher, and more public, rendering the richness and complexity of the observed world. The need for research that speaks to wider non-academic audiences is critical.

## Education as More and Better Questions

This book's focus is on ABR *in education*—where education is expansively defined as teaching and engaging with learners in a range of life circumstances across a variety of cultural contexts. Chapter authors work in a variety of education-related disciplines in contexts that are both chronologically and geographically "school" and "nonschool." What matters to us as editors and professors in education is to illustrate what creative and imaginative mergers between the arts and social sciences can teach us about improving access to high-quality education for all, including the training of new educational researchers. Rather than provide much desired answers, contributors to this edition raise new questions for educational research. Readers will find that what counts as an educational research site is as varied as an abandoned school, a men's prison, an orphanage, political street protests, a honky tonk bar, and college campuses. Words, photographs, drawings, song lyrics, and performances help us see and reconfigure our dependence on English language text at the expense of visual, and translingual thinking.

At a time when education obsesses with neoliberal goals of efficiency in reaching preordained educational objectives, scholartists remind us that the thoughtful engagement with our world is a messy, unpredictable affair. There is hurt, misdirection, and adaptation. Being constructively lost is a powerful situation for finding one's way and discovering one's own purposes. Such pedagogical and curricular moments are not a failure of education; they *are* education. The navigation of such moments is easily the most enduring lesson for addressing the complicated business of living an engaged life. Several contributors to this collection chart how curriculum is an opening to new becomings rather than a preordained course to be run. In this sense, the work of ABR is profoundly political, even when it begins in wonder or appears not to directly address a social justice educational concern.

## How This Book Is Organized

It was always our hope that the second edition, although entirely composed of new writing, would speak to the first. In both of these editions, we sought representations from a variety of artistic genres and different theoretical foundations that retained clarity of "translation" to social scientific audiences. Therefore, we are pleased that the third edition brings both volumes together, and the interconnections between the authors are now immediately visible. The reader will not be referred to an earlier edition that they may or may not have. Brought together over the span of almost two decades, we knew we had the best words, and our next questions were about the best order: in what sequence should these chapters appear?

In the first and second editions, we grouped authors thematically together, whether by artistic discipline, or by an inclination to either theory or practice. We debated a similar path in this volume and/or one that was chronological. In the end, we chose the neutrality of alphabetical order. By listing all authors, including the editors, in alphabetical order, we interweave chapters concerning varied arts practices, theoretical and methodological commentaries, and any characteristics regarding the authors' geographic or academic locations, subject matters, or career trajectories. Other than the editors' introductory and concluding chapter, each chapter is a world complete unto itself. The reader is invited to enter into the book at any point and move through the book as their interest guides them.

For those wishing for a map or guide, we provide a chart at the beginning of the text that maps major thematic threads that run through the individual chapters. If the reader so chooses, they can find a thread of particular interest and then move to the chapters that are related. Much like the doing of ABR itself, the reader does not follow a prescribed method, but creates their own journey through their reading (Figure 1.1).

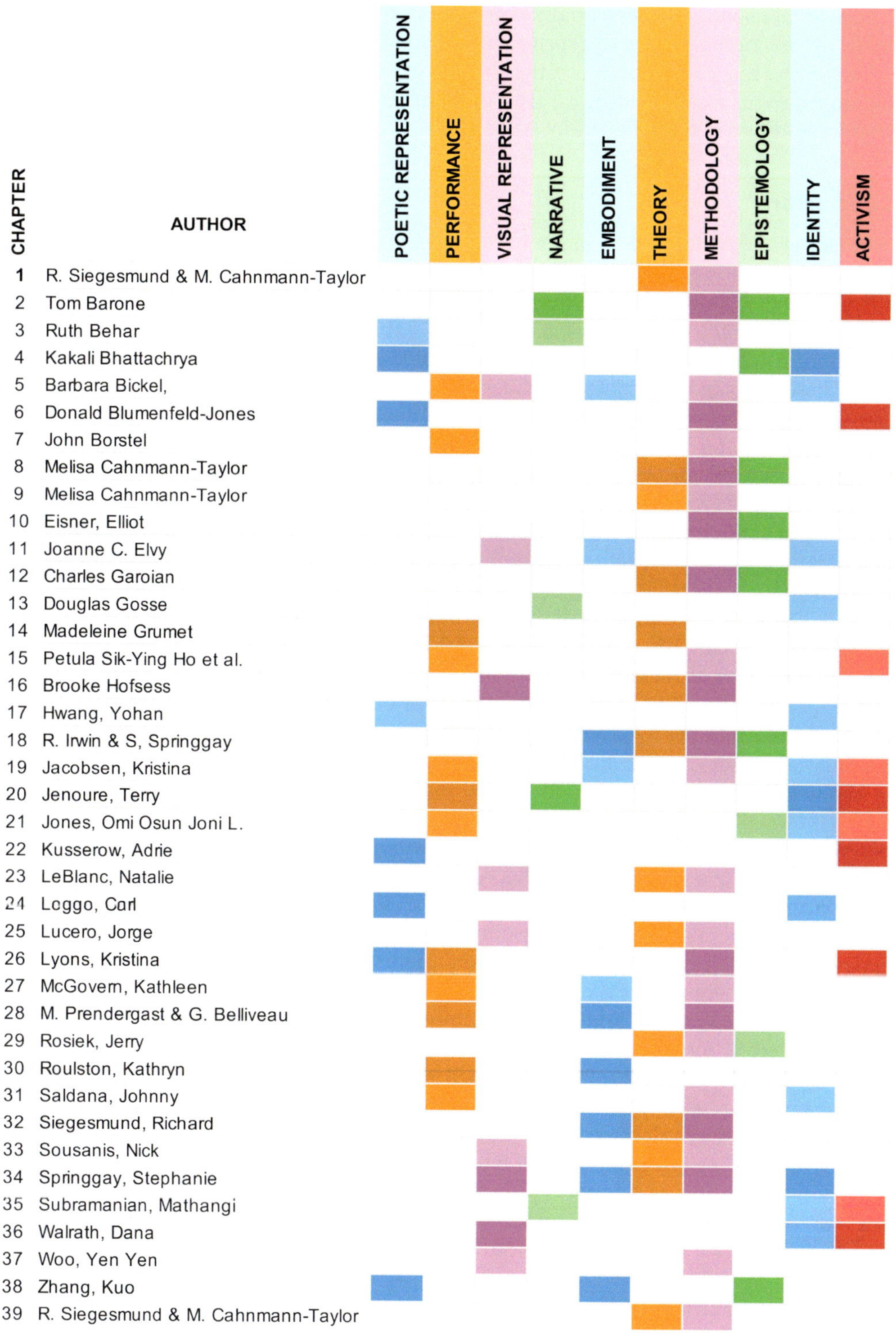


*Figure 1.1* Chart of major themes.

Individual chapters are essentially reprinted as they first appeared with modest changes made by the authors prior to reprinting. Authors were invited to provide a proscript to reflect on the space between when the chapter was first printed and where they are today. Far from a rogue methodology, we are particularly pleased with how many of the responses map a vigorous career sustained by ABR.

## Conclusion

In recent years, ABR has lost many of our greatest public intellectuals—individuals who reached out to nonacademic audiences. These include Maxine Greene (1917–2014), Augusto Boal (1931–2009), Carl Leggo (1953–2019), and Elliott Eisner (1933–2014), to name a few. Leggo (Chapter 24) and Eisner (Chapter 10) are represented in this volume. The pioneering work of Greene and Boal is cited and remembered in the pages that follow. These scholartists spent their lives as advocates for creativity in educational concerns and practices. Their legacy informs the work presented in this book, illustrating that the arts matter in the social sciences, and helps us rethink what we mean by inquiry altogether. We are pleased that this third edition of *Arts-Based Research in Education: Foundations for Practice* offers a comprehensive view of scholars who continue to build on a public, intellectual tradition to offer a vision for creative research that sustains democratic engagement, reflection, and thoughtful debate on what matters in teaching and learning.

Work represented in this book was not done by following an exact method to control for results. Rather, ABR scholarship was done by creative doing, informed through deep knowledge and/or attunement to the somatic qualities of tacit knowing nourished through artistic practice. Looking back over the contributions of scholartists over the past 20 years, the third edition comes together to show distinct pathways of thought. In summation, there are two important codas to make about ABR.

The first is how ABR is strongly rooted in the progression of qualitative inquiry. ABR builds on the past. It aspires to move us to new futures, even as these futures may be very different from what has come before. Each new beginning links to what has brought us to this moment. The second is that ABR's reconceptualization of inquiry has implications for our conceptions of educational curriculum. ABR shifts from a conception of education as the transfer of bricks of knowledge from teacher to student, to education as a co-creation: active and collaborative experience between teachers and learners, between the human and non-human, between the real and the virtual.

While many detractors and critics continue to question the pairing of "art" and "research," there is also increasing global activity where the creative turn is thriving. The scholars included in this book have opened the field that allowed new forms of research to blossom. Our selected contributors illustrate unique aspects of scholartistry within a broad conception of education and sites of learning. These authors continually challenge themselves to refine our definitions of what we feel ABR, particularly as it is applied within the field of education, *is*, what it *is not*, and what, with close attention and debate, *it might become*. A work of ABR is a journey into what is not yet. These are not findings; they are discoveries that open windows into future possibility. Those who pursue ABR must continue to ask and answer challenging and provocative questions regarding theories, research methods, artistic craft, and applications to education in order to engage with ever-expanding audiences.

## References

Bishop, C. (2012). *Artificial hells: Participatory art and the politics of spectatorship*. Verso Books.

Bishop, C. (2014, October 2). *In dialogue: Claire Bishop and Claire Doherty*, Lecture Series: A Lived Practice. School of the Art Institute of Chicago.

Cahnmann-Taylor, M., & Jacobsen, K. (Eds.) (2025). *The creative ethnographer's notebook*. Routledge.

Capps, J. M., & Capps, D. (Eds.) (2005). *James and Dewey on belief and experience*. University of Illinois Press.

Denzin, N. K., Lincoln, Y. S., Giardina, M. D., & Cannella, G. S. (Eds.) (2023). *The SAGE handbook of qualitative research* (6th ed.). Sage.

Dewey, J. (1989). *Art as experience* (J. Boydston, Ed.). Southern Illinois University Press. (Original work published 1934).

Ensler, E. (1998). *The vagina monologues*. Dramatist Play Service.

Erdman, L. (2021). The answerability of false hope: Examining the unexpected outcomes of the Finnexia® public art intervention. *Performing Ethos: An International Journal of Ethics in Theatre & Performance*, *11*, 55–75. https://doi.org/10.1386/peet_00037_1

Greene, M. (2001). *Variations on a blue guitar: The Lincoln Center Institute lectures on aesthetic education*. Teachers College Press.

Guggenheim-Bilbao (2018). *Ai Weiwei, dropping a Han Dynasty urn, 1995*. Guggenheim Bilbao. https://www.guggenheim-bilbao.eus/en/learn/schools/teachers-guides/ai-weiwei-dropping-han-dynasty-urn-1995

Harper, D. (2002). Talking about pictures: A case for photo elicitation. *Visual Studies*, *17*(1), 13–26. https://doi.org/10.1080/14725860220137345

Haskins, C. (1989). Kant and the autonomy of art. *Journal of Aesthetics and Art Criticism*, *47*(1), 43–54. https://doi.org/10.2307/431992

Institute of Education Sciences (n.d.). *What works clearinghouse*. https://ies.ed.gov/ncee/wwc/

jagodzinski, j., & Wallin, J. (2013). *Arts-based research: A critique and a proposal*. Sense.

Kuhn, T. S. (1970). *The structure of scientific revolutions* (2nd ed.). University of Chicago Press.

Latz, A. O. (2017). *Photovoice research in education and beyond: A practical guide from theory to exhibition*. Routledge.

Neilsen, L. (1998). *Knowing her place: Research literacies and feminist occasions*. Caddo Gap Press.

O'Donoghue, D. (2009). Are we asking the wrong questions in arts-based research? *Studies in Art Education*, *50*(4), 352–368. https://doi.org/10.1080/00393541.2009.11518781

Polanyi, M. (1967). *The tacit dimension*. Anchor Books.

Saldaña, J. (2010). Forward. In M. Cahnmann-Taylor & M. Souto-Manning (Eds.), *Teachers act up: Creating multicultural community through theatre*. Teachers College Press.

Shavelson, R. J., & Towne, L. (Eds.) (2022). *Scientific research in education*. National Academies Press.

Sullivan, G. (2010). *Art practice as research: Inquiry in visual arts* (2nd ed.). Sage.

Chapter 2

# How Arts-Based Research Can Change Minds

*Tom Barone*

Most of us for whom educational studies are our chosen field see ourselves as engaged in an ongoing quest to make the world of schooling a better place. Our efforts, simultaneously personal and professional, are fueled by hopes for an educational enterprise guided by our moral compasses, a felt need to realign its policy and practice, and therefore its outcomes, with our own sense of educational virtue.

I cannot more aptly describe the nature of my own quest than did Maxine Greene (1988, p. xi) in articulating hers. Greene characterized her own lifelong struggle as one of "connect[ing] the undertaking of education ... to the making and remaking of a public space."

But in recent times those with opposing interests, most from outside the field of education, have made the pursuit of that quest more problematic. Working diligently toward the downsizing of that public space, they have, from my point of view, moved to denigrate the public schools and to castigate those who live and work within them, in favor of a less expansive vision, one guided by a narrow, private, corporatist ideology.

As academic professionals, one of the most important outlets for pursuing our quest is our scholarship. And for some educational researchers, quantitative and qualitative alike, it is there more than anywhere, that frustration and even futility reign, with a sense that the realm of schooling has been largely untouched by our painstaking efforts to study that world and to reveal what we have found. Indeed, since the November 2004 elections, a few colleagues, in personal conversations, have expressed to me their doubts that progressive educational researchers, even in collaboration with like-minded academic colleagues and public-school educators, can ever effect the realignment of schooling in America with their aspirations for it.

Despite the ongoing trials and recent disappointments, my quest, and hopefully yours, is not easily retired. But, as we witness the educational landscapes of the public school and the academy devolving around us, I feel the need to support our longings, to revive our yearnings, for making a positive difference through our scholarly research. And to that end I quote the following words of Jean-Paul Sartre (1988): "The world and man reveal themselves," he wrote, "by undertakings. And all the undertakings we might speak of reduce themselves to a single one, *making history*" (p. 104).

Sartre was not, of course, directly addressing the world of educational research, but from those pithy words I extrapolate the following: As educational inquirers, parts of our professional selves are indeed defined by our notions of the educationally true, good, and beautiful. We do indeed reveal these parts of ourselves within, among other locations, our research projects. And it is through those undertakings that we must continue to strive to make educational history.

DOI: 10.4324/9781003412892-2

To that end, this essay represents a tentative foray into a realm of possibilities. In it, I explore merely one avenue for redressing the dire state of education through our work as educational scholars and researchers. It is divided into two parts. In the first, I attempt to more fully articulate the nature of the obstacles that we face as educational researchers in our efforts to make educational history. In the second, I suggest some features of qualitative research, especially arts-based research, that might serve us in our quest.

## The Problem

At the beginning of the twenty-first century, we have witnessed the greatest intervention of the federal government into the field of education in the history of the United States, a deep intrusion into the once public space of the classroom for the purpose of managing the transactions between those who live and work there. The consequences of this intervention, intended and otherwise – but largely, I believe, pernicious – are too varied and widespread to catalogue here. But among them has been the reinforcement of frame factors that have served to diminish the professional autonomy of teachers and administrators, deskilling them, as Apple and Teitelbaum (1986) would say, and severely hampering them from engaging in history-making practice, which is to say, praxis.

Among the available forms of resistance to this institutional oppression of educators is a quiet subversion of these externally generated policy mandates from behind the closed classroom door. But while some degrees of professional freedom surely remain for educational practitioners, the omnipresent standardized exam, like Foucault's (1977/1995) panopticon, renders subterfuge more problematical. Subterfuge, moreover, does little to alert non-educators to the extent of the damage currently being inflicted on the educational process. While signs of discontent with practices such as high-stakes testing have emerged among scattered clusters of laypeople, conventional suppositions upon which harmful policy mandates are based go largely unchallenged; within the general public, the confusion remains widespread.

Writing in the 1920s, John Dewey (1927/1954) observed that a "public that is organized in and through those officers who act in behalf of its interests," including policy-makers, is critical to the health of a democracy. He further noticed that the public of the time "is in eclipse, unsure and uncertain ... The public seems to be lost; it certainly is bewildered" (pp. 15–16). With other social and educational progressives, I detect nowadays a similar "eclipse of the public." The populace seems lost, distracted, and largely unconcerned as one of the last bastions of hope for what Dewey called the Great Community – the public school – is betrayed by policy-makers who are failing to act in the public's interests in ways that most do not fully comprehend.

Schneider and Ingram (1997) have identified the kind of politics that operates when the public is bewildered, lost, befuddled, and betrayed. They call it *degenerative* politics (pp. 2–3; quoted in Smith, 2004). Degenerative politics depends and feeds on an organized, usually public, display of entertainment. This theatrical display, designed to manipulate social reality toward a desired end, constitutes what Edelman (1988) calls *the political spectacle*. Of the several elements identifiable within that spectacle, I will mention three here.

The first significant element in this public pageant is that of skewed imagery, a series of distorting pictures lodged in the public consciousness. The second is a symbolic language, a set of abstract words, devoid of concrete referents, to which meanings are nevertheless assigned. Third, the words and images live in a mutually supportive relationship within an overarching storyline, similar to what the post-modern social critic Jean-Francois Lyotard (1979) would call a master narrative.

Master narratives are meta-stories that aim to bring final meaning to cultural phenomena. These are stories that we cling to for a comfort and familiarity otherwise denied us in an increasingly jarring and bewildering world. A narrative provides a kind of coherence to the symbolic language and images, just as the words and images drive and illuminate the story, free to operate within the political spectacle, to pervade public awareness.

The words, images, and meta-story that are serving to confuse the public about educational matters are, of course, part of a more inclusive cultural narrative about issues of childhood, race, gender, social class, intellectualism, and private initiative versus public good. In teasing out the ways in which this vocabulary, imagery, and narrative pertain to education, I blend my own ideas with those of Mary Lee Smith (2004), who has transported some of Edelman's (1985, 1988) notions about the political spectacle into the educational arena.

The public has been bombarded with images of indolent and insolent schoolchildren, especially children of color; of disinterested, incompetent, mostly female teachers who are responsible for those children's purported deficiencies; or of the rare, isolated hero-teacher who, on behalf of their students, combats, without a posse of colleagues, a corrupt and stifling school bureaucracy; and finally there are the manufactured images of the aloof, impractical, theory-obsessed teacher-educator, portrayed as the ultimate apologist for the self-serving educational establishment.

Meanwhile, conversations about education are riddled with words such as "accountability," "high standards," and "freedom of choice." Who, asks Smith (2004, pp. 12–13), could disagree with these words? And yet, she notes, the meaning of each term can vary within alternative contexts. For example, "accountability" suggests something quite different to accountants, to educators, and to testing experts. But those who use the term within the political spectacle "gloss over real differences in definitions and values" in favor of a privileged meaning that serves the narrow interests who seek to maintain the political spectacle.

Within the meta-story that flows from and through these words and images, children, public-school teachers, administrators, and professors of education are stereotyped and scapegoated. Members of the educational establishment are portrayed as not responsible to the motivational forces of the free market. Because they have placed our nation's social, cultural, and economic well-being in jeopardy, they themselves are in constant need of surveillance, or "accountability." Most importantly the public (a.k.a. "government") schools in which they work require a dose of private-sector competition to cure what ails them.

Because this master narrative is an artifact crafted within a degenerative politics it is not, ultimately, a useful one. This is because it draws its breath from within an air of unreality. Edelman (1985, p. 5) suggests that the pictures within the political spectacle "create a moving panorama taking place in a world the public never quite touches," its members never actually experiencing it for themselves. The images associated with words such as "accountability," and the meta-story they support, lack concrete referents and so "float free of specific meaning" (Smith, 2004, p. 13). "No tether ties these words [and images] ... to the world of experience and intractable concrete details." Nor are the meanings of the words, images, and story within the meta-narrative tied to debilitating cultural forces, details of which might reveal teachers and students as the victims rather than the perpetrators of social crimes. Instead, unwarranted meaning is arrogated to these words and images by those in a position to do so. The result is a public that is "held in a kind of thrall" (Smith, 2004, p. 13).

My favorite evidence of the extent of this psychological bondage continues to be the annual Phi Delta Kappa/Gallup Poll of the Public's Attitudes toward the Public Schools (Rose & Gallup, 2004). Year after year, the poll has demonstrated a sizable gap between the views held about the quality of schools with which respondents are directly familiar, and their views of those with which they are not. In the 2004 poll, 70 percent of parents from across the nation awarded an A or a B to the school attended by their oldest child. Asked to grade all public schools nationally, only 26 percent of the same parents chose an A or B (p. 44).

How to account for this paradox? Between the parents' direct experiences of the nearby schoolhouse and their impressions of the distant classrooms inhabited by other people's children, there toils the political spectacle churning out distorted language and clichéd imagery. These words and images are rife within the products of the commodified and banalized mass media, especially the electronic visual media (Males, 1999) such as film, TV sitcoms, and news magazines, the commercial aims of which are, paraphrasing Abbs (2003, p. 19), "as far removed from actual experience as an amusement arcade is from teaching philosophy."

Those aims are indeed to bewilder and befuddle, to mystify and indoctrinate. The evidence from that Gallup poll (and elsewhere) suggests that, while the flow from the popular media may be limited in its capacity to affect profoundly the meanings we derive from "actual" experiences, it remains sufficiently powerful to transform the benignly distant and unfamiliar into the fearfully strange and exotic. Unfortunately, however, it is within this anxiety manufactured within the political spectacle that much of today's educational policy is being fashioned.

The difficulties of removing the blindfolds should not be minimized. The political spectacle has allowed the seeds of misperception to be planted deep within the collective subconscious. Indeed, discussions in the media about educational matters almost inevitably betray assumptions built on the imagery within the master narrative. When even the National Federation of Teachers condescends to the language of educational standards and teacher accountability, the extent of the problem is more clearly registered.

The seeds are certainly buried below the cultural topsoil of political partisanship. While the 2004 campaign platforms of the two major parties in the United States surely reflected, to some degree, the interests of different constituencies, the rhetoric on both sides floated above the meaning of terms such as accountability, educational standards, and even the ways in which a child may be left behind.

Of course, in a political campaign the spectacle reaches its height; indeed, dueling pageants vie for center stage. A campaign hardly represents an opportune moment for educating an electorate. It may be in the cooler years, with the spectacle malingering but its fever diminished, that we find the most appropriate moments for our arduous efforts at intervening in history through our scholarship, all the while refusing to create a spectacle of our own.

## What To Do?

What are the various research approaches available to us for the kind of intervention of which I speak? The list of qualitative inquiry strategies has grown more extensive in recent decades, to include the various forms of case studies, participatory action research, phenomenological research, hermeneutical research, cultural studies, critical ethnography, postmodern, post-structural, and post-colonial approaches, autoethnography, narrative research, life history, performative ethnography, and so on.

Only to be recast, as we know, as a kind of *blacklist* of research methodologies (indeed, one that disparages all non-experimental forms of educational research). But recast by whom? Are the proponents of a new, aggressively retrogressive research orthodoxy, the same policy-makers and politicians who benefit from a degenerative politics? If so, does their disdain for these research approaches reflect a concern that the methodologies might facilitate a remaking of the history that they feel they own? The presence of such a fear would support my own beliefs about the potential of these alternative research genres, and so offer hope.

In addressing the possibilities of making educational history through alternative genres of educational research, I focus primarily on the kind known as *arts-based.* I am wondering about the potential of a research approach that, boldly but not rudely, humbly and not arrogantly, intervenes in the current state of educational affairs, one that expands the reach of our scholarship because of (*and not despite*) the fact that it is profoundly aesthetic, one that *both* finds its inspiration in the arts *and* leads to progressive forms of social awareness. I am thinking of an approach to research on educational phenomena that alters the world by raising questions, one that makes history by providing a catalyst for the changing of minds. And among the candidates whose minds might be changed are the members of the general public currently under the sway of the political spectacle.

This is, as we know, not the usual audience for educational researchers of any stripe. Instead, career success for members of the professoriate has largely depended on the degree to which our texts inform and persuade professional colleagues within our circumscribed discursive sub-communities. But some cultural observers have reinforced our discomforts with this narrow audience, expressing concerns about the tendency of academic writing to alienate readers unprepared to penetrate the opaque prose of disciplinary specialization. Russell Jacoby (1987), in particular, has insisted that even writings by academics with emancipatory intentions have not served to resist, but rather contribute to, a general decline in public discourse.

In the last few decades, some educational researchers have abandoned the traditional premises, procedures, protocols, and modes of representation of the quantitative and qualitative social sciences for those of the arts. But arts-based researchers have thus far only rarely abandoned the traditional conception of research audience. For those who have, the alternative audiences have included, among others, educational practitioners and policy-makers, the informants whose experiences have been represented in the research text, those who commission evaluations of educational programs, and the researcher herself.

I am – emphatically – not suggesting that arts-based researchers cease addressing any audience we desire to address. But I am imagining research projects that reach out to an audience that transcends one consisting only of colleagues and those alternative readers and viewers. Such an audience might include laypeople of all social categories, privileged and otherwise, those who may be identified as members of an intelligentsia or literati, and those who do not know the meaning of those words, all of us who are, or should be, active participants in the larger civic culture, and all of us who have been, in varying degrees, captivated by the spectacle.

I am envisioning educational inquirers who undertake the reclaiming and redirecting of history by communicating directly with the general public through research that is based on the arts. But which characteristics of art and arts-based research hold promise in this regard? Two will be highlighted here. First, I am recommending research that is *socially engaged*, and second, research that is *epistemologically humble.* I begin with the notion of social or political commitment in art and arts-based research.

## Socially Engaged Arts-Based Research

We have learned from various postmodern theorists that power relationships inevitably inhabit every human activity and cultural artifact. All science is, therefore, inherently political, as is all art. But like some science, art can be emancipatory, and in more than one sense. For Nelson Goodman (1968), art can free us from entrenched, commonsensical ways of viewing the world. By calling for and yet resisting "a usual kind of picture," writes Goodman, "it may bring out neglected likenesses and differences ... and in some measure, remake our world" (p. 33).

Goodman sees the emancipatory potential of art in its capacity to obviate and undercut facets of a prevailing worldview. Other definitions of art seem to emerge out of a more specific concern for inequities within the sociopolitical relationships in a culture. Art of this sort, more directly focused on the effects of social practices and institutions on human beings, operates out of what bell hooks calls (1994) an *outlaw culture*, one that promotes "engagements with ... practices and ... icons that are defined as on the edge, as pushing the limits, disturbing the conventional, acceptable politics of representation" (pp. 4–5).

Outlaw art represents a kind of assertively political project similar to what Sartre called socially engaged literature. Sartre (1988) also viewed the primary aim of art as a challenge to the established interests within society, seeing the artist as "in a state of perpetual antagonism toward the conservative forces which are maintaining the balance he needs to upset" (p. 81).

Both hooks and Sartre are recommending artistic projects that move to shape and influence the public consciousness by critiquing the politically conventional and the socially orthodox. And artists throughout the ages have succeeded in doing so. From Sophocles to Bertoldt Brecht, from Victor Hugo to Richard Wright, from Pablo Picasso to Judy Chicago, from Spike Lee to Gregory Nava, from photographer Lewis W. Hine to Dorothea Lange, to name but a few is to omit untold numbers of others.

Their work reflects the spirit of more recent activist art, which, as Nina Felshin (1995) put it, has attempted to "change the conversation" by "exposing issues to a public view as a means of sparking *public* debate" (p. 37), and ultimately to stimulate social change. That is the sort of artistic stimulus that stands tall against the *Zeitgeist* maintained through the political spectacle, one that offers hope that history can indeed be made through the personal quest of the artist.

I am obliged to report that I have, up to this point in the relatively short history of the genre, not been privy to a completely unblemished work of arts-based research, one sufficiently powerful, by itself, to redirect the educational conversation in the manner suggested by Felshin. But some, in their closely observed, imaginatively crafted renderings of the struggles of teachers and young people, have confirmed my beliefs about the potential of alternative research genres to upset the balance maintained within the spectacle.

Take, for example, the ethnodrama *Street Rat* (Saldaña et al., 2005), a piece of arts-based research that focuses on the lives of some homeless youths in New Orleans. The play was adapted by Johnny Saldaña, Susan Finley, and her son Macklin from a research story composed by the Finleys (Finley & Finley, 1999) and from poetry written by Macklin (Finley, 2000). In April 2004, I attended a production of this ethnodrama directed by Saldaña.

The script, based on participant-observer Macklin's experiences with his informants, moved briskly from an introduction of the two main characters, Roach and Tigger, to complications arising partly from their relationships with each other and their homeless friends, to a dramatic climax as violence nearly erupts, and finally a touching denouement, a scene in which Tigger and Roach, obviously filling a void in each other's lives left there by others, declared in their garbage-strewn living quarters, that they were, at least for the time being, home. The narrative drive of the story was punctuated by the recitation of poems of various lengths, composed by Macklin, who thereby became, himself, a character in the play.

Other touches added to the production's effective *mise en scène*. Absent a proscenium arch, audience members were seated in a black-draped, rectangular room, its floor shared with the actors. The minimal props, authentic costuming, and background music were all carefully designed and selected to advance the vision of the director and his collaborators.

The formal attributes of *Street Rat* were matched by its content. The telling details in the lives of Roach, Tigger, and their comrades enabled me to dwell within an otherwise, largely unavailable world of homeless young people. Through an array of concrete images, particular forms of intelligence were revealed to me, the structure of moral codes laid bare. Through a cascade of specific utterances and gestures I was granted access to their personal hopes, dreams, and motivations.

As an example of socially engaged research this play addressed sociopolitical phenomena that remain hazy within the spectacle. Indeed, it was willing to refocus on – that is *re*-search – a part of what the postmodern theorist Nelson (1987) lists a the neglected ... the forgotten, the irrational, the insignificant, the repressed, the borderline, the eccentric, the sublimated, the rejected, the nonessential, the marginal, the peripheral, the excluded, the tenuous, the silenced, the accidental, the dispersed, the disqualified, the deferred, the disjointed ... [all that which] the modern age has never cared to understand in any particular detail, with any sort of specificity (p. 217).

But the glimpse that this play affords us of a hidden or unfamiliar world is not an act of mere voyeurism. It is, rather, a work of what Stone (1988, p. 160) calls *moral fiction*, one that aims to "establish the connections between [debilitating] social forces and individual lives." The socially committed play accomplishes what good outlaw art can: It "open[s] up institutions and their practices for critical inspection and evaluation" (Lincoln & Denzin, 2003, p. 377). The play's carefully embodied observations, the results of the researcher's scrutiny and artistry, challenge the arrogation of meanings within the political spectacle. It is indeed potentially emancipating in the strong sense advocated by hooks (1994) and Sartre (1988).

## Epistemologically Humble Arts-Based Research

Still, an arts-based research project geared to subvert the master narrative and confound the political spectacle must be more than socially committed. It must also be epistemologically humble.

Of course, the master narrative that serves the political spectacle, operating within a modernist epistemology that gravitates toward final knowledge, lacks all humility. Master narratives possess a totalizing character as they aim to impose order on the world from a distinct, if often hidden, ideological point of view, one that appears to be authoritative, final, exclusionary of alternative viewpoints, all-knowing.

A disposition of this sort in the social researcher represents the attitude of an epistemological bully. (Note that I have dampened down Lyotard's (1979) overheated epithet of *epistemological terrorist*.) "Arrogant bully" is, I think, an appropriate term for an epistemological stance that attempts to impose its own singular view of the world on its audience.

But adopting a stance of epistemological modesty in projects of social inquiry entails more than the exchange of a social-science methodology for an arts-based approach. Artists, and arts-based researchers, however high-minded their emancipatory intentions, may produce works as exclusionary, monologic, and hegemonic as other sorts of projects. This happens whenever, to paraphrase Sartre, the would-be artist, eager to change minds, zealous to make history, forgets to make art.

Image, language, and story are indeed the tools and the products of artists. But socially committed research that evidences an interrogatory rather than an authoritative attitude must not resemble, on the one hand, the self-abnegation of political eunuchs, nor, on the other hand, the ersatz artistry of dogmatists, propagandists, ideologues, and rigid partisans. My hope is for a politically vital arts-based research, the kind that challenges the comfortable, familiar, dominant master narrative, not by proffering a new totalizing counter-narrative, but by luring an audience into an appreciation of an array of diverse, complex, nuanced images and partial, local portraits of human growth and possibility.

This implies arts-based research with the power to involve members of the public in history-making dialogue, or in what I have called *conspiratorial conversations* (Barone, 2000, p. 150). A conspiracy suggests a communion of agents engaged in exploratory discussions about possible and desirable worlds. When an arts-based work engenders an aesthetic experience in its readers or viewers, empathy may be established, connections made, perceptions altered, emotions touched, equilibria disturbed, the status quo rendered questionable. Individual voices of audience members may be raised in common concern – either within the artistic textual engagement itself (between reader and text), and/or afterwards, among members of an audience of readers or viewers. In these conversations, ideas and ideals may be shared for the purposes of an improved reality. Plots may be hatched against inadequate present conditions in favor of more emancipatory social arrangements in the future.

How can a piece of arts-based research effectively engender conspiratorial moments? To create the possibility of conspiracy the artist must first imagine what Wolfgang Iser (1974) calls an *implied readership*. Implied readers are those who "actively participate in the composition of textual meaning" (p. xii). But this term "incorporates both the pre-structuring of the potential meaning by the text, and the reader's actualization of this potential by the reading process" (p. xii).

*Street Rat* was pre-structured by the Finleys and Saldaña in a manner that pulled me, implied *viewer*, member of the public, into the world of the play, enticing me to reconstruct the illusion first imagined by the playwrights. In such a textual re-creation, wrote Dewey (1934/1958):

> there is an ordering of the elements of the whole that is in form, although not in details, the same as the process of organization the creator of the work consciously experienced ... Without an act of recreation the object is not perceived as a work of art.
>
> (p. 307)

In this process of formal reconstruction, the viewer lives momentarily in a virtual world, bracketed off from the world of experience external to the work. Phenomenologist aestheticians would argue that the viewer thereby experiences a piece of subjective life, partakes of the vision of the artist as embodied in the pre-structured work. But some works may not allow for an easy return from that vision into the world outside. Indeed, a work that is only technically accomplished can have an effect opposite to that of promoting conspiracy.

While beguiling formal qualities can lure an audience into imagining another world, this hypothetical space is a realm of fantasy, an aesthetic remove. Like the educational spectacle, a formal masterwork may create its own detachment as it bedazzles its viewers into acquiescence with its vision, offering a sublime illusion, never really, as Edelman would say, "touching the world."

Some works of propaganda are like this – technically marvelous, formally beautiful. But they do not emancipate. Lacking nuance, closed to disconfirming evidence, they seek only to indoctrinate, to lull into quietude. This kind of propaganda is, in fact, akin to kitsch, a debased kind of art that sentimentalizes everyday experiences.

Works of kitsch can evoke emotions that are based on nostalgia, or they may construct imaginary enemies. These elements of kitsch are found in the popular media's characterizations of teachers as either singularly heroic or collectively incompetent, their tales in which the intelligence and moral fiber of today's youth compare poorly to those of yesteryear, their images of public schools as out of control (Edelman, 1995, p. 31). In kitsch, as in propaganda, a clear, controlled, unsentimental rethinking of mainstream truths and realities is sacrificed on the altar of the meta-narrative. But in their privileging of form over substance, their refusal to attend to the blemishes on the face of the prevailing master narrative, both propaganda and kitsch are disqualified as art, as re-search, and as catalysts for conspiracy.

Conspiracy is more likely to result from engagements in which aesthetic content grounds a work of art in the closely observed particulars of experience. The merely beautiful, or otherwise kitschy, work is thereby conditioned, planted in virtual space and time. A work that is closed in on itself is opened up to previously unimagined meanings.

The particulars that constituted the aesthetic content of *Street Rat* are what a traditional social scientist would call *data*. But here those data were carefully selected, edited, shaped, fashioned, dramatized, with an artistic end in mind. The aesthetic content of the play, in close relationship to its theatrical qualities, advanced in a credible fashion an understanding of these troubled youngsters, kids who, throughout their lives at home and in school, and later on the streets, were rarely either seen or heard. And now, along with the previously transparent forces that served to deform their lives, they were.

But just as form can become an imperial presence in the arts-based text, so can substance. Indeed, in many of the pieces of socially committed educational research to which I have been privy, aesthetic substance has hardly been the victim of an aesthetic sin. It has been the sinner. In that sort of work a regard for bombast over seductiveness can mean that formal qualities are casualties of the unrestrained political outrage of the socially committed researcher.

Now, minor imbalances of substance over form can be found in even the best socially committed arts-based research, including *Street Rat*. In that work, the sources of the street kids' alienation from their families, schools, and society in general, suggested within the more prosaic dialogue of the script, were successfully reinforced and amplified by the vivid imagery and driving rhythms of the poems interspersed throughout the text. Occasionally, however, anger overtook artistry, and stridency and shrillness prevailed. The poetry, hovering above the dramatized display of particular, contextualized injustices, seemed too obviously designed for the speedy delivery of a facile social message.

Considering the other attributes of this ethnodrama, those unfortunate lapses are easily forgiven. But in encounters with other emancipatory-minded arts-based projects, I have sometimes found myself cringing at a heavy-handedness in pursuit of noble goals. And even those who enjoy being preached to in a choir should remember that sermonizing the likeminded does not a conspiracy make. At their best, socially engaged arts-based research projects aim to entice into meaningful dialogue not merely, on the one hand, the progressivist faithful, nor, on the other hand, politically entrenched neo-conservative ideologues. They aim to conspire, rather, with all potential allies who have been temporarily mesmerized by the spectacle.

A successful enticement of these co-conspirators requires more than mere emotional discharge, which as Dewey (1934/1958, p. 61) reminds us, "is a necessary but not a sufficient condition of expression." Emotion that is effectively expressed through art is the result of a thoughtful composition of significant subject matter into an aesthetic form in which that emotion is embodied. Absent the artistic expression to which Dewey has alluded, there looms a reduced capacity to persuade profoundly, to move viewers affectively and cognitively into a skepticism regarding social pieties and platitudes.

Instead there is the kind of alienation that Carol Becker (1994) suggests is the product of some activist art:

> Art may be focused directly on the issues of daily life, but, because it seeks to reveal contradictions and not obfuscate them, art works which should spark a shock of recognition and effect catharsis actually appear alien and deliberately difficult. Art easily becomes the object of rage and confrontation. [And artists], frustrated by the illusion of order and well-being posited by society, ... [may] choose rebellion as a method of retaliation ... [I] n so doing, they separate themselves from those with whom they may actually long to interact.
>
> (1994, xiii)

This alienation may in fact be seen as the mirror image of that produced by either the beautiful-but-clueless, or the kitschy. Again there are totalitarian tendencies, a disinterest in or failure to facilitate democratic engagement. While *Street Rat* is a largely effective, socially engaged work that managed not to alienate, but to compel the attention of a limited, localized public audience, a second politically committed work has managed to secure a wider audience, although not as a full-fledged work of art. Indeed, it may offer hope regarding the degree of artistry necessary for a piece of qualitative research to promote conspiracy.

The book is *Doing School* by Denise Clark Pope (2001). Its subtitle reveals its political interests: *How We Are Creating a Generation of Stressed Out, Materialistic, and Miseducated Students*. The book explores the culture of competition in a comprehensive California high school as it traces the tensions between the felt needs of students and the materialistic brand of success expected of them. And, at least at its narrative center, it avoids an authoritative stance, striking an effective balance between aesthetic form and substance. The author maintains an eye for telling detail, even as she wisely avoids the off-putting stridency of which Becker speaks. She transforms her informants into quasi-literary characters, transmuting her own concerns into the form of biographical portraits of five ethnically diverse students, fashioning for inspection the idiosyncratic life worlds of these students and the common social forces that operate to diminish them.

Still, in its student portraits, *Doing School* never really achieves the formal power of great literature. In reading the student stories, there is little danger of entrapment in sublime illusion. *Doing School* is therefore, unlike *Street Rat*, hardly activist art. In fact, its author makes no artistic claims for it at all. Instead, the book defies labels, serving, I suggest, as an example of the kind of genre blurring that, so prevalent nowadays, first emerged in social research in the 1970s, during Denzin and Lincoln's (2000) so-called "third moment" in the history of qualitative research. Still, if its quasi-literary center is seen as a core out of which the analytical content is extrapolated, then the project might indeed be identified, if not as artistic, then as arts-based.

The limited formal attributes of *Doing School*, like those of many qualitative research texts, certainly seem sufficient for facilitating readers' reconstruction of the text. Without feeling bullied by either textual form or content, this reader accepted the invitation to dwell vicariously in the lives of these young people. So it was that, through these portraits, I came to regard these students, not as "other people's children" who populate a vague and distant campus, but as specific human beings who harbor recognizable dreams in the face of debilitating circumstances.

Indeed, Denise Clark Pope (personal conversation) has suggested that, more than any other aspect of the book, the student stories account for its surprisingly positive reception among the lay public. A significantly better "seller" than most books about educational issues, *Doing School* has received much publicity, from interviews with the author on CNN, public television stations, national radio shows, and local news media, to the creation of a conference at Stanford investigating the possibilities of school change. During that time, Pope has addressed approximately 12,000 people who are primarily attracted, she says, to both the substantive topic and the readable style of the book. When it comes to hatching conspiracies, *Doing School* seems good enough.

Pope, and in a different way, Saldaña, have been able to entice members of the public into dialogues about meaning, about the nature of educational virtue, connecting that philosophical concern to features of the debilitating sociopolitical matrix in which young people live their lives. Appealing to a wide audience that apparently includes sympathetic "outsiders," they seem to have generated the kind of public discussion that cuts through the miasma of the political spectacle.

They have accomplished this, I believe, by effectively calling into form the particulars of human life, thereby opening up their readers and viewers to the multiplicities of experience in the lives of young people. But, to return to Iser's (1974) notion of the implied reader, there is always the corresponding responsibility of the percipient of the work to assert herself in the actualization of its potential. Conspiracy is – to repeat – a dialogue, not a monologue.

Again, when particulars are called into form by an artist, they can come to mean more than they originally meant in the so-called "real world" outside the work of art. But after reconstructing the meaning contained in the personal vision of the artist, the vigilant percipient may assert her own influence over the work. Sensing a pull toward a closed, formal meaning may produce a healthy skepticism of the work, and a desire to dismantle it. Finding her own voice as interpreter and critic, the percipient may, I mean, interrupt the illusion of the work. Becoming what Belsey (1980) would call a *revolutionary reader*, she moves beyond the role of textual consumer to speak back to the work, to assign her own meanings to it. No longer is it just "reality" that means more than it originally meant. By dismantling the work, and transporting it into her own experiential landscape, the percipient makes it mean something different than it meant to the artist.

This means, of course, that the artist has lost a degree of control over the work. Sometimes the loss is complete, the artist's original vision vandalized. Indeed, Marcuse (1964), Said (1993), and others remind us that, throughout history, once-radical artworks have been co-opted and tamed by conservative cultural forces for their own purposes. All texts are, of course, vulnerable to an audience free to engage in that which Stuart Hall (1980) characterizes as an *oppositional reading*, one that rejects what a *preferred* reading accepts. In this kind of reading from an oppositional ideological ground, hopes for a spectacle-confounding, conspiratorial engagement are dashed.

Because an artistic engagement depends on the *twin* responsibilities of the artist and the viewer, no matter how potent the pre-structuring of the artwork, the artist's reach is limited. Or as Herbert Read (1966) wrote:

> The eye is thoroughly corrupted by our knowledge of traditional modes of representation, and all the artist can do is to struggle against the schema and bring it a little nearer to the eye's experience.
>
> (1966, p. 71)

I hope that arts-based researchers will never abandon that struggle. Nor, having produced our broadly accessible work, should we fear relinquishing control of it to the public. For this is, I believe, a profound and necessary gesture of epistemological generosity wherein a deeply committed arts-based educational researcher, abandoning the monovocal text out of faith in the social imagination, invites others to engage in a truly dialogical conversation about educational possibilities.

This invitation represents a refusal to reach toward indoctrination, and is born of an understanding that as artists and arts-based researchers we can never, strictly speaking, change minds. We must believe that people, within genuine dialogue, change their own minds. So instead we move to *artfully* coax them into collaborative interrogations of stale, tired, taken-for granted facets of the educational scene.

It is, I believe, precisely our humble stance, our speaking in tentative tones, our refusing to parade around in the uniform of a master narrator, that justifies our projects of arts-based research. Wayne Booth (1961) made the point in writing about the rhetoric of fiction. "I am not," he wrote, "primarily interested in didactic fiction, fiction used for propaganda or instruction. My subject is the technique of non-didactic fiction, viewed as the art of communicating with readers" (p. 1). And we too refuse to advance our small, inviting, carefully observed portraits of school people from a stance of omniscience. Nor do we, in self-defeat, attempt to erase ourselves from our works, refuse to inscribe in them our educational visions, abandon our quests.

In our efforts to create history-making works of arts-based research, we continue to work toward a public expression of a personal *point of view*, even as we remain observers who, while committed, are open to the world. Convinced that a conspiracy must play itself out in its own dialogical space, may we arts-based researchers ask the trenchant questions rather than provide the easy answers, with no desire to replace a master narrative with a totalizing alternative, let alone one that is preconceived.

## Challenges and Possibilities

Of course, there are considerable challenges to what may seem like a grandiose, even quixotic, vision of an arts-based educational research community that has succeeded in cutting through the educational spectacle on behalf of genuine educational reform. Engaged in research that is not only (a) arts-based or (b) emancipatory-minded, but (a) *plus* (b), we are swimming against the current of traditional methodological orthodoxy now reinforced, in a fit of political nostalgia, by federal policy-makers. We are also working under the increasing weight of the corporate university, wherein those members of the professoriate who secure extramural grant monies to replace dwindling public revenues for higher education are rewarded with enhanced professional status. We are pushing against our own perceived lack of talent for crafting meaningful works of arts-based research, and against an academic culture that refuses to support the fostering of those talents in the next generation of educational researchers. We are choosing to ignore those, often otherwise enlightened, members of our own educational community who would suggest that we leave the generation of conspiracies to professional artists who are not educationists. And, perhaps most difficult, we are attempting to cut through a seemingly impenetrable, commodified popular culture that is antagonistic toward the thoughtful, challenging, non-kitschy, inexpensively produced artifacts, whether as films, novels, short stories, poems, television programs, or theater.

How can we keep hope alive in the midst of these challenges?

In his book, *Changing Minds*, Howard Gardner (2004) posits a spectrum of mind-altering creativity with two poles. Located at one end, Capital C change is the result of the capital C creativity of capital C change agents. Gardner's examples from the arts and sciences, and fields of public policy, include historical figures such as Einstein, Picasso, de Gaulle, Freud, and the like. At the other pole are the "teachers, parents, and storekeepers who are satisfied with 'lowercase mind change,' changing the mental representations of those for whom they have [direct] responsibility" (Gardner, 2004, p. 132). But Gardner credits his colleague Csikszentmihaly with suggesting (in Feldman et al., 1994) that while "most of us cannot hope to effect big C creativity, we might at least expect to be 'middle C' creators" (Gardner, 2004, p. 132). Understanding that we need not necessarily match the high art of the masters in order to make history might reduce the levels of performance anxiety of some arts-based researchers.

We might also eschew the "Great Man" model of capital C change in order to avoid the isolation of those geniuses who single-handedly turn history on its head, in favor of mutual support afforded within a collectivity of artists. Recall, for example, the politically committed American artists of the 1930s, the novelists, playwrights, cartoonists, photographers, and painters whose work, as Edelman (1995, p. 108) points out, "made poverty vivid for Americans and made them feel its miseries, so that public welfare came to be categorized by most of the public as a justifiable aid to the needy rather than a drain on the treasury."

The work of these artists served to question the prevailing cultural narrative and helped make possible the policy initiatives of the New Deal. Might individual arts-based researchers, each pursuing her own personal desires for the expansion of the public space through her own chosen art form, coalesce to interrogate the entrenched master narrative of our own era? And might we be joined by qualitative researchers of other genres, even social scientists, whose work, now similarly disparaged, has included, ever since its inception, elements of artistry?

Collaborative and group efforts have also been, since the 1980s, the modus operandi of many activist artists. And for those of us without sizable grant funds, the history of activist art may offer clues for feasibly penetrating the popular culture. While sometimes prone to sensationalistic excesses, these artists have nevertheless moved their work, including applied theater, exhibitions, installations, and media events, onto public sites (Felshin, 1995, p. 10). Some activist artists have focused on the creating of visual images designed for consumption by the mass media. More successful, in my estimation, have been those who have targeted specific constituencies within the public, often collaborating with members of marginalized communities. Most recently, activist artists have exploited the possibilities within the electronic media.

Finally, most encouraging is surely the knowledge that our work has, indeed, already begun. Let those apologists for the master narrative feel the need to clutch their tightly sealed version of educational history closer to their bosoms. For there are now, in the once politically subdued and artistically disinclined academic research community, those who would challenge their history. They include Pope, Saldaña, and a growing number of other socially engaged and epistemologically humble qualitative researchers, some of whom are found in this collection. The aim of their – of our – continuing quest is to politely but powerfully, that is to say, *artfully*, change the conversation, to persuade those to whom history and public policy rightfully belong to resist the "usual kind of picture" in favor of one that, in touching the world of education as it is, makes one wonder about what it should and can become.

## Editors' Postscript

Critical arts-based educational research explicitly seeks the remaking of public and educational spaces by exposing the implicit forces at work in society that intentionally seek to repress individuated thinking to maintain and expand their own influence (Foucault, 1966/1970, 1977/1995; Freire, 1970). Educator Susan Finley eloquently calls for forms of ABER that explore the "notion of possibility, the what might be" in order to establish "a research tradition that is postcolonial, pluralistic, ethical, and transformative in positive ways" (Finley, 2018, p. 561).

Research is more than a process of looking again (re-search), it is a process of struggling to think anew: to think what has not been thought; to feel what was present but never consciously felt. Thus, the standards of traditional empirical research (validity, reliability, and generalizability) need to be reconsidered. A new conception of research may need to be born that is incommensurable with early forms of qualitative research and even early forms of ABER (St. Pierre, 2024). However, with Elliot Eisner, Barone has continued a quest for forms of arts-based research, grounded in the praxis of education, that operate in the liminal edges of empirical inquiry, rather than advocating for a philosophically different conception of science that rejects outright the paradigm of traditional qualitative empirical research (Barone & Eisner, 2012).

## References

Abbs, P. (2003). *Against the flow: Education, the arts, and postmodern culture*. RoutledgeFalmer.

Apple, M., & Teitelbaum, K. (1986). Are teachers losing control of their skills and curriculum? *Journal of Curriculum Studies*, *18*(2), 177–184. https://doi.org/10.1080/0022027860180207

Barone, T. (2000). *Aesthetics, politics, and educational inquiry: Essays and examples*. Peter Lang.

Barone, T., & Eisner, E. W. (2012). *Arts based research*. SAGE.

Becker, C. (1994). Introduction: Presenting the problem. In C. Becker (Ed.), *The subversive imagination: Artists, society, and social responsibility*. Routledge.

Belsey, C. (1980). *Critical practice*. Methuen.

Booth, W. (1961). *The rhetoric of fiction*. University of Chicago Press.

Denzin, N., & Lincoln, Y. (2000). Introduction: The discipline and practice of qualitative research. In N. Denzin & Y. Lincoln (Eds.), *Handbook of qualitative research* (2nd ed.). SAGE.

Dewey, J. (1927/1954). *The public and its problems*. Swallow Press/Ohio University Press.

Dewey, J. (1934/1958). *Art as experience*. Capricorn Books.

Edelman, M. (1985). *The symbolic uses of politics*. University of Illinois Press.

Edelman, M. (1988). *Constructing the political spectacle*. University of Chicago Press.

Edelman, M. (1995). *From art to politics: How artistic creations shape political conceptions*. University of Chicago Press.
Feldman, D., Csikszentmihaly, M., & Gardner, H. (1994). *Changing the world*. Praeger.
Felshin, N. (1995). *But is it art? The spirit of art as activism*. Bay Press.
Finley, M. (2000). *Street rat*. Greenroom Press, University of Detroit Mercy.
Finley, S. (2018). Critical arts-based inquiry: Performances of resistance politics. In N. K. Denzin & Y. S. Lincoln (Eds.), *The SAGE handbook of qualitative research* (5th ed., pp. 561–575). SAGE.
Finley, S., & Finley, M. (1999). Sp'ange: A research story. *Qualitative Inquiry*, 9(2), 254–267. https://doi.org/10.1177/107780049900500302
Foucault, M. (1970). *The order of things: An archaeology of the human sciences*. Pantheon. (Original work published 1966).
Foucault, M. (1995). *Discipline and punish: The birth of the prison*. Vintage Books. (Original work published 1977).
Freire, P. (1970). *Pedagogy of the oppressed* (M. B. Ramos, Trans.). Continuum.
Gardner, H. (2004). *Changing minds*. Harvard Business School Press.
Goodman, N. (1968). *Languages of art*. Bobbs-Merrill.
Greene, M. (1988). *The dialectic of freedom*. Teachers College Press.
Hall, S. (1980. Encoding/decoding. In S. Hall, D. Hobson. A. Lowe, & P. Willis (Eds.), *Culture, media, language: Working papers in cultural studies, 1972–1979* (pp. 128–138). Hutchinson.
hooks, b. (1994). *Outlaw culture: Resisting representations*. Routledge.
Iser, W. (1974). *The implied reader*. Johns Hopkins University Press.
Jacoby, R. (1987). *The last intellectuals: American culture in the age of academe*. Basic Books.
Lincoln, Y. S., & Denzin, N. K. (2003). The revolution in presentation. In Y. S. Lincoln & N. Denzin (Eds.), *Turning points in qualitative research*. AltaMira Press.
Lyotard, J.-F. (1979). *The postmodern condition* (G. Bennington & B. Massumi, Trans.). Manchester University Press.
Males, M. (1999). *Framing youth*. Common Courage Press.
Marcuse, H. (1964/1991). *One dimensional man*. Beacon Press.
Nelson, J. (1987). *Postmodern meaning of politics*. Paper presented at American Political Science Association, annual meeting.
Pope, D. C. (2001). *Doing school: How we are creating a generation of stressed out, materialistic, and miseducated students*. Yale University Press.
Read, H. (1966). *Art and alienation*. Schocken Books.
Rose, L. C., & Gallup, A. M. (2004). The 36th annual Phi delta Kappa/Gallup Poll of the public's attitudes toward the public schools. *Phi Delta Kappan*, *86*(1), 41–58. https://doi.org/10.1177/003172170408600108
Said, E. (1993). *Culture and imperialism*. Knopf.
Saldaña, J., Finley, S., & Finley, M. (2005). Street rat. In J. Saldaña (Ed.), *Ethnodrama*. AltaMira Press.
Sartre, J.-P. (1988). *What is literature? and other essays*. Harvard University Press.
Schneider, A., & Ingram, H. (1997). *Policy design for democracy*. University of Kansas Press.
Smith, M. L. (2004). *Political spectacle and the fate of American schools*. RoutledgeFalmer.
Stone, R. (1988). The reason for stories: Toward a moral fiction. *Harper's*, 276(1657), 71–78.
St. Pierre, E. A. (2024). A primer for post qualitative inquiry. *Qualitative Research in Psychology*, *22*(3), 571–595. https://doi.org/10.1080/14780887.2024.2347579

Chapter 3

# Between Poetry and Anthropology

## Searching for Languages of Home

*Ruth Behar*

As a teenage girl growing up in New York, I wrote many poems. I wrote while staring at the moon from the bedroom in Queens that I shared with my younger brother. I had a pretty good view of the moon – our apartment was on the ninth floor of a brick building whose elevator only stopped on odd-numbered floors. We were immigrants from Cuba and my father told us that we ought to feel lucky to live on an odd-numbered floor. If you were a tenant living on an even-numbered floor, you had to get off a floor above or a floor below and take the creepy, hidden stairs either up or down to your apartment. But I tried not to think too much about the everyday circumstances of our lives. My poems tended to be abstract ruminations on the passage of time and the inevitable decay of things. I spent several weeks writing a poem about the cheap carnations that wilted too soon in the vase on our glass and chrome dining-room table. At the time I also loved drama and fiction, and was very drawn to philosophy, especially the Spanish philosopher Miguel de Unamuno's (1913) notion of the tragic sense of life. I had an absolutely huge admiration for Simone de Beauvoir, who it seemed to me could do everything – be a philosopher as well as a writer, and a smart, beautiful, and well-traveled woman. I didn't know in those years that this brilliant person I put on a pedestal suffered from truly wretched spells of depression, occasioned by an incessant lack of self-confidence that was aggravated in her adult life by her beloved Jean-Paul Sartre's various infidelities. At home, I didn't receive much encouragement for my poetic and intellectual daydreams. My mother and father worried that I was too studious, that I spent too much time alone with my books. They were both fun-loving people and on weekends they liked to splash a lot of cologne and perfume on themselves and go out to dinner with their Cuban friends and catch a movie or go dance salsa. Both had gotten as far as high school in Cuba, and they thought that was more than sufficient education for me, especially given the fact that I was a girl. My father had dreamed of becoming an architect, but his father forced him to work with him peddling blankets in Havana, so he went to night school and studied the only thing he could, which was accounting. The accounting degree served him well because he was able to find a job in New York City in a belt and handbag company, but he despised the work and always came home in a bitter mood. I know that he held a lifelong grudge against his father for having broken the wings of his ambition. But when I announced that I'd been accepted at various universities and intended to leave home to further my education, my father became furious and refused to let me go. He felt that I was betraying him and my mother by wanting to leave home. Even though it was the 1970s and the heyday of the feminist movement, he still thought like a man who'd come of age in Cuba in the 1950s and he declared that it wasn't proper for a girl to live anywhere but in her parents' house until it was time for her to be married. Somehow, after shedding many tears

DOI: 10.4324/9781003412892-3

at the glass and chrome dinner table, I got my way. I might have surrendered my will to my father had it not been for my high-school Spanish teacher, Mercedes Rodríguez, who was also from Cuba, and vigorously defended my desire to advance my education. I think she was living, vicariously through me, what she wished for her daughter, because her daughter, who was my age, had chosen to stay home and not study any further.

So I went off to college hoping to become a poet, or a philosopher-writer of some sort. But I continued to worry about having abandoned my family in New York, though I'd only gone as far as Connecticut. I missed home, missed it more than I dared admit, and was distressed about the economic burden that my education was placing on my parents, even with the scholarship I'd received. Before my first year of college was up, I'd arranged to graduate a year early through a combination of Advanced Placement tests, summer courses, and independent study. Being in a rush to get through school, the poems and stories I wrote were produced all too hurriedly. I was impatient, I wanted, as I say about myself in one of my recent prose poems, to rush my poems out into the street like peddlers who are anxious to be rid of their wares. "How quickly I want the poems to be written! How quickly I want to close the door in their faces! I write with a gun at my temple, I write like a prisoner" (Behar, 2001a, p. 23). Not surprisingly, the teachers I came into contact with in college failed to offer praise, or even just a dab of encouragement for my hasty poems and stories, and I took that to mean that I didn't have talent, didn't have the gift for writing.

There was one teacher, in particular, a philosopher by training who'd imbibed wisdom directly from one of the greatest minds of the twentieth century. And she also wrote poetry. Initially, she advocated for me, but I disappointed her when I did poorly on an important test graded by outside examiners. I hadn't studied for the test because I was too busy directing a production of García Lorca's play, *The House of Bernarda Alba* (1936/1945). I had expected to gain her admiration for putting Art above humdrum academic work. Instead, my favorite professor shunned me, just at the moment when I most needed her support. How I longed for even the most feeble words of recognition from her, a few whispered words of faith in my promise. But those words never came. And that was how I ended up seeking refuge in anthropology – the discipline which attracts all those who are either homesick or homeless, which these days often amounts to much the same thing.

When I began to write poetry again, I was an adult woman with a career, a child, a car, a mortgage, and a frequent flyer account. The second floor of my house sagged from the weight of all the books I'd read and the numerous ones I'd meant to read over the years. I'd published my own books, and I'd won fellowships. My name appeared in footnotes in other people's writing. Surely I was over the sadness of having left poetry behind for anthropology. But the sadness was still there, and it emerged unexpectedly in a poem I consider to be a kind of underside to my curriculum vitae. I called it "Obedient student":

> I was such an obedient student that when my teachers told me I wouldn't make a good poet, I stopped writing. I adored words more than anything else in the world and preferred to cut out my tongue than to insult the Muses with my sickly and impoverished language. That is why these poems are so timid: like the invalid who rises from her bed after a long convalescence and walks embracing the walls.
>
> (Behar, 1997/2001b, p. 4)

I did try hard to conform to the norms of academic writing in anthropology, and my dedication brought results. I got all the rewards that most people seek in an academic career. I was, after all, an obedient student. But the dreams of our youth never leave us. As the years passed, my writing in anthropology became haunted by my longing for poetry. Finally, I came back to poetry, to that intimate voice that had gone into exile, but the poems I wrote *were* timid. They revealed the uncertainty, the humility, the shame I'd come to feel about my abilities as a poet. Still, I wrote poetry anyway, because I needed poetry; it was the only way I could speak while I was restoring my ties with Cuba as a returning child-immigrant and as an anthropologist who couldn't think about her lost homeland as a field site. Overcome with emotions that were so powerful that they produced panic attacks, I discovered a voice etched with longing and regret in poems I wrote in English and translated into Spanish and published in Cuba. Many of these poems found a home in the handmade books of Ediciones Vigía, an artisanal publishing house in the city of Matanzas, where my family has roots.

I consider myself fortunate to have been able to acquire another life, a parallel life in Cuba. I've been reborn there as a poet. I can be a poet in Cuba because I left too young to be wounded by teachers who did not love me.

If this statement sounds rather too pained, I can't help wondering just how much pain lies buried unspeakably within the profession that takes as its subject matter the search for languages of home. Naturally, I don't want to over-generalize from my experience but as I reflect on the fraught relationship between poetry and anthropology in my own life, I've come to see that I am not the only anthropologist who has had frustrated, or at least hampered, poetry ambitions.

A special issue on "Poetry and anthropology," published in the journal *Dialectical Anthropology* in 1986 and edited by Stanley Diamond, anthropologist and poet, was framed by two telling epigraphs, both written in 1926. The first, by Franz Boas, the German-Jewish father of American anthropology, states: "I'd rather have written a good poem than all the books I'd ever written – to say nothing of a movement in a symphony." The second, by the American-Jewish poet and cultural linguist Edward Sapir, is part of a letter addressed to his friend, Ruth Benedict, a cultural anthropologist whose lyrical books, *Patterns of Culture* and *Chrysanthemum and the Sword*, are classical texts in anthropology. Sapir writes to Benedict, "It is no secret between us that I look upon your poems as infinitely more important than anything, no matter how brilliant, you are fated to contribute to anthropology" (as cited in Diamond, 1986).

The volume includes the poems of Ruth Benedict, the lone woman represented, as well as poems by various male anthropologists. Much as I hate to say it, the poems don't shine; they range from acceptable to dismal. For example, Benedict's three-stanza poem about her grandmother, entitled "Of graves," with its all-too-basic rhymes, describes her elder's carefree relationship to death in this way: "The rabbit nibbled at the grass/Will someday cover me." The closing stanza reads: "And days I shiver swift and strange/This still is what I see:/Sunlight and rabbit in the grass/And peace possesses me" (Benedict, 1986, p. 169). After reading this poem and others equally cloying, I, for one, have to disagree with Edward Sapir. I think we have to be very glad that Ruth Benedict wrote her anthropology books. Their importance, and certainly their influence, have been far greater than her poems, which have mercifully fallen into oblivion.

Of course, I feel terrible saying this, because I'm denying to Ruth Benedict, now in *her* grave, the words of praise and recognition for her poetry that I so wanted for my own poetry when I was a student, words that, even now, as I hesitantly return to poetry, I hunger for. But the truth is that Ruth Benedict's poems are a less significant achievement, not because she lacked talent, but because her poems, largely written in the 1920s and early 1930s, were simply not given the same chance to grow and flourish as her anthropological writings. The more she focused her energies on anthropology, the more her poetry writing became a secondary and secret pursuit. At her death in 1948, Benedict left many unpublished poems, and those which she published, in prestigious journals like *Poetry* and *The Nation*, didn't carry her real name. They were published under the pseudonyms of Ruth Stanhope and Anne Singleton, in an effort to keep them hidden from the eyes of her academic colleagues, and especially from the eyes of her revered mentor, Papa Franz, who she feared would scoff at her flings with the Muse. But as it turns out, while Papa Franz was busy building anthropology into an intellectual edifice that could speak to the ruins of the past and the racisms of the present, he himself secretly wished he could say what it all meant in a good poem, or, alas, being soulfully German, in the movement of a symphony, rather than in so many hundreds of tedious anthropology papers.

What more is there to say, if even Boas, the Big Daddy of modern American anthropology, longed to be able to write *the* poem that could metonymically stand in for all the bottles of ink he spilled to craft persuasive academic prose that might legitimize an always questionable discipline? It's no accident that I, and other ethnographers like me who are drawn to poetry and the literary and visual arts more generally, continue to struggle with the same conundrum. We didn't invent the fraught relationship between poetry and anthropology. We inherited it as part of the family romance of our discipline.

Poetry – not just the literal writing of poems but also the larger desire to speak from a deeper part of the self, which is the goal of all artistic expression – is the thing that we, that is, those of us who are still living out the family romance, thirst for but feel we can't, or rather shouldn't, admit we desire. To long for poetry is to cast doubt on our commitment to maintaining the sobriety and respectability of anthropology within the bureaucracy of the university system. To long for poetry is to want to throw caution to the winds. To long for poetry is irresponsible. To long for poetry is to be immature, self-centered. To long for poetry is to risk losing it all – losing the academic departments that teach us how to travel to other places and not be ugly Americans, or lately, that teach us how to go home and see something strange there; it is to risk losing the grants that actually pay for us to go to those places and learn about others and ourselves by becoming temporary nomads; it is to risk losing the jobs that allow us eventually to settle down surrounded by native rugs, clay pots, inlaid wood tables, and bark paintings that we are certain are of much better quality than the second-rate stuff sold to the tourists; it is to risk losing the conferences that try to awaken us from our poetry daydreaming and remind us of all the real intellectual work remaining to be done. To long for poetry, under these circumstances, with all these adult responsibilities and obligations, and commitments weighing on us, is to turn our backs on the long-suffering discipline that has stood by us through thick and thin descriptions and given a higher purpose to our wanderings. Dare I say it? To long for poetry is to want to commit adultery.

Now, if we consider representations in Western literature and film, adultery isn't necessarily a bad thing. It's often seen as a necessary evil to bring a burst of oxygen to a suffocating marriage, or to break away toward a necessary freedom from a marriage that has been outgrown, or never been grown into. Yet there isn't a Western representation of adultery that lets an adulterer off the hook without paying some penance. As my *comadre* Esperanza in Mexico always says, "Todo se paga en esta vida." You pay for everything in this life. Take, for example, Jane Campion's movie, *The piano* (1993). Her willfully silent protagonist, Ada, communicates her poetic longings through her elusive piano playing. The piano has come with her from Scotland across the deep sea, and it symbolizes the vestige of home she has carried to colonial New Zealand. Her father has sold her – as girls around the world are sold into prostitution today – into a miserable arranged marriage. But Ada finds understanding and passion in the arms of a lover, Baines, a European gone native, complete with facial tattoos. However, in the process of creating a new life with Baines, she calls forth the jealous rage of her husband, who chops off the index finger of her right hand in a scene whose violence is excruciating to watch. After their escape, Baines fashions a metal finger for Ada, and he patiently supports her efforts to speak normally again. But Ada's body is forever marked by the price of her liberation, and her piano playing ceases to be haunting and becomes drab and ordinary.

The first time I saw this movie, the tears poured out of me in buckets. I've since seen it many times and taught it many times, and it still makes me cry. I'll be watching the movie, analyzing it carefully and critically taking apart the stereotyped representations of the Maori, so I'll be ready to talk to my anthropology students about it the next day, and then it happens, the scene I know is coming ... Now, now ... Oh, God, it is so terrible. The scene is too perfect: the relentlessness of the piano music, the rage of the husband, his picking up the ax, the way he rushes to the house and shoves the delicate, birdlike, mute Ada, the way he drags her out to the chopping block and lays her pretty hand down flat and the way he yells at her to declare whom she loves and the way he lets the ax fall and the blood starts to flow and the way Ada crumples to the ground in the Victorian full skirt, the way she crumples, as if the air, the breath of life had gone out of her. I can't help myself: I cry, I cry as if my own finger had been chopped off, I believe that it is I who am Ada. I, too, will be punished if I dare surrender to such an immense passion ....

Now, obviously, the consequences are not going to be so dire for those of us who stray from anthropology to have a love affair with poetry. At least I hope not! And there are many ways to carry on an affair. I think Ruth Benedict provided a model that many of us, and I include myself, have followed. The poetic legacy she left us, I believe, is not in the words she wrote in verse and called poems and published under an alias, but in the poetry that she spun through her anthropology, the poetic sensibility that she brought to her scholarship and made inseparable from it. There is a certain pathos about this, to be sure. She didn't let the affair get out of hand. She kept it under wraps. She brought Poetry home and dressed it as something else, so that she could stay loyal to Anthropology. This was good for anthropology, very good for anthropology. But what was good for anthropology was not so good for Ruth Benedict's ambitions as a poet.

We could sit around, allowing ourselves to become depressed about Benedict's unrealized potential, but I think there's a positive lesson to take from this history. The lesson is simple and obvious: poetry is bigger than the poem. Poetry is much bigger than the poem. There is poetry to be found in every aspect of our lives. There is poetry to be found in all human endeavors to understand the world. The thing is to know how to see the poetry, how to hear the poetry, how to feel the poetry. More often, the thing is just to remember that it's there. In springtime in Michigan, which is always late and always too brief, I'm grateful for that sign a neighbor I don't know always puts up on Seventh Street, which is one of the main arteries through the town. "Slow down and smell the flowers," it says, and I do. I open my windows and bring my driving to a crawl and let the lilacs inside and dare the drivers behind me to honk – which they don't because they're way too polite in Michigan.

So I write my poems while doing my anthropology, just as Benedict did, and fortunately, I can do so openly. We now have a Society for Humanistic Anthropology that encourages the writing of poetry, fiction, and creative nonfiction by anthropologists. The Society has a magazine that publishes works in these genres and awards yearly prizes for the best works. All this is very positive, and no doubt in the future we'll have a larger group of anthropologists who are equally strong poets and writers. But I know that the more important work I'm doing right now is the effort I'm making to craft a poetic anthropology. After all, we have a lot of poetic poets out there, but tell me, how many poetic anthropologists do you know? Anthropology needs its poetic anthropologists. And the funny thing is that most anthropologists don't know that. Or don't want to know that.

What does it mean to be a poetic anthropologist? I can tell you what it has meant for me. It has meant allowing myself to experience the emotionally wrenching ways in which we attain knowledge of others and ourselves. In my ethnographic writing, I've made the case that the most charged intellectual insights occur precisely when one's ethnographic work and one's life crash into each other in a head-on collision, even though every effort has been made to keep them running smoothly in their own lanes.

One of the first such collisions I experienced was when I found myself doing research on attitudes toward death in rural Spain with people I'd known for years and come to love, while at the very same moment, my dearly beloved grandfather was dying of cancer in Miami Beach. The conflict between these two loves – the love for a soft-spoken grandfather whose hand I remembered holding in Cuba and despaired of losing forever, and the love for the strangers who'd let me become part of their lives – proved excruciating. I wanted to be in two places at once, and I couldn't be. I chose to be in Spain because my family thought it best for things to go on as normally as possible, so that my grandfather wouldn't fear his death. But then, when my grandfather died before I could return, I hated myself. It was the loving kindness of strangers in Spain that gave me the hope of attaining some self-forgiveness. Eventually, I was able to honor them and my grandfather in a piece of writing that brought them both together, though in real life, they inhabited worlds that were completely separate. That writing, a long essay called "Death and memory" (Behar, 1991), was a double ethnography. It was an ethnography of the way death was being commodified in a small, fiercely Catholic village in northern Spain and the pain this was causing people, and it was an ethnography of how the anthropologist who was making the observation had become so detached from her own Jewish roots that she didn't know how to mourn the loss of her grandfather.

After Spain, I spent a considerable amount of time in Mexico in the mid-1980s and early 1990s. It was there that I took the principle of head-on collision between ethnography and life in a different direction, by engaging in an extensive dialogue with Esperanza Hernández, a woman who couldn't be more unlike me, a street peddler, a woman of Indian heritage, an aggressive, self-assured single mother who'd survived both child abuse and domestic abuse and found strength in the veneration of the spirit of Pancho Villa. Esperanza's story became the foundation for my book *Translated Woman*, a feminist ethnography, in which I explored the conjuncture between her life and mine. What kind of observer was I? What was I willing to see and not see in her life? Why was she telling me her story? How would her story travel across the border, and what would it mean in the US academy? All these questions formed the framework for the account of our relationship, which produced new knowledge about the struggles and yearnings of a working-class Mexican woman. While very rooted in the particular life of one woman, this ethnography traveled well beyond its origins; it has been read by Latino and Latina students trying to understand the lives of their Latin American mothers, as well as by women in prison interrogating the violence in their lives, as Esperanza interrogated it in hers, so they, too, can move forward through empowered forms of storylistening and storytelling.

Most recently, I've turned to documentary filmmaking to try to make sense of my own unusual heritage as a Cuban Jew and to learn from others of the same background how they think about their identity. In my film, *Adio Kerida/Goodbye Dear Love* (Behar, 2002), I create a forum for Cuban Jews on and off the island to speak about what their heritage means to them. Although political and economic differences separate these Cuban Jews and are made evident in the film, a common search for history and memory unites them. The film becomes an imaginary homeland, a space to envision the reconciliation that has yet to happen fully in reality. It is fascinating to me that the character that Jewish Cubans on the island like the best is my father, who openly declares in the film that he has no wish to return to Cuba and doesn't care what Fidel Castro thinks about anything because he lives in the United States. Precisely because he's so genuine and so funny in a typically Cuban manner in the way he says what he feels, he appeals to Cubans on the island because they feel he's so much like them. In turn, my father, in watching the film, has been impressed by the struggles of the Cuban Jews on the island to maintain their faith and traditions in the midst of considerable hardship and isolation. Ethnographically speaking, the film allows both sides to recognize each other's humanity, which is always the first step toward the making of community.

These, in brief, are some of the ways I've tried to enact and embody poetry within anthropology during the last 20 years. If I had to say what is the thread that ties together these disparate ethnographic pursuits, it's the search, the unceasing search for connection across borders of nationality, ethnicity, class, religion, and ideology. And the search, the unceasing search, for languages of description and analysis that have not grown wooden, languages where the sap still flows. There are words I won't use in my writing, even though the concepts they were meant to express are still of great value. Words, for example, like hegemony and habitus, have been sucked dry by thoughtless overuse. But the bigger issue is that I often feel ill at ease in the presence of academic code languages, otherwise known as jargon. Believe me, I know the jargon, I could use it if I wanted to, but I choose not to, try not to.

For me, this is a moral and political decision. It comes from being a minority scholar, a Latina scholar, from coming to the academy as an outsider, without a sense of entitlement. Not that I had the words to articulate this position when I was a graduate student. I think my real education took place after I was done with my Ph.D. in anthropology. It was at this point, as I began teaching, that I connected what I'd learned in the academy with the world of Latina letters and philosophy, which initially developed beyond the academy because it was viewed as so radical. Gloria Anzaldúa, the Chicana theorist, poet, writer, and philosopher, was a key leader in the Latina movement for self-recognition. I know that she had a major impact on my rethinking. How I wish I didn't have to speak of her in the past tense. Gloria passed away recently, too young, and too soon. Gloria more than anyone understood the vitality and creativity of mixtures, of conjunctures, of crossroads. Her book, *Borderlands/La Frontera* (1999), brought into being a genre that blended poetry and prose, theory and family stories, manifesto and analysis, myth and history, English and Spanish that was left deliberately untranslated because she felt it was time for non-Spanish speakers to meet us Latinas and Latinos at least halfway. Gloria always worked on the edge of the academy; she was constantly on the verge of finishing her

Ph.D. at U.C.-Santa Cruz. But she struggled with language. She didn't want to use fancy language that would create a new borderland between herself and the Latino community. She advocated for other Latinas to find methods of analysis and research that would not alienate them from their histories and families. I was one of the Latinas who took up her call. Thanks to her example, as well as her gentle encouragement, I found the courage to write poetically, as I'd wanted to in college, but hadn't been able to. She gave me back not only poetry, but philosophy. She gave me back the identity I wanted to claim and wasn't sure I could, telling me that there was no contradiction in being Latina and Jewish. She was the loving teacher I'd been looking for, and I only wish I'd thanked her properly while she was alive.

No doubt, you might want to ask me, as students often have, whether I get a lot of flak for doing what I do, writing the way I write. Well, gratefully, I have my fans, and somehow I've managed to find a niche in anthropology and in the academy. It's amazing the range of things I get asked to speak about as a broken-hearted anthropologist. Lately, I've been writing a lot of forewords to other people's books – about autobiographical writing across the disciplines, about women on the verge of home, about wounded ethnographers. I think some sea changes are taking place. It's been shocking to me lately to have two male colleagues of mine at Michigan, who are known respectively for their rigorous work in demographic and linguistic anthropology, pass along manuscripts for me to read that are intensely personal and poetic accounts of the fieldwork stories they never told.

All this is immensely reassuring and does give me some confidence that what I'm doing isn't totally idiosyncratic, but I'd be lying if I didn't tell you that I also get plenty of flak. Serious flak. Flak that really hurts. Because flak hurts more when you've put yourself on the line. Let me share one story that I'm not even sure how to tell. After reading the special issue of *Dialectical Anthropology* on "Poetry and Anthropology" from two decades ago, I thought I'd look to see what they've published lately and, to my surprise, I came across a critical article that included a harsh reading of one of the essays in my book *The Vulnerable Observer* (Behar, 1996). The article (Ryang, 2000) was published in 2000, and no one had ever told me about it. What stunned me, and shouldn't have, was the castigating voice of our profession's gatekeepers, who aren't necessarily the old fogeys, but the young untenured professors made uncomfortable by the artistic flirtations of some of their elders. The writer expressed her wariness about work that is autobiographic and poetic and written in pretty language, because she feels it takes us away from our true mission – to raise up and to make known the voice of the Other. The voice of the People. I could see where she was coming from, because I've heard a million versions of this debate – that auto-ethnography is all about navel-gazing and fails to lift up the People. For me, this rhetoric always smacks of paternal notions of saving the Other because the Other cannot save himself or herself, and personally, very personally, I think it's an insult to the intelligence and independence and creativity of the people who are kind enough to let us into their lives. Anthropologists, though they detached themselves long ago from the well-meaning salvation enterprises of colonial missionaries, have still kept a strong, righteous streak. Criticism coming from that angle I could handle. From my perspective, anyway, I was still in the ring.

But the punch I wasn't prepared for was when she compared my efforts to write personally with those of Anne Frank and concluded that my texts didn't have the same urgency, and that my life wasn't as interesting as Frank's life. Of course, I had to agree with her on both fronts, but if every text we write has to measure up to Anne Frank's diary of a death foretold, I don't think most of us are going to be in the running for very long. This comparison, I have to say, struck me as absurd, as cruel to history. I tried to get angry, but I felt overwhelmed by sadness. I wanted to reply, but all that came was silence, a deathly silence. The writer, it was clear, meant to be earnest. She seems to be someone at the start of her career. It is well known that young scholars often try to make their mark by stabbing their predecessors in the heart and drawing blood. And I'll tell you, she succeeded. She succeeded.

You might want to know, because people always ask, is it necessary to have tenure to write the way you do? Some flak is to be expected, after all, but basically, what you're thinking is, she gets away with it. But to do what I do without tenure? Surely it isn't possible. Could a lowly student embark on a similar path?

The answer is no, you don't have to have tenure, and yes, you can do what I do, and you will do it, if you need to. You will reach a point, as I did, where there is no choice but to work from your poetic self. For me to work in any other way would be like pulling teeth. I can't do it. A day may come when I will be formally dismissed from the profession – excommunicated, you might say, or perhaps *desterrada*, deterritorialized, cast into exile. But until then, I will do what I do in the name of anthropology, and create the conditions for others who want and need to do the same.

After many, many years spent in the field, as we like to say in anthropology, I now spend much more of my time in the classroom. Those of us who come to teaching with any degree except for an education degree get absolutely no training in pedagogy, but we are magically expected to know what to do in the classroom. I've had to confront a good deal of ambivalence about being a teacher, as well as a good deal of fear. I am always afraid that I will break the transparent butterfly wings of my students, who grow younger and more delicate, it seems, with every passing year. The kind of teacher I am: too nice, because I'm absolutely terrified of causing harm. I know all too well, from my own life, that we are susceptible as students to the words of our teachers. So, as teachers, we need to be careful about our words. Nothing we say can be taken for granted.

I've developed a range of methods that I believe help to validate the role of the imagination in intellectual work. Every year I teach an undergraduate course about Cuba since the 1959 Revolution and examine both Cuban culture on the island and Cuban culture brought to the United States by Cuban immigrants. We read across the disciplines and consider a range of themes, including Cuban history, politics, race relations, the role of women, art, music, and Afro-Cuban religions. The course meets requirements at Michigan for courses focusing on race and ethnicity, and it also meets a writing requirement. The course is accompanied by a weekly film series and students are required to keep journals about the films. They write three papers that they're encouraged to draft and redraft. For their final project, they are given the option of writing a research paper or doing a creative project in any format they wish. The students almost always choose to do the creative project.

All the creative projects are presented in the final class during a four- to five-hour performance party complete with fresh tamales made by a local Salvadoran caterer. The last class is always a lively culmination to an intense semester of immersion in all things Cuban. The students love working on their final projects, and this love shows in their presentations. Last year I had two women students who were very moved by the stories of the *balseros*, the rafters who make the plunge into the sea and risk their lives to get to the United States. Their presentation consisted of building a life-size raft, before our eyes, using junked pieces of wood found at Home Depot, on which they painted an image of the Virgen de la Caridad, the patron saint of Cuba. This year I had a gay student from Peru who had fallen behind on schoolwork because of personal troubles and whom I feared wouldn't come to the last class. But he came and delighted us all, arriving cross-dressed in a tight gown and high-heeled platform shoes, beautifully impersonating the great Cuban diva Celia Cruz, who had just recently passed away. There were students who performed the work of Cuban poets, there were students who composed music inspired by Cuban rhythms, there were students who conducted interviews on what their peers think of Che Guevara; and there was a cigar-loving student who researched every aspect of cigar production in Cuba and made the rest of the students try their hand at rolling cigars. Students of Cuban origin in the class who'd never talked to their families about their heritage went home and discovered stories they needed to form their own identities.

On the graduate level, I teach a course each year on ethnographic writing. What began as a course for anthropology students interested in learning about creative ways to write their ethnographies has grown into an inter-disciplinary class that also attracts students in education, literature, history, creative writing, ethnic studies, nursing, and psychology, all of whom come to the seminar with concerns about the possibilities and limits of representing lived experience. All of them want to write more poetically and vividly, but they're not sure how far they can go. In the class we read poetry, fiction, everything from urban to feminist ethnographies, personal essays from the *New Yorker*. I give students writing assignments in the first few weeks to get them thinking about voice, place, and what kinds of observers they want to be. And then they do their own writing and we discuss it in workshop format in class. Ultimately, I hope the class gives students the courage to know what they know and speak what they think.

Two graduates of the class have recently defended their dissertations (Fosada, 2004: Lehrer, 2005), and they have both completed projects that were immensely brave and imaginative. Erica, whose Jewish family is of Polish origin, went to Poland, learned Polish, and studied the way the legacy of the Holocaust is being taken up by contemporary Polish people in Cracow, many of whom learn Hebrew and otherwise immerse themselves in things Jewish to seek reconciliation with their history. Her family thinks she's crazy for doing this, rather than doing something more Jewish herself, like learning Hebrew and going to Israel. Her dissertation is written as a series of moving vignettes that move between Jewish and Polish voices. In turn, Gisela, who is from Mexico and suffered sexual abuse as a young girl, chose to seek out a deeper understanding of masculinity by working in Cuba with gay men who sell sex to North American and European tourists. In addition to writing life stories of the men, placing side by side the contradictory views of the Cuban men and the sex tourists, she used video, often giving the men the camera to film themselves and each other. The result is an ethnographically rich portrait of the ways in which intersecting and conflicting desires come together in our globalized and highly unequal world. What impresses me about the work of both Erica and Gisela is how they released the poetry in their personal lives to move ethnography in new, more powerful directions, where what's at stake in the work is never just an intellectual exercise but knowledge that is essential, knowledge that you couldn't live without.

I am now at that stage in a teacher's life where I can learn as much from my students as they can learn from me. It's that stage where the students take your ideas and run with them a whole extra mile, a mile you're not sure you can run anymore. And maybe, though I wouldn't have expected it back when I was a student in search of a teacher who could love me, maybe that is the ultimate homecoming.

## Postscript

It's both exciting and a little embarrassing to see with what breathless energy I wrote about the fraught borderland between poetry and anthropology 20 years ago. The piece reads a bit like a manifesto. I guess that's not a terrible thing. But now that more anthropologists are concerned not just about *what* they write, but *how* they write, it may no longer seem necessary to be quite that fierce in the call for more creativity in our discipline. This may be so, yet let's not forget the long road some of us have walked to get to where we are today. At the time when I was writing, it was not easy to do creative writing and still be considered a serious anthropologist deserving of a position in the academy. The divide seemed immense and, as with Ruth Benedict, you felt the need to hide your poems, and make sure no one in anthropology knew you were playing with words instead of doing the important work of gathering data for social theories and cultural analysis. Fortunately, we seem to have moved beyond this stage of naivete in anthropology, as the vast numbers of books about ethnographic writing published in the last few years amply indicate. More and more anthropologists have literary agents and seek to write the kinds of creative nonfiction books that not only their colleagues but also the world will want to read. They may not all be writing poetry, but they are writing poetically, lyrically, with more heart than ever before. I think Ruth Benedict must be resting peacefully these days. Her journey wasn't for naught.

## References


Anzaldúa, G. (1999). *Borderlands/La Frontera* (2nd ed.). Aunt Lute Books.

Behar, R. (1991). Death and memory: From Santa María del Monte to Miami Beach. *Cultural Anthropology*, 6(3), 346–384. https://www.jstor.org/stable/656440

Behar, R. (1996). *The vulnerable observer: Anthropology that breaks your heart.* Beacon Press.

Behar, R. (2001a). Prisoner. In *Todo lo que guardé/Everything I kept: Poems by Ruth Behar* (p. 23). Ediciones Vigía.

Behar, R. (2001b). Obedient student. In *Todo lo que guardé/Everything I kept: Poems by Ruth Behar* (p. 4). Ediciones Vigía. (Original work published 1997).

Behar, R. (Writer/Director) (2002). *Adio kerida/Goodbye dear love* [Motion picture]. Women Make Movies.

Benedict, R. (1986). Of graves. *Dialectical Anthropology*, 11(2–4), 169. https://doi.org/10.1525/ahu.2007.32.2.145

Campion, J. (Writer/Director) (1993). *The piano* [Motion picture]. Miramax Films.

Diamond, S. (1986). Preface. *Dialectical Anthropology*, 11(2–4), 130.

Fosada, G. (2004). The exchange of sex for money in contemporary Cuba: Masculinity, ambiguity and love. Unpublished doctoral dissertation, University of Michigan.

García Lorca, F. (1945). *La casa de Bernarda Alba, drama de mujeres en los pueblos de España.* Editorial Losada. (Original work produced 1936).

Lehrer, E. (2005). "Shoah-business," "Holocaust culture," and the repair of the world in "post-Jewish" Poland: A quest for ethnography, empathy, and the ethnic self after genocide. Unpublished doctoral Ph.D. dissertation, University of Michigan.

Ryang, S. (2000). Ethnography or self-cultural anthropology? Reflections on writing about ourselves. *Dialectical Anthropology*, 25(3–4), 297–320.

de Unamuno, M. (1913). *Del sentimiento trágico de la vida*. Renacimiento.

Chapter 4

# Voices Lost and Found

## Using Found Poetry in Qualitative Research

*Kakali Bhattacharya*

During my dissertation study, I became increasingly vigilant of the multiple deconstructive arguments about voice and re-presentation from feminist, postcolonial, and postmodern perspectives. I acknowledged that the participants' voices are always mitigated through various academic filters, thus questioning our ability to really hear the participants. On the one hand, I identified with one of the purposes of qualitative research: to capture the experiences of the participants as told through their voices. On the other hand, how can those voices be really heard through/with/against the researcher's subjectivities and various processes of academic gatekeeping in peer-reviewed published spaces? I struggled with the purpose of data collection and re-presentation especially after I accepted that the participants' voices are always already partially or completely silenced in academic research. But the silencing of voices does not erase the everyday experiences and their effects on participants. Therefore, how should I negotiate voice and silence through the academic gaze that is on me, through the gaze that I put on my participants, and through the gaze that the participants put on me?

I looked toward re-presentations that blurred multiple genres of writing where the messiness of qualitative research was represented in the "findings" of research. I came across multiple poetic representations, one-act plays, and photo-elicitations. I attended some poetry readings and became familiar with a local political activist group in Athens, Georgia, who used found poetry to discuss issues of abortion, race relations, sexuality, and war. Drawn to the organic nature of juxtaposing participants' and researcher's dialogues especially in an insider–outsider researcher–researched relationship, thereby overtly acknowledging the researcher's subjectivities, I wanted the data re-presentation to be evocative. It cannot be assessed on merits of truth, accuracy, or holistic understanding of the participants' lives. It can only be re-presented as fragmented, contradictory testimonials of participants merging with my own, without any clear indication where the researcher's perspective begins and the perspective of the researched ends.

"*Small Small* Things" became a way for me to speak in multiple mitigated voices, of which two can be credited to graduate students from India who had been in the United States for less than six months during the timeframe of the study. Taking material from various parts of formal and informal conversations I had with the participants, I used the participants' words, our conversations, filtered through my subjectivities, and combined with the aesthetics of poetic re-presentation. Of course, such re-presentation is driven by my cognitive selection of issues of transnationalism, which at a rudimentary level, refers to the practices of migrants who live their lives across multiple nation-states if not in at least two nation-states. Consequently, I identified experiences that spoke of shuttling between familiar and

DOI: 10.4324/9781003412892-4

unfamiliar spaces where transnationals negotiate between multiple cultural values and expectations as they accommodate, resist, and re/author themselves. In writing about transnational experiences, I knew I was going to write about myself, my understanding of being in the middle, in constant motion, blurring lines between cultures and familiarity.

As I constructed the poem, I became aware of my complicated positioning as a transnational academic in a higher institution in the United States, trying to depict experiences of other transnationals. How do I negotiate my multiple contested loyalties between academic expectations, personal experiences of being a transnational, using de/colonizing frameworks that directly contest western academic ways of knowing, and participants' ways of knowing and understanding their experiences? Thus, the poem became a space for me to demonstrate these loyalties in their fractured forms while realizing that these loyalties will always be divided and pull me in multiple directions.

Strategically, while going through the text data, I selected phrases and ideas that appeared organic in their content and style. For example, the use of the term "*small small*" is indigenous to Indian transnationals and their ways of using the English language, as was the term "after some time." I kept many Hindi words in the poem, some without any explanation or translation, to depict to the reader(s) that the transnational voices and experiences are grounded in these organic emotions and identification that might not be universally understandable or transferable. So the reader(s) would have to be comfortable with the ambiguity, the unfamiliar, and draw on their familiar experiences to interact with the poem, much like the transnationals, shuttling between the familiar and unfamiliar. This poem also represents the contradictions of being a transnational. On the one hand, being away from a "home" culture, the participants crave something familiar in their "host" culture. On the other hand, the hybridized representation of cultural practices and symbols in the United States implores the participants to glorify various practices of their "home" culture, including religion.

I read the poem at a poetry reading where the participants were present to hear their fragmented voices in spoken words. At the end of the reading, both participants were in tears and stated that they were able to identify, remember, mourn, and personalize the poem to their experiences. Was I successful in capturing their voices? I don't really know. It was evocative and spoke to the participants in a way that was meaningful and real to them. Should that be the purpose of data collection and representation? Who are the intended audiences for research? Is it the researcher, academic circles, the participants, or all of the above? How do we come to negotiate which voices get heard and which silenced when considering a specific group or multiple groups of intended audience? When I imagined my primary audience to be the participants, my writing reflected the care and obligation I had toward them. While imagining an academic audience as a secondary audience, I struggled against being a "Third-World" broker for the United States academia who is tempted to exoticize the participants' experiences to consumable dishes of Indian curry. Thus, the only voice I can really "claim" is mine, re-presented through/with/against the contested voices of the participants, which inevitably leads to messy spaces of knowing and being known. These tensions are not easily resolved, but rather require sustained reflexivity and humility. As qualitative researchers, we must grapple with the complexities of representation, the politics of knowledge production, and our own complicity in systems of power. Arts-based approaches like found poetry offer generative tools for engaging with these challenges, not to arrive at tidy solutions, but to dwell in the productive discomfort of partial, contingent, and plural ways of knowing.

### The *small small* Things

Weekend fall breezes
remind me of autumn in India
even without wafting jasmines.
I match my *bindi* to my *salwar kameez;*
*sindur* red bangles bring out
the reddish pink *jhumkas*
dangling by my ears, eager to hear
puja drums, voices of Indian chatter
in a rented high school auditorium –
Desoto County Spring Valley Tigers.

Even when they are weekend festivals,
not on their actual auspicious dates,
even when they sing Bollywood songs,
not *bhajans*, but *antaksharis* during *pujas*,
holding on to these *small small* things
even when they are amplified, modified
not authentic as I remember,
they are still familiar.

Sometimes I don't like masked
Indian-ness with clothes, jewelry, cuisine,
all-you-can get buffet, for everything Indian.
Main course culture: side orders of religion
and socialization, generous helpings
of comparisons, gossips, and envy –
all in one weekend.

I'd rather pray like Papa, in Mumbai.
How to find God in a high school auditorium?
Unabashed walls roaring
with American football murals
draped with *saree* curtains.
Players, mascot, audience
cheerleaders in short skirts
peeking through silky folds.

In processions, like *Ganpati Visarjans*,
decorated brown bodies
in *sarees, kurtas, salwars*

*in Tikas, tilaks, and bindis*
*in Henna, alta, and mehndis.*
Slums and highrises, side by side,
hearts dancing on the streets.

I miss how I used to be one of them
at the crowded Churchgate station.
Daily passengers, languages blended yet distinct
Punjabi, Gujarati, Bengali, Hindi, Marathi.
Their colors, alta red, turmeric yellow, peacock blue
chiming like the silver bells
on an *adivasi* woman's anklet.

Memories glow like pearls
on the Queen's necklace.
Focusing, blurring
what used to be, what it is.
It's the *small small* things really;
after some time it feels natural.
Natural to forget them.

## Postscript: A Lifetime in Arts-Based Research and Beyond

To reflect on this chapter is to trace the rhythm of a life lived in arts-based research, a journey that has evolved from my early experiments with found poetry into deeper explorations of contemplative art-making and spiritual activism. When I first wrote this piece, I was navigating the terrain of qualitative inquiry, drawn to poetry as resistance against positivist traditions. I understood research was not neutral, but I had yet to fully articulate how arts-based methodologies could serve as necessary epistemological interventions against rigid academic conventions.

Since then, my work has expanded beyond textual poetics to embrace visual, performative, and multimodal storytelling. I have delved deeper into the intersections of transnationalism, de/colonial methodologies, and arts-based inquiry, developing approaches that recognize knowledge as embodied and relational. My scholarship has challenged sanitized notions of research, instead insisting on work that breathes, feels, and dwells in uncertainty.

I am humbled to see how these ideas have resonated across disciplines. Scholars have taken up and extended these contemplative arts-based approaches, using them to explore everything from trauma-informed pedagogy to environmental justice. My work on threshold theories has influenced researchers seeking to work beyond binary oppositions. Doctoral students tell me they find permission in my writings to pursue more embodied, spiritually informed approaches to inquiry.

Yet the fundamental questions remain: What does it mean to research with care? To witness with integrity? To write in ways that co-create rather than extract? These questions resist resolution. Arts-based research is not about arriving at definitive answers but about opening portals, making space for what is uncontainable, inviting multiple ways of knowing to coexist in productive tension. This remains our challenge and our invitation.

Chapter 5

# Who Will Read This Body?

## An A/r/tographic Statement

*Barbara Bickel*

An Artist Statement is a historical document written by an artist as accompanying text for an art exhibit. Each Artist Statement I have written over the years has challenged me to create text that will assist the viewers'/readers' understanding of my art. Most artists prefer to allow curators, art historians, and art writers/critics to take on the textual expanding of the art. I have to admit I have been one of these artists. As a spiritual feminist artist now situated within the academy, committed to add researching, teaching, and writing to my practice of art making, I am challenged to reach beyond my familiar artist practices. The practice of a/r/tography (Irwin & de Cosson, 2004; Springgay et al., 2004) has given me a framework to address this challenge. *A/r/t*ography calls for an inner collaborative relationship between my *a*rtist self, *r*esearcher self, and *t*eacher self. Each role engages a critical hermeneutic, self-reflexive practice of art-making and writing. The a/r/tographic work is offered to the public as an interwoven tapestry of art/research/education/writing.

The Statement (Exhibit 1) that accompanied my thesis art exhibition was my first A/r/tographic Statement. It was originally offered to gallery viewers within a gallery setting, similar to an Artist Statement. It was written just prior to the exhibition and before I began the written component of the thesis (Bickel, 2004). Within this chapter, I offer the A/r/tographic Statement with selected images of the art and performance rituals. I consider the Statement a time-specific historical archival document and because of this footnotes are added as hypertext to share my expanded thinking and writing beyond that moment in time.

### Exhibit 1: A/r/tographic Statement

> The more I delve into fleshing inquiry through the body, I am more deeply aware of the paradoxes resonant within me.
>
> Celeste Snowber (2002)

> I am an instrument in the shape of a woman trying to translate pulsations into images for the relief of the body and the reconstruction of the mind.
>
> Adrienne Rich (Yorke, 1997)

This body of work exposes a creative research process that began with a one and a half hour private performance ritual,[1] witnessed by two friends, in which I literally wrote on

DOI: 10.4324/9781003412892-5

my body. The documented private performance ritual launched the a/r/tographical inquiry that makes up part of my Master's thesis in the Faculty of Education at the University of British Columbia. The performance ritual was an intuitive[2] effort, undertaken in part, to embody and understand the numerous feminists who compellingly summon women to write from their own bodies and write with the body as a form of resistance (Cixous, 1997; Dallery, 1992; Irigaray, 1997; Lorde, 1984; Minh-ha, 1999; Rich, 2001; Snowber, 1997). My personal intention and desire in this performance ritual was to begin to externalize and embody writing as art. What has become apparent with the unfolding of the art and exhibition preparation is that it transgresses the boundaries between shame and freedom through the intimate and personal exposure of both the subconscious female mind and the naked female body, through the ritual process of a/r/tography. While I have felt at home with the method of a/r/tography, I have also struggled with the challenge of being conscious of and activating the often conflicting roles of artist, researcher, and educator this method demands.[3] Through this struggle I have come to recognize art-making as research and curriculum making, seen art as curriculum, experienced performance ritual as pedagogy and worked with the body as text. This statement is an attempt to articulate a complex, exciting, and emergent research journey.

*Who will read this body?* was preceded by a 13-year individual and collaborative (co-creative) art practice of (re)presenting the human body, predominantly the female body, in two-dimensional drawings and collages, and in the multi-dimensional medium of performance rituals. The process and experience of art-making is extremely important for my art and practice. I have attempted to bring the art-making process into the gallery setting through performance rituals co-created by myself and co-creators/models of the projects. The solo multimedia installation of *Who will read this body?*, which included video installation, sculpture, and two-dimensional collage (Figure 5.4), along with an artist talk and public performance ritual (Figure 5.3), reveals the raw, organic ritual process of a/r/tographic research and documentation, that has in the past been hidden from the viewer/reader/learner in my art exhibitions. I have come to learn through a/r/tography that my art has a complex agenda.[4] Not only does it encompass honoring and freeing the human body, but it also serves to challenge and bring to the surface a wounded patriarchal culture of shame and fear. I live within and embody this oppressive and hurtful culture on a daily basis and believe it is rooted in and perpetuated by the philosophical rupture between the mind and body[5] that has existed within western society for more than 500 years (Eisler, 1987). In this split, the mind is valued over the body, associated with the masculine and aligned with societal power, while the body is associated with the feminine and the natural world and is considered something to be controlled and brought into submission (Grosz, 1994). In admitting my own struggle within this philosophical split, I come to acknowledge myself as a microscopic part of a whole system.

I begin this journey with myself; with my own body and my own writing. I welcome the viewer/reader/learner into the exhibition space as witness to my a/r/tographic testimony; a testimony that has the potential to disrupt body/mind dualisms and illicit feelings of shame and discomfort.[6] Drawing upon the feminist phrase "the personal is the political," I invite the reader/viewer/learner to witness the personal with or without shame and to move with the personal to the larger, more complex challenge of re-forging the often dissociated and hurting elements of mind, individual, and language, with those of body, communal, and image.

In this work, I ask the viewer/reader/learner to ponder with me the questions[7] that have troubled my own a/r/tographic journey:

Am I not making art?
Am I not researching?
Am I not educating?
Am I not writing?
Am I not performing?
Am I not ritualizing?
Am I not learning?
Am I not my self?

The multimedia art exhibit and performance ritual, entitled *Who will read this body?* took place at the University of British Columbia in April 2004, at the AMS Gallery (Figure 5.1).

Upon entering the gallery, the visitor was shielded from the exhibition by a white veil. Before entering the gallery, they encountered a ritual table and were invited to take part in a ritual of placing their hands into earth (soil) and water. Consciously choosing or not

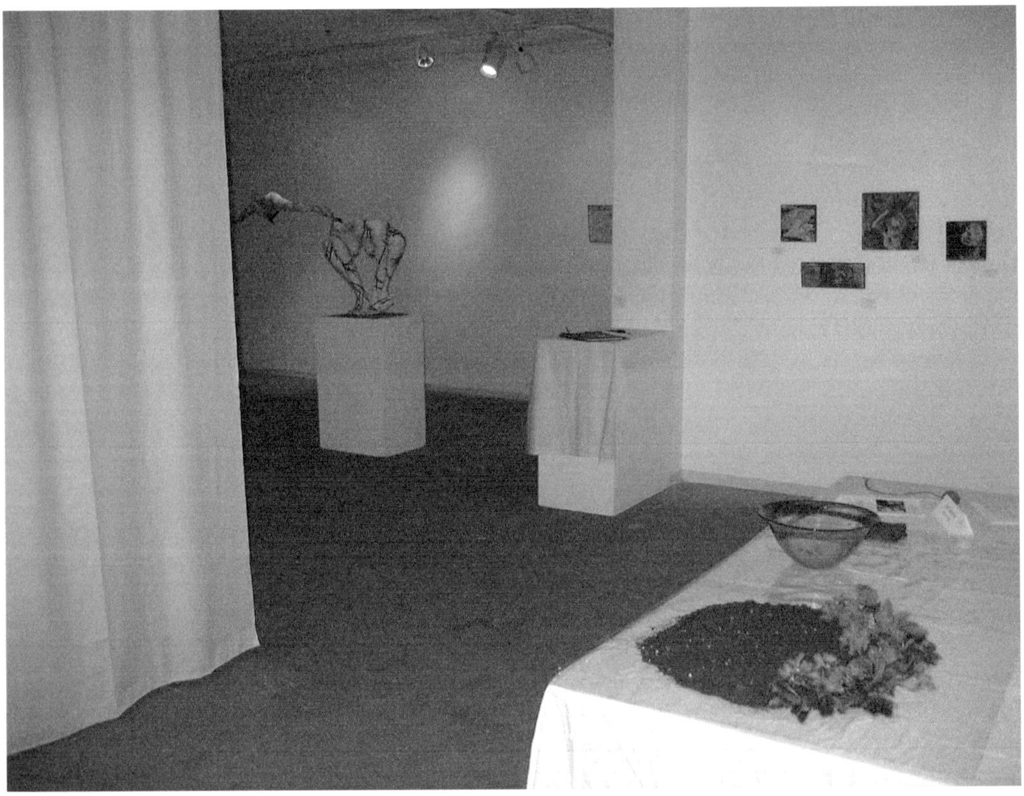

*Figure 5.1* Bickel, B. (2004). *Who will read this body?*, gallery entrance view. The University of British Columbia, AMS Gallery.

Photography by B. Bickel.

choosing to take part in the ritual prepared viewers to enter the gallery as "sacred space." Viewers not comfortable or not interested in the ritual turned away and left the gallery at the point of encountering the ritual invitation. On the other side of the veil, two TV monitors angled at opposite corners in the gallery, played looping videos of the ocean and its horizon at close range. The hypnotic sound of waves was accompanied by a woman's recorded voice sharing multiple trance journeys. Intimate and small art pieces appeared intermittently on the gallery walls, while body cast sculptures drew the viewer into the central gallery space. As the viewer approached the far end of the gallery another veil was encountered. Behind this veil the video of the outdoor forest performance ritual entitled *Who will read this body?* was projected onto a large piece of plywood.

Continuing the walk through the gallery, a floor installation piece brought the viewers' gaze to the floor. Within this installation, black-and-white photos documenting the ritual in the forest (see Figure 5.2) were displayed within two long rectangular containers filled with water and lit by four glass-encased candles.

The submerged photos were veiled thinly under the surface of water. A hand-bound book of poetry, written throughout the inquiry process, was part of the installation and was read by some viewers before fully engaging the gallery space or was looked at before they left the space.

I was present throughout the week-long exhibition, witnessing those that viewed the art. At times this was difficult as I was the exposed subject being "researched" in this exhibition, witnessing strangers witnessing me. Months of internal debate as to the vulnerability and risk of exhibiting this art as research, led to the creation of sacred space in the gallery installation and prompted me to have a pre-gallery opening ritual (Figure 5.3), where I invited close friends and family to witness the exhibition and offer their responses and supportive intentions just prior to opening the gallery doors to the public.

The path of the artist as researcher and educator is demanding on many levels. Not all artists have the support or guidance available to take on the multiply complex practice of a/r/tography. I have found it requires external support from others willing to be critical allies, as well as an internal personal practice that assists in working through the emotional, ethical, and spiritual issues that arise when engaged in this practice. Following my months of preparation, which included dialogues with my thesis committee and colleagues and the pre-gallery ritual within the sanctuary of the gallery, I was able to step beyond my personal discomfort. Being present as a witness and being witnessed in the exhibition allowed me to understand more deeply the embedded societal struggle of reuniting the body and mind.

As the final list of questions in my A/r/tographic Statement suggests, I was left with many questions at the completion of this exhibition. In the three months following the exhibition, I wrote the thesis and entered into these questions more deeply. The opportunity to stop and reflect critically on my art practice was a gift that many artists do not have the luxury of, as economics often require they immediately prepare for the next exhibition. The responses I received from those that saw the exhibition and the discussion and engagement that ensued at the end of the performance ritual in the gallery, offered further self-understanding of my work as a cultural worker (Giroux, 2000). Through this, I have come to fully acknowledge that my preferred teaching site for "transformative learning" (O'Sullivan, 1999) is within public spaces such as art galleries. The space of the gallery is transformed with each individual exhibition. Within the contemporary gallery setting there is an expectation of innovation and stepping beyond familiar understandings and representations, allowing the

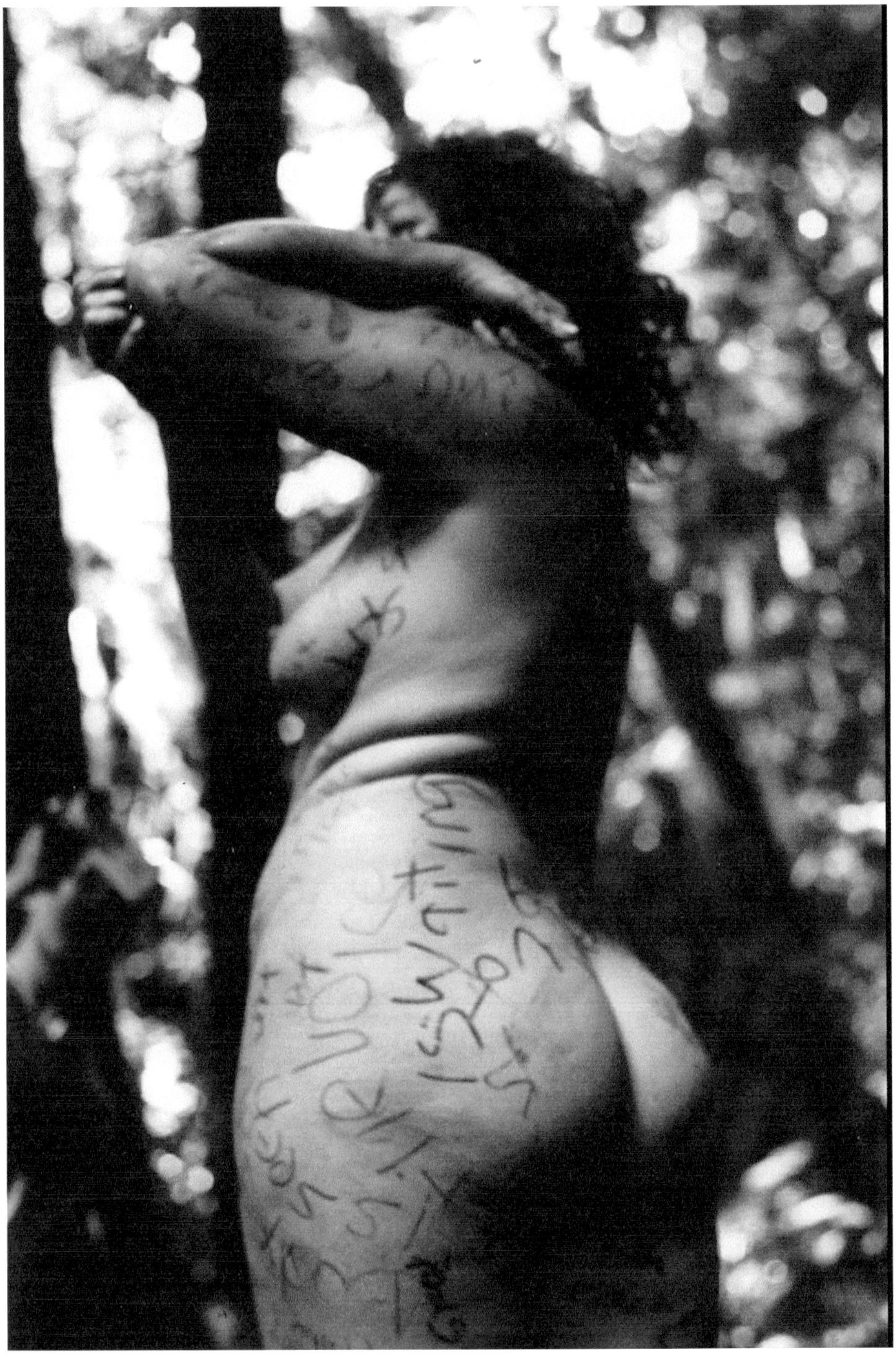

*Figure 5.2* Bickel, B. (2003). *Private performance ritual*. The University of British Columbia Endowment Lands.

Photography by C. Pulkinghorn.

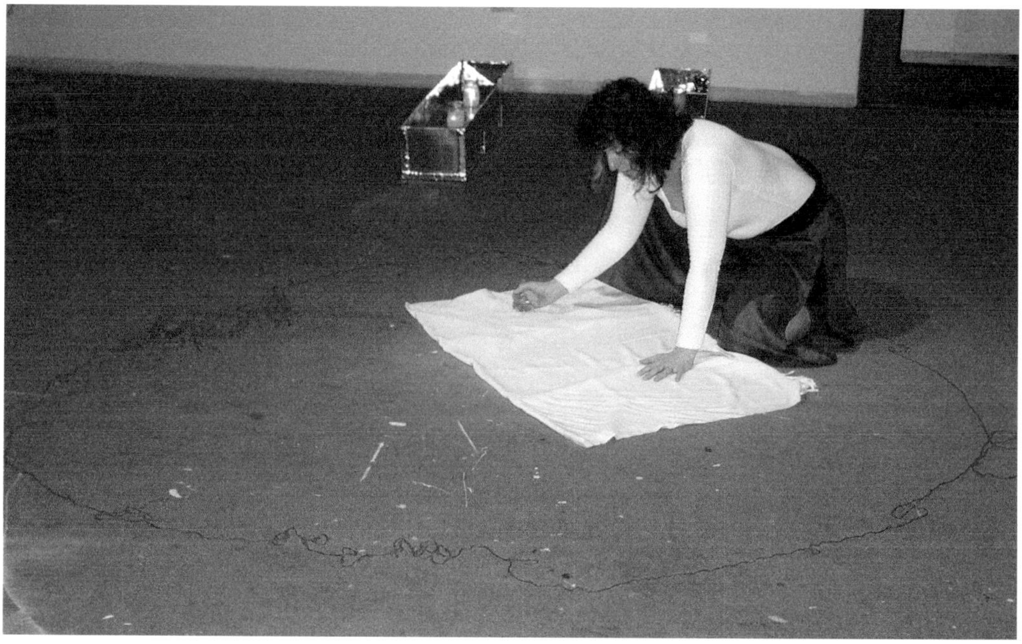

*Figure 5.3* Bickel, B. (2004). *Who will read this body? Public performance ritual.* The University of British Columbia, AMS Gallery.

Photography by D. Reicken.

beholding of new information and interpretations that can change patterned ways of knowing, seeing, and being in the world. Aesthetics as well as public interaction and learning can and should guide the presentation of art with an a/r/tographic intention of expanding understanding and knowledge.

Through multiple methods of inquiry, I engaged and collected data from processes that included art-making, ritual, the female menstrual cycle, trance, journal writing, and poetry (Figure 5.4). Drawing from these arational sources for the research allowed me to access material that my rational mind would have kept hidden or deemed inappropriate. Surfacing the hidden and unspoken caused me to rationally rethink and reassess the limiting assumptions that I was operating within. Critically reflecting through writing, and researching the work of other artists and writers, carried the inquiry to another level. My discoveries were not unique, yet my expression of the struggle between the body/mind dichotomy re-revealed the struggle and allowed an individual embodied understanding of it to unfold. This in turn offered an embodied location for others to reassess their own struggles and assumptions within the body/mind split.

The practice of a/r/tography led me, oftentimes reluctantly, into an expansive research process where I was making art, researching, educating, writing, performing, ritualizing, and learning while simultaneously expanding my notions of a self. This multi-modal and multi-perspectival research has made my commitment to arts-based research within the humanities and social sciences that much stronger and clear.

Offering arts-based research as a valid research method within the academy challenges a limited modernist lens that privileges rational ways of knowing over arational ways of

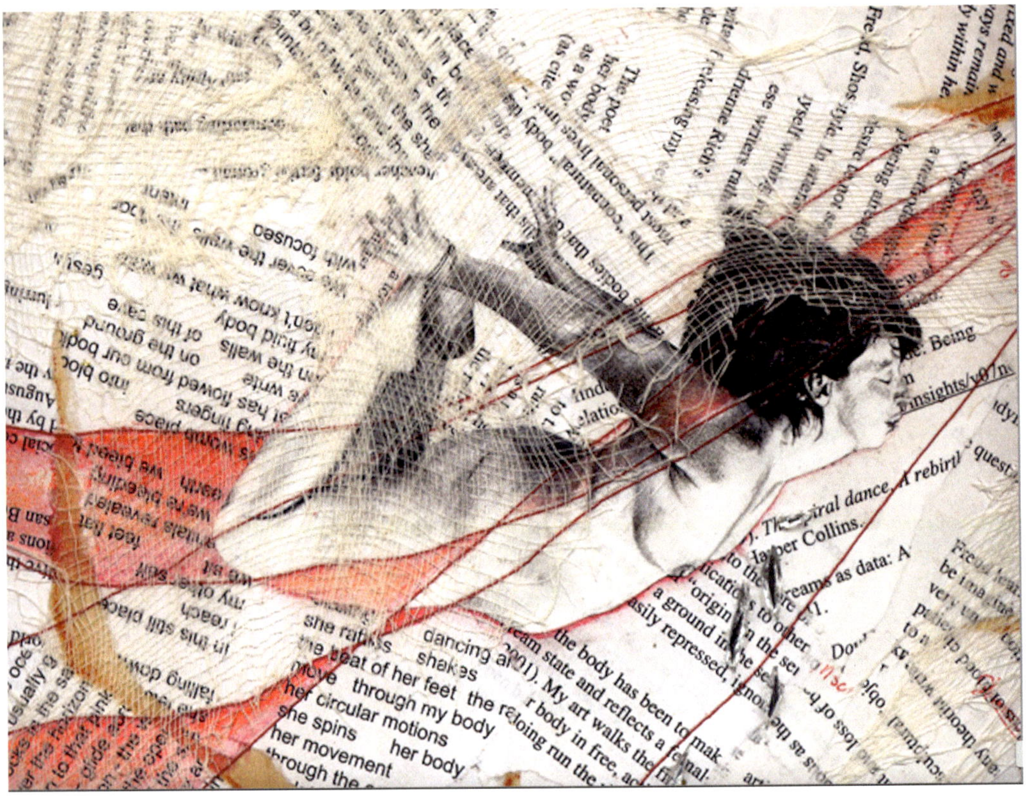


*Figure 5.4* Bickel, B. (2004). *Spinning red words on paper*, detail. The University of British Columbia, AMS Gallery (mixed media collage on wood, 12 × 24 inches).

Photography by B. Bickel.

knowing. As an artist interested in art as transformative learning, a/r/tography offers a location to engage an integral spiritual feminist practice that utilizes rational knowing alongside arational knowing. A/r/tography is not a path that everyone can travel easily. It is a disorienting practice that "shifts the relationship[s]" (Springgay, 2004) between, around, and within the mind and body, writing and art, ritual and education, and the rational and arational. In sharing my experience of the a/r/tographic inquiry, my desire is to intrigue as well as invite artists that are educators, artists interested in their art as research and education, arts educators, educators and scholars, to support and engage further explorations of the practice of arts-based research.

## Postscript

Revisiting my first a/r/tographic study summoned me to *com-passionately wit(h)ness* an earlier self who was following the seductive power of art as an inquiry and learning process. Responding to the nascent writing, I swell with *com-passion* for her struggle to write from Her body in a relational feminine language—a *fragilizing* encounter with herself at the start of an academic journey. "Com-passion," artist-philosopher-psychoanalyst

Bracha Ettinger (2009) explains, has three major "transformational affects": "primary fascinance," "primary compassion," and "primary awe". These affects bring the other and the subject into contact with the Cosmos through aesthetic and *proto-ethical wit(h) nessing* (p. 1).

In writing a recent a/r/tographic career reflection chapter, I traversed *carriance*, another word drawn from the feminine language of Ettingerian Matrixial Theory (EMT), telling my story of carrying and being "carried within the field of ABER in the academy" (Bickel, 2023, p. 107). When I began my artist-scholar journey I was buoyed by a spiritual feminist primary awe for and understanding of the Divine feminine in the Cosmos. What I did not have was spiritual feminist academic language to interrupt secular hegemonic phallic language. My body and journey with ABER led to seeking spiritual feminist scholars (e.g., Gloria Anzaldúa, M. Jacqui Alexander, Celeste Snowber), and finding EMT, which carried me into waters that lure me ever deeper into aesthetically, ethically and politically co-creating and learning with the Cosmos. To close this post-script, I flow together my early and co-becoming maturing self by sharing the art book (Figure 5.5), *Metramorphosis*

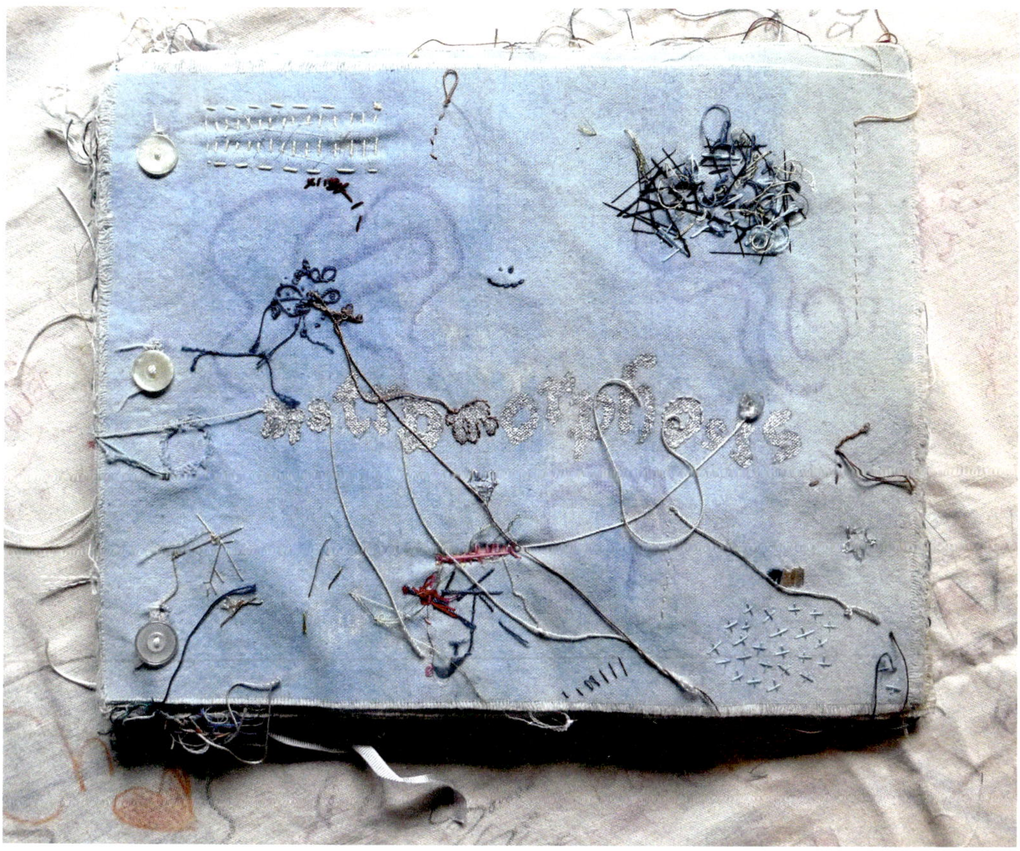

*Figure 5.5* Bickel. B. (2024). *Metamorphosis* book (canvas, acrylic paint, silk thread, buttons, lake stones, 16 × 11 inches).

Photography by Barbara Bickel.

(2011–) marking my early ABER study of Ettinger's lexicon, and a found poem from the *Carriance* chapter, weaving together the words of Ettinger and mystic Hildegard von Bingen.

The cosmos is born
revealed
by aesthetical
ethical
joining-in-differentiating
working-through
spiritual
knowledge of the Other.

The Divine feminine cannot be seen
but is known through
divine creation
artworking
art-works create such
knowledge.
(Bickel, 2023, pp. 125–126)

## Notes

1 *Ritual* creates the sacred space/context/container for entering the often disorienting and challenging work of a/r/tography. Ritual essentially includes an arational sacred practice of trans-egoic respect/awareness/openness to the creative interaction of physical, emotional, intellectual, and spiritual realities, within nature, culture, and self, for the purpose of transformation (for further reading on women's ritual see Northrup, 1997).

2 I have come to articulate the intuitive component of art-making as an arational process. To further explore the concept of the arational, I draw from the late philosopher Jean Gebser's theory (1984) of the arational. The arational as a form of knowing includes the body, emotions, senses, intuition, imagination, creation making, the mystical, spiritual, and the relational, alongside the rational. The concept of the arational viewed from the rational (mental) perspective, has most often been confused with the irrational, thus repressing it, pathologizing and disqualifying it from being seen as a valid and significant site of learning (Gebser, 1984). Contemporary philosopher, Ken Wilber (2002) draws from and expands Gebser's arational/aperspectival-integral view and offers a model of consciousness that embraces and integrates the arational with the rational. Wilber defines integral "Not in the sense of a uniformity, and not in the sense of ironing out all the wonderful differences, ... but in the sense of unity in diversity, shared commonalities along with ... wonderful differences" (p. 15).

3 At its best, a/r/tography encourages the combined creative freedom and risk-taking of the artist with the theory, rigor, and responsibility of the academic researcher, along with the ethics and compassion of the educator. Combining these three roles with the integrity and awareness of what is called for from each area, is a demanding undertaking. During my thesis art making and research process, I tended to privilege the role of the artist. It was often with resistance and struggle that I had to cede my familiar artist's lens to activate and give equitable authority to the roles of the researcher and teacher.

4 As an artist I have been content to trust an intuitive-like process. I have held onto an anti-intellectual stance in my research as an artist that has limited my ability to fully take in the complexity of the cultural politics embedded within my art practice and art.

5 I refer here to the Cartesian mind/body split that came with the age of the rational Enlightenment (Wilber, 1996). Philosophers (i.e., Derrida, Foucault) and feminists (i.e., Grosz, 1994; Irigaray, 1994) have and continue to deconstruct this dichotomy and its impact on the world.
6 Figure 5.1 is pulled from a larger installation piece in the exhibit entitled *To Find Traces of Her Estrangement*. Documentary photographs of the performance ritual in the forest, where I wrote on my body with menstrual blood and make-up pencils, were part of the installation. I chose to install them submerged in water within an aluminum container set on the floor. Glass-encased candles burned ritually, illuminating the photos. The water, along with floating red threads, embodied the metaphor of life's blood acting as a protective veil over the photos. Placing the photos under water required the viewer to leave the comfortable element of air and pass visually through to an alternate realm of water in order to gain access to the images. It was a risk to pull this individual image out of the installation and place it onto a page within my thesis text. I risk separating the image from its context again, offering the image within this essay as an exposed and integrated body as text.
7 In asking these questions I spun off the questioning lyrics of Canadian singer-songwriter Jane Siberry within her song, "Sail Across the Water" from her 1993 CD, *When I Was a Boy*.

## References


Bickel, B. (2004). *From artist to a/r/tographer: An autoethnographic ritual inquiry into writing on the body*. Unpublished Master's thesis. University of British Columbia.

Bickel, B. (2023). Carriance: Stitching an artist-scholar through cyclical time. In B. Bickel, R. Siegesmund, & R. L. Irwin (Eds.), *Arts-based educational research trajectories: Career reflections by authors of outstanding dissertations* (pp. 107–129). Springer.

Cixous, H. (1997). The laugh of the Medusa. In R. R. Warhol & D. P. Herndl (Eds.), *Feminisms: An anthology of literary theory and criticism* (pp. 347–362). Rutgers University Press.

Dallery, A. (1992). The politics of writing (the) body. In A. Jaggar & S. Bordo (Eds.), *Gender/body/knowledge: Feminist reconstructions of being and knowing* (pp. 52–67). Rutgers University Press.

Eisler, R. (1987). *The chalice and the blade: Our history, our future*. Harper & Row.

Ettinger, B. (2009). Fragilization and resistance. *Studies in The Maternal*, *1*(2), 1–31. https://doi.org/10.16995/sim.141

Gebser, J. (1984). *The ever-present origin* (Trans. N. Barstad & A. Mickunas). Ohio University Press.

Giroux, H. (2000). *Impure act: The practical politics of cultural studies*. Routledge.

Grosz, E. (1994). *Volatile bodies: Toward a corporeal feminism*. Indiana University Press.

Irigaray, L. (1994). *Thinking the difference: For a peaceful revolution* (Trans. K. Montin). Routledge.

Irigaray, L. (1997). This sex which is not one. In K. Conboy, N. Medina, & S. Stanbury (Eds.), *Writing on the body: Female embodiment and feminist theory* (pp. 248–256). Columbia University Press.

Irwin, R. L., & de Cosson, A. (2004). *A/r/tography: Rendering self through arts-based living inquiry*. Pacific Educational Press.

Lorde, A. (1984). *Sister outsider: Essays and speeches*. Crossing Press.

Minh-ha, T. T. (1999). Write your body and the body in theory. In J. Price & M. Shildrick (Eds.), *Feminist theory and the body* (pp. 258–266). Routledge.

Northrup, L. A. (1997). *Ritualizing women: Patterns of spirituality*. Pilgrim Press.

O'Sullivan, E. (1999). *Transformative learning: Educational vision for the 21st century*. OISE/UT and University of Toronto Press.

Rich, A. (2001). *Arts of the possible*. W.W. Norton.

Siberry, J. (1993). *Sail across the water. When I was a boy* [Compact Disc]. Reprise Records.

Snowber, C. N. (1997). Writing and the body. *Educational Insights*, *4*(1). https://einsights.ogpr.educ.ubc.ca/archives/v04n01/writing.html

Snowber, C. N. (2002). Bodydance: Enfleshing soulful inquiry through improvisation. In C. Bagley & M. B. Cancienne (Eds.), *Dancing the data*. Peter Lang.

Springgay, S. (2004). *Inside the visible: Youth understandings of body knowledge through touch*. Unpublished doctoral dissertation, University of British Columbia.
Springgay, S., Irwin, R., & Wilson Kind, S. (2004). A/r/tography as living inquiry through art and text. *Qualitative Inquiry*, *11*(4), 897–912. https://doi.org/10.1177/1077800405280696
Wilber, K. (1996). *A brief history of everything*. Shambhala.
Wilber, K. (2002). *Boomeritis: A novel that will set you free*. Shambhala.
Yorke, L. (1997). *Adrienne Rich: Passion, politics and the body*. Sage.

Chapter 6

# Wild Imagination, Radical Imagination, Politics, and the Practice of Arts-Based Educational Research (ABER) and Scholartistry

*Donald Blumenfeld-Jones*

I begin with an anecdote that situates my concerns. Several years ago, I met with an Arizona State University public health PhD student interested in using arts-based educational research (ABER) in her research. She didn't know much about ABER, but felt it was the ideal approach to do advocacy work for her participants. I demurred on this point, not because it can't be done or shouldn't be done, but because, in my estimation, this is not the heart of ABER work. ABER begins in making art and, along the way, is inevitably "political." Her desire was not art. Rather, she desired to tell her population's stories to get others to act appropriately toward her people; she saw art as a vehicle for her agenda. I assert that while all art might have a political dimension, it is not necessarily about persuading people to a point of view. Art-making is the exploration of questions for which there are no easy or obvious answers, revealing the human complexity of our situation and addressing the confusions among which we all, inevitably, live. This is political because "political," at its most basic meaning, is about the wielding of power and all human complexity is inevitably dealing with power. "Power" is not about political social movements, per se. Power is everywhere, and an artist's exploration of the world is an exploration of power without always naming it as such and being hemmed in as if power is the sum total of the human experience. ABER is well-situated to address that broader human experience *and* address power. Thus, my response was, if she wanted to do ABER, she must start with becoming an artist and understand how an artist thinks and practices.

Her desire is not an ABER anomaly. Barone (Chapter 2 this book) wrote that "art can be emancipatory," and in more than one sense, ABER work can "[move] to shape and influence the public consciousness by critiquing the politically conventional and the socially orthodox" (p. 19). This echoes the doctoral student's agenda and, in my estimation, has become a strong, if not dominant, voice in ABER, as indicated by Susan Finley's (2017b) chapter on Critical Arts-Based Research. That said, some of what Barone offers in his discussion of socially oriented ABER connects to what I will discuss in elaborating wild imagination. For instance, Barone (Chapter 2 this book) points out that:

> Artists, and arts-based researchers, however high-minded their emancipatory intentions, may produce works as exclusionary, monologic, and hegemonic as other sorts of projects. This happens whenever, to paraphrase Sartre, the would-be artist, eager to change minds, zealous to make history, forgets to make art.
>
> (p. 21)

Additionally, Barone cautions us to be "epistemologically humble." I agree with Barone as, for me, this means not knowing the outcome of my inquiry *avant la lettre*, which is, I

DOI: 10.4324/9781003412892-6

think, an important disposition for the artist. Barone also calls for ABER to critique "the politically conventional and the socially orthodox ... not by proffering a new totalizing counter-narrative, but by luring an audience into an appreciation of an array of diverse, complex, nuanced images and partial, local portraits of human growth and possibility" (p. 21).

While Barone and I agree on some important ABER dimensions, this notion of "luring" audiences discomforts me. Artists are not, in my estimation, in the practice of "luring" anyone. We are not training, tricking, nor luring them to know/see/feel ways of "human growth and possibility." I argue that this orientation loses something of great value in the practice of art-making. This chapter is dedicated to exploring this other way of understanding art-making and ABER.

## ABER and Social Justice, Are Arts a Means to an End?

Susan Finley (2003), an increasingly notable ABER spokesperson, focused on two leaders in the qualitative inquiry field, Yvonna Lincoln and Norman Denzin, to support her assertion that ABER should be involved in social justice issues. She noted that one of Lincoln's (1995) elements of a new qualitative inquiry paradigm was to "improve participants' lives," calling for, in part, a focus on "social justice" (Finley, 2003, p. 282). Finley then cited Denzin (2000), writing that qualitative inquiry should "take a stand against social injustice" (p. 293). More recently, she continued this focus in her keynote address to the 13th International Congress of Qualitative Inquiry titled "The Future of Critical Arts-based Research: Creating Political spaces for Resistance Politics" (Finley, 2017a). She writes, in her abstract, that Critical Arts-based Research "is a performative research methodology ... structured on the notion of possibility, the what might be, of a research tradition that is postcolonial, pluralistic, ethical, and transformative in positive ways." While in adding the term "critical" to her ABER focus she situates her work as a subgenre of ABER, her prominence may lead politics rather than art practice to being central to ABER.

Let me be more concrete with my concerns in this regard. Finley and her son published ABER work with homeless children (Finley & Finley, 1999). They wrote,

> It is the authors' purpose to provide an opportunity for homeless youth to tell their stories and to contribute their own voices to conversations among educators and policy makers who make decisions that influence the life histories of youth, homeless or otherwise. (p. 313)

The Finleys' emphasis is on influencing others, not on making art. Art is a servant of the project, not its heart. Their purpose is not to uncover something unknown, to deploy imagination as a way of new knowing, but rather, as a better way of helping social policy be formed. I will not argue with their motives, but I do suggest that subordinating art to social justice, social policy, and better relationships loses ABER's core value.

Political goals such as these miss what ABER can do for us when we focus upon what artists do: live imaginatively in a way free from knowing what our ends are and have something revealed that could not be revealed without such imaginative life. In an interview on National Public Radio, E. L. Doctorow (2014) illustrated this other approach to making art from the unknown while discussing his approach to his novels. He stated, "The ideal way to get involved in [writing] is to write in order to find out what you're writing. You don't start with an outline and a plan, you start with ... images that are very evocative to you" (n.p.). The writing helps him think. Doctorow doesn't start with a plan but with images that speak back to him and, eventually, begins to make sense of what the writing is telling him. Through the process of writing, he comes to know something of what he has observed.

Doctorow's ideas begin to elaborate my sense of what it means to be a scholartist: *putting the world into question with no expectation of what will answer that question.* Further, I am asserting that it carries us toward a vision of politics grounded in artistic imagination, not imagination in the service of political ends. This latter relationship is labeled by some social theorists as *radical imagination.* I consider this form of imagination problematic for the practice of ABER. I have written at some length about this (Blumenfeld-Jones, 2014), discussing the German Marxist playwright Bertolt Brecht, who worried about an approach to politically aware work that already knew what it thought. I will not rehearse that discussion here, but suffice it to say, he noted that in socially conscious art,

> Right and wrong courses of action were shown .... The theatre became an affair for philosophers, but only for such philosophers as wished not just to explain the world but also to change it. So, we had philosophy, and we had instruction. And where was amusement in all that? Were they sending us back to school, teaching us to read and write? Were we supposed to pass exams, work for diplomas?
>
> (Brecht, 1936, p. 2)

"[S]ending us back to school": for me, this is the problem with calls for social justice and activism. I, like Brecht, remain concerned that we will think that art is merely a teaching tool in which the teacher already knows the answers to the questions and the student (art receiver) must be shown the right way to think.

This isn't to say that we should know nothing in making art. Brecht suggests that he needs scientific understanding to perform his work. He does not feel that his own imagination is sufficient for imagining truths that need exploration. He made a practice of absorbing other kinds of literature as materials through which his art-making would proceed, making sure his art-making was grounded in reality of some sort, rather than only a fantasy world existing in his mind. This "grounded in reality" does not guide the art as if the art illustrates the "reality" (and is, thus, secondary to reality). Art as its own reality finds greater strength as it explores a world out of which it springs and illuminates that world in new ways. It is a back and forth between realities in which we live *and* making art that begins in those realities. As the art proceeds, we "check in" with those realities to see what is illuminated by the art-making, what has gone astray, and what is phantasmal and, in some cases, detached from reality in ways that do not help us know more about our world. There is a constant vibration between what I "see" and what I "make" (Blumenfeld-Jones, 2015).

## From Radical Imagination to Wild Imagination

This leads me to examine the previous idea of *radical imagination.* I begin with a non-ABER social justice example from a leader of the social justice community, Henry Giroux. Giroux (2013) employed the term "imagination" in critiquing schools:

> If ... right-wing billionaires and apostles of corporate power have their way schools will become "dead zones of the imagination," reduced to anti-public spaces that wage

> an assault on critical thinking, civic literacy and historical memory. Trust, imagination, creativity, and a respect for critical teaching and learning are thrown to the wind in pursuit of profits ... the unreformers kill the imagination.
>
> (n.p.)

Giroux seeks, instead of this assault on imagination, an "imagination and hope for a better world" (n.p.). Imagination, both as a dystopian use and as imagining a better world, is only invoked by Giroux but not described. Imagination appears to be only "critical thinking, civic literacy and historical memory," a truncated form of imagination, at service to the world but not inquiring into the world.

I now turn to scholars who use the term *radical imagination* to characterize their work. In the first citation, we are not yet in the area of art, but there is a bridge to be found. Haiven and Khasnabish (2014) write of radical imagination in a way that begins to move toward my notion of *wild imagination* (to be elaborated later):

> radical imagination is the ability to imagine the world, life and social institutions not as they are but as they might otherwise be ... to recognize that the world can and should be changed .... about bringing ... possible futures 'back' to work on the present ... about drawing on the past, telling different stories about how the world came to be the way it is ... remembering the power and importance of past struggles and the way their spirits live on in the present .... about imagining the present differently too ... radical imagination not as a thing individuals possess ... but as a collective process, something that groups do and do together.
>
> (emphasis added, Location 116 on Kindle Edition)

The italicized portions of this passage require us to see beyond what is, perhaps in radically different terms than those offered by the present circumstances. Here, imagination transcends the given world, reimagining the past as if it were a different story than the one we currently tell.

Haiven and Khasnabish are asserting that to find a thoroughly different, almost alien view of the past, we must transcend the past's and present's almost hypnotic hold upon us. We might invite marginalized versions of the past, "remembering past struggles" trying to "work across boundaries, real and imagined," but we must not trust those boundaries or past struggles to be any more real than the present. Those boundaries are manufactures of the present world, so why trust they are the boundaries we must transcend? Those struggles might be defined by the power structure, so why trust that these are the struggles in which we must engage? The task is to treat the past and the present standing outside of it, putting everything into question, even what we take to be radical truths and versions of that present. This suggests that the artist starts with as truly blank a canvas as possible, all the while understanding that one can never start with a blank canvas. This provides the kind of openness that I think is necessary for an artist to put the world into question.

This brings me to another scholar of radical imagination, who provides a bridge to the idea of wild imagination. Robin D. G. Kelley (2002), a distinguished scholar of African-American history, offers a vision of radical imagination, writing as follows:

> the map to a new world is in the imagination, in what we see in our third eyes rather than in the desolation that surrounds us. Now that I look back with hindsight, my writing and

> the kind of politics to which I've been drawn have more to do with imagining a different future than being pissed off about the present. Not that I haven't been angry, frustrated and critical of the misery created by race, gender, and class oppression – past and present. That goes without saying. My point is that the *dream of a new world*, my mother's dream, was the catalyst for my own political engagement. I came to black nationalism filled with idealistic dreams of a communal society free of all oppressions, a world where we owned the land and shared the wealth and white folks were out of sight and out of mind. It was what I imagined precolonial Africa to be. Sure, I was naïve, still in my teens, but my imaginary portrait, derived from the writings of Cheikh Anta Diop, Chancellor Williams, Julius Nyerere, Kwame Nkrumah, Kwame Ture, and others, gave me a sense of hope and possibility of what a *post*colonial Africa could look like. Very quickly I learned that the old past wasn't as glorious, peaceful, or communal as I had thought.
>
> (p. 3)

Kelley recognizes that he needed to move away from the presentism that centered his thought in the Marxism, socialism, and other radical political movements that "had little to say ... to a more elaborate dream of freedom" (p. 4). In his search, he discovered the surrealist movement "under my nose ... buried in the rich black soil of Afrodiasporic culture ... the ancient practices of the Maroon societies and shamanism ... the blues people of North America ... the likes of Aimé and Suzanne Césaire and Wifredo Lam" (p. 5). He found that surrealism in visual artwork celebrated "the emancipation of thought" focused on "resolv[ing] the contradiction of everyday thought and our wildest dreams ... to emancipate desire and supply it with new poetic weapons ... advanc[ing] ... the creation of a free society in which everyone will be a poet." (p. 5). "Wildest dreams": this is to what I am referring when I think about wild imagination. These dreams are not simply the desires of a different or better world, but are, themselves, worlds in which we live. They are wild in that they suborn thoughts that one could not have had while employing the usual radical imagination, because the poet does not live in "this world" but in an alternative world that turns over a stone and finds something in her life that was previously so hidden. When Kelley invokes the surrealists, he invokes, by his own testimony, those who not only imagined a different way of doing art that was not tethered to what "is" but also a different way of living together that was deeply connected to the way of making art. This provides a bridge to tracing some uses of the idea of wild imagination, followed by my approach to it, how I employed it in an ABER work, and how I link it to a form of politics.

## Wild Imagination

I must, now, begin to locate wild imagination. First, there is wild imagination that deals with hyperbole, a kind of "over-the-topness" that may also be a foil to the ordinariness and dryness of everyday life. Thus, in Lisa du Rose's scholarly article (1998) on the poet Wallace Stevens, Stevens creates a character, Victoria Clementina, a "Negress" who acts as a foil to stodgy white women. Du Rose writes:

> Stevens admires the wild imagination and savage beauty of Victoria Clementina, [but] he does not allow her to exist outside stereotypical and racist perceptions of African Americans .... the poet uses Victoria Clementina almost exclusively as a point of reference; her presence merely enables him to critique ... stuffy Victorian women; her

> sexuality foils their prudishness; her vibrant imagination, their stifled thoughts. She becomes the Other from which we can define the white women in the poem.
>
> (p. 14)

Du Rose notes, however, that while Stevens treats her in "a stereotypical fashion endow[ing] [her] with a primitive and wild sexuality," his "representation ... is ambivalent ... he uses her as a symbol of sexual power and freedom" but "also elevates her as an individual force, content and happy with herself" (p. 11). Here, we see Stevens allowing his imagination to both act conventionally and not conventionally (his ambivalence), an important characteristic of wild imagination. Further, du Rose points to Stevens endowing Clementina with "vibrant imagination," which he clearly admires. This vibrant imagination is grounded, in part, in her sexuality, in a visceral state, opposed to something more intellectual. The "visceral" characteristic is an important dimension of "wild imagination," but for now we can see that, according to du Rose, Stevens deployed it not for its own value but to say something about people who do not function from it.

Second, wild imagination may be viewed as a state in which one desires something that is impossible to obtain or attain and, thus, is wild because it is not reasonable. Thus, "I can imagine what it would be like to fly to the moon without need of a space ship" is a wild idea, but not a reasonable one. No logic will support the counterfactual character of the imagined object. It can be dismissed as foolish pie-in-the-sky thinking. It, too, is not what I mean by wild imagination, but it does contain a seed of what I do mean: wild imagination is the opposite of reason or reasonableness, just as Kelley's surrealists presented a world that might start from reason, logic, and "facts" but quickly undermined those entities by mixing them up in odd, fecund ways. It severs ties with the world as we live in it or even imagine we could live in it, imagining beyond what the world offers us. "Reality" and "fantasy" are never far from each other, and yet, the distance between them makes all the difference and creates the intense vibration between them necessary to wild imagination.

## Wild Imagination: An ABER Example Develops the Idea

*Hogan Dreams* (pronounced *HÓ-gone*, referring to sacred Navajo dwellings; Blumenfeld-Jones, 2004/2012) began as a curriculum project dedicated to strengthening the Navajo culture character of a BLM Navajo school's curriculum and life. The school was preparing to apply for a large grant to accomplish this work by first securing a planning grant. As project evaluator for the planning grant application, I was to report to the granting agency my evaluation of the planning grant process. Before beginning my work, I was told the Anglo principal of the school (also the PI on the grant) was "more Navajo than the Navajo." I didn't know what this could mean until I met him. I almost instantly felt the power of his personhood and his convictions as he sorted actual Navajos into three groups: (1) genuine Navajos, (2) those who aspired to be genuine Navajos, and (3) those who have betrayed the Navajo people and culture (for example, Navajos who had adopted Christianity or those who were not interested in speaking Navajo). Not Navajo himself, he felt yet that he knew more than the tribe as to what was needed. I couldn't just evaluate this project but needed to study it. At the same time as my study of this project, I was working on a project for Bagley and Cancienne's (2002) book, *Dancing the Data,* which resulted in a series of poems rather than a dance performance titled *Hogan Dreams* (Blumenfeld-Jones, 2002/2012). As an artist, I was aware of my judgment against the principal and sympathetic to the Navajo tribe experiencing his arrogant imperialism.

However, as an artist, I resisted a politically charged perspective. The art-making without a known answer helped me explore the organized chaos that created this situation, rather than trying to change the chaos with my poems. As with Doctorow (2014) who wrote in order to discover what he was writing and thinking, I had no idea what had happened, but I knew something had happened and that creative writing would be important to my coming to grips with the experience, whatever it was.

I took four different approaches to an analysis of the complexities of Navajo culture curriculum, including theoretical explorations based on the ideas of Bakhtin (1982) and Bourdieu (1972, 1993) as well as a straightforward narrative of the project. The ABER aspects allowed me to investigate the inner life of the people in this situation, as well as something about the resonances with a larger world that we each occupied in different ways, many of which went unseen even by ourselves. I wanted to know why I cared so much about this. I wanted to understand the swirl of feelings I encountered during these meetings. The "objective" analyses were illuminating, but almost too easy, too predictable. If they were social justice oriented, it was only so through my desire to show some ways people act in such fraught situations, so that we might better understand how to withstand power moves and, thereby, gain more "control" over a situation. But, with the poetic analysis titled *Hogan Dreams,* I wanted to know that "something else" that is elusive, inchoate, and yet, in some as yet unknown way, important to our humanness. In short, what else was there that I could not know through my intellectual self?

I must begin with an honest assessment of this work. As already stated, I felt angry with the principal of the school and the ways in which he discussed the Navajo people. The eponymous poem ("Hogan Dreams"), not the first poem I wrote for this work, has a political, almost social justice character. I was responding to my angst upon visiting the assistant principal's home and viewing the principal's building plans for a new school. I was deeply offended by what I took to be an imperialist reinterpretation of the hogan by the Anglo assistant principal and a perversion of the notion of the hogan by the principal. I had seen hogans for the last nearly 30 years as I drove through the reservation on numerous occasions. I had feelings about the hogan (and what I had read of the Navajos) from when I was a child in elementary school in New Jersey. But, for me, I found this poem one important dimension of my response that I needed in this writing.

*Hogan Dreams*

I – The Hogan dreams

The hogan – eight-sided wonder of the world
    knot of geography drawing the earth
    through its delicate threads.

The hogan – axis of the spinning earth
    Rough-hewn and mud daubed,
    settled into the dust of the desert.

The hogan – can the hogan be this axis –
    so small and heavy under
    the scudding sun?

The hogan – draws the sun
    through that knot,
    makes the sun work for its ends, is worked by the ends of the sun.

The hogan – an invention of time
    so old, no origin is known
    but reverence follows in a minute.

The hogan – in this life
    so much to do,
    to know and here, in the hogan, life is lived.

A life is lived – in the hogan –
    a life known by those whose life within the
    walls of the hogan streams out

    into the desert
    and the high pastures where, in summer,
    the sheep graze,
    the horses neigh,
    the dogs bark,
    the people breathe
    of Navajo.

II – The Assistant Principal dreams (of a home)
Or the postmodern hogan

Another hogan – this the invention of a mind –
    Knowing of the West
    (no north, no south, no east).

Another hogan – hoping to find
    In the eight walls,
    Amongst their smooth, roughed out timbers

Another hogan – this of the mind
    Of the liver in these walls
    Delivered from his own destiny.

Another hogan – rich and replete
    With new ideas, the hogan
    Updated, delivered from time.

Another hogan, rich with water, ladders,
    Stone and gleaming steel, beyond the hopes of
    The hogan dwellers who see this edifice.

Another hogan – this one owned –
    Can you own a hogan
    Or are you owned by the hogan?
        As your life is made
        Within the story-telling of your fires
        Made with wood and stone and, here,
        Made with another's money.

Another Hogan – stealing the desert land,
    Sweeping up its dust inside and
    Fortified with heavy walls – no streaming here.

Another hogan – anti-hogan –
    Another universe without the sun
    To guide and intervene its life.

III – The Principal dreams (of a school)
Or the institutional hogan

Many Hogans – the invention of a mind
    Which hopes to transform
    The mind of the people.

Many Hogans – massive roofed
    Green and tan,
    The colors of the desert perhaps.

Many Hogans – careering
    Through the sky,
    Linked and flowing as no sun could.

Many Hogans – the budding pictures of a dream
    Held by one for the people
    In hogans, understood by whom?

Many Hogans – restoring the people's dreams
    Forgotten, for there are no hogans,
    Or they are desert hidden.

These Many Hogans cannot be hidden,
    Nor will they be as
    They monument the moment.

Many Hogans – is it their eight-sided nature
    That makes them hogans
    Or the people inhabited by them?

Many Hogans – imitation of hope
    For living among the hogan
    That is lived in by the people.

I knew, however, before writing this poem, that there was more to this principal than his arrogance explored in this poem. In fact, the first poem I wrote—in thinking about the principal as a strange, dangerous, terrifying, mysterious character—was "The Principal's Regret." I identified something in him that was disappointed in himself, seeking something to make him anew, balanced against the accumulation of influence of the past self. Writing this poem alerted me to the complexity of the situation I couldn't simply "figure out." Here is the three-line poem:

"The Principal's Regret"

Apple trees are funny.
They grow up to find
They are not orange trees.

Initially, I didn't understand what I had written, only that these images (which were disconnected from the school, Navajo culture, the principal himself) somehow felt right. I refer to this as "wild imagination": this poem came to me unbidden and—as with coming upon wild flowers in an unexpected cranny of a rock or a small, almost hidden lichen and feeling the surprise and beauty—the poem presented a sudden revelation of which I didn't know its meaning, but I knew it felt significant, having something to do with the project, but I didn't, at the time, know what. Its resonance was concentrated in image. This is what artists have at their disposal: sensibility/sensitivity/antennae out for "something" that will enliven a response that "feels" before it "thinks."

Once I had this poem, I knew that I wanted more than one and proceeded to write four poems gathered under the title "The Principal's Songs," that constitute a "song cycle" (as Yeats [1933] had written his *Crazy Jane* poems). But, once those poems were drafted, what was to come next? Here, again, I relied upon wandering in my mind to pluck something not just from the data of this project but also from something that might concretize my many concerns about this project, that might situate *me* in the project (for, really, why should I care about this?). That "something" became the opening poem of the project.

*August in The Land (STONES)*

  A dry sky
Expands endlessly over brown mountains
    Cuddled by sage green grass
      Whose wisdom it is to survive.
    And those grasses, sparsely pocking the scraping dirt
      Dig deep, tapping their roots toward water.
            This is their survival.

  In a dry land,
The fog drips heavily over straight edged, gray mesas,
    Lipping the greener desert in an alluring kiss

That seems peaceful.
This fog is here
When the August skies are livid with rain.
For how else could things survive?

But be wary,
For the water that comes from the wet sky
Carries death
As the floods crash washes
With no resistance.
Those foreign borne feel the power
That greens the grass for a moment.
The moment kills the one, survives the other.

Amongst the great rock ridges
Shielding the grasses that greyly breath,
Block homes neatly align under clustered cliffs,
Appearing alone and happy.
Small, quiet dirt, having nothing, everything.
How do the people in the blinding flood?
They dig deep and quiet. Like the grass.

Yet I break through this land
On a fast running black highway slower
Than the still brown dirt that sweeps to a house,
A hogan, truck and sheep.
I feel wild in this blowing, fearful amidst the rocks
Who say "I am here" as God to Moses in the burning Bush.
He was afraid he could not survive.

Here the wet rock is vermilion,
Red, orange and mauve, the color of fire,
Coldly moist and seething with lichen life
Sitting for centuries waiting.
I know no waiting, as I am in but not part
Of this wet place, as I skitter across lightly
Which is danger to some, survival to others.

The grass is rooted,
But there are those weeds which find a route
Through the channels of earth
Fetching up against the railed pasture.
To live lightly in a dry land is to take
What is offered in the spirit of hope,
Seeing grandeur in the moments of survival.

But what else can I do? I am not light,
This rock, this grass, this spawning dirt

Which appears dead but is beloved with a life which belongs.
These are The People and I am, as always,
The skittering wanderer who knows no place like this
But respects the grass
That grows for their survival.

This poem was rooted in a trip I took with my family to the Grand Canyon North Rim through the Navajo Reservation, across a road ringed with cliffs upon which hung dark storm clouds. I thought about my own lostness in the project. I thought about being a Jew. What connected my Jewishness, the storm clouds, and people's homes? Nothing I knew intellectually, but a connection I felt that I could not (and cannot and will not) explain. This poem also connected, for me, with the film *Cat Ballou* and the insistence of the old gunfighter that the Indians were the lost tribe of the Israelites. Thoughts began to swirl. I brought together weather and the elements, my Jewishness, what it means to be in a land, and more. I allowed a swirl of seemingly disconnected elements to come together, to lead me forward in what it meant to be part of the land, how the weather and the land were part of the identity of human beings, and what this meant for the battle lines drawn in the curriculum project meetings (although, please note that in this poem the project is not mentioned). I didn't do this through any sort of straightforward assemblage of politically astute analysis. I allowed images to well up, spill forth, and then fashioned them into the final writing.

I want to underscore this description of my process, for I think it stands at the heart of wild imagination. It is surreal in the sense that nothing belongs together in a typically rational manner. It plays as children can play, who assemble an odd assortment of "things" and then make a world. It is personal and distanced simultaneously. These two elements, coupled with the unbidden "The Principal's Regret," begin to get at a way into wild imagination.

Wild imagination is not limited to the poetry. Even the theoretical musings were part of this inchoate process. When I came to examine the place for which this curriculum was destined, I wrote:

> The school, the place, the land. Geography matters, the human geography which wends about the corner its influence and meaning. The place, the school, the places in which the people live. Perhaps these are the most contested aspects of their lives. My mother-in-law lived in the house in which I knew her for many, many years. She chose that house, that place as her place, the place in which and out of which her life had most meaning for her. No other place would do, could speak of her or for her and she defended it fiercely against all encroachment and injustice. These days few of us know of such attachment to the land, the place, the buildings, the human geography of our souls. Indeed, I must say "souls" for that human geography (those buildings, the cobwebbed barn, the lofty house which settles one into the earth) touches something so deep in us that we know no rationality but only a love which binds us, which binds to us, which is ours. We dream in that geography, we dream of that geography as it carries our histories to us and sustains us, makes us melt with missing. But, whose geography shall it be? The place where she lived was not always her place or even the white people's place, but the place for hunting, for fishing, for farming, for sustenance of another people. And it was not their place either but, and yet, we feel attached to a place where we find the meaning of our lives in every stone and stream. We dream in that place. And that is, perhaps, most important,

> that we dream in that place, dream a life, dream of a life, dream for a life to be our own life. But, we cannot dream another's life, only our own, and how shall we know the life we dream is our own? By what meanings, traditions shall we recognize ourselves in the dream? Whose dream is it, anyway?

What has my mother-in-law to do with this project? Nothing, and yet I felt there was some connection between her love of her place in Cleveland, Ohio and the Navajo love of their place. I didn't think about the political implications of this, but only that there is something, perhaps in all of us, that taps into a rootedness in the land that we need for the sustaining of our lives. We do not notice, usually, that we may be standing on the land that was, at one time, someone else's home, which makes the situation more fraught and confusing. Whose land is it, and what does it mean to even think that the land belongs to anyone? Simultaneously, there is the sustaining of place that supports us. This sustaining is connected to dreaming.

Power play permeates the whole of *Hogan Dreams*, as characters vied for domination and/or control and/or a place in the project. There were the Navajos ("Voice") who deployed their hidden power in ways that protected them from the outsiders and yet kept their voice in the mix. There was the encounter between the "important academic expert in Navajo culture" and the Principal ("The Rooms of the Meeting"): immensely violent in a nonviolent way and yet, how? There was my own confusion as to my place in that world or any world. Through my writing I brought together the disparate elements of my own experiences outside the project, my wanderings into social theory, and the events of the project itself. Lastly, and unseen at the time, there was an exploration of weather as a unifying constant that I had not known until after finishing writing *Hogan Dreams*. I experienced "weather" as meaningful as we drove through the reservation to attend our first project meetings. We stopped at a pullout to look at the landscape. I remember feeling something about the air, the sky, the distant mountains, the flat, sere, seemingly empty desert that felt filled with portent for me. I didn't know what it meant, still don't know what it means, but I felt it and felt strongly moved by it in an inchoate way. But, with all this description, I worry that you might take *Hogan Dreams* as moralistic. I hope not. It is, for me, a sad, even tragic tale, with no clear judgment about what to do, but with strong hints of what felt wrong but, at the same time, what was beautiful and powerful and life-opening.

The whole of *Hogan Dreams* seems, in retrospect, to be profoundly political without being partisan or oriented toward social justice. I didn't know this at the time of the writing, but I engaged with creative writing in order to think about the context in a new form. As with "The Principal's Regret," I wrote to know what I think by sifting through my unconscious mind as a poet.

## Discussion

I have tried to situate the political as a ubiquitous character of all art-making, indeed probably of all inquiry. But, this ubiquity is no reason to insist that social justice concerns are necessary or even desirable when practicing ABER. If we insist on political certainty, then we forget about the affordances of art as a form of inquiry into the confusing world in which we live and lose what makes ABER invaluable. When we use art-making instrumentally for other ends, we open ourselves to superseding art as the preferred instrument of political action, when a "better" way is discovered for accomplishing social justice ends.

That is another reason I am asserting that ABER is first and foremost about making art, about problematizing the taken-for-granted world, about posing questions to that world for which there are no easy answers. We must help people reexperience that which has become frozen in their lives. Art-making provides the opportunity to become skeptical of what we know; in turn, we become skeptical of ourselves.

How do we accomplish what I have stipulated are the affordances of art-making and art-experiencing? We accomplish them through the deployment of beauty. Yes, beauty, a word so contested I almost dare not use it. But, I must. What is art, at its core, other than a deployment of beauty, which no other form of inquiry provides except tangentially, such as the beauty of a mathematical proof? I cannot tell you what constitutes "beauty," but I know that artists strive for beauty, even when others think that what has been accomplished isn't beautiful. Sometimes, the most overtly "ugly" art is beautiful. Beauty is no easier than wild imagination. But, it is also no less important.

Taken together, wild imagination and the deployment of beauty provide opportunities for imagining anew, for feeling not that we know (and so we don't have to feel) but that what we thought we knew, we didn't know. We disallow ourselves to feel for others (always at a distance), but feel ourselves discomforted. Wild imagination seeks beauty through putting unlikes together, being willing to encounter what we cannot expect, to be wild and not care about the outcomes, being sure *something will happen* that inevitably calls our truisms into question. That is not political in the sides-taking form of politics, but it is political in the way of feeling the ebb and flow of powers as the world swirls around us. ABER can leave the politics of side-taking to the political arena and provide the opportunity for everyone in that arena to reconsider themselves and their sureties. That is what beauty and wild imagination can provide.

## Postscript

Since writing this chapter, I have come to think in two ways about the state of the field. First, I continue to feel that the arts-based research (ABR) field is dominated by simply recording one's feelings in art-like language and image. I reject this idea as I have always done. I support art as "objective" inquiry through which something is discovered that surprises the maker. This involves an unstinting self-critique and objectivity applied to the emerging art-work, distancing oneself from what is emerging, while simultaneously continuing to be immersed in the sheer emotional embodiment of the making, living dialectically between two opposed motives. Second, however, there appears to be a hopefully emergent position of ABR as action taken from within a non-verbal embodied action that enacts work but with the necessary distancing to come to understand what one is doing in a way that strengthens the work through self-critique. As Hanya Holm, one of the founding Mothers of Modern Dance, put it to me many years ago "If you're stuck and have gone down the wrong road that 'felt' right, then you must go back to the fork in the road and make the work bleed again."

## References

Bagley, C., & Cancienne, M. B. (2002). *Dancing the data*. Peter Lang.

Bakhtin, M. M. (1982). *The dialogic imagination (four essays)*. University of Texas Press.

Blumenfeld-Jones, D. S. (2002/2012). If I could have said it, I would have. In D. S. Blumenfeld-Jones (Ed.), *Curriculum and the aesthetic life: Hermeneutics, ethics, body, and curriculum*. Peter Lang.

Blumenfeld-Jones, D. S. (2004/2012). Hogan dreams. In D. S. Blumenfeld-Jones (Ed.), *Curriculum and the aesthetic life: Hermeneutics, ethics, body, and curriculum*. Peter Lang.

Blumenfeld-Jones, D. S. (2014). Arts-based educational research serving the public good: A critical Brechtian perspective. *International Journal of Education and the Arts*, *15*(SI 2.1), 1–12. http://www.ijea.org/v15si2

Blumenfeld-Jones, D. S. (2015). The artistic process and arts-based research: A phenomenological account of the practice. *Qualitative Inquiry*, *22*(5), 322–333. https://doi.org/10.1177/1077800415620212

Bourdieu, P. (1972). *Outline of a theory of practice*. Cambridge University Press.

Bourdieu, P. (1993). *The field of cultural production*. Columbia University Press.

Brecht, B. (1936). Theater for pleasure and theater for instruction. In W. B. Worthen (Ed.), *Wadsworth anthology of drama* (4th ed.). Thomson.

Denzin, N. K. (2000). Aesthetics and the practices of qualitative inquiry. *Qualitative Inquiry*, 6(2), 256–265. https://doi.org/10.1177/107780040000600208

Doctorow, E. L. (2014, January 11). Doctorow ruminates on how a 'brain' becomes a mind. [podcast]. *Weekend Edition Saturday*. NPR. https://www.npr.org/2014/01/11/261450791/doctorow-ruminates-on-how-a-brain-becomes-a-mind

du Rose, L. (1998). Racial domain and the imagination of Wallace Stevens. *The Wallace Stevens Journal*, *22*(*1*), 3–22. https://www.jstor.org/stable/44884497

Finley, S. (2003). Arts-based inquiry in QI: Seven years from crisis to guerrilla warfare. *Qualitative Inquiry*, *9*, 281–296. https://doi.org/10.1177/1077800402250965

Finley, S. (2017a, May). The future of critical arts-based research: Creating political spaces for resistance politics. Plenary address at the 2017 ICQI Conference, Champaign, IL.

Finley, S. (2017b). Critical arts-based inquiry. In N. Denzin & Y. Lincoln (Eds.), *The SAGE handbook of qualitative inquiry* (5th ed.). Sage.

Finley, S., & Finley, M. (1999). Sp'ange: A research story. *Qualitative Inquiry*, *5*(3), 313–337. https://doi.org/10.1177/107780049900500302

Giroux, H. (2013, August 13). *When schools become dead zones of the imagination: A critical pedagogy manifesto*. Truthout. https://truthout.org/articles/when-schools-become-dead-zones-of-the-imagination-a-critical-pedagogy-manifesto/

Haiven, M., & Khasnabish, A. (2014). *The radical imagination: Social movement research in the age of austerity*. Zed Books.

Kelley, R. D. G. (2002). *Freedom dreams: The black radical imagination*. Beacon Press.

Lincoln, Y. S. (1995). Emerging criteria for quality in qualitative and interpretive research. *Qualitative Inquiry*, *1*(3), 275–289. https://doi.org/10.1177/107780049500100301

Yeats, W. B. (1933). Crazy Jane talks with the bishop. In *Collected poems* (pp. 294–295). Macmillan.

Chapter 7

# Finding the Progress in Work-in-Progress

## Liz Lerman's Critical Response Process in Arts-Based Research

*John Borstel*

### Critical Response Process (CRP): Choreographing the Conversation for Arts-Based Inquiry

Liz Lerman was vexed. In the late 1980s, at mid-career as a working choreographer, touring educator, and community facilitator, she found herself frequently at odds with usual practices in the arts for feedback and critique. She chafed at the one-sided nature of newspaper criticism. She doubted the merits of her own critical impulses when invited to assess the work of university students as a visiting artist or of peers as a grants panelist. She watched powerless as feedback sessions about artistic work (occasionally her own) stalled, collapsed, or spun out of control. Driven by dissatisfaction, Lerman, who went on to receive a 2002 MacArthur Fellowship, started her search for a new method for dialogic and nurturing feedback. Her first step was to define good feedback as the kind of response that makes you eager to get back to work on the project under consideration. Asking what creates the conditions for such feedback, she sought partners for experimentation, tried out some ideas, and within a short period had coalesced the structure she called the Critical Response Process (CRP) (Lerman & Borstel, 2003). Since its introduction in 1990, CRP has been embraced by practitioners and institutions in practically every arts discipline, in North America, Europe, and beyond. This chapter describes Lerman's method and its relevance for arts-based researchers in education.

I had my first encounters with CRP in my capacities on the staff of Dance Exchange, Liz's performance company, functioning as in-house writer, fund seeker, and communications project manager. I was soon facilitating, co-leading trainings, and partnering to write about the Process. In time, CRP infiltrated my own practice as an interdisciplinary artist and photography teacher. I've maintained a steady practice and continued to work with both Liz and the Dance Exchange (which have been independent of each other since 2011) to take CRP into diverse artistic, educational, and institutional settings, including the training of social science researchers.

### CRP and ABR: Emerging Conditions and a Common Path

The relevance of CRP for readers of this book is rooted in the common ground between Liz's lifelong focus and arts-based research (ABR) concerns. A boundary-buster from the start of her career, Liz invented the Process when she was working at the crossroads of art and social purpose, art and learning, and art and activism. It was a point when she was deeply invested in the "nonfiction" potential of dances about history, current events, and

DOI: 10.4324/9781003412892-7

cultural identity that engaged research collaborations with scholars and practitioners in those fields.

Both CRP and ABR have emerged and gained strength over the last 25 years in ways that reflect a larger phenomenon challenging the traditional separation between process and product. Not so long ago within the arts, product was the primary focus of consideration in education, public perception, and professional practice. Product was everything. But, the last two decades have seen a growing premium placed on process and its value as a source of learning, a useful commodity, a focus for documentation and analysis, and a locus of public encounter. Process, moreover, is increasingly perceived in an integrated rather than diametrical relationship to product, a both/and rather than an either/or. The emergence of ABR as a field partly reflects this understanding of the inherent value of process and the possibility of multiple outcomes extending from acts of making art.

This change in our perception of process has radically repositioned the concept of work-in-progress from the artists' secretive purview to a focus of public engagement, from a forum of feints, failures, and red pencil to a generative laboratory. In the neighborhoods of the art world where this new mentality has taken hold, artists can be more vulnerable, artwork more malleable, interim states of formation more exposed and appreciated, and an audience's role as a cocreator of meaning more active and overt. Work-in-progress has come out of its closet: rather than a focus for shame, apology, and inadequacy, it stands as an emblem for (just imagine!) progress.

You can observe this shift toward exposed and audience-engaged process in almost every art form, e.g., the emergence of ensemble-devised work in theatre, immersive productions, and public readings of scripts in progress; the fan fiction phenomenon, which offers an audience the opportunity to participate in the creation of a fictional world rather than simply consume an artistic product. The shift is evident in my own field of photography when, for example, National Gallery of Art's 2009 exhibition on Robert Frank's *The Americans* includes page proofs, marked-up contact sheets, and even the typewritten original of the photographer's Guggenheim Fellowship application (National Gallery of Art, 2009) or when Annie Leibovitz tours her *Women: New Portraits* collection to pop-up sites in ten cities, hanging test prints of her recent local work as the focus of public "talking circles" moderated by collaborator Gloria Steinem (Sheets, 2016). What might once have been thought of as devaluing a product through demystification of process now only adds to the wonder of art and diversification of its functions.

This repositioning of work-in-progress parallels a reconsideration of critique and its role in the art world. In *Beyond Critique* (Walters-Eller & Basile, 2013), a publication of Maryland Institute College of Art (MICA), faculty members offer a plurality of methods and mindsets for guiding visual art critique. Art School, Critique 2.0, a series of symposia at Teacher's College, Columbia University that began in 2014, is posing the question "How have the recent changes to the learning landscape—student-centered teaching models, collaborative ways of making and online classrooms—changed the nature and practice of critiques?" (Columbia University, 2014). At Arizona State University, David Tinapple's CritViz offers a computer-based platform for digitally connected learners in classes of 50–100 students, combining numeric peer ranking with challenges of articulation that benefit both givers and receivers of feedback (CritViz, 2017). These innovations in academe have been spurred by the realization that traditional, professor-driven, free-for-all art school-style "crit" sessions no longer serve a culturally diverse and technologically adept student body or offer preparation for the expanded and integrated roles that arts majors might assume in the 21st century. From almost every subsector of the arts, be it community engagement, arts-integrated K-12 education, or the tradition-bound (and tradition-grappling) conservatory world, Liz and I get queries from passionate practitioners who not only want to find better ways of doing critique, but also perceive functional feedback processes as central to improving collaboration, supporting interdisciplinary encounters, and enhancing learning.

Meanwhile, the climate for feedback is also shifting in scholarly domains beyond the arts, particularly in terms of how research is refereed, leading to innovations in the peer review process. In the 1990s, some science publications began to experiment with open peer review, which has entailed the publication of reviewer comments alongside scholarly articles (Van Rooyen et al., 1999). The emergence of electronic platforms for academic publishing has encouraged a transition from pre- to post-publication review, wherein research may be posted in an online journal without passing a review panel, but then is open for commentary, critique, and numeric rating, publicly displayed in a thread that follows the article (Marlow, 2013). Through the introduction of wikis, digital technology has made it possible for scholarly content to be vetted and modified in knowledge management systems that are collaborative, ongoing, and readily updatable. These changes reflect both a transition in thinking about critique and a more fluid understanding of the process/product relationship, offering some parallels to the shifts I've noted in arts fields.

What, then, are the ramifications for critique in ABR, particularly as a mode of exploration that occurs at the borders of art, social science, and education? How might a generative CRP mentality about work-in-progress be embraced as an asset for ABR? What are the multiple meanings of critique in the varied communicative, evidential, and exploratory ways that art and research intersect as artistic practice brings new methods to bear on the rigors of research?

## ABR as Work-in-Progress

If work-in-progress is the open field where ABR happens, then critique can be thought of as its centralized laboratory. And the most effective laboratory might be one equipped to address the unique modes of thinking and qualities of knowledge that artistic research deploys.

> Artistic research as form of knowledge production ... invites 'unfinished thinking.' Hence, it is not formal knowledge that is the subject matter of artistic research, but thinking in, through, and with art.
>
> (Borgdorff, 2010)

In contemplating these words of philosopher and music theorist Henk Borgdorff, consider the possibility of a critique method that exalts and harvests "unfinished thinking" and that engenders a process of "thinking in, through, and with art." Moreover, with the wide range and variation in what is defined as ABR, consider the number of purposes to which such critique might be put:

- To assess and help shape the artistic dimensions of the work in ways that encompass emotional, aesthetic, and conceptual qualities, both on their own merit and in relation to research aspects.
- To vet research-focus areas or models, processes, or outputs of research at various stages in the development of a project.

- To conduct research by surfacing response, testing questions, and harnessing dialogue to the development of ideas.
- To advance learning-through-research in formal educational contexts by pushing in the moment discovery and constituting formative assessment.
- To facilitate the cross-disciplinary collaboration frequently engaged in ABR contexts.

Among the options, CRP is uniquely equipped to meet these varied functions by virtue of its constructive, asset-based orientation, the mindfulness it engages to address the interpersonal dimensions of critique, and the probing role that it accords to disciplined inquiry. Rather than pausing the development of work-in-progress for a detour into feedback, CRP engages feedback for its active potential as creativity, learning, and research. The Process is described as follows with examples intended to elucidate its value in ABR contexts.

## The Critical Response Process

CRP's structure has held its form consistently over the 25 years since it was devised. In a brief description on paper (Figure 7.1), CRP can appear flat and procedural. Its essential points are fairly simple, but its principles run deep. As regular practitioners of this system, Liz and I are constantly surprised by the new subtleties, perspectives, and functions that we continue to discover within it.

### *The Setup*

CRP engages an (schol)artist, a group of responders, and a facilitator in a sequence of four steps, usually following directly on a showing of work-in-progress. (Note: As is our general practice, in the text that follows we use the word "artist" as a term of convenience to designate the person[s] receiving feedback regardless of discipline, but that individual can be the originator of work of any kind, in any discipline.) I refer to the inquiry into making as "research" and as an arts-inquiry ABR extension.

Even before CRP begins, questions with relevance to the research functions of critique often arise. "Should I say anything about the work?" an artist might ask. We ask artists to contemplate what they want to get from the feedback and to weigh how a preamble will color responders' experiences and the ways they engage with the work.

Consider the effects of a contextualizing statement like this:

> The human images that we've used on this quilt have been digitally reproduced from a series of posters on the theme 'This is America: Keep it free' released by the U.S. Government during World War II. Intended to promote patriotism, these posters depicted only white subjects who appear to live in all-white communities. In crafting the quilt with my collaborator, we have combined the images with whitework, a traditional technique featuring white stitching on white fabric.

This opener is likely to have two effects: (1) viewers are cued to look for something in particular, thereby potentially gaining greater insight to share with the artist about the relationship of their experience of the work to the intention behind it, and (2) it narrows the field of vision, and therefore the scope of commentary/inquiry. By telling responders to "look for this," such a preamble diminishes the likelihood they will perceive other things,

**The Critical Response Process**

**The Roles**

- The **artist** offers a work-in-progress for review and is prepared to question that work in a dialogue with other people.
- One, a few, or many **responders**—committed to the artist's intent to make excellent work—engage in the dialogue with the artist.
- The **facilitator**, initiates each step, keeps the process on track, and works to help the artist and responders use the process to frame useful questions and responses.

**The Steps**

The Critical Response Process takes place after a presentation of artistic work. Work can be short or long, large or small, and at any stage in its development.

1. **Statements of Meaning:** Responders state what was meaningful, evocative, interesting, exciting, striking in the work they have just witnessed.

2. **Artist as Questioner:** The artist asks questions about the work. After each question, the responders answer. Responders may express opinions if they are in direct response to the question asked and do not contain suggestions for changes.

3. **Neutral Questions:** Responders ask neutral questions about the work. The artist responds. Questions are *neutral* when they do *not* have an opinion couched in them. For example, if you are discussing the lighting of a scene, "Why was it so dark?" is not a neutral question. "What ideas guided your choices about lighting?" is.

4. **Opinion Time:** Responders state opinions, subject to permission from the artist. The usual form is "I have an opinion about ______, would you like to hear it?" The artist has the option to say no.

Liz Lerman's Critical Response ProcessSM


*Figure 7.1* Liz Lerman's Critical Response Process.

make other connections, or have experiences that do not relate to the artist's framing. Neither approach is right or wrong, and the artist's choice may be driven by multiple factors: where she is in the development of the work, the knowledge level of this particular audience, and what she hopes to learn from this particular round of dialogue.

The other principle CRP facilitators offer is that, for purposes of the feedback, "The art starts as soon as you begin talking," that is, everything you do or say in the act of presenting your work will be subject to response. Therefore, the more extensive the statement, the more likely the critique is to address the preamble's content and presentation versus critique of the artwork itself. The alternative to this framing is to allow context and intention to emerge over the course of the four steps. They inevitably will. When in doubt, I recommend trusting in that inevitability. Introductory statement or no statement, CRP follows four steps once responders have experienced the work.

*Step One: Statements of Meaning*

CRP begins with a question posed by the facilitator to responders: "What was exciting, meaningful, memorable, interesting, and/or provocative to you about the work you just witnessed?" "Statements of Meaning" filters out strong discomforts and negative opinions from the conversation. (Responders are encouraged, however, not to suppress those impulses from consideration, as they will be able to address them, to the possible benefit of the work, later in the sequence of steps.) A kind of microscope, kaleidoscope, and periscope for the work-in-progress, step one deepens and elaborates the varied lenses of as many responders as are gathered to receive and perceive the work. Meaning is manifold. Using some examples loosely, based on my recent encounters applying CRP to art at the intersection of research, social purpose, and education, step one responses might sound like this:

- In response to the preceding quilt example:
  - *"The handwork is exquisite ... beautifully done."*
  - *"A quilt makes me think of southern traditions that cut across racial lines."*
  - *"The fragmentation of the original artwork against a white background throws the faces into high relief."*
- In response to an interactive dance/theatre performance engaging dialogue about public health issues:
  - *"I was impressed with the performers' ability to create an improvisation based on a story from the audience."*
  - *"What really sticks with me is the idea that readily accessible dental care will improve overall public health."*
  - *"The story of the family that sacrificed to pay for the kids' dentistry really resonated with my own experience. I felt it in my gut."*
- In response to a lesson plan that engages middle school students in writing manifestos of personal belief and designing monumental sculpture:
  - *"The focus on manifestos is a great way to bring together art history with political history."*
  - *"I'm stimulated by the idea of building a monument to a value."*
  - *"Your students are lucky to have a teacher with so much conviction and enthusiasm."*

Step one mirrors and manifests the ways that we construct knowledge and meaning from any first encounter with new material. This is evident in two ways: (1) how people categorize particular attributes of the work (through aesthetic dimensions like color, dynamics, form, or metaphoric qualifiers); and (2) through personal filters, offering connections to states of stimulation, preference, individual affinities, and memory.

Broadly speaking, the categorization impulse is ordered and rational. The connection to personal experience is emotional and intuitive. These functions oscillate and inform the response to produce a series of richly served renderings of the artwork or research under consideration as subjective events, interspersed with qualitative information about past experience, interpretation, and emotional states. Considered as feedback on research-through-art, it captures the emotional, exploratory, and analytical aspects of artistic experience.

CRP's productive synthesis of multiple mental functions contrasts with the intentional separation of objective and subjective responses that is often featured in other systems for critique. For instance, Krafchek (2013) describes an eight-step process of "liberatory critique" that includes separate steps of "I see" (in which viewers strive to take an unbiased inventory of the work being considered) and "I feel" (in which they may give free rein to emotional reactions). It is interesting to contemplate how CRP's oscillation between rational and emotional compares to the separation of the functions in Krafchek's system to potentially yield a greater amount of unique value to the "unfinished thinking" referenced earlier.

For fellow responders, step one offers a level of replay, refocus, and a chance to reexperience the work, perhaps with fresh slants. For the maker, these reprojections of the work can be set against their own internalized image of the work in all of its dimensions of impulse, intention, and process. In sum, Statements of Meaning filters out strong discomforts, placing a broadly defined idea of meaning at the forefront to enrich developing work-in-progress in the following forms:

- A vein of response in which rational and emotional are enlightening one another.
- Externalizations and interpretations of the work that offer the artist a comparison with their vision, intention, impulse, or generative experience.
- An amplification of the work to precede the deeper interrogation through question and opinion that happens later in the process.

Usually step one promotes an atmosphere of goodwill, heightened potential, and forward momentum for the work under consideration. Applied to ABR in its early stages, step one can suggest paths of focus and inquiry.

#### *Step Two: Artist Asks Questions*

The next two CRP steps are about questions and responses. This is where CRP departs from many traditions in critique in which artists are either charged to keep silent or placed in a position to defend while other participants in the conversation are free to offer responses unchecked by reflection or any measure of the artist's own perspective. Step two also contrasts with traditional academic peer review, where communication tends to move in one direction from reviewer to scholar with the expectation that comments are to be addressed through revision rather than through discourse.

There is great power in artist-driven questions. When we ask a question, we surrender certainty, name what is unknown, and begin to negotiate its relationship to the known. This is demonstrated by a warm-up we often do near the start of a CRP workshop, a practice initiated by my colleague Margot Greenlee. We ask participants to talk about something in their lives that is a work-in-progress. (I have heard a range of responses from choreographing a dance about immigration policy, to launching a $5 million capital campaign, to "cleaning out my car.") Then, I'll invite participants to formulate questions:

- How can I facilitate and execute a collaborative mural with only one week for the process and $200 for materials?
- How can I inspire preteen girls to think critically about the images of women they encounter in the media?

- How do I get my staff excited about a new initiative that can transform our mission but may mean extra work for them?
- Am I in too far to back out now?

How such questions function for their framers is worth considering. Sometimes the question will already be sitting at the surface: "It's what I keep asking myself ..." At other times, question-making moves thinking forward by concretizing discomforts or sharpening uncertainties. "How" questions are frequent, sometimes of a technical nature, but often of a diplomatic turn. Other questions probe the maker's own reasons or impulses, or the role in the wider world of the thing being made. Optimally, questions change your brain and offer creative breakthroughs that can start immediately upon their articulation—preceding answers. As one participant told me: "When I talked about the project, I said all the things I already knew. When I tried to form a question, it shifted my mind into areas that I hadn't previously considered." The mind's unique capacity for inquiry surfaces the questions that open out of CRP.

But, the dynamics of inquiry exercised in steps two and three entail more than flatly stating a question and seeking its answer. Because there is a consciousness of how a question may influence an answer, artists and responders may be challenged to engage in a kind of elastic thinking about the question, in which they move the framework from general to specific, preliminary to follow-up, wide to narrow, and biased to neutral. To encounter art this way is to probe its potential, grasp its implications, and grapple with where the artist ends and the art begins. To encounter research this way—content that embodies information, elicits data, or expands knowledge—is to manage the relationship between method and means and to align evidence, intention, and interpretation. When art and research combine, the discourse can be incisive, deep, and occasionally challenging.

In the context of ABR, among other functions, step two offers the maker an opportunity to explore the critique as a form of research into the content, effect, and broader implications of their work. In forming questions, we encourage artists to rechannel what might be otherwise negative impulses of discomfort, uncertainty, apology, problem-finding, and gap perception. With these articulations augmented by opportunity to exercise curiosity in front of an invested audience, questions can take many forms, such as deepening a specific aspect of the work, surveying responders' connections, or vetting options for future phases.

- Since the focus of this project is to promote dialogue about public health, what insights or new knowledge did you gain about that subject?
- What struck you or stood out about the central figure of a woman wielding a sword? How did you identify with her?
- What was it like to switch back and forth between watching the performance and talking to your fellow audience members?
- What was your experience during the section of the work when the four actors were all telling stories simultaneously? What words, images, or ideas stood out to you?

Throughout, step two tests the artist's capacity for exercising elastic thinking and may challenge the facilitator to guide the artists to the question that will be both generative and pertinent to their concerns.

By asking questions, the artist drives the discussion of the work-in-progress. In the dialogue that emerges, step two can offer:

- A chance to test the premise(s) of the work;
- An exploration into the dynamics of the art or other content in relation to this audience, with a probe into the communicative power of the work;
- Depending on the stage of the work, if it has a research focus, a chance to extend the focus or the approach through the information gathered;
- In work with social relevance, a range of cultural viewpoints and language choices that can create or dissolve distinctions.

Considering its potential as a form of research, step two can expand knowledge about the subject matter as well as about the artistic form and the terms on which it addresses its audience. Often, the more innovative and out-of-convention that form is, the richer the research and the more we stand to learn.

#### *Step Three: Responders Ask Neutral Questions*

In step three, the dialogue is reversed. Responders ask questions that are *neutral*, meaning they do *not* have an opinion couched in them. For example, if you are discussing the lighting of a scene, "Why was it so dark?" is not a neutral question. "What ideas guided your choices about lighting?" is.

Responders' questions can be motivated by curiosity, a desire to get the artist to think and talk about a particular dimension of the work, or by a strong opinion, but, with neutrality prevailing, the question must be phrased as not to expose that opinion. This discipline affords dialogue on the topic of the opinion and allows the responder to be informed about the artist's perspective before exercising the opportunity to offer an opinion in step four.

Here's an example from a neutral question dialogue with a middle school visual art teacher developing a lesson plan about connecting personal convictions to monument design:

*Responder:* Before students create their scale models, you are having them do a two-dimensional rendering as a drawing. Can you talk about this aspect?

*Artist:* I'm influenced by the concept of drawing-as-thinking, an idea promoted by the famous graphic designer Milton Glaser and some others. The idea is that drawing is not just a tool for rendering reality but a way of experiencing the world, developing ideas, maybe connecting vision to reality. The students in the class are keeping drawing journals and I'm trying to work drawing-as-thinking into as many of our activities as possible.

Frequently in step three, follow-up questions are useful:

*Responder:* How do you see this idea of drawing-as-thinking playing out in helping the students get to their monument designs?

*Artist:* Doing a drawing in advance will require them to zero in on a vision in their mind and get specific, before they get their hands on sculptural materials, where a sense of improvisation can sometimes take over. I guess the idea is to focus intention.

Step three questions may also seek to guide the artist's thinking, while still remaining neutral:

*Responder:* Are there other ways to apply the idea of drawing-as-thinking in this project?
*Artist:* That's interesting. I'd have to think about it ... The first thing that occurs to me is that there might be an earlier step, maybe having the students make multiple thumbnails that translate ideas from the manifestos they are writing into visual form. But yes, that's worth exploring.

Step three's exchange takes place both as a verbal dialogue and as an intersection of thought processes. Knowledge is revealed, processed, and parsed in a variety of ways. The responder may be testing a hypothesis about the artist's work and its possibilities, which the neutral question exposes to deeper investigation. Because the questioner has taken time to reflect on how to frame the inquiry, neutrality builds a relationship between the two participants, and the dialogue may therefore assume more risk, potentially leading the artist into the fruitful unknown. When, as in the preceding example, a neutral question can have one or more follow-ups that probe deeper as information is revealed, the dialogue can take the form of a laboratory in which the artist is guided in actively seeking new options and potential solutions.

When defensiveness starts, learning stops. The neutral question re-sequences the dynamics of attack and defense—frequently encountered in conventional critiques—into one of inquiry and emergence. Rather than a negative opinion prompting a retort or a shutdown, neutral inquiry elicits an opening of information that informs, alters, or surgically narrows the focus of the responder's opinion to ready it for sharing in step four.

The curious and sometimes confounding challenge of framing a neutral question returns us to the idea of elastic thinking, as it exercises the mind's capacity to expand and contract a frame of reference. Or it can shift a frame of reference. Such a shift can recategorize the perspective to correct an assumption and challenge the way that categorization can limit understanding.

Distilling, refining, clarifying, and discerning: all are functions of step three, and all are relevant when work has a research component. In this context, step three can lead to:

- Constructive challenges to critical thinking;
- New articulations that may be helpful in advancing the work;
- Identification of points that need to be clarified and the exploration of ways to clarify;
- A model for collaborative thinking.

#### *Step Four: Permissioned Opinions*

Step four is opinion time, in which responders state opinions, subject to permission from the artist. The usual form is "I have an opinion about ______, would you like to hear it?" Artists may decline or accept.

Occasionally, in a formalized CRP training, someone new to the Process will call a time-out in step one and—thinking that any sort of personal viewpoint is to be withheld until step four—will say, "But aren't these opinions?" Indeed, opinion is with us every step of the way in CRP. And there's no denying that however much we might try to finesse, manage, or reformulate it, opinion is the first and most strongly sustained position many of us jump to when experiencing new work. Our opinions, when mined, are full of information that may be of genuine value to the maker of art or the purveyor of research. CRP allows us to winnow through that opinion to find the most useful to that purpose, as statements of meaning in step one, as honest responses that bear directly on artist's questions in step two, or as the motivator to neutral questions in step three. Step four—note, the end, not the beginning—is when we get the chance, if invited by the artist, to state it uncontrolled by such protocols. A responder who has employed the disciplines and filters of the Process in an engaged and mindful way leading up to that point is likely to encounter an artist eager to hear the opinion.

Much as we expect in-progress art to be pliant, malleable, and subject to change as a condition of meaningful critique, CRP makes an equal, complementary call to opinion. Are you, the opinionated, and your opinion open to change, development, revision, dismissal, or recalibration during the course of the Process's four steps? If the artist in CRP is engaged in a research process about the value and validity of their work, so equally is the responder engaged in research into the viability of their opinion, subjecting it to the scrutiny of the thinking disciplines engaged in the first three steps. So, by the time the step explicitly focused on opinion arrives, it may have passed through a refining fire, becoming more specific, more gauged to the expressed concerns or intentions of the artist, or more contextualized inside aesthetic, formal, or research-based terms that are meaningful to the maker. Or it may have resolved itself or discovered its own irrelevance.

The protocol, some would say ritual, of asking permission to state an opinion on a defined dimension or topic may strike CRP newcomers as its most arcane or even stilted feature. Relative to the refining functions of the Process, it calls on the responder to narrow, categorize, or recapitulate the subject of an earlier exchange and to renew the contract with the artist that has built the interpersonal relationship through the earlier steps.

*Responder:* I have an opinion about having students draw their monument concepts in advance and the idea of drawing-as-thinking. Would you like to hear it?

*Artist:* Yes, please.

*Responder:* I was initially concerned about the drawing requirement, because rendering a three-dimensional object out of imagination seemed like a somewhat advanced task for middle school and that it might be a source of frustration. I was going to suggest that you offer other options, like writing a description or doing preliminary sculpts in less permanent materials, because kids at that age are often hitting that "I can't draw" phase. But, when you described your drawing-as-thinking program, I got excited, because it seems to address that stumbling block head-on and offer a whole range of ways to think about drawing. So, my opinion is that you could incorporate drawing-as-thinking much more integrally. I loved your ideas about a whole series of conceptual thumbnails, and I think you could even expand on that.

Step four encompasses the goals of research and the exposure of new knowledge in a variety of ways:

- Externalizing an experience of the work-in-progress that builds and expands on step one and weighing in on the work relative to context, aesthetic value, and audience perception;

- Sharpening the focus on an aspect of the work, particularly if the responder has used step three to narrow the focus of the opinion;
- Functioning generatively either by posing suggestions (a phenomenon that can be addressed in a variety of ways) or, as in the example, by highlighting a new idea that the artist may have broached earlier in the exchange.

For teachers of artistic disciplines, the process of getting to step four may expose gaps in a student's technique and practice that can be addressed in curriculum. When art is engaged as research, it may surface valuable new questions and open paths within the field of study.

## CRP as Research Practice

Originating in artistic practice over 25 years ago, CRP has, in the last decade, made inroads into varied arenas where art intersects with research, education, and social purpose, as Liz Lerman and I have witnessed through numerous recent encounters. Baltimore Participatory Action Research (BPAR), a group of graduate students and emerging academics in social science and education fields, has employed CRP to nurture research projects, youth-development enterprises, and arts-based educational initiatives. In the spirit of participatory research, BPAR has especially welcomed the ways in which CRP breaks down some of the dominant hierarchies of academic review to create more open, egalitarian ways of advancing inquiry. Seizing on the educational possibilities of this feedback system, the New York City Department of Education is in a three-year project to introduce its 3000-odd arts teachers to CRP. It is currently exploring the ways that CRP can extend existing practices in formative assessment to enhance learning and instruction relative to such hard-to-measure components of arts learning as creative impulse, emotional expression, and individual intention. Dance artist Margot Greenlee, an alumna of Dance Exchange and veteran CRP trainer/facilitator, has been influenced by the Process in designing the response and dialogue aspects of her Perforum methodology, which uses movement, story, and image to facilitate public conversations with field experts about such topics as public health, child marriage, and food equity.

At intersections like these, we observe human creativity and aesthetic expression entering the stream of inquiry in beyond-arts disciplines at varied stages: during early concept and ideation, as the impetus for response, as data and evidence, and at the point where new knowledge is communicated to the public. At whatever point, CRP can offer unique value as art meets the empirical:

- Functioning as a form of peer review, capturing the discernment and rigor valued in scientific and scholarly work while affording room for personal expression and aesthetic response;
- Promoting what I've referred to in this chapter as elastic thinking: when the object of the critique is perceived as pliant and the minds of the participants remain agile, the result is a unique opportunity for shared learning and growth;
- Bringing a horizontal mode of feedback that offers a valuable alternative to hierarchical models, in which responders of varied backgrounds and differing degrees of expertise can participate on a level field;

- Affording a way for practitioners from different disciplines to find a common language through the emphasis on questions as a way to clarify understanding and probe assumptions;
- Allowing participants to gain practice in broadly applicable skills of inquiry.

The conjunction named in the title of this book, *Arts-Based Research in Education*, suggests a unique intersection of domains that are currently undergoing flux within themselves and in relation to each other. New roles for art emerge when creative products and aesthetic experiences are the vehicle for understanding, the measure of human experience, or the impetus for insight. Embracing research as the production of new knowledge that can happen in, through, and with the process and experience of art, ABR encourages broad participation, breaks down barriers between fields, and confounds the old process/product binary. As a mode of feedback imported from the arts, CRP offers distinctive empirical and pedagogical value.

## Postscript

Two significant developments relative to the CRP have occurred since the original publication of this chapter. In 2019, Liz Lerman's organization launched a certification program that annually engages ten to fifteen practitioners in intensive group study and independent practicum exploring the meaning, methods, and knowledge-production potential of CRP. In 2022, Wesleyan University Press published *Critique Is Creative: The Critical Response Process in Theory and Action*. Coauthored by Liz Lerman and John Borstel, this 238-page book features an in-depth survey of the principles of the Process, as well as articles contributed by over 20 guest authors about applications in varied arts, humanities, and teaching disciplines. Information on both the program and the publication are available at lizlerman.com.

## Acknowledgments

The author expresses his thanks to Frank Anderson, Sherella Cupid, and Liz Lerman for their consultation on this chapter and to Diane Kuthy and Margot Greenlee for consultation and permission to use their projects "Swaddled" and "Woman With Sword" as the basis of examples.

## Resources

Published by Dance Exchange, *Liz Lerman's Critical Response Process: A method for getting useful feedback on anything you make from dance to dessert* by Liz Lerman and John Borstel offers a comprehensive overview of the process, its inner workings, and variations. Soft cover and electronic versions are available at Amazon.com.

Information about facilitation and training in CRP is available at www.lizlerman.com.

## References

Borgdorff, H. (2010). The production of knowledge in artistic research. In M. Biggs & H. Karlsson (Eds.), *The Routledge companion to research in the arts* (pp. 44–63). Routledge.

Columbia University. (2014). *Art school critique*. www.tc.columbia.edu/critique20
CritViz. (2017). *Peer review and critique for engaging classrooms*. https://critviz.com/about
Krafchek, K. (2013). The liberatory critique. In S. Walters-Eller & J. J. Basile (Eds.), *Beyond critique: Different ways of talking about art* (pp. 20–25). MICA Press.
Lerman, L., & Borstel, J. (2003). *Liz Lerman's critical response process*. Liz Lerman Dance Exchange.
Marlow, J. (2013). Publish first, ask questions later. *Wired*. http://www.wired.com/2013/07/publish-first-ask-questions-later/
National Gallery of Art. (2009). *Looking In: Robert Frank's "The Americans."* https://www.nga.gov/exhibitions/looking
Sheets, H. M. (2016, October 9). Annie Leibovitz's Work on 'Women' Is Never Done. *New York Times*. https://www.nytimes.com/2016/10/09/arts/design/annie-leibovitzs-work-on-women-is-never-done.html
Van Rooyen, S., Godlee, F., Evans, S., Black, N., & Smith, R. (1999). Effects of open peer review on quality of reviewers' recommendations: A randomised trial. *BMJ*, *318*(7175), 23–27. https://doi.org/10.1136/bmj.318.7175.23
Walters-Eller, S., & Basile, J. J. (Eds.) (2013). *Beyond critique: Different ways of talking about art*. MICA Press.

Chapter 8

# Arts-Based Research

## Histories and New Directions

*Melisa Cahnmann*

### Introduction

With the acceptance of postmodern approaches to educational research in the last few decades including feminism, post-structuralism, critical theory, and semiotics, assumptions about what counts as knowledge and the nature of research have dramatically changed. Not only have multiple qualitative research methodologies gained more widespread acceptance, but also the tools we employ to collect data and display findings have been diversified to include artistic as well as traditionally scientific methods. As a researcher deploying a range of literary, visual, and performing arts through different stages of my own research, I begin this chapter with the assumption that the arts have much to offer educational researchers – challenging us to think creatively about what constitutes research; to explore even more varied and creative ways to engage in empirical processes; and to share our questions and findings in more penetrating and widely accessible ways.

When working with students, I find it helpful to draw on examples of the arts in educational research and related fields in the social sciences, particularly anthropology, to understand how they have been used, by whom, for whom, in what contexts and to what end. Therefore, this edited volume of arts-based research merges essays about arts-based research from both anthropology and education, along with specific examples of practice, to provide a lens for what arts-based educational research (ABER) looks like – i.e., when poetry, visual images, drama, music, and other artistic forms become integral to the empirical project. Reading through the first, second, and third editions of *Arts-Based Research in Education*, one might ask: what do the arts add to a researcher's project and to our general understanding of the topic under study? In other words, how are the arts used, by whom, for whom, for what purpose, and to what possible ends?

As co-editor of these volumes and an arts-based researcher myself, my aim has been to simultaneously explore what arts-based researchers do and identify what is to be gained from blurring the boundaries between the arts and the sciences. While I have long advocated for the increased application of the arts in educational research by highlighting some of the most fresh and exciting contemporary work, I have not posed arts-based approaches to inquiry as an either-or proposition to more traditional, scientific research paradigms. I believe arts-based researchers do no service to themselves to define creative methods in opposition to more traditional approaches to inquiry. Rather, the literary, visual, and performing arts offer ways to stretch a researcher's capacities for creativity and knowing, creating a healthy synthesis of approaches to collect, analyze, and represent data in ways that paint a full picture of a heterogeneous movement to improve education. Every research methodology is a

DOI: 10.4324/9781003412892-8

way of seeing the world – and every way of seeing is a way of not seeing (Eisner, 2002). No methodology is perfect; each comes with trade-offs. It is incumbent on each researcher to know what is gained – and what is lost – in the methods one chooses to employ.

That said, new forms that challenge traditional conceptions of research, can also change "the rules of the game;" and whenever the rules change, there is the possibility of new outcomes on the playing field. New talents are revealed; old talents may not seem as essential as they once appeared. My purpose in this chapter and as co-editor of this book has been to explore this new playing field of the arts and inquiry and to candidly look at what these new possibilities might reveal, increasing our attention to complexity, feeling, and new ways of seeing.

## Early Developments

Educational research has its roots in the late nineteenth and early twentieth centuries when innovators such as Elwood P. Cubberly envisioned building a science of education that emulated industrial practice (Tyack & Cuban, 1995). However, the modern field of education began at the beginning of the nineteenth century, particularly with the work of the Swiss educator Johann Pestalozzi and his German follower, Johann Friedrich Herbart. Both Pestalozzi and Herbart were influenced by the new field of aesthetics that had emerged in German philosophy. As Friedrich Schiller (1795/2004) suggested, aesthetics sought to explore the dimensions of experience that were hidden in the push to impose reason on all levels of human endeavor. For Schiller, aesthetics was a pre-rational understanding that formed the base for the sound and moral application of reason. Pestalozzi and Herbart – as well as followers like Friedrich Froebel and Maria Montessori – were to build educational theory and curricula on these ideas. Thus, the beginnings of educational curriculum theory and research are profoundly arts-based.

This connection is made even more explicit in the work of John Dewey. Writing early in the twentieth century, Dewey (1934/1958) argues that the impulse toward learning begins with *an* experience. However, Dewey is concerned that the kind of artistic experiences that Schiller, Pestalozzi, Herbart, and Froebel envisioned could no longer be termed aesthetic. Dewey feared that effete formalistic appreciation had ossified aesthetic experience (which T. S. Eliot captured so poignantly in "The Love Song of J. Alfred Prufrock"). Therefore, although writing in the spirit that animated the early nineteenth-century theorists – arguing for an emotional, experiential basis of knowing as critical to learning – he suggests that what was now called aesthetic experience was dysfunctional if it did not entail interaction and meaning making.

Dewey's concept of human beings being actively sentient creatures who assemble sensory experience has resonated across other disciplines concerned with the dynamics of learning. For example, the Sapir–Whorf (Carroll, 1956) theory of linguistic relativity, although largely discredited, had tremendous influence on early studies of language and culture, influencing the emergence of *ethnopoetics* as a field of study. Ethnopoetics, a field coined by poet-ethnographer Jerome Rothenberg in 1968 (Brady, 2000) focused largely on differences in aesthetics between Indigenous verbal artists and Western literary traditions. Ethnopoetics was of central concern to linguistic anthropologist, Dell Hymes in his research among Native American communities. Hymes (1964), an anthropological linguist and poet, was the first to propose the "ethnography of communication" as a merged field between linguistics, education, anthropology, and, implicitly, poetry.

Despite the unspoken connections between the arts and early research in education, anthropology, and linguistics, there were few, if any, explicit references to the arts in research before 1980. As to artistic products, there were fewer still. In fact, one of the first female anthropologists, Ruth Benedict (1934), whose book, *Patterns of culture*, was one of the first to introduce the public at large to cultural diversity, published her poetry under pseudonyms in order to keep them hidden from her mentor, Franz Boas, and other academic colleagues (Behar, Chapter 3). By mentioning the arts in academic study, one risked the impression that one's research was less a piece of scholarship than a fictive invention. For some researchers, these fears gave way to a postmodern turn in research, one that became disenchanted with absolute knowledge and objectivity in favor of "an epistemology of ambiguity ... [celebrating] meanings that are partial, tentative, incomplete, and sometimes even contradictory and originating from multiple vantage points" (Barone, 2001, pp. 152–153).

In the field of education, Elliot Eisner, with his graduate students at Stanford University, actively began to build on the discipline of art criticism to develop a new arts-based research methodology for conducting inquiry in the social sciences. This new methodology, which was applied to numerous dissertations, was called *educational criticism* (Eisner, 1991). Eisner's student, Tom Barone, took educational criticism and developed it into a new arts-based methodology, *narrative storytelling*. Where educational criticism called on the researcher to function as a connoisseur to see deeply into a situation and to reveal details that the casual observer would miss, narrative storytelling cast the researcher as a raconteur, who – if necessary – created facts to fill the holes in the story. Barone's (2001) landmark work of arts-based research, *Touching Eternity*, documents his personal research journey from educational criticism to narrative storytelling.

Eisner's work was controversial within the educational community, but provided a beacon that others followed. Within a short time, Sara Lawrence-Lightfoot (1983) published her arts-based methodology of *portraiture* that described her method of combining systematic, empirical description with aesthetic expression to describe the qualities of "goodness" in learning communities.

However, even with the growing adoption of arts-based methods by qualitative researchers, there was continued hostility to embracing the arts in the field of education – which since the time of Elwood P. Cubberly held aspirations of being considered a social science. Consequently, a special panel assembled by the National Academy of Science (Shavelson & Towne, 2002), which was charged with defining the new Federal mandate for scientific-based research, specifically denounced Eisner and Lawrence-Lightfoot's arts-based methods. Thus, by attempting to follow mechanistic models of inquiry from the early part of the twentieth century, educational researchers denied the intellectual arts-based origins of the discipline of education as represented in the work of Rousseau, Pestalozzi, Schiller, Froebel, and Dewey.

## Major Contributions, "Blurred Genres"

Nevertheless, education researchers and others in the social sciences began to embrace this postmodern turn, leading to the origins of what later came to be called "blurred genres," "arts-based inquiry," "scholARTistry," and "a/r/tography." In the last few decades, researchers and theorists have begun to explicitly draw upon blurred genres of the arts and sciences to analyze data and present their findings. In the 1980s these frontrunners in arts-based research – though not identified as such – paved the way for present-day arts-based researchers to take even greater risks, crossing entirely into artistic genres of fiction, poetry, painting, and drama. Because writing is a vital element of research inquiry, most of the initial contributions concentrated on the use and analysis of literary art forms in the human sciences with nods to music and the visual arts.

Other examples, besides Eisner and Lawrence-Lightfoot, include Heath's (1983) classic ethnography of children learning to use language in two different communities, one of the first studies in education to adopt a literary approach to ethnography that drew upon narrative structures and metaphor. Clifford and Marcus's (1986) book *Writing Culture* collected the first group of essays to address the poetic and political nature of cultural representation, drawing attention to the literary and rhetorical dimensions of ethnography.

Music theory and technique have also influenced some of the most noteworthy discourse studies in education, analyzing speech for its rhythm, meter, pitch, and tone. For example, Erickson and Shultz's (1982) study of counselor and student interactions used musical notation in analysis to discover that distorted rhythms in communication were heavily associated with cultural and racial differences. Erickson, who has experience in music composition and theory, used his creativity to enhance his ability to hear and make sense of discordance and harmony in everyday talk. Similarly, Foster's (1989) study analyzed the musical qualities of an African American teacher's classroom discourse to shed light on the qualities of her success in an urban community college classroom. In particular, Foster focused on the teacher's use of Church-influenced discourse patterns such as vowel elongation, cadence manipulation, and repetition. Edelsky (1981) addressed the visual as well as aural aspects of transcription, identifying areas of concern as to how to best represent the authenticity and dimensionality of an observed interaction for conversational analysis.

### Works in Progress, "Arts-Based Research" Is Born

The 1980s and early 1990s were critical for the expanded directions of arts-based inquiry today. However, arts-based research methodologies are still in conflict with conservative scholarly and political climates that emphasize traditional, scientific definitions of research. Thus, modern-day Ruth Benedicts may still exist: education researchers may still be invisibly producing poems as Benedict had, or, worse yet, discouraged from exploring creativity in their scholarship at all.

Despite plentiful deterrents, qualitative researchers in the social sciences, many of whom are represented in this volume – confident that alternative arts-based methods are rigorous, relevant, and insightful – continue to take even greater risks, exploring new dimensions of arts-based methods that experiment at the scientific perimeter to push research questions and methodologies outward and enhance the field.

There is tremendous variety in the ways the arts are incorporated into educational inquiry. For schematic purposes, we identify two major strands in contemporary arts-based research methodology today: those that embrace *hybrid forms* of artistic and scientific scholarship and those that produce *art for scholarship's sake*.

### Hybrid Forms

The hybrid arts-based research text was described by Barone and Eisner (1997) when they first introduced the concept of "arts-based educational research" in Richard M. Jaeger's co-edited book with Barone, *Complementary methods for research in education* that was published by the American Educational Research Association. In this chapter, Barone and Eisner focused largely on contributions of the literary arts in educational research producing blurred genres between the arts and sciences. Barone and Eisner laid out a theoretical framework for arts-based research, describing the qualities of arts-based texts: the creation of a virtual reality and a degree of textual ambiguity; the presence of expressive, contextualized, and vernacular forms of language; the promotion of empathetic participation in the lives of a study's participants; and the presence of an aesthetic form through the unique, personal signature of the researcher.

One of the first book-length examples of arts-based research in education is Tom Barone's (2001) merger of fiction and scholarship in *Touching Eternity*. The hybrid form allowed Barone "to play two games at once" in his study of a high-school art teacher and his former students:

> On the one hand, I assuaged a felt need to speak in an analytical voice about motifs confronted within my conversation with former students. On the other, I wanted to honor the life stories of participants before transforming them into life histories. So I experimented with a format in which life stories were presented extensively and physically distanced from the commentary of the researcher.
>
> (2001, p. 171)

Another impactful book-length work was Ruth Behar's (1993) feminist ethnography, *Translated Woman*, a blurred genre that integrates artistry and anthropology. Behar shares long, uninterrupted stretches of discourse from her informant, Esperanza's, *testimonio* about life experience as a single mother and peddler in Mexico. In addition, Behar shares her own reflections as an anthropologist *del otro lado* – literally from the other side of the border and figuratively from the other side of life in terms of race and class status. Behar's work as well as that of Carolyn Ellis (1997, 1999) has opened the territory of "autoethnography," a merger between autobiography and ethnography, highlighting the extent to which the researcher foregrounds his or her own reflections and experiences in a given study.

Blurred genres of arts-based research contextualize the creation of art – story, poetry, printmaking, sculpture, autobiography, and ethnodrama – within their experimental science, perhaps, as Barone (2001) suggests, "because many postmodernist innovators began their careers as ethnographers and sociologists (rather than as artists, literary critics, or art theorists)" (p. 153). Neilsen (2005) identified blurred-genre work as "scholARTistry," a hybrid practice which combines tools used by the literary, visual, and/or performing arts with tools used by educators and other social scientists to explore the human condition. Neilsen (2005) addresses three goals of scholar/artistry: "to make academic writing an area where virtuosity and clarity are valued, to make educational research an area where the arts are legitimate inquiry, and to infuse scholarship with the spirit of creative connection." Varieties of teacher research and action research also constitute forms of scholar/artistry where an educator uses narrative portraits to document her own literacy classroom (e.g., Hankins, 2003) or where an administrator autoethnographically documents her process to begin the first dual-immersion charter school in Georgia (e.g., Perry, 2005). In visual arts, Irwin and de Cosson (2004) published *A/r/tography*, a collection of work that explores curriculum as aesthetic text through visual renderings as well as prose interpretations.

Blurred genres share many of the same goals in their work. First, to incorporate tools from both the sciences and the arts to make new, insightful sense of data during and beyond the research project. New insights and questions take precedence over a desire for absolute answers to educational and linguistic questions. Second, these blurred genres all share an explicit recognition of the self–other continuum, where the researcher is explicitly recognized as the primary instrument for documenting and interpreting knowledge from participants or from a specific context which ultimately informs the researcher about him or herself as well. Third, blurred genres tend to have the goal to speak to diverse audiences both within and outside the academy. The use of accessible, vernacular, and aesthetic language and image, helps to explicitly reach out to larger, more diverse audiences and to engage in what Barone (Chapter 2) calls "truly dialogical conversation[s] about educational possibilities" (p. 25).

## Art for Scholarship's Sake

If hybrid art forms exist between two ideal forms of "art" and "science" then *art for scholarship's sake* as we define it exists just beyond hybridity in a place that plants itself more squarely in the realm of stand-alone artistry – poems, short stories, paintings, dance, and drama among other forms of artistic expression. Unlike those creating hybrid forms, most creators of art for scholarship's sake have years of training in their art form in addition to their studies in the social sciences. These scholar/artists use their experiences during education fieldwork to create pieces of art that capture the essence of their findings in emotionally penetrating ways. What distinguishes this work from art for *art's* sake is often the context in which this work is found and that the content is typically grounded in the experience of data collection and analysis.

Johnny Saldaña (Chapter 31) had used his 25 years of experience as a theater artist to produce what he calls "ethnodrama," transforming fieldwork data into scripts for live theater. One of Saldaña's best-known ethnodramas is his adaptation of educational anthropologist Harry Wolcott's research into a play called *Finding my place: The Brad Trilogy* (Saldaña, 2002). In this ethnodrama Wolcott, the researcher, and Brad, his research participant, become characters in a script that dramatizes the research findings as well as the complicated and, at times, controversial nature of the research process when the researcher becomes intimately involved with a participant.

Adrie Kusserow (Chapter 22) and Kristina Lyons (Chapter 26) are two cultural anthropologists who have extensive backgrounds as poets. Both use poetry and ethnographic writing separately to share findings from their studies in different ways with different audiences. Kusserow's research has appeared in traditional ethnographic books and journals; she regularly publishes ethnographically inspired poetry in a blurred-genre journal, *Anthropology and Humanism*, and has also written an acclaimed book of poetry, *Hunting Down the Monk* (Kusserow, 2002), which illuminates themes from her fieldwork in Nepal and northern India. Likewise, Lyons has placed her work in a range of venues from conventional ethnographic writing to her published poetry (Lyons, 2005, 2006). Through poetry Lyons's research in Central America comes alive through scintillating and unexpected language.

Stephanie Springgay is a visual artist working on projects that explore women's subjective experiences of bodied space through community-engaged art. Springgay (Chapter 34) describes her academic curriculum vitae which includes international shows of her art work alongside published papers and conference presentations. Springgay describes two works titled *Nurse-in* and *Spillage*. These sculptures created from felted human hair, glycerin soap, and parts of a breast pump are designed to illuminate the contemporary feminist negotiations between motherhood, breastfeeding, and work.

In sum, art for scholarship's sake is grounded in extensive artistic training and aims to imbue art with socially engaged meaning from research and imbue socially engaged research with art. Increasingly, education research journals such as the *Qualitative Inquiry*, *Harvard Educational Review*, *Journal for Latinos and Education*, and *Anthropology and Education Quarterly* formally exhibit creative reflections on fieldwork in non-traditional forms such as poetry and autobiographical prose. Other journals such as the *International Journal of Education and the Arts* and the *Journal of Curriculum and Pedagogy* feature an even wider array of representational forms and formats including musical, pictorial, and videographic, as well as verbal/print and multimedia. There are poetry readings, performances, and arts exhibitions at major research meetings such as those of the American Education Research Association (through the ABER special-interest group) and the American Anthropology Association (through the Society for Humanistic Anthropology). Examples of art for scholarship's sake in education research share renderings of inquiry in ways that are unexpectedly memorable due to their emotive and visceral impact.

## Problems and Difficulties

Due to degrees of risk – professional and personal – involved, the artistic aspects of education research have often been implicit, seldom acknowledged as such, and have often been achieved through luck rather than purposeful development. Consequently, there is very little explicit training for current and future researchers to practice methods of inquiry that embrace tools and techniques from the arts as well as the sciences. Without explicit training, there can be no critical community to establish what constitutes quality in arts-based research.

The problem that arises by not creating a critical community is that there are few measurements of quality in arts-based research. Without a critical community, arts-based research is at risk for an "anything goes" criteria, making it impossible to distinguish what is excellent from what is amateur. Accompanying the demand for arts-based approaches to inquiry must also be a call for tough critics, those who advocate alternatives but will not substitute "novelty and cleverness for substance" (Eisner, 1997, p. 9). To foster a tough critical community, more arts-based educational researchers need to share the techniques and aesthetic sensibilities they use to prepare other researchers to understand, sensibly critique, and further develop arts-based approaches to scholarship.

Jane Piirto (2002) has been especially critical in regard to the question of quality in arts-based research. She distinguishes arts-based exercises for personal creativity enhancement versus a higher level of scholartistry that requires extensive and disciplined training. Piirto prescribes a minimum of an undergraduate minor, preferably a major, and/or evidence of peer-reviewed success for those who wish to make art for "high-stakes" research purposes such as dissertations, theses, or publications (2002, p. 443). Critical of anthropologist Ruth Benedict's "cloying" attempts at verse, contemporary anthropologist, Ruth Behar (Chapter 3), advocates that scholars stick to genres that they know well, enhancing their artistic quality as she does in her own hybrid genre, which she describes as a *poetic anthropology*: "After all, we have a lot of poetic poets out there, but tell me, how many poetic anthropologists do you know?" (p. 34).

Aside from quality, another tension in arts-based research concerns the metaphoric novelty of the work versus its literal utility in a climate where our audience requires answers for practice rather than an additional set of ambiguous, beautifully stated questions (Eisner, Chapter 10). Eisner contends:

> Novelty is a part of creativity and creativity is important to have, but when it trumps instrumental utility ... namely that it contribute to the enrichment of the student's educational experience, it loses its utility as a form of educational research.
>
> (Chapter 10, p. 110)

Thus, an important concern for arts-based researchers in education is how to make the process and products of scholARTistry valid and useful to other researchers, educators, politicians, and others wishing to benefit from the outcomes of inquiry.

The challenges of distinguishing quality in arts-based research and creating arts-based forms of inquiry that matter, especially in a political climate insistent upon definitive, unambiguous, generalizable answers, are not to be taken lightly. There are still more researchers writing *about* arts-based research criteria than those producing examples of what it looks like in each area of the literary, visual, and performing arts. Thus, increased numbers of researchers need to experiment with hybrid forms and art for scholarship's sake, in order to continually refine our critical sensibilities. Increased numbers of scholARTists working with an established criteria for excellence will help others in the field of education research discover aesthetic forms that are valuable to educational inquiry as well as to diverse audiences of scholars and lay people outside the academy including teachers, administrators, politicians, and others involved in pedagogical practices and high-stakes decision-making in educational contexts.

## Future Directions and Possibilities

Among the value arts-based inquiry can afford a researcher's own imaginative thinking is that of sharing the process and products of ABER with a much larger readership than that of a typical education study, with more immediate and lasting impact. For example, sharing a poem may be a much more effective way to bring a discussion of research findings back to a group of students or teachers, than sharing a lengthy research article or book-length manuscript. Sharing a series of photographic images in the hallways of a college of education may disperse research findings to pre- and in-service teachers in more penetrating and immediate ways than any traditional text. Finally, hybrid forms and art for scholarship's sake may be more likely to find venues outside the immediate academy. For example, Jonathan Kozol's (2005) hybrid piece of journalistic ethnography found a large, influential home in *Harper's Magazine*, potentially reaching tens of thousands of readers about the conditions of under-resourced schooling in low-income areas of the urban United States.

Education researchers cannot lose by acquiring and applying techniques employed by artists as well as scientists. We must assume an audience for our work; one that longs for fresh language and imagery to describe the indescribable emotional and intellectual experiences in and beyond language-education contexts. We may not all be poets, dancers, or painters, but we can all draw on the arts to craft poetic discourse analysis or artful case studies – renderings that realize the heights of artistic as well as scholarly potential, challenging the academic marginality of our work.

We might decide to read more poetry, take a dance class, and thus find ourselves taking more risks in the ways we approach our research methodology – whether this means incorporating sketches of a field site in our notebooks, writing "data-poems" from interview transcripts, or creating a scripted dialogue between the "characters" of influential theorists such as Bakhtin and Vygotsky wrestling with theory and data. Our hope is for education researchers to explore the arts-based research methodologies mentioned here as well as others as a means to add more joy, meaning, and impact to our work. The arts have much to offer researchers as a means to make our thinking clearer, fresher, and more public in rendering the richness and complexity of the observed world.

## Postscript

Many of the future directions pointed to at the end of the first version of this chapter (published in 2008) have been realized – new scholartists find increased opportunities for creative training and practice as part of their doctoral studies in education related fields; and numerous opportunities to present and publish their work, attracting larger and varied audiences. Many contributors to this volume produce work they share in a variety of standalone creative contexts including creative literature, theatre, artwork, and film (e.g., Ruth Behar, Adrie Kusserow, Yen Yen Woo, and many others). Great strides have been made to include the arts in teacher and researcher training in vastly different fields from math and science education to foreign language, social science and art education. There have been dozens of books on arts-based research published in both smaller and larger presses; whole conference themes and journal issues devoted to arts-based research and pedagogy, and numerous dissertations authored with arts-based research methodologies and creative representations of findings. My own doctoral students have pushed the boundaries of what is possible, exploring educational inquiry through musical theatre (Thorne, 2018), poetry (Zhang, 2021), literary translation (Moscaliuc, 2023), improv theatre (Cahnmann-Taylor & McGovern, 2021) and visual arts pedagogies (Moreno, 2021; Wang, 2025), among others. Nevertheless, many of the concerns and worries about arts-based research written almost 20 years ago in this chapter still hold true. In a climate where educational research funding is in jeopardy and enrollments in Colleges of Education are in decline, the arts in teacher preparation and research training may be in greater jeopardy today than when this chapter first appeared. In times of uncertainty, precarity, and drought, I believe we will turn more fiercely to arts practices to help us seek creative solutions to complex problems confronting educator and educational researchers today.

## References

Barone, T. (2001). *Touching eternity: The enduring outcomes of teaching*. Teachers College Press.

Barone, T., & Eisner, E. W. (1997). Arts-based educational research. In R. M. Jaeger & T. Barone (Eds.), *Complementary methods for research in education*. American Educational Research Association.

Behar, R. (1993). *Translated woman: Crossing the border with Esperanza's story*. Beacon Press.

Benedict, R. (1934). *Patterns of culture*. Houghton Mifflin.

Brady, I. (2000). Anthropological poetics. In N. K. Denzin & Y. S. Lincoln (Eds.), *Handbook of qualitative research* (2nd ed.). Sage.

Carroll, J. B. (Ed.). (1956). *Language, thought, and reality: Selected writings of Benjamin Lee Whorf*. MIT Press.

Cahnmann-Taylor, M., & McGovern, K. (2021). *Enlivening education with drama & improv theatre: A guide for second and foreign language teachers. Routledge.*
Clifford, J., & Marcus, G. E. (1986). *Writing culture: The poetics and politics of ethnography.* University of California Press.
Dewey, J. (1934). *Art as experience.* Minton Balch.
Edelsky, C. (1981). Who's got the floor? *Language in Society, 10*(3), 383–421. https://doi.org/10.1017/S004740450000885X
Eisner, E. W. (1991). *The enlightened eye: Qualitative inquiry and the enhancement of educational practice.* Macmillan.
Eisner, E. W. (1997). The promise and perils of alternative forms of data representation. *Educational Researcher, 26*(6), 4–10. https://doi.org/10.3102/0013189X026006004
Eisner, E. W. (2002). *The arts and the creation of mind.* Yale University Press.
Ellis, C. (1997). What counts as scholarship in communication? An autoethnographic response. Paper presented at the Annual Meeting of the National Communication Association, Chicago, IL. https://files.eric.ed.gov/fulltext/ED416549.pdf
Ellis, C. (1999). Heartful autoethnography. *Qualitative Health Research, 9*(5), 669–683. https://doi.org/10.1177/104973299129122153
Erickson, F., & Shultz, J. (1982). *The counselor as gatekeeper: Social interaction in interview.* Academic Press.
Foster, M. (1989). It's cookin' now: A performance analysis of the speech events of a Black teacher in an urban community college. *Language in Society, 18*, 1–29. https://doi.org/10.1017/S0047404500013257
Hankins, K. H. (2003). *Teaching through the storm: A journal of hope.* In M. Cochran-Smith & S. L. Lytle (Eds.), *Practitioner inquiry series.* Teachers College Press.
Heath, S. B. (1983). *Ways with words: Language, life, and work in communities and classrooms.* Cambridge University Press.
Hymes, D. H. (1964). Introduction: Toward ethnographies of communication. *American Anthropologist, 66*(6), 1–34. https://doi.org/10.1525/aa.1964.66.suppl_3.02a00010
Irwin, R., & de Cosson, A. (2004). *A/r/tography: Rendering self through arts-based living inquiry.* Pacific Educational Press.
Kozol, J. (2005). Still separate, still unequal: America's educational apartheid. *Harper's Magazine, 311*(1864), 41–54.
Kusserow, A. (2002). *Hunting down the monk.* Boa Editions.
Lawrence-Lightfoot, S. (1983). *The good high school: Portraits of character and culture.* Basic Books.
Lyons, K. (2005). Then silence. *Anthropology and Humanism, 20*(2), 232–233.
Lyons, K. (2006). The first visit. *Anthropology and Humanism, 31*(1), 87–88.
Maynard, K. (2001). *Sunk like god behind the house, Wick Chapbook Series.* Kent State University Press.
Moreno, R. (2021). Shaping a critical study abroad engagement through experiential arts-based inquiry. *Teaching & Learning Inquiry, 9*(2), n2, 1–22. https://doi.org/10.20343/teachlearninqu.9.2.4
Moscaliuc, M. (2023). From *Records of Explosion*: Poems by Nianxi Chen, translated from Chinese by Melisa Cahnmann-Taylor and Kuo Zhang, with an interview by Mihaela Moscaliuc. *Plume Magazine, 144.* https://plumepoetry.com/from-records-of-explosion-poems-by-nianxi-chen-translated-from-chinese-by-melisa-cahnmann-taylor-and-kuo-zhang-with-an-interview-by-mihaela-moscaliuc/
Neilsen, L. (2005). *Homepage.* Retrieved March 6, 2005 from www.iirc.mcgill.ca/collaborators/collabln.html (Site Inactive).
Perry, D. (2005). *Unchartered territory: An autoethnographic perspective on starting a dual language immersion charter school in Georgia.* Paper presented at American Anthropological Association.
Piirto, J. (2002). The question of quality and qualifications: Writing inferior poems as qualitative research. *Qualitative Inquiry, 15*(4), 431–446. https://doi.org/10.1080/09518390210145507
Saldaña, J. (2002). Finding my place: The Brad trilogy. In H. F. Wolcott (Ed.), *Sneaky Kid and its aftermath: Ethnics and intimacy in fieldwork.* Altamira Press.
Schiller, F. (2004). *On the aesthetic education of man* (R. Snell, Trans.). Dover. (Original work published 1795).
Shavelson, R. J., & Towne, L. (2002). *Scientific research in education.* National Academy Press.

Thorne, M. (2018). #Schooled!: Understanding teaching and learning through ethnotheatre. Unpublished dissertation, University of Georgia.
Tyack, D. B., & Cuban, L. (1995). *Tinkering toward utopia: A century of public school reform*. Harvard University Press.
Wang, Y. (2025). A cootie catcher/fortune teller to recruit "English native teachers" to teach in China. *Anthropology and Humanism*, *50*(1), https://doi.org/10.1111/anhu.70017.
Zhang, K. (2021). Embrace the uncontrolled nature of poetry writing: A poetic ethnographic study on international graduate student mothers' intercultural discourses. *Qualitative Inquiry*, *27*(3–4), 429–443. https://doi.org/10.1177/1077800420920696

Chapter 9

# Four Guiding Principles for Arts-Based Research Practice

*Melisa Cahnmann*

When considering questions about who should or can engage in arts-based research (ABR) in education, why, and to what end, I have often referred to Eisner (Chapter 10) where he addressed "persistent tensions" regarding novelty, utility, and value of the work. He described these tensions as "a psychological state that creates a feeling of mild discomfort, a feeling that can be temporarily relieved through inquiry" (p. 105). Like Eisner, I have experienced tensions when teaching and speaking about ABR and have found this uncertainty, and the debates and discussions about it, productive. In students' dissertation processes, in ABR seminars, and with scholarly peers in conferences and visiting lectures, I have pressed this disequilibrium into my own words in the effort to create something useful for emerging and practicing scholartists. I present these four principles as follows not to define precise routes for ending up at a fixed or known destination—but rather as something to guide decision-making and self-reflexive questions. There's no "getting it right" in the arts. However, fundamental principles help. In this chapter, I share four principles that guide my own thinking and advisement when approaching art-making as a social scientist and social science as a poet. The reader will see threads of one principle interwoven with threads of another, and yet I find the separate naming useful. If they are of value to you, reader, then I have done my job. Yet, my job is also to share Hugo's (1979/2017) poetic wisdom where *write* might be replaced by *research*: "Every moment, I am, without wanting or trying to, telling you to write (research) like me. But I hope you learn to write (research) like you" (n.p.). These four principles may serve as a useful guide for readers on their own ABR journeys.

- The Principle of Subjectivity and Public Good
- The Principle of Attribution and Ethical Good
- The Principle of Impact and Aesthetic Good
- The Principle of Translation to Scientific Good

## The Principle of Subjectivity and Public Good

All arts-based researchers must ask: what and whom are the subjects of this work and to what extent does this project further some aspect of public good? By "public good," I do not mean luring the "others" (perceived as un[der]-educated or unaware) into the researcher's privileged point of view regarding what is "good"; rather, I mean luring oneself and others into seeing self-other connections that expand multiplicity and complexity. I believe "public good" can be obtained if the arts-based researcher makes a commitment to exploring the unknown with complexity, humility, bravery, and beauty.

DOI: 10.4324/9781003412892-9

hooks (1994) wrote passionately about the vitality of "outlaw culture" in the academy as one "disturbing the conventional, acceptable politics of representation" (pp. 4–5). Regarding ABR, Barone (Chapter 2) wrote it should disrupt master narratives that maintain status quo imbalances of power and promote "conspiratorial conversations" (p. 21). Disturbing the conventional and disrupting master narratives does not, however, mean luring audiences to a specific political view, as wisely discouraged by Blumenfeld (Chapter 6). Rather, an important ABR goal is to invite audiences to question hegemonic norms and to ask questions such as these that may have not been asked before: *Who or what is in the room, not in the room, defines the room, is the subject/object of art/research? What role does the human and organic or nonhuman play?* and always, *Why?* and *To what end?*

The postmodern turn has left many arts-based researchers with great confusion regarding what, if any, method can be used to understand or serve any group of "not me" individuals, including the nonhuman. The interview, participant observation, ethnographic field notes—this "conventional humanist qualitative methodology" is often critiqued by post inquiry scholars as tools that should be deconstructed and discarded (e.g., St. Pierre, 2014, p. 2). According to this theoretical framework, we cannot claim to know anything with certainty anymore. Thus, many in ABR take license to invent, compress, and use our imaginations in social scientific study to document multiple truths and perspectives. But, what public good is at risk if ABR scholars avoid all truth claims? My opinion is that art that responds to data can result in a more layered and resonant scientific truth as well as a more robust and impactful work of art. Additionally, I assert that ABR distinguishes itself from stand-alone "art" precisely because of its connection to data and truth claims data makes possible.

This collection invites readers to reflect on the principle of subjectivity and public good in each of these works appearing in the third edition. For example, Rosiek (Chapter 29) draws readers attention to "the relational modes of being generated between human and non-human agents," and Grumet (Chapter 14) to human thinking and discovery in the current politics of "cruel time." I stand by a principle that our labor as scholars and inquirers in education is to ask an applied question about the value of our work to others—from international graduate student mothers in Zhang's work (Chapter 38) to prison inmates in Prendergast and Belliveau (Chapter 28). Many arts-based researchers use the arts to work with a variety of human stakeholders in educational and community contexts—e.g., second-language teachers and writers, art educators, refugees, inmates, and many others. Others charge scholartists with purpose to include nonhuman agents such as abandoned school buildings and social media posts in conversation with educational concern. At the heart of educational concerns are human actors, and ABR achieves public good in education when the work is *human+*, as opposed to *posthumanism* (Appleby & Pennycook, 2017; Barad, 2003) in educational concerns.

Postmodern theory encourages us to question traditional binaries as to what counts as "art" and what as "research," and what as "self" and what as "other." This has led many scholartists to focus work on the self, work that integrates art with self-study and auto-ethnography. When scholartists begin a project that has art-making at its core or uses art to engage in a subject of great personal connection, I always ask: *so what*? In what ways does this arts-based study challenge established social interests and abide by what the famed linguist Labov (1982) referred to as the "principle of debt incurred," an obligation "to use the knowledge based on ... data [collected in and about any given community] for the benefit of the community" (pp. 172–173)? Labov claims scholars also must engage in "error correction," stating: "A scientist who becomes aware of a widespread idea or social practice with important consequences that is invalidated by his own data is obligated to bring this error to the attention of the widest possible audience" (p. 172). When scholartists want to do a self-study and render it in an artistic way—through the production of a series of poems, a play, a dance, or painting—I anticipate clear articulation of the relevance of their subjectivity to the surrounding community in which the self lives. Self-studies can and often should move beyond the self to make strategic use of a range of qualitative methods including participant observation, field notes or "heart notes" (Hankins, 2003), interviews, and multimodal arts methods to expand how they understand their own story and others who may, to some degree, share it. High-quality ABR matters when a clear reference is made outside the self, even (and especially when) the subject of the research is, in fact, the self. Exploration of the entanglements between human and nonhuman, self and other, may be one way to realize the agential realism to which Rosiek (Chapter 29) refers.

What does an ABR song, poem, or story—one's own and/or that told on behalf of others' lived experiences—add to commitments to expand perceptions (Dewey, 1934) of what *is* in order to explore what *might be*? ABR is uniquely suited to draw complex attention to an issue (e.g., aging, second-language acquisition, mothering, refugee status, etc.) through image, music, narrative, and metaphor. But, just because ABR is suited to disturb conventional understanding doesn't always mean that it will. We must be cautious of producing propaganda instead of research and/or of pushing personal agendas disguised as ABR. The arts and research, when deeply engaged, rise above facile "good/bad," "human/nonhuman," or "subjective/objective" binaries. Public good can be obtained when scholartists explore topics with complexity for more multifaceted understanding. Self-study ABR work might consider the role other human and nonhuman agents play. To conclude this principle with a metaphor, artists and arts-based researchers do not offer a wrench to fix our own subjective sink (though we may experience a great deal of repair through the work). Rather, through disciplined practices as artists and researchers, we observe particular phenomena to expand perceptions of the plumbing: how do human beings in educational contexts work, why, where, when, and to what end?

## The Principle of Attribution and Ethical Good

Ethics, attribution, and veracity in art and science have long been controversial subjects. Among the numerous controversies that have emerged over ethics in the art world related to "truth" was James Frey's admission three years after his best-selling "memoir" (Frey, 2003) *A Million Little Pieces* (second in sales that year behind Rowling's [2005] *Harry Potter*) was released that his memoir contained multiple fictions to make his addiction redemption all the more exciting. By calling this a "memoir" instead of a novel, readers believed what they read to be true and felt betrayed. More than three decades later, we find all nonfiction truth claims under question: memoir, history, journalism, and research. "Fake news," where divisions between what is true and what is fiction appear to matter less than what is provocative, entertaining, and politically convincing. For example, whether events in the United States on January 6, 2021 were described as an insurrection, a coup, a peaceful protest, race riot, domestic terrorism or the storming of the capitol was less about what took place and more about the ethical stance of the perceiver.

How big the crowds are, how wide the profit margins, how guilty or innocent the accused—we see the ways in which political, economic, and virtual fictions foster deception and abuses of descriptive language and power to manipulate a single worldview.

Scholar artists must steer clear from such propaganda. Rather, scholar-artists are tasked to awaken audiences to alternative points of view, helping us to ask more refined questions and be less certain of any single answer. Working creatively with what constitutes data and how to analyze and represent that to which we bare witness is to nourish a community of ethical and reciprocal scholarship in service to those who are most vulnerable. Making art with scholarship is an ethical mode of resistance.

"Historical fiction," "virtual reality," "creative nonfiction," and "docudramas" are some creative genres that have emerged to highlight the liberties many artists take to present emotional truth based on a mix of true and imagined details. Miranda's and Chernow's discussions of *Hamilton* (Miranda & McCarter, 2016), in which black and Latino actors play the Founding Fathers of the United States, is one such example of a radical artist and historian working together, inventing to present "a story about America then, told by America now" (Miranda & McCarter, 2016, p. 33). While many of these cutting-edge inventions are thrilling, I worry we have arrived at a frightening elevation of *factual relativism*, a time when the truth of overt acts of discrimination and foul play can also be called into question and re-storied. Blurring between fact and fiction can allow the public to question the veracity of events such as the Holocaust, Armenian genocide, racialized police violence, or FBI investigations of information leaks from the Oval Office.

ABR has often promoted the blurring of fact and fiction as a way to support invention and imagination in our own work. We employ the word "research" as a way to assure audiences that behind our imaginative processes and representations is a truth based on "systematic investigation, including research development, testing and evaluation, designed to develop or contribute to generalizable knowledge" (National Institutes of Health (NIH), 1979/2017). While this definition of research has lent itself to great debate regarding what systemic generalizable knowledge and research mean or might mean, those of us who use the word "research" benefit from the authority it implies.

Documents to codify ethics and ethical treatment such as the Belmont Report (NIH, 1979/2017) have been created to avoid recreating the horrific abuses of research in the past—from Nazi experiments on Holocaust victims to the 1940s Tuskegee syphilis study, which took advantage of rural black men. Universities uphold ethics through Institutional Review Boards (IRB) that guide scholars' empirical decision-making and help avoid lawsuits as well as ethical foul play. While fair use or abuse of empirical power may be political and contingent, researchers are long since aware that it can be abused and destructive without guiding policies. While scholartists might balk at lengthy and detailed IRB processes based on medical research paradigms, the principle of ethical good can help us see these processes in a new, favorable light. By attaching the word "research" to "art," we require scholartists to review the principles of sound, ethical practice when other (non)human agents are involved. We may play with forms of data collection and reinterpret what "data" means altogether. Nonetheless, we still encounter questions regarding attribution and ethics: Whose work? Who benefits? What risks are involved? For example, is it ethical for an art or language teacher to use a former student's work or interview transcript for their own creative rendering? Was the arts-based creation described in Chapter 1 of *Finnexia*, a fictional medication that purported to facilitate the acquisition of the Finnish language, fair to vulnerable immigrant populations who believed it to be true (Erdman, 2021)? While an artist might consider copyright, a researcher must consider human subjects' voluntary and informed consent, as well as the risks and benefits of others' participation.

When documenting a participant's words and rendering them, verbatim, in one's own poems or newly employing a scholar's previously published words (Giles, 2010) or police dash-cam footage in a script (Cahnmann-Taylor, 2017), it's important to ask questions about ethics and permissions. Scholartists make numerous ethical decisions moving between data and creative work with data, and it is imperative that we articulate how we make the decisions to which we adhere. Written descriptions of process, changing fonts for different voices, footnote citations, co-authorship and/or acknowledgement—these are some of the strategies scholartists in this book and elsewhere have used to attend to ethical attribution and decision-making.

ABR that is conceptual and does not include human subjects may be excused from many of these concerns and ought to more closely attend to the principle of public good discussed earlier. Many contributors to the third edition of *Arts-Based Research in Education* draw readers' attention to the ethics of research in virtual and/or openly public forums that inform new ethical considerations (Markham & Buchanan, 2015).

Because ABR is suited to push the limits of old qualitative inquiry tools (e.g., face-to-face interviews and field notes) and gravitate toward the new, this requires us to ask new and better questions regarding attribution and ethical good. For example, LeBlanc's (Chapter 24) startlingly fresh decision to create a visual installation of an abandoned school's interior on the same school's exterior walls reminds us to attend to the entanglement of human and nonhuman trajectories. ABR can lead the way for conversations about ethics and attribution that interweave human-subjects research to the nonhuman, expanding knowledge practices to enrich our ability to describe educative worlds.

## The Principle of Impact and Aesthetic Good

Eisner (Chapter 10) wisely advised in our first volume that "[ABR] deeds, not words, may be in the end the most persuasive source of support and the source that yields the highest levels of credibility" (p. 106). Eisner recognized the ineffable combination that mastery of technique and/or innovation would show itself by example. But, what guidance does this provide for those of us who work in so many different literary, performing, and visual arts genres which have such different parameters for excellence? What principles guide all of us in the pursuit of impact for aesthetic good? Mastery of technical skill in the arts (e.g., brushstroke, meter, dialogue, etc.), originality of concept and form, the mediums used, emotional complexity, timing, and social consensus—whether scholartistry is "good" or "persuasive"—is often determined by those whom Eisner (Chapter 10) refers to as "connoisseurs." Drawing inspiration from the art world's connoisseurs—individuals adept at discerning subtle qualities in artworks—Eisner applied this idea to education and later to ABR, emphasizing the importance of recognizing and appreciating the intricate aspects of teaching and learning and educational inquiry. Art world connoisseurs—curators, editors, publishers, producers—are those trained in making judgments regarding aesthetic criteria. Yet, we have come to question the connoisseurs' elitism, sanctioning and rewarding aesthetic qualities that often fit into a narrow purview implicated in unjust systems of sociopolitical and economic power. What is considered as aesthetically and educationally good and/or what will have impact are fluid and subject to power dynamics and other aspects of social circumstance at any given time. So, where do we turn for a guiding principle regarding ABR's aesthetic quality and impact in education?

Since Eisner (1991) began making ABR arguments, he and a growing number of arts-based researchers, including contributors to this volume, began pushing qualitative inquiry boundaries to embrace the arts as more than a metaphor for research practice but as research itself. Art-making became a conceptual and empirical practice where fiction, poetry, music, painting, film, or dramatic script/performance might represent the struggles observed and/or experienced and documented by the researcher and presented to audiences as works of art. Many of us have been calling for increased exemplars of high-quality ABR. While international ABR groups have grown in numbers as discussed in the introduction (Chapter 1), some of the most powerful work is still illustrated by artists who do not attend education meetings or publish their work in social science platforms. For example, Barone and Eisner's (2012) ABR text referenced famous fiction writers (Nadine Gordimer), filmmakers (Steven Spielberg), playwrights (Arthur Miller), performers (Anna Deavere Smith), and photographers (Robert Doisneau) as exemplary scholartists in the late 20th and early 21st centuries. Later in the 21st century, artists become researchers and researchers become artists to document urgent environmental and social concerns with impact and precision. For example, Erika Blumenfeld's artist studios have included laboratories and observatories; she has collaborated with scientists and research institutions to document wildfires, ocean health, and other pressing ecological concerns. Other artists incorporate self study and other research strategies to examine issues of race, class, violence and war around the world. For example, Danez Smith's poetic integration of inquiry is characterized by a profound engagement with what it means to be Black, queer, and HIV-positive in the U.S. Joanna Chen is a British-born Israeli poet, essayist, and literary translator whose work deeply engages with themes of empathy, coexistence, and the human dimensions of the Israeli-Palestinian conflict. This selection of artists who are also researchers showcases the highest quality of research artistry demands the highest attention to the art form itself.

But, where does that leave the majority of arts-based researchers who do not (yet) hold MFA degrees[1] or have extensive film budgets or connections to active professional writers, singers, dancers, etc.? Woo (Chapter 37) and Sik-Ying, Hoi-Yan, and Sui-Ting (Chapter 15) inspire scholartists to realize one's highest quality aspirations through a combination of creative funding strategies, collaborations, and engagement in rigorous self-study. While making a feature length, award-winning film as Woo has done may not be possible for all creative educational studies, this work inspires each of us to question the quality limitations we may self-impose.

Having engaged in ethnodrama (Cahnmann-Taylor, 2016b), applied theater focus groups (Cahnmann-Taylor & Souto-Manning, 2010), and ethnographic poetry (Cahnmann-Taylor, 2016a), I've striven for different thresholds of aesthetic excellence according to my own strengths, limitations, resources, and audiences. At times these engagements have illustrated ways in which arts practices change the entanglement with social science inquiry practices, leaving textual representations and traditions largely intact. On other projects, these entanglements have served as catalysts for major empirical and representational change. ABR educational scholars often engage in experiments of process and reward articulations of intentions as much as final products. Such support entails freedoms that nurture creative thinking and imagining. Viewing art only as a "product" overlooks training in creative thinking, living, and being that an arts-orientation produces. Hence, Lucero (Chapter 26) encourages "Jon," an emerging education scholar yet inexperienced artist interested in ABR, to feel warmly invited to the creative party and be unafraid to think about "art" as much more broad than an end product for [re]presentation. As I wrote in Cahnmann-Taylor (2003, 2009, 2017) and elsewhere, I still believe the "artistic" can come into play in rethinking and playing with conventional qualitative research methods and strategies—e.g., a focus group interview that builds on improv theater practices (Cahnmann-Taylor & Souto-Manning, 2010) or a choreographed dance of a teacher's school day (Goodrich, 2017). Critical of anthropologist Ruth Benedict's "cloying" attempts at verse, contemporary anthropologist, Ruth Behar (Chapter 3), advocates that scholars stick to genres they know well, enhancing them with what she describes as a "poetic anthropology":

> The more important work I'm doing right now is the effort I'm making to craft a poetic anthropology. After all, we have a lot of poetic poets out there, but tell me, how many poetic anthropologists do you know? Anthropology needs poetic anthropologists. And the funny thing is that most anthropologists don't know that. Or don't want to know that. (p. 34)

Scholartists must attend to playful and creative learning processes, but we must also attend to the much more discriminating art world if we are to take ourselves seriously as both scholars and artists. In professionally creative circles, the criteria for excellence may seem exhausting, arbitrary, ambiguous, and/or debilitating, as Borstel (Chapter 7) discussed in the dance world. Nonetheless, there are often basic foundational expectations for originality and/or technical skill. When students or colleagues ask me questions about how to develop aesthetic competence in ABR, I offer six ways one can engage in ABR along a continuum of high-quality art-making and artistic thinking. Is the emerging ABR scholar willing to do any or all of the following:

1 Spend systematic time with other artists working in the same genre (e.g., if writing poems, one should also actively read published poets, attend poetry readings, and participate in the poetry world).
2 Consult (and yes, compensate) more expert artists or connoisseurs for critical feedback and/or collaboration.
3 Experiment and take risks to *misperform* or *fail* (Prendergast & Belliveau, Chapter 28) and articulate the implications.
4 Exhibit creative work/thinking/imagination for public consideration and response.
5 Have a clear sense of the "so what?"—for whom/what does this matter, why, how, and to what end is the creative scholarship created—perhaps en route to more poetic anthropology or scholarship rather than a creative product itself.
6 Articulate entanglements when working across modalities, disciplines, and human/nonhuman agents to further inscribe and expand ABR as a methodology and field.

The first point may seem obvious: when practicing an art form, spend time with other artists in the same field. Too many times I have met aspiring scholartists who claim not to want their own creativity "affected" by the work of other artists, even teachers. For me, this attitude fails to honor and learn from traditions in art-making. To be a scholartist is never to have arrived but to be always searching for creative ways to employ old tools in service to the highest quality, impact, and implications of the work. There are endless opportunities on campuses, in communities, and on the internet to learn with great practicing artists and translate artistic craft into crafted inquiry.

## The Principle of Translation to Scientific Good

There are many paths by which educational scholars and artists may have arrived at this text, which uses the word "art" purposely with the word "research." If what we are doing is merging arts and science traditions, then we must not only pursue aesthetic good. We must also find ways to communicate the value and processes of our work to social science and practitioner audiences in the field of education. While some scholartists eschew the word "research" altogether, as it may limit the extent to which the artwork can speak for itself, I disagree. I embrace expanded definitions of what "research" might mean, and the roles language, image, and movement serve to help inscribe new meaning for broader audiences. How does ABR matter to educators, social science colleagues, and policymakers if we discard the empirical? ABR that communicates itself to larger social science and public audiences is well poised for impact and credibility.

Educational scholartists may respond to Braidotti's (2013) argument that to move beyond anthropocentrism, we need "resources of the imagination, as well as the tools of critical intelligence ... to be enlisted for the task" (p. 82) and Pedersen's (2010) argument that we must "transcend traditional disciplinary boundaries between natural sciences and social/humanist sciences" (p. 246). An ABR challenge is to find in art the tools to arouse others and ourselves to think more critically about new forms of becoming in the human, organic, and inorganic world (Appleby & Pennycook, 2017). In 2016, I'd met a biologist with a specialty in fireflies whose "communicating science" course asked students to research literary references to the "stars at heart" such as those found in Frost's (1928) "Fireflies in the Garden" poem. Scientists of climate change, genetics, biology, and other fields increasingly look to the human and social sciences to better understand their fields; ABR is likewise enhanced by scientific forms of communication, processes, and methods.

By communication, I do not mean scholartists need to explain or translate what the works of art "mean." Rather, ABR scholars provoke new forms of language to honor the original creative achievement and place it in its new context, just as the visual artist Marcel Duchamp surprised the art world by placing a found toilet, *Fountain*, in an art museum in 1917. ABR scholars will have greater impact if they articulate not only what they have "done" but also why their accomplishments matter in fields such as education, anthropology, ecology, and medicine.

## Conclusion

In sum, there's much to celebrate in ABR, and the composing of this collection invigorates new directions. The examples in this *Arts-Based Research in Education* collection have illustrated the ways in which empirical, theoretical, and philosophical research in education can be heightened through attention to the arts. Each chapter highlights the power of art in science and science in art to make "old themes" in education feel new and compel us to think and act differently. While there is much to celebrate, these four principles lead me to acknowledge ongoing tensions and contradictions regarding public, ethical, aesthetic, and scientific good. ABR must still be vigilant to Eisner's (Chapter 10) concern that we may overrate novelty and discount utility. In this same line of concern, I worry about scholartistry that overrates the self and discounts participants; overrates the conceptual and discounts practice; overrates the margins and discounts multiple centers; overrates instinct and discounts rigor and craft; or overrates science and discounts art or vice versa. While these are real ABR risks, this volume is full of risk-takers, those who know failure is an effort worth learning from and improving upon.

## Postscript

In the years since the second edition of this collection was published in 2018, I have continued to supervise arts-based dissertations and celebrate arts-based scholarship on a global scale I could never before have imagined. ABR workshops and keynote addresses are found regularly at many educational and social science conferences. Illustrations of ABR can be found in most major educational research journals. There are dozens of books across smaller and larger presses in a range of social science fields illustrating arts-based research. What was once a methodology on the margins has become much more central, attracting artists into educational inquiry and educational scholars to the arts. The descriptive and emotive powers of the arts (e.g., drawing, poetry, music, dramatic performance, and others) are no longer treated as mere illustrations of "real" inquiry but rather as essential empirical practices and products of representation. Scholartists, practiced in the arts of noticing, are well prepared to conceptualize new questions, redefine problems, and co-create knowledges with nuanced understanding.

I have continued to author arts-based work through poetry (e.g., Cahnmann-Taylor, 2022) and creative nonfiction, that incorporate ethnographic practices such as participant observation and interview. In this later stage in my career as Professor of Education, I seek literary and public audiences as well as academic. In collaboration with a former student and arts-based researcher, I authored an applied pedagogical text, *Enlivening Instruction with Drama and Improv: A Guide for Second Language and World Language Teachers* (Cahnmann-Taylor & McGovern, 2021), and with a colleague in anthropology published *The Creative Ethnographer's Notebook* (Cahnmann-Taylor & Jacobsen, 2024), a craftbook to guide others in creative social science practices. During and beyond the Covid epidemic I "traveled" to China through collaborative literary translation of Chinese poet, Nianxi Chen (Cahnmann-Taylor & Zhang, 2024, 2025). This has since become the basis of an empirical project inviting English monolingual teachers to engage in collaborative literary translations (children's songs, poems, short stories) with bilingual students in their classrooms. The movements between making art and making science feels more nourishing and fluid for myself and my students than ever before. In a political climate that moves toward increasing authoritarianism and restricts research, scholartists harness freedom, recording and telling dissenting stories from many different perspectives and through multimodal, aesthetic practices. Making art as a part of educational inquiry and engaging in collaborative art-making with teachers and students feels more important today than ever.

## Note

1 Scholartists take advantage of many newly available opportunities for arts study, including: "low-residency" MFA programs for distance-learning with highly accomplished artists as mentors; open access to take courses across education and arts departments rather than restricting creative writing or art-making to degree majors; and greater numbers of creative courses in community settings. Beyond the scope of this chapter is a discussion of how, with the increased access to arts training, many institutions are replacing MFA terminal degrees with PhD programs in the arts.

## References

Appleby, R., & Pennycook, A. (2017). Swimming with sharks, ecological feminism and posthuman language politics. *Critical Inquiry in Language Studies*, *14*(2–3), 1–23.

Barad, K. (2003). Posthumanist performativity: Toward an understanding of how matter comes to matter. *Gender and Science: New Issues*, *28*(3), 801–831.

Barone, T., & Eisner, E. W. (2012). *Arts based research*. Sage.
Braidotti, R. (2013). *The posthuman*. Wiley.
Cahnmann-Taylor, M. (2003). The craft, practice, and possibility of poetry in educational research. *Educational Researcher*, *32*(3), 29–36.
Cahnmann-Taylor, M. (2009). On finding original and transformative ethnographic voices. *Etnofoor*, *21*(2), 101–104.
Cahnmann-Taylor, M. (2016a). *Imperfect tense*. Whitepoint.
Cahnmann-Taylor, M. (2016b). Imperfect tense: An ethnodrama of American adults learning Spanish in Mexico. *Reunion: The Dallas Review*, *6*(1), 110–169.
Cahnmann-Taylor, M. (2017). "I'm not talking to you!" "You don't have to!" Trans/scripting the Bland-Encinia case. *Pedagogy & Theatre of the Oppressed Journal*, 2(Summer), 1–26. http://scholarworks.uni.edu/ptoj/vol2/iss1/2/.
Cahnmann-Taylor, M. (2022). Eighteen ways of looking at property. *Lilith*. https://lilith.org/2022/04/poetry-eighteen-ways-of-looking-at-property/
Cahnmann-Taylor, M., & Souto-Manning, M. (2010). *Teachers act up!: Creating multicultural learning communities through theatre*. Teachers College Press.
Cahnmann-Taylor, M., & McGovern, K. R. (2021). *Enlivening instruction with drama and improv: A guide for second and foreign language teachers*. Routledge.
Cahnmann-Taylor, M., & Jacobsen, K. (2024). *The creative ethnographer's notebook*. Routledge.
Cahnmann-Taylor, M. & Zhang, Kuo (2024). 4 translations [Nianxi Chen] and introduction Southern Humanities Review. https://www.southernhumanitiesreview.com/nianxi-chen-poetry-month-feature.html
Cahnmann-Taylor, M. & Zhang, Kuo (2025). 5 poems in translation [Nianxi Chen] Los Angeles Review. https://losangelesreview.org/five-poems-by-nianxi-chen-translated-by-kuo-zhang-melisa-cahnmann-taylor/
Dewey, J. (1934). *Art as experience*. Minton Balch.
Eisner, E. W. (1991). *The enlightened eye: Qualitative inquiry and the enhancement of educational practice*. Macmillan.
Erdman, L. (2021). The answerability of false hope: Examining the unexpected outcomes of the Finnexia® public art intervention. *Performing Ethos: An International Journal of Ethics in Theatre & Performance*, *11*, 55–75. https://doi.org/10.1386/peet_00037_1
Frey, J. (2003). *A million little pieces*. Anchor Books.
Frost, R. (1928/2017). Fireflies in the garden. *The poetry of Robert Frost*. www.poetryfoundation.org/poems/42892/fireflies-in-the-garden
Giles, D. P. (2010). *"Unchartered" territory: An auto ethnographic perspective on establishing Georgia's first public two-way immersion school* [Unpublished doctoral dissertation]. University of Georgia.
Goodrich, A. (2017). *Necessary trouble: Dancing a teacher's story [video]*. www.youtube.com/watch?v=0N2rvj4esWg
Hankins, K. H. (2003). *Teaching through the storm: A journal of hope*. Teachers College Press.
hooks, b. (1994). *Outlaw culture: Resisting representations*. Routledge.
Hugo, R. (1979/2017). *The triggering town: Lectures and essays on poetry and writing*. WW Norton. https://www.poetryfoundation.org/articles/69402/the-triggering-town
Labov, W. (1982). Objectivity and commitment in linguistic science: The case of the Black English trial in Ann Arbor. *Language in Society*, *11*(2), 165–201.
Markham, A., & Buchanan, E. (2015). *Ethical decision-making and internet research: Recommendations from the AOIR Ethics Working Committee (version 2.0)*. Association of Internet Researchers, 2012.
Miranda, L. M., & McCarter, J. (2016). *Hamilton: The revolution*. Grand Central Publishing.
National Institutes of Health (NIH). (1979). The Belmont Report. *Belmont Rep. Ethical Princ. Guidel. Prot. Hum. Subj. Res* (pp. 4–6). Retrieved from www.hhs.gov/ohrp/regulations-and-policy/belmont-report/index.html#xethical
Pedersen, H. (2010). Is 'the posthuman' educable? On the convergence of educational philosophy, animal studies, and posthumanist theory. *Discourse: Studies in the Cultural Politics of Education*, *31*(2), 237–250.
Rowling, J. K. (2005). *Harry Potter and the half-blood prince*. Scholastic.
St. Pierre, E. S. (2014). A brief and personal history of post qualitative research: Toward "post inquiry". *Journal of Curriculum Theorizing*, *30*(2), 2–19.

Chapter 10

# Persistent Tensions in Arts-Based Research

*Elliot Eisner*

I write today about persistent tensions in arts-based research. In many ways, it should be expected that an approach to research that employs new assumptions and methods and has a short history should generate tensions. We would lack vitality if we were cocksure of everything we do. Tensions can be motivating. But before describing them, let me address what I mean by tensions. By tension I mean a psychological state that creates a feeling of mild discomfort, a feeling that can be temporarily relieved through inquiry. A tension is close to what Dewey (1934) means by "disequilibrium." It can be produced by a sense of uncertainty about one's work. It can be stirred by the vague feeling that in one's work something is just not right. It can be the result of being attracted to two incompatible values. But, it can also be motivating, and it can evoke a sense of vitality.

Yet the presence of tension in doing one's work, though it may engender vitality, does not, by itself, guarantee that as a result one's work will be either theoretically cogent or practically useful. There are tensions that virtually all of us experience in doing arts-based research and my aim in this chapter is to explore a few of the tensions that I believe to be among the most persistent.

But first, a little history.

It was in 1993 that the first Arts-Based Research Institute was offered to members of the American Educational Research Association (AERA). The Institute was held at Stanford and has been offered at Stanford and at Arizona State virtually every other year since then. In initiating the Institute, I was driven by a tension that I felt personally as a scholar and as someone immersed in the arts. That tension pertained to the idea that we might apply the arts in some productive way to help us understand more imaginatively and more emotionally problems and practices that warrant attention in our schools. At the same time, the idea that the arts could be at the core of research seemed a bit oxymoronic.

In another life I was a painter, so it is not surprising that I was interested in the ways in which the arts generate awareness – wide-awakeness as Maxine Greene (2001) might say. At the same time, I did not expect arts-based research to culminate in the creation of paintings, poems, or pirouettes. I thought that the crafting of evocative forms might enable us to address aspects of educational life that normally get neglected. I also hoped our social-science colleagues would find such work credible.

The initial iteration of this conjecture of mine about the relationship between the arts and educational research had been expressed earlier in the concepts of educational connoisseurship and educational criticism (Eisner, 1991), two notions rooted in the arts. Could there be, I asked myself, an approach to educational research that would rely upon the imaginative and expressive crafting of a form in ways that enlarge our understanding of what was

DOI: 10.4324/9781003412892-10

going on, say, in teaching, or in the school cafeteria, or in the high-school mathematics classroom? Educational connoisseurship and educational criticism were in most ways marginal rather than central to the production of an art form. To be sure, criticism and connoisseurship acknowledged, and indeed, employed aesthetic criteria in making judgments about how something was to be rendered, but it was a tool for seeing and for describing far more than an effort to craft a work of art as such.

In many ways, this ambition of mine, to develop an approach to the conduct of educational research that was rooted in the arts and that used art forms to reveal the features that mattered educationally, was a central ambition. This ambition had ramifications. For example, it led to considerations regarding the role of fiction in educational research. The AERA debate that Howard Gardner and I had about whether a novel could function or serve as a dissertation is an example of the position that I embraced (Donmoyer et al., 1996). Gardner argued that doctoral training was essentially that, a training program designed to prepare skilled journeymen in the use of conventional research methods. My argument was that universities ought to be places in which doctoral students could explore imaginatively new methods and concepts and if universities could not provide such a setting, there were few places that could. You might say I was interested in pushing the boundaries of possibility. It is not necessary to get into the details of the debate, but I will say that it was spirited and that it represented two perspectives on how research might be undertaken. In neither case, I believe, was either of us looking for a single hegemonic orientation to research methods. I have always embraced pluralism in method, and I think Gardner does as well, even if he didn't argue that position when we shared a session in AERA in New York.

To make the case for arts-based research, especially in a research climate of the kind we have today, is as daunting as it is important. The federal government, as almost everybody reading this knows, has embraced field-based experimental trials as the "gold-standard" for supporting educational research (Shavelson & Towne, 2002). What this means is that arts-based research, as a "soft-form" of qualitative research, will have an uphill battle to fight to maintain its place as a legitimate form of inquiry in the educational research community. At the same time, the very position articulated by the federal government concerning what it calls "evidence-based research" (Shavelson & Towne, 2002, p. 1) (implying that other kinds of research do not provide evidence) may ironically strengthen the acceptance of approaches to research that are closer to arts-based research than we have ever had. When your own ox is being gored, you tend to become somewhat more tolerant, maybe even more sympathetic to approaches that you once found problematic. I am saying that the very pressure upon traditional researchers to do experiments may warm them toward non-experimental approaches to research.

In any case, it is still necessary to have arguments that offer support for arts-based research. This is not a new requirement, but it may be, at present, particularly important.

At the same time, the greatest source of security concerning arts-based research is not in tight rationales articulated by academics who have a vested interest in its use, but exemplary arts-based work which is difficult to dislike. In other words, deeds, not words, may be in the end the most persuasive source of support and the source that yields the highest levels of credibility.

So much for establishing a grounding of where I and the field have been. Let's turn to tensions. Earlier I discussed the existence of tensions. I want to identify them now. One of these tensions pertains to a deep dilemma. This dilemma relates, on the one hand, to the desire to work imaginatively and, on the other hand, as a result of doing so producing material that does not communicate.

How shall we arbitrate differences in our interpretive response to materials that have no clear referents? Surely one of the functions of educational research in general, and arts-based research in particular, is to make vivid certain qualities encountered by the researcher normally, but not necessarily in the context of schools. Will the images made through arts-based research possess a sufficient degree of referential clarity to engender a common understanding of the situation being addressed, or is a common understanding of the situation through arts-based research an inappropriate expectation? If so, what are we to make of the well-crafted but ambiguous poem or painting, for example, the expressive painting that we want to connect to the situation we intend to render but which works more like a Rorschach test? Put another way, how do we deal with referentiality when we do not have a means that enables us to make the needed connections? Should we worry about this?

Just what are the other tensions in arts-based research?

A second tension is located between the particular and the general. By this I mean that there is a tension between focusing on the particular conditions of an educational situation in order to illuminate its distinctive features and, at the same time, developing observations and insights that extend well beyond the particular that was addressed in the first place. As you well know, in conventional forms of generalization in the social sciences, generalizations can be made *if* the sample drawn from a population is random and, if it is, one is able to draw conclusions from the sample to the larger population of which it once was a part. The procedures are straightforward and almost universally applied in studies that attempt to generalize using statistics.

In arts-based research, we have no comparable set of conditions. The very conditions that make a study arts-based are conditions that personalize the study or the situation by allowing an investigator's thumbprint to work its magic in illuminating the scene. Furthermore, the samples in arts-based research are typically convenience samples, i.e., idiosyncratic sites that are most often intuitively selected rather than randomly identified or otherwise rule-governed. How, then, given these conditions, is generalization possible? One answer, which doesn't satisfy everybody, is to argue that the general resides in the particular and that making general observations from particular circumstances is precisely what we do in life. We formulate generalizations on the basis of particular instances, none of which have been randomly selected. But as I said, that explanation, which I find congenial, does not satisfy all investigators. At the same time, it should be remembered that conclusions drawn in statistically based research that purport to generalize are often generalized to populations that were not a part of the population from which the sample was drawn. In other words, generalizations in the social sciences are often over-generalized given the rules of the game that statistically oriented researchers play. Nevertheless, the fact that statistically oriented studies are often generalized beyond their appropriate limits does not grant permission to arts-based researchers to generalize from particulars, *unless* one's conception of generalization adheres to a different model.

The different model about which I speak is a model that is much closer to literature than to statistical analysis. It culminates in an icon that, let us say, edifies or illuminates. Great works of literature teach their lessons in ways that go well beyond the particular circumstances they address. Their lessons are general. In fact, intelligence itself might be regarded as a process that enables one to see connections between the instance and aspects of the world that were not initially a part of that instance.

As I write these lines in this chapter, I feel comfortable with a literary conception of generalizability, and yet I well know that for many in the field of educational research this conception is not persuasive. Hence the tension.

It may be the case that the tension is inevitable and will be enduring. "You can't generalize from an N of 1" is an unquestioned mantra in the educational research community. Do we really know that other situations will be illuminated by what we find in the one that we select to study? But perhaps that's all we can get. Perhaps the function of educational research is not to draw near-certain conclusions about states of affairs that generalize, but rather to secure technologies of mind that will enable us to peer more deeply into situations that might not be the same as the one that we study. In short. we might say that useful research enlarges our intelligence. In any case, a tension is there, and it is one that we need to acknowledge and address with the aid of the best conceptual work we are able to muster.

A third tension in arts-based research is the tension between the desire to achieve a work product that has aesthetic properties and the desire to achieve at least some degree of verisimilitude in our work. It is so attractive and satisfying to shape a line or a paragraph so that it sings even if it portrays in questionable ways the situation we are attempting to address. In other words, there is a tendency to allow aesthetic considerations to trump the need for an epistemic orientation to disclosure or, if not epistemic, at least one that is phronetic. True and certain knowledge – the aspiration to achieve episteme – is, according to Stephen Toulmin (1982), too demanding and unrealistic an aspiration for inquiry into human affairs. It is simply too much to ask for. Nevertheless, aesthetic achievement places its demands upon us; statements about states of affairs can be attractive and wrong. Indeed, the more attractive they become, the more they might mislead. Consider advertising.

But perhaps this, too, is something we should not worry about. After all, in the theater the individuals portrayed by actors are often larger than life. It is their overwhelming character that awakens us to qualities in the human condition that we often neglect in daily life. In other words, the drama on stage can be more vivid than what one might normally find. Is this a problem? One could argue that it is in the very exaggeration of the features of a situation through which we come to grasp its significance. Put another way, exaggeration can promote understanding.

Perhaps the problem or tension that we experience between the aesthetic and the world it portrays is our belief, often unexpressed, that a correspondence theory of truth is the model that should guide our work. And yet, if it is not the model that should guide our work, just what is? And if it is something other than a correspondence theory of truth, is it likely to be accepted by our colleagues who have grown up on such a model?

But what if we neglected aesthetic considerations in doing arts-based research? If we did, could we still call it arts-based research? I have my reservations. For me, the distinguishing feature of arts-based research is that it uses aesthetic qualities to shed light on the educational situations we care about. Arts-based research is not simply the application of a variety of loose methods; it is the result of artistically crafting the description of the situation so that it can be seen from another angle. To talk about the desirability of seeing a situation from more than one angle is to tacitly acknowledge what I will make explicit.

In promoting the practice of arts-based educational research, I seek no new hegemony in matters methodological. What I believe we need in educational research are multiple perspectives. Each template or lens one engages to see can make vivid what other lenses obscure. Unlike our brethren at the national level who believe that randomized experimental field trials are the only way to go, I believe there are many roads to multiple Romes. Put another way, I don't think there is one destination that several roads will lead you to, but that there are, rather, multiple destinations which require multiple roads.

A fourth tension in arts-based research is related to the features of its "product." For some arts-based researchers, the results of arts-based research pertain to the formulation of new, more interesting questions than the ones one started with. You might say that arts-based researchers are interested in generating puzzlements. Now the generation of puzzlements is an intellectually attractive thing to do. Many claim that questions are the most significant form of intellectual achievement, not answers. What arts-based research should do is to raise fresh questions.

For many of us who love to participate in the life of the mind, this conception of the products of arts-based research has an attractive ring. It suggests an emphasis on inquiry, a tolerance of ambiguity, a preference for what is open-ended, a desire for what is fluid rather than what is rigid. These are all values that most of us here could subscribe to. At the same time, we must not forget that policy-makers, teachers, and parents are not primarily interested in better questions; they would like to have some answers to questions about the ways in which teaching affects learning, about what their children have learned, or about the discovery of better ways to teach reading. The point is that, while questions are just fine for those of us in the academy, they are not necessarily fine to people who have a problem and who wish to solve it and who believe that research may be one way to provide better answers than the ones they had before. Can arts-based research furnish answers to complex educational questions? Will those answers stand up in court? Is arts-based educational research essentially a reconnaissance effort to generate questions that "real research" can secure answers to? Just what is our stand concerning our ability to present reasonably confident answers to educational questions through arts-based research, or is our mission to provide interesting new leads for other educational researchers to pursue?

I know that in making a distinction between answers and questions I am walking on thin ice. One could clearly argue that conventional research is also interested in better questions; that aspiration is not owned by arts-based researchers. And yet the kinds of answers that arts-based research yields, if any at all, seem much more ethereal, global, impressionistic, than those secured through conventional forms of research. Now it could be argued that what I have called the ethereal character of arts-based research products is a much more congenial fit between situations and ideas about them than the misleading implications that come out of much traditional research that answers are known and that schools should simply implement "what works."

Although I am in favor of implementing what works if what works, works, I do believe that there is a difference and a tension between ideas that culminate in propositional assertions about empirical starts of affairs and those that culminate in qualitative metaphors that may not have the same kind of precision that traditional research offers. Thus, I think there is a tension between the more literally oriented conclusions of conventional research and the more metaphorical conclusions, if they can be called that, of arts-based research.

Now many of us here have an affinity to metaphor. I certainly do. Yet research is more, or at least should be more than a Rorschach test. If arts-based research culminates in little more than a delightful poetic passage or a vivid narrative that does little educational work, it is not serving its function. In other words, I am trying to remind us here that in the end research is an instrument, whether arts-based or not, that is supposed to contribute to the quality of education students receive and that arts-based research must ultimately be appraised on the extent to which that aim is realized.

That this can be accomplished, I have no doubt. When Powell et al. (1985) write of shopping mall high schools and of students and teachers making *treaties* to enable them to get through the school year peacefully, they employ metaphors. These metaphors have a purpose. They do call our attention to relationships and to infrastructures that we might not otherwise notice. Metaphors can do educational work. We must try to resolve this tension by trying to make sure that they do.

I mention this consideration because in arts-based research there is at times a tendency, I believe, to mistake the novel for the useful. Since research is related to art, I get a sense that there is a tendency to want to make sure that the form and method employed is novel. Put another way, there is a tendency to want to make the work creative. Now novelty is a part of creativity and creativity is important to have, but when it trumps the instrumental utility I just described, namely that it contribute to the enrichment of the student's educational experience, it loses its utility as a form of educational research. Put in still another way, arts-based research needs to pursue novelty without sacrificing utility. It needs to be more than a projective test. And this creates a tension between achieving the shock of the new and, at the same time, genuinely communicating. When novelty out-distances a reader, the reader's delight may reside in the aesthetic rather than in the usefulness of the work.

Now it must seem strange to you to hear someone like me talk about the potentially distracting effects of the aesthetic and my belief that the practical utilities of arts-based research need to remain salient. I do so because I do not think the future of arts-based research will be well served unless its utilities are achieved. Novelty, or should I say "near novelty," is simply not going to be enough to sustain interest and engender high regard among our colleagues.

Another, fifth tension relates to the recognition that objectivity is always beyond reach and at the same time the desire that most of us have for our work not to be a projection of whatever we want it to be. Put another way, I am seeking a constructivist orientation to knowledge but a constructivist orientation within constraints. How do we resolve the tension between our correct belief that meanings are made and that they are made in part with our life histories while at the same time recognizing that, if in arts-based research anything goes, nothing will.

The "solution" that I have wrought in my own work pertains to the relationship between what Stephen Pepper (1942) calls "structural corroboration" that is a kind of circumstantial evidence, a form of triangulation, and referential adequacy, which is the empirical test of one's observations with respect to the situation that has been described and interpreted. For me, these concepts are helpful, although I must confess that structural corroboration is seldom adequately provided for in the arts-based research that I have seen. I think the field of law, which in part deals with matters of evidence, can furnish some useful leads on how to think about matters of objectivity and matters of verification; circumstantial evidence comes close.

We know that we cannot ever get a comprehensive view that is objective in any definitive sense, and we also recognize that verification – if that's the right word in the first place – will never be complete. At the same time, we don't want to be pushovers for procedures that will not bear what our colleagues call rigorous scrutiny. Can arts-based research be rigorous? If so, what would it look like if it was?

These five tensions, and I remind you of them now, penetrate our work – first the tension between using open forms that yield diverse interpretations and forms that yield common understandings is one such tension. A second is that between the particular and the general. We want our single case research to extend beyond the single subject studied. A third tension is between the desire to aesthetically craft form and the desire to tell it like it is; aesthetic considerations can trump epistemological ones. A fourth tension is between the desire to pursue new questions and puzzlements and the need in the practical world for answers. Finally, there is the tension for arts-based research to seek what is novel or creative and the need to create work that has verisimilitude to the furniture of the world.

What are we to make of this analysis and can we learn anything from it? I would make three concluding observations about the tensions that I have identified and their significance in education. First, it strikes me that the tensions experienced in the conduct of arts-based educational research are not like the tensions that traditional researchers encounter in doing their own work. The tensions we experience, in some sense, are the tensions of an underdog working in a universe in which we are "the smallest kid on the block." As a result, it has taken considerable courage on the part of arts-based researchers to stick their necks out in order to do work that fits their way of thinking about education.

A second observation pertains to the tensions about beliefs regarding the nature of knowing and the processes of the mind. Convictions about verification, generalization, reliability, and replicability participate in a hard-nosed universe of beliefs that we probably know all too well. The concepts and processes that we have employed in arts-based research are much more likely to work at the edge of possibility and address questions of meaning and experience that are not likely to be as salient in traditional research. Put another way, our basic concepts and methods participate in a new universe. Knowing, for example, takes on the attributes of a verb, that is, a process rather than an object or product that is fixed and definitively knowable. Mind, for us, is much more likely to be a fluid stream rather than a fixed rock. Our minds are always a work in process.

Finally, the tensions and procedures that I identify I believe can produce a general model that, if applied in our classrooms, could reshape and advance the practice of education and reform our conception of its proper aims. Regarding mind as a cultural achievement, knowing as a process that yields tentative resolutions, objectivity as an aspiration rather than a realization, the impact of forms of representation beyond the literal use of text, recognizing the power of form to inform, yet realizing that every form of representation both reveals and conceals, such ideas might broaden our perspective regarding what is worth teaching and learning and through a broadened perspective change the scope of the curriculum and enrich the practices that teachers employ to promote student growth.

Let me conclude by saying that, if only a portion of such aspirations were realized, our efforts would certainly be more than worthwhile. After all, the aim of research is not to advance the careers of researchers but to make a difference in the lives of students. That aspiration is realized not only by sharing conclusions about matters of fact but also by changing perspectives on how we see and interpret the world. Arts-based educational research can contribute significantly to a re-visioning of education. That contribution could be, in the long run, its most important.

## Editor's Postscript

Up until his death in 2014, Elliot Eisner remained a pioneering advocate for applying the arts as a tool in educational research. His 2012 book that he co-authored with Tom Barone, *Arts-Based Research*, remains a benchmark in the field.

In this chapter, Eisner states that he originally conceived of arts-based educational research as drawing skills from the arts – particularly the critical description of artistic events, as a critic does when describing a concert, a performance, or art exhibition. He was among the first to identify the value and validity of the arts and research, but did not anticipate that arts-based educational research would result in works of art. Furthermore, he aspired for arts-based research to be accepted within the paradigm of qualitative research. He wanted to stay at the edges of an empirically grounded world.

Much has changed since he wrote these words. Today, a significant literature in the arts explicitly claims that expressive visual and performative *making* is research (jagodzinski & Wallin, 2013). These may not be acts of building and forming, but tearing apart, breaking open, or monstrously mutating. These approaches do not seek to form but to undo. These are acts of using the arts to *unlearn* the past (Baldacchino, 2019).

Eisner never went this far. It is open to conjecture if his thinking would have continued to evolve and concur with these iterations had he lived longer. What is clear in this chapter from the first edition is that he asks us to *take* from the arts an attention to fine-grained qualitative distinctions. Seeing such distinctions in educational settings allows the educational researcher to create new *forms of representation* (Eisner, 1994) through which we gain insight – emotional resonance – into specific educational dynamics. This is an empirical process grounded in close attention to the world. It is a reporting of what has been present but previously gone unnoticed. Forms of representation brings into vision empirical evidence that heretofore has been ignored.

As Eisner claimed in his chapter, this is an effort to rejuvenate the process of science, what Patti Lather describes as "the quest for the science possible after the critiques of science (Lather, 2016, p. 125)." However, Eisner might disagree with Lather that this is a *post-epistemological* project. For Eisner, ABER does not come *after* epistemology. It is *neo-epistemological*: it makes epistemology and empiricism new (Manning, 2016).

## References


Baldacchino, J. (2019). *Art as unlearning: Towards a mannerist pedagogy*. Routledge.

Dewey, J. (1934/1958). *Art as experience*. Minton Balch.

Donmoyer, R., Eisner, E. W., Gardner, H., Cizek, G. J., Gough, N., Tillman, L., Stotsky, S., & Wasley, P. (1996). *Can a novel be a dissertation?* Panel presented at the American Educational Research Association Annual Meeting.

Eisner, E. W. (1991). *The enlightened eye: Qualitative inquiry and the enhancement of educational practice*. Macmillan.

Eisner, E. W. (1994). *Cognition and curriculum reconsidered* (2nd ed.). Teachers College Press.

Greene, M. (2001). *Variations on a blue guitar: The Lincoln Center Institute lectures on aesthetic education*. Teachers College Press.

jagodzinski, j., & Wallin, J. (2013). *Arts-based research: A critique and a proposal*. Sense.

Lather, P. (2016). Top ten+ list. *Cultural Studies/Critical Methodologies*, *16*(2), 125–131. https://doi.org/10.1177/1532708616634734

Manning, E. (2016). Ten propositions for research-creation. In N. Colin & S. Sachsenmaier (Eds.), *Collaboration in performance practice: Premises, workings and failures* (pp. 133–141). Palgrave Macmillan.

Pepper, S. C. (1942). *World hypotheses, a study in evidence*. University of California Press.

Powell, A. G., Farrar, E., & Cohen, D. K. (1985). *The shopping mall high school: Winners and losers in the educational marketplace*. Houghton Mifflin.

Shavelson, R. J., & Towne, L. (2002). *Scientific research in education*. National Academy Press.

Toulmin, S. (1982). The construal of reality: Criticism in modern and post modern science. In W. J. T. Mitchell (Ed.), *The politics of interpretation*. University of Chicago Press.

Chapter 11

# Notes from a Cuban Diary: We Believe in Our History

## An Inquiry into the 1961 Literacy Campaign Using Photographic Representation

*Joanne C. Elvy*

In 1961, the Revolutionary government in Cuba initiated a Literacy Campaign of great magnitude that became the vehicle for social change in the country; a vision that affirmed to Cuban citizens the value of education, health care, citizenship, professional development and the conception of family and community. With educational reform a high priority in the early years of the Cuban Revolution, more than 100,000 middle-class urban youth between the ages of 10 and 19 traveled to remote areas of the country as literacy *brigadistas* as part of this Campaign, facing challenges that were not "easy, safe or immediately rewarding" (Kozol, 1978, pp. 348–349). They lived with peasant families for months at a time, sharing in the manual labor by day, and teaching reading and writing at night. More than half of those who volunteered as *brigadistas* were young women.

*It was the first significant Revolutionary event for those of my age.*
*Myself, I was only 13 years old.*

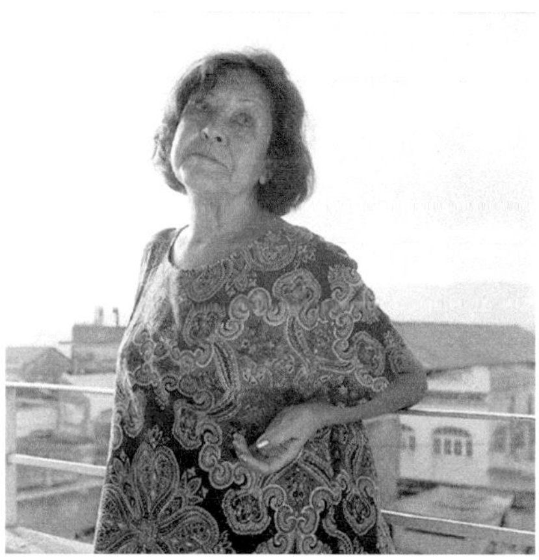

*Carmen*, Santiago de Cuba

*Being in this massive undertaking*
*was a point of departure for me,*
*in respect to my personal independence & identity, and*
*the responsibilities I took on as a young woman ...*
*Rosa*, Havana

DOI: 10.4324/9781003412892-11

As artist-researcher, I explore the transformation that occurred in Cuban women who reflect upon their role as *brigadistas*; in how the self-actualization that happened at that time spurred them to contemplate broader ways of viewing their own lives. My practice of photography has been a valid way for me to engage in and present my findings.

The cultural and social values of pre-Revolutionary Cuba provided little opportunity for women beyond the expected familial role of wife/mother, and traditionally parents made decisions on behalf of unmarried daughters to ensure their futures as "good" wives. For the young woman away from the family home for the first time, how she would perceive and envision possibility in her own life would no longer be the same.

As a photographer outside the fixed event from times past, I am now invited into their homes, and inside a poetic moment. As each woman names the limited opportunities they once had, I am "filled with fear and with joy," observing and responding "as faithfully as I can" to their memories (Cixous, 1991a, p. 52, 91). As women, we know how our stories – and those of our mothers, and those before – have been historically undervalued or overlooked by patriarchal constructs of one form or another; ones "written on the body ... the accumulations of a lifetime" (Winterson, 1995, p. 89). With my own body, "a human instrument" and an integral part of the research process, my perceptions of and interactions with these women are tools I use to record and interpret our exchange (Winterson, 1995, p. 89). Together our voices claim space, as we take steps not to forget.

This Literacy Campaign was one grand life lesson.
As a brigadista, this was the moment I took charge of my life.

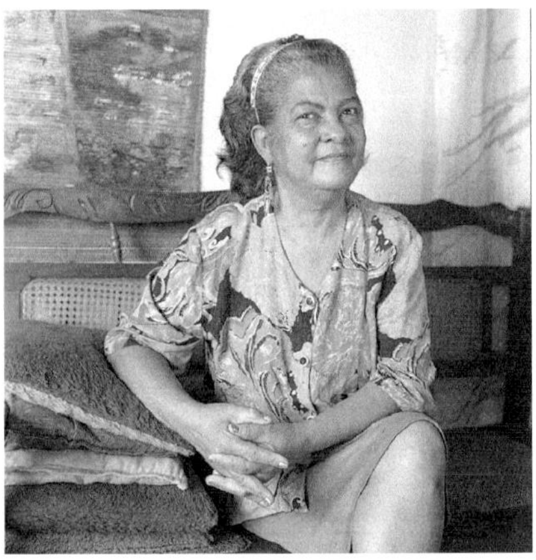

*Eneida*, Santiago de Cuba

I became outgoing ... I became conscientious.
I wasn't going to be tied down again!
*Dora*, Santiago de Cuba

How can one measure a "knowing" that does not fit within a prescribed format? The broader success of this Campaign cannot be merely fixed as "data," as it reverberates in the lived presence of these women in how its fundamental principles and ideals carry from their past into the present. If I contain myself within the margins of traditional knowledge production, I struggle with conventional forms of representation: "I would have liked to hear a sentence with room for me in it" (Cixous, 1985, p. 83). As human experience is dynamic and meanings shift over time, I relocate the photograph within poetic space, beyond the limitations of its own history and its "decisive" moment.

With the language of photography evoking an ideological lens that captures, frames, contains, and regulates subjective experience within the mere click of the shutter, I thus redefine this patriarchal hold on the construction and interpretation of photographic images. As a woman I turn inside, "further into the birth-voice" (Cixous, 1991b, p. 52); the darkroom, a familiar space, alchemic and visceral, where technique and intuitive knowing embrace as visual text. "Led beyond codes," history unravels and "meanings flow … no longer enclosed in the maps of social constructions" (Cixous, 1991b, p. 52). The academy similarly dictates an institutional standard for information gathering and thesis presentation that collides with the spirit of the lived everyday; in how research is defined and implemented, in which knowledge holds value … and in what can be tolerated.

*An illiterate woman is chained to her responsibilities at home.*
*She takes care of her husband & attends to the children.*
*But an illiterate woman can't participate in society*
*as a person & as a human being.*
*It's clear to me, she can be taken advantage of,*
*if she can't defend herself. Someone who is illiterate just doesn't know.*
*And THAT's exploitation.*
*Humbelina*, Pinar del Rio

Further, with the Cuban everyday reinventing itself in relation to exterior forces, what outsiders to these events see as problematic may well be assumptions held hostage; ideological renderings framed, fixed, and analyzed through a particular lens by those who hold the power and privilege to do so. The blur of technical boundaries of and with digital media also requires that I acknowledge my own moral and ethical responsibilities as a photographer on image production, and on no uncertain terms. Winterson argues that "if we admit that language has power over us, not only through what it says but also through what it *is*, we come closer to understanding the importance of poetry" as a tool for transformation, one that can take us further than we could have ever imagined; "the poet will not be satisfied with [simply] recording data" (1995, p. 76).

*As a Revolutionary event, the Literacy Campaign sparked the consciousness in the Cuban people to then help others.*
*Certainly, as we became educated as a people,*
*we came to realize*
*what we had achieved as a people.*
*Alida*, Ciego de Avila

In reconciling with the visual, Barthes describes how seeing, feeling and noticing are part of a collective memory woven into the broader script of our being human, "a carnal medium, a skin I share with everyone" (1981, p. 42). With reflective quotes written by the women I interview reaffirming the Campaign's significance, onlookers draw from their own embodied memory to become active participants in the research "findings."

Purveyors of a knowing we are able to *feel*; a visceral mediation as we are "moved by what we see in images," as we are touched (Robins, 1995, p. 39). As a visual gesture that can appeal to diverse audiences and reflect experiences above and beyond the walls of the academy, I argue that the photograph as a language holds the potential to transcend linear thought as an intimate, poetic document. As humanity continues to face fragile and uncertain times, I propose that this knowing, a *felt* knowledge, will carry through past the immediate, when words alone fall short.

This Literacy Campaign was such a gesture of humanity.
I believe it could not have happened
without the participation of women.

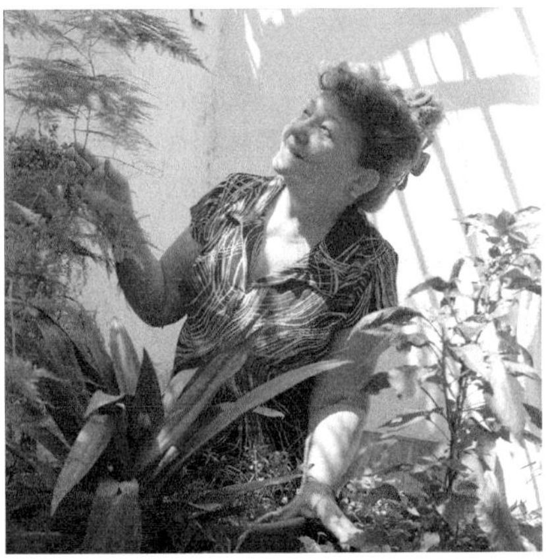

*Nuria*, Santiago de Cuba

Those of us who were part of it, we proved that
together we could overcome obstacles,
despite all the challenges we would undoubtedly face,
socially or economically.
Yes, women ARE capable of taking on such tasks.
*Zeida*, Pinar del Rio

Outside a fixed point in time, I believe that the stories of these women are not yet finished and cannot be finished; and that history can be impermanent to allow for the possibility of a world not yet realized. In this case, history comes alive as a kind of performance, inside the collective memory of a people, shifting the Literacy Campaign from a nostalgic event in the past to a vision for the future, intellectually, emotionally, and ethically. Such stories give light to Cuban women; and they who already have it, points out Lizette Vila, noted Cuban television producer and filmmaker, as "the illuminator of her surroundings" (Morris, 2001). And together our voices claim space, as we take steps not to forget.

## Postscript

This arts-based project marked my last time using a film camera in the face of digital innovation. As a Canadian scholar taking on this research on a contested island off the coast of America in late 2001, I could never have imagined the degree of uncertainty that the new millennium would confront in the aftermath of 9/11. Instead of fostering understanding toward engagement and reconciliation, the ease of technology has come to fuel suspicion and distrust, distancing human interaction and often in inexplicable ways. Social networks began to distort media events into a kind of white noise, the reality of the lived everyday far removed from incongruency of data bits and sound bytes.

I photographed these women to remember their stories. Invited into their homes and into their lives, I now look back at these fleeting times with great nostalgia. The photographs themselves represent actual lived moments. As historical documents they recall our exchanges over coffee, the camera's decisive moment, the hours I later spent in the darkroom, each frame filled with hope and anticipation for a better world. While I was once suspicious of photographs "evoking an ideological lens" to contain and regulate subjective experience, I now embrace them as visual text, testimonies capable of transcending time and space, steadfast as memories, visceral in how I am touched by their timeless gaze. Her-story as history now moves beyond the complexity of politics and personalities. As years go by I can now say aloud how "I photograph to remember," a knowing that defies scientific logic and any need to explain further. As historical documents that exist in real time and are undeterred by an uncertain future, these photographs are concrete proof of lives lived, as an urgent reminder that we must never forget.

## References

Barthes, R. (1981). *Camera lucia: Reflections on photography*. McGraw-Hill Ryerson.
Cixous, H. (1985). *Angst* (J. Levy, Trans.). John Calder.
Cixous, H. (1991a). *The book of Promethea*. Routledge.
Cixous, H. (1991b). *Coming to writing and other essays*. Routledge.
Kozol, J. (1978). A new look at the literacy campaign in Cuba. *Harvard Educational Review*, *48*(3), 341–377. https://doi.org/10.17763/haer.48.3.u51x64052k47jr06
Morris, H. (Writer & Director). (2001, March 30). Cuba: Paradox found, host Lizette Vila (Season 1, Episode 4). [TV series episode]. In H. Morris & J. Morris (Executive Producers), *Adventure divas*. Public Broadcasting Service.
Robins, K. (1995). Will images move us still? In M. Lister (Ed.), *The photographic image in digital culture* (pp. 29–50). Routledge.
Winterson, J. (1995). *Art objects: Essays on ecstasy and effrontery*. Alfred A. Knop.

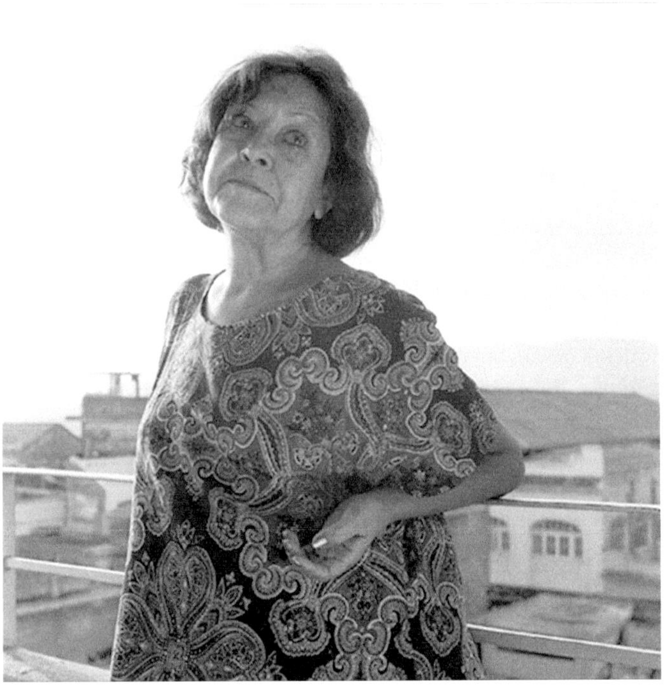

*Figure 11.1* Elvy, J., *Carmen*, Santiago de Cuba

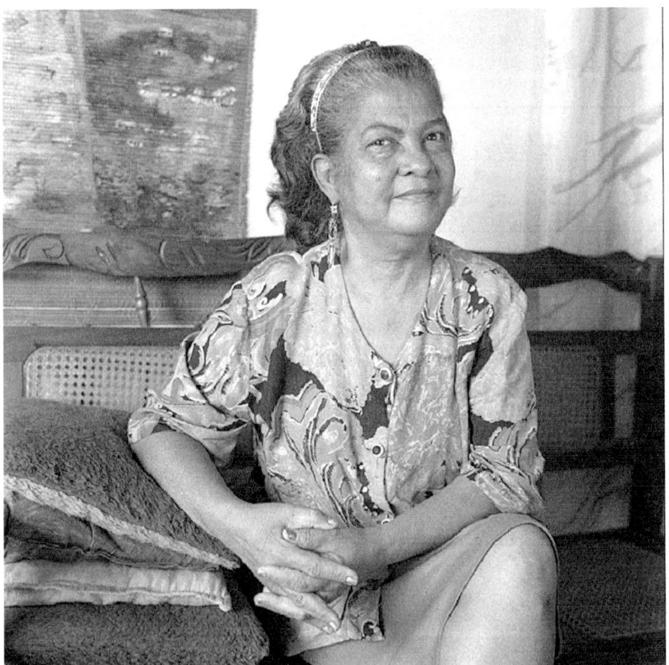

*Figure 11.2* Elvy, J., *Eneida*, Santiago de Cuba

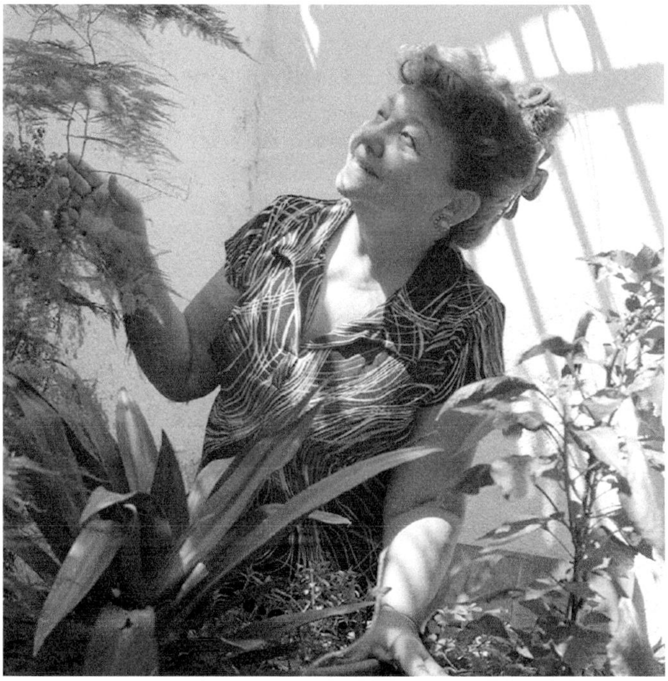

*Figure 11.3* Elvy, J., *Nuria*, Santiago de Cuba

Chapter 12

# Happenings

## Allan Kaprow's Experimental, Inquiry-Based Art Education

*Charles R. Garoian*

> Only because the artist operates experimentally does s/he open new fields of experience and disclose new aspects and qualities in familiar scenes and objects.
>
> John Dewey (1934/1958, p. 144)

> The word "experimental" is apt, providing it is understood not as descriptive of an act to be later judged in terms of success and failure, but simply as of an act that the outcome of which is unknown.
>
> John Cage (1961, p. 13)

> It might be that in paying too much attention to what we want art to be and do for society, we have made of it an enormous "lesson plan" full of bad acts.
>
> Allan Kaprow (1966b, p. 82)

### An Impulse Toward Experimentation

In his introduction to the collected writings of the American artist Allan Kaprow, *Essays on the Blurring of Art and Life*, art critic Jeff Kelley (Kaprow, 1993) describes a small well-worn black book, circa 1949, that then belonged to Kaprow, a 22-year-old artist and graduate student in philosophy. Within the next two decades, Kaprow would go on to achieve international recognition for his invention and theorization of the contemporary art forms of assemblage, environments, and happenings. What Kelley found in that well-worn copy of Dewey's (1934/1958) *Art as Experience* were Kaprow's underlining of particular words and passages, scribbled notations on the margins, and his penciled-in thoughts between the lines of its yellowing, oxidized pages. After having carefully examined Kaprow's fragmented inscriptions, Kelley likens them to "subheadings for pages *not yet written*" (Kaprow, 1993, emphasis added, p. xi). Considering the fragments' immanent potential, Kelley then writes: "One feels the tug of re-cognition as it pulls the artist away from the philosopher's text and toward the margins, where his own thinking begins to take shape ... ground[ing] himself in American pragmatism and forecast[ing] the themes of his career" (p. xi). The "*re-cognition*" that Kelley speculated about Kaprow's engagement with *Art as Experience* is not a *recognition* of what is already known by the artist, but that which—in its virtual, yet unknown figuration—accords with philosophers Deleuze and Guattari's (1987) conceptualization of the *body without organs* (BwO): an indeterminate body, a dynamic assemblage of disjunctive concepts resisting signification and organizational and institutional totalization.

DOI: 10.4324/9781003412892-12

The vibrant assemblage that Kelley encounters in Kaprow's notations affirms such *a body*, comprised of contiguous, *a*-signifying concepts extracted from Dewey's theory entangling with each other on a plane of consistency unrestricted by any organizational principles. Experienced virtually, the *a*-signifying potentialities of immanence occur as precognitive and prelinguistic figurations (Semetsky, 2003). They open and actualize thinking outside foundational knowledge through an incipient, radical experiential process that Deleuze refers to as *transcendental empiricism*. Un-grounding knowledge to repeat it otherwise, the immanent potentiality of transcendental empiricism resists anchoring the contingent happenings of experience to ideal subject positions. It is an empiricism that is committed to the "flow or multiplicity of experiences [of immanence] *from which* any being or idea is effected" (Colebrook, 2002, pp. 86–87).

Kaprow (1993) refers to such an unrestricted impulse in experimental art as "a free-for-all meaning nothing and everything" (p. 69). Put differently, what Kelley's encounter with Kaprow's notational assemblage suggests is the artist mapping *an* experience—his event encounter with Dewey's theory—is *a happening*. An archipelagic singularity, Kaprow's notational mapping constitutes a dynamic, ideational ecology expressing a multiplicity of movements, encounters, and alliances that Deleuze and Guattari (1994) refer to as a *plane of immanence* (p. 35).

Deleuzian scholar Claire Colebrook (2002) characterizes immanence as "giving 'consistency' to chaos ... to *constantly reopen thinking to the outside*, without allowing [interpreting] a fixed image [representation] of that outside to act as one more foundation" (emphasis added, p. 77). In giving chaos consistency, *immanence coheres as a vital, irreducible unity* that continually inflects, mutates, and affirms foundational texts and understandings while repeating them otherwise.

In what follows in this chapter, I characterize the irreducible and affirmative relationship between Kaprow's notational inflections and Dewey's writing in *Art as Experience* that later inspired Kaprow's research and practice as artist and writer. To activate the vital coherency and potentiality of their betweenness, I situate Dewey's theory of experience and Kaprow's experimental art-based practice adjacent with each other, not to reduce and conform their differences, but to initiate between them ideational encounters and alliances that cohere an immanent irreducible unity about inquiry-based art and its education.

The empirical inflections of Kaprow's scribbling, underlining, penciling outward into the marginalia, and his "having *an* experience" (Dewey, 1934/1958, p. 35) with *Art as Experience* accord with what Dewey characterizes as an experimental "consummation" that never terminates (p. 35). As such, the encounters and alliances between and among Kaprow's writerly gestures, and Dewey's text, function as an irreducible unity in which their differential attributes retain their character while remaining in appearance (Dewey, 1934/1958, p. 36). Their perpetual interplay alongside and with each other evoked in Kaprow ways of exploring and experimenting with the contingencies and immanent potentialities of art, education, and everyday life that forecasted, as Kelley (in Kaprow, 1993) suggests, the themes of his entire career (p. xi).

Kaprow pulling away from Dewey's text and moving toward, out, and into its margins with a multiplicity of markings constitutes an experimental playing-with the philosopher's writings on *learning by doing*—a pragmatics of art research and practice. Hence, I argue Dewey's pragmatism as the guiding force that moved Kaprow away from the center of the art world and toward its margins, where the experimental ethos of his assemblages, environments, and happenings unsettled the institutionalization and professionalization of art, and landed him an invitation to participate in the pivotal 1965 Penn State Seminar in Art Education. In mapping the trajectory of Dewey's influence on Kaprow's art practice, creative art, art education proposal at the Seminar, and his subsequent writings on "The Education of the Un-Artist" (1993), I conceptualize Kaprow's impulse toward experimentation, which continues to pulsate within contemporary art-based research and practice in challenging the instrumental assumptions and practices driving today's neoliberal art and educational politics.

## But What Do We Do Now?

When Kaprow arrived at the Penn State Seminar, his influential essay on Jackson Pollock (Kaprow, 1993) had been published seven years before. For Kaprow, Pollock represented a watershed in art history, as his experimental process of painting constituted an unsettling disavowal of art's disciplinary traditions and an affirmative turn toward "ritual, magic, and life" (Kaprow, 1993, pp. 6–7). In this essay, Kaprow describes Pollock's frenetic painterly actions over and around, in and across the canvas uncommonly placed on the floor of his studio, constituting the art of painting as a diaristic, performative gesture (p. 4). What he found compelling was Pollock's foregrounding of the experiential *process* of art—that is, the *work* of art, its *doing*, how art *affects* experience that is too often overshadowed by what it represents and especially its commodity status as an object.

Pollock's flicking, pouring, spattering, and spilling household paints with dried brushes, sticks, twigs, and his entangling various minute objects between and among the strewn lines and layers of paint hinted at the unremarkable events and materialities of everyday life. Uncommon to the orthodoxy of painting, they had greater affinity with the vicissitudes and contingencies of ordinary experiences, of existence outside the rarified confines of the professional art world. By disavowing "the confines of the rectangular field in favor of a continuum going in all directions simultaneously, beyond the literal dimensions of any work" (Kaprow, 1993, p. 5), the indeterminate, chance landings of pigment spilling toward and across the margins of Pollock's canvases and onto the surrounding studio floor, combined with their enormity, constituted "mural-scale paintings [that] ceased to become paintings and became environments" (p. 6). With these and other such characterizations in his essay, Kaprow suggests Pollock's movements over and around the canvas served as a mapping process that opened radically different paths for inquiry-driven art practice that differs from symbolic representation.

For Kaprow, Pollock's turn from representationalism to contingent embodiments created a predicament that begged: "But what do we do now?" Left with two choices, "to continue in [Pollock's] vein [or] to give up the making of paintings entirely" (Kaprow, 1993, p. 7), Kaprow did both! He turned away from historically established forms of art research and practices and, in his pursuit of new directions into the everyday world, he wrote:

> Pollock, as I see him, left us at the point where we must become preoccupied with and even dazzled by the space and objects of our everyday life, either our bodies, clothes, rooms, or ... Forty-second Street ... we shall utilize the specific substances of light, sound, movements, people, odors, touch ... objects of every sort are materials ... paint, chairs, food, electric and neon lights, smoke, water, old socks, a dog, movies, a thousand other things that will be discovered ...
>
> (pp. 7–8)

Reading much like a taxonomy, the preoccupations with everyday life about which Kaprow refers suggest a foreshadowing of his assemblages, environments, and happenings that by 1965 had established him as a major international artist. However, before addressing his involvement in the Seminar, I now turn to John Dewey's aesthetic pragmatism as it accords with Kelley's assertion of the philosopher as Kaprow's "intellectual father" (Kaprow, 1993, p. xxvi). The problematic of patriarchal designation aside, I nevertheless contend that it was by way of Dewey's theory of art experience that Kaprow articulated his insightful conceptualization of Pollock's exploratory, experimental, and improvisational process of *action* paintings.

### *Dewey's Instrumental Pragmatism*

In his essay "The Development of American Pragmatism," Dewey (1925) traces the origins of pragmatism from Charles Sanders Peirce's monistic, deductive conceptualizations of variation as simple, congealed realities to the dynamic, mutable pluralism of William James (Dewey, 1925). While Peirce sought single, uniform determinations from experimental consequences in the laboratory, James argued that conceptual truths emerge as a plurality from human interactions and social behaviors. Following his predecessors, Dewey differentiated between two approaches of experimentation: a monistic "rigid universe [suggestive of Peirce] where everything is fixed and immutably united to others, where indetermination, free choice, novelty, and the unforeseen in experience have no place"; and a pluralistic pragmatism, suggestive of James, that

> leaves room for contingence, liberty, novelty, and gives complete liberty of action to the empirical method, which can be indefinitely extended. It accepts unity where it finds it, but it does not attempt to force the vast diversity of events and things into a single rational mold.
>
> (pp. 8–9)

A significant characteristic of James's pragmatism with which Dewey aligned himself was its break from experiential determinism in which utilitarian *aspirations* were given precedence over a plurality of experimental *consequences*. Dewey (1925) writes: "Pragmatism, thus, presents itself as an extension of historical empiricism, but with this fundamental difference, that it does not insist upon antecedent phenomena but upon consequent phenomena; not upon the precedents but upon *the possibilities of action*" (emphasis added, p. 12). Thus, it was from James's theory of pragmatism—with the liberty that it afforded from preexisting truths and its basis from which future observations and experiences could be predicted—that Dewey developed *instrumentalism* as his own version of pragmatism. Dewey wrote:

> consideration of the future takes us to the conception of a universe whose evolution is not finished, of a universe which is still, in James' term, 'in the making,' 'in the process of becoming,' of a universe up to a certain point still plastic.
>
> (p. 13)

As such, based on James's consideration of *concepts as instruments*, or tools for "the experimental determination of future consequences" (Dewey, 1925, p. 14), his instrumentalism gave prominence to the intellectual participation of a plurality of individuals:

> It is s/he who is the carrier of creative thought, the author of action, and of its application … And the individual which American thought idealizes is not an individual per se, an

individual fixed in isolation and sets up for him/herself, but an individual who evolves and develops in a natural and human environment, an individual who can be educated.

(p. 20)

Considering the constitution of the social as a sphere of individual carriers and authors of creative thought, action, and application, as Dewey suggests, clearly aligned with James's contingent and agential pluralism. More importantly, such an instrumental understanding of experimentation relocates it from the artificial conditions of a laboratory into the natural, human, everyday world, where an intellectual multiplicity coexists and prevailing truths are learned and continually challenged.

At the end of his essay on American pragmatism, Dewey (1925) argues against reductive, positivist understandings of instrumental experimentation that "regard intelligence as a mere mechanism of belief ... [that] attempt[s] to re-establish the dignity of reason by making of it a machine for the production of beliefs useful to morals and society" (p. 21). He otherwise clarifies that instrumental experimentation does not constitute a narrow, teleological production of useful utilitarian and positivist outcomes and beliefs, but instead a pluralistic, consequential intelligence that is immanent between all participants' experiencing life and living in a society (p. 21). What Dewey suggests in this pluralistic characterization of instrumental experimentation comports with his earlier writings on democracy and education, and foreshadows his later turn to aesthetics.

## Dewey's Unexpected Turn

With *Art as Experience*, Dewey's instrumentalism took an *aesthetic turn* toward the immanent potentiality of art: "The unexpected turn, something which the artist him/herself does not definitely foresee ... gives the spontaneity of the unpremeditated ..." (Dewey, 1934/1958, p. 139). The felicitous, unpremeditated spontaneity to which he refers comports with the contingent and immanent forces of art experience. Resisting dualistic determinations, Dewey (1934/1958) describes two consummatory phases of art experience and situates them alongside one another in a performative relationship: the finality of "mechanical production" and the potentiality of "esthetic creation and perception" (p. 139). When these phases are synchronized, "there is *no final term* in appreciation of a work of art. *It carries on and is, therefore instrumental as well as final*" (emphasis added, p. 139).

According to Dewey (1934/1958), the phasal synchronicity of consummation occurs rhythmically: "doing and undergoing [*an* experience] ... in relationship ... like breathing" (pp. 44–56). With "no final term" (p. 139), he is referring to the paradox of art experience—its aporetic, undecidable performativity. Consistent with Dewey's non-dualistic characterization of mechanical finality and creative potentiality, philosopher Thomas M. Alexander (1987) clarifies an oft-misunderstood relationship between Dewey's notions of instrumentalism and aesthetic experience: "The same theory of experience underlies both aspects of his philosophy, but instrumentalism only gains its significance because of the aesthetic possibilities of experience to have directly funded consummatory meaning and value" (p. 184). In other words, the consummatory experience of art denotes instrumentalism as a vibrant, performative process differently than conventionally understood, merely in terms of practical, utilitarian objectives.

Dewey's (1934/1958) characterization of consummation as *carrying on* both *instrumentally and finally* accords with his notion of art as a dynamic process of *undergoing* where the "closure of a circuit of energy is the opposite of arrest, of *stasis* ... [and] 'taking in' in any vital experience ... *involves reconstruction [of thought] which may be painful*" (emphasis added, p. 41). Here again, denying narrow, mechanistic understandings of art's instrumental experimentation, Dewey points to its performative aspects: "The work ... of art does not cease when the direct act of perception stops. It continues to operate [instrumentally] in indirect channels" (p. 139). Such indirection is unsettling and *painful*, according to Dewey, inasmuch as it short-circuits foundational representations and understandings. In other words, *undergoing* constitutes suffering and enduring the experiential contingencies of art, and *taking in*, perceiving the *working* of art, more than adds to recognizable knowledge. The perceptual synchronicity of undergoing and taking in experience reconstructs and repeats the comforts and assurances of "bare recognition" in ways that initiate thinking and doing otherwise (p. 53).

## Having *an* Experience

The indefinite article "an" is key to understanding Dewey's concept of experience. It is significant as well to understanding the performative, inquiry-based research of Kaprow's assemblages, environments, and happenings. In Chapter III of *Art as Experience*, Dewey (1934/1958) characterizes the din of everyday *continuous* experience as distracting, dispersive, and at odds with each other. Such experience, he contends, is "inchoate" (p. 35) inasmuch as it constitutes the steady, chaotic rumble of everyday living in which we are always already immersed. He contrasts this rudimentary notion with "hav[ing] *an* experience when the material experienced runs its course to fulfillment" (p. 35).

Unlike the utilitarian, moralizing objectives of pragmatism, what Dewey (1934/1958) is suggesting about *fulfillment* is an experience that "is so rounded out that *its close is a consummation and not a cessation*" (emphasis added, p. 35). Accordingly, *an* experience is "whole and carries with it its own individualizing quality and self-sufficiency" (p. 35). A singularity, it occurs as a "continuous merging ... [and] continued acceleration [that] prevents [its] parts from gaining distinction" (p. 36). For Dewey, these consummatory characteristics of *an* experience function as aesthetic occurrences that resist intellectual closure. That is, the relationships between and among the individual parts of *an* experience are mutable and dynamic. They are performative inasmuch as its parts are contiguous, interdependent, and irreducible to one another.

Indeed, it is by way of art experience that Dewey (1934/1958) conceptualizes aesthetic performativity. Reiterating consummation as a continuous process, he writes: "In a work of art, different acts ... fuse into unity, and yet do not disappear and lose their own character ..." (p. 36). Consummation thusly occurs as a unifying aesthetic experience with its own distinctive quality (p. 38). More succinctly, "If a conclusion is reached [in an experience], it is that of a movement of anticipation and culmination, one that finally comes to completion" (p. 38). Ironically, it is by way of the aesthetic performativity of art that Dewey associates consummation with even the mundane, non-art experiences in life, such as being handed a receipt by the cashier at the grocery store, as being aesthetically unified. "A 'conclusion' is no separate and independent thing; it is the consummation of a movement" (p. 38). Dewey further elaborates on the closure of an experiential "circuit of energy." Contrary to a static conception of closure, consummation initiates a contingent process of *undergoing* and absorbing experiences beyond what was understood or conceptualized up to this point (p. 41). As mentioned previously, Dewey refers to such contingent reconstruction as *painful*, inasmuch as it unsettles past understandings to initiate thinking and experiencing them in qualitatively different ways.

As I alluded to earlier, what Kelley (in Kaprow, 1993) describes as Kaprow's "pull[ing] away" [and] "toward the margins" (p. xi) of *Art as Experience* suggests the artist riffing on Dewey's text just as Dewey riffed on Peircean and Jamesian theory. In doing so, both Kaprow and Dewey were moving in their respective directions away from the narrow, utilitarian understandings of instrumental experimentation. By attending to the unanticipated experience of art, Kaprow conceptualized instrumental experimentation in ways that were consistent with Dewey's defense of aesthetic experience. In pointing out the hypocrisy of those who dissociated instrumental experimentation from art, Dewey (1934/1958) writes:

> Persons who draw back at the mention of "instrumental" in connection with art often glorify art for precisely the enduring serenity, refreshment, or re-education of vision that are induced by it .... Such persons are accustomed to associate the word with instrumentalities for narrow ends—as an umbrella is instrumental to protection from rain ....
>
> (pp. 139–140)

For Kaprow (1993), a narrow, utilitarian understanding of Deweyan instrumentalism reduces art to its content, glorifies its institutional value, and assumes professionalization as the ultimate objective of art practice. According to Kaprow, the dominance of utilitarian understandings of instrumentalism, which is evident in the institutional and professional estrangements and confinements of art, its museumization, runs contrary to the contingent circumstances and happenings of everyday life.

#### *Kaprow's Response to a Field*

In *Assemblage, Environments, and Happenings*, Kaprow (1966a) describes the trajectory from painting to "The New Forms, Materials, and Attitudes" much like his characterization of Pollock painting beyond the pictorial margins of the canvas and onto the open floor of the studio as mural-like environments:

> unless one works out in the open, it must be admitted that old responses geared to a canvas's dimensions and character are probably now transferred to the three-dimensional measurements of the room, and this may be a response to a 'field.'
>
> (p. 160)

That field of response, about which Kaprow is referring across the historical and social margins of the canvas, foregrounds the spatial phenomenon of proximity—that is, a "fuller involvement with actual space" (p. 160). Such proximal involvement is experimental. It spills over academic and institutional margins, and continuously merges and consummates with the contingencies of everyday life to open new possibilities of action, as Dewey (1934/1958, p. 144) asserts in the first epigraph that begins this chapter. This would be an inquiry-based art education.

That Deweyan principle of experience is also evident in the exploratory, experimental, and improvisational processes and materials that Kaprow (1966a) initiated in his assemblages, environments, and happenings. To open the institutional parameters of the art world, he included "memoirs, objects of everyday use, industrial waste" (p. 166) and other such commonplace materials of everyday life. His objectives for material usage were threefold: to "represent a further enlargement of the domain of art's subject matter"; to "practically guarantee a new range of forms not possible with conventional means"; and to "introduce materials that are of the greatest fragility" (pp. 166–167). The spatial and temporal range of these materials situated the art world in an aporetic, paradoxical relationship with the circumstances of everyday life—a foreshadowing of Kaprow's writings on the education of the un-artist. That paradoxical relationship, unlike the contemptuous critique of negation, initiates an affirmative criticality that riffs and improvises on academic and institutional assumptions to conceptualize and render them otherwise. Kaprow's assemblages, environments, and happenings constituted an irresolvable, aporetic performativity from which the relational potential between art and life could be experienced through immanence.

While differences existed between Kaprow's assemblages, environments, and happenings, their performative characteristics nevertheless overlapped. "Assemblages can be handled or walked around, while environments must be walked into" (Kaprow, 1966a, p. 159). He described the differences between environments and happenings as the "passive and active sides of the same coin" (p. 184), which are in paradoxical proximity and irreducible to one another. Kaprow provides the following attributes of happenings (which also apply to his assemblages and environments and constitute inquiry-based art):

A The line between art and life should be kept as fluid, and perhaps indistinct, as possible.
B The themes, materials, and actions of Happenings are taken from anywhere but the arts, their derivatives and milieu.
C The performance of a Happening should take place over several widely spaced, sometimes moving and changing locales.
D Time, which follows closely on space considerations, should be variable and discontinuous.
E Happenings should be performed once only.
F It follows that audiences should be eliminated entirely.
G The composition of a Happening proceeds exactly as in Assemblage and Environments, that is, it is evolved as a collage of events in certain spans of time and in certain spaces.

(Kaprow, 1966a, pp. 188–198)

The performative attributes of Kaprow's assemblages, environments, and happenings are implied in his essay "Experimental Art" (Kaprow, 1993, pp. 66–80), which was first published in *Art News* in 1966, a year after his participation in the Penn State Seminar. Arguing the teleology of art as "developmental rather than experimental" (p. 68), Kaprow (1993) conceptualizes the latter as a playful process: doing "something never done before, by a method never before used, whose outcome is unforeseen" (p. 69). Such an unanticipated outcome is experimental insofar as it is not measured in terms of success and failure, but as "an act that the outcome of which is unknown," as experimental composer John Cage (1961, p. 13) asserts in the second epigraph of this chapter.

While affirming the immanent potentiality of experimentation, Kaprow (1993) nevertheless reaffirms the developmental figuration of history in terms of an unbound assemblage, an experimental situation in which "historical references ... [are] missing, even for a short time ... *where certain lines of thought would be cut or shorted out*" (Emphasis added, p. 69). Such short circuiting inflects the chronology of historical time-out-of-joint—that is, a boundless assemblage. Inversely, when valued as instrumental methodologies, historical references are more likely to inhibit the immanent potential of art by interpreting and rendering its creative force manageable. Kaprow writes that historical references "are useless ... for experimental artists except as points of departure ... for them all existing values are equally good and equally unconvincing. To affirm any one of them requires discovering it anew by some as yet unknown method" (p. 74). Accordingly, Cage's and Kaprow's *unknown* is that which emerges as an inflected, differential way of thinking from the immanent potentiality of art experience.

### *An Immanent Inquiry-Based Art Education*

It was in accordance with the experimental impulses of his assemblages, environments, and happenings that Kaprow addressed the topic of research and curriculum development in art education at the 1965 Penn State Seminar in his paper entitled *The Creation of Art and the Creation of Art Education* (Kaprow, 1966b). Expounding on those impulses, he situated "the creation of art" and "the creation of art education" in proximity with one another. In doing so, he made a case for an immanent, inquiry-based art education curriculum inspired by "the artist's decision-making process as s/he works [experimentally], her/his creative growth [through experimentation], and her/his [experimental] relation to the cultural past" (Kaprow, 1966b, p. 74).

Kaprow (1966b) advised against systematic investigations of creativity that would control teaching and art making, and merely add to existing academic expectations. He advocated for "ignorance and uncertainty" as ways of unsettling and inflecting institutional rules and lesson plans (p. 74), that is, "an attitude of childlike curiosity and intellectual curiosity ... rather than analytical investigative procedures" (p. 81). Critical of prescriptive teaching and learning methodologies, he questioned, as in the third epigraph at the beginning of this chapter, whether instrumentalist attitudes and practices had turned the creative force of art into an "enormous 'lesson plan' full of bad acts" (p. 82). Contrary to academic and institutional dispositions toward art and education, he called for "the artist's sense of being ... [an] active participation in the life of the imagination ... that simply exists as a way to be alive" (p. 84). Then, having exposed, examined, and critiqued the foundational assumptions of art making alongside those of art teaching, he recommended three potential sources for qualified art teachers:

> The large roster of American artists of acknowledged reputation, the even greater number of art majors graduating from universities and professional schools, and a hard-to-estimate number of generally ignored but often gifted, men and women conducting community art classes, slum-reform recreations, and "Y" or church activities.
>
> (p. 84)

While seemingly simple, Kaprow's proposal for a pluralistic source of art educators corresponds with the social assemblage of Jamesian and Deweyan pragmatism. Understood within the context of Kaprow's art practice, it suggests that the immanent, creative potential of art education is contingent upon source teachers' and artists' individual immersive practices and their willingness to work alongside and with each other. Ostensibly, what emerges from the constitutive *assemblage* of immersive teaching and art making is an alliance, a coherent ecology, that is an *environment* of images, ideas, materials, and actions spilling over, crossing their presumptive margins, converging, entangling, and incubating with the contingencies of everyday life. Regarding the immanent potential of immersive experience, Dewey (1934/1958) writes "incubation goes on until what is conceived is brought forth and is rendered perceptible as part of the common world" (p. 56). Indeed, what is conceived is rendered perceptible, but as a perceptual culmination that is nevertheless in perpetual movement, resisting foundational ways of seeing and thinking as it engages with the world (p. 35). Hence, homologous with Dewey's consummation of *an* experience, Kaprow's *happenings* short-circuit foundational understandings of art and education, and in doing so, inspire inquiry-based art practices that blur the margins between art and everyday life.

The absurd coherency of Kaprow's assemblages, environments, and happenings—or, what some might consider incoherent—aligns with Dewey's continuous merging of *an* experience and with what poet David Antin (2011) refers to as *radical coherency*. While coherence is ordinarily associated with conformity, Antin's particular conception is similar to the field of proximal involvement that Kaprow ascribed to Pollock exceeding the margins of the canvas to the actual spatial contingencies and vicissitudes of everyday life. In a zigzagging, assemblage narrative similarly entitled, Antin queries

> ... the idea of what we consider coherent ... why we consider it coherent ... and the different ways of thinking things are coherent that are based on different organizing principles ... taking pieces of things that were once parts of certain larger things ... usually continuous things you would consider coherent ... and putting them together ... or next to each other ... as looking to see what happened ...
>
> (pp. 227–228)

Antin's "Looking to see what happened" suggests *paying attention* to the contingent encounters and alliances of Kaprow's radical coherency. Deleuzian scholar Laura Cull Ó Maoilearca (2015) refers to such attentiveness thusly: "observation as a kind of participation" (p. 145). As such, she describes Kaprow's "pursuit of participation ... [as] allow[ing] an audience to inhabit a creative and co-authorial relationship to the work" (p. 159). In his essay "Allan at work," Antin (2011) associates co-authorial participation with the radical coherency of Kaprow's assemblages, environments, and happenings as

> real if absurd achievement[s] ... [that] derives from the way a given action, situation, or utterance fits or, more precisely, fails to fit, dislocates or disrupts some conventional stable cultural and social understandings, *to which it must be referred to have any effect at all.* [emphasis added]
>
> (p. 151)

Such is the contingent performativity of experimental art from which Kaprow's inquiry-based art education emerges and unsettles cultural and social predeterminations, the "bad acts" of traditional conceptions of art research and art curriculum.

Approaching the problem of art education from his radically coherent practice as an artist, Kaprow advocated for an experimental approach to research and curriculum development that was centered on art practice's immanent potentiality. Within the scholarly milieu of the Penn State Seminar, he presented a strong case for experimentation that was, and is still, often overlooked by those who are consumed with instrumentalist approaches in art and education. In all probability, it was Kaprow's contribution to and participation in the discursive assemblage of the Penn State Seminar that inspired his three essays on "The

Education of the Un-Artist" (Kaprow, 1993), which were subsequently published in the international journal *Artforum* between 1971 and 1974.

## The Artless Work of the Un-Artist

In his first iteration of those essays, "The Education of the Un-Artist, Part I," Kaprow (1993) asserts: "Artists of the world, drop out! You have nothing to lose but your professions" (p. 109). Kaprow backs this humorous invocation with three evocative passwords, *non-art, anti-art,* and *Art-art,* with which he challenged the overly determined classifications of the art world. His use of "password" as a professional designation suggests having access to a private, privileged organization, which in this case implies the rarified, cloistered space of the art world. He characterizes the first password, *non-art,* as "whatever has not yet been accepted as art but has caught an artist's attention with that possibility in mind" (p. 98). In other words, while *non-art* may suggest aversion and nonconformity, it nevertheless seeks recognition and accommodation within the organizational systems of art. His second password, *anti-art,* is already bound historically, as it associates with the *avant-garde* provocations of the Dadaists that are easily coopted by a market that fancies novelty in art. With his third password, *Art-art,* he admonishes the art world for "tak[ing] art seriously" (p. 101), for extolling its academic and institutional significance at the expense of art's relationship with everyday life.

It is with Kaprow's fourth password, *un-art,* that the exclusivity of the previous three is deferred, thus blurring the margins between the foundational systems of the art world and the plurality of the everyday world by situating them alongside one another to entangle, intermingle, and evoke from their in-between an immanent art, an art of persistent plurality, an "art which can't be art" (Kaprow, 1986). Instead of taking art seriously, the contingent performativity of un-art is mischievous and playful. Its work unsettles and inflects the professionalization of art

> to become, for instance, an account executive, an ecologist, a stunt rider, a politician, a beach bum ... different capacities in which different kinds of art would operate indirectly as a stored code that, instead of programming a specific course of behavior, would facilitate an attitude of deliberate playfulness toward all professionalizing activities well beyond art. *Signal scrambling, perhaps* [emphasis added].
>
> (p. 104)

The playful, signal scrambling about which Kaprow refers renders reductive, moralizing assumptions of professionalization *useless.* It perturbs regressive, neoliberal inclinations that assume the goals and objectives of creative and intellectual agency purely in terms of profit driven, institutionalized outcomes: their *usefulness.*

### *The Co-Optation of Art-Based Experimentation*

While Kaprow's inclusion in the Penn State Seminar represented a serious effort on the part of the organizers to bring Dewey's aesthetic theory into art education, during the next two decades (1965–1985) his compelling contribution, and those of the other participating scholars and artists, was diverted toward strengthening the National Art Education

Association (NAEA) and establishing its research goals and objectives. The basic research that emerged from the Penn State Seminar was thereafter interpreted and applied toward asserting art's disciplinary usefulness alongside those of the other disciplines in American schools. That instrumentalist application of art and its education eventually led to the marketing of Discipline-Based Art Education (DBAE), which was backed by the Getty Education Institute for the Arts. With the cultural credibility and massive financial support from the Getty secured, proponents of DBAE envisioned making art an academic imperative in schools.

With disciplinarity and equitable accessibility as their justification, proponents of DBAE research and curriculum aspired to elevate art from what in the past was pejoratively stigmatized as its "handmaiden" status to an esteemed position in schools. The four curricular "buzzwords" of DBAE, *art studio, art criticism, art history*, and *aesthetics*, were endorsed by the NAEA and promoted to teachers, administrators, and schools nationwide based on their instrumental affordances. Dewey's experimental pragmatism notwithstanding, this move toward institutionalization ironically occurred while the influx of French poststructuralist thought was already taking effect in challenging monistic disciplinary practices with the academy. As art education scholar Richard Siegesmund (personal communication, April 16, 2016) has astutely asserted:

> ironically the Penn State Seminar is now more commonly associated with the emergence of DBAE, which for most scholars in the field is perceived as a regressive curriculum ... there is a progressive, pragmatic way of wrestling with Dewey's aesthetics ..., and then there are reified conceptions of aesthetics that flatten learning to appreciation of a canon.

The flattening about which Siegesmund refers accords with the reduction and disciplining of experimental impulses to easily conform with neoliberal, canonical impulses that define art, teaching, and learning according to a consumerist ethos that elevates utilitarian benefits and applications. Such an ethos values the creative impulse of art solely in terms of interpreting and labeling a recognizable advantage: whether it makes sense, whether it means something, whether it is a sound investment, whether it will sell, whether it promises a job, whether it benefits learning in math and the sciences, whether it will raise test scores, etc. (Garoian, 2016). Dewey's (1934/1958) criticism of *recognition* correlates with neoliberal instrumentalist thought: "Bare recognition is satisfied when a proper tag or label is attached ..." (p. 53). Unlike the mischievous *artlessness* of the un-artist, the aim of the neoliberal professionalization of art and the artist is *artful* opportunism: to market "American Exceptionalism," a cunning ideology that selects and expropriates resources from around the world for the exclusive benefit of those living within its tightly secured borders. It is against the grain of such exclusivity that Kaprow advocated for an experimental inquiry-based art and art education, a pragmatic vision toward which art-based research and practice aspires.

## Editors' Postscript

In this essay, Garoian stresses the importance of Deleuzoguattarian theory and its concept of immanence to understanding the avant-garde art of the late 20th century. He particularly stresses the parallels to this Poststructural philosophy and the late aesthetic theory of John

Dewey. As Elliot Eisner argues (Chapter 10), arts-based educational research can help us revisit, revise, and reconceptualize our thinking. Deleuze and other Poststructural philosophers can help us to think with Dewey in new ways (Siegesmund, 2013).

However, Garoian challenges Eisner's claim that arts-based research needs to show utility. He argues instead for a need for *useless* creative practice to resist the neo-liberal commodification of education. Jorge Lucero (Chapter 25) similarly argues for arts-based research as a conceptual form of critical resistance to the regimentation of education.

In social science qualitative research methodology, educator Elizabeth St. Pierre argues that Poststructural theorists like Deleuze, Foucault, and Derrida have brought us to *post qualitative* inquiry. St. Pierre observes that "what we *find* in the world is what our system of thought claims exists and enables us to recognize" (2024, p. 8). Thus, it's easy to categorize something that we don't recognize as useless. Our existing theory will not let us see outside of theory's own blinders. We must tear the blinders apart. New theory may help us to discover the significance and value in what previously was dismissed as worthless. It is thus through pressing into these places of supposed worthlessness that we might re-imagine new possibilities for education.

## References

Alexander, T. M. (1987). *John Dewey's theory of art, experience, and nature: The horizons of feeling*. State University of New York.

Antin, D. (2011). *Radical coherency: Selected essays on art and literature 1966 to 2005*. University of Chicago.

Cage, J. (1961). *Silence*. University Press of New England.

Colebrook, C. (2002). *Gilles Deleuze*. Routledge.

Cull Ó Maoilearca, L. (2015). *Theatres of immanence: Deleuze and the ethics of performance*. Palgrave Macmillan.

Deleuze, G., & Guattari, F. (1987). *A thousand plateaus: Capitalism and schizophrenia* (B. Massumi, Trans.). University of Minnesota.

Deleuze, G., & Guattari, F. (1994). *What is philosophy?* (H. Tomlinson & G. Burchell, Trans.). Columbia University.

Dewey, J. (1925/1984). The development of American pragmatism. In J. A. Boydston & B.A. Walsh (Eds.), *John Dewey: The later works 1925–1953 (Volume 2: 1925–1927)* (pp. 3–21). Southern Illinois University.

Dewey, J. (1934/1958). *Art as experience*. G.P. Putnam's Sons.

Garoian, C. R. (2016, March). A Useless Leadership in Art and Its Education. Paper presented at the National Art Education Association Annual Conference, Chicago, IL.

Kaprow, A. (1966a). *Assemblage, environments & happenings*. Abrams.

Kaprow, A. (1966b). The creation of art and the creation of art education. In K. R. Beittel & E. L. Mattil (Eds.), *A seminar in art education for research and curriculum development* (pp. 74–89). The Pennsylvania State University.

Kaprow, A. (1986). *Art which can't be art*. In the exhibition catalog Allan Kaprow. Museum am Ostwall (August 24–October 5).

Kaprow, A. (1993). *Essays on the blurring of art and life* (J. Kelley, Ed.). University of California.

Semetsky, I. (2003). Deleuze's new image of thought, or Dewey revisited. *Educational Philosophy and Theory*, *35*(1), 17–29. https://doi.org/10.1111/1469-5812.00003

Siegesmund, R. (2013). Dewey, a/r/tography, and ab-use of global dialogue. In N. Denzin & M. Giardina (Eds.), *Global dimensions of qualitative inquiry* (pp. 137–155). Left Coast Press.

St. Pierre, E. A. (2024). A primer for post qualitative inquiry. *Qualitative Research in Psychology*, 1–25. https://doi.org/10.1080/14780887.2024.2347579

Chapter 13

# Queering Identity(ies) and Fiction Writing in Qualitative Research

*Douglas Gosse*

While I share common research goals with many qualitative researchers, such as attempting to better understand subjectivities, social conflicts, and cultural contradictions, arts-based educational research using queer theory and fiction writing is highly imaginative, reflective, and singularly provocative. *Jackytar* (Gosse, 2005b), the first educational novel published in Canada originally written as part of a doctoral dissertation (Gosse, 2005a), responds to a desire in education to inquire into diversity in new ways that more effectively provoke empathy and deeper learning (Parsons & Brown, 2001). The imaginative data for this research derives from my own implicit and explicit experiences and knowledge as an educator, researcher, and bilingual, working-class, disabled gay man who grew up in rural Newfoundland, where a steady exodus of Newfoundlanders continues, people leaving the struggling island in droves to explore better opportunities elsewhere.[1] In Newfoundland, "jackytar" refers to a person of mixed *Mi'kmaq* and French origins and carries pejorative connotations, such as laziness and moral decrepitude (Charbonneau & Barrette, 1992, p. 48). In the novel, the protagonist, Alex Murphy, is both gay and a "jackytar." While teaching in Toronto, he receives a phone call informing him that his mother is dying. Upon returning to rural Newfoundland, situations and people from his past incite him to a gradual re-examination of societal beliefs, customs, and practices. Through the lens of sexuality, I creatively investigate the intertwining identity markers of race, class, gender, sexual orientation, geographical location, ablebodiness, geographical location, and language and culture, in the lives of the fictional characters. Since *Jackytar*'s publication by Jesperson Press, and distribution in bookstores and libraries across Canada, we have contributed to a needed bridge between the academy and the public, a core goal of much arts-based (Barone, 1995) and arts-informed educational research (Cole & Knowles, 2001). Rather than invest in the ubiquitous uncertainty reduction of positivists and limit the sharing of my research to an academic elite, I seek to poststructurally challenge status quo assumptions, provoke further questionings, and shed light on intricacies of the human condition to as expansive a readership as possible.

This queer theoretical perspective is stylistically and figuratively embodied in the fiction writing itself but also evoked through judicious use of footnotes that act as marginalia or a kind of hypertext. To those interested in becoming writer researchers, my temperate use of footnotes may prove stimulating. In the dissertation version of *Jackytar*, footnotes serve five fundamental purposes. First, they serve to reference stories I adapted from others and to heighten awareness of the subjective construction and intertextuality of all knowledge and research. In particular, I footnote several contemporary and poignant parables told by Rev. Dr. Brent Hawkes, social activist, pastor of the Metropolitan Community

DOI: 10.4324/9781003412892-13

Church of Toronto,[2] and stirring storyteller. These stories derive from sermons I observed and contain themes of compassion and perseverance in the face of adversity which mirror *Jackytar*'s social justice foundation. Second, footnotes provide additional academic sources on key themes related to race, class, gender, sexual orientation, ablebodiness, geographical location, and language and culture for interlocutors[3] who wish to complement their reading of the fictional text in this way, although it is not a necessity for comprehension or engagement. Third, I sometimes trace the genealogy of certain words as part of my queer resistance (Jagose, 1996) and reference these in footnotes; this occurs most flagrantly towards the end when the character of Rev. Heather Byrne queers[4] Biblical scripture in a sociolinguistic manner. Fourth, I employ footnotes to articulate specific thoughts on the creative research process tied in with parts of the text.[5] Helping interlocutors understand my creative research process so that they might engage in similar writing was one of my primary motives. Fifth, I explain words and expressions indigenous to Newfoundland to highlight linguistic domination (Gosse et al., 2000). *Jackytar* explores how the acceptance or legitimization of knowledge and power in society depends largely upon subordination of certain groups, particularly those from rural, working-class, ethnic, and linguistic minority backgrounds, and how individuals and groups may resist marginalization.

The published version of *Jackytar* does not contain footnotes because the publisher initially felt this might compromise the public's appreciation, but the published novel remains identical to the dissertation version in all other respects. However, plans for another edition containing footnotes are now in progress for both academic audiences and what has been a convivial, enthusiastic public readership. I used the dissertation version of *Jackytar* which includes footnotes with great success in a fourth-year cultural anthropology course I taught at the University of Toronto, entitled "Sexualities and Dissident Narratives." My students read *Jackytar* and journaled their critical interpretations regarding identity(ies) and linguistic and cultural domination in particular; *Jackytar* also proved a powerful platform for critical discussion with reference to other course readings. At Nipissing University where I teach in the Faculty of Education, a number of students continue to read the version published without footnotes, and to share their interpretations with me. One such reading by a straight woman spurred an empathetic dialogue after several years of silence with her gay brother. In several cases, the intertwining nature of identities and power in the published *Jackytar* spawned thoughtful debates among colleagues and students that led us to re-examine our beliefs and practices about what constitutes acceptable research and the intricacies of power in our relationships: Is not all knowledge a subjective construction and sharing of stories? Do we not all drift in and out of sites of privilege and subjugation that studies of intersectional identity (rather than traditional binaries such as male/female or bourgeois/plebs, for instance) may elucidate? Should not heterosexuality, like research historically on homosexuality, be more rigorously studied via intersectional identity analysis, as a constructed social phenomenon with its own rituals, rigid codes of behaviour, and shaky hold on what is commonly enforced and viewed as "normal" and "acceptable?" I continue to receive personal emails from interlocutors in the broader public which lead me to believe that, with or without footnotes, the story is a catalyst for critical self and social reflection. Ultimately, interlocutors seem to identify with the fictional characters and provocative themes in a myriad of ways for I strove to provoke multiple interpretations and reflections throughout the entire reading process, including the ending, unlike in many traditional novels which focus on developing a central conflict and then leading readers towards resolution (Gosse, 2006). I hope that *Jackytar* may continue to function in provocative ways in a wide gamut of settings, not only for its propensity to generate critical debate, but also for its qualities and form as an example of arts-based educational research using queer theory in an accessible way.

So what might *queer* mean in the context of *Jackytar*, and what are some connections to analysis of identity/ies?[6] People tend to grapple uneasily with queer theory but its strength lies in shocking our sensibilities and generating debate. The queer research focus in *Jackytar* challenges the status quo of positivist research by providing more questions than answers, especially via persistent analysis of language (including tracing the genealogy of words) and sexualized cultural representations. *Jackytar* also inquires into ways in which queer identities seem partially constituted and reconstituted by acts of symbolic violence, particularly silencing. For instance, as queers we may be silenced from contributing our opinions for fear of psychological reprisal, including disapproval, taunting, and ignoring. Likewise, queer symbolic violence may take the form of invisibility in institutional culture, such as an absence of affirmative job action initiatives or equity policies. Indeed, despite official policies from government and school boards against racism and sexism, and sexism has become synonymous with bias against females (O'Beirne, 2006), thereby often obliterating the multiple ways many males are marginalized; furthermore, homophobia remains a virulent epidemic in our schools and is largely ignored. To illustrate, drop-out and suicide rates for queer students are significantly higher than that for their heterosexual peers, as well as incidents of reported physical and psychological violence (Dorais & Lajeunesse, 2004). Initiatives to counteract bullying rarely consider the widespread homophobic components of much male socialization. Schools tend to assume that everyone is heterosexual when in fact there are many educators, administrators, support staff, parents, and students who self-identify as queer, or have members of their families, colleagues, and larger community who do. Furthermore, Francophones like Alex who are also queer, an ethnic and linguistic minority, and from a working-class background, may experience increased violence within social, educational, familial and work spheres and the workplace (Labrie & Gosse, 2003). Still, representations of queers in popular culture would lead us to believe that most queers, if not all, are White (upper) middle-class, stylish, urban, ablebodied, wry gays and lesbians, whereas the so-called homosexual population is every bit as diverse as the heterosexual population. The use of the French language and Newfoundland dialect in *Jackytar* may trouble many interlocutors to reflect upon such linguistic and cultural domination. Significantly, the negotiation and regulation of normalized heterosexual identities are also stringently troubled in *Jackytar* in keeping with queer theoretical analysis (Namaste, 1996). In *Jackytar*, I have attempted to create revisionist telling(s) and reading(s) of stories that provoke, disarm, disrupt, and transform.

## *jackytar* Excerpt: Chapter 3

*This dream sequence/flashback occurs while the adult Alex is on board a plane heading to Newfoundland. The use of third-person limited narrative creates a sense of distancing and contributes to a mood/theme of alienation.*

"Well, now, looky who we got here!" sang Jeremy. "Whatcha doin today?" asked Sandra, her voice syrupy. "Just gettin some stuff at the shop," said Alex.

"What? Tampons?" said Jeremy.

Sandra snickered.

"Ya got a pussy in those jeans, Alex?" said Austin, their cousin, a teenager a few years older, stocky and strong from working in the local lumber mill. Alex commanded his legs to move but they felt like jelly. He tried to remain expressionless.

*On répond aux imbéciles par le silence.*

A rough hand fastened on his shoulder. "Hey, I was talkin to ya!"

"Ya fancies un, don't ya Austin? Maybe ya wants to date un, eh?" Sandra said. "Take un up in the alders then and have some fun!"

The redness spread from Alex's ears down to his neck.

"No fuckin way!"

"Whatcha holdin on to his shoulder for then?" Sandra sneered. "Luh, he's in heat. All flushed like a bitch. Go fer it, Austin."

Austin let go of his shoulder like he had leprosy. Then he spat on the dusty road and stepped back. "Goddamn gay[7] pussy faggot!"

"Ah, now you'm hurtin his feelins. Leave Alex alone, youse. He's m'friend. Ain't ya Alex?" Jeremy grabbed him by the arm and tried to kiss his face. "Wanna play hoist-yer-sails-and-run[8] wid us?"

Sandra and Austin pretended to gag.

"Watch out! Ya might catch AIDS," Sandra said.

"Let's git the fuck outta here," Austin said. "Leave the little Jackytar pussy alone."

"O' revwraaar!" drawled Sandra.

They sauntered off, giggling.

The boy walked alone. Past saltbox houses. He looked at the landwash. Remembered having spent time there with Sandra two years ago when they were ten years old. They had poked at a gigantic cobweb. The biggest spider they'd ever seen scurried away from their sticks. Sandra had toyed with the spider until she got fed up and squished it with her stick. He'd hidden his squeamishness from her. Voicing it might have risked her friendship.

Not that it mattered anymore.

He thought about Nanny. Every morning, she used to have toast and tea[9] ready for him at the kitchen table, overlooking the bay. Toast cooked over the wood stove and real butter. Delicious hot jam, what some called blueberry, picked on the Bond Cove barrens. He missed her. The Atlantic Ocean used to look so peaceful from the kitchen window. Now it just reminded him that he had to escape, that somewhere out there he might find happiness. And be safer.

"Why do things have to change?" he muttered aloud.

He spied Ole Man Howell working in his garden, using an old-fashioned sickle to cut the grass like in the olden days. He faked a smile and waved. Someone was always watching. Except when he needed them most. Through parted curtains. From a shed. From a passing car. This was an old people's town. Young people moved to the Mainland to get jobs—Toronto or Fort McMurray.

To escape maybe like he had to. One way or another.

He walked along Brigg's Road. The curving dirt road hugged the ocean side. The houses were pretty colours. Red. Blue. White. Beige. Red was his favourite. Especially the faded red of Johnson General Store. Boarded up now for years. He remembered shopping there as a small boy with his Nanny and Poppy. Mannequins loomed overhead, and more than once, he could have sworn their limbs stirred, or a head slightly cocked in his direction.

"Git some candy popcorn, m'ducky, if ya wants," she used to say.

Once, his Poppy Murphy had called him over for a special gift.

"Look, m'son, let's git ya some t'igh rubbers, awright?"

Poppy did indeed buy him thigh rubbers and he had worn them proudly that whole evening, until bed.

"Ya gotta go to sleep, now," Poppy cooed. "Wear em for just anot'er little while."

But he had never really enjoyed trouting. Poppy would have liked spending more time with him trouting in silence on the ponds and sometimes spinning yarns. He enjoyed the yarns, but trouting was boring. And he hated it when Poppy Murphy killed a trout.

"What's the matter, b'y?" Poppy Murphy had asked him the first time. "That don't hurt em none, luh!"

And he'd bashed the struggling trout on the head against a rock to prove his point and then tossed it in the basket. "Trout don't feel not'in a t'all!"

But he'd always suspected that trout did feel pain. And he couldn't bring isself[10] to do it. Eventually, his grandfather stopped coaxing him along.

And he didn't like the rough softball games on the field either. The older boys swore. They grabbed each other by the bum or balls. They talked dirty about girls. And that always made him feel ashamed.[11] The younger boys strove to copy them. But not him. "What's wrong? You idden[12] a girl, is ya?" "You should go play wid the girls' team!"

Or sugar sweet tones. "Leave un alone. He's m'buddy. Alex prefers the books. Right Alex? You idden into the girls yet, is ya? I can't blame ya. No time for that when ya gotta study, right?"[13]

More often than not, he'd try to laugh it off, or ignore it, hoping it'd go away. His mother had taught him, "On répond aux imbéciles par le silence!"

One by one, most of his local friends started imitating the older boys. This past summer had been agony, even though he had a couple of friends visiting from Ottawa and a few other outsiders who still chose to hang out with him. Alex thought about crossing Jeremy, Sandra, and Austin Smith for the hundredth time.

He wished he had no feelings like the trout.

Being treated like he was a piece of shit hurt deep down, and there was physical pain. He stopped and held his stomach for a moment. There was only so much he could take. Funny how they never went after him when they were by themselves. Never when he was with his few remaining friends. Just when he was outnumbered.

The past two weeks in Bond Cove had been pure torture.

How he loved Shepherd's Bluff, where away from the others, he felt safe. He used to love hearing about the pirate legends from Poppy Murphy, but Poppy told him he was getting too old for that now. He still spent hours wandering the mossy footpaths, conscious of the blue bay and its small boats sailing in and out, day after day. He heard sheep close by, and was mindful not to step in dung. Just last summer, he had spent hours here playing space warriors with friends. Now most of them avoided him like the plague and joined the likes of Sandra, Austin, and Jeremy Smith. Drinking and getting into mischief started early in Bond Cove. He crouched down almost flat, feet first, and slid over the edge of the cliff. Rocks and pebbles rolled to the bottom, but he wasn't afraid. He'd climbed down this same drang[14] tons of times.

At the bottom, he sat on the rock.

"My Rock," he thought. Shaped like a chair with armrests. Facing the Atlantic Ocean. While it was summertime, the wind felt chilly. His bum grew numb on the icy seat.

"I hate being called Jackytar. I hate being made fun of because I speak French! Oi'm[15] not a lazy half breed Indian! I'm not a faggot!" he said aloud, starting to weep. "I hate my life!"

He reached down and gingerly picked up a piece of broken beer bottle. He twisted the amber glass back and forth.[16] The sun was bright but he was seated in shadows. Alone. Miserable. He pressed the pointy tip of the shard to his wrist ...

Déclic![17]7

"Excuse me sir, would you like a snack?"

I heard metallic sounds: clicking seatbelts and clanging utensils. "Pardon?" I said, waking up and opening my eyes.

"Would you like a snack? Perhaps some bottled water? A soft drink?"

I removed my hand from my wrist where the tiny scar remained and recalled bits and pieces of the dream I'd just had. Memories to be more precise. My mouth felt dry and gritty.

"Yes, some water, please."

"Then please put your laptop away. I'll be back shortly."

The flight attendant, an athletic man with a narrow waist and broad shoulders, worked his way down the aisle, serving right and left. I pressed a button and my seat righted itself. The interior of the plane was bathed in gentle grey shadows. I put my laptop in its case and stored it underneath my seat. The flight attendant arrived and handed me bottled water, a glass, and a napkin.

"Are you from here?" he asked. "Huh?"

"You just visiting?"

"I'm originally from Newfoundland but I moved to Toronto.

How long until we land?"

"Oh won't be too long now. We left Montreal a few minutes ago and you fell asleep like a baby. Maybe another hour and a bit? We have the winds behind our sails as the Capt'n says. Excited?"

"Yeah, it's been a few years."

"Well, nothing ever changes on the Rock!"

I smiled but the knot in my stomach worsened.

## Postscript

There is now a growing plethora of theories, methodologies, and examples of fiction as research. Two of my graduate students have written progressive novels as the core part of their doctoral dissertations. Dr. Kari Janz (2022) wrote *Blondie: A narrative existential inquiry* (2022), in which she investigates an epistolary Bildungsroman titled *Blondie*, to explore the complexities of mental illness and its treatment. Dr. Janz was influenced by the dirty realism style of Charles Bukowsko. Dennis Barrow (2025) has written the Bildungsroman, *Finding Grace,* as the central part of his doctoral dissertation, to research how 2SLGBTQ+ identities of formal educational leaders influence their leadership roles in Newfoundland and Labrador. Barrow's distinctive writing style, honed from Newfoundland and Labrador's rich literary fiction, dialects, and tropes of the raw coastal landscape, offers a groundbreaking lens to a minority group in the province. While Barrow intends to publish his novella with a traditional publisher, Janz opted to use digital forums, such as her own blog. The means of disseminating research via fiction writing are ever expanding but one core element remains consistent—fiction writing allows the writer-researcher to gain readers/interlocutors both within and beyond the academy in unprecedented numbers and innovative ways.

## Notes

1 Higgs (1996) suggests that, while various research methods have utility, the subjective experiences of an educator may also be construed as legitimate knowledge. Similarly, he uses tacit knowledge as data for the construction of stories that explore questions relevant to education and psychology.
2 The worldwide Metropolitan Community Church counts predominantly queer congregations and is under-acknowledged in queer studies (Altman, 2002).
3 I use the term *interlocutor*, derived from French, rather than reader. I choose this term because it denotes taking part in dialogue or conversation with another (Rey, 1988, p. 551), a more analytical, (inter)active connotation than r*eader*, in my mind, which suits the reflexive nature of what I aspire *interlocutors* to do.
4 Queer researchers examine how heterosexuality is made to seem normal, and who and what is excluded when polarized terms such as man-woman or gay-straight are used. In this case, *queer* is used as a verb to designate this type of analysis which may lead to *ruptures*, where troubling of knowledge or knowing occurs.
5 For instance, the Author's Note at the start of the *Jackytar* is inspired by Jean-Paul Sartre's ruse at the beginning of *Nausea* (1964), in which he similarly claims the editors found notebooks and papers belonging to his fictional character, Antoine Roquetin, a historical researcher. My fictional character, Alexandre Murphy, an educator, similarly makes journal notes, but that he later uses to (re)construct his own story in a hybrid journal-novel.
6 The excerpt from Chapter 3 of *Jackytar* contains footnotes which detail several more interpretations of "queer" to ponder.
7 *Gay* may be used to refer to homosexual males only. For some, *gay* carries a White, middle-class, urban male stigma (Hogan & Hudson, 1998). It may also be used as a problematic umbrella term, like queer, for people who do not identify as straight (St.-Hilaire, 1999). *Queer* generally carries a more political, confrontational connotation and may be associated with queer theory (Halperin, 1995). Ultimately, although they must be used, these terms need to be challenged in light of who and what is left out and *Why?*
8 Hoist-yer-sails-and-run: tag or hide-and-seek (Story, 1959), that in this instance may carry a threatening, sexual overtone.
9 *Tea* may be pronounced *tay*.
10 *Himself* may be pronounced *isself or hisself* (Lowell, 1974, p. 124).
11 Shame is a leitmotif throughout this educational novel and closely linked to invisibility and silencing (Armstrong, 2002). Males and females may dissociate or repress memories of abuse.
12 *Idden* may be used instead of *isn't* or *aren't*, and *tidden* for *it isn't*, parallel to Western England usage (Story, 1977).
13 Heterosexuality is often defined in relation to dissonant sexualities (Ghaill, 2000); hyper-masculine and misogynist qualities imbue homophobia, so that even being studious may be viewed as *gay* or *unmasculine*. This is a troubling reality for educators to confront.
14 Drang: a long, narrow path (Story et al., 1990).
15 The Newfoundland pronunciation of *I'm* as *Oi'm* has British parallels (Story, 1977).
16 Queer youth are at a greater risk for suicide because they often lack familial, peer, school, and community support compared to straight youth (Dorais & Lajeunesse, 2004).
17 *Déclic*, French for *snap* or *click*, signals some ruptures in this educational novel (interlocutors are free to interpret others), as well as flashbacks.

## References

Altman, D. (2002, October 29–30). *30 Years of gay liberation in Australia*. Paper presented at the Queer Studies Conference, Out from the Centre, University of Newcastle, Australia.
Armstrong, M. (2002). The price we pay for shaming little boys. Paper presented at the Canadian Boys, Untold Stories, Colony Hotel.
Barone, T. (1995). The purposes of arts-based educational research. *International Journal of Educational Research*, *23*(2), 169–180. https://doi.org/10.1016/0883-0355(95)91500-G

Barrow, D. (2025). *The experiences of 2SLGBTQ+ formal educational leaders in the Newfoundland and Labrador K-12 education system: A qualitative critical/transformative study* (Unpublished doctoral dissertation). Nipissing University.

Charbonneau, P., & Barrette, L. (1992). *Contre vents et marées, l'histoire des francophones de Terre-Neuve et du Labrador*. Les Éditions d'Acadie.

Cole, A., & Knowles, J. G. (2001). Qualities of inquiry: Process, form, and "goodness." In *The art of writing inquiry* (p. 321). Backalong Books.

Dorais, M., & Lajeunesse, S. (2004). *Dead boys can't dance: Sexual orientation, masculinity, and suicide* (P. Tremblay, Trans.). McGill-Queen's University Press.

Ghaill, M. M. a. (2000). The cultural production of English masculinities in late modernity. *Revue canadienne de l'éducation/Canadian Journal of Education*, *25*(2), 88–101.

Gosse, D. (2005a). *Breaking silences, an inquiry into identity and the creative research process* (Unpublished doctoral dissertation). Ontario Institute for Studies in Education at the University of Toronto.

Gosse, D. (2005b). *Jackytar*. Jesperson Publishing Ltd.

Gosse, D. (2006) *Deconstructing queer theory and literary devices in Jackytar, the Canadian Bildungsroman*. Paper presented at the Arts-based Educational Research (ABER) Special Interest Group of the American Educational Research Association (AERA), San Francisco.

Gosse, D., Labrie, N., Grimard, M., & Roberge, B. (2000, September 23). *Violence in discourse of gay and lesbian Francophones*. Paper presented at the Lavender Conference, Washington, DC.

Halperin, D. (1995). *Saint Foucault: Towards a gay hagiography*. Oxford University Press.

Higgs, G. E. (1996). *Jordan, an allegorical novel exploring meaning and educational counseling psychology* (Unpublished Ph.D. thesis). University of Tennessee, Knoxville.

Hogan, S., & Hudson, L. (1998). *Completely queer: The gay and lesbian encyclopedia*. Fitzhenry & Whiteside Ltd.

Jagose, A. (1996). *Queer theory*. Melbourne University Press. Labrie.

Janz, K. (2022). Blondie: A narrative existential inquiry (Unpublished doctoral dissertation). Nipissing University.

Labrie, N., & Gosse, D. (2003). *Multiple identities and resistance to marginalisation: Bilingual French-speaking gays, lesbians, and bisexuals in Ontario*. Paper presented at the Department of Sociology and Equity Studies in Education Speakers Series, Ontario Institute for Studies in Education of the University of Toronto.

Lowell, R. (1974). *The new priest in Conception Bay*. McClelland and Stewart.

Namaste, K. (1996). The politics of inside out: Queer theory, post-structuralism, and a sociological approach to sexuality. In S. Seidman (Ed.), *Queer theory/sociology* (pp. 194–212). Blackwell Publishers.

O'Beirne, K. (2006). *Women who make the world worse and how their radical feminist assault is ruining our schools, families, military, and sports*. Penguin Group.

Parsons, C., & Brown, P. (2001). Educating for diversity: An invitation to empathy and action. *Action in Teacher Education*, *23*(3), 1–4.

Rey, A. (Ed.) (1988). *Le Micro-Robert, langue française*. Dictionnaires le Robert.

Sartre, J.-P. (1964). *Nausea* (L. Alexander, Trans.). New Directions Publishing Corporation.

St.-Hilaire, C. (1999). Le paradoxe de l'identité et le devenir-queer du sujet: de nouveaux enjeux pour la sociologie des rapports sociaux de sexe. *Recherches Sociologiques – Rapports sociaux de sexe*, *3*, 23–37.

Story, G. M. (1959). *A Newfoundland dialect questionnaire, Avalon peninsula*. Memorial University of Newfoundland.

Story, G. M. (1977). The dialects of Newfoundland English. In H. J. Paddock (Ed.), *Languages in Newfoundland and Labrador* (preliminary edition, pp. 74–80). Memorial University, Department of Linguistics.

Story, G. M., Kirwin, W. J., & Widdowson, J. D. A. (1990). *Dictionary of Newfoundland English* (2nd ed.). University of Toronto Press.

Chapter 14

# Celebrating Monkey Business in Art Education and Research

*Madeleine Grumet*

Admittedly, we have, for some time, worked in an environment hostile to arts education.[1] In response, arts educators and researchers have promoted arts curricula as providing the expressivity, humanity, sensuality, and community desperately missing in schools haunted by assessments, dredged in technology, and starved for funding. For us, the arts agenda is obvious and so necessary that we will justify it as generating the creativity required by entrepreneurship or science and technology if those accommodations will wedge it into the schedule of classes. As arts researchers, often funded by foundations or school districts, we also accommodate, asking questions of arts practices that will reassure funders or accreditors that academic standards and progress are being met.

Some years ago, I examined these compromises in an essay "Where the Line Is Drawn" (Grumet, 1988), where I asked that we acknowledge the oxymoron of art education: a discourse and tradition that challenges the status quo and normative processes of schooling with questions of everyday experience that spring from subjectivities expressed through aesthetic forms. It is this insistence on subjectivity that still thrills me in Herbert Marcuse's work, *The Aesthetic Dimension* (1978), where he takes on the Marxist aesthetic that locates the liberation of consciousness only in works that would depict the lives of the proletariat. Marcuse argued that in advanced capitalism, proletariat consciousness had already been integrated into the ideologies of the capitalist system, and so it could no longer generate a vision of liberation. Instead, it would be the subjectivity of an individual person that would reveal the dimensions of freedom: "The work of art is a universe of colors, sounds, and words and concrete characters. There is no death, there is only Phèdre dying" (Goldmann as cited in Marcuse, 1978, p. 25).

Rest assured, I am not calling for Marcuse's vision to be our standard, for one of the jobs of schooling is to introduce children to the categories that organize our world. But, it is also our job to reveal them as just that, only abstractions that invite their understanding as well as their doubt, their exceptions, their repudiations. Marcuse's paean to subjectivity in *The Aesthetic Dimension* challenges us to clarify what we are proposing and defending in our support for the arts in education.

I recall telling this story to a group of elementary school teachers who were ardent supporters of arts in their classrooms, convinced that they invited expression and delight. I told them that after a visit to a museum with her family, my friend's seven-year-old daughter drew a picture during art class of a girl that, in her mind, resembled the images that she had seen in a trip to the museum over the weekend, only to be sharply scolded by her enraged teacher, "Don't you ever, ever do that again." She had drawn a nude figure with breasts and pubic hair. The teachers in the workshop were clearly uncomfortable with the harshness of that

DOI: 10.4324/9781003412892-14

rebuke, but when I asked them how they would respond to that same situation, they giggled nervously and guessed that they would call the guidance office—a code blue for failing propriety. Personally, I prefer rage to diagnosis.

If we were only dealing with rambunctious thoughts, we could resort to the literature on critical thinking or cognitive dissonance, but art issues from our bodies as well as our minds. The word "aesthetics" comes from the Greek word *aisthetikos*, meaning sentient, perceptible to the senses. And it is because art expresses embodied knowledge informed by sensation and perception that it can enrich the discursive systems that dominate knowledge and education. But, without grappling with the gorgeous complexity that aesthetics offer, I fear that rage and diagnosis or avoidance is all we have.

Perhaps it was always so, but I think that our frustration with contemporary schooling has led to a sentimentalization of art in the experience of children and a failure to acknowledge what Marcuse is saying when he insists that only when art interrupts the daily configuration and musings of our lives does it bring the freeing of consciousness that he calls "art."

> Mimesis is representation through estrangement, subversion of consciousness. Experience is intensified to the breaking point; the world appears as it does for Lear and Antony, Berenice, Michael Kohlhass, Woyzeck, as it does for the lovers of all times. They experience the world demystified. The intensification of perception can go as far as to distort things so that the unspeakable is spoken, the otherwise invisible becomes visible, and the unbearable explodes. Thus, the aesthetic transformation turns into indictment—but also into a celebration of that which resists injustice and terror, and of that which can still be saved.
>
> (p. 57)

The distance that stretches between the classic literatures in this paragraph and the contemporary classroom may be too great to sustain this application, so let me turn to less august company, the performers and audience for a cheesy musical that is the center of Francine Prose's recent novel *Mister Monkey* (2016). The performance of this children's theatre piece provides focus for the lives of the children and adults who live in this novel. I have often wondered why it is so difficult to find literature that addresses teaching and the relation of curriculum to the lived world of the teachers, children, and families it meets. But, Prose carries it off, and even though her interest is not school, *per se*, this art event, ostensibly for kids, gathers them and their families and teachers up in a satire of the languages we use to lie to our children and to ourselves about our experience. Although this is a novel and not research, Prose has crafted a narrative of arts experience that challenges the generalizations of social-science research with the specificity and emotion of the humanities, "there is only Phèdre dying."

The play "Mister Monkey" has been adapted from a book written by a Vietnam veteran who writes to exorcise the horrors of the war that haunt him. Scoured of these improprieties by his publisher, it becomes a well-known children's book and is then turned into a garish musical production that opens with this number:

> *Monkey Tango.*
> *Orangutang-o.*
> *You rang? Oh tango.*
> *King-King Kong-o. Mighty Joe Young-o.*

No Lear or Antony here. But, the characters in this demented dance live through it to touch the truth of their lives. There is the Yale-trained actress in her 40s, costumed in a clown's wig and tight purple skirt, who dreams of playing Chekhov; a twelve-year-old gymnast who plays the monkey in a costume of brown chenille; the author who lives off the royalties of this travesty; a widowed and grieving grandfather who takes his five-year-old grandson to the play; and the boy's family and teacher, among other performers and audience members. Prose uses the play and its performance to move her characters between layers of language and to bring them from their split-off preoccupations into relation with each other. As the author uses this primate as a screen for our projections, I read the novel as arts education and arts research.

In an early chapter, the hush of the theater is broken by a little boy's question: "Grandpa are you interested in this?" His question brings the suspension of disbelief down like a deflated balloon. The audience is shocked, the actors insulted and defensive. This is not a welcome question in the theater or in our classrooms, particularly when posed by a student. But, if the audience members are not interested in the play, *per se*, the rest of the novel reveals how very interested they all are in their own experiences of it. They are interested when the lead actress drops her cell phone and then, instead of picking it up, kicks it right into the wings, for Prose imagines that many of the adults, and maybe some of the kids, would like to do the very same thing to theirs. They are interested in evolution. They are interested in the sexually inappropriate behavior of the boy playing Mister Monkey.

So, here is the first question that we might ask of arts education curricula and arts research: Is it interesting? And if it is, then we probably have to admit to ourselves what it is that interests our students. According to Freud, it is sex and by that he meant life—how we got to be here—and death. And then other, perhaps related, interests that Prose uncovers as she develops the characters and their responses to the play. Her characters—all of them—desire recognition and honest communication and relationships. Their interest in the play is tethered to their interest in the world they live in.

The actor who takes it most seriously is Adam, the twelve-year-old who plays Mister Monkey and who reads books on Darwin and evolution that his mother provides as part of his homeschooling:

> Does his mom have any ideas what's *in* these monkey books that she's so happy he's willing to read? It's always the same story, the scientist getting down with the monkeys, overjoyed to make friends with them and be accepted in their gang. And then things start to go south ... A mother and a daughter monkey turn into psycho serial cannibal killers, kidnapping and murdering monkey children. The chimpanzees in one habitat divide themselves into groups based on bloodlines or kinship ..., and start bloody wars that involve killing and eating each other's babies. When Adam read that, he'd wanted to give up. What was the point? The really bad shit that people do is still there, ... deep in our brains, from way back when we used to be monkeys.
>
> (Prose, 2016, p. 39)

Like so much of the world that we offer children scoured free of the details and meanings that fill us with guilt, dread, or disgust, the director instructs his cast to ignore evolution and vicious primate tales. Adam recalls Miss Julia's take on Mister Monkey when she taught the book to his fourth-grade class: "*What is a stereotype class? Mister Monkey shows us that stereotypes aren't true*. The brave Latina housekeeper. The crusading woman lawyer.

Animal rights" (p. 46). Adam, intuiting the imposition of ideology, no matter how righteous, realizes how much of what was interesting in the story was obliterated in the teacher's politically correct questions. In their thoughtful text, *Curriculum in Abundance* (2006), this deadly editing is deplored by David Jardine, Sharon Frieson, and Pat Clifford. They engage curriculum moments to explore the ways that what goes on in school might open up to the world, touching its beauty and complexity. They cite David Smith's concern:

> It is as if young people ask for, above all else, not only a genuine responsiveness from their elders but also a certain direct authenticity, a sense of that deep human resonance so easily suppressed under the smooth human-relations jargon teachers typically learn in college. Young people want to know if, under the cool and calm of efficient teaching and excellent time on task ratios, life itself has a chance, or whether the surface is all there is.
> (as cited in Jardine et al., 2006, p. 235)

We might have found something beneath the surface in the original manuscript of *Mister Monkey* that the author brought forth, wishing to make reparation for the brutality he witnessed, but in the playscript, the Mister Monkey we meet is emphatically cute, dependent, and impotent. But Adam, the boy who plays the part, not so much. Stimulated by his readings, his hormones, his fears that global warming is about to destroy the world and drown his apartment house, his father's remarriage to a younger wife—who knows?—he humps Margot, who plays his lawyer, to her distress and to the titillation of the audience, some of whom correctly perceive his assault, others who are just excited to see him attack the mother figure who is working to help him throughout the play.

As Prose plays out the reactions of cast members to Adam's tasteless aggression, we recognize the abstentions that we know all too well in classrooms. Some label Adam as an incorrigible adolescent, as if the developmental label is sufficient. Others pretend that there is nothing that can be done and just hope to make it to the end of the run before something worse happens. Only toward the end of the novel does one of the performers take him aside to ask him to be kind.

The grandfather and his grandson, Edward, return from the play to the boy's home, where his parents are entertaining neighborhood friends. There is no room for Edward and his grandfather in the conversation, which revolves around the parents' complaints about their children's preschool. The grandfather's attempts to join the conversation are deflected. Sidelined and isolated in a group that celebrates multigenerational families, he knows that "they just don't like being reminded that being a grandparent means being *old*. His grandson doesn't mind. The child knows who is old and who is young. The child is aware of everything happening in the room" (Prose, 2016, p. 93).

The grandfather is grieving and dreading his own death. Stranded without his wife in a world of cell phones and political correctness, he is passionately interested in the unedited and vulnerable thoughts and feelings of his grandson. The little boy is interested in dinosaurs and in his conviction that we evolved from them. His new teacher is interested in coping with her insomnia and keeping her job. Edward is also aware of everything going on in the new school his parents send him to, when, prompted by the teacher who is trying to let him shine, he steps up in show-and-tell to talk about the play he went to with his grandfather. When he mentions that we descended from dinosaurs, he is challenged by the class know-it-all who says that he is lying; we descended from monkeys. Sonya, the teacher, isn't sure. She pauses in anguish and then comes down on the side of the monkeys, tumbling herself into guilt and worry. Prose realistically portrays the pressures on this young Teach for America teacher. She worries that she did not know enough about Darwin to turn the conflict into learning; she worries that the parents will complain that evolution is not in the kindergarten curriculum, which they do; she worries that her principal will call her in and regale her with "depressing examples of hardworking teachers and administrators axed for having imparted actual knowledge or expressed a reasonable opinion" (Prose, 2016, p. 125), which she does.

In this novel, gathered around this piece of children's theatre, Francine Prose exposes both the dilemmas and aspirations of drama in the lives of children and in their classrooms. We celebrate the capacity of the arts to engage us, and Prose uses *Mister Monkey* to show us that the meaning of what we compose or receive is layered and associative and informed by our lives. Her novel reminds us that art is simultaneously sensuous and intellectual. It is this compelling combination that challenges art education and our research. Does the art education curriculum contain the artwork within the studio, the special project, or does it open out onto the world that children are interested in, bringing in information that may seem to be owned by other disciplines? Who owns evolution? Anthropology? Science? History? Religion? And those conversations can acknowledge the discursive cultures of all the places we and the children we teach live in: homes, schools, TV and film, museums, churches, and dreams.

Toward the end of her novel, Francine Prose brings many of her characters in touch with each other through their shared experience of the world that the play has created. Her resolution of the novel comes after the conversation in the coffee shop between Eleanor, the actress who plays Janice, a character who wears false fingernails, and the assaulting monkey Adam:

> Eleanor and Adam have been doing something together, creating a world, the illusion of a world, the world that is .... It transcends Roger's tyranny and vagueness, transcends Adam's feeling for Margot; transcends the group nervous breakdown occurring backstage. It is the consolation and the reward for what Adam is suffering at home. Janice's fingernails and Adam's monkey suit are all they need to make them, and the people who watch them feel less alone.
>
> (Prose, 2016, p. 249)

Eleanor is able to talk to Adam about his behavior because they share this world, a world they have made together. Under the dome of this intimacy, difficult conversation is possible and persuasive. Intellect and sensuality are not always joined as we relate to each other in our theaters or our classrooms, but when we weld this fragile triangle together, we have created good art and good education.

As qualitative research methods became established, I often mused about the processes and stances they shared with the arts and humanities. I objected when their creativity and specificity was arrogated to the instrumentalism and generalization of social science. On the other hand, I objected when the reference of the artistic narrative or evaluation could not be pulled beyond its pages to inform educational policy or practice. Now, in the second month of the Trump administration, the latter no longer bothers me. As we confront proposals to eliminate the National Endowment for the Arts, after-school programs, to undermine public education with proliferating charter schools and to ostracize immigrant populations, work that honors the range, depth, and novelty of our human experience offers a refuge from a cruel time.

## Postscript

In the years between the beginning of Trump's presidency (2016), when this chapter was written, and this moment of his return (2025), we have seen arts and humanities education even more constricted than we had previously imagined. Fear and antagonism accompanying the polarization of our politics have provoked calls for censorship of public school curricula and libraries, and have inhibited and discouraged teachers, already exhausted by the pandemic. It is my hope that this third edition will encourage stalwart researchers and educators to redouble our efforts and capacity to welcome the world back into our classrooms, celebrating the interests and concerns of students as well as the sparkling surprises of their unfettered imaginations. Theatrical performance extends the school curriculum into the community, engaging children and parents, and realizing the rich promise of the public school to include all of our families in experiences and discussions that inform our democracy.

## Note

1 Editor's note: As an example, a national study on the effects of the No Child Left Behind legislation on art educators in K-12 schools found that 89% of art teachers surveyed reported lower morale and 67% reported that school administrations were disrupting regular art classroom instruction to accommodate testing demands (Sabol, 2010).

## References

Grumet, M. R. (1988). *Bitter milk: Women and teaching*. University of Massachusetts Press.
Jardine, D. W., Friesen, S., & Clifford, P. A. (Eds.) (2006). *Curriculum in abundance*. Lawrence Erlbaum.
Marcuse, H. (1978). *The aesthetic dimension: Toward a critique of Marxist aesthetics*. Beacon Press.
Prose, F. (2016). *Mister monkey*. Harper Collins.
Sabol, F. R. (2010). *No child left behind: A study of its impact on art education*. National Art Education Association and National Art Education Foundation.

Chapter 15

# Expanding Paradigms

## Art as Performance and Performance as Communication in Politically Turbulent Times

*Petula Sik-Ying Ho, Celia Hoi-Yan Chan, and Sui-Ting Kong*

This chapter documents the creation of a critical arts-based research (ABR) methodology, employing a collaborative focus group analysis plus theatre. We describe the experiences of female activists in Hong Kong's 2014 Umbrella Movement, a protest movement for greater democratic participation, and how this evolved into devised theatre and research connected to feminist movements in Hong Kong and Mainland China. This chapter raises questions about how scholars not primarily trained or engaged in artistic pursuits can adopt artistic forms to further their empirical and political goals: specifically, in this case, providing a platform for female activists to communicate issues of concern. Do those who engage in arts-based educational research (ABER) without any training in "art" risk creating "shoddy" art? What can be gained by accepting and defying this risk? This chapter addresses these questions.

### ABER as a Means of Political Activism and Change

To a significant extent, pursuing change through social activism requires shifting audiences' perceptions and beliefs. This is an act of education in its broadest social context: the production of democratic forms of knowledge. Filmmaking has long been argued as one of the most provocative and effective ways for initiating social dialogue (Benjamin, 2003). To take up this challenge, Petula Ho, a social work educator-researcher-practitioner and her qualitative researcher colleagues, sought to acquire a new skill set with the aid of young filmmakers. Since 2008, this collaboration has produced 58 documentary films, covering topics ranging from the self-reported experiences and views of middle-aged housewives to married men and families in Hong Kong—groups largely unexamined by the public. Shown to students as well as public audiences, these films have raised local and international understanding of the complexity of Hong Kong society. They are examples of visual/auditory ethnographic practice, combining the camera as a research tool with the practice of an intimate dialogue of action-reflection-participatory engagement (Berry, 2013; Enria, 2016). The first author, Petula, calls the recording of data for knowledge exchange and the creation of a permanent record of personal experiences at a particular moment in time *dialogic filming* (Ho, 2013a, 2013b).

### The Umbrella Movement and Gender Bullying

Hong Kong united in protest in 2014 when a Chinese government proposal threatened to unravel universal suffrage. In March 2013, the group Occupy Central with Love and Peace (OCLP) organized seminars, conducted a referendum, and planned to block roads in the

DOI: 10.4324/9781003412892-15

central business district if the government did not provide an electoral system that satisfied the international standard of universal suffrage. In August 2014, China ignored these calls for democratic participation and instead insisted that only candidates approved by the government-controlled Nomination Committee could be put forward on the ballot for the position of Hong Kong's Chief Executive (Kaeding, 2015). Deeply disappointed by this decision, civic organizations resorted to civil disobedience, and the Umbrella Movement was born.

Student protesters were first to take to streets in late September 2014. Once riot police fired rounds of tear gas on September 28th, many more citizens joined them, turning Occupy Central into a decentralized movement. Protesters set up tents, stocked up on supplies, and protected their territories with makeshift barricades in several neighborhoods. Impressively, the protests lasted for 79 days until police cleared the last occupied site on December 15 (Chan, 2015).

In Hong Kong, individuals who support independence and separation from the People's Republic of China are called "radical localists." The "Left Plastics" (LPs) took a rational, peaceful democratic approach, and the "Right Plastics" (RPs) wanted to escalate conflict and chaos to bring about a revolution. An RP group, the Passion Times, composed mostly of male activists, coined the term LP as a derogatory reference to the belief that LPs were useless obstacles to real revolution. These accusations unleashed greater sexist discourse, gender and sexual harassment, cyberspace bullying, and vilification from progressive forces seeking greater political autonomy and from conservative forces seeking to maintain the status quo.

## From Film to Multimedia Theatre: A Response to Turbulent Political Times

Our presence in this Movement afforded us the chance to interact with other activists deeply involved in the organizing processes, including those critical of our views. Our feminist stance allowed us to identify, respond to, and critique the gendered nature of harassment against female activists, committed by their male counterparts. The splits in views among activists escalated over time, with harassment against women becoming increasingly hostile. A number of those harassed formed an online group known as The Young Girls' Heart and reached out to Petula in recognition of similar online ridicule received from male localists.

As the early 20th-century critical theorist Benjamin (2003) noted, film provides the opportunity to communicate the reality of social conditions to a wide spectrum of people. Nevertheless, with film, direct feedback/interaction between performers and audience is limited. The multiple social splits that came out of the Umbrella Movement appeared to call for a more authentic form of direct dialogue. Participants in The Young Girls' Heart felt a need to connect with audiences, resulting in our critical action research evolving into critical arts-based, multimedia theatre. We organized the *Labouring Women Devised Theatre Group* to understand how sexist attacks affected the experience of female activists, their self-image and relationships, and their social movement participation.

## Labouring Women Devised Theatre Group (2016) 辛苦女協作劇場

Theatrical performance provided a new type of democratic space that we hoped would collaboratively generate a greater in-depth understanding of personal political trauma and combine different talents and skills more directly connected to drama than documentary filmmaking to create our own research-based theatre method. Such a nontraditional space for teaching, learning, and documenting the process through the arts, existing outside formal political institutions, might also serve to influence democratic movements (Cornwall & Goetz, 2005, p. 789).

Data generation began in August 2015 at the University of Hong Kong with an initial focus group involving six members of the Young Girls' Heart: four university students, one NGO worker and long-term activist, and one research assistant. Petula was admitted to the Young Girls' Heart group as the seventh member because of her shared experiences of being harassed for her political stance.

In this first session, we worked collaboratively with all participants to identify the barriers to women's political participation. Specifically, we focused on the intra-movement stigmatization, especially regarding the conflicts between the LPs and RPs. We investigated their experiences in the Umbrella Movement and its ensuing consequences for their body image, self-presentation, performance in the media sphere, and intimate relationships. In addition, group members identified injustices previously overlooked in their personal relationships and social movement participation.

The group reflected on its members' own experiences in light of recurring incidents where female activists were fiercely criticized not only by opponents but also by democrats and feminists who felt they had not been outspoken enough. Some (outside our group) felt we should fight back by being even more vocal rather than feeling depressed and shameful. Others felt we should just ignore the attacks to show we would not be affected by them. Any sign of unhappiness would appear to indicate that one is weak, only providing our opponents with satisfaction! It was in these discussions the idea of a theatrical performance emerged as a means for educating the community, and the Labouring Women Devised Theatre Group was born.

Inspired by Boal's (1979) *Theater of the Oppressed*, we believed theatrical performance could encourage our own and others' (e.g., the general public, comrades, friends, family, and so forth) reflections on the difficulties facing women brave enough to participate in public and political spheres of life.

## The Focus Group Plus Reflecting Team

To create a more dialogical space for interpreting and reflecting, we created a reflecting team (Andersen, 1987, 1995) to provide rapid interpretation of the experiences discussed in the focus group. This allowed these female activists to immediately reflect on and agree or disagree with interpretations in focus group-reflecting team joint sessions and helped provide a credibility check on the initial focus group. Through expanded dialogue, a reflecting team helps foster the democratization of the process of knowledge creation (Owton & Allen-Collinson, 2014). Ours was composed of six additional participants, including the remaining two authors and one representative each from two feminist Non-Governmental Organizations (NGO): Association for the Advancement of Feminism and HER Fund.

By combining focus group interview with the reflecting team's simultaneous analysis of the interview, we generated a Collaborative Focus Group Analysis (Ho, 2016). Through this process, the female activists were first invited to share their stories while the reflecting team observed them (Clark et al., 2009). After hearing the participants' stories, the reflecting team swapped roles and shared their analysis while observed by the participants. Participants were then invited to discuss the analysis of the reflecting team. This data collection and analysis method aims at leveling the power differences between the researcher and the researched by engaging the female activists as coresearchers (Bergold & Thomas,

2012; Caretta & Riaño, 2016; Kong, 2015). The process increases the transparency of the research process, provides a mechanism for incorporating alternative perspectives from the research participants (Heron, 1996), and creates a more enriched and holistic body of data for analysis.

To provide a richer context for presentation of our findings, Petula proposed a theatrical performance to share the experiences of gender-based harassment. This was received enthusiastically, resulting in the *Labouring Women Devised Theatre Group*. The reference to *labour* was an attempt to encapsulate different kinds of work in which women engage but is often dismissed as insignificant (Grumet, 1988): physical and emotional, on and off the stage, inside and outside the social movement. Through devised theatre, participants who lacked dramatic training cobbled together a performance as *bricoleurs*.

### Devised Theatre to Professional Edu-Tainment

This work led to a performance for an audience of more than 100 at Studio 303, HKU on April 22, 2016. The research process itself was built into the performance, as the members of the reflecting team took the stage following the performance to provide their perspective on the presentation. We came to understand that they had collectively achieved, through the performance, a specific form of critical action research drawing on traditions in participatory research and performance ethnography (Kong, 2015; Sewell & Harris, 2015) as well as critical arts-based inquiry (Finley, 2008).

Members of Young Girls' Heart suggested names of additional female activists and politicians who might be willing to be recruited to our theatre group, leading to 13 female activists agreeing to participate in the production of a multimedia performance. We invited two young artists, graduates of the Academy of Performing Arts in Hong Kong (one female and one male), who became the assistant director and director, to facilitate the production of this research-based theatre. Two young musicians were also recruited to help create the mood needed for storytelling. These performing artists had university training in their arts discipline, but were not full-time performers. They embraced participation as a venue for their own artistic professional development and cross-disciplinary collaboration (Mok & Ho, 2013).

Rehearsals were script-writing workshops. The directors provided dramatic exercises to elicit expanded narratives about participants' experiences, helping performers to share ideas and encouraging empathy, reciprocity, and openness among people who previously had been strangers. This helped performers to reveal themselves and accept their own hurtful experiences resulting from political participation (Enria, 2016, p. 327). These female activists had been lampooned. Editorial revisions, annotations, and modifications made to photos and texts had been filled with pornographic innuendoes. Furthermore, members of The Young Girls' Heart had a hard time coping with misunderstandings from their families, partners, and other social movement activists who had different judgments about their roles and their strategies for responding to these online and offline attacks and criticisms.

Two days after the performance, a half-day evaluation workshop was held involving everyone who participated. Everyone was invited to give feedback in creative ways using mini performances, songs, prose readings, and drama. Thus, together the focus group, the reflecting team, and artistic participants (directors, musicians, and performers) were in dialogue. Each had the opportunity to both act and create. Participants were not simply limited to discursive analysis. Out of this expanded format for evaluation, members of the reflecting team responded emotionally as they recalled how personal experiences affected their analysis of other people's stories. This extended to the performers as well. For example, some became upset because they had not anticipated that their political activism would leave them open to online harassment or affect their personal relationships. Social support within the group helped ease some of the emotional pain, consequences of political oppression. The evaluation session generated further dialogue between researchers, participants, and artists, which was video recorded. All data were analyzed to develop a theatrically reflexive research methodology, focusing on encouraging political participation and managing injury resulting from political violence.

While the theatre production was one attempt to reach new audiences, the whole production process itself was video recorded to create another medium for sharing our research with stakeholders in the Umbrella Movement, the Young Girls' Heart, The Labouring Women Devised Theatre Group, and the general public. Two new documentary films were produced and screened on several occasions. During the fall of 2016, we extended our discussion of women's experiences and the consolidation of female power in public and political participation in the Gender Plus Politics seminar series at the University of Hong Kong.

## Learning to Make "Good" Art and Redefining Impact

Permitting the complexity of people's life stories, especially the ignored and subjugated aspects of their experiences, to be presented enabled theatre members and the public to see what could not previously be seen. Just as social science interviewing is a task of allowing participants to find words for what has previously not been said (Glesne & Peshkin, 1992), critical arts-based performance allows participants to actualize what has been previously felt but repressed (Saldaña, 2005). While we had realized the empirical and political goals of our project, we also asked how we might ensure our work was a well-enough crafted piece of theatre. Our goal, shared by both social science and the fine arts, was to reflect real human experience and concerns, to touch people's hearts in order to generate dialogue around social change. In the end, we were left to answer this question: was the work any good?

As for addressing this question, we have had to devise alternative ways of understanding the arts and aesthetics. The theatre piece had emotional power for the performers as they all testified to its positive therapeutic impact. The audience may also have found it moving, as indicated by reactions such as applause (however, applause could also simply be a social courtesy). Researching the post-performance emotional resonance with an audience could be a test done in the future for assessing the impact of ABR.

Did our work together result in a good enough piece of art? Who should make that judgment? If, as a performance, its "raw" character and relevant content lent it authenticity and made it a powerful agent of dialogue between stakeholders and new audiences, why ask that it also meet an arbitrary standard of artistic professionalism? Professional beauty is not relevant to the context and purpose. The goal was to make it possible for neglected voices to be heard and to give life and breath to undervalued people and their experiences. In our inclusion of professionally trained theatre personnel and musicians, we, as novices, engaged with drama and film. In our case, attention to the basics of scholartistry was sufficient to achieve our goals of fashioning new forms of communication through which our social concerns were seen and heard. We did not feel a need to achieve an externally imposed standard of taste and beauty.

## Learning to Redefine Impact and "Measure" It

What "evidence" could we share to show what we, outsiders to the arts, have accomplished? What are both new and conventional ways of assessing "value," "validity," and "impact"? Conventional ideas of impact factors and citations may not be the best ways to elucidate pioneering methods or to measure the social impact of the rich body of empirical work that remains outside mainstream academia. Thus, we have to create new ways of assessing ABR's social impact. A greater diversity of knowledge, public platforms for sharing arts-based representations of findings (e.g., public performances, Facebook screenings, open-dialogue forums), reaching diverse audiences (e.g., feminist groups who came to watch the show)—this arts-based project resulted in outcomes in the real, as opposed to the strictly academic, world. Generally speaking, far more people see documentary films than read academic articles. Although we have not done so because of privacy and consent issues, films and seminars can be advertised on social media, an important forum for discussion and opportunity for ongoing data collection and analysis. We continue to document audience responses on Facebook. Our various sources of data from real and virtual spaces have helped us triangulate sources and influenced our understanding of processes and impact (Pain et al., 2016). Here, impact is not a separate stage or endeavor, but built into research processes. The participants involved are well-placed to define impact, which happens throughout coproduction and is partly produced through people existing together in shared spaces (embodied connection) rather than the fact of collaboration.

## Conclusion

This chapter highlights a methodological innovation in ABR that developed in the context of Hong Kong's struggle for democracy. This approach shed light on the possibilities of creating new platforms for facilitating understanding of research participants' experiences and opinions because of the empathetic atmosphere and spirit involved. It was also a more democratic way of engaging the researcher and the researched in different types of exchanges useful for critical reflection, dialogue, and our understanding of emotion and narrative in the participatory research process and democracy movements (Constable, 2013; Presser, 2005; Rattine-Flaherty & Singhal, 2009). Finally, it helped us rethink the nature of art, aesthetics, and the impact of ABER.

A willingness to experiment with conventions of social science research led to the development of a useful, innovative arts-based method called "collaborative focus group analysis plus theatre." The personal struggle for democracy with all its concomitant frustrations in pursuing the goal of constitutional reform inclined many of us to think deeply about how we should undertake "deep ploughing and careful cultivation" (a fashionable phrase used by Umbrella Movement activists to refer to what people can/should do to educate their own communities about the importance of democracy and resistance) through channels outside formal institutions. The experience of our struggle for democracy in Hong Kong made it important for us to think about how knowledge should be produced in a democratic way. It became intrinsic to our fight for democracy.

Within the context of this democratic knowledge production project, our social movement participants were reconstructed as knowledge producers rather than passive research participants (Enria, 2016). The issue of impact was important to us all and encouraged thinking about how collaboration impacted individuals.

But, was it art? And, if it claims to be art, was it "good"? Our methods were creative and very possibly original in the context in which they were used. We can make no claim for the beauty of our theatrical and filmic end products, but we do put our hands up for emotional power. Under the guidance of those more skilled, we saw the experiences of those who in our society lack a voice and a platform translated into a form that is lasting, accessible, and able to influence. It was useful and meaningful for those who participated in creating the performances and films and, we hope, to those who viewed them in whatever form; but no, not high art. However, we can lay claim to an approach that could be called pragmatic art that engages, informs, entertains, and challenges (and maybe changes) society's entrenched perceptions and beliefs about fellow citizens whose lives, needs, and views are frequently ignored. It is an honest and honorable interpretation of ABER.

## Postscript: Collaborative Focus Group Analysis Plus Theatre: Recent Developments

Our exploration of collaborative focus group analysis as a research methodology has provided valuable insights into the experiences of diverse groups in Hong Kong, particularly during the anti-extradition movement of 2019. However, we have not utilized theatre in our recent work.

One notable project, titled "Dialogues and Dialogues about Dialogues: Collaborative Focus Group Analysis on the Intergenerational Conflict, Dyadic Coping, and Reconciliation among Families in the Social Movement 2019 in Hong Kong," was supported by the Public Policy Research Funding Scheme (Special Round) 2020–2021. This project focused on the perspectives of parents and their adult children regarding the impact of the protests on family dynamics.

Through collaborative focus group analysis, we facilitated open dialogues that allowed participants to share their experiences and the conflicts stemming from differing political views within families. This was possible because the research materials were not made public, and discussions occurred in online and face-to-face meetings rather than through theatre. These dialogues revealed how tensions affected relationships and emotional wellbeing, highlighting the complexities of navigating familial bonds in a politically charged environment.

As we approach 2025, the landscape for such explorations has shifted dramatically due to the national security law. The climate in Hong Kong poses significant challenges for participatory methodologies, especially those involving public expression. The fear of repercussions has made it increasingly difficult for individuals to engage in performances that critique or reflect on their roles in social movements.

Given these challenges, we are considering applying our methodology to the Hong Kong diaspora in the United Kingdom or Taiwan, particularly for those who do not expect to return. While there may be a desire for artistic political expression, encouraging research participants to perform in theatre remains a significant difficulty. This highlights the ongoing challenges of fostering engagement and expression amid a climate of fear and uncertainty.

## References


Andersen, T. (1987). The reflecting team: Dialogue and meta-dialogue in clinical work issue. *Family Process*, *26*(4), 415–428. https://doi.org/10.1111/j.1545-5300.1987.00415.x

Andersen, T. (1995). Reflecting processes: Acts of informing and forming. In S. Friedman (Ed.), *The reflecting team in action: Collaborative practice in family therapy* (pp. 11–37). Guilford Press.

Benjamin, W. (2003). The work of art in the age of its technological reproducibility. In H. Eiland & M. W. Jennings (Eds.), *Walter Benjamin: Selected writings, volume 4, 1938–1940* (pp. 251–283). Harvard University Press. (Original work published 1938).

Bergold, J., & Thomas, S. (2012). Participatory research methods: A methodological approach in motion. *Qualitative Social Research*, *13*(1), Art. 30. https://www.jstor.org/stable/41756482

Berry, C. (2013). Agent provocateur: The camera as a social work research tool. *Sexualities*, *16*(1–2), 102–112. https://doi.org/10.1177/1363460712471017

Boal, A. (1979). *Theater of the oppressed* (C. A. & M. Leal McBride, Trans.). Theater Communications Group. (Original work published in 1974).

Caretta, M. A., & Riaño, Y. (2016). Feminist participatory methodologies in geography: Creating spaces of inclusion. *Qualitative Research*, *16*(3), 258–266. https://doi.org/10.1177/1468794116629575

Chan, K. M. (2015). Occupying Hong Kong: How deliberation, referendum and civil disobedience played out in the Umbrella Movement. *Sur International Journal on Human Rights*, *12*(21), 1–7. https://sur.conectas.org/en/occupying-hong-kong/

Clark, A., Holland, C., Katz, J., & Peace, S. (2009). Learning to see: Lessons from a participatory observation research project in public spaces. *International Journal of Social Research Methodology*, *12*(4), 345–360. https://doi.org/10.1080/13645570802268587

Constable, N. (2013). Conference as feminist ethnography and the blurring of boundaries. *Sexualities*, *16*(1–2), 113–120. https://doi.org/10.1177/1363460712471019

Cornwall, A., & Goetz, A. M. (2005). Democratizing democracy: Feminist perspectives. *Democratization*, *12*(5), 783–800. https://doi.org/10.1080/13510340500322181

Enria, L. (2016). Co-producing knowledge through participatory theatre: Reflections on ethnography, empathy and power. *Qualitative Research*, *16*(3), 319–329. https://doi.org/10.1177/1468794115615387

Finley, S. (2008). Arts-based inquiry: Performing revolutionary pedagogy. In N. K. Denzin & Y. S. Lincoln (Eds.), *Collecting and interpreting qualitative materials* (pp. 95–113). Sage.

Glesne, C., & Peshkin, A. (1992). *Becoming qualitative researchers: An introduction*. Longman.

Grumet, M. R. (1988). *Bitter milk: Women and teaching*. University of Massachusetts Press.

Heron, J. (1996). *Cooperative inquiry: Research into the human condition*. Sage.

Ho, P. S. Y. (2013a). Introduction to the special section – Remapping the erotic: Interrogations from Asia. *Sexualities*, *16*(1–2), 3–11. https://doi.org/10.1177/1363460712465556

Ho, P. S. Y. (2013b). Researching with a broken arm: Finding sisterhood in injury. *Sexualities*, *16*(1–2), 78–93. https://doi.org/10.1177/1363460712471014

Ho, P. S. Y. (2016, June 27–30). Hong Kong politics and gender: A collaborative focus group analysis. Paper presented at Joint World Conference on Social Work, Education and Social Development, Seoul, South Korea.

Kaeding, M. P. (2015). Resisting Chinese influence: Social movements in Hong Kong and Taiwan. *Current History*, *114*(773), 210–215. https://www.proquest.com/openview/04c0a2658dde29cd562ca1bca9a6735f/1.pdf?cbl=41559&pq-origsite=gscholar

Kong, S. T. (2015). Social work practice research innovation, implementation and implications: A case of 'Cooperative Grounded Inquiry' with formerly abused women in Hong Kong. *Qualitative Social Work*, *15*(4), 533–551. https://doi.org/10.1177/1473325015595856

Mok, J., & Ho, P. S. Y. (2013). Advice to a 24-year-old: Wisdom from a middle-aged woman. *Sexualities*, *16*(1–2), 94–101. https://doi.org/10.1177/1363460712471015

Owton, H., & Allen-Collinson, J. (2014). Close but not too close: Friendship as method(ology) in ethnographic research encounters. *Journal of Contemporary Ethnography*, *43*(3), 283–305. https://doi.org/10.1177/0891241613495410

Pain, R., Askins, K., Bank, S., Cook, T., Crawford, G., Crookes, L., & Vanderhoven, S. (2016). *Mapping alternative impact: alternative approaches to impact from co-produced research*. Centre for Social Justice and Community Action, Durham University.

Presser, L. (2005). Negotiating power and narrative in research: Implications for feminist methodology. *Journal of Women in Culture and Society*, *30*(4), 2067–2090. https://doi.org/10.1086/428424

Rattine-Flaherty, E., & Singhal, A. (2009). Analysing social-change practice in the Peruvian Amazon through a feminist reading of participatory communication research. *Development in Practice*, *19*(6), 726–736. https://doi.org/10.1080/09614520903026884

Saldaña, J. (2005). *Ethnodrama: An anthology of reality theatre*. AltaMira Press.

Sewell, S., & Harris, N. (2015). Exploring women's care for the local environment: A community-based feminist participatory research approach. *Community Development Journal*, *51*(2), 195–211. https://doi.org/10.1093/cdj/bsv012

Chapter 16

# Turning Toward

## Materializing New Possibilities through Curating

*Brooke Hofsess*

> There is a fundamental similarity to the act of curating, which at its most basic is simply about connecting cultures, bringing their elements into proximity with each other – the task of curating is to make junctions, to allow different elements to touch. You might describe it as the attempted pollination of culture, or a form of map-making that opens new routes through a city, a people or a world.
>
> (Obrist, 2014, p. I)

### A Curator's Essay[1]

Arts-based educational research (ABER) does not require that we launch questions from a singular vantage point, but rather anticipates how our queries reverberate within a complex network of identities. As philosopher of aesthetic education, Greene (2001) articulated,

> It is a matter of posing questions on both sides and of loving the questions that merge with one another, questions about living in the world and creating communities and collectivities, caring for each other, making each other feel worthwhile.
>
> (p. 159)

One of the complicated questions I love is this—*what does teaching do to teachers?* (Britzman, 1991). This is a question I have lived in and examined from multiple sides, as my career has shifted between locations in K-12 art teaching, community art education, visual art practice, teacher education, and qualitative research. This is a question embedded in my past and, at the same time, reaches for the future as I seek new possibilities for preparing and sustaining art teachers in an era that emphasizes standardized outcomes for learning, and therefore for teacher preparation and professional learning. A deep engagement with philosophy pushes my thinking and inspires me to experiment with theories that provoke a reimagining of our assumptions and ways of seeing. Playing with the form of a curator's essay, in what follows I turn toward contemporary issues in curatorial practice and to new materialist philosophy. Offering examples from my teaching engagements in a university teacher preparation program, where I work with preservice art teachers, I consider how curating materializes new possibilities for ABER researchers working in visual arts modalities.

DOI: 10.4324/9781003412892-16

## Turning Toward Curatorial Impulses

> (C)uriosity and collecting are basic animating impulses for everyone.
>
> (Obrist, 2014, p. I)

As it turns out, I was engaging with curating research well before I could articulate my impulses. They arose as I grappled with how exactly to express the materiality inherent in visual art practice within the constriction of text-based forms of scholarship, namely, the dissertation I was trying to write. Looking back, I can see that my first curatorial impulses occurred during the process of transcription—a seemingly ordinary practice in the life of a qualitative researcher. Even now, I can recall the frustrating impossibility of transcribing handcrafted letters—composed of words certainly, but also of paint, collaged pieces, tiny sketches, and more. Even the textual information ranged from individual characters stamped in ink to the soft velvet bleed of a marker. This study (see Hofsess, 2016) advocated for more complex understandings regarding how educators become renewed as artists and as teachers through a yearlong exchange of monthly correspondence art. This exchange occurred in the form of letterpress-printed postcards sent by me and handcrafted letters mailed in response from a group of K-12 art educators (see Figure 16.1).

In the act of holding the letters in my hand while I typed, I found myself reveling in what vital materialist Bennett (2010) called "Thing-Power: the curious ability of inanimate things to animate, to act, to produce effects dramatic and subtle" (p. 6). I vividly remember how this reductive act of stripping the materiality of the letters away by working solely with characters punched on a keyboard alone troubled and exasperated me. The root of my discontent was a salient loss—as the light from the window, the address labels, the stamped ink, the old wood desk, the torn-open envelopes, the different shapes of handwriting, the drawings, and the time of day all quietly escaped as I worked through words alone (Hofsess, 2016). You see, I wanted not only to revel in this materiality but also to share it with my readers.

Once struck by the vibrancy of matter (Bennett, 2010), the question of how to express it in the text-based form of scholarship followed. This is where I got stuck. Not knowing what to do, I began to experiment. I photographed the letters in my hands, allowing the space in which I was working to frame the periphery. In hindsight, I see now how I longed to treat my reader as a visitor dwelling in my studio or lingering at an exhibition of my work. I began to thread these images into my transcriptions, along with embodied memories, snippets of conversations with these art teachers, and quotes from theorists. My transcriptions evolved into chapters; chapters dissolved into individual letters to a "Dear Reader" as I clung to the words of Bourriaud (2002), curator and philosopher of relational aesthetics: "Each artwork is a proposal to live in a shared world, and the work of every artist is a bundle of relations with the world, giving rise to other relations, and so on and so forth, ad infinitum" (p. 22). A lush, invitational space was becoming crafted on the typed page. Curating had offered me a potential way to begin moving again, although I couldn't have named it so at the time.

Considering these impulses as curatorial came much later. In fact, it was through conversations with colleagues and mentors that I first began to refer to my analytical process as curating. As they listened over tea and tilted their heads, I was encouraged to further enflesh my tentative understandings. How could I describe the complex work of analyzing research (St. Pierre, 2011)? For me, the word that always came up first was curating. So, I had some reading and mulling over to do.

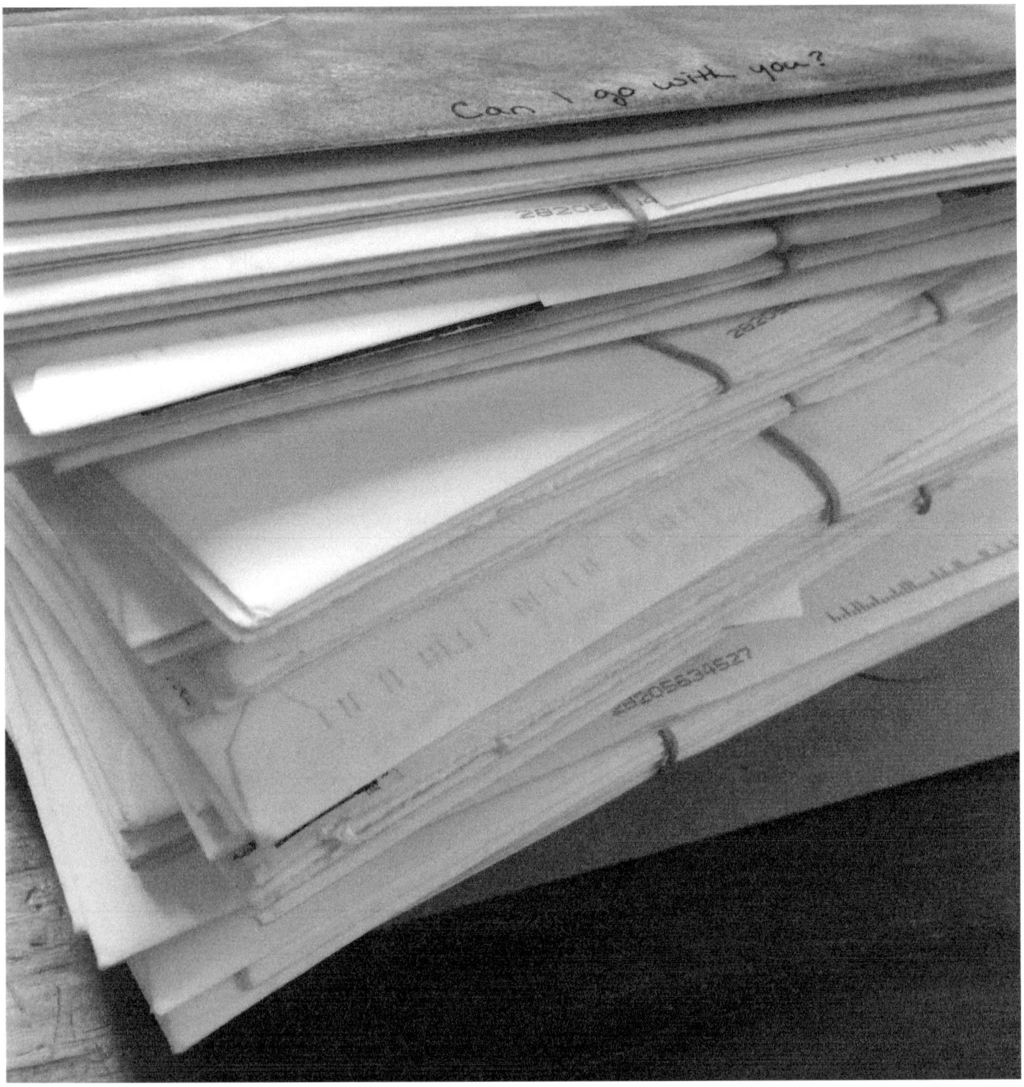


*Figure 16.1* A stack of letters awaiting transcription.

## Turning Toward the Pedagogical

> Curating changes with the change in art.
>
> (Obrist, 2014, p. 33)

Curating comes to us from the Latin *curare*, meaning to care—as in "to care" for a collection of artwork (Plagens, 2013). Historically speaking, the primary responsibilities associated with curating have been the preservation and care of a collection, selecting and acquiring artworks, contributing to art historical discourses, and making exhibitions by arranging art in a space (Obrist, 2014). Yet, paradigmatic shifts in contemporary art practice have invited a reimagining of the curatorial (Obrist, 2014; Plagens, 2013).

I feel compelled to pause briefly here, as the word curating is perhaps too-often evoked to mean something very different than my use of the term. Curating has been folded into our everyday vernacular. In conversational language, curating speaks to how we go about choosing, selecting, and personalizing a handful of things from the overwhelming sea of options available to us in a globalized economy (Balzer, 2015). Yet, curating as a creative practice—and not merely a popular verb—goes beyond grouping objects together, making lists or recommendations, gleaning preferences, and so forth.

My particular interest lies in the reimagining of curatorial practice with the educational turn (or "pedagogical turn") in the early 2000s. This was a notable movement in the contemporary art world that pulled "discursive interventions" (O'Neill & Wilson, 2010, p. 12)—talks, debates, discussions, and other collaborative and democratized forums for engagement—away from the periphery. This movement proved capable of renegotiating the pedagogical nature of art from a supplemental to a central component of artistic and curatorial practice. With this turn, the curator's role expanded. Curating became less about *informing* the public and more about *activating* "a permeable space that offers more questions than answers—produced by artist, curator, educator, participant, and audience" (Johnston, 2014, p. 23). These dynamic transformations offered me pause and spark. Over the next several years, I continued to explore the curatorial in various theoretical and pedagogical contexts (see Hofsess, 2015a, 2015b; Hofsess, 2016; Hofsess & Thiel, 2017). Next, I situate how I see contemporary understandings of the curatorial in relationship to new materialist philosophy and specifically to relational ontologies—or the entangled nature of knowing, being, doing, and responsibility (Barad, 2007).

## Turning Toward Relational Ontologies

> Curatorial acts intend to bring the various determinations of the individual elements with which they work into relation with one another, and in so doing do not create any fixed images or stills, but ... generate processual events that are set in motion by way of relational tensions and crises, acts of reception, or the mobility of what is collected.
>
> (Von Bismarck, 2007, p. 164)

As a visual artist working primarily in papermaking and book arts, I feel an urgency regarding the role materiality plays in my work that led me to explore curating in the first place. When I speak of curatorial impulses, I am attempting to name the embodied "analytical inclination to revel in the materiality of the data arts-based researchers exercise in their thinking through research questions" (Hofsess, 2015a, p. 7). Following such impulses as a researcher requires listening and attending to how materials *intra-act* (Barad, 2007). For example, how individual pages of a preservice teacher's visual journal allow us to see something different when layered, combined, and recombined in various mapping configurations as shown in Figure 16.2 (see Hofsess, 2015a). *Intra-action*, or how differences arise when matters comes together, is but one new materialist concept envisioned by Barad, a theoretical feminist physicist.

Which brings me to mention how my interest in the curatorial overlaps with my interest in new materialist philosophy, specifically to the lexicon of concepts Barad imagined at

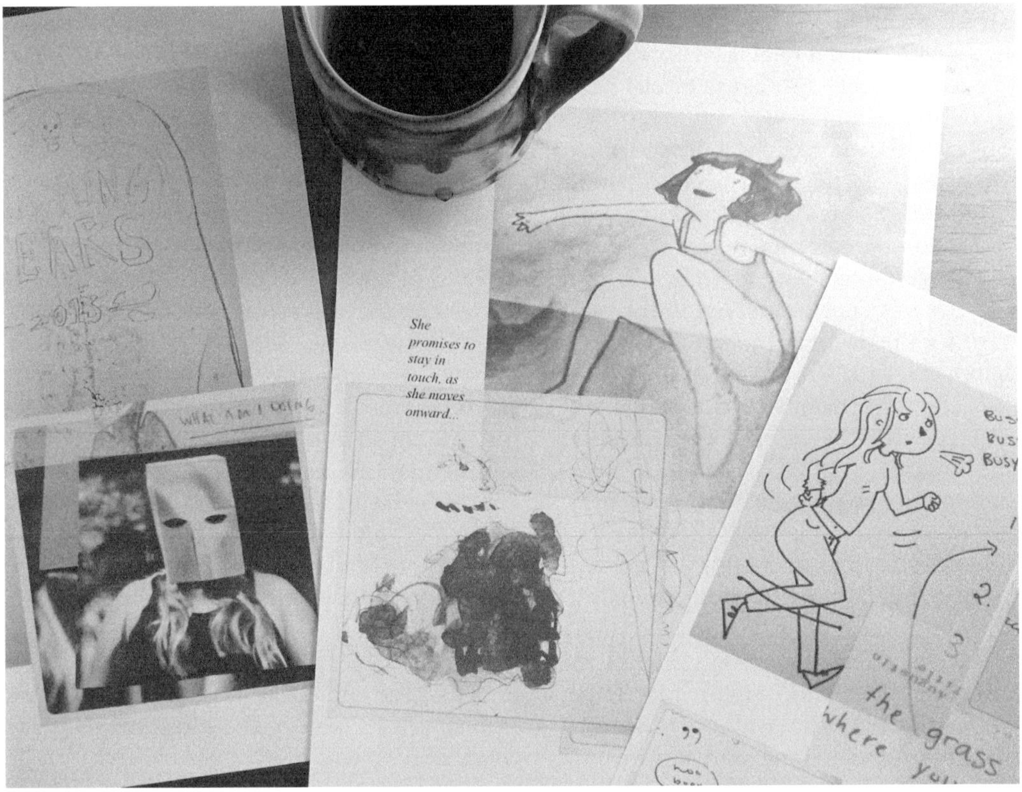


*Figure 16.2* Following curatorial impulses in the mapping of a preservice teacher's visual journal.

the intersection of quantum physics and feminist theory. These concepts, frequently called upon to activate new materialism in educational research and practice (see Taylor, 2016), coalesce through her larger conceptualization of *relational ontology*—or, how matter and meaning are always, already threaded through one another and, therefore, inseparable (Barad, 2003, 2007). Broadly speaking, waves of new materialist thought have rippled through philosophy, social and cultural theory, art, feminism, and onto education—unsettling *how matter comes to matter* (Barad, 2003) in the production of knowledge (see Barad, 2007; Braidotti, 2013; Coole & Frost, 2010; Haraway, 1997). These waves have been set in motion to trouble, unsettle, and reimagine alternative courses for knowing (and therefore doing and being) when it seems "language has been granted too much power" (Barad, 2003, p. 801). Let me pause here briefly to contextualize how such an entanglement applies to art education spaces.

Learning in and through the visual arts involves complex ecologies of visual, material, affective, spatial, and discursive insights. For example, rendering the fullness of the world on flat paper, becoming lost to time in a flow with sensuous art media, being stung by a harsh criticism or buoyed by warm affirmation, or recognizing that soft vine charcoal makes a distinctly different mark from hard graphite pencil. From a new materialist perspective, the art student and teacher are tangled up in, not above or in front of, all of these matters. In other words, thinking with new materialism invites an exploration of art classrooms as lively spaces where *who* and *what* play a vital role in how we conceptualize pedagogy and research (Springgay & Zaliwska, 2017).

My various theoretical and pedagogical experimentations with the curatorial have involved crafting narratives in epistolary form, representing interview conversations and embodied memories of those encounters as letterpress broadsides, piecing together rhizomatic mappings (Deleuze & Guattari, 1987) of a preservice teacher's visual-verbal journal pages (see Figure 16.2), to name a few projects. Through this work, I have found that following curatorial impulses and creating curated forms of representation resemble diffractive practices. The new materialist concept of diffraction comes out of the feminist theories of Haraway (1997) and Barad (2007) to emphasize the shifting and relational qualities of difference. In other words, diffraction relates to how someone or something becomes different in relation with and to another. Further, diffractive practices go beyond locating *where* differences occur to emphasize the *effects* of those differences and why they matter to how we come into knowing, being, doing, and responding (Haraway as cited in Barad, 2003).

The very spirit of curating is to bring "different elements to touch" (Obrist, 2014, p. I) in the creation of something new, something yet unseen. The curatorial offers arts-based educational researchers a way to conceptualize and communicate their queries and findings by allowing various insights to be read through one another in ongoing reverberations of meaning and interpretation. Such insights can be visual, material, affective, textual, theoretical, and/or practical in nature. Further, they can clash, brace, mingle, balance, conflict with other insights, rather than be tamed by codes, categories, or themes. The research, research participants, researcher—even the theoretical framework—are gifted permission to become different on the written page (as in life) as the inquiry unfolds (Hofsess, 2016).

Curating, as a process of inquiring, is not merely to collect, care for, acquire, or arrange "data." Rather, evoking the curatorial invites researchers to explore how individual moments or elements (theories, field notes, embodied memories, interview conversations, and visual documentation, for example) might be culled together to create invitational and relational spaces in which the effects of differences perpetually and playfully rebound. Further, curating releases the assumption that these elements become stabilized in the writing up of research (see Hofsess, 2016). As Cahnmann-Taylor and Siegesmund (2008) articulated, "(a) rts-based visual research reminds us that data (sic) is not found; it is constructed. It emphasizes the authority of both researchers and reader to create personal meaning from a work of research—rather than relay or receive an external meaning" (p. 101). Curated spaces are made possible and powerful through a curator *and* an audience—not to mention matter, things, materiality, and so on.

## Turning Toward Evocative Critique

> (A) way of seeing is also a way of not seeing.
>
> (Eisner, 2002, p. 25)

Curating is not only about what is constructed and archived but also about what has been omitted; the very word implies selection—and, therefore, exclusion. Integral to the curatorial process is the decision-making that determines content, form, sequence, participation:

Who and what generate the curated space? What criteria were employed to make these choices? And, who and what determined the criteria? In other words, curatorial processes bound what materializes, and new materialisms encourage scholars to engage with how "the cuts that we participate in enacting matter" (Barad, 2007, p. 178).

Leading me to ask, what are the broader implications for ABER work when *scholARTists* (Knowles et al., 2008) bring curating into the mix of art practice, research, and teaching? As Barone and Eisner (2012) articulated, politics and ethics become "intimately intertwined" in ABER as constructs such as *voice, power, point of view, responsibility, member checking, and truth* are embraced, avoided, and manipulated by the artist/researcher in various aesthetic forms (p. 121). Obrist (2014) recognized at least one potential foil when he warned:

> Artists and their works must not be used to illustrate a curatorial proposal or premise to which they are subordinated. Instead, exhibitions are best generated through conversations and collaborations with artists, whose input should steer the process from the beginning.
>
> (p. 33)

Communicating research findings through arts-based forms of representation offers a unique capacity to spark imaginative conversations with those who generatively inspire educational research—teachers, teacher educators, and those learning to teach. Obrist's caution inspires me to explore the potential of curating in ABER to enfold research participants in collaborative and co-constructive ways from the start. Next, I turn toward imagining how all of this informs new possibilities for art education curriculum.

## Turning Toward Imagining

> Ultimately, ABER not only shifts the focus to how we inquire, but also models a new vision of curriculum. Arts-based research demonstrates strategies that might inform our thinking about how we allow students to exhibit their coming to know.
>
> (Siegesmund & Cahnmann-Taylor, Chapter 39, p. 396)

For me, the porousness of curating after the educational turn opens possibilities for how "the curatorial can be employed, or performed, by people in a number of different capacities within the ecosystem of art" (Hoffmann & Lind, 2011–2012, para 20), leading me to wonder: How do teachers always, already perform curatorial acts and set curatorial criteria in classrooms? What would preservice teachers glean and adapt for K-12 art education, museum education, and community arts education if given the chance to explore the curatorial more explicitly in teacher preparation programs? And, how might curating evoke new possibilities for documentation practices?

My experiments with curating in ABER have become interwoven in the way I think about my work educating and sustaining art teachers. For example, a recent collaborative project invited preservice teachers to view themselves as *curators* in addition to artists, researchers, writers, and educators by cocurating a virtual exhibition using social media platforms (Hofsess & Thiel, 2017). Inspired by this project, I started using a class Instagram account for students to post still and moving images that speak to particularly salient moments of

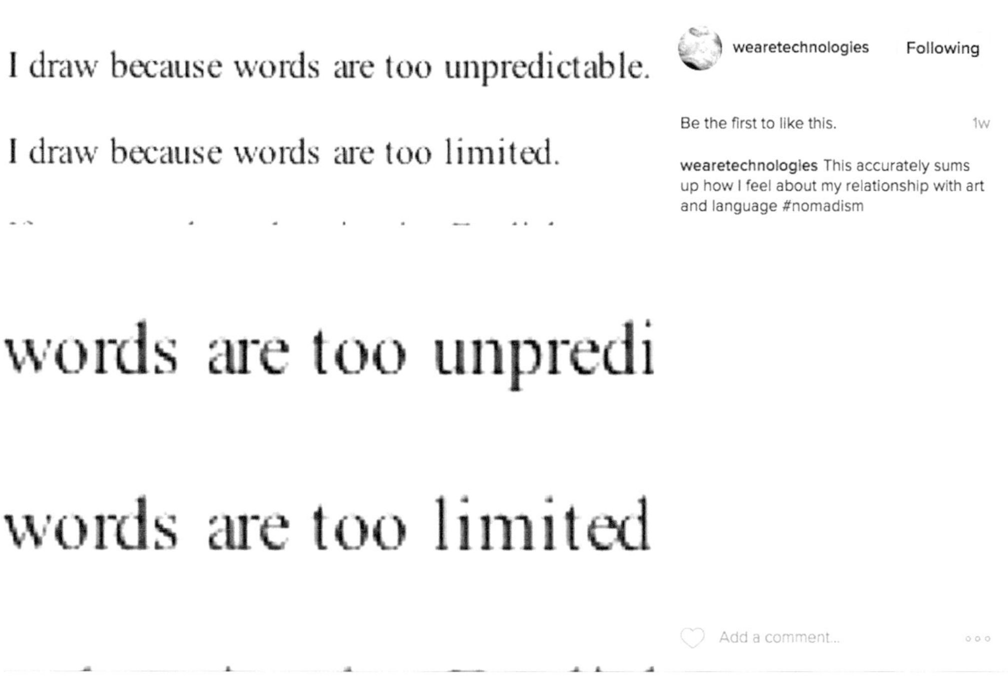


*Figure 16.3* Curating salient teaching-learning moments (screenshot of a preservice art educator's Instagram post).

our class sessions. This curated feed is projected at the end of each class, allowing the entire group to contemplate not only the individual images but how each image can also be read diffractively through the other responses (see Figure 16.3).

To close, as I delve into these questions regarding how curating activates curriculum, new possibilities for putting the curatorial to work in art education spaces become visible: possibilities that stir me to explore new questions about being and becoming art educators at this particular moment in time. My hope is that this chapter has revealed my intrigue with the premise that curating seeks "to imagine the world other than it is" (Thea, 2009, p. 9) and that my musings might spark new imaginings for other arts-based educational researchers.

## Postscript

Since first composing this essay, I've deepened my engagement with curatorial processes, finding myself increasingly immersed in the blurring of ecological, material, and social realms as a *scholartist* (Knowles et al., 2008; see Hofsess & Thiel, 2017; Hofsess et al., 2019). In the blur, I have come to see curating as a practice that unfolds in the dynamic interstices between what is visible and what resonates beneath the surface—conjuring connections and creating openings that invite difference to emerge and escape conventional boundaries. Less about fixing meaning and more about inviting processual becoming, curating interweaves learners, educators, environments, and imaginations into ongoing entanglements.

To *curate-with* is to immerse oneself in dissolving the boundaries that traditionally separate inquiry, artistry, and life. Here, matter and meaning continually shift and inform one another: landscapes become teachers, art flows into story, and stories open new possibilities for collective and individual growth. This heightened sensitivity to the interdependencies that sustain our practices cultivates an embodied awareness that feels both urgent and generative. Rather than offering conclusions, curating invites the world to seep into practice, perforating rigid structures and allowing new ways of knowing, being, and doing to emerge. Ultimately, curating has become for me a way of living inquiry—an approach that honors the relational vibrancy of the world and our role within it as educators, learners, and creatives.

## Note

1 My sincere gratitude extends to Melisa Cahnmann and Richard Siegesmund for their insightful feedback on the initial draft of this chapter. My articulation of the curatorial was strengthened by their keen questions and provocations. Further, like many emerging scholars I imagine, the first edition of this edited volume emboldened me to experiment with curating in and through ABER to begin with—so it is especially meaningful to be among the contributors invited to this project.

## References

Balzer, D. (2015). *Curationism: How curating took over the art world and everything else*. Pluto Press.

Barad, K. (2003). Posthumanist performativity: Toward an understanding of how matter comes to matter. *Signs*, *28*(3), 801–831. https://doi.org/10.1086/345321

Barad, K. (2007). *Meeting the universe halfway: Quantum physics and the entanglement of matter and meaning*. Duke University Press.

Barone, T., & Eisner, E. W. (2012). *Arts based research*. Sage.

Bennett, J. (2010). *Vibrant matter: A political ecology of things*. Duke University Press.

Bourriaud, N. (2002). *Relational aesthetics*. Le press du reel.

Braidotti, R. (2013). *The posthuman*. Polity Press. (Originally published in 2011).

Britzman, D. P. (1991). *Practice makes practice: A critical study of learning to teach*. State University of New York Press.

Cahnmann-Taylor, M., & Siegesmund, R. (2008). *Arts-based research in education: Foundations for practice*. Routledge.

Coole, D., & Frost, S. (2010). *New materialisms: Ontology, agency, politics*. Duke University Press.

Deleuze, G., & Guattari, F. (1987). *A thousand plateaus: Capitalism and schizophrenia* (B. Massumi, Trans.). University of Minnesota Press. (Original work published 1980).

Eisner, E. (2002). *The arts and the creation of mind*. Yale University Press.

Greene, M. (2001). *Variations on a blue guitar: The Lincoln Center Institute lectures on aesthetic education*. Teachers College Press.

Haraway, D. (1997). *Modest_Witness@Second_Millennium.FemaleMan©_Meets_OncoMouse™: Feminism and technoscience*. Routledge.

Hoffmann, J., & Lind, M. (2011–2012). To show or not to show. *Mousse*, *31*. https://www.mousemagazine.it/magazine/jens-hoffmann-maria-lind-2011/

Hofsess, B. A. (2015a). The map of true places: Moving onward in art teacher preparation. *Visual Arts Research*, *41*(1), 1–15. https://doi.org/10.5406/visuartsrese.41.1.0001

Hofsess, B. A. (2015b). Do with me: The action orient of aesthetic experiential play. *Visual Arts Research*, *41*(2), 1–17. https://doi.org/10.5406/visuartsrese.41.2.0001

Hofsess, B. A. (2016). *Unfolding afterglow: Letters and conversations on teacher renewal*. Sense.

Hofsess, B. A., & Thiel, J. (2017). Pause/Play: Curating as living/aesthetic analysis. *Reconceptualizing Educational Research Methodology*, *SI 8*(3), 31–52. https://doi.org/10.7577/rerm.2549

Hofsess, B. A., Ulmer, J., Carlisle, J., & Caldwell, S. (2019). Curating with: Walking and making ecologies of girlhood. *International Journal of Education through Art*, *15*(3), 357–368. https://doi.org/10.1386/eta_00008_3

Johnston, M. (2014). Slow curating: Re-thinking and extending socially engaged art in the context of Northern Ireland. *Oncurating.org, after the Turn: Art Education beyond the Museum, 24*, 23–33. https://www.on-curating.org/index.php/issue-24-reader/Slow_Curating_Re-thinking_and_Extending_Socially_Engaged_Art_in_the_Context_of_Northern_Ireland.html

Knowles, J. G., Promislow, S., & Cole, A. L. (2008). *Creating scholartistry: Imagining the arts-informed thesis or dissertation*. Backalong Books.

O'Neill, P., & Wilson, M. (2010). *Curating and the educational turn*. Open Editions.

Obrist, H. U. (2014). *Ways of curating*. Faber and Faber.

Plagens, P. (2013). Cool curating. *Art in America, 101*(1), 41–44.

Springgay, S., & Zaliwska, Z. (2017). Learning to be affected: Matters of pedagogy in the artists' soup kitchen. *Educational Philosophy & Theory, 49*(3), 273–283. https://doi.org/10.1080/00131857.2016.1216385

St. Pierre, E. A. (2011). Post qualitative research: The critique and the coming after. In N. K. Denzin & Y. S. Lincoln (Eds.), *The Sage handbook of qualitative research* (4th ed., pp. 611–625). Sage.

Taylor, C. (2016). Edu-crafting a cacophonous ecology: Posthumanist research practices for education. In C. Taylor & C. Hughes (Eds.), *Posthuman research practices in education* (pp. 5–24). Palgrave Macmillan.

Thea, C. (2009). Introduction. In C. Thea & T. Micchelli (Eds.), *On curating: Interviews with ten international curators* (pp. 6–16). D.A.P./Distributed Art Publishers.

Von Bismarck, B. (2007). Unfounding exhibiting: Policies of artistic curating. In M. Schavemaker & M. Rakier (Eds.), *Right about now: Art & theory since the 1990s* (pp. 157–166). Valiz Publishers.

Chapter 17

# What Is an Artist-Teacher When Teaching Second Languages?

*Yohan Hwang*

Recently, there has been renewed interest among teachers, researchers, and school administrators in a reconciliation of the artistic and educational enterprises as complementary partners. Daichendt (2010) and Eisner (2002) have been proponents of creating, appreciating, and sharing artful works in both the school and the world in which students and teachers live. Eisner (2002) argued

> the distinctive forms of thinking needed to create artistically crafted work are relevant not only to what students do, they are relevant to virtually all aspects of what we do, from the design of curricula, to the practice of teaching.
>
> (p. 208)

According to Booth (2003), a variety of titles have emerged that refer to artists working in classrooms; these include "artist-in-residence," "artist-educator," "visiting artist," "arts expert," "arts provider," and "teaching artist." While these terms are used elsewhere interchangeably, in my research I prefer the term "artist-teacher," adopting Uptis's (2005) definition referring to "those teachers with substantial professional training in one or more art forms, who are otherwise active in art-making, but whose primary vocation is teaching" (p. 2). Specifically, I use the term "poet-teacher," similar to an apprenticed artist and referencing a prospective language teacher who recognizes the importance of creative inquiry, expression, and manifestations in the second language (L2) classroom.

The movement toward arts partnerships in education is prevalent in the field of Teaching English to Speakers of Other Languages (TESOL). Many L2 teachers and scholars have documented the positive outcomes from arts-based learning as applied to TESOL (Chappell & Cahnmann-Taylor, 2013; Chappell & Faltis, 2013; Hanauer, 2010). This movement draws attention to the considerations of creativity and artful engagements in teacher preparation and practice, making connections between language teachers' identities and those of artists (Cahnmann-Taylor et al., 2015).

## Central Phenomena and Sociocultural Landscape of English Education in East Asia

My inquiry into the influence of creative writing and poetry in TESOL teacher preparation was motivated by some of the drawbacks and limitations I experienced as an L2 learner in traditional English classes in South Korea. Although I considered myself a creative writer, having written more than 80 poems in my first language, I had never thought about writing

DOI: 10.4324/9781003412892-17

a poem in English when I began my doctoral studies. Most of the English courses I took restrained my creativity switch from turning on during the process of L2 writing. I thought that this difficulty resulted from my lower level of proficiency in English, but as a poet-teacher, I now realize that the lack of creativity and personal voice in L2 writing were connected to grammar and translation-oriented pedagogies.

I must admit, I'm not a representative of all English learners in Korea, but studies have shown that the grammar-translation method, which focuses mainly on practicing interpretation and/or translation from a native language to the L2, is still common in many East Asian countries (Pan & Pan, 2012). These kinds of "controlled composition lessons" (Matsuda, 2003) do not allow L2 learners space to make any grammatical mistakes, which does not improve their ability to explore new meanings and produce creative works in a new language. Rather, this pedagogy is directly connected to the neoliberal landscape influencing English teaching in East Asia.

According to Gray (2000), neoliberal ideology has attempted to "make all spheres of social life play by the rules of the market" (p. 21), and the English education of many East Asian countries where teachers and parents are making extreme efforts to make their students/children be more "native-like" is no exception (Anderson & Kohler, 2012; Bacon & Kim, 2018; Choi, 2021; Kubota, 2011; Park, 2010). Take contemporary Korean society, where the private English-education industry earns 15 trillion won ($15.8 billion) per year (Jeon & Choi, 2006), as an example. In my native country, the drive and even lunacy to have native-like accents is everywhere, as English ability is valued as a neoliberal project to maintain class status quo (Choi, 2021). Of course, overcoming our natural pronunciation difficulty, such as the "R/L" and "P/F" distinction, is important for better communication (e.g., "rice" vs. "lice" or "pool" vs. "fool"). However, the aspiration and competition for the "native-like" have often gone too far, purportedly resulting in operations on children's tongues (Demick, 2002; Park & Abelmann, 2004). Park (2010) argues that English education in South Korea, represented by a current "English Frenzy," structures a stable elite system that privileges only a few highly proficient English speakers who have social privilege. In this ultracompetitive setting, L2 is a form of capital with high exchange value, rather than a means to develop individual thinking and learning (Bourdieu & Passeron, 1990). When English learners make efforts to improve their speaking and writing skills in the classroom, they may often find that their own cultural and linguistic identities turn out to be obstacles that stand in the way of the goal of being "native-like."

This erasure approach grounded in neoliberal ideologies in many East Asian countries has been justified by large classroom size and standardized testing culture. However, neoliberalism's tendency to commodify language and reduce English to a mere tool for global competition overlooks the deeper, humanistic value of language learning as a process of self-discovery and identity formation (Bacon & Kim, 2018). Under neoliberal ideology, English is treated as an economic asset—a means of securing better jobs, higher social status, or elite privileges—rather than a medium for personal expression or critical engagement with the world (Choi, 2021). This instrumental view of English can suppress individuality and creativity, particularly when learners are pressured to conform to "native-like" standards that may alienate them from their cultural and linguistic roots.

This issue must be reconsidered, because L2 learners' first language, past experiences, and cultural backgrounds are what make them unique and significant, serving them as a means to critically reflect upon their own culture and to foster multicultural perspectives (Agar, 1994). In this context, poetry writing offers a powerful counter-narrative to the neoliberal commodification of English. Unlike traditional grammar-translation methods or standardized test preparation, poetry allows learners to engage with language on their own terms, weaving their linguistic identities and life experiences into creative expressions. It becomes a space where their voices, shaped by diverse cultural and linguistic histories, can be fully realized and appreciated. This is one of the most important reasons for L2 learning, as Pavlenko (1997) argues: "the process of successful L2 learning necessitates re-construction of one's linguistic, cultural and social identity, or at the least the development of new ones" (p. 80). Too much emphasis on "native-like" aspirations may fail to deepen the quality of L2 education, in that English becomes oppressive and L2 learning could be confined to mindless and automatic copying of someone else, not developed as a means to rebuild the self. Poetry, in contrast, invites learners to step away from these rigid, market-driven demands and reclaim their agency as creative thinkers and meaning-makers. As a way of facing the challenges of creatively and critically thinking in my L2, personally, I found poetry to be a possible solution.

## Poetry Writing for Creative L2 Education in the ABR Tradition

In this study, I examined the experiences and interactions of TESOL graduate students who, like me, had enrolled in a creative writing poetry course at a Southeastern US university TESOL program that attracts large numbers of Asian students preparing to teach English in their home countries. The Research Map (Figure 17.1) portrays the overall research context, including my own roles in the course as student and/or participant observer and the chronology of the course from the first through fifteenth week of the semester. All participants held similarly novice experiences with poetry and advanced knowledge of English as they completed their second and final year in the Master's program.

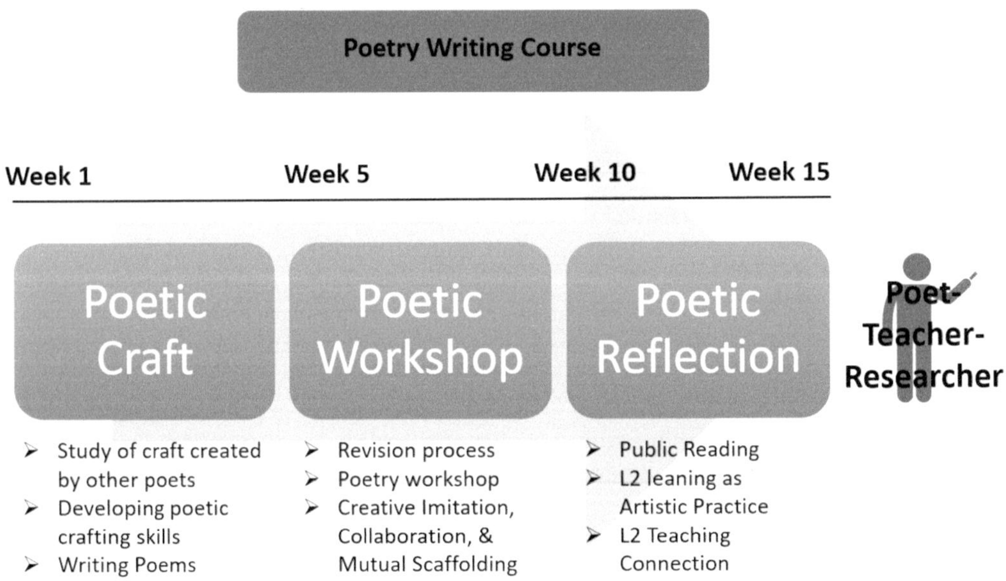


*Figure 17.1* Research Map.

During the study, I interacted with students as their fellow-poet, which gave me membership in the participant group. For instance, one of the important features of the research context was a poetry revision workshop. The observation and participation in the workshops encouraged me, as a scholartist, to create my own poem, expressing the surprise of how hard L2 writers strive to be creative in their own writing. This form of artful engagement and manifestation made my data representation process more creative and connected with the participants. Specifically, at the end of the semester, I recited my poem (appearing as follows) at the poetry reading night. This gave other students the opportunity to laugh and to co-witness, which created a unique relationship between myself and the research participants.

*Poetry' Door*

Trembling hand chaps the door, "Knock, Knock, Knock."
".........." Nobody answers. We crumble our poem draft,
titled Mountain, and put it into the paper-key door lock.

"Beep, Beep, Beep." Lock scowls at our paper
"Big abstraction, Boring cliché, Bad craft."
Rejection letter crawls out: "Novice! Come later."

Sigh! We are lost in thought with our eyes shut
dreaming of a *"That's great!"* hunter chasing a fresh
prey at the Mountain. Creative Thoughts initialed *by the teacher*.

We insert the revision and cast our fear away.
"Clank." We shove the knob and make our entry.
Creaking of the hinges whispers on our way.

"Welcome to the world of poetry"
The door becomes open spouting its sheer joy.
by Yohan Hwang

I saw that poetry writing often became a mechanism for other Asian TESOL graduate students to exorcise negative and/or painful emotions, turning frustrations into more positive feelings and outlooks toward their identities as non-native speakers of English. For example, in poetic form, one participant vented her frustration as an L2 speaker in an English phonology class, which provides alternative ways to view non-native speakers' sound systems. With her permission, I include her poem-draft to illustrate how poetry was personally meaningful to others:

*Physics of Sound – Non Native Speaker's Linguistic Homework*

The diagram is too cool for me to understand,
*Sinusoid, millisecond, frequency of sound.*
This is science,

familiar to me in high school, now
we are strangers.

Put it aside, save me from a glimpse.
Sinewaves, like snakes.
Cover it with textbooks, as if I
cunningly escaped from tangling with homework.

I am sensitive to the sound spectrum's
delicateness, unique.
Like water sleeves for *Tsing Yi**;
going through time and space is sweet and soft singing.
I don't wear a calculator on my sleeve.
I can't figure out the sound spectrum.
But I can speak English.
Play with it, rock it, make fun of my Chinglish.
I can't make every sound right,

Well, not a big deal-
the accent is the postcard of identity.

* *Water sleeves: actress's long sleeves in opera.*
*Tsing Yi: one kind of actress role in Beijing opera.*
by Zihan Lin

Sharing this poem in the revision workshop encouraged her peers, who had experienced similar issues, to appreciate the unique value of being a non-native speaker. An excerpt of classroom discourse between Chengyuan and Xiao illustrates this: "I think even though you make a wrong sound, it is not so important because it is your identity ... so this is identity ... could help others understand ourselves well." "I don't think it's a shame to admit that we are non-native speakers. Maybe we have accents but, it is okay, I mean it is natural, we're in the process of learning ... we can do better, we can grow." These are just some of the examples that showed how poetry writing provided opportunities for L2 writers to appreciate the value and validity of non-nativeness while living in a dominant culture and language. Understanding this helped me rethink and recast the extreme ways in which striving to be native-like means cutting out non-native sounds, making L2 learners "fix" their original identities.

Analysis of Zihan's poem also inspired me to investigate the connection between poetry and my own L2 writing voice and identity. During my graduate studies in the United States, I could feel my English writing skills had improved, because I had to write for *survival* in a new academic context, as my poem reveals in the following. However, as an L2 learner of English raised with the habit of passive learning of grammatical rules, I was always concerned about perfect grammar and had to fight to write the way native speakers do. As a result, I frequently went to the writing center on campus and even paid money for grammar revisions, looking for a native speaker who could "fix" my papers' grammar and forms. The editors' corrections were very helpful, indeed, so much so that they not only kept my language from being deficient but also helped me learn about the formal conventions of academic writing. However, one day on the way out of the writing center, while reviewing the excessive number of red marks on the rough draft of my paper, I felt tired of forcing myself to adhere to the rigid rules of grammar, of mindlessly copying how native speakers write. I sat down in front of the building and wrote the poem:

*On the Way Out of the Writing Center*

Teacher's red nib scours,
teases, and commands:

*Write as natives write.*
*Speak as natives speak.*
*Think as natives think.*

It pokes me. But how
I can be what I'm not?

I need to ink my
정체성 (Jung-Chae-Sung)* somewhere.
I tap at Poetry's door where:

*I write as I write.*
*I speak as I speak.*
*I think as I think.*

* *Identity*

by Yohan Hwang

There are many conventional rules in poetry that must be followed and correct grammar matters, but writing poetry was a different experience. It allowed me a different type of freedom that I was seldom permitted in academic English contexts. Poetry asked me to pursue alternative hybrid identities, embracing my L1 identities in and through creative L2 uses. Specifically, I found that poetry was an artful genre where non-native values and L2 validity could be appreciated, where bilingual identities could be praised and loved in the process of revealing writers' voices as who they are. Thus, I came to poetry as a great work of art as opposed to following someone else's rules, just filling the words in the five paragraphs of a paper. By revealing my own voice and identity, I came to poetry truly filling the world from my past/current experiences, linguistic/cultural backgrounds, and even with my first language, often finding myself bridging two worlds.

## I Am a Poet-Teacher-Researcher

As of the time of this writing, I am in my home country, South Korea, teaching courses in English Education and Sociolinguistics. I returned to find that English (and other) departments still regard high scores on standardized tests and native-like aspirations as unquestioned trends. As a TESOL professor, I hope to help my students come to English writing as a place to develop as creative and productive meaning-makers, rather than just mimicking someone else and remaining passive receptors of grammars and language forms. As poetry writing helped me to arrive at this point, I deeply ponder how I can be a language teacher who invites students to view the study of L2 as a fundamentally creative process that manifests future possibilities (Vygotsky, 2004). I want to be a poet-teacher who highlights a need for different pedagogical approaches that understand English teaching and learning as forms of artistic practice/performance, where English learners speak, write, think, and, most importantly, are valued for who they are. In addition, I want to be a poet-researcher who engenders new connections and relationships in the classroom, exploring students' refined experiences and unrefined feelings through poetry writing. I aspire to be a scholartist, engaging in "a hybrid practice that combines tools used by the literary, visual, and/or performing arts with tools used by educators and other social scientists to explore the human condition" (Cahnmann-Taylor, 2008, p. 247).

I know artful, creative teaching and study might not be easy in a context where new faculty with new ideas are teaching too many courses and have too many students. I understand that creative training could be considered impractical within an English education system that still looks for high scores on the standardized tests. Changing the education system in any society might be difficult, but we must remember that every turning point of history has required an initial step. Poetry is my literary suggestion for TESOL educators and a literacy key for myself to take that first step in this endless, challenging, but joyful and rewarding journey of teaching and researching.

## Postscript

Since the time of this writing, the intersection of arts-based research and English language education has continued to evolve, offering new insights into how creative practices can empower L2 learners. Recent studies have critically examined the impact of neoliberal ideologies on English language education, revealing how these forces shape perceptions of language proficiency and success (Bacon & Kim, 2018; Choi, 2021). This scholarship underscores the importance of resisting the commodification of English and instead promoting pedagogies that value linguistic and cultural diversity. By aligning creative writing with identity-building, educators can challenge oppressive systems that reduce English to a tool for economic gain, highlighting its potential as a medium for personal and social transformation. Reflecting on these developments, I am convinced that poetry writing in the L2 classroom is not merely an exercise in creativity but a radical act of reclaiming linguistic agency. Through poetry, learners can articulate their hybrid identities and resist the erasure of their unique voices. As we move forward, the integration of arts-based research (ABR) into TESOL offers promising pathways for fostering more inclusive, reflective, and empowering educational practices.

## References

Agar, M. (1994). *Language shock: Understanding the culture of conversation*. William Morrow.

Anderson, T. M., & Kohler, H. (2012). *Education fever and the East Asian fertility puzzle: A case study of low fertility in South Korea*. PSC Working Papers, 38.

Bacon, C. K., & Kim, S. Y. (2018). "English is my only weapon": Neoliberal language ideologies and youth metadiscourse in South Korea. *Linguistics and Education*, *48*, 10–21. https://doi.org/10.1016/j.linged.2018.09.002

Booth, E. (2003). Seeking definition: What is a teaching artist? *Teaching Artist Journal*, *1*(1), 5–12. https://doi.org/10.1080/15411796.2003.9684265

Bourdieu, P., & Passeron, J.-C. (1990). *Reproduction in education, society and culture (theory, culture & society)*. Sage.

Cahnmann-Taylor, M. (2008). Arts-based approaches to inquiry in language education. In K. A. King & N. H. Hornberger (Eds.), *Encyclopedia of language and education. 2nd edition, Research methods in language and education* (pp. 243–254). Springer Science and Business Media.

Cahnmann-Taylor, M., Zhang, K., Bleyle, S., & Hwang, Y. (2015). "Searching for an entrance" and finding a two-way door: Using poetry to create East-West contact zones in TESOL teacher education. *International Journal of Education & the Arts*, *16*, 1–30. http://www.ijea.org/v16n21/

Chappell, S., & Faltis, C. (2013). *The arts and emergent bilingual youth: Building critical, creative programs in school and community contexts*. Routledge.

Chappell, S. V., & Cahnmann-Taylor, M. (2013). No child left with crayons: The imperative of Arts-Based Education and research with language "minority" and other minoritized communities. *Review of Educational Research*, *37*(1), 255–280. https://doi.org/10.3102/0091732X12461615

Choi, L. J. (2021). English as an important but unfair resource: University students' perception of English and English language education in South Korea. *Teaching in Higher Education*, *29*(1), 144–158. https://doi.org/10.1080/13562517.2021.1965572

Daichendt, G. J. (2010). *Artist-Teacher: A philosophy for creating and teaching*. Intellect.

Demick, B. (2002, March 31). Some in S. Korea opt for a trim when English trips the tongue. *The Los Angeles Times*. http://articles.latimes.com/2002/mar/31/news/mn-35590

Eisner, E. W. (2002). *The arts and the creation of mind*. Yale University Press.

Gray, J. (2000). *Two faces of liberalism*. The New Press.

Hanauer, D. I. (2010). *Poetry as research: Exploring second language poetry writing*. John Benjamins.

Jeon, H., & Choi, H. (2006). The economics of English. *Samsung Economic Research Institute(SERI)*, *578*(15), 2.

Kubota, R. (2011). Questioning linguistic instrumentalism: English, neoliberalism, and language tests in Japan. *Linguistics and Education*, *22*(3), 248–260. https://doi.org/10.1016/j.linged.2011.02.002

Matsuda, P. K. (2003). Second language writing in the twentieth century: A situated historical perspective. In B. Kroll (Ed.), *Exploring the dynamics of second language writing* (pp. 15–34). Cambridge University Press.

Pan, Y., & Pan, Y. (2012). The use of translation in the EFL classroom. *Philippine ESL Journal*, *9*, 4–23.

Park, J. S. (2010). Naturalization of competence and the neoliberal subject: Success stories of English language learning in the Korean Conservative Press. *Journal of Linguistic Anthropology*, *20*(1), 22–38. https://doi.org/10.1111/j.1548-1395.2010.01046.x

Park, S., & Abelmann, N. (2004). Class and cosmopolitan striving: Mothers' management of English education in South Korea. *Anthropological Quarterly*, *77*(4), 645–672. https://doi.org/10.1353/anq.2004.0063

Pavlenko, A. (1997). "To speak a foreign language is to depart from yourself": Late bilingualism as (re)construction of identity. In X. P. Rodríguez Yáñez, C. C. Pereiro, & A. M. Lorenzo-Suárez (Eds.), *Comunidades e individuos bilingües*. Paper presented at the Actas do I Simposio Internacional sobre o Bilingüismo, Universidade de Vigo, Galicia-Spain, 21–25 October (pp. 80–88). Servizo de Publicacións da Universidade de Vigo.

Uptis, R. (2005). Experiences of artists and artist-teachers involved in teacher professional development programs. *International Journal of Education & the Arts*, *6*(8), 1–12. http://www.ijea.org/v6n8/

Vygotsky, L. S. (2004). Imagination and creativity in childhood. *Journal of Russian and East European Psychology*, *42*(1), 7–97. https://doi.org/10.1080/10610405.2004.11059210

Chapter 18

# A/r/tography as Practice-Based Research[1]

*Rita L. Irwin and Stephanie Springgay*

We're waiting for the bus that travels south on Granville Street in Vancouver, British Columbia. For weeks we've been staring down the street from the bus stop at a storefront window that appears to function as a type of shelter for the public – sometimes seemingly random people stop and step inside only to emerge again and continue on their journey. It dawns on us one morning, when the coffee is extra strong and frothy, that what we've been witnessing is in fact a recent exhibition by the Canadian artist Germaine Koh at the Katriona Jeffries Gallery. *Shell* is one of Koh's recent explorations into the behaviors and situations that define and construct public and private space. Fashioned from aluminum, plexiglass, and plywood, Koh has modified the glass-fronted private space of the gallery. An enclosure is built on the inside of the space, attached to the existing glass front of the gallery, but with a pane of glass removed in order to create free access to the structure from the street. In contrast to the gallery, the public has access to this space 24 hours a day. Resembling a bus shelter, and conjuring up metaphors of crustacean shells (Szewczyk, 2005) this in-between space which is both and neither private or public, exposes the vulnerability of private space, the fragility of safety, seclusion, and property (Koh, 2005). As Monica Szewczyk (2005) writes in the exhibition text, Koh's space accentuates both the contemplation of time, and the wasting or killing of time. Koh's architectural intervention is a transitory space, waiting to be filled and acted upon, inviting participation in the in-between. It is this openness, uncertainty, and exposure of meaning that situates this work and others like it, as potential acts that allow us to inquire into and create new models for thinking and conducting research. Just as Koh's art presents a vulnerable space between private and public, how might we begin to think of research methodologies as relational situations that provoke meaning through contemplation, complication, and as alternative models of space and time?

In this chapter, we introduce the features of a/r/tography. We draw on scholarship from philosophy, phenomenology, educational action research, feminist theories, and contemporary art criticism to theorize the methodology of a/r/tography, with an attention to the *in-between* where meanings reside in the simultaneous use of language, images, materials, situations, space, and time.

A/r/tography is a research methodology that entangles and performs what Gilles Deleuze and Felix Guattari (1987) refer to as a rhizome. A rhizome is an assemblage that moves and flows in dynamic momentum. The rhizome operates by variation, perverse mutation, and flows of intensities that penetrate meaning, opening it to what Jacques Derrida (1978) calls the "as yet unnamable which begins to proclaim itself" (p. 293). It is an interstitial space, open and vulnerable where meanings and understandings are interrogated and ruptured. Building on the concept of the rhizome, a/r/tography radically transforms the idea of theory

DOI: 10.4324/9781003412892-18

as an abstract system distinct and separate from practice. In its place, theory is understood as a critical exchange that is reflective, responsive, and relational, which is continuously in a state of reconstruction and becoming something else altogether. As such, theory *as* practice becomes an embodied, living space of inquiry (Meskimmon, 2003).

In turn, rhizomes activate the *in-between*; an invitation to explore the interstitial spaces of art making, researching, and teaching. According to Elizabeth Grosz (2001):

> The space of the in-between is the locus for social, cultural and natural transformations: it is not simply a convenient space for movements and realignments but in fact is the only place – the place around identities, between identities – where becoming, openness to futurity, outstrips the conservational impetus to retain cohesion and unity.
>
> (pp. 91–105)

Like Koh's *Shell*, the in-between disrupts dualisms (private and public or neither). Similarly, it is not merely a physical location or object but a *process*, a movement and displacement of meaning (Grosz, 2001). Contemporary art criticism argues that the relationship between artist and place is a complex discourse where place is re-imagined as "situation." Site moves from a fixed geographical category to a relational constitution of social, economic, cultural, and political processes (Doherty, 2004; Kwon, 2002). Process becomes intertextually and multiply located in the context of discursive operations. It is a process of invention rather than interpretation, where concepts are marked by social engagements and encounters. Again we turn to Deleuze and Guattari (1994) and their arguments: "[c]oncepts are centres of vibrations, each in itself and every one in relation to all the others. This is why they all resonate rather than cohere or correspond with each other" (p. 23). Meaning and understanding are no longer revealed or thought to emanate from a point of origin rather they are *complicated* as relational, rhizomatic, and singular.[2]

A/r/tography as practice-based research is situated in the in-between, where theory-as-practice-as-process-as-complication intentionally unsettles perception and knowing through living inquiry. Our chapter will examine the constructs and conditions of a/r/tographical research: as practice-based research, as communities of practice, as relational aesthetics, and through six renderings of engagement. The chapter further complicates the space of doing a/r/tographical research, unfolding a series of questions about the possibilities and challenges of practicing this form of qualitative research.

## Practice-Based Theoretical Underpinnings

Our understandings of practice-based research are informed by feminist, post-structuralist, hermeneutic, and other postmodern theories that understand the production of knowledge as difference thereby producing different ways of living in the world (St. Pierre, 2000). One way of understanding this is through theories of touch and intercorporeality (Springgay, 2003, 2004a, 2004b, 2005a, 2005b, 2006, 2022; Springgay & Freedman, 2007). Western thought has been primarily influenced by Cartesian rationalism which isolates the distinct and autonomous subject, whose "vision" of the world is separate and distanced from the object perceived. "I see" is commonly understood to mean "I know." Thus, distant, objective vision is a means by which to judge or examine phenomena. However, a phenomenological, feminist, and/or a/r/tographical approach to understanding through touch reconfigures the ways in which we perceive objects, providing access to depth and surface, inside and outside

(Grosz, 1994; Merleau-Ponty, 1968). Touch expresses active involvement with the subject matter. Touch becomes a mode of knowing through proximity and relationality and poses different ways of making sense of the world, challenging the mechanisms of visual perception. Similarly, it draws attention to sensory experiences and knowledge that is interconnected with our bodies and with others.

In contrast to rationalist thought which imposes system and order, classifying and categorizing the world in dualistic terms, where individual consciousness is viewed as private, self-contained, and invisible, theories of touch propose that subjects are interconnected. According to Maurice Merleau-Ponty (1968) "to comprehend is to apprehend by coexistence" (p. 188) and Jean Luc Nancy (2000) reiterates this concept, maintaining that meaning is constituted between beings. A/r/tography resides in this intercorporeal space, and attends to the forms and folds of living bodies. It is a thinking that reflects on interembodiment, on being(s)-in-relation, and communities of practice. Research becomes a process of exchange that is not separated from the body but emerges through an intertwining of mind and body, self and other, and through our interactions with the world (see Springgay & Irwin, 2004; Irwin et al., 2024).

What emerges from such considerations is an understanding of embodiment as "being in motion" (Ellsworth, 2005). Yet this "being in motion" is not the act of a hand moving a paintbrush, or a dancer's limbs being catapulted across the stage. Such understandings of the arts and embodiment are limiting and superficial, akin to Gardner's theories of multiple intelligences. While "movement" can be embodied, it isn't always. Likewise, a painter can sweep their arms across a canvas and it can be a disembodied action. Rather, embodiment is constituted through the self/body's movement, force, action, and transformation "in the making" (Ellsworth, 2005). Accordingly, Elizabeth Ellsworth (2005) contends: "embodiment puts us into a moving relation with forces, processes, and connections to other in ways that are unforeseen by consciousness and unconnected to identity" (p. 121). This immediate, living, and unfolding body is enmeshed with an understanding of the cultural location and the specificity of the body (Garoian & Gaudelius, 2007).

> Embodiment is not about identity per se, a topic of earlier performative representations, but about subjectivity. As such, embodiment is not an immutable signifier of identity, but is a signifier of multiplicity existing within a complex web of cultural understandings and significations.
>
> (Garoian & Gaudelius, 2007, p. 9)

Likewise it is dangerous to suggest that the arts are more suited to embodied forms of learning and research. This continues to perpetuate a cognitive/bodied divide between the arts and other (the "serious" or "hard") disciplines. Rather, as Ellsworth (2005) argues, "some knowings cannot be conveyed through language" (p. 156) and as such invite us to "acknowledge the existence of forms of knowing that escape the efforts of language to reference a 'consensual', 'literal', 'real' world" (p. 156). This knowing, Ellsworth purports, moves us beyond "explanation" that can be commodified, captured, and in essence "taught," toward a way(s) of knowing that is rooted in embodiment as being in motion, relational, and singular. The arts, or a/r/tographical research, we argue, provide potential time-space intervals for the "coming of a knowing" (Ellsworth, 2005, p. 158).

For instance, recent bodies of literature in the arts and education are exploring how practices inherent in the work of artists and educators are indeed forms of research. The intellectual, imaginative, and insightful work created by artists and educators as practitioners is grounded in ongoing forms of recursive and reflexive inquiry engaged in theorizing for understanding. This perspective is in contrast to long standing traditions – that have enveloped both the arts and education – in which research is perceived as a means of gathering and interpreting data using traditions steeped in social-science disciplines such as sociology, history, and anthropology, or in natural-science disciplines such as biology. Though these traditions and their research paradigms address questions of great interest to society, they have a particular orientation to knowledge that is quite different from inquiry steeped in the practices of many artists and educators. Whereas the disciplinary-based science traditions perceive research and theory as a means of explaining phenomenon or revealing meaning, practitioner-based research perceives research as a disposition for knowledge creation and understanding through acts of theorizing as complication. In the earlier instance, theory and research serves to find answers to questions. In practitioner-based research, theorizing through inquiry seeks understanding by way of an evolution of questions within the living-inquiry processes of the practitioner. In other words, practitioners are interested in an ongoing quest for understanding, a questing if you will. This active stance to knowledge creation through questioning informs their practices making their inquiries timely, emergent, generative, and responsive to all those involved.

Many people see artists as practitioners (see Brown, 2000) and educators as practitioners (see Britzman, 2003). Graeme Sullivan, an advocate of art practice as research, argues for practice-based research and states that theorizing for understanding through practice is "grounded in the praxis of human engagement and yield[s] outcomes that can be seen to be individually liberating and culturally enlightening" (2004, p. 74). He goes on to state: "If a measure of the utility of research is seen to be the capacity to create new knowledge that is individually and culturally transformative, then criteria need to move beyond probability and plausibility to *possibility*" (italics in original, p. 72). These ideas resonate with the work of Terrance Carson and Dennis Sumara (1997) who talk about action research as a living practice. In educational circles, teacher research is a practitioner-based form of action research. Carson and Sumara talk about educators who, as action researchers, are deeply committed to meditative and contemplative practices: "lived experiences that permit an openness to the complexity of the relations among things and people" (1997, p. xv). Although they suggest that a commitment to writing is required in living a life of awareness, they also acknowledge the potential of an artistic commitment to changing habits of expression. In this way, practices are not comfortable taken-for-granted ways of being but are rather the challenging practices of learning to perceive differently within our everyday practices. Carson and Sumara state:

> As all artists know, the greatest challenge to producing works that interrupt normalized ways of perceiving and understanding is to learn to perceive freshly .... Learning to perceive differently, then, requires that one engage in *practices* that, in some way, remove one from the comfortable habits of the familiar.
>
> (1997, italics in original, p. xvii)

When asked how one conducts a life committed to educational action research, they suggest:

> Who one *is* becomes completely caught up in what one knows and does. This effectively eliminates the tiresome *theory/practice* problem that continues to surface in discussions

> of educational action research, for it suggests that what is thought, what is represented, what is acted upon, are all intertwined aspects of lived experience and, as such, cannot be discussed or interpreted separately.
>
> (1997, italics in original, p. xvii)

We would go a step further by saying that knowing (theoria), doing (praxis), and making (poesis) are three forms of thought important to a/r/tography (see Leggo, 2001; Sullivan, 2000). Relationships between and among these ways of understanding experience are integral to an intertextuality and intratextuality of ideas and form a foundation for a/r/tography (see Irwin, 2003; 2004). All three ways of understanding experience, theoria, praxis, and poesis, are folded together and form rhizomatic ways of experiencing the world. This is important as we come to appreciate how a/r/tography is conceived as research. Thus,

> action research [and a/r/tography] practices are deeply hermeneutic and postmodern practices, for not only do they acknowledge the importance of self and collective interpretation, but they deeply understand that these interpretations are always in a state of becoming and can never be fixed into predetermined and static categories.
>
> (Carson & Sumara, 1997, p. xviii)

Whereas many forms of research are concerned with reporting knowledge that already exists or finding knowledge that needs to be uncovered, action research and a/r/tography are concerned with *creating the circumstances* to produce knowledge and understanding through inquiry-laden processes (see Irwin et al., 2006).

### Communities of Practice

Practitioner-based research is necessarily about self but it is also about communities of practice. Individuals committed to inquiry are situated in communities of practice. Deborah Britzman suggests that for teachers:

> To theorize about one's experience means to engage one's reflective capacities in order to be an author of that experience .... The sources of theory, then, are in practice; in the lived lives of teachers, in the values, beliefs, and deep conviction enacted in practice, in the social context that encloses such practice, and in the social relationships that enliven the teaching and learning encounter.
>
> (2003, pp. 64–65)

Through a dialogical perspective teachers are able to engage in independent and socially transformative activities by theorizing practice.

Relations between and among teachers, students, and society are important to this dialogical perspective. Yet, this is also true for artists, audiences, and institutions. Relations in artistic communities of practice are equally important. Artists do not create in a void. Their work is necessarily related to the work of others, and their theorizing happens within communities of affiliation. Whether as an artist, educator, or researcher, a/r/tographers acknowledge the work of others in the documentation of their own work. For many this would mean attending exhibitions or performances or reading about artists and sharing this knowledge in one's a/r/tographic work. It would also mean reading about research in education and sharing the work of educational researchers. Citational practices are important for a community of practice-based researchers wanting to understand a body of literature and work in their fields while positioning their own work within those and potentially other fields. Furthermore, as a/r/tographers work with others, the potential exists for many individuals and groups to become a/r/tographers in a way that is appropriate for them. Thus, primary teachers can be a/r/tographers working with young children who may engage in age-appropriate forms of a/r/tographic practice. Alternatively, community-based artists could be a/r/tographers working with community members who in turn become a/r/tographers as they rethink taken-for-granted ways of being in their communities. In essence, it is the intertextual situations that provoke a/r/tographical research, not necessarily academic intentions (Irwin et al., 2008).

A/r/tography is steeped in the practices of artist-educators committed to ongoing living inquiry and it is this inquiry that draws forth the identity of a researcher. Artist/researcher/teacher identities contiguously exist in relationship to one another (see Springgay et al., 2005). In communities of a/r/tographers, it may be that separate communities of artists, educators, and researchers exist yet it is more likely that hybrid communities of artists, educators, and researchers locate themselves in the space of the in-between to create self-sustaining interrelating identities that inform, enhance, evoke, and/or provoke one another. It is here that a definition of artist and educator should be considered.

A/r/tography as living inquiry necessarily opens the way to describing and interpreting the complexity of experience among researchers, artists, and educators, as well as the lives of the individuals within the communities they interact with. As a result, it also opens the topics, contexts, and conditions of inquiry. Although a/r/tography privileges the identities of artist, researcher, and teacher within its name one needs to be thoughtful about how these identities might be conceptualized. For instance, educator may be a more inclusive title for the identity of the individual we are imagining. Many artists and educators have questioned the boundaries placed upon their identities and as such have interrupted the hegemony of schooling as a primary location for education (see Barone, 2001) as well as the hegemony of art-world establishments as primary gatekeepers to art and art institutions. With this said, it is important to point out that education in the context of a/r/tography is broadly conceived to mean any contexts concerned with learning, understanding, and interpretation. Therefore, educators who consider themselves a/r/tographers are those individuals who are committed to acts of learning, teaching, understanding, and interpreting within communities of learners. Similarly, within a/r/tography, art is broadly conceived to mean sensory-oriented products understood, interpreted, or questioned through ongoing engagements and encounters with the world. Artists are therefore committed to acts of creation, transformation, and resistance. Artists engaged in a/r/tography need not be earning a living through their art, but they need to be committed to artistic engagement through ongoing living inquiry. Educators engaged in a/r/tography need not be K-12 educators, nor educators within higher education, but they need to be committed to educational engagement that is rooted in learning and learning communities, through ongoing living inquiry. In this way, both artists and educators can be found in many contexts employing a range of ideas and materials. Perhaps more importantly, the relationship between artists and educators becomes somewhat blurred using our definitions. Both artists and educators are concerned with learning, change, understanding, and interpretation. It is in this complex space of the in-between that the disposition of inquiry brings us to a researcher identity through an implicit and explicit commitment to ongoing living inquiry across the domains of art and education. Earlier, we stated that action research is concerned with creating the circumstances to produce and complicate knowledge and understanding through inquiry-laden processes. In effect, a/r/tographers are concerned with creating the circumstances that produce knowledge and understanding through *artistic and educational* inquiry-laden processes.

## The Relational In-Between of Space and Time

A/r/tography is a process of unfolding image and text together (image in this sense could mean poetry, music, or other forms of artistic inquiry). As a research methodology that intentionally unsettles perception and complicates understandings, how we come to know and live within space and time is subsequently altered. Since the 1960s artists have engaged in what has commonly come to be understood as site-specific work. Miwon Kwon (2002) identifies various permutations of this form including site- determined, site-oriented, site-referenced, site-responsive, and site-related. All of these various terms are concerned with the relationship between the art work and its site; how the production, presentation, and reception of the work incorporated the physical conditions of a particular location (Kwon, 2002). However, as Kwon argues, the term "site" itself needs to be redefined not through physical or local terms, but as a complex figure in the unstable relationship between location and identity. In other words "sites" are not geographically bound, but informed by context, where "context [is] an impetus, hindrance, inspiration and research subject for the process of making art" (Doherty, 2004, p. 8). Site is not a fixed category but constituted through social, economic, cultural, and political processes, which Nicholas Bourriaud (2001, 2002, 2004) calls *relational aesthetics*. Like Kwon, Bourriaud contends that in "site-specific" art or "situations" (see Doherty, 2004) both process and outcome is marked by social engagements. These encounters breakdown the conventional relationships between artist, art work, and audience. The artists and art works that are the subjects of Kwon and Bourriaud's investigations create art as a socially useful activity:

> The forms that [the artist] presents to the public [does] not constitute an artwork until they are actually used and occupied by people.
>
> (Bourriaud, 2004, p. 46)

In this instance the audience moves from beholder of art (interpretation) to interlocutor (analyzer). In many instances audiences are actually called to a specific time and place where they become active participants in the art work, and thus argues Bourriaud (2004) alternative modes of sociality are created. *Shell* exemplifies this slippage between time and space, a condition of relational aesthetics. Meaning making within relational aesthetics is embodied in the intercorporeal negotiations between things.

Another theoretical way of understanding relationality of space and time is through complexity theory. According to Carson and Sumara (1997) complexity theory "suggests that the world is organized and patterned in ways that can be mathematically modeled but not in a predictive, linear, or deterministic manner" (p. xviii). Understandings emerge "from the associative relations among complex interactions" (p. xix). Therefore how we make meaning of images and texts is contingent upon the relations between artist (or in this case let us say a/r/tographer), art work, text, and audience and social, cultural, economic, and political contexts, and the ways these relations are altered by what Derrida (1978) calls the "as yet unnamable which begins to proclaim itself" (p. 293) – that which is not readily apparent. Thus, relationality is more than just the contexts that are brought to bear on particular "sites" but the potentialities and the "other thans" (Springgay, 2004a, 2004b) that continuously evolve and provoke meaning. Merleau-Ponty (1968) writes of this intertwining between self and other, inside and outside, as a way of becoming folded together in a porous encounter that leads to openings between subjects. Each subject is created through encounters *with* others and it is this *with* that creates the contiguity and distinctiveness of aesthetic forms (see Nancy, 2000).

In western cultures, time is typically perceived as uniformly flowing without regard for individuals, events, or contexts. Space is typically perceived as a container or even a vast emptiness (outer space). Yet artists, poets, performance artists, novelists, and musicians perceive time and space differently. They often speak of time as pausing, enduring, changing, interrupting, and pacing, and speak of space as openness, fragmented, endless, confined, and connected. Artists see time and space as conditions for living, conditions for engaging with the world through inquiry. After all, how we perceive time and space in the world affects how we engage with the world.

Educators also see time and space in particular ways. Complexity theories of learning (Davis et al., 2000) describe learning as participatory and evolutionary. Learning therefore is never predictable and is understood to be a participation in the world, a kind of co-evolution of those learning together. Thus, learners would be interested in keeping pace with their changing yet evolving circumstances. One might call this relational learning in that contiguous entities such as mind/body, theory/practice, or artist/researcher/teacher are not separate or dichotomous but are "enfolded in and unfold[ed] from one another" (p. 73) as learning becomes more sophisticated, flexible, and creative within acts of relationality. The notion of a fold (see Springgay, 2003, 2004a, 2004b) is important to a/r/tography as it suggests an infinite number of undulating entities unable to be separated into parts: in fact, through un/folding more folding may result. Understanding a/r/tography as un/folding the phenomena and/or identities being studied "can be simultaneously seen as a whole, a part of a whole, or as a complex compilation of smaller wholes" (Davis et al., 2000, p. 73). Therefore, learning becomes concerned with critical concepts rather than isolated facts, and the interconnections between concepts – learning as rhizomatic.

## Conceptual Practices: Renderings

The research conditions of a/r/tography reside in several notions of relationality: relational inquiry, relational aesthetics, and relational learning. Mieke Bal (2002) and Irit Rogoff (2000) have informed our work through their discussions of interdisciplinarity. Rogoff suggests that an emphasis upon process rather than method allows an active space for participation that lies between existing disciplines and their methodologies while resisting the formation of new methodological criteria. It is this process space that alludes to the conditions for research. Furthermore, we look to Bal for an understanding of how to engage with these relational aspects. She suggests that interdisciplinarity "must seek its heuristic and methodological basis in *concepts* rather than *methods*" (italics in original, 2002, p. 5).

We interpret concepts to be flexible, intersubjective locations through which close analysis renders new understandings and meanings. These concepts or renderings, as we prefer to call them, guide our active participation in making meaning through artful, educational, and creative inquiry. Renderings offer possibilities for engagement and do not exist alone but in relation to one another. Though it is tempting to suggest these renderings are criteria for a/r/tography, they are better perceived as rendered possibilities.

Renderings are embedded in the processes of artful inquiry (in any art form such as music, dance, drama, poetry, and visual arts) and writing. To be engaged in a/r/tography means to inquire in the world through both processes, noting that they are not separate or illustrative processes but interconnected processes. Relational inquiring through relational aesthetics and relational learning is constitutive rather than descriptive and may represent the work of a single a/r/tographer, a community of a/r/tographers and/or an audience member's process of meaning making. Each individual and group informs and shapes the living inquiry. Therefore, renderings are concepts that help a/r/tographers portray the conditions of their work for others. Elsewhere, we have interpreted each rendering in great detail (Springgay et al., 2005). For the purpose of this chapter we would like to briefly describe each of the six renderings: contiguity, living inquiry, metaphor/metonymy, openings, reverberations, and excess.

## Contiguity

Contiguity is a rendering that helps us understand those ideas within a/r/tography that lie adjacent to one another, touch one another, or exist in the presence of one another. This happens in several ways. First of all, contiguity is found with the artist, researcher and teacher identities existing simultaneously and alongside one another. The forward slash or fold portrays this act of contiguity. Secondly, contiguity is found in the relationship between art and graphy, that is, between the art form and writing with, in, or about the phenomenon. And thirdly, contiguity is found in the act of double imaging between art as an activity or product and a/r/t as a symbolic representation of the three constituent identities. To live the life of an a/r/tographer is to live a contiguous life sensitive to each of these relationships and particularly to the spaces in-between. Being attentive to the in-between spaces opens opportunities for dynamic living inquiry. A/r/tographers may visualize these in-between spaces as parts of an endless fold, or folds within folds, or as concepts linked together. A/r/tographers may or may not choose to include text as part of their art forms but they will always include textual materials and writing in their ongoing inquiry processes (Richardson, 1994). This includes citing and engaging with the work of other artists, researchers, and educators as a/r/tographers pursue their inquiries. These acts of contiguity ensure relational inquiry and learning amid an attention toward relational aesthetics.

## Living Inquiry

Living inquiry, another rendering, refers to the ongoing living practices of being an artist, researcher, and educator. Elsewhere we have defined living inquiry as "an embodied encounter constituted through visual and textual understandings and experiences rather than mere visual and textual representations" (Springgay et al., 2005, p. 902). Though this definition privileges the visual, any sensory form can be applied. Living inquiry is a life commitment to the arts and education through acts of inquiry. These acts are theoretical, practical, and artful ways of creating meaning through recursive, reflective, responsive yet resistant forms of engagement. A/r/tography is a methodology of embodiment, of continuous engagement with the world: one that interrogates yet celebrates meaning. A/r/tography is a living practice, a life-creating experience examining our personal, political, and/or professional lives. It uses a fluid orientation within the contiguous relationships described earlier. Its rigor comes from its continuous reflective and reflexive stance to engagement, analysis, and learning. This can include any qualitative form of data collection such as interviews, journal writing, field diaries, artifact collections, and photo documentation, yet it can also encompass any form of artistic inquiry such as painting, composing music, and writing poetry, and educational inquiry such as student journal writing, teacher diaries, narratives, and parent surveys. The reflexive and reflective stance to analysis will be ongoing and may include aspects from traditional ethnographic forms of inquiry such as constantly comparing themes that emerge from the data. What is important is the attention given to ongoing inquiry through an evolution of research questions and understandings. It is here that the difference between thesis and exegesis is important. Most research is designed to answer, address, or create a proposition that is advanced through an argument. This is called a thesis. In a/r/tography and other arts-based or arts-informed types of research, an exegesis is more suitable. An exegesis is a critical explanation of the meaning within a work. In the arts, an exegesis is often extended to include any documentation that contextualizes the work (see Sullivan, 2004) and helps to critique or give direction to theoretical ideas. Some theorists suggest that this documentation should not be considered research but rather the method by which ideas are conceived (see De Freitas, 2002). We prefer to see the process of living inquiry, as well as the understanding created through the inquiry, as comprising the full research enterprise. An exegesis provides opportunities to do just that.

From time to time, a/r/tographers may choose to share their inquiries with others and it is here that products are refined and shared. These living-inquiry moments are not end results but rather understandings of experiences along the way. Thus, a/r/tography needs to be pursued continuously over time while searching for ways to disseminate aspects of the work at particular moments in time. Artists may wish to display or perform their artistic works in particular venues while educators may wish to share their scholarly engagements in other venues. Though these endeavors are not separate, there are times when particular aspects may be highlighted for unique audiences.

## Metaphor and Metonymy

A/r/tographers will naturally favor the third rendering: metaphor and metonymy. Through metaphors and metonyms, we make sense of the world and we make relationships accessible to our senses (see Richardson, 2002). Both tropes open possibilities for meaning making: metaphor through its substitution of signifiers and metonym through its displacement of subject/object relations (see Aoki et al., 2001). Metaphors and metonyms exist as intertwined relationships in which meaning un/creates itself. There is at once a loss of meaning, a realization of meaning, or neither. Just as there is contiguous movement between other concepts so too is there between metaphor and metonymy. This movement reverberates in and through each rendering as struggles in understanding emerge and shifts in awareness take place. It is in these struggles that openings are created.

## Openings

One purpose of a/r/tography is to open up conversations and relationships instead of informing others about what has been learned. Another purpose of a/r/tography is to open up possibilities for a/r/tographers as they give their attention to what is seen and known and what is not seen and not known. Openings are not necessarily passive holes through which one can see easily. Openings are often like cuts, tears, ruptures, or cracks that resist predictability, comfort, and safety. It is here that knowledge is often created as contradictions and resistances are faced, even interfaced with other knowledge. Meanings are negotiated by, with, and among a/r/tographers as well as with their audiences. It is in these conversations that multiple exchanges co-exist and reverberate together.

### Reverberations

Reverberations refer to a dynamic movement, dramatic or subtle, that forces a/r/tographers to shift their understandings of a phenomenon. Reverberations often take us deeper into meanings or they shift us toward a slippage of meaning. Pollock talks about nervous performative writing in a similar fashion, suggesting that it "anxiously crosses various stories, theories, texts, intertexts, and spheres of practice, unable to settle into a clear, linear course, neither willing nor able to stop moving, restless, transient and transitive" (1998, pp. 91–99).

### Excess

Research then becomes an evocation, a provocation, calling us to transformation. This transformation often happens with some attention to the final rendering of excess (see Bataille, 1985). Excess is that which is created when control and regulation disappear and we grapple with what lies outside the acceptable. Excess may deal with the monstrous, the wasteful, the leftover, and the unseen, as well as the magnificent and the sublime. It is also the "as yet unnamable" the "other than" – those aspects of our lives and experiences that are potentials and filled with possibility. Excess opens up opportunities for complexifying the simple and simplifying the complex by questioning how things come into being and the nature of their being.

Renderings, as the conceptual practices of a/r/tography move into the boundaries between theory, practice, and creative activity and allow each to impact one another. A rigorous attending to the renderings will result in deep interactions within the relational conditions of relational inquiry, relational aesthetics, and relational learning. An assessment of any a/r/tographic work will depend upon its compelling ability to yield access to, and new insights about, a particular phenomenon.

## Practicing A/r/tography: Contributions and Challenges

If encounters like the work of *Shell* embody an a/r/tographical position, how does one engage in a/r/tographical educational research? Without appearing pedantic in responding to this question, we firmly believe that a/r/tographical work entails living and inquiring in the in-between, of constantly questing, and complicating that which has yet to be named. The transformative power of theory as practice changes our understandings of research methodologies beyond the bounds of specificity and objectivity, toward an articulation of research as intercorporeality, relationality, and process. Residing at the in-between, a/r/tographers dwell in the space and time of contemplation insisting on the openness of everyday phenomena (see Irwin, 2006). Like *Shell*, a/r/tography is an interstitial process, where encounters between subjects, thoughts, and actions propose new assemblages and situations. Furthermore, a/r/tographical research calls for an interrelation between image (or any artistic and creative form) and text, not that one is descriptive of the other. Visual encounters exist simultaneously with textual understandings. Thus, the construction of a/r/tographical research goes beyond the insertion of images into a research paper or dissertation. It is a way of living, inquiring, and being that is relational.

This last point however, enters us into another struggle, namely that of assessment and measurement. How do we evaluate and judge an a/r/tographical work? Once again we turn to philosopher Jean Luc Nancy (see 2000) to assist us with this task. In his essay *Human Excess*, Nancy contends that the engagement with measurement is a matter of bringing a certain responsibility to light. Rather than an understanding of excess as a numerical equivalent (10, 400, or 2 million) we need to think of excess as elements of discourse in its totality. Measurement is not a degree of magnitude, but rather magnitude itself is the infinite totality of Being – the measurement of no other. Excess becomes an unheard of measure. In other words measurement is not qualifying something against something else – the setting of criteria or an established norm. Rather the conditions for measurement (assessment) are contingent upon and exist within the structure itself – an absolute measure.

In this sense an a/r/tographical act is its own possible measure. Instead of thinking of our actions, encounters, and thoughts – our living inquiry as substance that can be arranged in discrete moments, counted, and subjected to normative evaluations, we need to understand living inquiry as responsibility. However, "To be responsible is not, primarily, being indebted to or accountable before some normative authority. It is to be engaged by its Being to the very end of this Being, in such a way that this engagement or *conatus* is the very essence of Being" (Nancy, 2000, p. 183). We are not responsible *for* our own actions or the actions of others (a passive approach that separates and distances) but our very Being, our subjectivities, identities, and ways of living in the world are gestures and situations that struggle with, contest, challenge, provoke, and embody an ethics of understanding and a responsibility. Responsibility itself resides in the in-between. Stepping outside the glass front of the gallery – our personal shell – turning a corner onto the city street, we may be hailed by other situations; unexpected gestures and invitations to all responsible persons.

## Postscript

Gathering over zoom, Irwin and Springgay discussed the saliency of the original chapter, and the central concepts explored. While written almost 20 years ago, in-betweeness, living inquiry, site specificity and place, and renderings are pliable propositions that continue to invoke an a/r/tographical practice that is intimate, process oriented, and expressive. A/r/tography emerged at a time when arts-based forms of research were emerging, and there was much debate as to its value, accountability, and artistic merit in the academy. A/r/tography prioritized the living nature of inquiry, as opposed to a static artistic form of dissemination, and sought to rupture binary oppositions that continue to dominate colonial knowledge systems. Emphasizing a research and pedagogical practice committed to transcorporeality and materiality a/r/tography was never a "how to" manual, but rather an orientation to living in the world affectively and ethically. The renderings were meant to expand, transform, and become un/done in various iterations, where scholars could emphasize their own linguistic, cultural, and place-based contexts. While the concepts expressed in the chapter are still relevant to a/r/tography in this moment, the authors discussed how the significance of a/r/tography is its commitment to living inquiry, which means reckoning with the past, present and future including decolonial and anti-oppressive research practices. In re-printing an almost 20-year old publication, the authors thought about the future of a/r/tography as pliable propositions that are responsible to, and accountable to a future yet-to-come.

## Notes

1 "A/r/tography as practice-based research," by Rita Irwin and Stephanie Springgay first appeared in Springgay, S., Irwin, R. L., Leggo, C., & Gouzouasis, P. (Eds.). (2008). *Being with a/r/tography*. Sense. Permission to republish provided by Brill.

2 Singularity in this usage is derived from Jean Luc Nancy's (2000) theories of "being-singular-plural." For Nancy (2000) to be a body is to be "with" other bodies, to touch, to encounter, and to be exposed. In other words, each individual body is brought into being through encounters with other bodies. It is the relationality between bodies that creates a particular understanding of shared existence. Relationality depends on singularity. A singular body, argues Nancy (2000) "is not individuality; it is, each time, the punctuality of a 'with' that establishes a certain origin of meaning and connects it to an infinity of other possible origins" (p. 85). Peter Hallward (2001) substantiates this with: "The singular proceeds internally and is constituted in its own creation. The singular, in each case, is constituent of itself, expressive of itself, immediate to itself" (p. 3). Criteria are not external but are determined through its actions. Nikki Sullivan (2003) provides us with a further explanation: "Each 'one' is singular (which isn't the same as saying each 'one' is individual) while simultaneously being in-relation" (p. 55). Singularity, as a theoretical construct, demands that self and other no longer hold opposing positions. Bodies/selves cannot exist without other bodies/selves, nor are the two reducible to one another.

## References


Aoki, T. T., Low, M., & Palulis, P. (2001). *Re-reading metonymic moments with/in living pedagogy*. Paper presented at the American Educational Research Association Annual Meeting.

Bal, M. (2002). *Traveling concepts in the humanities*. University of Toronto Press.

Barone, T. (2001). *Touching eternity: The enduring outcomes of teaching*. Teachers College Press.

Bataille, G. (1985). *Visions of excess: Selected writings 1927–1939* (A. Stockl, Trans.). University of Minnesota Press.

Bourriaud, N. (2001). *Post production*. Les presses du réel.

Bourriaud, N. (2002). *Relational aesthetics*. Les presses du réel.

Bourriaud, N. (2004). Berlin letter about relational aesthetics. In C. Doherty (Ed.), *From studio to situation* (pp. 43–49). Black Dog Publishing.

Britzman, D. P. (2003). *Practice makes practice: A critical study of learning to teach*. SUNY Press.

Brown, N. (2000). The representation of practice. Working Papers in Art and Design (vol. 1). https://www.herts.ac.uk/__data/assets/pdf_file/0016/12283/WPIAAD_vol1_brown.pdf

Carson, T. R., & Sumara, D. J. (Eds.). (1997). *Action research as a living practice*. Peter Lang.

Davis, B., Sumara, D., & Luce-Kapler, R. (2000). *Engaging minds: Learning and teaching in a complex world*. Lawrence Erlbaum.

De Freitas, N. (2002). Towards a definition of studio documentation: Working tool and transparent method. Selected Working Papers in Art & Design (vol. 2). https://www.herts.ac.uk/__data/assets/pdf_file/0011/12305/WPIAAD_vol2_freitas.pdf

Deleuze, G., & Guattari, F. (1987). *A thousand plateaus: Capitalism and schizophrenia*. University of Minnesota Press.

Deleuze, G., & Guattari, F. (1994). *What is philosophy?* Columbia University Press.

Derrida, J. (1978). *Writing and difference*. University of Chicago Press.

Doherty, C. (2004). *From studio to situation*. Black Dog Publishing.

Ellsworth, E. (2005). *Places of learning: Media, architecture, pedagogy*. Routledge.

Garoian, C., & Gaudelius, Y. (2007). Performing embodiment: Pedagogical intersections of art, technology, and the body. In S. Springgay & D. Freedman (Eds.), *Curriculum and the cultural body* (pp. 3–20). Peter Lang.
Grosz, E. (1994). *Volatile bodies*. Indiana University Press.
Grosz, E. (2001). *Architecture from the outside: Essays on virtual and real space*. MIT Press.
Hallward, P. (2001). *Absolutely postcolonial: Writing between the singular and the specific*. Manchester University Press.
Irwin, R. L. (2003). Towards an aesthetic of unfolding in/sights through curriculum. *Journal of the Canadian Association for Curriculum Studies*, *1*(2), 63–78. https://doi.org/10.25071/1916-4467.16859
Irwin, R. L. (2004). A/r/tography: A metonymic métissage. In R. L. Irwin & A. de Cosson (Eds.), *A/r/tography: Rendering self through arts-based living inquiry* (pp. 27–38). Pacific Educational Press.
Irwin, R. L. (2006). Walking to create an aesthetic and spiritual currere. *Visual Arts Research*, *32*(1), 75–82.
Irwin, R. L., Beer, R., Springgay, S., Grauer, K., Gu, X., & Bickel, B. (2006). The rhizomatic relations of a/r/tography. *Studies in Art Education*, *48*(1), 70–88. https://doi.org/10.1080/00393541.2006.11650500
Irwin, R. L., Lasczik, A., Sinner, A., & Triggs, V. (Eds.). (2024). *A/r/tography: Essential readings and conversations*. Intellect.
Irwin, R. L., Springgay, S., & Kind, S. (2008). Communities of a/r/tographers engaged in living inquiry. In G. J. Knowles & A. L. Cole (Eds.), *International handbook of the arts in qualitative social science research* (pp. 83–92). Sage.
Koh, G. (2005). *Shell* [Public Installation]. https://www.germainekoh.com/works/shell
Kwon, M. (2002). *One place after another: Site-specific art and locational identity*. MIT Press.
Leggo, C. (2001). Research as poetic rumination: Twenty-six ways of listening to light. In L. Neilsen, A. L. Cole, & G. J. Knowles (Eds.), *The art of writing inquiry* (pp. 173–195). Backalong Books.
Merleau-Ponty, M. (1968). *The visible and the invisible* (A. Lingis, Trans.). Northwestern University Press.
Meskimmon, M. (2003). Corporeal theory with/in practice: Christine Borland's *Winter Garden*. *Art History*, *26*(3), 442–455. https://doi.org/10.1111/j.0141-6790.2003.02603007.x
Nancy, J. L. (2000). *Of being singular plural*. Stanford University Press.
Pollock, D. (1998). Performative writing. In P. Phelan (Ed.), *The ends of performance*, (pp. 73–103). New York University Press.
Richardson, L. (1994). Writing. A method of inquiry. In N. Denzin & Y. Lincoln (Eds.), *Handbook of qualitative research* (pp. 516–529). Sage.
Richardson, L. (2002). The metaphor is the message. In A. P. Bochner & C. Ellis (Eds.), *Ethnographically speaking: Autoethnography, literature, and aesthetics* (pp. 372–376). AltaMira Press.
Rogoff, I. (2000). *Terra infirma: Geography's visual culture*. Routledge.
Springgay, S. (2003). Cloth as intercorporeality: Touch, fantasy, and performance and the construction of body knowledge. *International Journal of Education and the Arts*, *4* (5). http://www.ijea.org/v4n5/
Springgay, S. (2004a). Inside the visible: Arts-based educational research as excess. *Journal of Curriculum and Pedagogy*, *1*(1), 8–18. https://doi.org/10.1080/15505170.2004.10411470
Springgay, S. (2004b). *Inside the visible: Youth understandings of body knowledge through touch* [Unpublished doctoral dissertation]. University of British Columbia.
Springgay, S. (2005a). Thinking through bodies: Bodied encounters and the process of meaning making in an email generated art project. *Studies in Art Education*, *47*(1), 34–50. https://doi.org/10.1080/00393541.2005.11652812
Springgay, S. (2005b). An intimate distance: Youth interrogations of inter-corporeal cartography as visual narrative text. *Journal of the Canadian Association of Curriculum Studies*, *3*(1), 107–122. https://doi.org/10.25071/1916-4467.16959
Springgay, S. (2006). Small gestures of the un/expected and the "thingness" of things. *Arts and Learning Research Journal*, *22*(1), 163–183.
Springgay, S. (2022). *Feltness: Socially-engaged art, research-creation, and affective pedagogies*. Duke University Press.
Springgay, S., & Freedman, D. (Eds.). (2007). *Curriculum and the cultural body*. Peter Lang.

Springgay, S., & Irwin, R. L. (2004). Women making art: Aesthetic inquiry as a political performance. In G. J. Knowles, L. Neilsen, A. L. Cole, & T. Luciani (Eds.), *Provoked by art: Theorizing arts-informed inquiry* (pp. 71–83). Backalong Books.

Springgay, S., Irwin, R. L., & Wilson Kind, S. (2005). A/r/tography as living inquiry through art and text. *Qualitative Inquiry, 11*(6), 897–912. https://doi.org/10.1177/1077800405280696

St. Pierre, E. (2000). *Working the ruins: Feminist poststructural theory and methods in education*. Routledge.

Sullivan, G. (2000). *Aesthetic education at the Lincoln Center Institute: An historical and philosophical overview*. Lincoln Center Institute.

Sullivan, G. (2004). *Art practice as research: Inquiry in the visual arts*. Sage.

Sullivan, N. (2003). Being, thinking, writing "with." *Cultural Studies Review*, 9(1), 51–59. https://doi.org/10.5130/csr.v9i1.3583

Szewczyk, M. (2005). *Chronocidal citizens*. https://germainekoh.com/content/press/szewczyk-cjg2005.html

Chapter 19

# Songwriting as Ethnographic Practice

## How Stories Humanize

*Kristina Jacobsen*

As a touring singer/songwriter,[1] ethnographer,[2] and honky-tonk artist living on the Navajo Nation for many years, songwriting and ethnography in my own work are two ends of a continuum linked through the central role of storytelling in our lives. Rather than two isolated and sometimes polarized domains—one "artistic" and the other "analytic"—I see songwriting and ethnographic writing as mutually feeding one another, not only as forms of artistic expression but also as genres that offer the capacity for what I call empathetic analysis. As a cultural anthropologist and Assistant Professor[3] of Music and Anthropology (Ethnology) at the University of New Mexico, I use empathetic analysis to inform my approach to teaching in classes such as the anthropology of music, Navajo (Diné) expressive culture, songwriting, and the student-led honky-tonk ensemble (http://www.facebook.com/UNMHonkyTonkEnsemble/; for videos, visit: https://vimeo.com/search?q=unm±honky±tonk±ensemble).

In this chapter, I reflect on my own work as both ethnographer/researcher and singer/songwriter to show how I use ethnography and songwriting to share my love and appreciation for a place I've now lived on and off for 20 years, the Navajo reservation in Arizona and New Mexico. As an Anglo (in this context, the local terminology to refer to someone who is white and non-Native) anthropologist, these roles are complicated and sometimes fraught. Drawing on my own roles in this sovereign space as a high school social studies teacher, volleyball coach, radio station deejay, park ranger, sheepherder, singer/lapsteel player in an all-male country band,[4] language learner, tribal college instructor, and, much more recently, as an anthropologist and songwriting facilitator, I reflect on how these experiences are channeled and then refracted through an original song, "Inez," from a recent solo album, *Three Roses* (to hear songs from this album, visit https://soundcloud.com/kristinajacobsenmusic/sets/three-roses-album-preview) and also through an ethnographically immersive songwriting retreat I led from 2016 to 2019 on the Navajo Nation. I then discuss my sense of connection to another part of the world that is more heritage-driven, reflecting on a show I recently played in a men's prison outside of Stockholm, Sweden. Here, I delve into a cowrite, "No Man's Land," a newer song inspired by the Syrian refugee crisis and its impact in suburban Sweden, performed while on tour in October 2016.[5]

I conclude by reflecting on the ways that songwriting and ethnographic writing are different tools that serve to narrate and humanize a small sliver of human experience for outsider (and sometimes insider) eyes and ears. I argue that paying as much attention to emotional authenticity and alchemy in our ethnographic writing as we do in our songs and paying as much attention to specificity, detail, and cultural nuance in our songs as we do in our

DOI: 10.4324/9781003412892-19

ethnographic writing serves to enliven our songs and broaden the resonance and applicability of our ethnographic work, as well.

## Ethnography

Long-term ethnographic fieldwork is used to get to know a community or culture from the inside out. As a methodology, it is by definition deeply immersive—"deep hanging out" (Geertz, 1998)[6]—and, at its best, serves to humanize communities that we as readers might not otherwise come to know or even care to know. The vehicle for this work, however, is the self. Ethnography, Ortner (2006) reminds us, "has always meant the attempt to understand another life world using the self—as much as it is possible—as the instrument of knowing" (p. 42). Ethnographic writing is the product of ethnographic fieldwork, a genre unique to anthropology that combines storytelling—thick description—with analysis.

Specificity, disturbing what we think we know, and crafting meaningful, sense-bound descriptions that invite an audience into a story are also central tenets of anthropological writing. Sense-bound writing—focusing on taste, touch, smell, hearing, sight, and what Pattison (2009) calls the kinesthetic sense—invites us immediately into a story and a lifeworld. If ethnography is understood not as a science but as an interpretive art (L. Meintjes, personal communication, October 1, 2012), then it is in the interpretation and the craft of writing about a lifeworld with compassion, depth, and nuance where the greatest skill—and challenge—arguably lies. At the same time, getting the facts right—down to the brand of someone's western boots, the spelling of someone's maternal clan, and knowing where the mutton was raised in the stew you ate the day before—and accurately reflecting the worldview of one's interlocutors is essential to one's credibility as an ethnographer. Thus, ethnographic writing—like songwriting—is a delicate balance between art and accuracy (a key difference, of course, is that songwriters have an artistic license to alter the details of a story that ethnographers do not).

Storytelling and narration are essential to both songwriting and ethnography, and utilizing visceral,[7] sense-bound imagery to invite the listener or reader deeply into a story (e.g., Fox, 2004; Samuels, 2004)—showing not telling—is part of what distinguishes a good song or ethnography from a great one. It is also part of what determines a listener's desire to enter the world that you create, as either songwriter or ethnographer, and their subsequent emotional investment in that world. Ethnographic writing—like songs—has the potential to change the way human beings respond to and treat one another, and in this way, does "real" work in the world, when and if we let it.

## Songwriting

Following Ortner (2006), my own songwriting uses the self as an instrument of knowing. In contrast to ethnographic writing, however, as songwriters we are also given license to make a more personal commentary on our subject, with the focus often on lived experience, using sense-bound writing to access that experience.[8] Here, telling an emotionally authentic story is the focus, creating investment from the listener's perspective to stay with the artist through the entire duration of a three-minute song.[9] This is labor intensive. "Getting to truth and beauty," Americana songwriter Mary Gauthier (2013, 2014, 2021) reminds us, "is effortful, hard work."[10]

Artfully crafted songs also humanize their subject. Gauthier's (2012) "Karla Faye,"[11] about executed death-row prisoner Karla Faye Tucker, is one example. Another is Gretchen

Peters's (2012) "Five Minutes,"[12] a story of a middle-aged waitress who is a single mom with a broken heart reminiscing on her life, and Steve Earle's (2002) "John Walker's Blues," about U.S. Taliban fighter John Walker Lindh,[13] is yet another (also, to my knowledge, the only country song incorporating Koranic chant). Songs also humanize, because the best songs help us as songwriters to connect back to our own sense of humanity in live performance; in the process, they allow listeners to connect back to their own humanity and to connect to each other, as well (Gauthier, 2013, 2014).[14,15] There can also be tremendous personal healing and catharsis through the songwriting process: through learning to write songs in our own authentic voice, we go from feeling narrated to learning to effectively and powerfully narrate our own stories, instead. The self as an instrument of knowing becomes the way to create narratives from our own stories and lived experience.

Songs take the particular and make it universal. Ironically, this universality—and what distinguishes a song with limited circulation from one that has the potential to universally resonate—is often grounded in specificity: this is what allows someone to identify a song as "their" song. Well-written songs allow others to latch on at whatever entry point they're able, and each richly descriptive line, each phrase that shows rather than tells, is a potential jumping-on point; conversely, each predictable rhyme and tritely described woe or joy (sometimes the critique of contemporary pop-country songs) is a potential jumping-off point, an exit sign where you lose your listener before your song—and your story—are fully heard.

## Songwriting and Ethnography

Songwriting and ethnography have the potential to feed one another—and feed me—in central ways. Operating in two genres allows me, as an educator, to reach a much broader audience than I might if I put my energies into one orbit, alone. For example, in thinking through an issue for an article—civic estrangement, heritage language politics, assimilation policies, or performances of masculinity by steer wrestlers on the Navajo Nation—these same issues often simultaneously show up in songs I'm writing. The empathy that I'm able to convey in the song—the ability to live into the lived experience of the character in the song—then translates back into the article or chapter, changing the way I frame my interlocutors and the argument I'm making. But, this is also true in reverse: the historic and ethnographic specificity I gain in the research process also surfaces more organically in the song lines, helping me to narrow down what the "point" of a particular song really is. In this way, the two genres co-craft one another.

Specificity is central to songwriting and ethnographic writing, where sense-bound imagery and specific places, times, and identities are essential to bringing listeners into a story. Specificity also matters because, as I like to tell my songwriting students, *stories* matter. As Glynn Washington (2016), host of the radio show *Snap Judgment* recently put it, referencing the Trumpian moment in the United States, "There is no way to hear someone's story and to continue to hate that person at the same time." Stories humanize.

## "Inez"

In my own ethnographic work, I focus on the politics of difference on the contemporary Navajo Nation, and in my first book, *The Sound of Navajo Country* (2017),[16] traced how these politics of difference are expressed by Diné citizens through choices about language use, musical taste, place of residence, recording technology, and musical equipment. My songwriting also focuses on many of these same issues, often narrated through the life experience of one person—or composite portraits of several people—I've come to know, care for, and feel connected to.

This is the case with the song "Inez," which focuses on a mentor, the first woman I learned to call mom or "*shimá*" in Navajo. Inez was my supervisor when I worked as a Ranger-in-training at Canyon de Chelly National Monument, the summer I also began to learn to speak Navajo. In these instances, sometimes the more analytic tack of ethnographic writing feels inadequate: expressing someone's story in song form provides catharsis, and performing a song provides a sense of shared connection with others that ethnographic writing, a less performative genre, rarely provides.[17] What songwriting and other expressive arts give us more tangibly is lived experience, from the inside out, produced within the formal and thematic constraints of a three-minute story (Fox, 2004, p. 242). If a song is well written, it gives us a direct line to an individual's personal pain, loss, triumphs, and stories of hope and regeneration, too.

The preamble, or stage patter, offered before a song to set it up is part of a singer/songwriter's performance toolkit. As I tell my songwriting students, this part of the performance is as important as the song itself and should be carefully planned and thought out. Rather than "explaining" what the song is about—like a poem or short story, a well-written song should always stand on its own—the stage patter should get the listener in the proper emotional frame of mind to hear the song. The preamble becomes the setup for deeper learning and emotional growth, creating a space where both listening and feeling heard can occur simultaneously. So, when I set up "Inez" in live performance, I typically offer one of three preambles[18] depending on the audience, my educated guess about what they already know about indigenous histories in the southwest, and their own potential political sensibilities.

The first talks about the Mormon Placement Program,[19] run by the Church of Latter Day Saints from 1947 to 2000, in which southwestern Indigenous children, because they were seen as being part of the "lost" tribes of Israel (also known as the "Lamanites"), were sent to live with Mormon families in Utah with the hopes that their skin would lighten or even become "white" in the process (Nephi 2:30, Book of Mormon).[20] Inez lived with an Anglo, Mormon family in Brigham City, Utah, a family she became very close to and refers to as her foster family.

The second introduces traditional *Diné* foodways, such as the word I use in the song for roasted corn, *neeshjízhii*—typically served in mutton stew. Thus, I'm able to teach my non-Native audience words of this beautiful but challenging tonal language. In contrast, when performing the song for Navajo audiences, *neeshjízhii* becomes an inside word, a secret language that only Diné listeners share and understand. In fact, the bandleader of the Navajo country band I played in, *Native Country Band*, refers to this song as the "*Neeshjízhii*" song.

Finally, I sometimes preface the song by discussing the popular T-Shirt that inspired the first line of the chorus, "homeland security, fighting terrorism since 1492." Featuring a black-and-white photograph of Chiricahua Apache leader, Geronimo, holding a rifle and flanked by other Chiricahua men, the caption is an ironic commentary behind the notion of "homeland security," a reappropriation of settler colonialism's reach into contemporary indigenous communities (Smith, 2009) and a redefining of who the "real" terrorists are from an indigenous perspective.

*"Inez"*[21] *(Kristina Jacobsen, copyright 2006, BMI)*

Inez, big smile, crooked teeth
White T-shirt, a Ranger's watchful eye
Foster parents in Brigham City
Stolen Generation, black hair and white lies

A Latter Day Saint, but she drinks pop and whisky
She loves spam, mutton stew with *neeshjízhii*
A sailor's gut, she's as calloused as they come
Oh Inez, she's American (she said I'm proud to be:)

**Chorus:**
Homeland Security
Fighting terror since 1492
Oh but our history
Is bittersweet
But this I know:
She said I'm proud to be a Navajo

She was born in Cameron, Arizona
Trading Post, selling Navajo rugs
Boarding School, ugly marks left upon her body
Hell, she's bitter, but she's also full of love (She's the backbone of)

**Chorus**
Who came first, what does that mean?
Politicians fight over who
Will defend our homeland under siege
She said: "we've already been doing that, for centuries"
She's proud to be:

**Chorus**
Oh but our history
Is bittersweet
But this I know:
She said I'm proud to be Diné

Perhaps most importantly, "Inez" allows me to paint a portrait of Indigenous resilience—one that feels emotionally authentic to my ethnographic experience living on the Navajo Nation—of a feisty, fiercely loving Diné woman with a bawdy sense of humor who loves mutton stew and who, as one music reviewer put it, has perhaps "been beaten down but not conquered" (Minter, 2015, n.p.).

Perhaps unsurprisingly, resilience is also the lens I use to frame the Navajo Nation in my writing and teaching. Resilience and a sense of connection to place are the central tenets of a cultural immersion-focused songwriting retreat on the Navajo Nation that I offered for the first time in June 2017, held on top of an Arizona mesa on a working ranch with no running water and hosted by a Navajo family.[22] Following the mantra that all stories happen somewhere (Basso, 1996, p. 143; Camus, 1955, p. 188), our workshop is guided by the principle that "all songs happen somewhere," and songs written on sovereign *Diné* land inevitably reflect the place in which they are written.[23] The second guiding principle for the workshop is that paying attention on purpose, a guiding tenet not only of ethnographic fieldwork but also of mindfulness meditation and songwriting, is essential for writing deeply immersed, place-based songs. An anglicized Navajo word such as "Yatahey" ("hello") is not the same as the Navajo word "Yá'át'ééh," and getting these differences and their nuances correct in a song—if one is brave enough to try to sing using glottal stops!—can mean the difference between a song resonating with a *Diné* audience member or feeling parodied by that same song. These nuances are particularly important, since the final concert, held in a Navajo hooghan, is performed explicitly for community members, a form of reciprocity for allowing us to offer the workshop as guests on sovereign land.

## "No Man's Land" or When a Song Comes Home to Roost

In another geographic context, as an anthropologist focusing on senses of belonging, social citizenship, and civic estrangement, I've been closely following the Syrian refugee crisis as it has unfolded and differentially impacted various European countries where I've lived. In January 2016, I wrote "No Man's Land" with Swedish singer/songwriter Lina Horner,[24] a song first chronicling the Okie dustbowl migration to California from the perspective of the woman in Dorothea Lange's (1936) famous photo, "Migrant Mother,"[25] then describing another migration experience from the perspective of a Syrian refugee (Moutafis, 2015),[26] Amina, to the suburb of Göteborg (Gothenburg), Sweden. In the writers' room, the birth of the song itself was fundamentally anthropological: to give names, stories, and ethnographic specificity to anonymous faces in widely circulating photographs that have visually come to stand in for the displacement and suffering of entire groups of people (émigrés from Oklahoma and Syria).

*"No Man's Land"[27] (Kristina Jacobsen; Lina Horner, Copyright 2016, BMI & STIM)*

Chiseled face
Buried in her worried hands
Migrant mother
In a burlap dress

Kids a-cryin'
Hungry all day
Asking questions you can't answer
Anna Mae

California ain't
what it seemed
buried in the Tulare dust
Lie your broken dreams

**Chorus**
I won't pretend
To know what you've been through
But as I look at your picture
I'm trying to
I won't pretend
To know what you've been through
But I want you to know
I see you

Covered head
Cried-out eyes
Firm hand
Comforts the child at your side
Strange new city
Temporary home
People all around, Amina,
Yet you're all alone.

A Swedish suburb
Wasn't what you planned
But here you are, now,
In a no man's land.

**Chorus**

**Bridge**
Our forefathers
once were immigrants, too,
And someone threw them a lifeline when they needed passage through

**Chorus**
I will remember this window into
what you've been through
And I want you to know
I see you
I will remember this window into
And I want you to know
I see you

**Tag**
And I want you to know
I see you

In October 2016, ten months after writing this song, I performed it in a Swedish prison to a room full of Syrian immigrants. Thus, I was singing the song in the exact place and to the community about whom the song had been written. Since 90 percent of inmates in Swedish prisons are apprehended on drug-related charges at Arlanda Airport in Stockholm and then transported directly to the prison, very few of them speak Swedish or have been integrated into Swedish society. Moreover, upon release, a similar percentage return immediately home to their country of origin. Thus, these inmates live in a betwixt-and-between, liminal space, and their greatest crime, as the warden himself phrased it, "is being poor" (L., 2016, personal communication at Mariefred Men's Prison, Mariefred, Sweden, October 25, 2016). Inside the prison, as I introduced the theme of a "No Man's Land,"[28] an inmate from Nigeria interjected, "We know what that's like. We live in the ultimate no man's land, here." Although I didn't know I'd have the opportunity to perform this song at Mariefred Prison at the time I wrote it, the song had, literally, come home to roost.

But, performing this was also an opportunity to experience the way a song can change the chemistry of a room. At the beginning of the performance, the men were talkative and lively, some joking with each other and continuing to talk through part of the song. As I continued, however, a quiet began to descend upon the room, and, by the end, some of the inmates began to squeeze their eyes shut in an effort to cover up tears. As we all drank coffee and ate sweets, afterwards (a traditional Swedish "fika"), the openness of the men—many Syrians but also eastern European Roma, West Africans, and southern Europeans—was palpable. What was perhaps most remarkable in this hypermasculine space was the permission they gave to one another during the performance to express emotion, in general, and sorrow, in particular. (This was expressed most visibly through side nudges and rough pats given to one another on the shoulder or back.) This was—and is—one of the most powerful performance experiences and senses of connection with the audience I've had to date.

Although I'm proud of this cowrite, I'm also not under any illusion that our song on its own is so powerful that it moves mountains. Connecting with an audience is a marriage of craft, practice, tenacity, and serendipity. A well-crafted song, performed with power to the right audience on a theme they can relate to, can chemically change the composition, mood, and emotional space of a room, palpably and sometimes dramatically, within a matter of minutes. This is the serendipitous marriage of openhearted listening and the possibility of being and feeling truly heard as a songwriter. As songwriter Laurie Hyde-Smith (2004) has put it, you really can "take a crowd of rowdy drunks and hush them with a song."[29]

There is also something about alchemy in moments like these. As truth teller Gauthier shared with a group of songwriters:

> The art [of songwriting] is not about singing, guitar playing, or mastery of any instrument. It's not about performance, show business, or even entertainment. It's not about reading or writing music. The art of song is about combining vision, ideas and truth in an effort towards wholeness. At the end of the day, songwriting is conjury. The conjurer is often as mystified as anyone as to where our creations come from. We often can't explain how we do what we do because we don't fully understand it ourselves. But in the right mood, with the right frame of mind, there's a feeling of being an antenna, receiving, then transmitting, receiving, then transmitting. Great songs are more than words and music. Welded together just right, they become emotional electricity.[30]
>
> (Gauthier, 2013)[31]

## Conclusion

Ethnography and bringing someone alive through ethnographic writing is another form of conjury, a combination of vision, ideas (using the toolkit of social theory), life experience, and emotional authenticity. As anthropologists, we are charged with being the antennae, ears, and eyes always to the ground within a given community of practice. Welded together by equal parts storytelling, accuracy, and connection to one's interlocutors, ethnographic writing, like songs, can become emotional electricity. I've seen this in my classrooms in the process of teaching a poetically written, powerful ethnography, where attitudes toward an unknown group can change dramatically over the course of a single text. As scholars, humanists, and educators, we should take—in fact, we must take—the aesthetics of our ethnographic work as seriously as we take the aesthetics of our songs. Concomitantly, as songwriters, we are obligated to use the specificity of ethnography to create richer, fuller, and more nuanced portraits of the lives and human communities we share through both sung and spoken forms of storytelling.

Songs—and expressive cultural forms more broadly—give us the ability to voice the ineffable, allow listeners to access emotions we didn't even know we had or were capable of feeling. Tightly crafted art forms take us to the liminal cracks that exist betwixt and between the analytic realm of the head and the spaces of the heart. Songs let us reach and then connect through those spaces, places even the most fine-grained and nuanced analysis might not ever take us. To get there, we need to pay attention on purpose, take artist dates, create the space in our daily lives to produce the art we are inspired to create, set time aside to focus on our art and to trust that it's worth it, and continually remind ourselves and our students that songs and expressive forms matter because they create human empathy and connection across racial, socioeconomic, and cultural divides. And that is powerful and important work.

As ethnographers, songwriters, artists, and social scientists, it is these moments—of the profound connection achieved through alchemy, conjury, and storytelling—we strive for. We aren't always successful, but knowing what a story is capable of and how it can change the social fields around us is this potential reward that keeps us writing, singing, and sharing stories in the rawest, most humane way we know how.

## Postscript: "My Own Creative and Scholarly Practice Since 2017"

Publishing "Songwriting as Ethnographic Practice" was my first invitation to think holistically in an academic forum about the ways that my songwriting and anthropological practice directly influenced one another. It was a timely invitation which served as a catalyst for the creative and ethnographic work I have continued to explore.

### *Recent Work*

In 2019, I received a Fulbright Artist-Scholar grant to live on the Italian island of Sardinia for one year in order to write collaborative ethnographic songs with poets, shepherds, storytellers and musicians across the island, released as an album called *House on Swallow Street* in 2021[32] with the Sardinian label, Talk About Records.

Since 2016, I have recorded and released four new albums, including songs inspired by walking the Camino de Santiago in northern Spain, my own mindfulness practice, and the ways in which mindful walking, songwriting and creative practice intertwine. These are songs I now perform with my duo, Heartstrings (https://kristinajacobsen.weebly.com/heartstrings.html), where we especially love playing acoustic house concerts. These songs are also part of my newest album of nine songs, called The South Valley Sessions,[33] released in January 2025.

My scholarship also now intersects more directly with my own creative practice. In fall 2024, I released two new books. The first is an edited craftbook called *The Creative Ethnographer's Notebook*,[34] co-edited with Melisa Cahnmann-Taylor (2024), featuring 33 creative prompts offered by our favorite scholartists around the globe. This book includes prompts from myriad artistic genres and is designed by emerging and experienced ethnographers to think more deeply about creative practice in ethnographic work through honing their craft as artists.

The second book is a musical ethnography, *Sing Me Back Home: Ethnographic Songwriting and Sardinian Language Politics* (University of Toronto Press, 2024).[35] This book is a multi-sensory ethnography, set on the Italian island of Sardinia, and explores language and culture through songwriting as an ethnographic method. *Sing Me Back Home* features original songs from *House on Swallow Street* as QR codes at the beginning of each chapter, where songs serve as ethnographic vignettes in their own right. *Sing Me Back Home* was also published in Italian in 2025 with the Italian publisher, NeoClassica.[36] Also in spring 2025, I toured across Sardinia and continental Italy with the Italian translation during a month-long tour, offering a combined reading-concert, reading vignettes from the book and performing songs featured in each book chapter.

Last, what started as "Songs from the Rez" in 2016 has now become a fully-fledged, culturally immersive retreat and workshop business, called Sing Me Back Home Songwriting,[37] where I offer culturally immersive, place-based songwriting retreats in places where I have lived, done ethnographic fieldwork and speak the language. These retreats are open to anthropologists, musicians, poets, and mindfulness practitioners. Currently, I offer retreats in Sardinia, on the Camino de Santiago, and in the mountains of northern New Mexico.

### So What's Next?

My next creative projects fuse collaborative songwriting and ethnography. The first, "Together at the Table," brings together songwriting, the anthropology of food, and community building. "Together at the Table" connects food to songwriting, and sound to taste and smell, through the performance of a song cycle of six original songs, each inspired by cultural encounters with food. The performance is followed by a meal shared around a long table with members of the audience, where the menu is crafted around the foods referenced in the songs. The songs will be used to craft a state of the art, multi-course menu and an ethnographic cookbook, designed together with a professional chef who is my chief collaborator on this project. Through this multi-sensory sonic and culinary adventure, guests are transported to other places that they otherwise might not think, or care, to know in a deeper way. Thus, food and song become portals to greater cultural curiosity and interpersonal connection. You can now listen to the first song from this song cycle, "Salt, Fat, Acid, Heat,"[38] and learn more about this project on my website: https://kristinajacobsen.weebly.com/together.html.

The second project, "Three Miles an Hour" is an ethnography of mindful walking and collaborative songwriting on the storied Camino de Santiago in northern Spain, a route I first walked in 2022. In it, I'll be cowriting songs with support staff and service workers on the Camino, many of whom hail from outside of Spain, to document and relay their own experiences participating in the "Camino" economy.[39]

## Notes

1 www.kristinajacobsenmusic.com.
2 www.kristina-jacobsen.com.
3 http://music.unm.edu/faculty/kristina-m-jacobsen/.
4 To hear songs from the main band, Native Country, with whom I played and chronicle in *The Sound of Navajo Country* (2017), visit: https://myspace.com/nativecountryband.
5 This essay is conceived of as an interactive work encouraging readers to engage directly with sound and video clips provided.
6 www.nybooks.com/articles/1998/10/22/deep-hanging-out/.
7 I'm grateful to ethnographer/poet Adrie Kusserow (2013) for highlighting the importance of visceral experience in poetic writing as a means of teaching about the human experience, as seen especially in her book of poems, *Refuge*.
8 Although not my primary lens of analysis here, much of what I write regarding songwriting also applies to the genre known as ethnographic poetry. For published exemplars, see Faizullah (2014), Kusserow (2002, 2013), Rosaldo (2013), Stone (2008), and Cahnmann-Taylor (2016).
9 Along these lines, I appreciate the following as a guiding principle for both songwriting and storytelling: "Think of songwriting as lowering someone down the side of a mountain, methodically. Make too big a movement and you're going to lose the person" (Gauthier, 2013).
10 For excellent texts on creative practice, see Cameron (1995/2002), Goldberg (1986/2005), Ueland (1938/1987, 2010), and LaMott (1995).
11 www.youtube.com/watch?v=hbioUv_1fPY.
12 www.youtube.com/watch?v=17s_aJfSrrI.
13 www.youtube.com/watch?v=ISFNTRaXRiI.
14 Something similar happens with ethnography, where, as a by-product of entering the narrative world of someone else, we are also rehumanized in the process.
15 www.marygauthier.com.
16 https://uncpress.org/search-results/?keyword=The+Sound+of+Navajo+Country+.
17 I'm struck, here, by ethno-poet Ather Zia's reflection on the possibility of song-writing and poetry in the field as forms of "self-care" tools used to process the intensity of the immersive fieldwork experience (American—Anthropology Meetings, "Ethnographic Poetry," 11/17/2016).
18 For an example, please visit: https://vimeo.com/172336891.
19 https://ictnews.org/archive/assimilation-tool-or-a-blessing-inside-the-mormon-indian-student-placement program.
20 In the *Book of Mormon*, it states: "Their scales of darkness shall begin to fall from their eyes; and … they shall be a pure and a delightsome people" (Second Book of Nephi, Chapter 30). www.lds.org/scriptures/bofm/2-ne/30.6?lang=eng.
21 https://soundcloud.com/kristinajacobsenmusic/sets/three-roses-album-preview.
22 http://kristinajacobsen.weebly.com/navajonationsongwriting.html.
23 An example of this is retreat participant Alicia Stockman's song "AM 660,"a reference to the local country music AM radio station: https://soundcloud.com/kristinajacobsenmusic/am-660-alicia-stockman.
24 https://soundcloud.com/linahorner.
25 The Dorthea Lange (1936) photo is of Florence Owens Thompson of Tahlequah, Oklahoma, taken in a migrant camp in California. To view the photo, visit: www.loc.gov/rr/print/list/128_migm.html.
26 For the specific image from Giorgos Moutafis' photojournalist series on Syrian refugees fleeing to Europe that I refer to here, see https://soundcloud.com/kristinajacobsenmusic/no-mans-land-introduction. The woman in the photograph is unnamed.
27 https://soundcloud.com/kristinajacobsenmusic/no-mans-land-introduction. Thank you to engineer Stefan Lindvall, cowriter Lina Horner and Anfallszonen Recording Studio of Göteborg, Sweden, for permission to share this track. Thanks for Drake Hardin for the mastering.

28 One way that I introduce this song can be heard here: https://soundcloud.com/kristinajacobsenmusic/no-mans-land-introduction.
29 Lyric from "Me and Willie," Laurie Hyde-Smith, recorded by Emmylou Harris, *Luxury Liner*, 2004.
30 For a more recent version of this work, see Gauthier, Mary. *Saved by a song: The art and healing power of songwriting*. St. Martin's Essentials, 2021.
31 www.marygauthier.com.
32 https://talkaboutrec.bandcamp.com/album/house-on-swallow-street. Also available on all digital streaming platforms.
33 https://distrokid.com/hyperfollow/heartstrings4/the-south-valley-sessions. Available on all digital streaming platforms.
34 https://www.routledge.com/The-Creative-Ethnographers-Notebook/Cahnmann-Taylor-Jacobsen/p/book/9781032429915.
35 https://utppublishing.com/doi/book/10.3138/9781487553869.
36 https://www.neo-classica.com/catalogo/fuori-collana/sing-me-back-home-songwriting-etnografico-e-politica-della-lingua-sarda/.
37 https://www.singmebackhomesongwriting.com/.
38 https://www.youtube.com/watch?v=H4fsMrOoQWg.
39 Both projects are supported by a two-year long residency (2025–2027) in Helsinki, Finland, at the Helsinki Collegium for Advanced Studies, an independent institute of advanced study within the University of Helsinki.

## References


Basso, K. (1996). *Wisdom sits in places: Landscape and language among the Western Apache*. University of New Mexico Press.

Cahnmann-Taylor, M. (2016). *Imperfect tense*. Whitepoint Press.

Cahnmann-Taylor, M., & Jacobsen, K. (2024). *The creative ethnographer's notebook*. Routledge.

Cameron, J. (1995/2002). *The artist's way: A spiritual path to higher creativity*. Pan Macmillan.

Camus, A. (1955/1991). *The myth of Sisyphus: And other essays* (J. O'Brien, Trans.). Vintage Books. (Original work published 1942).

Earle, S. (2002). John Walker's blues. *On Jerusalem* [CD]. E Squared/Artemis.

Faizullah, T. (2014). *Seam*. Southern Illinois University Press.

Fox, A. (2004). *Real country: Music, language and working-class culture*. Duke University Press.

Gauthier, M. (2012). Goodbye Karla Faye. *On live at Blue Rock* [CD]. In the Black.

Gauthier, M. (2013). Rocky Mountain Song School. Masterclass.

Gauthier, M. (2014). Kerrville Folk Festival Song School, Kerrville, TX, 5–20.

Gauthier, M. (2021). *Saved by a song: The art and healing power of songwriting*. St. Martin's Essentials.

Geertz, C. (1998). Deep hanging out. *New York Review of Books*, *45*(16), 69. http://www.nybooks.com/articles/1998/10/22/deep-hanging-out/

Goldberg, N. (1986/2005). *Writing down the bones: Freeing the writer within*. Shambala Press.

Hyde-Smith, L. (1976/2004). Me and Willie [Recorded by Emmylou Harris]. *On luxury liner* [CD]. Warner Bros.

Jacobsen, K. (2024). *Sing me back home: Ethnographic songwriting and Sardinian language politics*. University of Toronto Press.

Jacobsen, K. (2025). *Sing me back home: Songwriting Etnografico e Politica della Lingua Sarda*. NeoClassica.

Jacobsen, K. (2017). *The sound of Navajo country: Music, language, and diné belonging*. The University of North Carolina Press.

Kusserow, A. (2002). *Hunting down the monk*. Boa Editions.

Kusserow, A. (2013). *Refuge*. Boa Editions.

Lamott, A. (1995). *Bird by bird: Some instructions on writing and life*. Anchor Books.

Lange, D. (1936). *Migrant mother* [photograph]. http://www.loc.gov/resource/fsa.8b29516/

Minter, M. (2015). *Three roses* [CD review]. http://www.melminter.com/2015/11/04/mixed-bag-flash-reviews-of-harvey-valdes-mike-holober-and-kristina-jacobsen/
Moutafis, G. (2015). Photos: Syrian refugees on the way to Europe: Refugees search for safe passage to Greece. *Al Jazeera*. https://www.aljazeera.com/features/2015/9/25/photos-syrian-refugees-on-the-way-to-europe
Ortner, S. (2006). *Anthropology and social theory: Culture, power, and the acting subject*. Duke University Press.
Pattison, P. (2009). *Writing better lyrics: The essential guide to powerful songwriting* (2nd ed.). Writer's Digest Books.
Peters, G. (2012). Five minutes. *On hello cruel world* [CD]. Scarlet Letter Records.
Rosaldo, R. (2013). *The day of Shelly's death: The poetry and ethnography of grief*. Duke University Press.
Samuels, D. (2004). *Putting a song on top of it: Expression and identity on the San Carlos Apache Reservation*. University of Arizona Press.
Smith, P. C. (2009). *Everything you know about Indians is wrong*. University of Minnesota Press.
Stone, N. (2008). *Strangers notebook*. Triquarterly Press.
Ueland, B. (1938/2010). *If you want to write: A gook about art, independence and spirit*. Graywolf.
Washington, G. (2016, November 17). Gratitude [radio show]. In G. Washington (Producer), *Snap judgment*. WNYC Studio.

Chapter 20

# Hearing Jesusa's Laugh

*Terry Jenoure*

*Jesusa's Laugh* is a dramatic musical performance created to report findings from educational research I conducted in South Africa. It combines live and pre-recorded music with dance, poetry written by my students and me, journal entries, taped interviews, and visual imagery. Through my trip, I was looking to understand two things: How might I apply arts-based pedagogy to a cultural context much different from my own? What have been some of the experiences of ten teenage boys from a South African township? Then, through the performance that ensued, I was hoping to find ways of sharing what I learned, some of which were related to my original inquiry, but most of which were not. The entire endeavor has propelled me toward ongoing investigations into my professional practice and family history, and has stirred up longings among many parts of myself. Like a ball of yarn with its strands of fibers wrapping and spiraling all around each other, the many facets of this project come together through seemingly unrelated, yet connected people, places, and events configured and reconfigured in New York City, Puerto Rico, and South Africa.

In this chapter, I am attempting to reconstruct the route I took in merging educational research and this performance. Although this all may seem quite tidy and straightforward, it is far from that. By my own admission, I did not originally view this as a research project. A newcomer to the field, and an outsider by my own recognizance, I am looking at what occurred from a bird's-eye view. It does not follow a linear route, and may be better appreciated as an amorphous entity with tentacles in odd and unlikely events and conversations. Only as I continue to watch and question it, as I have here, am I better able to define and find a place for it.

This chapter is explored in four parts. The first part is about my trip to South Africa in 2001—what prompted it and what transpired once I got there. The second describes some of my process as I went about bridging research with art. The third part is a script of the text from my performance. Then following are concluding thoughts about the meaning and purpose of the project as well as implications for its application.

## Ikhwezi

My trip to South Africa has firm, solid roots. I was a little girl, living on the fourteenth floor of a high-rise in New York City's fierce Bronx. Examining braids and scars, lip plates and scooping breasts, I lovingly and carefully turned the pages of my father's large coffee-table books that carried me off to a continent he always regarded with tremendous dignity and reverence. I knew the quickening in this little girl had something to do with a deep, complex "me." Another root: The album cover for singer and South African icon Miriam Makeba

DOI: 10.4324/9781003412892-20

that I saw at age twelve, and the inimitable sound of her clicking Xhosa tongue. I looked and listened studiously. Her close-cropped, unstraightened, naturally kinky hair was not yet a common sight in my neighborhood, nor in the America I had come to know in my brief years. But it was 1965 and I had my adolescent ear to the ground. I was getting wind of the "Black and Proud" storm that was sweeping America, in which, just a few short years later, I would be gleefully swept away. And in my home, where aesthetics and politics were inseparable, "Natural" and "Pride in Self" were mottoes that reigned supreme. So, I admired the self-assuredness of this Miriam Makeba while I was reminded over and over by my family of a priceless teaching that would last me at least another forty years: confidence in expression is ultimately where all beauty lies.

There were aspects of my current professional work that inspired the trip. I am a musician who often collaborates with artists in other media, including dance, poetry, and visual art. I am also the director of a university art gallery that produces visual and performing arts events. And, for ten years I have been a teacher educator at another university, with many earlier years spent as an educator in secondary schools and private instruction.

Oddly, it was my growing frustration as an educator that initially played the most significant part. I teach through the arts in a Master's degree Education program that has distance sites, with students in many parts of the country. Most of them are in-service public school teachers who are learning to apply the creative use of the arts in their classrooms. In addition to guiding them in developing curriculum strategies, I talk a lot about the need for creative teachers to think and function more like artists, shaping people, places, things, and ideas in unprecedented ways. We mostly agree that the arts are good medicine for an ailing, flailing system. But *why* make art? Here is where we seemed to part ways all too often.

It was the teaching of my mostly White, mostly middle-class, mostly women—my kindergarten through twelfth-grade teachers from Oregon to Georgia to Wisconsin to New Mexico to Maine to Montana to South Carolina to Idaho that troubled me. More and more frequently, I found myself wondering what had happened to me? What had happened to my sixties' Black Power, working-class, bent on "revolution by any means necessary" self? It had always been a part of me that burned when I taught, and that taught me to keep burning. It had initially been my entry into this work. I was certain and driven about the connectedness of art and cultural identity. But lately, I had begun to feel myself buckling inside when my students quietly snickered at my proclamation that America is a racist nation, or were horrified by my critical condemnation of blind national patriotism. Many of these women resented the readings I assigned about the insidious nature of sexism in education. I had begun to cringe when they snarled into my exclamation that we are slaves to a patriarchy, our mutual resistance and disdain, politely tucked behind our deadpan expressions.

A child of the sixties, I had never quite shaken my first political lesson: question authority. And, a child of parents whose biographies had come together from two different countries, economic class associations, and languages, I was raised to honor cultural distinctions, to value questions and to question values. But now, our worlds, my students' and mine, collided and crashed again and again. I had become hypersensitive, so I saw the smirks before they were formed. I felt their desire for the course to be over before it had begun. They didn't want these topics approached, and definitely not by me. Yes, most of them were terribly frustrated with their schools, and with the politics of standardized testing and the daunting repercussions in their classrooms and other parts of their lives. And yes, their schools had become increasingly more diverse. To some degree, many had a desire to understand more about the nature of change in regard to multiculturalism as an educational mandate and a social reality, and the role that the arts could take in reforming schools. But in one course after another, as I attempted to respond to these needs, I seemed to be meeting fewer of mine. I was beginning to see them through the eyes I had so often cautioned them against. They had become one loud voice. A "them."

When I teach, I want to be heard. I want to breathe into a warm receptacle instead of shouting into what was feeling like such a cavernous vacuum. Granted, there was a part of me that still loved what I did, and even *needed* to do it. But, there was also a growing part of me that was angry at them, at *us*, really, for being so smug. So complacent. So bored with yet another method for teachers to bandage their classrooms. The Arts in Education. Another antidote. Like a new improved mouthwash or laundry detergent. And I was tired of being the traveling saleswoman. There was nothing left of me to give. Ultimately, it was a good thing because this wall that I hit helped me make my move.

When I went to South Africa, I was looking to find out whether I could apply my experience and skills in arts integration to a very different cultural context: South Africa, a Black-ruled country that had been rebuilding itself for about ten years, following centuries of the enforced racial segregation and minority rule called Apartheid. But I had other questions: What would I learn about my relationship to Africa that would be fresh and personally uplifting? Would I meet people with similar professional and sociopolitical interests? So, at first, when the trip was still just in the realm of "a good idea" and not quite yet "a plan," I received a grant. Without a template or suggestions on how to proceed, I trusted my hunches and my excitement. I began to focus on what I wanted from the trip. And I wanted a lot. I wanted to teach; to find out more about people's lives; to meet and collaborate with other artists; to find educators who use the arts for the purpose of bringing about social awareness and change in their communities; to pursue a very old emotional connection to Africa; to explore whether South Africa might be a place where I could return and establish professional roots and partnerships; to fortify myself in order to continue my teaching at a more developed, profound, and satisfying level.

I had no roadmap for this inquiry. I simply began talking to a wide range of people about the seed that was germinating. Colleagues, students, as well as strangers with indirect connections to me offered helpful contacts through email addresses. They'd say things like, *Get in touch with him. He teaches at this university and knows lots of people.* Or they'd say, *I know someone who received a grant to go to South Africa a few years ago. Maybe you should contact her.* Or a couple said, *Here is the name of an organization in South Africa that is somehow connected to arts and AIDS awareness.* The associations were broad and varied, but almost all of them led me somewhere. So, I launched my emails introducing myself, explaining some of my interests, what I wanted to do, why the trip was important, always offering myself as a volunteer speaker, teacher, or musician. Before I knew it I was receiving responses: *I don't know much about arts education but I know someone at a local university who has a similar curriculum. I'll send your email to a few people.* My letter was being shared among academics, artists, social workers, people with compatible interests. I felt vulnerable. I felt strong. I had imagined something and had taken steps to make it real, like when God told Noah how to build the ark, dimensions down to the minute details. The hammer and nails were my thoughts, emails, lists, and conversations. Then there was more pondering, more lists, more emails. This boat felt impenetrable, and the flood ended up being more like a cleansing downpour.

In 2001, I spent a frightening, exhilarating, exhausting month in South Africa, resigned to the heat, the newness of everything, the way English sounded so smooth in other people's mouths—so smooth I caught my head nodding to the melodies and often missing the questions and answers. My calendar was packed. I crammed in as much as I could. I met scholars from Johannesburg's prestigious Witwatersrand University, and the founders and coordinators of the renowned Art against Apartheid movement, which had become popular for its radical political stance. I led art and poetry classes with two groups of children. I interviewed Princess Francina the elder artist from Siyabuswa, in the countryside near Pretoria, who has assumed leadership in retaining and teaching an important Ndebele painting style. Her art has restored a nearly lost tradition whereby the exteriors and interiors of homes are painted in bold, geometric patterns. She spoke with me about her views on teaching young people. Dr. Jackie Phahlamohlaka graciously invited me to be a keynote speaker at the graduation of a college preparatory school, the Siyabuswa Educational Improvement and Development Trust, in a rural technology program. At the close of one particularly long, strenuous day, I was honored to have met the Ndebele cultural leader, King Mayisha, at his home. But shortly before I was about to leave, I fell under his harsh inquisition. Without hesitation he cornered me and probed about my trip to this community that continually attracted curious tourists: *What have you brought?* I felt myself shrink. By then, I had been wondering the same thing. What could I possibly have to offer in a country where 20 percent of the population suffers from AIDS, water is precious in rural areas, and drugs ease the nagging, unbearable pain of unemployment, hunger, and disillusionment? Art? I felt like a glutton. For one very long and painful moment my visit felt trite. Even today, I wrestle with this jumbled mix of feelings.

My trip culminated in a five-day workshop that I led in Cape Town. Sias Sabelo Dyani, David Magidigidi, Vuyani Mahalwana, Lindela Sydwell Ndzulu, Zweli Tukayi, Sizwe Mfecone, Phumlani Nkoyi, Richard Mzwamadoda, Nqgongwa, and Luwandh Melikhaya Tana. They were a group called Ikhwezi, which means "the morning star" in Xhosa. They were ten kids from Khayelitsha, a nearby township, who would be in my class. My friend Ingrid Askew, a theater artist and community activist, had formed the organization when she left Massachusetts to live in Cape Town about five years earlier. It was Ingrid's apartment, where I stayed, which overlooked Table Mountain, at the tip of Africa where the Indian Ocean meets the Atlantic intimately and inevitably. During Apartheid apartments and houses with this glorious view in Cape Town had been a privilege reserved for Whites. My new acquaintances, these living witnesses of such profound shifts in their destinies, reminded me and each other of this fact often, and with a mix of disgust and pride.

Ikhwezi already knew I had come to them not only as a teacher, like Ingrid, who vibrated with energy and devotion about art and the building up of their communities. I explained that I had come in two capacities: as an educator and as the director of a university art gallery. I would be teaching them, using collage and poetry as part of our ongoing explorations. I would then take their art back with me to my gallery and display it in one of the upcoming exhibitions as part of our Young Artists Series, which features visual art by a diverse population of young people interested in delving into topics related to cultural identity.

And so, it is time for us to begin. I have some vague idea about what might happen—what could happen. My teaching style tends to be both tight and loose at the same time. I love the precision and choreographed rhythms, but I also need the clutter. On the first morning, as they arrive and we introduce ourselves, we wind our way through the wooded area along the rim of the manicured botanical gardens abutting the National Gallery of Cape Town, just across the street from Ingrid's apartment. We're going to work with "found" materials from the park, so we begin to collect things. Odds and ends. Junk. Leaves and candy wrappers, dirt, sticks, matchbooks, grass, bugs, and newspapers. Although I'm not exactly certain what we will do with them, as we hunt it becomes clearer. The group is timid and I'm feeling the same way. Still, we are excited to be together. The weather is hot and dry. The park in the summer is full of visitors. Luckily, none of them are even slightly interested in us. Our group breaks up into twos and threes while some wander off by themselves into other sections of the park. They gather more than I expect they will and far more than I figure they need. I'm enthusiastic because they are. These beautiful young men, old enough to be my children, almost young enough to be my grandchildren. I announce that we will now go inside and look a little closer at these things we've gathered. They're curious, and all of us are amazed, laughing at what we've found, putting our treasures in brown paper bags as we head indoors.

Our classroom is in an annex of the National Gallery of Cape Town. It is a formidable institution in what seems to be a relatively affluent area. Some of the young men already know each other from Khayelitsha, their home town, but many of them met for the first time when Ingrid formed the organization. They are accustomed to getting together regularly in her drama course and have already grown close. They call her Mama Ingrid. A bus picks them up at a central location in their neighborhood and brings them to Cape Town. Then after class, the bus takes them back home. Some of the members of the group have dropped out of school. Some of them have night jobs that barely help feed families. Some have had drug problems. Some are plagued by circumstances I know nothing about, and can't even imagine. Their spirits are enormous and profound.

I'm suddenly so moved, so overwhelmed by what they are giving me in the form of attention and commitment. I'm impressed and warmed by it. Ingrid did a wonderful job of developing this kind of trust long before I arrived. I announce that I want to share a song with them. We go into a more spacious room and I explain, *I have songs from the African American Freedom Movement of the 1950s and '60s that I want to share. These songs mean a lot to me. This one is called "I Woke Up This Morning with My Mind on Freedom."* They watch me closely and listen. I'm encouraged. When I finish singing, they applaud with excitement, and I feel completely centered and certain.

The investigation through the arts that I've planned in this workshop continues, as I wonder: *How can we speak to each other? What is it about ourselves that we feel others may or must know? How can we tell those stories? Who do we want to tell them to? How will they be heard? What will happen to these stories once we tell them? Once we hear them ourselves?*

We settle at desks that are arranged in a square around the room with large white poster boards, one for each person. There is plenty of room behind them to stretch and move around, and room in the center for me to move among them. Materials are spread out on the tables: paint, large sheets of white paper, colored construction paper, glitter, markers, yarn, glue, and tape. *Use the materials that you've found in the park as well as the supplies that I've brought. Also, look around and see if anyone else might have things that they've collected that they wouldn't mind sharing—things you may want to use. Create images and marks that represent something important to you—it should tell us something special about you. Maybe it's something you want people to know about you. It can tell us about something you think about often, or that frightens you. It might be someone very special in your life, or an event that is meaningful, or maybe a desire or dream that you have. Maybe it's some experience you've had or some advice you want to share with others.*

The room is completely quiet. The boys stare out in front of them. I wonder: *Will they go along with this direction? Does it even interest them?* I'm beginning to feel tense and self-conscious. They move very, very tentatively. I wonder if they understand my directions, so I repeat them slowly. Then, I invite them to ask me questions. I explain, *I love questions. I'm not always as clear as I'd like to be, so if you ask me questions, it may be one that someone else is thinking about too. In fact, it probably is.* But I soon realize that they do understand my directions and are just thinking quietly, deeply, carefully. Slowly, they begin talking to each other and working, and I can suddenly feel the room get warmer and brighter. Relieved, I'm feeling light and giddy as I think about the days that lie ahead and realize how fast they're going to go by.

On the second day, we move from handling these materials to examining how we might incorporate words too. I direct them: *Write one sentence that tells us about the image you've created.* When they have done this, I instruct them to take a word from their sentence and free-associate new words for as many of the words in their original sentence as they can. Then, from that huge list we'll use as many of the words as we can in order to create a poem. This encourages the writers to accumulate words that they may not have employed if writing in a more linear fashion. It invites contributions from the mind's subconscious reserve, finding new meanings and applications for common words. I demonstrate this with a sentence of my own. We generate a long list of amusing associations, laughing at their incongruity, all of us wondering where we might be headed. This large list of freely generated words becomes like the artist's pallet of colors. We dip in, arrange, and rearrange them for my sample poem. I say: *As you do this on your own, you will find that you have lots of words that don't seem to make sense for the poem you want to write. Don't worry about that. Use them anyway, and use as many as possible. Use them even if you think that no one will understand its meaning.*

The poems are then integrated with the visual representations in whatever way they choose. Some put the poem on the back of the image, some blend it into the body of the visual art, while others attach it to their painting or collage with tape or staples. Three days have gone by. And in the busy, noisy room, in between the pasting and writing and drawing, they individually, throughout each session, call me over to their tables. They whisper things about their personal lives to me. They understand that we may not meet again. They ask my opinion and even suggest their own wisdom about some of their predicaments. The more I hear, the less I understand. This is an important, unexpected moment for me.

As they work, I encourage them to step back and take time away from what they're doing—make some distance—get another perspective—another approach perhaps. *Go visit other stations—go see other people's construction—get inspired.* As they do this, their interest in each other's processes grows. Again, I ask them to borrow an object from their neighbor's bag and incorporate it somehow in their own work. I continue to encourage the intentional use of new or unintended materials. It is this element of surprise and the ability of the mind to operate below the surface of consciousness and cognition that often offers the most meaning to us and to each other. They complete their art on that third day. The collages are magnificent, with no two even remotely alike.

There is a lot of detail in Richard's picture. It is arranged like a story-board into a few different segments, and divided with lines to separate the portions and lead us through the events. It has a surreal quality, with fragments and characters and scenes in odd dimensional relationships to each other. His poem helps us follow the trail:

*Suddenly the Sun Shines Like a Foretold*

*Mirror on the wall story*
*The dog is creating a great deal of noise*
*Under a big shade tree while mumbling and chatting to itself*
*It growls and enjoys some sweet bones.*
*Suddenly a hungry wolf is making ugly music*
*Of its own character not caring who dares*
*To not enjoy it and suddenly its targets*
*Human, sheep and beetles murmured with fear*
*As their ears witness the music of the good*
*Bad one.*

*Suddenly nature observes the matter*
*By sending the dawn of the day*
*Suddenly it's night again, and the day*
*Is gone and it shades bad image.*
*Suddenly an elder is telling a story to*
*The grandchildren, uncles, and aunts, sons, and daughters,*
*A story of secret long-lost tribes of Africa.*
*But it was not an end for them*
*They continued to struggle for their*
*Tribal voices and not forgetting who*
*They were and where they come from and*
*Deep in my heart I am one of them.*

In contrast, Phumlani tells about a life that's been very hard. His message is personal, candid, and introspective. He seems withdrawn and is observant and determined. His image is striking. A boy, his large blue face covers almost the entire surface of the paper about three-feet square. The face looks straight out at me. There is a huge teardrop falling from his eyes. I wonder why he is crying:

*This boy was sad*
*He was yelled*
*He was shouted*
*Sent to shops when it was raining outside*
*People were taking advantage of his kindness*
*Life was not fair for him*
*He made one big mistake*
*He is down on his knees*
*Begging for forgiveness*
*Oh Lord won't you see him*
*Let the road be clear*

*Of Satanism.*
*He is pushed*

*To force to face the ground*
*Those who know say*
*"Don't kiss the ground."*
*Just push them aside.*
*Your journey is only beginning.*

I see from their responses that many have faced the grip of drugs directly or indirectly. Luwandh has produced two pictures and poems. They have a mixture of materials, but with no representational images. They make references to themes I am unable to connect. He writes punitively, didactically, and urgently about the importance of not using drugs:

*Many things break hearts*
*But most broke are unexpected, Hard or easy*
*Black or white heart now*
*Be broken if use drugs.*

*We always have someone to blame.*
*Who is to be blamed for broken hearts*
*You hurt us why can't you heal us*
*What is it that makes a heart?*
*We have to heal each other.*
*Stop Drugs*

His second poem is more emotionally revealing and has the desperate feel of someone holding on to a lifesaver:

*I've lost my love I lost every thing*
*But my body is still my body*
*I've lost my love but my friends*
*Brothers, relatives and family are not lost.*
*So I'm still a human*
*I can't use drugs to heal my wounds.*
*I can't eat vitamins to heal my wounds.*
*Yes I can survive without drugs.*

Vuyani's poem is a wonderful mix of literal and metaphoric ideas. He talks about travel in physical and emotional terms:

*I took a ride on the horseback*
*To Africa where I belong*
*I flew by jet flight*
*I took a ride on the elephant's back*
*Sometimes on the rhino's back*
*I passed many rivers by ship*

*I traveled by train without tickets*
*I saw places and faces on my way*
*I learned new cultures and customs*
*I got caught by police and traveled by police van.*

*It was confusion without fear*
*I used a bicycle as my vehicle without feast*
*I have no clothes, shelter, and direction*
*I spent many years in foreign countries*
*By dedication I'm home again*

When Sydwell writes about Nelson Mandela, his references remind me of ones we've come to associate with the leader, including Mandela's contributions to cultural and racial reconciliation and progress. The painting is grand, exaggerated, and explodes with pride. There is a noble-looking man in a house with ferocious animals as he rests with ease in his surroundings. From the words, we get a real sense of what is valued, as well as a tribute he's created with reverence and satisfaction. He calls it, "The Home of a King or a Hero":

*The king's home is symbolized with its beauty.*
*The doors are decorated with bars*
*The house with shiny diamond*
*Fire pot also shows that it is a hero's house.*
*The man who had been won the battles.*
*The man who had been stopped the violence,*
*Discrimination itself.*
*People are forgiving each other because of that man.*
*It is something*
*As you see his home is very beautiful with*
*Flowers, trees and the tiger.*
*The tiger shows his braveness when the time*
*Of wars*
*The bones of ancestors helped him to abolish*
*The violence, bad behavior and discrimination.*
*The sky and the sun shows that the king*
*Is the man who had worked hard so he*
*Deserved to have such beautiful home.*
*Heavy rains were raining to this man*
*Trying to eradicate him with his roots*
*This home itself signifies it is owned by the man*
*Who had worked hard for people*
*This home is the reward for his attempts*
*To freedom.*
*I'm talking about the home of a hero here you see.*

On the fourth day we finally hang the art works up across the length of the room's very long wall in order to view them as a whole. I want them to talk about themselves—the stories they are telling, and anything else they may care to share. I want them to own the presentation—to lecture, to teach, to take full control of the colors, shapes, textures, words, and feelings that cover the walls—to bring these tales to even larger life.

But now there seems to be a glitch in my plan. The National Gallery has a resident photographer who covers special events like ours in order to announce and promote the institution's programs. I'm told that she will be here this morning to photograph. I reluctantly agree. I tell the group that we will simply continue with what we're doing when she comes. We have already mounted the art on the walls for our final viewing. We have lined up these large mixed-media configurations one next to the other to examine them—to see them from a distance and up close. And, mostly to understand each other better and celebrate this special time we've had together. We are so pleased with the results, which we spread out over the walls like a map to our pulses, lifestyles, and moments in our collective stories.

The photographer arrives about halfway into our morning. She is a small, young, White woman, very polite and excited to be taking pictures. She assures me she will not interrupt. After taking a series of shots of the group while we continue our viewing and discussing, the young woman asks if she can take a picture of the group standing together. It is now beginning to feel like an intrusion. I had hoped that our last day of production would be spent completely focused on the task of critical examination. It is crucial that we summarize and make meaning of our efforts. Nevertheless, I agree to her suggestion. We stop and they huddle for the shot. Then, in an instant that now seems both distorted and strangely lucid, she puts her camera down. She has a good idea. Will those who are wearing baseball caps please turn them around? Will they please turn their hats around and smile really big for the camera? I am frozen. In fact, the memory is a fractured one. It is a collage of arms and breath, eyes, breath, adrenaline and hats, browns, blacks, and heat, more breath, fear, and a raw rage. She has seen the group of young men in this room and now has a picture in her mind that she wants to reproduce. As she directs them on how to pose, I now see the picture too. It's that stereotypical, media-driven, hip-hop image of rappers. Her instructions are an assault on our work—the strenuous task of claiming our voices and choices. Of acknowledging the political implications of what it means to "be yourself," and what it means to rule ourselves as human beings—to be "free" and "new" as is suggested by the common phrase, "The New South Africa." Some of them take their hats off and begin to turn them. *Don't do that. Turn your hats back around.* I shout it. And in that one split instant my mind collapses as I retrieve a forty-year-old memory:

> *It's Saturday. We're on the outer edges of the Bronx River Projects, my mother, my brother, and me. We walk down Sound View Avenue toward Westchester Avenue where all the shops are located. The elderly Jewish storeowners in our neighborhood, a long way from their own families, who live anywhere but here. We go to the hardware store, where my mother wants to purchase something. But now, the old man is talking strangely to her. Like she's worthless. She's a bother. She's a despicable child. I hear his impatience and scorn, his clipped speech and tone. And there's his small, wrinkled wife who stands hunched and gray and sour, smugly and just slightly behind him. How dare they talk to her that way? My beautiful mother, always gracious in private and in public. Slim, dignified, her skin, just a shade darker and warmer than my own. In an instant, she's changed. Only moments ago, she was light as a feather, now everything inside her is condensed, solid. Her eyebrow raised, mouth tight and pursed, she turns and quickly ushers my brother and me out the door.*

And today, I feel like my mother as I call Ikhwezi to attention in that little basement room in the National Gallery of Cape Town decades later and on the other side of the world. I need to draw the line. I also need to let these young men know what I'm seeing, hearing, and feeling. I have a desperate need to break this down for them and for me. They have been telling their stories all week. And though the opportunity has presented itself in an oddly unexpected and awkwardly painful way, I now have a chance to tell mine. *Keep your hats on the way you're wearing them.* I hear myself say. But I'm disappointed. I have nothing more. The photographer packs up and leaves. We are alone. There's a huge echo in the room. Some look at me gently, respectfully. Others seem to not be thinking at all about what has just happened. While others look hopeful, expecting me to say something. I know I *want* to say something. I know it is part of my teaching —part of our learning. I need to translate the experience—to scream it really loud. I want to say that the stench that lingers is what remains of a dead thing. The stink of cruel and hideous agreements that are made between people. Of assumptions and frustrations—all of ours—the photographer's, theirs, and mine.

It's quiet. They're waiting on me. I'm accosted by the memory of an old man who had set up his shop in my neighborhood, then decided who my mother was and how we must behave. I'm disgusted, appalled, at what just took place in what had been our sanctuary, and probably not much less, at what it evoked, this intense moment that binds us in a common wretched history. But our workshop is nearly ended, and to my surprise, I resist my urge to follow the Race trail. It seems too ominous and will undoubtedly lead us to parts of this dense place with insufficient time or resources with which to find our ways home. *Don't you ever let anyone tell you how you should look or act.* Again, my voice disappoints me. Surely I must have something more to say. But what is burning on my heart is so huge that now it's stuck in my throat. It chokes me. And here in South Africa, like back home, my desire to talk Race with my students is still not quenched. There remains that part of me that wants to be fully revealed to my students, whoever they are. To walk with them down this decrepit place of our shame and rage with its wretched stink and mildew. I want to uncover and release that monster we keep trying to appease with our ignorance, and that keeps me feeling, whether here or back home in Georgia, Montana, and Oregon, like Isaiah, the barefoot prophet who cries deep from his soul: Save yourselves now. The end is near.

The next morning, we sit in our circle for one last time. I ask their permission to record our conversations. We make speeches to each other. To my complete surprise, they read poems to me—poems they've written on their own over the past few days, mostly at home or on the bumpy bus ride from Cape Town to Khayelitsha. The poems are about me. Some are naked and raw. Some are formal and contained. They tell me the things they've learned. They tell me what they plan to do with what they learned, and about how they care for me. They'll miss me. We sing our Freedom songs. David leads the group with his full tenor voice as they present me with a gift: a traditional Xhosa Initiation Song with accompanying dance that is sung in their communities when boys turn to men. It seals a promise, or at least a hope. We'll meet again.

Ikhwezi disbanded less than a year later due to the many changes in Ingrid's and their lives, as well as problems with funding for the project. They never saw pictures or videos of the exhibit I curated at my gallery, with their magnificent paintings and poetry filling the walls. They never saw their collages again, or even heard about the excerpts from their art that I used in my own performance piece where I attempted to make meaning of our profound journey together.

I returned home to teach my teachers. They were impressed by the story, wondering what it's like to be me, and to be Ikhwezi. They speculated. I insisted that their schools and communities are sites of meaningful culture no greater or lesser than Khayelitsha. Still, I'm conflicted and greatly troubled. To this day, I wrestle with it—how much I gained. I had wanted to know if I could apply my teaching methods in a cultural environment that was this unfamiliar to me. And yes, at least on the surface and to varying degrees, the learning had been valuable to us all. I wanted to know about the experience of these young men, and I had discovered many rich and unexpected things through their art and the relationships that had been formed. Still, I had other things on my mind. I had turned one visit into an invaluable and complex array of lessons and opportunities for myself. But had Ikhwezi been able to do the same? If not, how could I have facilitated that learning? If so, where had it taken them? What had *they* done with the results of our five days? My heart is loaded with these questions. They are burdens to this researcher. I struggle with what sometimes feels like a thwarted enterprise. I can still hear King Mayisha interrogating: *What have you brought?*

Ingrid reminds me that some of the young men, now fully grown, still sing the Freedom Songs I taught them, and occasionally ask about me on their way to the places they travel to day after day. I hold on tight to those bold eyes and compassionate smiles. There's a flutter in my deep self.

## Ikhwezi Meets Jesusa

It took time to settle myself upon returning home. So much had happened in a month. I had taught children, met artists, activists, teachers, old people, seen the countryside, the cities, conducted interviews and lectures, witnessed suffering and a lot of laughter. The wind and smell of the air had felt so drastically different from anything I had ever known. The way I seemed uninteresting to people in the streets occurred in high relief to my usual blistering presence in the small New England mill town where I now live. And although the project had been catapulted by my long-held attraction to Africa, my desire to escape the painful, strained race discourse with my students, and my passion for international travel and collaborations, I was far from finding closure or having definitive answers about much of anything.

It was almost a year before the idea of merging that experience with my life as a performer occurred to me. Upon initiating the research, my most prominent question had been whether I could translate skills as a teacher educator in the area of arts in learning to another, vastly different cultural context. However, the full answer was far more complex and unrecognizable than what I could possibly discuss, write about to others, or even make sense of for myself. In fact, I was at a loss about how to express what had happened and was still happening. The notion of performing my findings happened easily, enjoyably, and to my relief in the best way I could imagine, which was without intention or a plan. It happened when I was invited to perform at a venue where I would ordinarily work with my jazz ensemble. However, now, my mind was on this project. Those worlds began to come together as I prepared to share events and thoughts and conversations and insights and observations that had seemed so complicated.

I first began letting my mind wander freely for very long periods of time over the course of many days and weeks. I took notes for a while. And I noticed my mind's patterns, but I didn't try to make sense of what I was feeling or thinking. As I began to see and hear images and sounds, I noticed and marked those that emerged and were most prominent or lasting, and those that seemed to have less energy or made less of an impression on me. I made notes about important experiences in South Africa that I had managed to document, either in my journal, photographs, on audio tape, or through the children's poems and paintings. There were lists and comments and questions and short melodies and visual images and shapes, and then hunches and connections, and eventually, some stories I thought I might want to tell.

In sorting out the many pieces that seemed to be presenting themselves, I didn't try to make meaning of them or coordinate or organize them in any way. I simply let them come. I welcomed everything. The incongruent and unlikely ideas remained in the pages of my notebook. I trusted that I would at some point know what to do with them all. Eventually, things began to come together and make sense.

For me, the most profound part of my process was how I had all of a sudden and seemingly out of nowhere begun to think about my maternal grandmother. This was surprising and emotionally jarring. For reasons unknown to me at that time, I found myself aching as I reached inside myself for memories of her. In fact, I hadn't thought a great deal about my grandmother in the ten years since her death. I don't think I had even allowed myself to miss her in the way I now seemed to be doing. My grandmother's image and our conversations that immediately preceded her death were becoming more vivid as I retrieved memories of South Africa. She seemed peripheral but somehow related to this work. It was odd, but I completely trusted what was happening and allowed it. I even expected it to lead me, which it did. I began keeping journal notes about my grandmother in order to coax the question that felt lodged inside: *What is the relationship between my experience in South Africa and my grandmother?*

This sudden, unplanned focus on her is very appropriate in retrospect. As I began to explore her role in the performance, she began to take center stage. My grandmother, Jesusa Calcano Lanzo Lopez was born and raised in Loiza, Puerto Rico. This small rural province on the northeast coast of the island was the main port where enslaved Africans were forced to live by the Spanish who had brought them to the island. Loiza has retained its identity as an important cultural site, nurturing many of its memories of West Africa through music, visual arts, religion, and language.

It all came together when I decided to use an interview that I conducted with my grandmother for the performance I was creating. The interview had taken place, about ten years earlier, when my grandmother was eighty-nine, only a few days before she died. At the time, I remember feeling conflicted about interviewing her since she had recently been hospitalized and was deteriorating rapidly from cancer. But it turned out to be a powerful exchange. I selected a brief excerpt from our conversation where she is talking to me about her mother and father. Those few moments eventually become a key segment that opens the performance. Our voices can be heard while the stage is still dark. Also, in the process of listening closely to that interview, studying it in order to decide what I wanted to include, I remembered something so wonderful about her. My grandmother had been a joyful person who always found it within herself to laugh. Joyful, not in the sense of being jovial, but her soft laughter was part of a reserved and shy demeanor. My interview captures this signature laugh in spite of her physical condition at the time. When I went into the recording studio to have the engineer place the segments of our talk that I had selected on a compact disc for use in the performance, I did some experimenting and eventually found a moment in it that reveals her wonderful laugh. I had the engineer lengthen it and create a feeling of timelessness through the use of recording technology. I employed this effect to punctuate sections in the piece, hence, the title, *Jesusa's Laugh*.

As I began feeling clearer about what was coming together, I vacillated between listening to the interview with my grandmother and listening to the interviews and songs I had collected in South Africa. By then, I had fully given over my work habits to my intuition, which serves me very well, and upon which I always depend for this exciting and crucial part of my process. As I did this, I also began writing with more assurance, and that writing became the foundational narrative for the performance. It was also to be the first of many subsequent essays and poems about my family. I wasn't sure what I had on my hands. Was it something I would want to perform? Was it any longer part of my South Africa project? What were the data I was reporting? What had been the research? Where were the facts, and where was the fiction? Where were the boundaries between all my explorations? Who would determine this? And how? And why? Eventually I knew that I would do what I always do, which was to trust myself and the certainty I was experiencing. Then, at a later date, perhaps I would figure out what it was I had.

I began making theatrical decisions. I would integrate Ikhwezi's poems. Some of them are woven through the music, either spoken or sung with instrumental accompaniment. The interview with Francina in South Africa was on cassette tape. She spoke Ndebele and had an interpreter with her on the day we met. By listening to his simultaneous translation as she and I spoke, I was able to choose a segment that was directly related to teaching. Her ideas inferred the sort of spiritual ancestral and cultural teaching I was now also receiving from my grandmother. For me, Francina becomes a type of Jesusa. This three-minute segment was edited in a recording studio, where a huge echo was placed on Francina's melodic voice. As it reverberates and the piano synthesizer plays rich "washes" of sound beneath the recitation, it creates a dreamy, mesmerizing, haunting effect that is at once both ominous and intimate. I put this in a section where the dancer moves slowly and with exaggerated gestures in a central location on stage. There is a clothesline that runs diagonally and is draped with flowing, silky fabric reminiscent of the bright, bold colors Francina employs when she paints. The dancer moves from behind this wall of color with large motions, suggesting that she is communicating an array of tasks, directions, and feelings. The clothesline is a metaphor for women and traditional work. I ignore my usual critical, feminist inclinations, and feel very comfortable and settled with this association as I think about my grandmother, an immigrant who spoke mostly Spanish—a proper and strict, but kind, generous woman who stayed at home to raise her four children.

I chose a few brief sections from my journal notes, although, as the piece came together it became more difficult to decide what to include without it feeling too much like a travelogue. I wanted the audience to sense my wonder and awe, and finally decided on three short excerpts. The Initiation Song that Ikhwezi sang for me on our last day together in Cape Town, and which I had fortunately recorded, became such a powerful element in the performance. Their adolescent voices are right on the verge of manhood. I placed their singing at the very end and composed live music that plays simultaneously. It is a collage, with the juxtaposition of their slow, steady, rhythmic traditional song against the live musicians with their stark, extremely fast, free-swinging jazz ideas forged by the bass and drums. It is a fevered layering of musical styles, time zones, periods in our histories, traditions, and inventions. It becomes a force that drives us home—the performers, the audience, Ikhwezi, Francina, my grandmother, and me.

## Jesusa's Laugh

The following is the narrative for the performance of *Jesusa's Laugh*. It is the core around which the music, poems, dance, and interviews, revolve in this seventy-five minute work. In the quest to report what I found, I create a mythical bond between the South African township of Langa, and Loiza, the town in Puerto Rico where Jesusa was born and raised. This bond, alongside a tribute to her laugh, and my farewell at her bedside constitute the essence of the text.

(Pre-recorded interview segment)

| | |
|---|---|
| *Me:* | *So Grandma, when are you going to let me do my interview with you?* |
| *Jesusa:* | *[laughs] ... I don't know. I don't remember [laughs]* |
| *Me:* | *What did you tell me your mother's name ...* |
| *Jesusa:* | *se llama Florentina* |
| *Me:* | *[pronounces carefully] Florentina? Is ...* |
| *Jesusa:* | *... is my mother* |
| *Me:* | *Your mother.* |
| *Jesusa:* | *Y my father, Balbino Lanzo [pronounced slowly and clearly]* |

[Tape fades]

*#1*

*I heard her laughing as I landed in Cape Town. There she was waiting for me. Jesusa, in the late afternoon wind that whips around the flat-capped mountain. I'd know her laugh anywhere, but this time it was charging through Langa, the township that cannot keep a secret. It's tin roofs and clogged toilets. It's ferocious appetite and relentless pulse. Disgrace and ascension, gathered on this one piece of ground.*

*Africa is a come-and-go, here-but-not-always, there-but-not-really kind of thing for me. Like the trip I took. Like my hair, my nose, my behind and calves and feet that keep on tripping me, tricking me, changing and growing, then shrinking, then spreading. Africa will never be like I knew it before—pictures in my mind, through national geographic or nationalist rants and romance. And it all just keeps me wondering: about me, about you. Like, when I say "Africa," I can't say for sure, but I suspect you may be disturbed by your own not-so-free association shaped like a hammered, chiseled thing that protrudes like fibroids out the middle of this putrid American shame. To my own surprise and relief, but not without a lot of fighting that same hammer, when you say "Africa," I think about my grandmother. Listen. Can you hear her laughing? Because if you're lost, she may lead you through this fog that seductively drapes la montana de la mesa como una cubierta. I'm coming to understand so much of what I saw and heard and felt in South Africa through Jesusa's laugh.*

*#2*

*Even when we were young my grandmother's laugh sounded like it had stones in it. Not gravel, but stones the size of marbles. Her laugh was never loud or even bubbly. It started tight, high up in her throat, and ended in short, syncopated lows down in her chest.*

*Jesusa laughed all the time. It chased all her remarks that tumbled out in her own English that my mother figured only she understood. We understood grandma perfectly, my brothers and me. Her few words ... her huge heart. But whenever she came to visit, mommy would habitually translate anyway. Grandma would say [with heavy accent] "Eh mira, I think-eh I go-eh shop-eh down-town a Sound View Avenue" and Mommy would override the end of grandma's sentence, look at us and say: "Grandma's going shopping down at Sound View Avenue today." Even in her last days, through the cancer, her unmistakable laugh made its way through the pauses in her stories on a bed in a sterile death room on Jackson Avenue.*

*#3*

*I spent a lot of time with grandma when I was growing up, but I knew almost nothing about her life as a young woman in Puerto Rico. I did know she was from Loiza. I remember when I found out that she was from the African section of the island—what a gift that was—Imagine!—To discover that when I was so high on being Black and coming into my beauty in 1960 something. It's always been my lifesaver. Claro que si! Loiza, of course, Loiza. That made perfect sense to me. Loiza is the part of me that ignites like a brushfire when I hear the [rhythmically] kette tung-ke-pa-paaa/to-dun-to dun,dun kung of my own footsteps. Loiza is the part of me that spins incessantly when I hear the [rhythmically] kette tung-ke-pa-paaa/to-dun-to dun,dun kung of my feet. But I wonder why grandma never danced. We'd grab her hands and pull and pull, trying our best to get her on the floor to dance with us. But she would just make her body real heavy, and she'd laugh and laugh. If by some miracle we managed to pry her loose while she was already up on her feet and sweeping, she shook her hips two or three times, laughed some more and went on about her business cleaning. I knew she loved it, and we did it to hear her laugh. Now, I wonder if she ever waited for us back then, waiting, hoping we'd want to dance with her.*

*And, why and how did grandma keep Loiza, who never stops dancing, locked up like a criminal? When Loiza's only crime had been to push Jesusa through her womb and down the canal! Even hours just before Jesusa's birth, Loiza had been out dancing all night again. I suspect she might have been with Langa. Langa, who sits at the foot of Table Mountain, king that he is. Langa, who reclines against Table Mountain waiting, so cocky and confident, for his mamacita Loiza. It wasn't Loiza's fault that Jesusa never danced. Who can blame her? No, Loiza tried to teach her Bomba. But anyway, Jesusa slid from her womb and down her canal and through her legs. Maybe grandma got her directions all mixed up. Someone must have whispered Spanish Harlem to Loiza's belly before Jesusa slid from her womb and down her canal and through her legs and she landed on 102nd St. & Lexington Avenue.*

*#4*

*Jesusa's story isn't a story in the "once upon a time" sense of having a beginning and an end. It's more like the way I am inside. It's the weaving in and out of my understanding as best I know, so I don't get scorched or drowned. So I don't get overwhelmed or buried under the weight of it all. Her story takes me in and out of myself just enough for me to pull up bits and pieces of recall ... tiny bits and pieces of this love, this honor, this obedience to God and self and abuela. Through her soft skin and infectious laugh and strong hands, and heavy breasts and wavy hair and thin wrists and broad hips and slim ankles, and the way she always smelled like talcum powder, I'm deep in the sub-Sahara making sense of us—me and grandma.*

*#5*

*She tells me simple things. I can't believe I didn't know them before. And why had I waited until now? I stand and look at her. I want to hold her and bury myself in her. The best I can do is to hurry and catch her words as they fly and flutter and sputter and float and wade. Then, there are the words that have waited, wondered, wrapped themselves with such great care around these delicate breakables. These memories: Her mother Florentina who had one eye. Her father Balbino who was White, "but he was a very, very nice man" she assures me. She carefully unpacks and offers them to me. Her shrunken fingers tremble. Her breathing says she won't be needing these memories anymore. I think there's something about dying ... like childbirth where no one has to tell us to push ... When it comes, no one will need to tell us to travel light.*

*So, in a cold, metal-sterile hospital room. White sheets, white covers, white walls, white door, huge, cold, windows that look so mournfully sad out onto Jackson Avenue. Blaring TV overhead. My grandmother's sickness shaking hands with Good Morning America, The Price is Right, and Days of Our Lives ...*

*Jesusa laughs. I can hear the little stones rolling around in her chuckle. She tells me names and who wore them. We listen back. She laughs some more.*

*#6*

*What do I know? I know that from the Bronx to Cape Town, from Loiza to Langa, I am led and followed by myself. I take all that I am wherever I go!*

*I know how strange it is that we should meet here like this, under the stars and beneath the street lamp. Us. Yes, it's* your *story too. There is no seam, no pause, no here and there, no this and that. No line between marriage and death, sickness and health, Loiza and Langa, you and me. We're here, together, in this one moment ... all dressed up and ready for dancing Bomba well into the night.*

## The Laugh Resonates

The way I know that something is successful is by measuring how fruitful it has been. Has it opened doors for me and for others? Has it been inspiring and motivating? Has it been a source of revelation? Does it lead to unexplored frontiers? When I can answer "yes" to these questions, then I know I am headed down the right trail. My trip to South Africa and the resulting exploration of its meaning through this performance have helped me to define and value many things. These include how arts-based research has made its way into my current teaching, how it has affected other professional ventures as an arts administrator and performing artist, and some of the ways in which it has profoundly influenced my personal life. Perhaps the most abstract but transcendent finding for me lives in the last section of *Jesusa's Laugh*, which tells us that ultimately, everything is connected.

When I first pursued the idea of traveling to South Africa, its purpose seemed so entrenched in personal needs that it was difficult to see how something so self-serving could be useful to anyone but me. I slowly came to realize that in searching for a venue to express my composite voice as an artist and educator there might be some value for others in this project. A novice in the field, there were a few incidents that introduced me to arts-based research. None of which were rooted in my knowing about "a field" or even about others doing such things. There are two incidents that seem particularly responsible for my direction.

Right before I left for South Africa, I had a timely conversation with a graduate student at my university. He knew that I had traveled a great deal, and in particular, knew that I had spent two years, during the 1970s, living in the Middle East. He strongly encouraged me to write about that experience in particular, but my other numerous international travels in general. He insisted that they would benefit my work as an educator. A student of African American literature, he reminded me that there is a scarcity of our voices in the area of travel essays and related literature. There is an even greater lack of African American women in the field. I was excited by the prospect of documenting my experiences, and valued it as a new arena for me with much promise. In fact, I vaguely envisioned possibilities for the merger of my travels with my interest in pedagogy. This encouragement from a graduate student may have marked the clearing of a soil in which yet another seed was planted.

It happened some time just before I left for South Africa, as I found myself performing the results of my dissertation research at conferences. My dissertation, which had been published and had since become a book, had centered on understanding the experience of African American artists who teach in higher education. Upon its completion, I had begun to experiment with ways I might participate more genuinely and with greater authority at conferences in which I was being asked to share my research. Because I had spent so much time with my participants' stories and really missed performing on a more regular basis as I had in past years, I began to entertain the idea of transposing my research to the stage. This transition happened quite organically. I looked for new outlets to share my experiments, and eventually met and collaborated with others who were also examining similar possibilities.

Another benefit of this project is how it has pushed me to look at the personal implications of my professional experiences in greater depth. I don't know if I would have made the connection between my family, and my trip to South Africa had I not decided to create the performance. Hearing Francina's voice alongside the voice of Jesusa, offered me an unusual chance to join them in that unparalleled sensual dimension where art lives. Even today, I am not confident in my ability to verbally articulate what their relationship *is*. Yet, I feel sure in my attempt to discover it through performance, as well as in my ability to unravel it in the messy but fully satisfying way that art allows. Nowhere in this process am I more convinced of Jesusa's connection to Francina, or Loiza's with Langa, or with the sound of Ikhwezi's singing voices with my own than when I perform this. Efforts to understand it through discursive means fall short and reveal huge holes in their knowledge bases. It is through the process of knowing and sharing the research through an artistic medium that new, previously obscured avenues make themselves apparent.

I especially love to introduce this world to my students. Since returning from South Africa, my increased patience and resolve with all of our struggles with "otherness" and the enormous job of creating more caring educators and communities, and addressing sociopolitical inequities has resulted in a new enthusiasm for teaching. I have picked up where I left off, insisting that my students investigate their relations, real and imagined, to people they may view as "other," and that this happen for the sole purpose of creating a more equitable society. Only now I focus on formalizing my performance research methods. I apply my approach to developing *Jesusa's Laugh* in my teaching, and I want to see my students find their own distinctive ways into this limitless inquiry. The journey we take is invigorating. In fact, I find myself going to those places within me that I previously thought were only possible through my own art making. The excitement and freshness of students' discoveries about themselves and others, as well as their willingness to venture into aesthetic languages that may help them articulate more vague or dangerous or locked realms of knowing have proven to be rewarding.

A sample assignment throws light on one way I have applied arts-based research in the classroom. At the beginning of one course, my students are required to explore their own notions, biases, and assumptions about culture. We look at how those ideas may have been formed. Mainly, we begin to understand how we have all, in our own ways, consented to these notions. At the same time, in the early portions of the course, we experiment a great deal with the arts. We investigate ways of "speaking" about ourselves through visual art, sound, movement, stories, and poetry. Here, I am certainly not interested in or expecting to provide training in any art medium. On the contrary, students get to look at their own stumbling blocks, previously held and often debilitating self-images as art makers, as well as the potential that art wields for penetrating areas of discourse that are uncomfortable, unusual, or simply unexplored, such as notions about culture.

After some inquiry about how we create cultural and aesthetic knowledge, and as we begin imagining how they mingle with and serve each other, I give an assignment: *Identify someone you believe is different from yourself in some markedly clear way*. They must interview that person. I give some very pointed suggestions and encourage them to practice phenomenological interviewing methods. This approach is intended to help their participant to speak fluidly and in detail about their experience. I am asking students to avoid "flat" questions that might simply evoke "yes" or "no" answers. For example, "Tell me about growing up in Mississippi?" is preferable to "So, you grew up in Mississippi, didn't you?" Or "Where did you grow up?" I also do some in-class exercises to develop listening skills. They need to differentiate between "a conversation," where they are having an exchange with the participant, and "an interview," where they are looking to glean as much data that are neither tainted by their own biases and judgments, nor filtered through the shape-shifting of casual discourse.

Students must then use a combination of arts to present their findings. I ask them not only to offer information about their participants but also to identify new insights into their own growth. I encourage the exploration of tensions and inconsistencies, their own preconceived ideas about this "other" person, and some of the ways in which they are both different and alike. They need to describe those social, economic, and political forces that are in motion in both of their lives. They should consider the implications as educators. The results promote changes in thinking and lead us into discussions about the role arts can play in reporting data.

Then we go even further. The next phase is undertaken in order to refine their presentations. I want them to recognize the many aesthetic forms that are possible and that may be applied in the service of arts-based research. To do this, I ask them to tell a story. It should be one that is surfacing to their awareness as a result of the presentation that they have just done. I have no preconceived notions about what this story should be. Fiction? Non-fiction? Science fiction? A mystery? They write their stories down. This stage helps them travel even further, retrieving data that they may have missed—to unravel the stories that may be hiding, tucked beneath the surface. These findings are often about themselves. My method leads students into a comfort level and a welcoming of this highly distinctive part of the trek. Finally, the last phase is to determine what parts of the writing might lend themselves to movement, or perhaps puppetry, or use of pre-recorded music, or comedy. Any range of creative modes is possible. They can amalgamate interviews, their writing, and these art forms in any way they like. At this point, they are functioning in "studio" mode, without my direction and at their own pace. I function as a consultant and encourage them to show their ideas and to get feedback from the other "artists."

This is an extraordinary time for me. I get to immerse myself in what I love more than almost any other activity in which I engage: performance. I thoroughly enjoy watching my students awaken to the fear and power that accompany the stage. In those precious moments, there is no other place I want to be. At those times, even the professional stage, where I "entertain," feels slightly dimmed compared to being able to introduce and merge these lives, these worlds.

The trip to South Africa led me to venture into other areas I had not anticipated entering. Upon return to my gallery, I exhibited the paintings and poetry of Ikhwezi as part of our Young Artists Series, as I told those young men I would. The response from my university community was overwhelmingly supportive. My appreciation for international travel in the mutual service of communities was growing. I decided to establish a program called Arts International Residency Project (AIR), which would support artists in doing something similar to what I had done. Through this program, the gallery now sponsors artists to live and teach overseas, exploring the boundaries and limits of their philosophies and methods in these new contexts, and returning to us with their findings. They report these in their respective media in the form of exhibits or performances as part of the gallery series. Since my trip to South Africa, I have also traveled to Mexico, India, Germany, and Colombia to teach young people and community leaders through the arts, sharing what I know about arts integration, and to establish a broader range of partner sites and colleagues for this new initiative.

There are still other areas that have been affected. For one, my explorations have broadened both my performance style and self-identification as an artist. Before entering this arena of arts-based research, my professional performing persona was defined as a musician. A jazz improvising violinist, vocalist, and composer, I performed exclusively with music ensembles, occasionally collaborating with dancers, or taking poems and adapting them into lyrics. The focus has shifted. I am currently integrating my own writing, painting, and movement, all of which was done for my own enjoyment for many years, into my performances. The shift being that although I still identify as a musician, I feel quite comfortable publicly employing a wide range of materials, much as I have encouraged my students to do over the years.

Finally, some of the resounding effects have been more personal in nature, such as this particular story that seems to have pointed me toward a large corridor with even more open doorways. As a result of creating *Jesusa's Laugh* and having revisited the taped interview with my grandmother, my emotions were exposed and raw. Around that same time, I learned that my grandmother's sister, my great aunt or "titi" as Spanish-speaking people say, had recently entered a nursing home. Titi Yaya is 100 years old and in unusually strong mental health, though blindness in one eye and difficulty walking led the family to agree that she could no longer care for herself in her apartment. She had never married or had children and, since much of our family is spread out, she was pretty much alone, barring occasional visits from her nephews. I began visiting her last year on my trips to New York City. Titi Yaya has talked to me about being a young girl in Loiza, Puerto Rico. She talked about her one remaining sibling, my Great Uncle Amador who still lives there. I knew that I must finally make the trip I had put off for so long. So, I went to Puerto Rico in 2004 for the first time and reconnected with my family. I returned to Loiza again this year, this time taking my mother for *her* first visit to the small, rural town where her parents were born. The following month, Titi Yaya's ninety-year-old brother came from Puerto Rico to visit her in the nursing home. It was the first time they have seen each other in close to fifty years.

Something magical and priceless has taken place simply because I walked through the right doors: unknowingly, my students pushed me to my travels in South Africa. South Africa led me to Jesusa, who guided my performance. The performance prepared me to carve out opportunities for new endeavors with international partners, my art, and teaching. All those paths pointed homeward to Loiza, Puerto Rico where I met uncles and cousins, conducted more interviews, painted pictures, wrote poems, took photographs, and now, have learned that my family has land in Loiza, which we inherited from Jesusa, and which is waiting to be claimed. The lawyers' papers sit on my office desk, and I'll be calling him next week. These worlds are the wooly, fragmented threads in that ball of yarn that spiral and coil and twist upon themselves. They even seem to unravel at times, though I always pick up a loose strand or two and begin wrapping again. My sharply honed instincts tell me that I may only be able to make sense of all of this by diving into yet another performance.

## Editors' Postscript

With the publication of her dissertation research (2000), Terry Jenoure was an early champion of arts-practice as research. Her keynote address to the University of Georgia's Qualitative Interest Group (QUIG) conference (Jenoure, 2002), incorporated puppetry performance, and marked a new direction in how qualitative research could be reported and the role of the arts in communicating to new audiences.

Having served as the Director of Augusta Savage Art Gallery at the University of Massachusetts in Amherst for three decades and curating over 200 exhibitions and performances, she is now living fully as a musician and moving even deeper into her arts-based research practice (see Jenoure, 2015). She is a 2023 award recipient from the Creative Capital Foundation, a non-profit organization committed to funding the creation of new works by visionary artists. She maintains both an active musical and visual arts practice.

Video examples of her performances, along with a gallery of her visual work, exhibition, performance and workshop schedule can be found at https://www.terryjenoure.com/.

## References

Jenoure, T. (2000). *Navigators: African American musicians, dancers, and visual artists in academe*. State University of New York Press.

Jenoure, T. (2002). *Navigators: An Interdisciplinary Performance Collage*. Keynote Presenter, Qualitative Interest Group (QUIG) conference, University of Georgia.

Jenoure, T. (2015). Mysterious humanity. In D. R. Renate & W. Parker (Eds.), *Giving birth to sound: Women in creative music* (pp. 105–111). Buddy's knife.

Chapter 21

# *sista docta*, Redux

*Omi Osun Joni L. Jones*

Since I first performed *sista docta* in 1993 at the National Communication Association conference in New Orleans, I have added several new moments to this seriate collage of my experiences as an African American woman at predominantly White universities. These new moments reflect my evolving understanding of academic life and my developing clarity about my role within that world. As a sista docta – a Black woman with a Ph.D. – my experiences are my own, and they also exist as "collective autobiography," that particular brand of storytelling that is at once specific and individual as well as representative of group realities (Cudjoe, 1990). I believe these experiences also constitute a kind of collective scholarship that joins the many conversations around race, gender, and politics. This chapter is not collective in the sense of collaboration, but rather in the sense of comradeship. While I did not create *sista docta* with E. Patrick Johnson, D. Soyini Madison, Oloye Ajidakin Aina Olomo, Daniel Alexander Jones, Sharon Bridgforth, or Edmund T. Gordon, the performance is intimately linked with conversations, print scholarship, workshops, dinners, meetings, and celebrations I have shared with them. We work together every time we work individually.

The possibility of collective scholarship that occurs across time and place is one lesson I have learned in the intervening years between that first terrifying public exposure of my frustrations and fears presented at an academic conference and this current private moment as I write this commentary and attempt to live up to the complexity and richness that my intellectual/spiritual/artistic comrades have given me.

In the world of Black art, much time has been given to discussing the burden that Black artists bear as we respond to a muse who some feel makes us accountable to our diverse array of often competing forces – our ancestors, the NAACP, the Black Panthers, the Black Muslims, Lucumi traditions, the White academy, and all manner of Black Christian church groups. Regardless of our backgrounds, this is the swirl of political/spiritual realities that envelope our creativity. In Langston Hughes's (1926) often quoted essay "The Negro Artist and the Racial Mountain," Hughes admonishes a young artist for wanting to be "just an artist, not a Negro artist." While I understand and concur with Hughes's insistence that the young man is suffering from the rejection of his racial identity and a subsequent self-hatred, it is also true that Black artists walk onto the stage as interlocutors conversing with a host of invisible end men and women. Our freedom is not an unfettered creativity but instead resides in the courage and audacity to raise our voices at all.

Collective scholarship works as a buoy rather than a weight. Even as I write this commentary, I am envisioning another addition to *sista docta*, a praise song/dance in which I identify those who have shaped my art, scholarship, and activism. And as I review the

DOI: 10.4324/9781003412892-21

above list – Johnson, Madison, Olomo, Jones, Bridgforth, Gordon – I realize that only one of those collective scholars is indeed a sista docta.

Another important lesson learned between 1993 and now is the necessity for returning to the same terrain again and again. Rather than embarking on a new solo project, I have revised, adapted, edited, and massaged *sista docta* from a 30-minute companion piece with E. Patrick Johnson's *Back on the Auction Block Again* to a 90-minute performance complete with audience collaboration and self-defense demonstrations. Initially, I presented *sista docta* as a kind of museum piece – repeating it rather than inhabiting it anew. Soon, it became clear that the work was becoming more for the audience than for me. I'd be invited by an institution to present *sista docta*, often with the hopes of stimulating dialogue in their communities about education and representation. Rather than continuing to research the subject of academic identity through my own embodied experiences, I settled for presenting the same research over and over, denying performance the very spontaneity and immediacy that is its strength.

I would do this work for them with little attention to my own experience inside of the work. This choice was born more from an underdeveloped activist impulse than from an artistic one. Revolutionary poet Raul Salinas reminds us that when engaging in social change work, we should ask "How does this help me, not how will it help *them*" (personal communication, February 12, 2006) Salinas's wisdom is also apt for performance. After that dramatic and transformative first performance, I went on to perform *sista docta* as a challenge to racism and sexism, and slowly the power of the original truth telling began to dim. The work moved from being an urgent declaration of my role as an academic misfit to a commodity that was used to demonstrate an institution's forward thinking and progressive posture.

As a performer, my job is to be present with my own experience through the work being shared. I found myself consumed by the fight – the ongoing struggle to bring equity to academic institutions – at the expense of the very spark that makes art vital. bell hooks (1995) warns of the danger of mass duplication of Black art; conceived as a product for general consumption, Black art loses its insurgency and its transgressive power. In order to reinvigorate the work, I had to continue to ask terrifying questions – What am I most afraid of saying right now and why? What do I gain from this performance critique? How am I reinscribing the very images I hope to challenge? The most critical questions were the ones I had to pose to myself, not the ones I rather arrogantly presumed the audience needed to ask. I had to commit once again to truth telling because truth telling changes with time and circumstance. In 1993, it was courageous to have audience members read aloud the racially obtuse comments that had been made to me, but by 2000, especially after the work had been published and widely available to the performance studies community, *sista docta* became an act of predictability devoid of much of its potential power. Post-performance discussions suggested that audiences were still challenged and provoked by the piece. However, by not fully investing my current questions and discoveries into the work, I limited the understanding available both to the audience and to myself.

Being a scholar artist in the academy had already created constraints on my ability to access my art heart; the cramping of my artistic impulses was compounded by envisioning the work as the audience's instead of as mine. I reclaimed the urgency and danger that fueled *sista docta* by creating new segments about life in the academy.

After many of the performances, audience members would offer comments that pushed me to add to or amend the work. After a student challenged me about why I remained in the academy if it was so frustrating, I created a series of improvised moments in which I talk to myself and the audience, entitled "what I like about my job." This segment of the performance remains one of the most difficult as I attempt to articulate what joy I find in academic life. Would my honest answers to this question root me too deeply in a satisfied/satiated middle-class position that would undermine the very critique I was hoping to make? I am still grappling with this one.

When a former colleague from Howard University asked me why I had not mentioned my experience at an HBCU (Historically Black College or University), I wondered what I was avoiding by omitting these experiences from the performance. Was I reluctant to offer as stiff a critique of an HBCU as I was of White institutions? What lens might it uncomfortably shine on me to expose my feelings of sexism and homophobia at an HBCU? Had *sista docta* become that familiar space of assumed Black kinship that really masks a host of unspoken wounds? In answer to these questions, I created a chant done to movements reminiscent of a Black sorority step show routine.

*We are the sista doctas from the HBCUS*
*But when we talk about our differences Blacks give us the blues*
*At Black colleges they preach unity*
*But forget feminism and sexuality*

*When a sista docta says what about women's rights*
*They tell her she's been hanging out with too many whites*
*When her analysis includes sexuality*
*They say, "Hey, that sista docta sho nuff must be gay!"*

And when a White woman asked me why I hadn't included a segment on being a woman and being a mother, I initially dismissed her comments – after all, I thought, my very physical presence makes my womanness a given. My Black femaleness was a spectacle that could not be missed. As K. Sue Jewell, Deborah Gray White, and Sander Gilman have illustrated, my Black female body is the very essence of the grotesqueries and excesses ascribed to the construct called Woman. Was this yet another White person unable to see inside of an experience that did not overtly include her? Could she only connect with me and my work if I specifically mentioned sexism? What else could I do to invite her into my world, and was that my job anyway? Didn't my very body serve as a critique of the academy's sexism? It was not until after completing a Fulbright Fellowship at Obafemi Awolowo University in Ile-Ife, Nigeria that I was moved to comment on what being a woman in the academy felt like to me. Perhaps in a location where Black was more subtly set in bas-relief against Whiteness, the issue of gender was foregrounded.

## Never Tell a Woman to Wear Lipstick

and she sprang forth
fully formed
limbs lean
torso taut
feet sturdy nimble
a mind like quick silver

darting at the speed of light
a heart open yielding
a soul (her best feature)
large like the Sahara
dense like the Amazon
ancient like the Nok terracottas in all the Western museums
a natural work of art
her self package was not Kmart
but kente and asoke
courageous conscious marketing
counter hegemonic moves at every turn
crafted by the master carver
whose medium is always spirit, not flesh
if paint adorned her face
it would chart the course of the moon and the stars
in copper kohl across her brow
trace the lotus of her cheek and the yoni of her lips
in indigo cream
map the shadow of the goddess lurking on her lids
her face a canvas on which to play
but her mirror conjures Alice, not Diana
no ruby mouth and apple cheeks
no synthetic locks or press on nails
no magazine poses and visionless visions
for a righteous sista
would Beloved move you more if Toni's lips were red?
would the slaves have been more free if Harriet had pinched her
cheeks?
would the revolution have been stronger if Angela wore mascara?
so when you tell her
out of
friendship
that she could really use a little lipstick
know what vast beauty
you seek to erase

My response to the question of motherhood in the academy was to invite my daughter Leigh Gaymon-Jones, then in high school, to write about her experiences of being my daughter. This may have been skirting the issue of speaking my own truth about motherhood, but at least my reality as a mother would be firmly positioned within the performance.

Although "Leigh's Version" was published in 2003 in *Voices Made Flesh* (Miller et al.), I had not yet performed the piece (Jones, 2003). It was Leigh's story, not mine, and it seemed to lose power and authority when I attempted to perform it as her. Then, in 2005, I was invited to perform *sista docta* at Spelman College while Leigh was living in Atlanta. It was the perfect opportunity to give life to those words through Leigh's voice, body, and spirit. Before an auditorium full of Black women in Spelman's elite "Women of Excellence Leadership Series," Leigh and I shared her experience of being my child. The drummer that evening was

Omelika Kuumba, founder and director of the women's drum and dance company, Giwayen Mata. Her mother was in the audience. Through the performance, the women of Spelman could see a legacy of achievement and struggle and possibility, of individuality and solidarity as two generations of Black women made an offering of sweat and art.

### Leigh's Version

"Concentration
ishi-oshi-ation
thinking of (clap, clap)
starting with ..."
Moma
she *is* superwoman
and there is no kryptonite
soaring over private schools to save me
diving into fires, says prayers for me
knocking out ignorant boys who act crazy
and this is how my moma raised me
all praise to thee

class/rehearsal/out of town/meeting/
rehearsal/*ile* work/office/performance/
out of town
wait, what day is it?
right:
meeting/dinner/performance/class/
meeting
is it Thursday?
oh yah, out of town ... "Don't forget to take out the trash"
rehearsal/class/performance/office
me ... me ... me
but you're late ...
let's eat out ... rent a movie

never neglected
opinion always respected
forever protected
moms
never alone
always felt at home
even when I thought I was grown
moma
stressed, always
busy, maybe
careless, never
mommy

rock, rock
non-stop
in her arms wrapped up
always big hugs
kisses on eye lids
like Eskimo love

you think I'm pretty? ...
i know, my mother shines through well
my spirit's beautiful? ...
it's an inherent gene passed through her cells

"am I doing this right?"
"is this what a mom is supposed to be?"
yes, you lift me to infinite heights
and teach my light how to flow free

class/rehearsal/meeting/class/performance
out of town ...
superwoman
soaring
forever protected
infinite heights
eskimo love
rock, rock
even when I thought I was grown
and this is how my moma raised me.

Fourteen years later, I am very aware of my mortality as I perform *sista docta*. Ann DuCille (1994) has been conducting research on health issues related to Black women academics. We seem to be dying at an alarming rate. Cancer and heart disease have become common – more for us than for our sista doctas of other racial backgrounds. I recently completed an essay about the work of Laurie Carlos and Robbie McCauley in which I addressed the stresses of being an artist in academic institutions (Jones, 2007). After I had submitted the essay for publication, I was shocked when I realized that I had forgotten to mention that Robbie suffered a heart attack a few years ago, which she attributed to contingencies such as diabetes along with the internal unspoken tensions that come from being a Black woman artist in White institutions. She believes her life is threatened by the very experience that pays her bills and buys her food. At the beginning of this academic year, I was hospitalized with an unexplained cramp in my heart that pushed the pain down my left arm. In fact, I had been suffering from shortness of breath, this aching heart, and other symptoms of overwork and stress for at least five years – but doctors found nothing and sent me home without medicine or advice or answers. What I know is that my rounded shoulders, bulbous waist, and thickly calloused feet are evidence of living, and my being alive – a Black woman academic – is something worth celebrating. Even in 2006, Black women comprise less than 5 percent of tenured faculty in the United States. I created "imperfection" as an unconscious response to the White woman's question about my gendered presence in the academy as I have come to understand sexism all the more as my body ages.

"Imperfection" premiered at the University of Georgia in 2004. As my taped voice read the text, the audience watched a series of random slides that created a loose genealogy of the interpretation of Black women's bodies/images – Hattie McDaniel with Vivien Leigh in *Gone with the Wind*, Saartje Bartmann, Florence Mills, Freddie Washington, Hilda Simms, Louise Beavers in *Imitation of Life*, Josephine Baker, Ethel Waters with Julie Harris in *Member of the Wedding*, and the deeper abstractions of Romare Beardens's nudes, Betye Saar's *The Liberation of Aunt Jemima*, and Lyle Ashton Harris and Renee Valerie Cox's *Hottentot Venus 2000*, along with family photos – me accepting the National Merit Scholarship, my parents Dorothy Mae Brown and William Edward Jones on their wedding day, me with fellow high-school speech-team winners, me in the marching band, my mother pregnant with my oldest sister and my father laughing his huge laugh at the camera, me as an infant. And as the audience watches this montage and listens to my story of fear regarding the impossibility of perfection, I sit below the photos, my back to the audience, take off my top and wash/cleanse myself with water from a white bowl.

I knew the audience could see the rolls and creases around my waist, the way in which time had marked my body. And this is what I wanted. I wanted the women not to be afraid of the changes that time will inevitably bring; I wanted everyone to come into contact with their notions of beauty and desire, power and fragility. I wanted to free myself of the shame and terror of my own mortality. I hoped my bare torso would say "This is what middle age looks and feels like. Can you see the beauty in it? Do you avert your eyes in shame? Does my exposure encourage you to fold your arms across your own bellies in protection and defiance?" With "imperfection," my live, exposed body against the Mammies and Hottentots and Jezebels, and my words of fear and longing further tensed the poles of real versus imagined Black femaleness.

## Imperfection

When I was little, I used to bring my report card home to my father for approval. He respected education. It was a sign of status, of class – and so I wanted him to be proud of me. He had said how beautiful my oldest sister was, and he seemed to really have a special fondness for my second oldest sister – and I also wanted a place in his heart.

For my mother – I cleaned the kitchen. I went down on my knees with an old rag and Comet cleanser and scrubbed all the wax off of the yellow tile floor. Wiped up all the gritty cleanser, then put down a new thin layer of Johnson's wax. I cleaned the greasy film from the top of the refrigerator, I neatly arranged the salt and pepper shakers, the napkin holder, the toothpick holder and the odd nick-nacks on the yellow formica kitchen table. I made the kitchen really shine. This I did for my mother – I knew she would love it, and gasp at how clean it was, "Ooo Joni you have done such a good job! You are the one I don't have to worry about" – and I knew that the more my knees ached from the scrubbing the more she would be pleased, the more painful it was for me the more love I would get from her. That's the love formula.

But the report cards were for my father. The camera of my memory sees me walking from the kitchen into the living room where my father sat waiting to see my grades. The camera is right over my right shoulder so that the audience – me – can see my hands holding the folded thick paper stretched toward my father seated on the couch like a judge or a king or both. I walk slowly toward him, past the piano that my oldest sister played, and past the carpeted staircase that led to the bedrooms, and past the wooden mural my father had made for the wall.

On one occasion, daddy was sitting in the living room after having been in a car accident. He had broken some ribs and was sitting stiffly in the center of the couch with the glow of the picture window behind him. Or maybe this didn't happen at all and I just want this movie to be true – daddy there – the man who could bestow upon me my worth, sitting in judgment, doling out approval or condemnation. Smiling that almost menacing smile, and I float toward him, like in a Spike Lee film – the grades were my offering, my veiled dance, my tap dance and coon song, surely this would be enough, surely he would love me unquestioningly then, surely I could rest now.

Then there was high school and hours of overachieving – the band, the speech team, the precision dance team, the honor societies, national merit scholar, valedictorian, the graduation address – the sleepless push for perfection. Surely daddy could see, surely I was as beautiful as Regina and as sensuous as LaVerne. Smarter than Moma, more entertaining than Willetta. Surely I could rest now.

I float toward him with my sacrifice in my hand, a moment of perfect pain, of delicious horror – my worth scribbled in blue ink by teachers who always commended me for being nice – a nice colored girl – and one teacher, Mr. Finnegan, who had gone to Vietnam or was at least drafted and sent a letter to our class with instructions for me to read it – me! – and I stood before the class with the sheets of white paper outstretched before me, confirmation of my worth, of my superiority.

And in the memory movie, I am always walking toward daddy and I never quite get the report card to him – my king, my god to whom I bowed in submission and devotion. Always outstretched but never arriving. Never there.

And I prepared my credentials, the sum of my worth – these essays, these book reviews (of much lesser value), these productions (of almost no value at all). And I bound them neatly, beautifully in folders – clearly marked so my worth would not be missed, beautifully packaged so I would shine above the rest.

And there I sat on a shelf waiting for daddy to review me, to confirm me, to say "it's ok. You will never be as good as me, but I can see that you work hard. Hard work is not as good as intelligence but it is something. Such good work for a Negro." There I sat on the shelf waiting, still, quiet, terrified. The sum of me typed on sheets, gashed with three ring holes and strapped to folders.

And I hated myself as I gave away my power. And I hated the floating walk, my faceless self. I hated the man who smiled almost menacing smiles – "it must be nice to be a performer." "How about a little sugar." "I just want what's best for you." And Leigh just said "fuck 'em" and Reggie said "why do you choose pain" and Laurie said "they don't have to like you." But I stretched my hand out to my daddy and I never quite arrived.

The most recent addition to *sista docta* came in 2006 during a time when I was serving as Acting Director of the Center for African and African American Studies (CAAAS) at the University of Texas. For the previous five years, I had been Associate Director of CAAAS, but in 2006 the Director, Edmund T. Gordon went on a much deserved leave of absence. This left me at the helm and fully in charge of aspects of CAAAS that I had been happy to leave in Ted's command.

This administrative position gave me a new window into academic life. Hegemony is powerful. The struggle to challenge the status quo, to turn from the path of least resistance, to speak even the most obvious truths is depleting and demoralizing. I saw more clearly that the White elite were not the only impediment to the intellectual and political advancement of Black people. My one-semester stint as Acting Director of CAAAS prompted me to write "the off center blues." I first performed this piece at the CALARTS "Impunities" conference in October 2006. I invented a blues rhythm and melody, and proceeded to safely critique people and circumstances that were unknown to that audience.

Sometimes you get called to service
And you think you really want to go

Sometimes you get called to service
And you think you really want to go

But sometimes that service makes you more Blue than you knew
you could go

When you working with your people
You think – this is good – we all playing the same game

I say when you working with your people
You think – yeah, this is good – we all playing the same game

But the way your own people treat you is a low down dirty shame

Now I'm not talking about them HBCUs
I done taught at Howard and know those Black on Black Blues

What I'm shouting about now
Is those Negroes at those white Research One Public Schools

Whoa UT – You sho nuff killing me
Whoa UT – You sho nuff killing me

You put them Black crabs in a barrel
And laugh as we bring each other to our knees

Now Negroes can spout Omi and Winant, we know Gilroy chapter and Verse
We quote from Kobena Mercer, Joy James, Patrick Johnson the First
But when it comes to supporting each other we couldn't act no worse

I say, Whoa Black UT – You sho nuff killing me
Whoa Black UT – You sho nuff killing me

You talk about how white people treat you
You say you not getting your due
The critique you aim at others should be aimed at you

Whoa Black UT – You sho nuff killing me
Whoa Black UT – You sho nuff killing me

Research is a life project, not a one-time exploration – no matter how grand that exploration might be. The artist returns to the work to push further and deeper into that initial investigation. Each performance is a step in the development of an idea rather than a definitive resolution. I have been fortunate enough to have the opportunity to revisit *sista docta* through performance, like communing with an old feisty friend – and the conversation expands with each visit. In this way, each performance is truly redux, something that is restored to its former importance and prominence.

## Postscript

In the 17 years since this piece was originally published, my knowings have changed. Today, I reference identity markers differently. I do not capitalize "white" when referring to people or institutions because "white" does not require the political and psychic amplification that comes from capitalization. I now offer more nuance when discussing "women," acknowledging the range of ways someone might wear that identifier. And now, rather than solely naming Lucumi, I'd speak of Yoruba-based Spiritual practices thereby acknowledging common impulses across such traditions.

More broadly, I now question how asserting the fixity of such markers can collude in the fear, violence, and separation from Spirit that promotes illnesses, greed, and warmongering. Now, my exploration of identity is rooted in a Spiritually informed critical journey that wonders how identity markers might be wholly reimagined. I am guided in these contemplations by the work of Báyò Akómoláfé ("On Doors and\cracks\"),[1] Kaylynn Sullivan TwoTrees ("Indigenous Mind"),[2] and Zenju Earthlyn Manuel (*The Way of Tenderness*).[3]

As I re-read the article, I was most surprised by the glaring absence of Queer sensibilities and references! It is my Queerness that has encouraged me to reexamine my relationship to all identity markers. The work of E. Patrick Johnson (*Sweet Tea: Black Gay Men of the South*),[4] Omise'eke Natasha Tinsley (*Black Atlantic, Queer Atlantic*),[5] and the homeplace provided by allgo (the Texas Statewide Queer People of Color Organization)[6] profoundly shaped my sense of connection, of academic possibilities and limitations, and of the necessity to consider realities well beyond what we already know. What remains most salient for me in the original writing is the caution around the commodification of creative work which can dampen the work's Spiritual and political potency. I would now add that the strategies of artmaking – improvisation, innovation, collaboration, virtuosity as courage, and vulnerability as truth telling – not only help ward off the dangers of commodification, but also provide a way for all of us to imagine and create the worlds we want to inhabit.

For raúlrsalinas' poetry and essays, see *East of the Freeway: Reflections De Mi Pueblo*,[7] *raulrsalinas and the Jail Machine: My Weapon is My Pen*,[8] and *Experiments in a Jazz Aesthetic*.[9]

## Notes

1 https://www.bayoakomolafe.net/post/on-doors-and-cracks
2 https://ktwotrees.com/writing/
3 https://zenju.org/the-way-of-tenderness/
4 https://uncpress.org/book/9780807872260/sweet-tea/
5 https://read.dukeupress.edu/glq/article-abstract/14/2-3/191/34590/BLACK-ATLANTIC-QUEER-ATLANTICQueer-Imaginings-of?redirectedFrom=fulltext
6 https://allgo.org/
7 raúlrsalinas. (1995). *East of the Freeway: Reflections De Mi Pueblo: Poems*. Red Salmon Press.
8 https://www.degruyterbrill.com/document/doi/10.7560/712843/html
9 https://www.degruyterbrill.com/document/doi/10.7560/722040/html

## References

Cudjoe, S. (1990). Maya Angelou: The autobiographical statement updated. In H. L. Gates, Jr. (Ed.), *Reading Black, reading feminist: A critical anthology*. Meridan.

duCille, A. (1994). The occult of true Black womanhood: Critical demeanor and Black feminist studies. *Signs: Journal of Women in Culture and Society*, *19*(3), 591–630. https://doi.org/10.1086/494914

hooks, b. (1995). Performance practice as a site of opposition. In C. Ugwu (Ed.), *Let's get it on: The politics of Black performance*. Bay Press.

Hughes, L. (1926). The Negro artist and the racial mountain. *The Nation*, *122*(3181), 692–694. https://www.jstor.org/stable/26432664

Jones, J. L. (2003). sista docta. In L. C. Miller, J. Taylor, & M. H. Carver (Eds.), *Voices made flesh: Performing Women's autobiography* (pp. 237–257). University of Wisconsin Press.

Jones, J. L. (2007). "Making language": The jazz aesthetic and feminist foundations. In K. Juhl & A. Armstrong (Eds.), *Radical acts: Feminism, theater, and transformation*. Aunt Lute Press.

Chapter 22

# Ethnographic Poetry

*Adrie Kusserow*

After years of forcing myself to perfect rigid academic writing while getting my graduate degrees in anthropology and religion at Harvard, I came to a point where I was miserable enough to consider dropping out. Although I did end up finishing my Ph.D. and now teach cultural anthropology to undergraduates, I did end up actually writing my dissertation away from Harvard (in Northampton, Massachusetts), and it was at that time that I really embraced poetry and admitted that, if I were to stay engaged and committed to anthropology, I had to practice, read and write a kind of poetic anthropology, an anthropology that moves beyond a mere intellectual exercise and becomes an anthropology of the hips and soul. After Divinity School, I was two years into my Ph.D. in social anthropology when I started having trouble with my eyes. Whether this blurred vision was psychosomatic or not I'll never know. I'd been reading so much for my general exams, every time I tried to sit down and read, words became blurry. I was worried I wouldn't be able to see well enough to work on the computer during my general exam dates. After I confessed this to one of my senior anthropology professors, she looked at me with indifference and said, "Well, maybe you're just not fit for this profession. It does require a lot of reading." I left her office feeling ashamed, but also slightly liberated. In trying to impersonate a stiff, male, British scientific approach to the field, I knew more than ever that I had to leave. After years of milking dry academic readings for the soul and poetry of anthropology, I'd had enough. I had to get out. I was tired of feeling imprisoned, stifled, sick, scientific, stale. Tired of presenting and reading the juiciest parts of anthropology in cachectic, formal, half-dead language.

When I first started to write poetry, it felt like a bloodletting. All of the color, moods, feelings and nuances I'd wanted to gush for some time, came out easily. Ironically, despite the miles of bad confessional poetry I initially produced, when I tried to write about cultural concepts, I felt poetry, rather than being some overly subjective fiction, finally accurately represented what I wanted to explore anthropologically. Humans, in all their stickiness, chaos and confusion, their fluidity and subtlety, their unpredictability and color, were suddenly three-dimensional again, through images, smells, looks and metaphors I never dared use before. In this way, poetry not only followed data collection, as a way to focus on my notes and digest what I had observed after hanging out with Sudanese refugees, but it also influenced the kinds of data I chose to gather. Poetry and data collection became mutually informative. The act of writing a poem was a deep meditation on my field notes where I tried to focus on all of the subtleties of what I had observed. And yet a poem sometimes took me to new places, not necessarily places of "fiction," but places of new anthropological insight about Sudanese culture. In allowing a rich, full spectrum of language and

DOI: 10.4324/9781003412892-22

metaphor to describe and understand the Lost Boys of Sudan, I came to know them in a more subtle way than had I written them up academically for publication in a journal article. From here I would go back to my participant observation with the Lost Boys and focus or ask questions about some aspect of Sudanese culture or their adaptation to American culture that I had not fully appreciated before. For the first time, I felt I was doing justice to the anthropology I'd encountered and practiced over the years. The whole human, reality in all its wildness, once out of the procrustean bed of academic writing, never wanted to obediently march back in.

And yet I did make it march back in, briefly, until I got tenure and had my flat, stiff dissertation, replete with tiny footnotes, turned into a book. Until then, I kept my poetry hidden. I didn't attempt to cross any lines or blur any boundaries. I never let my professors know I was writing poetry, or initially even my other colleagues when I got my first academic position. Thankfully, I am now at a college where it is safe for me to come out as a poet. And the two now, poetry and anthropology, exist in a dialectic, like they always should have. I write about what moves me, what fascinates me, what confuses me, what I haven't yet even named. I write about what can't be statistically counted or scientifically verified except through simile and metaphor.

Poetry, in all its subtlety and fluidity, has had a profound impact on where I choose to place my anthropological gaze. Because of poetry, I not only write about obvious formal rituals, but what is underneath and beside them. I now sit with them longer, and lift them up, feel the warmth of the soil underneath, smell the matted leaves around them—I write about the light on them, the shadows that cross them. Poetry, insofar as it is a fierce meditation, has taught me to uncover layers of reality and subtlety that any good thick description should include, in the same way we get to know the main character in a great novel. I now "study" a Sudanese refugee in all his dimensions, his confusions, his embarrassments, his jokes, favorite videos, longings and failures. Nonverbal behaviors, the spirit or energy of a moment, are all legitimate fodder for my fieldwork.

Recently, I was in Dharamsala, India, the home of the Dalai Lama and Tibetan Government in Exile. Since most of my academic interests now involve working with refugees, I was there to explore setting up a student program to help Tibetan refugee children. While I was there, I gave a lecture on postmodern ethnography to some American Tibetan Studies students on a semester abroad with the School for International Training. I read my poems, poems about the most wretched and elating parts of field work, about the 10,000 shades of meaning and emotion that occur between myself and the "Other," about my own encounter with Buddhism, about other Westerners seeking meaning in the East, about Nepali child prostitutes, Sudanese refugees, about taking my daughter to India, watching my son in a refugee camp in Uganda, lady slippers, Catholicism, the mountain I live underneath.

Through my own poetry, where science and confession, art and social science all feed off each other, I tried to call into question the objective science they were supposedly practicing with the native Tibetans. Every time they tried to pin me down in some category, some four-walled room, some strict definition, I found myself wriggling out, noting how my own emotions influenced my interviews, how my love of colliding cultures influenced my poetry, how my poetic gaze influenced what I chose to study. As much as they were frustrated, I could tell they felt liberated because the range of what they thought could be included in anthropology had just widened and deepened considerably. Art and emotions, thick wild description, the whole messy terrain of the unsaid, the subjectivity they had already learned to wall off from their undergraduate papers, were allowed back in.

### Lost Boy

*The Lost Boys refers to the 17,000 children in southern Sudan who fled their homes in 1987 seeking refuge from the civil war. They walked 1,000 miles before they finally found protection in a Kenyan refugee camp, Kaukuma. By the time they reached there, half of the boys had died from starvation, thirst, soldiers, lions and bandits. About 3,700 have recently been resettled in America.*

Deng Majok sits inside his apartment,
heat cranked up to 80, curtains closed,
a pile of chicken boiling on the stove.
He slides another Kung Fu movie
into the VCR, settles back into the smelly,
swaybacked couch, a Budweiser between his legs.
He giggles.
In half an hour he'll ride his bike
to Walmart, round stray shopping carts
from the cracked grey lot,
crashing them back into their steel corrals.

He remembers joining
a black river of boys,
their edges swelling and thinning
as they wound their way
over tight lipped soil, sun stuck to their backs.
He remembers dust mushrooming
around a sack of cornmeal as it thudded, slumped over, like a fat woman crying in sand.

In America
they took him to a store,
bought him fresh sneakers
soft and white
as wedding cake.
The next day he walked through whole aisles
of dog food.

At first they dropped by all the time,
church ladies, anthropologists,
students, the local reporter.
They all left elated, having found something real
like yoga and organic food.

The first Thanksgiving, three families booked him.
Leaning hungrily across
the long white table,
they nibbled at his stories,
his lean noble life.

Over and over he told them about lions,
crocodiles, eating mud and urine.

The Americans came alive, with a sad,
compassionate glow, a kind of sunset inside them.
After dinner, he heard them berate their children,
twitching over a second straight hour of Game Boy.

Two years later, November again,
he's dropped out of high school –
he can't take
the kids staring, the tiny numbers and letters
he can't keep straight,
the basketball team he didn't make
despite his famous height.
All night he'll clean the toilets at the hospital
as silent tvs splash their images
over the bodies, into their open mouths.

Now he looks like a too tall gangster,
all gold-chained and baggy-trousered.
He's channel surfing,
listening to Bob Marley on his walkman,
his long legs awkwardly pushed out
to each side, the way giraffes
split their stilts
to drink of water.

Africa's moved inside him,
all cramped and bored, sleeping a lot.

He cracks another beer,
starts to float, the reggae
flooding the vast blue-black continent
of his body now limp and warm,
draped like a panther
over sides of the sofa.

His cousin calls, she needs more money,
her son has malaria. She can't afford school fees anymore.
His uncle gets on the phone to remind him to study hard,
come back and build a new Sudan.

Later he stumbles into the bathroom
to brush his teeth. Groggy Africa
flinches at the neon light, paces
then settles in the corner

of its den, paws pushing into the walls
of his chest with a dull pain.

The next morning he wakes,
stubborn Africa still shoved up against his ribs,
refusing to roll over, back into the middle
of himself where he can't feel it anymore,

back into some open place
where he ends
and America finally begins.

## Postscript

Since writing this chapter I have published two books of ethnographic poetry. *REFUGE* (BOA Editions, Ltd, New American Poets Series, 2013) and recently, *THE TRAUMA MANTRAS: A Memoir in Prose Poems* (Duke University Press, 2024). *The Trauma Mantras* has been reviewed in *Anthropology and Humanism; Current Anthropology; Anthropologica; SAPIENS; The AutoEthnographer; American Ethnologist; Social Anthropology; Culture, Medicine and Psychiatry.* My creative nonfiction memoir of taking care of my mother during her last year of life entitled *The Lonely, The Dogged* is forthcoming with Duke University Press (Fall 2026).

I have served as poetry co-editor for *Anthropology and Humanism* and *Green Mountains Review* and read my work at the PEN New England Freedom to Write Conference, the Mind and Life Institute, Harvard's Center for the Study of World Religions; Harvard Divinity School; School for Advanced Research; The Loden Foundation; William Joiner Institute for the Study of War and Its Social Consequences, The Democracy Center and taught poetry in South Sudan and Bhutan on behalf of the Iowa International Writers Conference/US Department of State. I continue to be a supporter of Africa ELI (Education and Leadership Initiative) along with the Lost Boys of Sudan resettled in Vermont which supports refugee girls education. My ethnographic poetry and writings on poetry as an ethnographic tool have also been featured in *Crumpled Paper Boat: Experiments in Ethnographic Writing* (Duke University Press), *The Creative Ethnographer's Notebook* (Routledge); *A Different Kind of Ethnography* (U Toronto Press); *HIMALAYA*. Aside from teaching classes on Anthropology of Refugees, I am also now working with Afghan refugees and a board member of the Vermont Afghan Alliance. I continue to rely on creatively written ethnographies for students in my anthropology classes because of the way their poetic language draws students to a foreign world in a more visceral and emotional way than most academic conventionally written ethnographies. I am also convinced that poetic devices are essential in any ethnographic writing because of the degree of subtlety and complexity they can convey. Poetic devices, particularly metaphor, can take ethnographic thick description to a whole new level of nuance and multidimensionality that any description of culture must convey.

My recent work has also been featured in *The Best American Poetry*, *American Poetry Review*, *The Kenyon Review*, *Harvard Review*, *Harvard Divinity Review*, *New England Review*, *Los Angeles Review*, *Prairie Schooner*, *Plume*, *War, Literature and the Arts*, *The Common* and numerous other poetry journals and anthologies.

Chapter 23

# The Abandoned School as an Anomalous Place of Learning

## A Practice-Led Approach to Doctoral Research

*Natalie LeBlanc*

As a visual artist, I have always been drawn to the abandoned: to empty lots, boarded-up homes, buildings that have fallen into disrepair. Places sinking into the land, or alternately, standing tall like shadowy ghosts. In these sites, foundations are crumbling, driveways and yards are overgrown with weeds, and windows sit vacant like hollow eye sockets. Growth is lodged between cracks, bordering walls and ledges, and literally trying to fill every crevice in its way. There are holes in fences, broken shards of glass, wet, rotten, and moldy materials; peeling paint and objects scattered haphazardly. Locks are hacked while cobwebs linger on doorknobs and in corners. Graffiti covers walls in layers, painted over (and under) each other like a palimpsest.

My preferred subject matter is abandoned architecture because it is a reflection of economic, cultural, and political history. My photographic practice, informed by the discourses of deindustrialization (Cowie & Heathcott, 2003; High & Lewis, 2007), urban exploration (Garrett, 2010; van der Hoorn, 2009), and the aesthetics of decay (Edensor, 2005; Trigg, 2006), demonstrates my fascination of towns and cities in North America, where places sit boarded up, desolate, and falling apart. The "deindustrial sublime" (High & Lewis, 2007) is a term used to describe the places that have become synonymous with the expressions "no-man's land" (High & Lewis, 2007, p. 8) and "dead zones" (Edensor, 2005, p. 13). In the discourse of art and aesthetics, they are commonly referred to as "modernist ruins" or "post-industrial sites"—symbols for transition and impermanence (Dillon, 2011; Hell & Schönle, 2010). Comparable to these places are abandoned farms, foreclosed homes, and closed schools—extensions of the direct ramifications of deindustrialization that have just as much (if not more) allure due to their everyday or mundane quality (LeBlanc, 2008, 2015).

In the context of history, culture, politics, philosophy, and art, abandonment is a rich and evocative concept (Armstrong, 2011; Dewar & Manning Thomas, 2013). It does not simply refer to things that have been discarded; it refers to the objects and the places that people have been forced to leave behind (Carswell, 2012). Social theorist Roger Salerno (2003) defines abandonment as "the estrangement from home" (p. 157). This idea implies a separation or a detachment between people and place, and as such, holds an ability to evoke a powerful source of human anxiety (Figure 23.1).

How might abandoned places direct us toward a time in the past while simultaneously revealing that there is a change—an interruption, or a tear, in the fabric of the built environment of today. This interruption has a future "directedness"—a future that is unseen, but felt—a future that is unknown and uncertain (van der Hoorn, 2009). And thus, my questions become: *What will happen when these places are demolished to the ground? What*

DOI: 10.4324/9781003412892-23

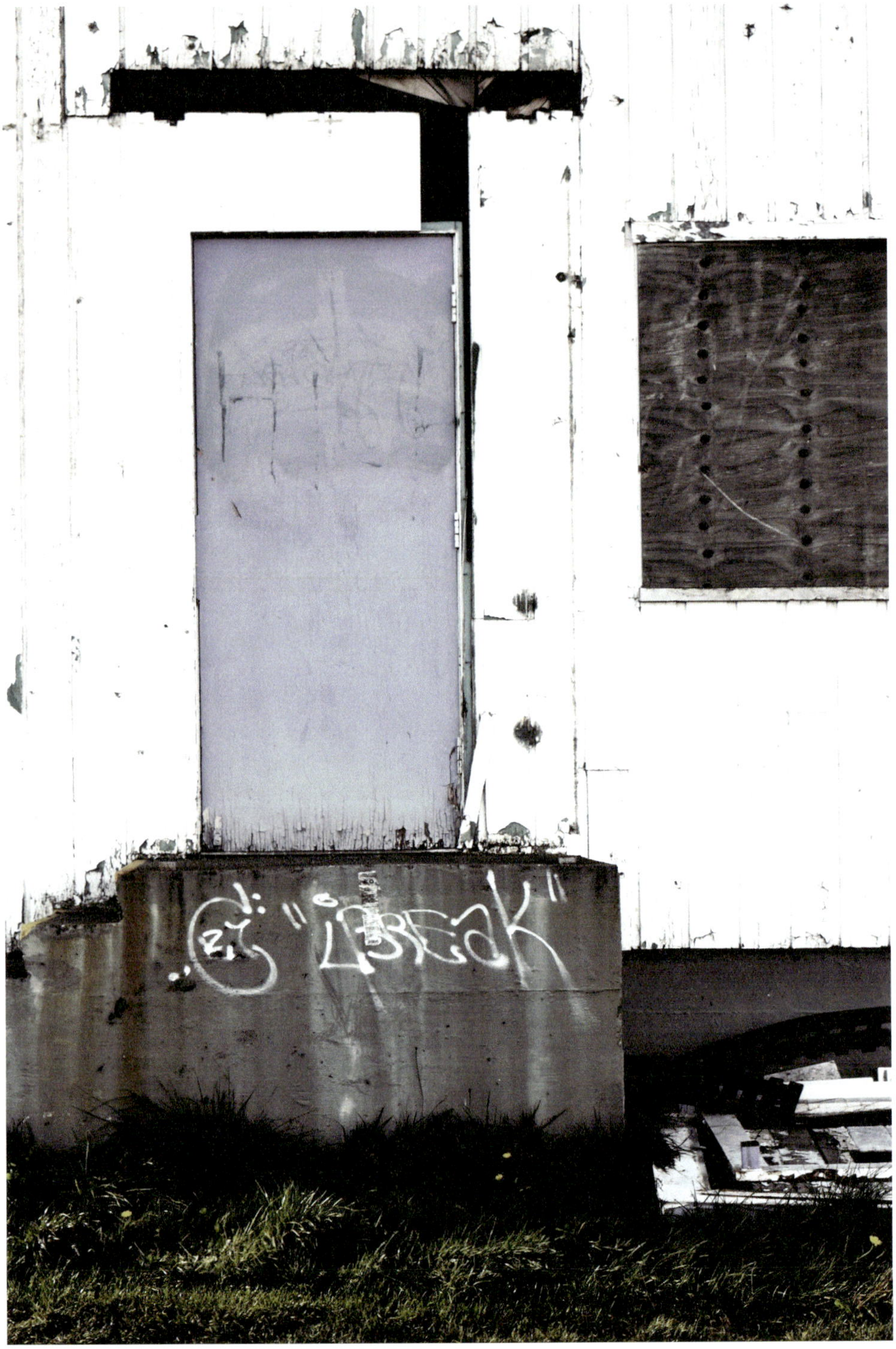

*Figure 23.1* Dead School.

Digital photography by Natalie LeBlanc, 2011.

*will happen to the stories, to the narratives, to the myths, and to the meanings that are attached to them? What will happen to the possibility for exploring some of the complex relationships between these places and the people who (used to) inhabit them?*

## Introduction to the Abandoned School

In this chapter, I explore the ongoing work of becoming an arts-based researcher through the processes and practices of photography that open artistic, autobiographic, conceptual, and theoretical sites of inquiry. My project focused on the abandoned school because it is a deinstitutionalized and decommissioned place that had not yet legally been rezoned, resold, or repurposed. Once inside the abandoned school, the reader/viewer may revisit an abandoned site of educational dwelling: to consider what has failed and what remains. They are invited to ponder the residual presence of schools in their imaginative lives so that with proper attunement, the abandoned school may become a "transitional" space, producing unanticipated ways of relation (Ellsworth, 2005). As my work attests, this space is generative and educational because the spatiotemporal (re)configurations that it asks readers/viewers to navigate and provoke palpable experiences where response, affections, afflictions, reflections, and perceptions create the conditions for new and creative thought.

Inspired by visual artists such as Zoe Leonard and Martha Rosler who also document architecture on the brink of vanishment, my project—comprising 2,487 photographs—is a visual archive that taps into the traditions of documentary and conceptual photography. Each photograph, carefully selected and arranged, holds a specific place within the larger photo-essay that comprises this work. Drawing on the photo-essay arts-based research of visual art educators Ricardo Marín-Viadel and Joaquín Roldán (2010), my research lends itself to multiple interpretations by exploiting the rhetorical or narrative potential of images as well as their figurative or representational functions. Purposively staging the photographs in and through the text extends, and at times disrupts, writing.

Like a *wunderkammer—a cabinet of curiosities*—(Suderberg, 2000), the abandoned school is a collection of things that, rather than being chosen for their historical or monetary worth, have been selected for their evocative qualities. Once inside the abandoned school, you may encounter things not normally regarded as being aesthetically pleasing, things that may appear overly ambiguous or excessive. As was the case of a Renaissance cabinet of curiosities, it is somewhat an interdisciplinary hybrid that lacks homogeneity. Its power resides in the uncontrolled imagination that, as a (virtual) space, it makes possible. As such, it is an offering: an invitation to enter inside this virtual abandoned school (a compilation of the 16 closed schools that I visited and documented as part of this research project). However, the geographical location of each place is intentionally withheld (Figure 23.2).

Entering the abandoned school, the reader/viewer encounters overexposed, blurred, and intimately close-up images. They are invited to navigate the myriad, fragmented, and fragile ways that they unfold. For some, these impressions may have a hallucinatory quality, while for others they may trigger partial or mixed recollections of (past) memories or experiences, calling a series of inner images or sensations to come forth. In any case, they may entertain these "unmoorings" (Farr, 2012)—especially if perforated, raw, or formless. Creating intersections between dreams and reality, memory and imagination, and authority and dissent, the abandoned school presents a somewhat disorienting experience, provoking illusions and/or things that don't necessarily speak to reason (Greene, 1990, as cited in Pinar, 2009,

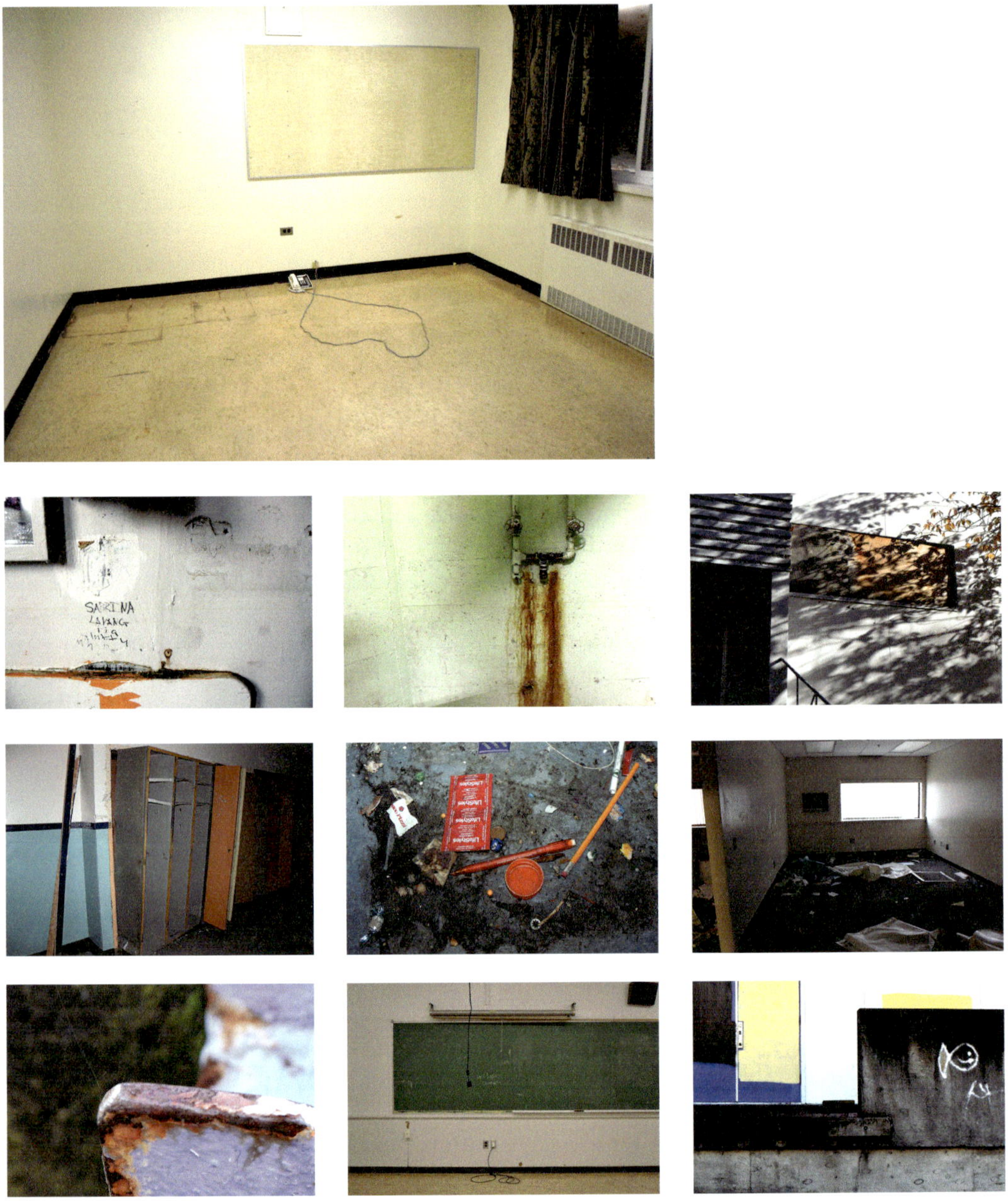

*Figure 23.2* Select images from *In/visibility of the Abandoned School: Beyond Representations of School Closure.*

Digital photography by Natalie LeBlanc, 2010–2015.

p. 125). As such, it is an invitation to focus on the effect that this experience provokes—to the "monstrum," the subterranean, or the unusual phenomena that lie beneath the surface of existence (Pinar, 2009, p. 124, 190).

Encounters with the abandoned school are brought forward in five *concessions*, as a provocation for (re)imagining relationships between space, time, place, and memory: *The Void*, *The Ghost Town*, *The Crypt*, *The Corpse*, and *The Wake*. Concessions refer to the right to use land or property for a specific purpose, normally granted by the government or other controlling body. Each concession, sounding like both *session* and *confession*, is a written and visual act of disclosure, leading the reader into a different, yet relational world. Each one, framed by a concept that emerged during my inquiry, allows the work, as a collection, to resist a chronological or linear ordering system. Through the five concessions, the reader/viewer is led on a journey as a provocation for understanding the abandoned school as a being with generative possibility.

Taking spatial form, each concession is an opening, a fragment, and an experience that invites the reader/viewer to encounter the ambiguous and changing relations of the work. This format intentionally challenges the traditional research structure and the preconceptions of an artist as a sole creator. Instead, the artist is a collaborator or even co-laborer (Irwin, 2013). Informed by arts-based researcher Graeme Sullivan (2010, 2011), the exegesis places photographic practices from the perspective of the artist: allowing my sense of visuality to drive decisions of selecting what images to take and how to arrange them in archives and publication. The methodology that I employed was practice-led research (Barrett & Bolt, 2007), a mode of "material thinking" (Bolt, 2007), in which understanding was realized through the handling of materials. Allowing my photographic practice to lead the inquiry, the questions that I researched emerged in and through my visual doing. Framed by a continual process of questioning that consistently challenged my artistic, theoretical, and educational interests, what I sought to understand was not predetermined. As such, understandings were realized *through* my artistic practice and *in* material thinking, and my final realizations were presented artistically as potentials for new insights.

The work of art critic Jane Rendell (2010)—whereby bringing together art and writing shifts the focus from the artwork, as an objective artifact, to the spaces *between* the artist, the artwork, and the viewer—also informs this research. As a spatial practice, or *spatial morphology* (Trigg, 2012), it provokes an interpretation and produces "a shift in thought itself" (Bolt, 2007, p. 29). Unlike a thesis, my exegesis does not answer or advance a hypothesis, nor does it explain the artwork. Rather, it provides "a forum to reconfigure theoretical positions" (Bolt, 2007, p. 33). It asks that the reader/viewer become attuned to the photograph, to my photographic practice, and consider unusual or unfamiliar places of learning that, like my exegesis, is a movement away from closed forms of exchange toward new and/or divergent modes of relation.

Although my research shares commonalities with qualitative or post-qualitative social science methodologies, it differs in that art practice is "the core around which inquiry unfolds" (Sullivan, 2010, p. 102). As such, I avoid utilizing art instrumentally *in order to* come to understandings, one of which being research (although the nuances of research were better understood) as a result of my inquiry. Therefore, it can be best described as a form of study (Pinar, 2015), an invented site of education where, situated as a learner, understandings about research were made retrospectively.

## Concession 1: The Void

The void is a metaphor for a non-school—a school that once was, but is no longer. The void refers to the emptiness of the once-was-school—a place that was central to the community, but now stands in the periphery or in the margins of society. In science fiction, a void sometimes describes an ambiguous place in the distance (Hamilton, 2010). In astronomy, a void can describe a large volume of space between filaments such as cosmic voids, which are the largest structures in the universe (Bharadwaj et al., 2004). Again, these spaces are ambiguous. Some scientists believe that voids are devoid of matter, while others believe they contain a smooth distribution of dark matter, which, as their name suggests, remain invisible (Zitrin & Brosch, 2008). The void presents us with the perplexing questions: is an empty space equivalent to nothing? If we are unable to see something, does it mean that it is not there? The prior definitions simultaneously point to the discourse of nothing (or no-thing) in philosophy and to the ontology of wanting or needing to know more about something that we are unable to see.

The void also emphasizes the physical and emotional complications related to school closure, while suggesting the ambiguous role that emptiness plays in its abandonment. I utilize Martin Heidegger's philosophy of the *nothing* (2000), what I understand as an abandonment of preconceived notions and a continual process of un/learning, to frame my work. Coming to arts-based research as an artist, un/learning is not about forgetting my artistic practice, it is about entertaining an alternative paradigm, allowing myself to recognize what my arts-practice brings to my research.

Through the specificity of my own experiences as an artist, I readily entertain the unknown, trust the process, and ultimately pursue an inventive methodology for my research. Beginning with my experiences photographing decommissioned schools, I engage with a Heideggerian nothing, provoking me to wonder about the very nature of my own being and doings. As my exegesis attests, the nothing draws attention to the things that cannot be seen and to the things that are imagined or conjured with/in the presence of absence. The nothing also speaks to the stance and the disposition that this process required, where—as a mode of inquiry—I focus on questions as they emerge instead of concerning myself with an end goal or outcome. I present my research in a similar vein, staging it into what Barone and Eisner (2012) refer to as an *aesthetic remove*, described as a *virtual world* designed to coax readers/viewer into having an experience that is analogous to (if not necessarily the same) as the experience of the researcher/artist.

## Concession 2: The Ghost Town

When a school is closed, where does everyone go? What remains left behind in the school that once played such a pivotal role in housing the community's social and educational encounters? For John Dewey (1907), education is a process of living. His belief was that the school should be a form of life: a unity of relations, an extension of the home, a stimulative environment, and "embryonic" community (p. 15). A closed school, having more in common with a place that has been deserted after war or a natural disaster, is a stark contrast to the image painted by Dewey. *When the closed school becomes one abandoned, does it haunt the community with its presence? Rejected from the people who commissioned it, from the activities it hosted, and from the period to which it refers to, does it become unwanted or unnecessary?*

Being inside, things are unnaturally still. There is a consistence of absence. There are no people, no paperwork, no books, no voices, and no footsteps in the halls. All of which become a set of signifiers that somehow become more powerful than if these things were present. The interior of the abandoned school presents us with a challenge; it tests our abilities of interpretation, creativity, and perception. How are we ever to make sense of this place when there is "nothing" to see? In this concession, the abandoned school demands careful observation. It asks that we take into consideration what is included in its visual and spatial composition and what is excluded. It requires paying attention to the subtle nuances of the place while taking into consideration our implicit assumptions. However, on closer inspection, the photographs in this concession present a multidimensional place, where countless cultural, historical, political, and social lineages are at work in a single image. With this stance, we might begin to see how the abandoned school begins to tell an alternate story to that of "closure."

## Concession 3: The Crypt

During this project, I had the opportunity of participating in multiple exhibitions that displayed several of my photographs and photographic series. However, these events left me feeling somewhat disappointed—somewhat unfulfilled. After exhibiting my photographs in the traditional mode for two-dimensional work (on a wall at which viewers looked from a distance), I wanted to do something different from what I had done before—I wanted to invite my viewers to see and to feel the abandoned school in a way that was similar to how I had experienced it as an urban explorer dwelling with/in an ambiguous place.

As such, I conceptualized an art installation in which photographs taken inside of a decommissioned school were projected onto the outside's physical structure, and I invited the public—community members who experienced the closure of the decommissioned school—to take part in an immersive experience in which they could, in turn, project their own stories and imaginations onto the artwork. One of the most defining features of a closed school is the meticulous window boarding that protects the unoccupied site from thieves and vandals. The photographic interiors projected onto the outside walls were conceptualized to evoke large, oversized windows and to disrupt the static building by creating openings into new spaces, new thoughts, and new worlds. Influenced by the work of Elizabeth Grosz (2001), the projected photographs intentionally addressed the binary of outside/inside, linking the two disparate physical spaces together by bringing the viewer "in" through virtual means. The projected interior, with its larger-than-life objects and empty rooms, became more dreamlike than actual. They were an invitation for imagination and for reflection, provoking viewers to engage with the closed school by putting their own fantasies, memories, and experiences into play.

The dialogue that took place on-site between the decommissioned school, the viewer(s), the landscape, and myself, the artist/researcher, who was present during the installation, refused to let the abandoned school "settle" into the background—rather, it became the topic of our conversation. Furthermore, the event produced a layering, or a folding of time and space into one place. As a re/imagined space (and as seen in Figure 15.3), the abandoned school is rendered as partial and open. No longer fixed, static, or whole, it is visually positioned as to connect with other spaces, places, people, and events. Like a palimpsest, it is an invitation to imagine other cracks, crevices, and cavities into (over and under) things that normally go unseen or unnoticed.

However, as the crypt attests, the installation brought forth a world lost and a history buried underneath the surface of the everyday. Some viewers revealed that they had a past greatly connected to the decommissioned school. For one individual, it spanned over 100 years, back to its very beginning when her great-grandfather donated the land that the school was built upon and for 70 years of which she lived next door. As Derrida (2005) argues, the crypt is a metaphor for a lost object that resides inside an individual, where it forever remains preserved. In this sense, the crypt is something that cannot truly be revealed to anybody else. As an invisible being, it is *felt*—and this feeling has an uncanny ability of haunting our thoughts, dreams, and imaginations (Figure 23.3).

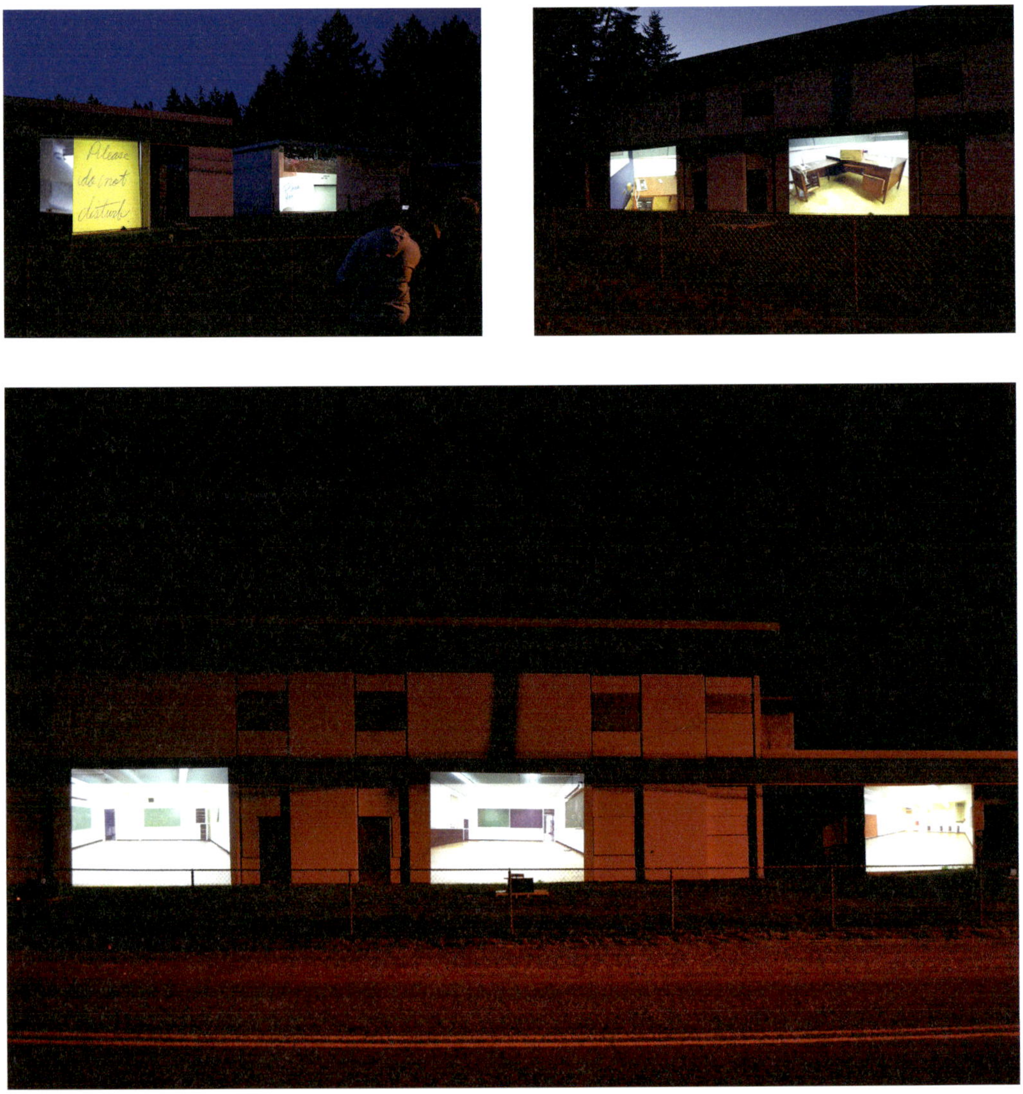


*Figure 23.3* Documentation of the installation *In/visibility of the Abandoned School.*
Digital photography by Natalie LeBlanc, 2014.

## Concession 4: The Corpse

Utilizing Hannah Arendt's (1998) notion of storytelling, this concession speaks to what it felt like, for me alone, to be part of and bodily present on the night that *In/Visibility of the Abandoned School* was installed. Focusing on some of the textures that the event opened up through feelings, memories, illusions, and reverie—a "tangled, murky zone where fantasy and images, desire and loss reside" (Morris, 2009, p. 92)—it is an invitation to contemplate life, death, dead space, live space, and spaces between.

In *The Corpse*, the abandoned school speaks to its humanized remains. Delving into the issue of school closure, an epidemic spreading throughout North America and other parts of the globe as a result of a neoliberal agenda based on educational reform, it raises issues and questions intersecting with, and relating to, social justice, citizenship, and human rights. *The Corpse* renders the abandoned school as something that has been terminated or killed—a place that has become invalid and worthless because the sovereign power that controlled its fate has deemed it so. The term is purposefully meant to conjure a disturbance, yet it is also meant to signify the sense of spirit that the abandoned school embodies.

*The Corpse* is an ironic nod to Hannah Arendt (1973) and how she utilized the term to denote a dead, non-thinking being. In my work, it speaks to the human capacity to act, what Arendt (1998) refers to as "the political activity par excellence" (p. 9), something that can only occur between people and is held in this connection. In meeting a community affected by a decommissioned school, individuals vocalized to me their opinions, concerns, and fears about political events, including diminishing school enrollment and the changing and mutating role that their civil and social institutions were playing with/in their community. The witnesses invited me to think with them about the complexity of school closure, while the installation provided an opportunity for interpersonal relationships.

Therefore, instead of "a dead zone of imagination" (Giroux, 2016), the abandoned school (re)entered the context of the living, where it exceeded beyond its limits. Instead of succumbing to the perspective that there was nothing left to do (but to give in) (Greene, 2010), the site-specific installation enabled spatiotemporal relations and connections between representations of the abandoned school and the actual decommissioned building, to produce an emergent space in which the decommissioned school could be (re)examined and (re)critiqued.

It is in this concession where Heidegger's theory experiences a death in my work and where his pupil Hannah Arendt and her counter-concept of *appearance* grows in importance. Rather than rendering being as a *being-towards-death* (Heidegger, 2010), the installation drew attention to being as appearance (Arendt, 1998). This is echoed in the very way that the installation appeared and disappeared in the night. Its ephemeral quality echoes the very nature of life itself: emerging out of darkness and disappearing back into darkness. In this way, and in its simplicity, the abandoned school extends beyond art, beyond research, beyond the academy, beyond the institution, and beyond the community where it will forever remain open, indeterminate, and mutable.

## Concession 5: The Wake

It is in *The Wake* where all five concessions come together as a commemoration of life. As a deferral, *The Wake* collects and in turn disseminates the ripples from the previous concessions producing new images of thought. Although *The Wake* is a series of traces, as a (continual) form of provocation, it is not the outcome of thinking, but a process of thinking itself. *The Wake* is primarily concerned with the close-up: a reduced frame of reference that paradoxically broadens perspective. This stylistic rendering is an analogy for how, in looking more deeply into things, "a wider constellation of memories and associations can emerge" (Rendell, 2010, p. 121).

The close-up—such as a thick spider's web found in a dark corner, a large flake of peeling paint, an abyss formed by cracked concrete—presents an abstract, micro universe out of an object that may rarely be glanced at or given attention to in the context of the everyday. In a close-up, things are severely cropped so that in their ambiguity, they may provoke a mix of feelings, sensations, and emotions. This characterizes my experiences of being-in and being-with the abandoned school as an unknown and uncertain event. These images, producing joy and excitement, work against the transcription of memory by offering *fragments* of memories, which as Jill Bennett (2005) argues, can be read only in reference to the viewer's bodily sensation. To be moved by them—not in the sense that one is touched by the plight of a character in a fictional narrative, but on the more literal sense being affected, stricken with affect (p. 29).

These photographs deny a static or fixed "truth." Provoking affect, all the sensations, uncertainties, and questions that surface refuse to adopt a language of external, common memory. Blurring the line between photography and painting, the photographs presented in this concession are the most abstract of the whole archive. They demonstrate my process as an active search *for* language.

As Bennett reveals (2005), images "evince a process of coming into view" (p. 31). I particularly take issue with what Bennett (2005) posits is the "unspeakability" of an image, which pertains to a realm of sense memory in which the unspoken is contained within everything that is un/heard, un/seen, un/touched, un/felt, un/smelled, and un/tasted with/in the photograph. This emphasizes the photograph's fragmented quality while drawing attention to the idea that the "thingness" of the abandoned school is something that can never be seen. As such, the photograph situates the viewer as a witness to an unknown story.

Drawing on Gilles Deleuze's (2000) notion of affect, Bennett (2005) argues that art produces intensity or *a dynamic encounter* rather than a narrative. She addresses the limitations of a narrative while drawing attention to the corporeal, in which art is more than one *thing* simultaneously. As Bennett (2005) argues, the form "provides a means of reading encounters between ||insides_ and ||outsides_—as between sense memory and common memory—within any given pictorial or performative field" (p. 32). As such, my photographs of the abandoned school depict memory as something poised at a point of entry *into* common language. They emphasize an expression, or rather, an emergence into what Bennett (2005) argues is *a rupture* within the field of common representation. As such, the photograph tests the limits of the viewer. It is an invitation for the viewer to enter into an ambiguous space where they, too, may feel the work before recognizing its "contents." Staged as an encounter (Bennett, 2005; O'Sullivan, 2006), this experience may be difficult to articulate.

In staging my work in this manner, it is my intention to trigger an affective response, where the reader/viewer can feel the photograph viscerally. Drawing on Deleuze's (2000) work, *Proust and Signs*, Bennett (2005) further explains the phenomenon of the "encountered sign," which "agitates, compelling and fueling inquiry rather than simply placating the subject" (p. 36). As an encounter, my intention is to link the affective actions of the image with a thinking process without asserting the primacy of either one. Drawing further from Deleuze (2000), Bennett (2005) argues that an artist thinks in sensations; therefore, what is depicted before the audience is a *body*, "not insofar as it is represented as an object, but insofar as it is experienced as sustaining this sensation" (Bennett, 2005, p. 37). The photograph, in turn, may be understood as a fragmented body that is undergoing sensation during an affective response.

In photographing the abandoned school and not what causes the abandoned school, as the viewer, you are presented a moment, yet you are unable to see the cause of this moment. Bennett (2005) reminds us that thinking in sense memory is a mode of thought, where the sensation is brought forth by the artist who does not reflect on a past experience, but registers the lived process of memory. As opposed to a representation of feeling, it enacts a state or an experience that more aligns with a post-memory. It asks that you shift your attention from asking, *what does the photograph represent?* to *what does the photograph do?* This idea relates to Elizabeth Ellsworth's (2005) concept of "a pedagogical pivot point" (p. 37). Drawing from Winnicott's (1989) concept of a transitional object, Ellsworth (2005) describes art as capable of putting the self in relation to others and the world and similar to a transitional space in that it is intentionally designed "to keep questions unanswered in any once and for all way" (p. 56). The pedagogical significance of the transitional object resides in the ambiguous and paradoxical characteristics of the experience, which ultimately resists a singular definition. To borrow the words of Elizabeth Ellsworth (2005), the abandoned school is intentionally "designed not to be the kind of answer that brings thinking to an end, but an 'answer' that provokes us to keep thinking" (Ellsworth, 2005, p. 59).

As a transitional space, it creates the possibility for the reader/viewer to become a participant in the work. Staged as an affective and/or sensorial experience, my photographs render the abandoned school as being somewhat unintelligible to thought, because their affective character is something that is not simply looked at, but something that, as Bennett (2005) reminds us, involves bodily responses that may lie outside verbal-semantic-linguistic representation.

## Conclusion

My photographic research theorizes a new structure for approaching visual arts-based research. The Void, The Ghost Town, The Crypt, The Corpse, and The Wake present a methodology for visual inquiry by offering a new model of knowledge that can work with/in the academy (Arnold, 2012) because it creates new dimensions and new definitions of arts-based research. Led by practices of art-making, my exegesis situates art as the driving force of the inquiry while making it the focal point of both my process and my findings. By analyzing my practice as a mixture of historic research, philosophy, theory, and art-making, the exegesis is presented as a spatial practice, or "spatial morphology" (Trigg, 2012), an invitation for readers/viewers to engage in the text, the photographs, and the spaces between, so that at times they are abandoned to navigate the decommissioned school alone. This approach directly counters more traditional dissertation formats while mirroring my process in which, as an urban explorer (Garrett, 2010; High & Lewis, 2007; van der Hoorn, 2009), flâneur (Benjamin, 1999) and dérive (Debord, 2002; Smith, 2010), I found myself working in an unchartered and ambiguous space.

The five concessions presented here do not refer to the abandoned school as nothing. Rather, they make reference to the contradiction that the abandoned school has come to be. Removing the emphasis from the building—from its architecture and from its mere objective qualities (that have been made remote and strange through a loss of identity)—it places emphasis on us as urban dwellers/explorers/modern day flâneurs and dérives and how we experience it as *part* of our landscape and, as such, a part of life.

Each concession also helps speak to the difficulty that visual arts-based research entails, in which understanding can only be gained through the repetition, variation, reflection, and reflexivity that art practice makes possible. Allowing my art practice—my professional training in how to see and how to apply the techniques of photography to expanding perception—to lead my inquiry, emerging and unfolding in space and through time, contributes to the performative research paradigm, which Barbara Bolt (2009) and Brian Haseman (2007) argue differs from the more dominant qualitative or quantitative paradigms in research.

By exploring the relations *between* the living and the abandoned school, this project not only emphasizes the qualities of a deinstitutionalized place but also renders these qualities as embodied and perceptually felt. These relations are both spatial and temporal in that they locate a space between the self and the abandoned school, and a space between the past and the future. As a deferred action, they prompt a mode of being in which the *in* and the *through* become necessary conditions for the production of the new. My arts-based research not only documents what is dis/appearing from the postindustrial landscape, but it also actively explores the generativity of loss and the possibilities of art as a form of remembrance within a context shaped by history, power, and memory. Furthermore, as an exegesis (exhibition and theoretical engagement), rather than a thesis (argument), the final form moves beyond the traditional boundaries of dissertation research, an invitation for the academy to rethink the nature of dissertation research in art education.

## Postscript

As a practicing artist and art educator, I ask my students to focus on what art can do and to think about ways that we can integrate it into our curricula and in our everyday lives to increase desirable qualities and skills such as empathy, morality, creativity, critical thinking, resilience, and so on without creating an instrumental justification for the arts—or in other words, validating art because of "its potential significance to impact 'something else'" (Biesta, 2018, p. 12). This is the conundrum of art and education, one that curriculum scholar Gert Biesta (2018) has described as a conundrum of *what matters*—because "what matters is not whether there is attention for the arts, but what kind of attention there is" (p. 12). In this chapter, I have attempted to demonstrate what arts-based educational research can look like and I would like to use this as an opportunity to emphasize what it can do. In my opinion, this is the kind of attention that matters.

My dissertation work, for which this chapter is based upon, demonstrates how *scholartistry* is not merely a matter of transferring art or implementing art within a research study, rather, it is concerned with creating new opportunities to engage in exploratory, experimental, emergent, affective, and improvisational processes that can question and problematize knowledge, learning, and pedagogy, even—and especially if this disrupts with more traditional approaches for conducting, writing, and reporting on research. This is the stance that I encourage my students to adopt in their own artistic-scholarly work for which the actual doing of art is imperative. It is through the material processes of making art that we learn about ourselves, others and our relationships in and with the world in which we inhabit. Moreover, art practice keeps these relationships in motion, fostering relational ways of thinking, knowing, being, and living.

## References

Arendt, H. (1973). *The origins of totalitarianism.* Harcourt Brace. (Original work published 1948).

Arendt, H. (1998). *The human condition* (2nd ed.). The University of Chicago Press. (Original work published 1958).

Armstrong, J. (2011). Everyday afterlife: Walter Benjamin and the politics of abandonment in Saskatchewan, Canada. *Cultural Studies, 25*(3), 273–293. https://doi.org/10.1080/09502380903579001

Arnold, J. (2012). Practice-led research: Creative activity, academic debate and intellectual rigour. *Higher Education Studies, 2*(2), 9–24. https://doi.org/10.5539/hes.v2n2p9

Barone, T., & Eisner, E. W. (2012). *Arts based research.* Sage.

Barrett, E., & Bolt, B. (Eds.). (2007). *Practice as research: Approaches to creative arts enquiry.* I. B. Tauris.

Benjamin, W. (1999). *The arcades project* (R. Tiedemann, Ed.; H. Eiland & K. McLaughlin, Trans.). Belknap Press of Harvard University Press. (Original work published 1972).

Bennett, J. (2005). *Empathic vision: Affect, trauma, and contemporary art.* Stanford University Press.

Bharadwaj, S., Bhavsar, S. P., & Sheth, J. V. (2004). The size of the longest filaments in the universe. *The Astrophysical Journal, 606*(1), 25–31. https://doi.org/10.1086/382140

Biesta, B. (2018). What if? Art education beyond expression and creativity. In C. Naughton, G. Biesta & D. R. Cole (Eds.), *Art, artists and pedagogy: Philosophy and the arts in education* (pp. 11–20). Routledge.

Bolt, B. (2007). The magic is in the handling. In E. Barrett & B. Bolt (Eds.), *Practice as research: Approaches to creative arts enquiry* (pp. 27–34). I. B. Tauris.

Bolt, B. (2009). A performative paradigm for the creative arts? Working Papers in Art and Design, 5. Retrieved from: https://www.herts.ac.uk/__data/assets/pdf_file/0015/12417/WPIAAD_vol5_bolt.pdf

Carswell, A. T. (Ed.). (2012). *The encyclopedia of housing* (2nd ed.). Sage.

Cowie, J., & Heathcott, J. (2003). *Beyond the ruins: The meanings of deindustrialization.* Cornell University Press.

Debord, G. (2002). *Society of the spectacle* (K. Knabb, Trans.). Rebel Press. (Original work published 1967).

Deleuze, G. (2000). *Proust and signs: The complete text* (R. Howard, Trans.). University of Minnesota Press. (Original work published 1964).

Derrida, J. (2005). Foreword. In N. Abraham & M. Torok (Eds.), *The wolf man's magic word: Cryptonymy: Vol. 37. Theory and history of literature* (pp. xi–xlviii). (B. Johnson, Trans.). University of Minnesota Press. (Original work published 1977).

Dewar, M., & Manning Thomas, J. (2013). *The city after abandonment.* University of Pennsylvania Press.

Dewey, J. (1907). *The school and society.* The University of Chicago Press.

Dillon, B. (Ed.). (2011). *Ruins: Documents of contemporary art.* MIT Press.

Edensor, T. (2005). *Industrial ruins: Space, aesthetics and materiality.* Berg Publishers.

Ellsworth, E. (2005). *Places of learning: Media, architecture, pedagogy.* Routledge.

Farr, I. (Ed.). (2012). *Memory: Documents of contemporary art.* Whitechapel.

Garrett, B. L. (2010). Urban explorers: Quest for myth, mystery and meaning. *Geography Compass, 4*(10), 1448–1461. https://doi.org/10.1111/j.1749-8198.2010.00389.x

Giroux, H. A. (2016). When schools become dead zones of the imagination: A critical pedagogy manifesto. *The High School Journal, 99*(4), 351–359. https://doi.org/10.1002/9781119082316.ch24

Greene, M. (2010). Pedagogies of thoughtfulness and imagination. In J. A. Sandlin, B. D. Schultz, & J. Burdick (Eds.), *Handbook of public pedagogy: Education and learning beyond schooling* (pp. 28–31). Routledge.

Grosz, E. A. (2001). *Architecture from the outside: Essays on virtual and real space.* MIT Press.

Hamilton, P. F. (2010). *The evolutionary void.* Del Rey Books.

Haseman, B. (2007). Rupture and recognition: Identifying the performative research paradigm. In E. Barrett & B. Bolt (Eds.), *Practice as research: Approaches to creative arts enquiry* (pp. 147–157). I. B. Tauris.

Heidegger, M. (2000). *Introduction to metaphysics* (G. Fried & R. Polt, Trans.). Yale University Press. (Original work published 1953).
Heidegger, M. (2010). *Being and time* (J. Stambaugh, Trans.). SUNY Press. (Original work published 1927).
Hell, J., & Schönle, A. (Eds.). (2010). *Ruins of modernity*. Duke University Press.
High, S., & Lewis, D. W. (2007). *Corporate wasteland: The landscape and memory of deindustrialization*. ILR Press.
Irwin, R. L. (2013). Becoming a/r/tography. *Studies in Art Education*, *54*(3), 198–215. https://doi.org/10.1080/00393541.2013.11518894
LeBlanc, N. (2008). *An investigation of the space between the painting and the photograph: Deconstructing the process and reflecting on the two media that constitute my art practice* [Unpublished master's thesis]. Concordia University.
LeBlanc, N. (2015). *In/visibility of the abandoned school: Beyond representations of school closure* [Unpublished doctoral dissertation]. The University of British Columbia.
Marín-Viadel, R., & Roldán, J. (2010). Photo essays and photographs in visual arts-based educational research. *International Journal of Education through Art*, *6*(*1*), 7–23. https://doi.org/10.1386/eta.6.1.7_1
Morris, R. (2009). The present tense of space. In C. Doherty (Ed.), *Situation* (pp. 27–28). Whitechapel.
O'Sullivan, S. (2006). *Art encounters Deleuze and Guattari: Thought beyond representation*. Palgrave Macmillan.
Pinar, W. F. (2009). *The worldliness of a cosmopolitan education: Passionate lives in public service*. Routledge.
Pinar, W. F. (2015). *Educational experience as lived: Knowledge, history alterity: The selected works of William F. Pinar*. Routledge.
Rendell, J. (2010). *Site-writing: The architecture of art criticism*. I. B. Tauris.
Salerno, R. A. (2003). *Landscapes of abandonment*. SUNY Press.
Smith, P. (2010). The contemporary dérive: A partial review of issues concerning the contemporary practice of psychogeography. *Cultural Geographies*, *17*(1), 103–122. https://doi.org/10.1177/1474474009350002
Suderberg, E. (2000). Introduction: On installation and site specificity. In E. Suderberg (Ed.), *Space, site, intervention: Situating installation art* (pp. 1–22). University of Minnesota Press.
Sullivan, G. (2010). *Art practice as research: Inquiry in visual arts* (2nd ed.). Sage.
Sullivan, G. (2011). The artist as researcher: New roles for new realities. In J. Wesseling (Ed.), *See it again, say it again: The artist as researcher* (pp. 79–101). Valiz Antennae.
Trigg, D. (2006). *The aesthetics of decay; Nothingness, nostalgia, and the absence of reason*. Peter Lang.
Trigg, D. (2012). *The memory of place: A phenomenology of the uncanny*. Ohio University Press.
van der Hoorn, M. (2009). *Indispensable eyesores*. Berghahn Books.
Winnicott, D. W. (1989). *Playing and reality*. Routledge.
Zitrin, A., & Brosch, N. (2008). The NGC 672 and 784 galaxy groups: Evidence for galaxy formation and growth along nearby dark matter filament. *Monthly Notices of the Royal Astronomical Society*, *390*, 408–420. https://doi.org/10.1111/j.1365-2966.2008.13786.x

Chapter 24

# The Ecology of Personal and Professional Experience

## A Poet's View

*Carl Leggo*

Because so much of my teaching, writing, and researching emerge from the intersections of the personal and the professional, I contend that autobiographical writing is always both personal and professional, and that we need to write autobiographically in order to connect with others (see Irwin & Springgay, Chapter 18). I live in the world as a poet. The word poetry is derived from *poiein*, "to make." As a researcher I am a poet or maker. I do not stand outside experience and observe experience like a video camera recording an objective reality. Instead, I seek to enter lived experiences with an imaginative openness to the people and activities and dynamics at work and play. I seek to make a story in collaborative dialogue with others, always aware that the story is one of many stories, one of many versions of the story.

My understanding of so much scholarly writing has been shaped by teachers and academics intent on filling the world with five-paragraph theme papers that prattle with predictable and pedantic persuasiveness, teachers who fear poetry with its subversive search for the strange. Still, I contend that my poetry and my poetic ruminations on teacher education, teacher well-being, pedagogic imagination, and creative living are scholarly writing, even though it might not always look or sound like the scholarly writing that fills academic journals beyond counting. In fact this kind of poetic research might be closer to the meaning of *scholar* than much writing that claims the label "scholarly writing." *Scholar* is derived from the Greek *schole* which signifies "leisure employed in learning." In much scholarly writing, "learning" is defined as research, explication, logic, reason, argument, and persuasion. The emphasis is on conclusions, implications, and recommendations. There is frequently a tone of world-weary urgency, akin to a military operation or corporate venture or political strategy convention. In most scholarly writing, learning is not born out of leisure. My research is the fruit of leisure, and it bears the sun-washed, moon-drawn, shadow-written lines of light where it has lingered. Like the familiar traditions of scholarly writing, my writing includes research, explication, logic, reason, argument, and persuasion, but the ingredients are mixed in unfamiliar ways, in a ruminant, poetic brew of learning sought and gained in the employment of leisure, of lingering in the world and in words.

So, in my autobiographic and poetic research, I proceed with a convicted understanding that the personal and the professional always work together, in tandem, in union, in the way of complementary angles. Only when they are together can two complementary angles compose the right angle. All my autobiographical research is devoted to my own professional development and the professional development of other educators (Leggo, 2004a; 2004b; 2004c; 2004d; 2004e; 2004f; 2004g; 2005a; 2005b; 2005c; 2005d; 2005e; 2005f; 2006a; 2006b). But for me to grow professionally, I also need to grow personally.

DOI: 10.4324/9781003412892-24

Autobiographical writing is both transcendent and immanent, both inside and outside, both internal and external, both personal and professional.

It is not easy to write autobiographically, especially in the academy, especially with honesty about many issues, including experiences of failure, fear, and frustration. We need a different culture, a culture that supports autobiographical writing that is marked by an understanding that writing about personal experiences is not merely egoism, solipsism, unseemly confession, boring prattle, and salacious revelation. We need to write personally because we live personally, and our personal living is always braided with our other ways of living – professional, academic, administrative, social, and political.

I constantly ask, why is it important that I write and tell my stories as a poet, teacher, and teacher educator? Why is it important that others write and tell their stories? Writing autobiographically is like echolocation. By means of echolocation, bats can navigate their nocturnal flights. They send out sound waves which then bounce off distant objects and reflect back to the sender. In a similar way, autobiographers are seeking to locate themselves in a rapidly growing network of contexts, including family, neighborhood, community, profession, and school, by sending out resonances from one embodied and personal location to other embodied and personal locations. There is no separating the personal from the professional. As a teacher, I do not leave my home and family experiences behind me when I drive to campus or when I enter the classroom. And I do not leave my past either. I am the person I am because of the experiences and people and places that comprise my life and living.

All my autobiographical research is about the construction of identity, especially in the spaces between self and subjectivity. As Griffin (1995) observes, "the self does not exist in isolation" (p. 50). Instead, "to know the self is to enter a social process. One does not know oneself except by being mirrored" (p. 51). I find this a very powerful notion for understanding issues of self-identity, especially the ways that we are often mirrored and represented, and hence shaped, in the discursive practices of the dominant culture. I agree with Griffin's comment about "a desire that is at the core of human imaginings, the desire to locate ourselves in community" (p. 146). The challenge that we constantly face is the challenge to fit into the community but not be swallowed up by the community; to live communally while also developing our individual talents and personalities. All of this is accomplished in telling stories, as Griffin understands, "for each of us, as for every community, village, tribe, nation, the story we tell ourselves is crucial to who we are, who we are becoming" (p. 152).

I often write about family, always seeking to know who I am, to gain a clear sense of identity and positionality in the midst of memory, desire, heart, and imagination, especially in relation to others. For many years, I have been writing autobiographical poetry about growing up on Lynch's Lane in Corner Brook, Newfoundland. So far, I have published three books of poems, and I acknowledge that I will never research, remember, and recreate all the stories of my backyard. I write about people and experiences that I never wrote about in school where I tried to imitate the writing I read in thick textbooks. For many years I heard a persistent voice of warning that it is not sufficient to write about ordinary people, places, emotions, and experiences. It took me a long time to appreciate the extraordinary in the ordinary. If we do not learn to appreciate the significance of our own lived experiences, then we will always live in the frustrating illusions of fictive creations shaped in the images of popular and dominant cultures. In order to know the possibilities for our unique presence in the world, we need to be connected to words that represent as well as challenge our daily understandings of who we are and who we are becoming. We need to know our stories before we can attend to the stories of others with respect and care. Education is a process of becoming in the world, a process of becoming in language and discourse. In *Pedagogy of the Heart*, published posthumously, Freire (1997) acknowledges from the perspective of a long life drawing to a close that the space of his childhood backyard was connected to many spaces:

> My childhood backyard has been unveiling itself to many other spaces – spaces that are not necessarily other yards. Spaces where this man of today sees the child of yesterday in himself and learns to see better what he had seen before. To see again what had already been seen before always implies seeing angles that were not perceived before. Thus, a posterior view of the world can be done in a more critical, less naïve, and more rigorous way. (p. 38)

In my poetry I seek to know the spaces of my childhood backyard, and how this specific geographical space represents a location for locution in the bigger world because Freire (1997) encourages me that "the more rooted I am in my location, the more I extend myself to other places so as to become a citizen of the world. No one becomes local from a universal location" (p. 39). Educators and learners need to attend to the specific local locations, the places that they know intimately, in order to see those places with creative and critical imagination, and in order to see how those places are connected to intricate and complex interrelationships with many other places located at lines of latitude and longitude throughout the earth.

I agree with Griffin (1995) who contends that "poetry does not describe. It *is* the thing. It is an experience, not the secondhand record of an experience, but the experience itself" (p. 191). Therefore, I offer the following few poems as exemplars of my autobiographic research, poems that represent part of my ongoing efforts to learn to live well in the world, to learn to live well in relationships with others, with the past, with the earth, with all creatures, seeking always the lines of connection that transcend the personal and the professional, and generate in all the creation a dynamic energy.

## SCRATCH IN MY THROAT

Four black birds sit in snow on the fence
inscribing my backyard.
Snow is rare in Steveston.

For a breath I linger in distant
Newfoundland where I lived
long winters in a sacred often scary land.
Wallace Stevens might ask
where are the other nine black birds.

I feel so close to a poem, its breath
a scratch in my throat in the tangled
midst of memories. I live with the past

trailing like a train of U-Hauls stuffed
with stories I no longer need, always hard
to clean the closet, especially in winter
when the stories might still be missed

like homespun sweaters, though this morning
while running on the dike I heard thousands
of snow geese write their way into the dawn
with a raucous eagerness for light.

## RHIZOME

Newfoundland is far away.
Lynch's Lane lingers
in imagination and poetry,
bulldozed daisies of memory.

Last night my mother called.

  Cindy Mercer, my third or fourth cousin perhaps,
  but definitely a Mercer like my grandmother and mother,

  met a man through the Internet,
  moved to Australia and married him

  while Cindy Mercer's father said,
  *Nice as you could meet anywhere*,

like there was doubt, some
need to defend Australian niceness,

and in an April morning with a muffled breath
of spring, my mother's aunt Sal Mercer
who liked shopping but never spent a cent

hiked the Heights to the new Wal-Mart
but collapsed as the automatic doors opened,

dead before the ambulance arrived,
the end to nine decades of Mercer stories,
few Mercers left, except

there are Mercers everywhere
married in Australia
  on their way to Wal-Mart
  seeking poems in British Columbia

rhizome connections in the earth,
the sheer certitude of lives spelled in
fields of wild plump strawberries
and sturdy crabgrass beyond counting.

## ECOLOGY

In the solitude of sabbatical retreat
in York Harbour on the Atlantic cusp,
I learn to hear the heart's light
borne on titanium filaments,
strong and resilient, beyond breaking.

I live without a clock, in the heart's time,
no longer a crone's gigolo beating
the incessant whine of chronos
measured precisely like cement blocks.

Instead of rushing from task to task,
without end or satisfaction, compelling
my body to catch up when it can,
I now move slowly, feel my feet,
grounded, taste the heart's rhythm.

In my old life, I had little time for grief
or prayer, God lost in the frantic crowd,
but now I hold others in the heart's space,
in the quiet time of imagination's bounty.

In the still silence of York Harbour
like a monastery in moonlight on the edge
of the snowlight sea, I hold friends
on lines of latitude throughout the earth,
friends with hearts, both swollen and splintered.

In the half dozen months I have dwelled
here, one friend has died with cancer,
another has received the dread news,
two more are regaining health after cancer.

I hold each one like wind in trembling aspens
including my pastor who no longer knows God,
claims God no longer knows him, lost in middle age
like a tangled forest where he can't be found,

and Clive, scholarly and cantankerous,
who taught me Wittgenstein while I taught him
the basics of teaching grade 9's the novel,
whose heart stopped in Japan, my age, now gone.

In today's e-mail I learned Bill died
in his sleep. Could Bill have stayed up all night
and beat death like a Stephen King novel?
He sat daily on the rock outside our office building
with a tender smile for everyone hurrying by.

If I can believe in an invisible net of worldwide
interconnections in cyberspace, surely I can
believe in the ecology of words and lines of care
borne lightly in the heart, even the unbearable.

I will hold my friends through the blustery
winds of winter into the promises of spring
as I know they will hold me, in blood-beating
heart and imagination and memory beyond
all counting of tense time, in tenderness only.

## Editors' Postscript

Carl Leggo (1953–2019) explored not just relationality but entanglements that draw one into the full complexity of the world. This concern manifested into moments of phenomenological attentiveness and lingering that Leggo would inscribe both into his poetry and his daily life. He held a profound respect, admiration, and trust for the presence of the in-between (Irwin & Springgay, Chapter 18) that emerges in these ephemeral moments.

Leggo actively challenged himself to stretch to new possibilities of relatedness. A generous teacher and mentor, Leggo brought forth the voices of his students and other arts-based educational research (ABER) scholars. With Monica Prendergast and Pauline Sameshima (2009) he co-edited a book on poetic inquiry. Collaboratively, he also explored arts-based research (ABR)'s turn to the phenomenological and spiritual (Walsh et al., 2015). His cross disciplinary work was exemplified by a "pedagogy of listening" that he wrote about with ABER musical scholar Peter Gouzouasis (Gouzouasis & Leggo, 2016). As he said here in this chapter, the personal "is always braided with our other ways of living – professional, academic, administrative, social, and political."

## References

Freire, P. (1997). *Pedagogy of the heart* (D. Macedo & A. Oliveira, Trans.). Continuum.

Gouzouasis, P., & Leggo, C. (2016). Performative research in music and poetry: A pedagogy of listening. In P. Burnard, L. Mackinlay, & K. Powell (Eds.), *The Routledge international handbook of intercultural arts research* (pp. 454–466). Routledge.

Griffin, S. (1995). *The eros of everyday life: Essays on ecology, gender and society*. Doubleday.

Leggo, C. (2004a). Listening to the silence: Honouring the complexity of the narratives we live. *Brock Education, 14*(1), 97–111. https://doi.org/10.26522/brocked.v14i1.59

Leggo, C. (2004b). Living poetry: Five ruminations. *Language & Literacy*, 6(2), 1–14. https://doi.org/10.20360/G2D307

Leggo, C. (2004c). The curriculum of joy: Six poetic ruminations. *Journal of the Canadian Association of Curriculum Studies*, 2(2), 27–42. https://doi.org/10.25071/1916-4467.16899

Leggo, C. (2004d). Light and shadow: Four reasons for writing (and not writing) autobiographically. *Vitae Scholasticae: Journal of Educational Biography, 21*(1), 5–22.

Leggo, C. (2004e). The poet's corpus: Nine speculations. *Journal of Curriculum Theorizing, 20*(2), 65–85.

Leggo, C. (2004f). The curriculum of becoming human: A rumination. *International Journal of Whole Schooling, 1*(1), 28–36. https://www.proquest.com/scholarly-journals/curriculum-becoming-human-rumination/docview/61840647/se-2

Leggo, C. (2004g). Tangled lines: On autobiography and poetic knowing. In A. L. Cole, L. Neilsen, J. G. Knowles, & T. C. Luciani (Eds.), *Provoked by art: Theorizing arts-informed research* (pp. 18–35). Backalong Books.

Leggo, C. (2005a). Autobiography and identity: Six speculations. *Vitae Scholasticae: Journal of Educational Biography, 22*(1), 115–133.

Leggo, C. (2005b). Alphabet blocks: Expanding conceptions of language with/in poetry. *TESL Canada Journal, 23*(1), 91–110. https://eric.ed.gov/?id=EJ924081

Leggo, C. (2005c). Pedagogy of the heart: Ruminations on living poetically. *Journal of Educational Thought, 39*(2), 175–195. https://www.jstor.org/stable/23767223

Leggo, C. (2005d). An archipelago of fragments: Writing other gendered lines of connection. *Men and Masculinities, 8*, 195–207. https://doi.org/10.1177/1097184X03257862

Leggo, C. (2005e). The letter of the law/the silence of letters. In P. Trifonas (Ed.), *Communities of difference* (pp. 110–125). Palgrave Macmillan.

Leggo, C. (2005f). The heart of pedagogy: On poetic knowing and living. *Teachers and Teaching: Theory and Practice, 11*(5), 439–455. https://doi.org/10.1080/13450600500238436

Leggo, C. (2006a). Attending to winter: A poetics of research. In W. Ashton & D. Denton (Eds), *Spirituality, ethnography, and teaching: Stories from within* (pp. 140–155). Peter Lang.

Leggo, C. (2006b). End of the line: A poet's postmodern musings on writing. *English Teaching: Practice and Critique, 5*(2), 69–92. http://education.waikato.ac.nz/research/files/etpc/2006v5n2art5.pdf

Prendergast, M., Leggo, C. D., & Sameshima, P. (Eds.). (2009). *Poetic inquiry: Vibrant voices in the social sciences*. Sense.

Walsh, S., Bickel, B., & Leggo, C. (Eds.). (2015). *Arts-based and contemplative practices in research and teaching: Honoring presence*. Routledge.

Chapter 25

# For Art's Sake, Stop Making Art

*Jorge Lucero*

Re: For art's sake, stop making art
From: Jorge
To: Jon

Dear Jon,

I heard from Hannah that you had additional questions about last night's conversation. Hannah said you don't consider yourself an artist in any conventional sense and you were wondering if a non-artist could still use art as a method of inquiry. I'm responding to that question, not because I have an answer that's specific to you, but because lately I've been looking at creative practices that utilize *deskilled* modes of working, *amateur-practice*, and *dematerialization* in scholarship. I'm looking at these modes of working in relation to teaching, the academy, and research; so naturally, my interest was piqued by your question. I hope you don't think that I'm being too forward by sending you this lengthy email. At the very least, I anticipate that this email will give you something to bounce your own ideas off of and perhaps the next time we meet we can tease it out further.

I'm getting ahead of myself here. "Deskilled," "amateur," and "dematerialization" are terms that get thrown around in different ways depending on context, so I'll explain how I mean them. Artists working through "deskilling" purposefully use lo-fi and counterintuitive construction methods, clumsiness, lack of refinement, everyday actions, simple gestures, and movements in their art. These artists are keenly aware of art's allegiance to craftsmanship and actively counteract those traditions. The art critic Michael Kimmelman wrote about the "amateur," not as a person in direct contrast with the so called "professional," but rather as "a lover, someone who does something for the love of it." In his 2005 *The Accidental Masterpiece*, Kimmelman alludes to the etymology of the word "amateur" to make his point (Kimmelman, 2005). You might recognize the word's Latin root found in *amor*, *amorous*, and *enamor*, among many others. Dematerialization is the trickiest of these concepts to think about, especially if you don't identify as an artist or if your definitions of art don't seriously consider the impact of conceptual art on art practice. Dematerialization in art was first identified by critics Lippard and Chandler in 1968. Dematerialization emerged when artists began deemphasizing the presence of archival materials in their artworks. Sometimes they would do this by using materials that were difficult to preserve and sometimes these artists made artworks that used no actual materials at all, frequently leaving little physical evidence of the artwork's existence.

DOI: 10.4324/9781003412892-25

All these modes of working propose that art (even as research method) is predominately a thinking process and needn't require a practitioner to make conventional art in order to claim the identity and license of an artist. Taken to its logical extreme, we can look to artists like Marcel Duchamp (in his 1979 interview with Cabanne) or choreographer Merce Cunningham (in his 2006 interview with Montagne) who both—on separate occasions—declared *mere breathing* as artworks equal to, if not more important than, the physical artworks for which they're celebrated!

To think about whether scholars, teachers, and researchers can work "through" art even though they don't identify as artists, let's examine the relation of art to definition/concretization. When too surely defined, art becomes stagnant. Art's vitality is dependent on its perpetual redefinition. Art's potential energy as a process of investigation is propelled by its wildness, instability, and unpredictable metamorphosis. Until now, many examples of arts-based research are caught in the same trappings around definition that most art and art education is truncated by. For lack of a better way to put it, art—particularly among art educators, but also among arts-based researchers—is defined narrowly enough that its deployment as a method of inquiry can sometimes appear passé and unadventurous. This will sound more cynical than I intend it, but—frankly—I suspect that *art itself is the problem.*

I know it sounds like I'm talking in riddles, but that's only because I'm not really talking about art proper. I'm talking about making the gestures, inquiries, and energies in the world that will *eventually* be called art. These are actions and queries that at their moment of enactment have no proper category! As the artist Allan Kaprow pondered in his germinal 1993 experimental art essay *Just Doing*, "Today, we may say that experimental art is the act or thought whose identity as art must always remain in doubt" (Kaprow, 1993). Here Kaprow hints at the intellectual calisthenics required to expand the field, since strategic doubt—which is useful for this way of making—is a function of the intellect. To bring this one step further, if our intellectual instinct is to categorize/finalize our findings and to answer definitively our questions, then we may become limited by the hard edges that inevitably emerge from that process of acquiring and retaining newness/knowledge. If, though, we can hold on to the promise that blurred genres elicit and sustain an open approach to discovery, maybe we can continue to reconfigure the "parts" into iterations that never would have occurred to us otherwise.

Kaprow also notes that broadening the definition of art is a moving target. He stresses that

> the experiment [of keeping the definition of art in doubt/flux] is not to possess a secret artistry in deep disguise; it is not knowing what to call it at any time! As soon—and it is usually very soon—as such acts and thoughts are associated with art and its discourses, it is time to move on to other possibilities of experimentation.

I like how Kaprow highlights that this ambiguity is not external. In other words, it's not like I know that I'm making art and the "public" (whoever that is) doesn't. It's that sometimes, even *I* don't know that I'm making art. Kaprow puts the onus and power of deciding *what is* and *what isn't* art on the passage of time and the art historical conversations that are had around certain actions and objects. The artist is free! Take, for example, this long email/letter that I'm writing you: it started as a mere email, then it was an epistle, and perhaps one day—depending on the reader—it might be scholarship, maybe even art, but—thankfully—that doesn't need to be up to me.

To further my point about the stranglehold of definition(s) on the potential of art-making as a means to acquire knowledge, I will tell you a story about something that happened recently on a Facebook page called "Art Teachers." The thriving network has more than 12,000 members in it. Everything you can imagine gets posted to this page (from complaints about administrators to philosophical questions about art and teaching), but once in a while someone posts something to the page that ignites the members of the group into a furiously sophisticated—even scholarly—discussion that plays out in real time and demonstrates the breadth of expertise among art educators. What I love about these FB threads is that they're a democratic representation of the art-education spectrum and that any member can come back to the thread repeatedly and study it regardless of whether we're actually in the conversation. It's the ultimate "fly on the wall" experience! I return to these "hot" threads continuously, particularly when I'm thinking about a prickly issue that I know classroom teachers have expert thoughts about. Those threads are a type of "data" and also an unruly collaborative performance/socially engaged art piece that cannot be ignored. As a quick aside here—in case your IRB antenna just went up—I've looked into using FB posts as material for either art or scholarship. FB's policy is that public posts are in the public domain and therefore fair use, but I think it also depends on how you're using them. There is a pretty clear article published in the March 2016 journal of *Monitor on Psychology* where the authors (Kosinski et al., 2016) stated, "that mining public data is equivalent to conducting archival research, a method frequently employed in disciplines, such as history, art criticism and literature, which rarely involve rules for the protection of human subjects," and this is exactly how I use the "work" that we all contribute to on FB *as* an art source. FB is an archive that I work from.

But back to the FB thread in the "Art Teachers" group that alerted me to the problem of definitions held—first among art teachers and second among anyone who might want to take up the charge of art as a method from a non-pedigreed approach (e.g., a social scientist such as yourself). A young teacher on that FB thread posted a comment about how art teachers should be making their own art and clearly stated that if art teachers don't make their own art, then they are doing their students a disservice. Needless to say, the nearly 200 responses to this post covered the gamut of possible thoughts on the matter. Some teachers agreed wholeheartedly, demonstrating a passion for the "right" side of this argument in a way that I recognized from the days when I zealously upheld the sanctity of the traditional studio above all other priorities in my life. Others admonished the original contributor by rightfully calling out the blind spots of his under-considered declaration. His detractors brought up topics such as: family, job integrity, tough schools, teaching different age groups, classroom space, summer breaks, and whether "teacher samples" can be considered "personal" art. Whether the critical rebuttals were based on a close reading of the original post or on what readers were inferring from that first statement, all of the reasons why teachers didn't make art bore equal parts sincerity and internal conflict. Although the participants' stances on the issue proved to be all over the place, two things were uniform across the entire thread: The first was that art teachers are acutely alert to the special tension that exists in art education when it comes to the mythic dichotomy between so called "doers" and "non-doers." The second thing was that unequivocally everyone was talking about the plastic/traditional arts (i.e., clay, paint, graphite, plaster, wood, ink, etc.) or some version of manipulating physical materials for the sake of expression through the making of objects.

So Jon, after a day's worth of reading the FB comments—which again wasn't really a "research" action, but more of a discovery based on being a part of the conversation—I chimed in with two posts to the thread that I felt offered a counter-narrative to the momentum of the conversation. If you don't mind, I'm pasting abridged versions of those comments as follows, because I think they capture what I'm saying about the potential of expanded definitions for the sake of doing our work as artists and scholars through experimentation and ultimately for the sake of art and scholarship of blurred genres, which consistently disrupts the expectations—and "products"—of its more conventionally and expected distinct and concrete parts.

**This was the first post:**

> ... I'm sure other "types" of teachers share this dilemma also, but I've noticed in my—almost—twenty years of being an art educator that the question of "practice what you preach"—no matter what side you're on—is wonderfully unique to art teachers. So many of us started our artist-teacher careers as undergraduates within very specific and tight models of what an artistic practice was, is, and can be. This idea—that the artist needs to have a studio, prolonged engagement with their work, and that our practice primarily involves the manipulation and mastery of "plastic" materials (e.g., paint, clay, paper, wood, etc.)—has colored the way that we teach art and consequently the way we see ourselves as artists within the very real constraints of being excellent at our occupations [as instructors]. The anxiety around this "practice what you preach" problem is magnified once we are teaching, having families, and living adult lives and no longer have the same luxury of the three- to eight-hour studio sessions that are so typical of college-level art courses. What is valued most in those college studio courses and ultimately valued most in our romantic imagination about what an artist should be are things like craftsmanship, refined skill sets, meditative making, solitude, vision, invention/problem solving, and expression. I looked up and down this FB thread to see if I could identify any inkling of art being conceived of in other ways that don't have to do with working with so-called "traditional" media or studio habits of mind (meaning the rich processes that unfold as part of a conventional studio practice), and I didn't come across any. I find this curious, because depending on who you ask, Western art has about 85 to 100 years of art history that gives us permission to enact our artistic urges, questions, and potential in ways that are—not only STILL cutting edge—but also aligned with the activities we're asked to fulfill as professional educators in schools. Conceptual art, performance art, time arts, social practice, activist art, text-based art, and other forms of what is known as "dematerialized art" give us cues—or what I have been calling "permissions"—to behave in ways that don't require some of the demands of an art practice that puts an unnecessary burden on many teachers who are already enacting one of the most significant WORKS known to culture.

**After several participants on the FB thread thought my original post was about curriculum, I posted this response:**

> Oh, I'm not talking about changing your curriculum. I wasn't meaning that an art teacher would substitute a painting project for a time-arts lesson (although that might be something too!). What I'm talking about ... is that teaching itself is a creative practice. Now, here I'm not talking about the craft of teaching or the so-called "art" of teaching.

> What I'm proposing is that the teacher (who thinks of themselves as an artist) never ceases being an artist just because they're not actively engaged in a studio activity. I'm proposing that switching the focal point of where "art" happens from the "hand" to the "mind" opens up the possibility that all sorts of school tasks become filled with potential to have art thoughts, "make" artworks, and feel fulfilled as an artist. [Under this way of thinking] something like giving out directions can be an artwork as is the case with Sol Lewitt's instruction-based paintings (Weber, 2000, p. 90); or giving advice/critique to students on their work can be an artwork as we see in the performance/participatory project *60 WRD/MIN* of art critic Lori Waxman (see Waxman, 2013); or cleaning up can be an artwork as we see in various multiyear projects called "maintenance art" by Mierle Laderman Ukeles (see for example Phillips, 2016); or doing a demonstration as artwork following the "aesthetics" of a cooking show like in Martha Rosler's emancipatory *Semiotics of the Kitchen* from 1975; or eating lunch with your students can be an artwork as in the relational events/meals of Rirkrit Tiravanija (see Kellein, 2010); or playground duty can be an artwork, not unlike the movement based Bruce Nauman performances that on first sight appear to be pure nonsense (see for example Nauman's 1967–68 *Dance or exercise on the perimeter of a square*); or like Andrea Fraser's 1989 *Museum Highlights: A Gallery Talk*, giving a lecture to your students about Van Gogh can be an artwork; or even the monotony and banality of calculating your students' grades can be an artwork in the style of Hanne Darboven's daily notations (see Enwezor, 2015); or even clocking into work every morning can be an artwork like in the notoriously arduous and repetitive year-long performances of Taiwanese artist Tehching Hsieh (see Heathfield & Hsieh, 2015); or organizing your supply closets can be an artwork as in the taxonomy-focused readymade arrangements called *Asterisms* by Gabriel Orozco (2012); or fighting for teachers' and students' rights can be an artwork such as many artists have demonstrated, and one example of this is Nicolas Lampert, who wrote about how so many artists have done this in 2013. ETC. ETC. Like I said, there's about a hundred years of—let's call it undervalued—art history that points to the fact that we can do the serious work of teachers, but think of those activities as art processes, and it is this minor—but gutsy—move that really flips the script.

So we return to your question about whether someone like yourself—who doesn't have an art pedigree—can participate in arts-based research or what I would more comfortably call arts-based scholarship, taking my cue from a Canadian colleague's examination of the differences between research and scholarship (in case you're curious about that distinction, read Donald O'Donoghue's "Art, Scholarship and Research: A Backward Glance," in the 2014 *Routledge International Handbook of the Arts and Education*). To be frank, my answer might not satisfy you if you haven't started to rethink your definition of art. As a lifelong artist, art teacher, and now university professor in an art school, I can tell you this: I know that you can make art and that you don't have to be "good" at it. Awhile back I worked out this phrase: "For art's sake, stop making art." And this, as much as anything can possibly be, has become a motto that actively prompts me to test out the pliability of the concretized world. It's for the sake of art that I want to do something else. If you can accept the premise, at least for a while, that conceptual approaches to making art are valid forms of inquiry and serious behavior, then we can really move to the question of how someone who doesn't have art skills or an art pedigree can still engage, not only in arts-based research, but ultimately in art (which many would argue is a form of scholarship to begin with). As a quick example, think back to the blurbs I just presented to you from that recent FB exchange I was a part of. For me, that exchange became the material that I could work with to compose you this letter, which—to be honest—I can't help but think of as a full-blown artwork now that it's reached this length. Without a doubt, this email/letter/manifesto (maybe) isn't a painting or a sculpture or even a piece of creative writing. But, as a conceptual artist, I understand what I've made in this email as something that carries the complexities and the proposals of what is important to me as an artist. What is important to me is the strengthening and valuing of relationships (particularly pedagogical relationships) and I would argue that you've helped to do that. Also, I'm interested in artworks that pull a "sleight of hand" and what I mean here is that in the past I've conceived of, made, and presented a lecture as a performance; a series of paintings as a curriculum; a syllabus as a "love" letter; a museum as a stage; and even a teaching career as a collage. Among many other things—if you allow me to be really optimistic/absurd—this letter is a sculpture, a bridge if you will.

Some final thoughts before I let you go and again, thanks for taking the time to read all of this. I know that long emails are the worst!

The conceptual artist, performer, and teacher Joseph Beuys has a famous dictum that is frequently dismissed because it comes across as too sentimental. He said, "everyone [is] an artist." What might make it too saccharine for some is that it's usually read, used, or spoken out of context, free-floating, like a bumper sticker slogan or a mantra you use to convince yourself of something you don't actually believe. What Beuys was talking about is an imagined manifestation of art that is yet to be, but filled with potential, mostly detached from the history of art and focused on "the invisible materials used by everyone." These are the notes Beuys wrote where we find this "everyone an artist" quote from the 2004 book *What is Art?* I've italicized some key words, but I would still advise that you read it carefully. The bold letters are from the original.

**Thinking Forms**—how we *mold* our thoughts or
**Spoken Forms**—how we *shape* our thoughts into words or
**SOCIAL SCULPTURE** how we *mold* and *shape* the world in which we live: Sculpture as an *evolutionary process*; everyone an artist.

Of course, Beuys was not talking about sculpture as we—even seasoned artists, educators, and scholars—might imagine. He was not talking about special art skills, pedigree, histories, objects, or know-how. He was talking about an approach to the world that involves testing the pliability ("mold," "shape," "evolutionary") of those things the imagination doesn't readily identify as lending themselves to pliability, for example, the rhythmic and attentive work of a data collector; or the preparation of a teacher; the collaboration in a family; the involvement of an activist/involved citizen, even politician; the inventions or—even—recipe-following of an amateur chef; the considerations of a quotidian grocery list-maker; the flourish *or* automatism of a note-taker, etc.

Beuys's proposal was a call to test the materiality—both formally and conceptually—of institutions, work and labor, relationships, time and space, scholarship, the cosmos, mythology, poor taste, boredom, objects, science, and the everyday. Beuys's call to an "evolutionary process" was not a call to make art objects, rather a call to think of art as a "science of freedom," by which I'm not wanting to imply that the making of objects wasn't critical to Beuys's and ultimately *my* arrival at this idea. This is something Beuys described as actions and inquiry taken within the motivations of an artist especially when one had no specific training, no refinement of skills, and no particular interests in continuing the legacy of art as it's recognized in relation to its antecedents. Beuys places art at the "beginning," with science as a first act of everything else. And if we think of research as the first act of *anything*, then we can think of art as the first act of research. What artists, teachers, and other social practitioners have done with Beuys's permission to seek out the pliable is more than he ever imagined. And in the end, I suppose that's why he said it.

After you take a look at what I've laid out here, feel free to write me back so we can continue thinking about this together. I hope that I've made enough interventions throughout the paper with an eye toward the question we started with, which I'm hoping I've answered in the affirmative. Yes, you can do arts-based research without having art skills, but not necessarily as a conventional artist, rather as "for art's sake, stop making art." As a final example, you can, as I have with this letter, refuse to write an academic paper—even though you know that's what's expected of you—and instead through a conceptual art turn of mind, write a super long email, which turns into an epistle, which turns into a manifesto. I'm working on the extended version of the manifesto by the way, and I'll leave you with this last little motto I've developed—I'm thinking about it as the title for that book on conceptual art and pedagogy—"In all things BE CONCEPTUAL."

Until then, please take care.
—Jorge

p.s. Please see the attached images in conjunction with my everyday efforts to make art out of what I'm not supposed to (Figures 25.1 and 25.2). Both of these images emerge from

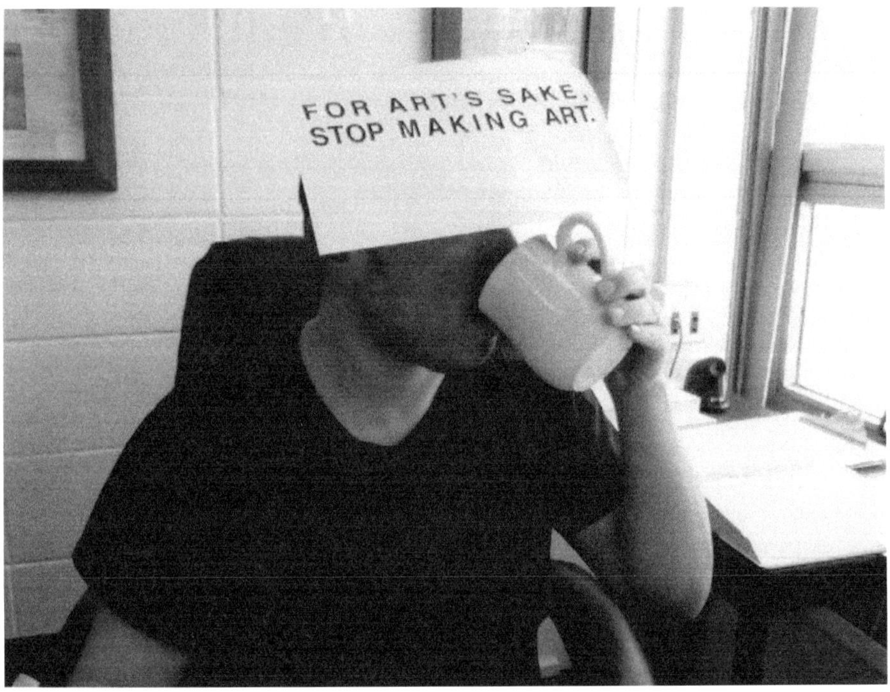


*Figure 25.1*

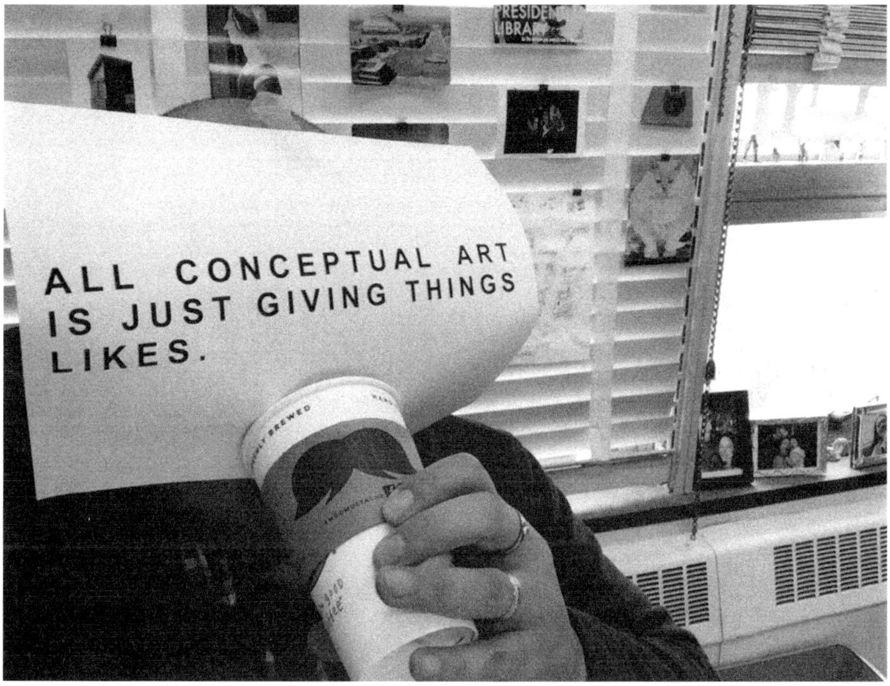


*Figure 25.2*

my thinking around this subject, but they also feed into it. p.p.s. Here is a list of references to things I've cited in the letter (Figures 25.3 and 25.4). I've taken my cue from the conceptual artist William Powhida and sent this part of the email as an APA-style drawing! Want to see more of Powhida's work? Take a look at his drawings that look just like mere notes on a piece of paper, like his 2009 drawing *Artists Statement (No One Here Gets Out Alive)*.

## Postscript

I have been writing and enacting a version of *For Art's Sake, Stop Making Art* for 25 years. In every bit of writing, artwork, lecture, workshop that I've done, I'm working through the questions, "what can art be?" and "what does it mean to be an artist?". I'm asking these two ancient questions over and over because I want to know what permissions their potential answers offer to the act of being in the academy as a scholar/researcher, teacher, administrator, and colleague. I have found that the more elastic my definitions of *art* and *the artist* are, the more liberated my scholarly inquiry/expression and academic labor becomes. One of the proposals I make in this chapter is about rethinking the everyday gestures we enact in our teaching and research jobs through the permissions of conceptual art. Since conceptual art has a long history of taking up—among other non-art things—ritual, ephemerality, deskilling, bureaucracy, documentation, relationality, and citizenry, studying it becomes a key to further understanding how an academic/teaching practice is perhaps one of the most progressive, impacting, and artistic things we do as humans.

The work of discovering and mapping the permissions of conceptual art over our tasks in the academy is interminable, but the perpetuity of this engagement also reveals how much each activity is like the other. Good artists are in continuous discourse with their

Cunningham, M. and Montagne, R. (2006). Merce Cunningham: Dance at the Edge. ~~Retrieved on July 24, 2011 from www.npr.org/templates/story/story.php?storyid=66~~ https://www.npr.org/2006/12/29/6692356/merce-cunningham-dance-at-the-edge

Duchamp, M. and Cabanne, P. (1979). Dialogues with Marcel Duchamp. Paris: Da Capo Press.

Enwezor, O. (2015). (Ed.). Hanne Darboven: Enlightement-time Histories, a retrospective. New York: Prestal Publishing.

Heathfield, A. and Hsieh, T. (2015). Out of Now: The Lifeworks of Tehching Hsieh. Cambridge, MA: MIT Press.

Kaprow, A. (1993). Just Doing. In Essays on the blurring of art and life (pp. 247–51). Berkley, CA: University of California Press.

Kellein, T. (2010). Rirkrit Tiravanija: Cook Book: Just Smile and Don't Talk. Bangkok, Thailand: River Books.

Lampert, N. (2013). A people's Art History of the United States: 250 Years of Activist Art and Artists working in Social Justice movements. New York: The New Press.

Lippard, L. and Chandler, J. (1968/1999). The Dematerialization of Art. In Alberro, A. and Stimson, B. (Eds.). Conceptual Art: A Critical Anthology, (pp. 46–50). Cambridge, MA: MIT Press.

O'Donoghue, D. (2014). Art, Scholarship and research: A backward glance. In Fleming, M., Bresler, L., and O'Toole, J. (Eds.). The Routledge International Handbook of the Arts and Education, (pp. 345–58). Abingdon, Oxon, UK: Routledge.

*Figure 25.3*

Orozco, G. (2012). Gabriel Orozco: Asterisms. New New York: Guggenheim Museum Publishers.

Phillips, P.C. (2016). Mierle Laderman Ukeles: Maintenance ART. New York: Prestal Publishing.

Rosler, M. (1975). SEMIOTICS OF THE KITCHEN (VIDEO). RETrieved from ~~http://ubu.com/FILM/Rosler_Semiotics.html~~ https://www.eai.org/titles/semiotics-of-the-kitchen. New York: Electronic Arts INTERMIX.

WAXMAN, L. (2013). 60 WRD/MIN ART CRITIC. PARIS: ONESTAR Press.

weber, J.S. (2000). Sol Lewitt: THE IDEA, THE WALL drawing, AND the public SPACE. IN GArrels, G. (ED.). Sol Lewitt: A RETrospective. San francisco, CA: SAN Francisco Museum of Modern ART.

## POSTSCRIPT

Chamberlain, C. (2024). *Fluxus Administration: George Maciunas and the Art of Paperwork.* University of Chicago Press.

*Figure 25.4*

contemporaries and antecedents; always trying to expand the limitations of the imagination by investigating what others have done both in form and content. In the chapter, I draw parallels between academic tasks and conceptual art practices in order to show how they can inform each other. Here's a new one to add to your quiver: The art historian Colby Chamberlain (2024) generously foregrounds Fluxus founder George Maciunas' activities as an "administrative author" (p. 13) working through entrepreneurial, real estate, and familial "apparatuses" (p. 2); testing the pliability of policy and red tape, and being a manager, whose most notable artifacts are piles of paperwork, "the bureaucratic protocols of editorial mastheads and newsletter distribution lists" (p. 15). Chamberlain's exploration of Maciunas' bureaucratic creative practice makes pliable the piles and files we keep as part of our occupation, potentially translating them into more than just the grease that makes the gears turn. The conceptual transformation of this ignored component of what we do then opens the possibility that other banalities might also be art.

## References


Beuys, J. (2004). *What is art?: Conversations with Joseph Beuys* (V. Harlan, Ed.). Clairview Books.

Chamberlain, C. (2024). *Fluxus administration: George Maciunas and the art of paperwork*. University of Chicago Press.

Cunningham, M., & Montagne, R. (2006). *Merce Cunningham: Dance at the edge*. NPR. https://www.npr.org/2006/12/29/6692356/merce-cunningham-dance-at-the-edge

Duchamp, M., & Cabanne, P. (1979). *Dialogues with Marcel Duchamp*. Da Capo Press.

Enwezor, O. (Ed.). (2015). *Hanne Darboven: Enlightenment–time histories, a retrospective*. Prestel.

Heathfield, A., & Hsieh, T. (2015). *Out of now: The lifeworks of Tehching Hsieh*. The MIT Press.

Kaprow, A. (1993). Just doing. In *Essays on the blurring of art and life* (pp. 247–251). University of California Press.

Kellein, T. (2010). *Rirkrit Tiravanija: Cook book – just smile and don't talk*. Edition Hansjorg Mayer.

Kimmelman, M. (2005). *The accidental masterpiece: On the art of life, and vice versa*. Penguin Press.

Kosinski, M., Matz, S. C., Gosling, S. D., Popov, V., & Stillwell, D. (2016). Facebook as a research tool: A look at how to recruit participants using Facebook-and the ethical concerns that come with social media research. *Monitor on Psychology*, *47*(3), 70.

Lampert, N. (2013). *A people's art history of the United States: 250 years of activist art and artists working in social justice movements*. The New Press.

Lippard, L., & Chandler, J. (1999). The dematerialization of art. In Alberro, A. & Stimson, B. (Eds.), *Conceptual art: A critical anthology* (pp. 46–50). The MIT Press. Original work published 1968.

O'Donoghue, D. (2014). Art, scholarship and research: A backward glance. In Fleming, M., Bresler, L., & O'Toole, J. (Eds.), *The Routledge international handbook of the arts and education* (pp 345–58). Routledge.

Orozco, G. (2012). *Gabriel Orozco: Asterisms* [Exhibition]. Guggenheim Museum.

Phillips, P. C. (2016). *Mierle Laderman Ukeles: Maintenance art*. Prestel.

Powhida, W. (2009). *No one here gets out alive*. https://williampowhida.com/no-one-here-gets-out-alive/

Rosler, M. (1975). *Semiotics of the kitchen* [Video]. Electronic Arts Intermix https://www.eai.org/titles/semiotics-of-the-kitchen

Waxman, L. (2013). *60 wrd/min art critic*. Onestar Press.

Weber, J. S. (2000). Sol LeWitt: the idea, the wall drawing, and public space. In Garrels, G. (Ed.), *Sol Lewitt: A retrospective* (pp 89–99). San Francisco Museum of Modern Art.

Chapter 26

# Understanding and Writing the World

*Kristina Lyons*

*Upon Traveling to Nosara* emerged from an incident I observed on a highway while leaving the Greater Metropolitan Area of San José, Costa Rica. At the time I was teaching in the Nicoya Peninsula and working on my undergraduate thesis – a compilation of poems reflecting on experiences of everyday violence in Costa Rica, Cuba, and Chile. While I was not studying anthropology then, this poem, and poetry in general, has continued to help me think about and write against the social production of death in Colombia, the site of my doctoral work.

This poem is meant to be performed by a group of four people. Read horizontally it is one single poem. However, each of the three vertical columns is also meant to stand alone. I chose this form after listening to a poetry reading by G. E. Patterson at the 2001 Breadloaf Writers' Conference.[1] The performative nature of the poem is meant to convey the overlapping voices and the variety of sensory components at work in the public bus. It is also meant to imitate the ordering of disorder that people engage in as they make sense of the crash. The notion of space is also important in this piece, for example, the space between living bodies and the corpse, between the passengers and what lays outside, as well as the connections or disconnections between people's disparate reactions to the everyday presence of death.

I believe that poetry's use of images, slices of conversation, repetition, and affect allow it to present both a literal and metaphorical way of seeing the world. By taking up sensory and material components, it creates a visual language in which the written text visualizes philosophical ideas as well as material objects, people, and events. In my opinion, this is the goal of good ethnography as well. The textual integration of poetry in ethnographic writing can mobilize affect, analysis, and imagination to help the reader or researcher see and make a theoretical or philosophical point through a different set of lenses. It allows us to grapple with distinct modes of storytelling, silence, and material conditions that cannot be conveyed through the measured realism of much traditional ethnographic writing and research methodology. This is not to say that poetry as a form of analysis or methodology is more "real" than documentary realism, but that it may provide a window into multiple perceptions and distinct experiences of reality that can mutually inform theoretical analysis. For me, poetry emerges from material objects, events, and conversations that I encounter in my research, and these things anchor me as I filter them through my analytical interpretation. Precisely because of this link, I believe that poetry can help us pay attention to local narrative modes and the quiet work of stitching together everyday life that occurs in contexts of violence but is often overlooked in metanarratives of suffering and redemption.

The process of writing has been important to me for as long as I can remember. In my mind, there is no separation between the work of scholars and scientists and the poet or

DOI: 10.4324/9781003412892-26

storyteller. All are telling stories; although these stories may assemble different audiences and obtain differential power and ability to travel and exert influence in the world. I see anthropology as a field from which to understand how others, as well as how we, tell stories to remember and use the past, to witness, to resist, and to mute experience. From my perspective, poetry provides an alternative form of conceptualization from which to address these stories as they continue to circulate among us.

### UPON TRAVELING TO NOSARA

– Thanks to G. E. Patterson

for four voices

| | | |
|---|---|---|
| I am sitting | on a bus | seven hours |
| with a dead man | Savanna trees | in the dry season |
| strung together | outside | a haze of mid-day heat |
| paper cut figures | scraping against the window | The blown-out tire's prayer |
| *arriba abajo* | *adentro* | A man is dead |
| leaning | (*chin chin …*) | beneath a stained curtain |
| against a vinyl seat back | Still more | people climbing in |
| No one knows | voices colliding | their shoulders almost touching |
| A man is dead | then silence | stepping on his head |

## Postscript

Reading over the short essay that accompanied my original poem, *Upon Traveling to Nosara*, makes me rethink the title of the piece. Today I do not see anthropology as primarily "understanding and writing the world" through our ethnographic and literary inspired texts. I think we are being asked, obligated, and required to do more in the sense of being publicly engaged, ethically committed, and politically motivated to have impacts on addressing historic injustices, ongoing discrimination, climate change, and other pressing social and environmental issues that have life and death consequences for diverse human and more-than-human communities. This entails continuing to expand the genres we engage with, and consequently, the methodologies that may result in more public and politically meaningful work. The question for whom and for what ends social scientific research is being produced is a recurrent debate in our field along with the critical challenges posed by decolonial propositions, and anthropology's interfaces with the interdisciplinary work of feminist, critical race, Indigenous, disability, and science studies scholarship among other fields.

Most recently, I see the environmental, digital, and medical humanities providing social scientists with important methodological and conceptual tools to broaden our transdisciplinary collaborations and public engaged commitments. These fields invite us to merge arts and science-based practices, which often results in multimodal approaches to communicate and share research results, engage in popular education strategies, and respect nontraditional learning styles. My current research interests include the memory and mourning of water, hydrogeological processes, participatory forms of territorial planning, socio-natural disasters, and water-inspired subjectivities. Along with publishing conventional academic texts in English and Spanish, I have also worked on the creation of documentary films, soundscapes, street performances, photographic essays, graphic novels, community radio programs, digital storytelling platforms, cocreated journalism projects, and various forms of literary writing.

Certain editors of academic journals still place obstacles and police the use of poetic and literary techniques in social science texts, restricting ethnographic experimentation and narrowing the narrative options in empirical-based writing. However, other mediums, such as audiovisual, performative, digital, and immersive approaches that may include the use of literary and poetic genres have significantly broadened our conceptual, sensorial, affective, and political registers, and in turn, our forms of public engaged social scientific and humanities praxis beyond solely textual publications. While multimodality may still require much translation at the privileged institutional level for professionalization, promotion, and tenure, it is widely embraced by many community partners and diverse interlocutors, interdisciplinary colleagues, and nonacademic publics.

## Note

1 Patterson was reading from his first book, *Tug* (Graywolf Press, 1999) at the 2001 Breadloaf Writers' Conference in Middlebury, Vermont.

Chapter 27

# A Researcher Prepares

## The Art of Acting for the Qualitative Researcher

*Kathleen R. McGovern*

> We bring to life what is hidden under the words; we put our own thoughts to the author's lines, and we establish our own relationships to other characters in the play, and the conditions of their lives; we filter through ourselves all the materials that we receive from the author and the director; we work over them, supplementing them out of our own imagination.
>
> Stanislavski (1936, p. 56)

In the opening of Chekhov's (1999) *The Seagull*, Medvedenko asks Masha, "Why do you always wear black?" Her response, "I'm in mourning for my life" (p. 111), is often pronounced by the actress in a depressed fashion. Yet, I once heard a director enthusiastically describe the choice to portray these lines flirtatiously. An actor's job of representing her character is full of choices that deeply impact the audience; the possibilities for representation are almost limitless.

Similarly, educational researchers are faced with multiple options for analyzing and representing their participants in given contexts. At the core of educational research, particularly qualitative research, lies the study and representation of participants; in this way, the goals of theater and qualitative research are aligned. All the work we do as actors or researchers has as its final goal the representation/interpretation of another (person, group of people, context) for a particular audience (the spectators/readers of our research). In this chapter, I intend to highlight parallels between the crafts of acting and educational research and provide readers unfamiliar with the world of theater with tools and ways of thinking about the world that transfer to a variety of research contexts, asserting that techniques used to train actors have the potential to enhance research processes from data collection and analysis to representation.

The idea that art and science can work together in innovative and complementary ways is central to arts-based educational research (ABER), viewing art as "inherently part of any scientific process" (Cahnmann-Taylor et al., 2009, p. 2536). In Chapter 8 of this volume, Cahnmann argues

> the literary, visual, and performing arts offer ways to stretch a researcher's capacities for creativity and knowing, creating a healthy synthesis of approaches to collect, analyze, and represent data in ways that paint a full picture of a heterogeneous movement to improve education.
>
> (p. 84)

DOI: 10.4324/9781003412892-27

Other contributors to this volume demonstrate how poetry, music, performance, writing, and visual arts enhance researchers' understandings of themselves and their participants, opening possibilities to reach audiences beyond the academy. Like researchers, artists of all kinds typically go through rigorous training to learn techniques that allow them to develop their craft. Cahnmann (2003) calls for artist-researchers "to share the techniques and aesthetic sensibilities they use to prepare other researchers to understand, sensibly critique, and further develop arts-based approaches to scholarship" (p. 29). Despite such advocacy, few works present these techniques in straightforward ways that allow researchers to adapt and apply them to their own contexts. Further, though the arts have been used as metaphors in qualitative inquiry, less work illustrates the potentials the arts offer to researchers' creative, narrative practice.

Performance, in particular, has long been used as a metaphor for life, and the study of it and performance theories are frequently drawn on by educational researchers. Social scientists from various fields discuss the "performance" of language (e.g., Butler, 2006; Gee, 1996), identity (e.g., Goffman, 1959; Norton, 2000), and research (e.g., Saldaña, 2005; Saldaña & Wolcott, 2002).[1] "Performance," however, takes on different and highly specified meanings in different fields, leading to what Saldaña (2016, p. 121) critiques as the overuse of the term. For actors, performance has a specific meaning associated with representing a character for an audience in film or theatre. Much of the ABER in the performing arts focuses on adapting research into scripts of some kind (e.g., Saldaña, 2003, 2005; Woo, 2008), as a promising avenue for reaching audiences wider than those of research journals. This chapter takes a different approach, exploring how the craft of acting can be useful throughout the research process.

Saldaña (2005) illustrates the connections between acting and research, pointing out that through training, theatre practitioners gain "prerequisite skills for qualitative inquiry" (p. 29), including:

> the ability to analyze characters and dramatic texts, which transfers to analyzing interview transcripts and field notes for participant actions and relationships; ... enhanced emotional sensibility, enabling empathic understanding of participants' perspectives; ... scenographic literacy, which heightens the visual analysis of fieldwork settings; ... and an aptitude for storytelling, in its broadest sense, which transfers to the development and writing of engaging narratives and their presentation in performance.
>
> (p. 29)

How do actors learn these techniques? What exactly do coaches teach actors that enables them to embody another in much the same way as a qualitative researcher aspires to understand one's participants from an emic, or insider's, perspective? There are diverse and varied approaches to training actors, just as there are to gathering and analyzing qualitative data. Individuals develop their own adaptations that spread through word of mouth throughout communities. Some methods, however, have had considerable influence on those that came after them. Stanislavski's "Method" of actor training is one such approach.

## Examining Stanislavski's "Method" as a Qualitative Researcher

Founder of the Moscow Art Theatre (MAT), Stanislavski realized his dream to share his theory and practice underlying the craft of acting with the publication of several books and the founding of the MAT School, where I had the pleasure to study for one summer (at their Massachusetts campus). In this chapter, I share some techniques from one of Stanislavski's (1936) seminal books, *An Actor Prepares*, along with other training techniques I have learned in the years during which I studied and worked as an actor and director, connecting them to work in the social sciences to discover possibilities along the border of these two complimentary fields.

Actors are trained to cultivate (1) the awareness of the self and the other, (2) their powers of observation, (3) a facility with textual analysis, and (4) the ability to develop a character through character analysis. Only after an actor has developed these abilities is she able to skillfully portray or represent a character in performance. I explore these four areas of actor training in terms of the possibilities they open for qualitative researchers generally and ABER in particular.

## Cultivating Awareness of Self and Other

Positionality, or the relationship of the researcher to the researched, is a core element of a researcher's epistemology. Freire's (1970) widely adopted notion of reflexivity hinges on the importance of a teacher or researcher's self-awareness as cultivated through the lens of theory. Likewise, actors "filter through ourselves all the materials that we receive from the author and the director; we work over them, supplementing them out of our own imagination" (Stanislavski, 1936, p. 56). Actors, too, concern themselves with epistemology: how do we come to know and represent another, working with the fundamental material of our self? Educational researchers would do well to heed Stanislavski's admonition, "if you only knew how important is the *process of self-study*! It should continue ceaselessly, without the actor even being aware of it, and it should test every step he takes" (p. 143). This process of self-study is equally important for the researcher: "Teaching is working with human beings—not the least of which is the complex human being we are as teacher (or learner) in the classroom" (Siegesmund, 2013, p. 239). In these quotations, we see the need for the educational researcher to engage in self-investigation, as well as the power of the theatre to bring such awareness to light.

On the ethical question of representing others, Conquergood (1985) critiques the performer/researcher who flatly declares: "I am neither black nor female: I will not perform from *The Color Purple*," pointing out, "it is a fact of life of being a member of a minority or disenfranchised subculture that one must and can learn how to perform cultural scripts and play roles that do not arise out of one's own culture" (p. 8). Axiology, "the role and place of values in the research process" (Ponterro, 2005, p. 127), demands that researchers examine their own ways of being along with their ethical positioning, just as actors must, especially when endeavoring to represent those of different backgrounds or culturally sensitive materials. Actor-training techniques emphasize that to do so we must cultivate self-awareness before we may begin to understand or represent another.

Theatre artists approach the development of self-awareness in a dualistic way, focusing on our bodies as well as our inner, emotional world. Stanislavski asks us to observe how our muscles move and our body feels at various moments. Many actors are trained to do this through the Alexander Technique and the Feldenkrais Method. The former, created by actor Frederick Alexander, develops awareness of how bodies store tension and specific ways to release that tension (see http://alexandertechnique.com). The latter, developed by engineer Moshe Feldenkrais, develops kinesthetic mobility through heightened self-awareness and specific movement sequences (see www.feldenkrais.com/about). Such bodily work has also been embraced by educational researchers. In his article on somaesthetics, Shusterman (2006) advocates the use of the Feldenkrais Method and Alexander Technique in order to integrate the study of the body into the fields of the humanities and social sciences. The aim of somaesthetics is

> to enrich not only our abstract, discursive knowledge of the body but also our lived somatic experience and performance ... to enhance the meaning, understanding, efficacy, and beauty of our movements and of the environments to which our movements contribute and from which they also draw their energies and significance.
>
> (Shusterman, 2006, p. 3)

Shusterman advocates that developing more bodily awareness can benefit researchers because "body, mind, and culture are deeply co-dependent" (p. 2) and becoming more attuned to our own embodiment and that of those around us can create a less one-sided view of the human experience.

For researchers, developing "control of an unusually responsive, excellently prepared vocal and physical apparatus" (Stanislavski, 1936, p. 17) may be of less import than the work of our "inner equipment." For actors, trained to draw on their own sensory memories, developing this inner equipment consists of fostering imagination, creativity, observation, ability to access emotion, and awareness of how our inner worlds are enacted through our physicality and conveyed to (or hidden from) others. For the researcher, developing inner equipment enhances our ability to recognize the roles that our imagination, emotions, and creative processes play in our research endeavors. Self-awareness on the part of the researcher is key in recognizing how our lived histories impact our research and our ways of being affect our participants.

Self-awareness facilitates awareness of others and helps us to build trustful relationships. For actors, embodying a character entails interacting with co-actors in character. This necessitates a relationship of trust akin to that between researchers and participants. Stanislavski (1936) instructed actors: "If you want to exchange your thoughts and feeling with someone you must offer something you have experienced yourself" (p. 222). This advice, meant for co-actors, is directly applicable to educational researchers. Paris (2011) describes the importance of sharing his own life experiences with his youth participants:

> This sharing of self in dialogic process, I believe, led youth to share their selves in more genuine and honest ways ... led to richer and truer data than the model of the somewhat detached, neutral researcher that echoes across the decades from more positivist-influenced versions of qualitative inquiry.
>
> (p. 139)

In communicating with participants during fieldwork or interviews, researchers may find that sharing their own experiences opens further avenues of exploration. Stanislavski bemoans "what torture to play opposite an actor who looks at you and yet sees someone else, who constantly adjusts himself to that other person and not to you" (p. 219). What torture must it be for research participants to feel that they may be seen as living iterations of the researcher's preconceived, rehearsed notions? To remedy this phenomenon in actors, Stanislavski forbade his students from developing the bad habit of reciting lines to inanimate objects (such as their mirror) and instead to focus on their co-actors in the moment. From this, educational researchers might remember that, no matter our theoretical orientations to the context we are studying, it is our job to remain receptive to the perceptions of those who live in those contexts, not to write that which we have rehearsed in our minds long before we began collecting data. Actors are constantly told to "remain in the moment," to remember "acting is reacting." These dictums hold relevance for scholartists as well. Saldaña and Wolcott's (2002) play, *Finding My Place: The Brad Trilogy*, illustrates a researcher's personal, ethical struggle conducting research with a young man with whom Wolcott had developed a close and contentious relationship. Their writings clearly illustrate this tension in educational research between our coexisting roles as researchers and as human beings in an authentic and intimate relationship with our participants. Like actors, qualitative scholars enhance our acting and reacting when we remain in the moment of fieldwork, mindful of our own lens.

## Observation

This brings us to the central task of interpreting and representing another's way of being. Like researchers, actors must develop keen observation of people and the world around them. Stanislavski (1936) reminds us that attention to the smallest detail is important and asks us to cultivate it through studied observation. He asks, "How can we teach unobservant people to notice what nature and life are trying to show them? First of all, they must be taught to look at, to listen to, and to hear what is beautiful" (p. 100). A common activity in acting classes is to observe someone and perform that person, imitating their walk, how they store tension in their body, how they laugh and talk, hold a coffee cup, sustain or break a regard, and so on. Another common activity is to sit in silence and listen to the sounds surrounding the class; in debriefing afterwards, it becomes apparent that a multitude of sounds surround us in "silence" and that each person has had different noises drawn to their attention. Why not try these activities as researchers, not just observing but embodying our participants? Take the time to notice what is truly going on in our surroundings and how our perceptions differ from those around us, not just looking for something but seeing what is there, not only listening for something we wish to hear but also hearing that which emerges organically from the space.

To observe, alone, is not enough; we must interpret our observations drawing from theory and our own positionality:

> When the inner world of someone you have under observation becomes clear to you through his acts, thoughts, and impulses, follow his actions closely and study the conditions in which he finds himself. Why did he do this or that? What did he have in his mind? Very often we cannot come through definite data to know the inner life of the person we are studying, and can only reach towards it by means of intuitive feeling ... Our ordinary type of attention is not sufficiently far-reaching to carry out the process of penetrating another person's soul. If I were to assure you that your technique could achieve as much I should be deceiving you.
>
> (Stanislavski, 1936, p. 102)

Though a researcher's job is to convey the meaning of data rather than imagining (or fabricating) it, intuitive feeling and imagination are still useful tools to develop. Several academics have argued that all research is an act of making, an act of fiction (e.g., Siegesmund, 2013). It may initially strike readers that the interpretation of fictitious characters is a far cry from the analysis of qualitative data, but as Siegesmund (2013) points out, fictions in ABER "are legitimate to the degree that they help us understand the world-as-it-appears to be in the lives of students, teachers, and stakeholders in education" (p. 236); he argues "our fictions are in the service of becoming facts. One might argue, that this is all that is possible in any kind of scientific research ... (ABER) is just less conceited about hiding this unpleasant truth from its audiences" (p. 240). The skill sets related to the imaginary that actors must develop provide a systematic way of analyzing the historical, sociocultural, and psychological worlds of their subjects.

In order to build understanding of characters and their world, actors are encouraged to use the magic "*if*" to imagine how their character might act in situations not present in the script: "all action in the theatre must have an inner justification, be logical, coherent and real ... *if* acts as a lever to lift us out of the world of actuality into the realm of the imagination" (Stanislavski, 1936, p. 49). In the same vein, researchers might use the *if*: how might a participant have responded *if* we had asked a question differently? What might we revisit *if* we had the chance to reenter the field for clarification? *If* one part of our research context changed, how might that affect the whole? These *ifs* can be examined on our own or brought up with participants. In fact, these questions are integral to most research already. In discussion of limitations and implications, researchers imagine how our own methods and findings might be useful to broader audiences. We reenvision our process by asking what might change to produce different results. This is at the root of praxis, the process in educational research of acting and reflecting, then allowing our reflections to influence our future practices as informed through both experience and theory. We are always filling gaps in reality through our imagination; as anyone who has attempted to transcribe data knows, on a second listen we find we have sometimes written what our brains have imagined rather than what our ears have heard. Theatre training cultivates awareness of our empirical imagination.

## Textual Analysis

In gathering data from participants, are we limiting ourselves to what they say? Privileging the spoken word over manner, movement, and intonation? Even if our original data source were three-dimensional, we most often transcribe it, analyzing text in the end. Even in multimodal analysis, text is most often the unit analyzed, as well as the medium of the final product. In ABER, however, researchers are encouraged to embrace multimodality (visual, auditory, kinaesthetic, etc.). Theatre artists, similarly, bring a text to life through the literal embodiment of it. To do this, actor-training methods provide tools for textual analysis to bring the play to the realm of three dimensions. These tools include the discovery of the *given circumstances*, the breaking down of a text into *units*, the discovery of *objectives*, and the systematic analysis of a character.

Through careful analysis of a play's *given circumstances*, an actor works to create a character coherent with how the playwright presents it, yet at the same time adding their own interpretive spin. Actors and researchers both work to triangulate data from different sources to ensure that their representation, though filtered through their own lens, is borne out by data. As Stanislavski (1936) puts it, "*If* gives the push to dormant imagination, whereas the *given circumstances* build the basis for *if* itself" (p. 54). Stanislavski encourages actors to first gather all materials that have any bearing on their role in a play (p. 57), then

> study it from the point of view of the epoch, the time, the country, condition of life, background, literature, psychology, the soul, way of living, social position, and external appearance; moreover, you study character, such as custom, manner, movement, voice, speech, intonations. All this work on your material will help you to permeate it with your own feelings. Without all this you will have no art.
>
> (p. 23)

The *given circumstances* of our research context are also important. How do historical factors, social positioning, and geography influence the research? Stanislavski claims that all feelings "are the result of something that has gone on before" (p. 43); in the same way, the moments observed in fieldwork, our participants' utterances, are influenced by historicity.

For Stanislavski, at the core of every unit lies an *objective*, meaning what the character is trying to achieve, do, or get in a particular moment. A character's objective is the motivation for each action taken over the course of the play, and the changing of the objective or tactics to reach an objective marks a new *unit*. This concept can be useful in the analysis of research participants' actions, as well as the writing of research reports as it calls attention to the fact that motivations, feelings, and intuitions may not be directly stated. This is particularly important to keep in mind when considering how participants respond to interview questions, why they choose some word and not another, or how they act under observation.

Of course, it is impossible to embody or represent a culture and its history in its entirety. To help with the monumental task of breaking the whole down into manageable parts, actors break a script into *units* or *beats*. In this endeavor, Stanislavski (1936) cautions us against getting bogged down in details, advising actors to instead break the play into units to determine, "*What is the core of the play—the thing without which it cannot exist ... go over the main points without entering into detail*" (p. 126). This is a necessary task for the researcher too, having accumulated dozens, hundreds, or thousands of pages of data. At the point(s) of analysis (rather than paralysis), the researcher might take comfort in Stanislavski's advice: "do not break up a play more than necessary, do not use details to guide you. Create a channel outlined by large divisions, which have been thoroughly worked out and filled down to the last detail" (p. 127). In the same vein, a researcher may first endeavor to construct major themes, locating details to support them, rather than allowing a thousand themes to emerge from each individual detail.

In writing, we would also do well to heed his advice on clarity and simplicity of communication:

> The people who talk most about exalted things are the very ones, for the most part, who have no attributes to raise them to a high level. They talk about art and creation with false emotions, in an indistinct and involved way. True artists, on the contrary, speak in simple and comprehensible terms.
>
> (p. 172)

There has been much debate on the usefulness of clarity in academic writing. Lather (1996), as an example, asserts:

> to speak so as to be understood immediately is to speak through the production of the transparent signifier, that which maps easily onto taken for granted regimes of meaning. This runs a risk that endorses, legitimates, and reinforces the very structure of symbolic value that must be overthrown.
>
> (p. 528)

However, one of the great strengths of ABER is that it allows researchers to broaden the work's reach to audiences who may have been typically denied access. Writing clearly need not imply writing (or acting, embodying) simply; rather, it necessitates audience awareness. One of the clichéd faux pas in the theatre is for a director to underestimate the audience's intelligence. Yet, with theatre, we can complicate and nuance in ways other than the elevated academic language of research papers through gesture, intonation, lighting, staging, and sound. Furthermore, it is of utmost importance that before we can convey (as researcher or actor) our analysis to our audience, we must have a clear view of it in our own right. Clarity in acting entails distilling our presentation to that which is born from the *given circumstances*: our data and context. Stanislavski advises us to "avoid straining after the result. Act with truth, fullness and integrity of purpose" (p. 128). Like actors, we must ensure that research assertions are grounded in evidence and communicated in terms appropriate for whatever audience we aim to reach.

### Character Analysis

After analyzing the world of the play, actors must build a character. To accomplish this, they may construct biographies of their characters, combining textual analysis with their imagination. In rehearsal, actors are encouraged to construct answers to common questions that may also be useful for researchers: Where was the character before they entered the scene?; What is their relationship with the other characters?; What impelled the character to enter the scene, speak, or take a particular action at that specific moment?; What happened in the moment preceding their entrance?; What do other characters in the play say about your character?; What does your character most fear/hope for?; What object is most dear to your character?; What is your character trying to conceal from others in the scene? The answers to these questions may not be present in the text, but considering them can give an actor, or researcher, a more textured purpose.

Considering these questions in the data collection, analysis, and representation phases of research can deepen both our understanding of participants and an audience's understanding of our research. During data collection, these questions might help us construct interview questions and attune to moments we might not have initially considered as data. They can encourage us to revisit our participants as we gather further data to probe more deeply, allowing the themes we uncover to generate new questions that take us back to the field. In the analysis phase, they ground us in the given contexts of our research and the historicity of our participants while encouraging us to take risks and engage in our analysis with imagination and depth. They remind us not to make easy choices in building our character (for the actor) or identifying themes (for the researcher), but rather to honor the nuances of each given situation. Poststructural theories remind us to trouble the notion of researchers knowing/

understanding their "subject." Stanislavskian methods of character analysis encourage us to further trouble the knowledge we construct, turning toward interactiveness in research. These questions can both lead us to self-awareness and complicate our representations of research.

The possibilities of character analysis in research representation have already been explored (e.g., Saldaña, 2003, 2005), in that they offer opportunities to create monologues, plays, or screenplays for performance based on our data. This enables us to reach a wider public and requires that we become so confident in our understanding of our participants that we feel able not only to *write about* them but also to *embody* and be *changed* by them. It requires the selection of moments that both encapsulate our themes and resonate with our readers on an emotional, intuitive level. In embodying, rather than only writing about an educational context, we are forced to consider the relationship between ourselves, our participants, the audience, and the various sociocultural forces that work upon all of these agents in confluence. We are required not only to think about our data but also to experience it bodily and emotionally. Of course, the saying that *no two actors play the same Hamlet* applies to researchers as well. We will not become our participants or truly understand their circumstances and experiences through theatre, but through actor training methods, we might further bring ourselves into the work and explore others' experiences through the full, somaesthetic capacities of our bodies, minds, and imaginations.

## Conclusion

Of course, there are key differences between theatre and educational research. Saldaña (2003) remarks, "Theatre's primary goal is neither to 'educate' nor to 'enlighten.' Theatre's primary goal is to entertain-to entertain ideas and to entertain for pleasure" (p. 220). Imagination and entertainment play a stronger role in theatre than in research. Stanislavski (1936), likewise, notes this difference: "I am not a census taker, who is responsible for collecting exact facts. I am an artist who must have material that will stir my emotions" (p. 101). Yet, much of the advice he meticulously set down for actors applies directly to research contexts. For instance, "Never begin with results. They will appear in time as the logical outcome of what has come before" (p. 20). Geertz (1975), along similar lines, reminds ethnographers of the necessity of collecting and analyzing a range of data to create a thick description of the participants and cultural context, and Rist (1980) cautions against swiftly conducted, shallow, and impressionistic work. Stanislavski's advice on portraying a character might, thus, easily have been taken from a research methods textbook.

Both theatre and research are inherently interdisciplinary and involve extensive collaboration and relationship building. Educational researchers draw from many fields to conduct their research, just as teachers must develop skills across different pedagogical and content areas. Because acting also involves a content area (the world of the play learned about through dramaturgy) and the development of expertise in the craft of theatre, the two can learn from each other. Not all researchers may want to present their research in the form of art, nor should they. However, by integrating some of the principles of actor training into our practice, we can strive to engage our full powers of observation and imagination to develop nuanced understandings and render our research artfully.

## Postscript

Re-reading this chapter, I find that Stanislavski's words (1936) continue to resonate with me as both a researcher and educator. Yet, his theories and techniques are just one out of so many approaches that have been developed to help actors explore themselves, their characters, texts, and the world around them and to represent their analyses for a public audience.

Since writing this chapter as a PhD student, I have relocated to Maine to serve as an Assistant Professor where I have found an exciting community of improvisational artists who inspire me with their creative energy and ability to whip new worlds seemingly out of thin air. I have also had the incredible privilege to collaborate with Vahdat Yeganeh, at the American Repertory Theater at Harvard University, exploring devised drama with immigrant and refugee communities (McGovern & Yeganeh, 2023; McGovern & Yeganeh, 2024). Through these new experiences, I see even further potential in drama, in all its forms, as inquiry.

Another chapter might easily be devoted to Jerzy Grotowski (2002) whose experimental theatre focused on actors' bodies in exploring character and text and expressing emotion, to engage in "detailed investigations of the actor-audience relationship" (p. 15). Another could draw from the work of Augusto Boal (1979) whose use of drama with actors and non-actors to fight systems of oppression aligns nicely with critical approaches to qualitative research. Another might yet explore how training in the skills and tenets of improvisational comedy, like saying "yes, and," can enhance researchers' relational and observational skills. In reflecting on this chapter a few years later, I want to say, "yes, and ..." the field of drama offers so many practical techniques and theoretical lenses to further our ways of knowing. Yes, to studying Stanislavski's craft and considering how it might enhance our skills and understanding as researchers, and yes also to exploring and developing the myriad ways in which drama, and art more broadly, gifts us with the means of experiencing and exploring the world through fresh perspectives.

## Note

1 For an example, see Chapter 31, "The drama and poetry of qualitative method" by Johnny Saldana.

## References

Boal, A. (1979). *Theater of the oppressed* (C. M. McBride, Trans.). Theater Communications Group (Original work published in 1974).

Butler, J. (2006). *Gender trouble: Feminism and the subversion of identity*. Routledge.

Cahnmann, M. (2003). The craft, practice, and possibility of poetry in educational research. *Educational Researcher*, *32*(3), 29–36. https://doi.org/10.3102/0013189X032003029

Cahnmann-Taylor, M., Wooten, J., Souto-Manning, M., & Dice, J. L. (2009). The art and science of educational inquiry: Analysis of performance-based focus groups with novice bilingual teachers. *Teachers College Record*, *111*(11), 2535–2559. https://doi.org/10.1177/016146810911101107

Chekhov, A. (1999). The seagull. In *The plays of Anton Chekhov* (P. Schmidt, Trans.) (pp. 109–164). Harper Perennial.

Conquergood, D. (1985). Performing as a moral act: Ethnical dimensions of the ethnography of performance. *Literature in Performance*, *5*(2), 1–13. https://doi.org/10.1080/10462938509391578

Freire, P. (1970). *Pedagogy of the oppressed* (M. B. Ramos, Trans.). Bloomsbury.

Gee, J. P. (1996). *Social linguistics and literacies: Ideology in discourses* (2nd ed.). Taylor & Francis.

Geertz, C. (1975). Thick description: Toward and interpretive theory of culture. In C. Geertz (Ed.), *The interpretation of cultures: Selected essays* (pp. 3–30). Hutchinson and Basic Books.
Goffman, E. (1959). *The presentation of self in everyday life*. Anchor Books.
Grotowski, J. (2002). *Towards a poor theatre*. Routledge.
Lather, P. (1996). Troubling clarity: The politics of accessible language. *Harvard Educational Review*, *66*(3), 525–545. https://doi.org/10.17763/haer.66.3.6qxv1p081102560g
McGovern, K. R., & Yeganeh, V. (2023). Drama for dialogue of civilizations: Performance as storytelling in the adult ESOL classrooms. *TESOL Journal*, *14*(4), 1–19. https://doi.org/10.1002/tesj.745
McGovern, K. R., & Yeganeh, V. (2024). Devised drama as social-emotional learning. *Anglica: An International Journal of Language Studies*, *33*(1), 19–41. https://doi.org/10.7311/0860-5734.33.1.02
Norton, B. (2000). *Identity and language learning: Gender, ethnicity, and educational change*. Longman.
Paris, D. (2011). 'A friend who understands fully': Notes on humanizing research in a multiethnic youth community. *International Journal of Qualitative Studies in Education*, *24*(2), 137–149. https://doi.org/10.1080/09518398.2010.495091
Ponterro, J. G. (2005). Qualitative research in counseling psychology: A primer on research paradigms and the philosophy of science. *Journal of Counseling Psychology*, *52*(2), 126–136. https://doi.org/10.1037/0022-0167.52.2.126
Rist, R. C. (1980). Blitzkrieg ethnography: On the transformation of a method into a movement. *Educational Researcher*, *9*(2), 8–10. https://doi.org/10.3102/0013189X009002008
Saldaña, J. (2003). Dramatizing data: A primer. *Qualitative Inquiry*, *9*(2), 218–236. https://doi.org/10.1177/1077800402250932
Saldaña, J. (2005). *Ethnodrama: An anthology of reality theater*. AltaMira Press.
Saldaña, J. (2016). *Thinking qualitatively: Methods of mind*. Sage.
Saldaña, J., & Wolcott, H. F. (2002). Finding my place: The Brad trilogy. In H. F. Wolcott (Ed.), *Sneaky kid and its aftermath: Ethics and intimacy in fieldwork* (pp. 167–210). AltaMira Press.
Shusterman, R. (2006). Thinking through the body, educating for the humanities: A plea for somaesthetics. *The Journal of Aesthetic Education*, *40*(1), 1–21. https://www.jstor.org/stable/4140215
Siegesmund, R. (2013). The use of fiction in arts-based educational research. In F. Hernández-Hernández & R. Fendler (Eds.), *1st conference on arts based and artistic research: Critical reflections on the intersection of art and research*. University of Barcelona.
Stanislavski, C. (1936). *An actor prepares*. Routledge.
Woo, Y. Y. J. (2008). Engaging new audiences: Translating research into popular media. *Educational Researcher*, *37*(6), 321–329. https://doi.org/10.3102/0013189X08324229

Chapter 28

# Misperformance Ethnography[1]

*Monica Prendergast, and George Belliveau*

Performance ethnography is well-established, focusing as it does on a live performance of some kind (see Alexander, 2005; Denzin, 2003; Hamera, 2011; Madison, 2012; Pollock, 2006). Within the hybrid field of performance studies, the notions of *mis*performance and the poetics of failure focus on the intrinsic qualities of ephemerality and contingency present in performance. More specifically, these concepts highlight how (un)planned mistakes, errors, and even disasters may befall those who perform. How do these aspects of performance affect both performer and spectator, whether intended or not? And how might these concepts be of value and interest to an arts-based researcher? This chapter presents performance studies' theories of failure. We then place theory in action, examining our recent applied theatre projects with federal inmates (Monica) and military veterans (George).

In *Ethnotheatre: Research from Page to Stage*, Saldaña (2011) observes that too often discussions of performance in the social sciences feature "unhealthy, incestuous inbreeding when it comes to ... citations of the scholarly literature related to performance studies" (p. 35). He goes on to strongly advise: "Don't just write about performance, write a play script" (p. 35). Saldaña's goal is to increase the quantity and quality of performance-based research. Common talking points in arts-based research (ABR) discourse are raising questions of artistic qualifications and perceived accomplishment of the work. However, in this chapter, rather than accomplishment and success, we are interested in the twin notions of *misperformance* and *performing failure*. Our hope is that those who have created, or may intend to create, various kinds of performance ethnographies may benefit from the aesthetic and critical possibilities that emerge from embracing and exploring vulnerability, mistakes, and failure in performance.

We begin this chapter by highlighting key concepts drawn from performance literature on misperformance and failure. In the second section, we consider how they might apply in the context of performance ethnography by "staging" a dialogue with each other based on these ideas. Our recent applied theatre projects with a male prison theatre company (Prendergast, 2013, 2016) and a group of military veterans (Belliveau & Lea, 2020; Belliveau & Prendergast, 2019) give us the opportunity to revisit our work with a different lens and focus. What were the silences, hesitations, mistakes, and misperformances we encountered in this work? How do we negotiate the challenges of intimacy that creating performance invites when working in vulnerable participant communities? What are the stories we, as arts-based educational research (ABER) researchers, resist telling? What can we learn from revealing what we try to keep hidden—our fears, our vulnerabilities, our sense of otherness in relation to participants whose lives are so different from our own?

DOI: 10.4324/9781003412892-28

The invitation to readers (and to ourselves) is to take on the productive tensions made available, to both performers and audiences, in the encounter between performance and audience framed as "successful" versus "misperformed" or "failed." We argue that in making ethnographic experiences of failure invisible—in a pursuit of seamless beauty and aesthetic resolution—we fail to create the most transparently and (perhaps ironically) aesthetically powerful work possible. As the master playwright of failure Samuel Beckett reminds, "Ever tried. Ever failed. No matter. Try again. Fail again. Fail better" (Beckett Archive, n.d.).

## Part One: Theorizing Misperformance Ethnography

### *Embracing Stage Fright and the Failure to Perform "Well"*

After many years of training, an actor's key goal is to present oneself at ease onstage, to ensure that audiences feel comfortable with the mastery of voice, body, and interpretive performance of character and situation. Matthew Goulish (2010) comments on this status quo scenario:

> Theatrical narcissism, [is] a tendency of performance, or performing, to be about itself, while pretending to be about something else. The something else that the performance claims to investigate retreats to a sentimentalized background, lurking behind the foregrounded act and presence of the performers. *Let us consider instead presence as mobility; not a thing made, but a thing in the making.*
>
> (p. 36)

Portrayal of the Other, or of the Self, that reveals hesitation, fear, the inability to fix the interpretation, to "get it right," all become not only aesthetic choices made available through an embrace of stage fright, but also an ethical stance made visible. Intentionally awkward performance style offers the chance to engage directly with an audience around the omnipresent pressures of performance and research representation, and to find creative ways to make these processes clear and present. Examples of companies that explore this aesthetic are Goat Island in the United States and Forced Entertainment in the United Kingdom (see Bailes, 2011; Goulish, 2000). The hesitancy and fear of the performer transmits itself to an audience that, in turn, cannot sink comfortably back in their seats, waiting to be entertained/enlightened by somebody else's labor power. Instead, akin to a loving parent attending their small child's first school play, the audience is in terror and in thrall to what is being played out for them, heartfelt yet painful at one and the same time.

There is something very much at stake for audiences subjected to the portrayal of amateur performance. Their choices are: to accept, tolerate, and/or support the weakness portrayed; reject it in overt ways (by heckling or leaving the performance space); or covertly reject (by tuning out, exchanging horrified glances with others, resisting engagement, refusing to suspend disbelief). In misperformance, a pretense lack of artistry is an aesthetic choice on the part of the performer or ensemble. This tactic enacts a resistance to theatrical narcissism and the risk of an audience being lulled and pacified by the perception of talent and expertise.

### *Engaging with Silence and Incoherence*

Silence in performance, which is never entirely silent (as composer John Cage notes, we can still hear the blood rushing through our bodies, the sound of our hearts beating; Gann, 2010), and stillness, which is never actually still (the body rebels and begins to shiver, shake, tremble, collapse), open up some provocative points of connection with performance ethnography. We are challenged as both performers and audience members to address stillness and silence that may occur as a result of performance mistakes: lines dropped, memory and rehearsal inexplicably failed. Yet, silence and stillness can also serve as points of reflection, filling space and time with opportunities to consider the nature and limits of human action and interaction.

What does silence and stillness make available in ethnographical contexts? An honoring that communication is really hard work and that the most challenging dialogues demand passages of silence, for those engaged to process, reenergize, and recommit themselves to the ongoing process, the attempt (doomed to failure?) to truly understand one another, oneself. This demand pushes us the way good visual art does: to interpret, fill in the blanks, take in, open up, become wider awake in the world.

Incoherence and unintelligibility is another aesthetic choice performance artists may embrace. A branch of performance art practice that has had currency in both modern and postmodern art practices is the *lecture-performance*. In Milder's (2011) essay on this topic, she notes:

> Twentieth-century artists ... have used lecture-performance to blur the lines separating art from discourse about art. ... The best lecture-performances always seem to originate from artists who believe that teaching itself is a central component of their artwork. (p. 13)

One tactic taken by a number of lecture-performers is that of performing failure to make oneself understood. Milder notes a 2009 lecture given by artist Terence at the National Arts Club, titled *Art History: 1642–2009*, that was delivered entirely in gibberish (p. 18): "Speaking to a packed house of art-world sophisticates in a completely unintelligible language, he railed, whispered, gestured, and danced his way through a visually entertaining lecture about art since the time of Goya" (Laster, 2009, n.p.).[2] Linsley (2012), in another essay surveying performance lecture praxis, mentions a lecture given at the Tate Gallery in 2003 by artist Pope L.:

> When Pope. L takes his place at the lectern he stands for a moment, then steps away to have a sip of water. He returns, and seems to clear his throat. He keeps clearing his throat. It slowly becomes obvious that he is not clearing his throat, but intentionally producing guttural sounds punctuated with heavy consonants. 'FFFFFFFFFFFFFFFFF FFFFFFFFFFFFFFFF', he intones, and 'SSSSSSSSSSSSSSSSSSSSSSSSSSSSSSSSSSSSS'. (p. 60)

The author finds out after this unintelligible event that Pope L. was actually delivering his lecture in Klingon, the fictional language derived from the *Star Trek* film and television series. Linsley comments on her response,

> There is something gleefully silly about delivering a lecture at a prestigious symposium in a fictional alien language, particularly without preamble or postscript. I snorted in

> approval on learning about the Klingon dimension of Pope L.'s performance and said, without thinking but with sincere appreciation: that's so stupid.
>
> (p. 61)

These case studies of lecture-performances rendered intentionally obtuse and imperceptible hold some interesting provocations for performance ethnography. Intelligence, effective knowledge production and transmission, scholarliness, and mastery are all desirable traits to be demonstrated in order to "succeed" within research contexts. Yet, what might occur if a performance ethnographer makes a conscious decision to translate her stories into "stupider," stuttering, nonlanguage forms? How might these choices open up the layers of hesitation, false starts, wrong turns, and dead-end disasters that are a "natural" part of the process of both performance creation and research? Alongside amateurism, stage fright, silence, and stillness, the qualities embodied in the failed attempt to communicate described in this section add more levels of possibility, a critique of the "expertise" status quo found in the vast majority of research, however it is performed.

## Part Two: Practicing Misperformance Ethnography

The following two misperformance ethnographies were created dialogically between Monica and George in a storytelling exchange carried out between the two of us in October 2016. We experimented with the technique of tabletop theatre, introduced to us by Forced Entertainment's project *Table Top Shakespeare* ("Complete Works," 2015). Company members performed adaptations of every play in Shakespeare's canon in 40-minute versions using a solo storyteller, household objects, and a table. We used salt and pepper shakers, some mugs, and a few other household items, manipulating these objects to assist our improvised storytelling. Our focus was to attempt to put misperformance principles—Embracing Stage Fright, the Failure to Perform "Well," Silence and Incoherence—into practice by sharing stories of difficulty or of failure. These are stories we had not told, or were resistant to telling, about our recent applied theatre projects. Here is what unfolded.

### *George's Story*

#### *Holy Shit! What Just Happened?*

Note on context: Tim is one of four veterans performing in a play called *Contact!Unload*, and his story is central to the play. The script weaves his journey from not wanting help to eventually seeking support and going through a therapeutic enactment (Westwood & Wilensky, 2005), sharing his psychological injury with the group. This interactive therapeutic approach asks participants to revisit past injuries in hopes of correcting neural pathways, mending parts of themselves that have become broken or separated from the person. Tim's story is one of feeling responsible for the death of an Informant during an attack in Afghanistan in 2006. As a signals operator, Tim was several kilometers away from the incident and receiving various messages from military personnel who were nearby the attack. His intent was to evacuate the ten wounded and four casualties who were lying on the ground as quickly as possible. However, the rescue helicopter cannot fly in until there is clearance that enemy fire has ceased. There was a man on a roof with an RPG who posed a threat. The messages Tim received were that this enemy had to be eliminated to allow the helicopters to fly in. Tim gives the green light to kill the man on the roof. The man on the roof was the Informant. Like Tim, this man was trying to save those bleeding on the ground. It took Tim six years to deal with his stress injury. In 2012, he had reached a low point where his life was at risk.

> I don't know what to do anymore. I'm at the end of my rope. Nothing I'm doing is working. I'm thinking about killing myself. I don't know what to do. I need help. I don't need help tomorrow. I need help now.
>
> (Tim in Dennison, 2014, p. 1)

TIM: FUCK! That fucking sucked!

*(Tim storms out of the rehearsal space. One of the counselors follows him.)*

GEORGE: It's Wednesday 5 pm, dress rehearsal night, and we just finished doing an Italian run through: everyone picking up the pace so we could get our lines out as quickly as possible. The cast didn't quite have their lines down, so I figured, as Director, it was necessary to take 40 minutes and run through the show as quickly as possible. The cast of 12 enjoyed the repartee of trying to get their lines out as quickly as possible and moving around the space, playfully doing the blocking. Despite it being a very serious show about traumatic moments veterans experienced during and post deployment, the Italian was very light with plenty of laughs. Only four cast members had previous theatre experience, however everyone was quick in picking up the pace so we could get our lines out as quickly as possible.

What took Tim six years to process, we zipped through in our Italian in forty minutes. We were playing around on stage, laughing, talking very quickly with little or next to no emotion. What we didn't realize was that we were ripping his soul apart again. That 40-minute Italian rehearsal was torture for Tim to witness.

COUNSELOR: *(addressing the group)* Tim would like to speak to the group in the dressing room.

GEORGE: At this point, I figured he's quitting. He's had enough of our artsy stuff. I knew I'd done something awful, but I didn't know what at the time. How could I have prevented it? What was "it"? However, it didn't matter, damage was done. Maybe bringing the theatre world inside a therapeutic process is not possible. It's maybe more damaging.

TIM: *(addresses the entire cast, as we were all tightly squeezed inside the small dressing room)* What happened out there fucking sucked. I'm not blaming anyone. But, I need you to know that every second sucked. Fucking bullshit. My heart was racing and pounding, still is.

COUNSELOR: Just breathe Tim. When you're ready, continue.

TIM: To go through this shit as fast as we could. It made it all into a big joke. I know your intent, George, was not that. I'm not blaming you.

*(Pause)*

COUNSELOR: Tim, you've just shared your feelings, your frustrations with us, and that's important. You've released some of the anger.

TIM: And you know what, as much as it sucked, going through that anger, pent-up frustration allowed me to release a little.

GEORGE: After some more conversation, we regrouped and got ready for our dress rehearsal. Tim's performance stepped up, as his authenticity in his role was near electric. I had no idea what would emerge out of this incident, how much damage I might have inflicted. The three shows went fine and Tim became stronger and more convincing with each show. Each night he cried, during or after the show, releasing emotions, something he'd seldom done for eight years.

The misperformance of the Italian rehearsal was a pivotal point in the development of the production. Arguably, it was an awakening for us all. What we were doing by presenting these very personal, difficult stories was exposing the veterans' souls to an audience. Souls that had been shattered and now gradually being rebuilt. This was not fiction, instead reliving, so we needed as a company to tread truthfully, respectfully, to try and get it "right." However, no matter how much one plans and is prepared for the inevitable, we can fail. We fail to fully appreciate the challenges of human interaction, and we fail to know what is the best choice in any given circumstance.

I came to understand a little more as to what Tim's stress injury was about. His decision to eliminate what appeared to be the enemy in Afghanistan on August 3, 2006 was made with the full intention of saving the bleeding soldiers on the ground. He went with his instinct and desire to save his mates. The decision he made in that moment was the best decision he could make under the circumstances, yet Tim demanded more of himself. He could not forgive himself for his decision. He felt responsible for that man's life.

I made a near mockery of Tim's story, his life, by doing an Italian. As the Director, I was pushing the performers to go faster and faster. It's unforgiveable what I did. This wasn't a French farce we were rehearsing, but rather, we were working on incredibly difficult stories of injured men.

However, this is where Tim's self-understanding and character comes through. Despite the pain he was going through in the Italian run-through, he could detect potential pain inflicted on others. Others who didn't mean to hurt, but simply failed, made errors in judgment.

Tim knew I had no intentions of belittling him by doing an Italian. As a human being of remarkable insight, he was able to first acknowledge his pain and then have the courage to share it openly with others. Remember that he didn't share his pain for six years, and it nearly killed him. This is a testament to the power and impact for change the therapeutic work had on Tim.

Immediately after sharing his feelings to the cast members about how he felt in doing the Italian, he forgives. He forgives me right away, so that I don't even have time to feel guilty and process my failure. His self-awareness and awareness of others was so attuned that in a moment of complete upheaval he reversed the outcome. This is something he had to do for himself and continues to do each day.

TIM: My trauma is not going away ... it's part of who I am. I deal with my shit every day. But every day, it gets a tiny, tiny bit better. This whole VTN and theatre project has fundamentally changed me.

The beauty of this misperformance is that our play is based on forgiving ourselves. Tim showed me and the company how we have to forgive ourselves for our mistakes, otherwise it will eat us alive. This sounds like a simple lesson, but many of us, as Thoreau suggests, live "lives of quiet desperation" because we can't forgive others or ourselves. Tim did both, and for that he has gifted us.

### *Monica's Story*

*The Story I Cannot Tell: A Storytelling Misperformance Within a Prison Theatre Project*

Note on Context: This story occurred during rehearsals of a prison play project within which I was working as a mentor actor. In this federal, minimum-security prison for men, female actors from the community take on women's roles as a method to work alongside inexperienced inmate performers. This form of theatre education is unique in its demands; our goal as "outsider" theatre artists and educators is to cocreate an effective piece of theatre for public audiences, as well as to transmit a meaningful theatre education experience to inmates in the program. The constant risk is of something going wrong that may threaten the continuation of this theatre project, the only one of its kind in Canada (see Prendergast, 2013, 2016). My story is about my experience of something potentially going wrong and what I did about it.

MONICA: I was the only person in the room when this happened. But there was a lot going on elsewhere. This was during , so during . So, uh … OK. So, what happens at the prison is that building when the performances happen … the gymnasium, if you've been out there to see any shows at  …

GEORGE: Yeah, yeah, I have. Yeah.

MONICA: And so, um, obviously it's a male, it's a prison for men, but the women's washrooms are locked because women are only there as volunteers or some staff members, and staff members have their own, um, washrooms and, um, the women's washrooms are only locked, only opened up when women volunteers are in the building. OK? So, when we come to rehearse or to perform, the women's washrooms are unlocked, [and] most of the women that I've worked with out there, including me, feel more comfortable changing in the women's washroom because it really is, you know, that's something we have to be very careful about, is in terms of, you know, regular dressing room behavior, because they don't have a separate dressing room for women. We're all in this same room together. So yes, I've seen plenty of inmates in their skivvies, their underwear, and it's kind of like, alright, you know, I just sort of have to avert my eyes and try to, you know, especially last year's show where we had so many costume changes, I mean it was absurd to think about how we were going to (cough) do all those things. Often, I was helping a guy—

GEORGE: Right.

MONICA: Helping him pull his pants down, pull his arms up, you know, just for quick changes. So that's the … the kind of ridiculousness, the absurdity of, you know, training us as volunteers to keep our boundaries and—

GEORGE: Right.

MONICA: You know, to not get too close to the guys, and they really are very concerned that we don't form personal attachments and that we don't have contact with them on the outside and all that kind of stuff, and yet, they have no idea. "They" being the administration, the institution, you know, uh, the bureaucracy of the prison that they really have no idea what the nature of theatre is. One of the things that theatre can do and does do is, is create intimacy.

GEORGE: Right.

MONICA: Right? Um, so that is built on trust and that is built on, you know, creating ensemble, and it takes time, and it doesn't happen overnight, and we all know that. OK.

So, obviously, so when I'm working with, working out there, this was my first show, I was having to get over all of my kind of nervousness and about … about who I am and being a middle-aged, privileged white woman and working with these guys who all have these horrendous life stories of abuse and addiction and violence, and abuse and addiction and violence, and just various iterations of, you know, variations on a theme. OK?

GEORGE: Yeah.

MONICA: But, you know, you can't help but build trust and connection, especially when you're invested in the storytelling as we were, and we ended up creating a really you know, lovely show, we were proud of it. So, I was there one night and we were, um, before the show, and I had to go to the bathroom. And so, I walked into the bathroom, and there are two stalls and it's very penitentiary-like, they are like solid metal doors, and it's you know, no aesthetics. It's not a nice washroom at all, but, you know, and um, and I walked into the larger stall and there was a little table where I could put costumes down to get changed. And I looked over into the ████, and in the ████ was ████ ████ and it was a ████. (Pause). So, I had this moment of standing over this ████ seeing something completely unexpected that I knew immediately shouldn't be there, and then I felt violated because I knew that someone had been in this women's bathroom and had used it to have a sex act—

GEORGE: Mmmhmm.

MONICA: And then disposed of ████ but hadn't ████. Just kind of left it ████, so then I sort of was a little paranoid for a second. My heart is going 150 miles an hour because I am so shocked to see it, and my head is going 300 miles an hour just processing what, what do I, like, what does this mean? And what do I do?

GEORGE: This was a rehearsal?

MONICA: This was during … I can't remember if it was … it was close to opening—

GEORGE: And before the rehearsal started?

MONICA: Yes.

GEORGE: OK.

MONICA: So, one of the guys had unlocked the door obviously, so I'm looking into … You know, it's a horrible image. You know, I'm looking at a ████ in a ████ ████, which I have to say, in my … protected life is not something that I think I've ever seen before. And so, it's not a very, you know attractive … aesthetic image that I'm looking at, but again, it was a moment that for me was frozen in time because, you know, I had those emotions of "something happened here that shouldn't have happened" … in the women's washroom … a space which I feel is my space … and the other women … a space that the guys respect and that they'd only come in here to clean or to change the toilet paper, um, you know, but would never ever set foot in, um, has been disrespected—

GEORGE: Mmm.

MONICA: On some level. So, I felt … that sense of violation and then I felt at the, at the higher level, this, this is an infraction. So, I'm not naïve, nor is the prison naïve, about ████. They provide ████. They don't want guys to be spreading ████ ████, and I've even heard some gossip over … a few years I've been out there that, you know, there are ████ who sometimes ████ with the guys and, you know, and or ████, um, and I have no idea of knowing this was a ████ or homosexual ████. It could have been one or the other.

GEORGE: Yeah, yeah.

MONICA: And obviously, I had no way of knowing. I just know that some kind of ██ ██ happened in that cubicle, in that women's washroom. So, all that is rattling through my brain at a million miles an hour, and the next thing I'm thinking is "I should report this." Right? Because as a volunteer, it's part of my responsibility to let, let the institution know if an infraction has happened, and again, it's like if I withhold that information and something, you know, blah blah blah, that domino effect of just feeling like I've gotta be a good girl, you know, I do what I'm supposed to do here, and yet my loyalty of course was with the guys, and again, being very aware that if I walked out of that bathroom and found a guard and, ironically I probably would have had to have done a bit of looking around to find a guard because they're not hovering during rehearsals. They pretty much let us, they check in every now and again, but they're not actually there all the time. But, you know, if I had walked out and said to ███ the director like, "I gotta show you something and we've got to deal with this," you know, it ... there could have been consequences, right? And because there clearly was an infraction, it would have embarrassed the prison, certainly would have gotten the guys in trouble, guys who are responsible with keys, you know.

GEORGE: Yeah.

MONICA: Because they definitely would have been able to track who has the keys. Um, and it could have led to somebody being shipped, because ultimately the, it could lead to if they had really done an investigation and found out what had happened, a guy could have been shipped back to medium. Um, which we've had happen, for various infractions that guys have had outside of the theatre program, but we've lost actors.

GEORGE: Mmmhmm.

MONICA: We'll just come to rehearsal, and it's like "Where's so and so?" "He got shipped." "Why did he get shipped?" Nobody knows. Nobody's going to tell you.

GEORGE: Yeah.

MONICA: You never are gonna know. Right? There's always the gossip of maybe it was this or maybe it was that, you know, but unless it was something that was public enough that people knew about, then you're never gonna know why somebody got shipped. So, all of this, George, is happening. All of this that I've just described to you is happening in my head in a matter of five seconds as I'm looking at this █████ in a ██████, and I'm just having this hugely emotional response, um, because on the one hand, I'm feeling betrayed and I'm feeling frightened for myself and for the program, for the show, for the guys. I'm feeling violated. I'm feeling loyal. I'm feeling, um, you know, many, many levels of emotion. And then, I kind of come to my senses, and I say to myself "Monica. You have a choice. You can reach over and ██████████ and get on with your life and what you're doing here, or you can step out of this room and go talk to—I would have talked to ███ the director—And everything will stop, and there'll be a shitstorm." This is not something that's gonna be some minor thing. It's gonna be a shitstorm. And I reached over and I ███████████.

GEORGE: Mmmhmm.

MONICA: But I was wobbly for the rest ... And I was perfectly comfortable with that decision, and at that point my loyalty was like, and also, I think that in my own personality is that I'm a fairly liberal person and I'm not, again as I said earlier, not naïve about what happens in a prison. Like, these men, just because they become inmates doesn't mean that they stop being █████████.

GEORGE: Yeah.

MONICA: So, you know, my objection was the location.

GEORGE: Yeah.

MONICA: Where this ████ happened where I felt was, was insulting, to me, a little bit, you know, um, um, but, but, ultimately in these few seconds, I was like "I gotta make this go away. I literally have to make this go away." And so, I ████████. But, um, and we went on with rehearsal, and ███, who I'm very close to, she could see I was not quite myself, but we have lots of kinda codes in that context when we're looking out for each other, because most of our energy is looking out for the guys.

GEORGE: Mmmhmm.

MONICA: So obviously, you know, when we women left the prison that night, we often we don't just debrief in the car on the way back to Victoria, we also often will stand in the parking lot, which can be a windy nightmare in the late fall out in ██████. But we often will just stand by somebody's car and have our own circle and debrief and check in.

GEORGE: Because you don't always drive together, all of you?

MONICA: Yeah. We're often going in different vehicles, so, so, you know, sometimes there are nine or ten of us out there—all women. Both these projects, all women, which is an interesting dynamic in terms of the risk of failure and misperformance [...] in this hyper-masculine environment space, right?

GEORGE: Yeah. Oh yeah.

MONICA: So, I told my colleagues what had happened, and they were very supportive, and they all said "Oh my God, Monica, if it had been me I would have felt exactly what you felt," because I was quite emotional when I told them.

GEORGE: For sure.

MONICA: You know, I wept a little bit, you know, because it was frightening for me, you know, I actually felt quite frightened for a moment about all the consequences of this ... should I decide to report it. And so, you know, we really do support each other a lot, you have to out there. The women. [...] But anyway, that was my story and I felt very, very supported by my women colleagues and, and, um, they took care of me, but for a few days, I have to say I was quite troubled by it. Because I felt that kind of lingering sense of betrayal.

GEORGE: Yeah.

MONICA: Small betrayal, but betrayal nonetheless of, you know, of their promise to us to have a protected space in the building for women and then that, that being ... You know, I guess what bothered me was, if, if, why didn't they ██████ themselves? Right? It was almost left there for someone to see, to find.

GEORGE: Oh yeah.

MONICA: And that, that, that's the part that kind of bothered me, you know? Because you'd think it would have been in their interests, whoever the ██████ were, to have gotten rid of that evidence.

GEORGE: That's right.

MONICA: But it was not gotten rid of, right?

GEORGE: Yeah.

MONICA: So that's the part that sort of bothered me, but um, to this day, um, I haven't shared that story with any ██████████, and I don't think I ever will.

GEORGE: Yeah.

MONICA: You know. Which makes me, you know, I now have the █████ problem of, you know, if I ever write this and put it in a book chapter you know, it is a kind of ████████, so I need to kind of think about that too, so. You know, sort of, sort of, an interesting kind of misperformance failure story, but it really is one of the ones, ones that from my time out there that I do find quite difficult to tell.

## Reflections: Lessons Learned

**George:** I knew the moment Tim left the rehearsal that day, something pivotal took place, a turning point. However, I didn't know the significance of the moment until I told the story verbally to Monica and eventually wrote about it. Through the telling, an understanding emerged as to how an artist's intentions can be misaligned with participant collaborators. In applied theatre, we bring a set of tools that are not always compatible and congruent with the group we're working beside. As theatre artists working within a research environment, our aim is to find the balance between honoring the research and providing aesthetic theatre (Belliveau, 2014). Our practices are well-intentioned, but our inability to fully know the context we're working in can fail us. What I discovered, though, was that through my failure came a deeper understanding, an insight that I would not have discovered otherwise.

**Monica:** What has been useful for me in the story I tell is the permission given in misperformance to include all of the awkwardness, hesitations, and stuttering that appear in the transcript of our conversation as aesthetic choices. Also, the silencing (in this case, a kind of self-censoring) of erasure is another aesthetic choice that allows me to tell the story I cannot tell—imperfectly, fragmented—in a more ethically conscious way. Redacting sections of the text protects the men I have grown to cherish and the theatre program we have participated in together. Unlike George's more intentionally polished and dramatized story, mine is more closely taken from the transcription of the audio recording, rougher by design; sitting perhaps closer to "failing" as "good" arts-based representation. This contrast between our stories functions as separate manifestations of our shared exploration of misperformance.

The prison theatre work that I have done, and hope to continue, is equal parts rewarding and demanding. The complexities of both teaching and creating theatre in a prison environment are very real and at times overwhelming. The emotional energy takes its toll. Holding both educational and artistic objectives in balance within this kind of risk-laden context can feel like trying to control a set of spinning plates destined to collapse. The story I share is one I've kept hidden for reasons I trust are made clear in the storytelling itself. The invitation to focus on failure (its potential or actuality) rather than success is the invitation made via the aesthetics of misperformance. I bring it (partially) into light as a way to experiment and explore the potential of misperformance in ABER and ethnographic performance practice.

## Postscript

Since the first version of this chapter, a special issue on the "Ethics in Research-based Theatre" was published in *Qualitative Inquiry* 29.2 (Cox et al., 2023) where issues related to this chapter are discussed by several international contributors. Also, the edited book

*Contact!Unload: Military Veterans, Trauma, and Research-based Theatre* (2020) and the chapter "Collaborating with soldiers in devising *Contact!Unload*" (2023) have been published, which provide new perspectives around the development and reception of the play shedding further light on aspects of this chapter.

## Notes

1 This chapter includes excerpts from "Misperformance ethnography" (Prendergast, 2014). Reprinted with permission from Intellect Books.
2 Brief excerpts of Koh's lecture on YouTube: www.youtube.com/watch?v=8Pu9vrgF4QE.

## References

Alexander, B. K. (2005). Performance ethnography: The reenacting and inciting of culture. In N. K. Denzin & Y. S. Lincoln (Eds.), *The Sage handbook of qualitative research* (3rd ed., pp. 411–442). Sage.
Bailes, S. J. (2011). *Performance, theatre and the poetics of failure*. Routledge.
Beckett, S. (n.d.). *Worstward ho. [MS 2602] Beckett collection*. University of Reading.
Belliveau, G. (2014). Possibilities and perspectives in performed research: A portrait of an artist/scholar within the academy. *Journal of Artistic Creative Education, 8*(1), 124–150. https://jace.online/index.php/jace/issue/view/13/Special%20Edition%20on%20Performed%20Research
Belliveau, G., & Lea, G. (Eds.). (2020). *Contact!Unload: Military veterans, trauma, and research-based theatre*. UBC Press.
Belliveau, G., & Lea, G. W. (2023). Collaborating with soldiers in devising *Contact!Unload*. In J. McKinnon & H. Fitzsimmons-Frey (Eds.), *Off book: Devised performance and higher education*. Intellect Books (pp. 335–351).
Belliveau, G., & Prendergast, M. (2019). Shadows of history, echoes of war: Performing alongside veteran soldiers and prison inmates in two Canadian applied theatre projects. In M. Finneran & M. Anderson (Eds.), *Education and theatres: Beyond the four walls*. Springer (pp. 211–225).
Complete Works: Table Top Shakespeare. (2015). www.forcedentertainment.com/project/complete-works-table-top-shakespeare/
Cox, S., Guillemin, M., Nichols, J., & Prendergast, M. (Eds.) (2023). Special issue: Ethics in research-based theater. *Qualitative Inquiry 29*(2), 247–402.
Dennison, B. (2014). A soldier's tale: 'Nobody understood what I'd done'. *The Tyee*. http://thetyee.ca/News/2014/11/10/Soldiers-Tales-Told/
Denzin, N. K. (2003). *Performance ethnography: Critical pedagogy and the politics of culture*. Sage.
Gann, K. (2010). *No such thing as silence: John Cage's 4′33″*. Yale University Press.
Goulish, M. (2000). *39 microlectures in proximity of performance*. Routledge.
Goulish, M. (2010). First, second, third. *Performance Research: A Journal of the Performing Arts, 15*(2), 34–38.
Hamera, J. (2011). Performance ethnography. In N. K. Denzin & Y. S. Lincoln (Eds.), *The Sage handbook of qualitative research* (4th ed., pp. 317–330). Sage.
Laster, P. (2009). *Terence Koh speaks in tongues at the National Arts Club* [video]. http://flavorwire.com/52771/terence-koh-speaks-in-tongues-at-the-national-arts-club
Linsley, J. (2012). Stupid, paranoid, wonderful: Staging non-knowledges in the pedagogical encounter. *Performance Research: A Journal of the Performing Arts*, *17*(1), 59–67. https://doi.org/10.1080/13528165.2012.651864
Madison, D. S. (2012). *Critical ethnography: Method, ethics and performance* (2nd ed.). Sage.
Milder, P. (2011). Teaching as art: The contemporary lecture-performance. *PAJ: A Journal of Performance and Art*, *33*(1), 13–27.
Pollock, D. (2006). Marking new directions in performance ethnography. *Text and Performance Quarterly*, *26*(4), 325–329. https://www.jstor.org/stable/41309686

Prendergast, M. (2013). Running around with inmates, maps and swords: A reflective poetic-narrative autoethnography of a prison theatre production. *Research in Drama Education: The Journal of Applied Theatre and Performance*, *18*(3), 313–323. https://doi.org/10.1080/13569783.2013.810927
Prendergast, M. (2014). Misperformance ethnography. *Applied Theatre Research*, *2*(1), 77–90. https://doi.org/10.1386/atr.2.1.77_1
Prendergast, M. (2016). Tracing the journey to here: Reflections on a prison theatre devised project. *Theatre Topics*, *26*(3), 343–349. https://doi.org/10.1353/tt.2016.0059
Saldaña, J. (2011). *Ethnotheatre: Research from page to stage*. Left Coast Press.
Westwood, M. J., & Wilensky, P. (2005). *Therapeutic enactment: Restoring vitality through trauma repair in groups*. Group Action Press.

Chapter 29

# Art, Agency, and Inquiry

## Making Connections between New Materialism and Contemporary Pragmatism in Arts-Based Research

*Jerry Rosiek*

An emerging movement in the philosophy and sociology of science is beginning to exert considerable influence on contemporary qualitative researchers generally and arts-based researchers specifically. The movement is referred to by many names, such as the ontological turn in social inquiry (Rosiek & Gleason, 2017), posthumanism (Alaimo & Hekman, 2008; Braidotti, 2013), post-qualitative research (Lather & St. Pierre, 2013), the new empiricisms (Clough, 2009; MacLure, 2013), and, the term I will use here, the new materialisms (Barad, 2007, 2010, 2011; Coole & Frost, 2010).

What the philosophies gathered loosely under these terms have in common is a frustration with well-worn debates between realist and constructivist philosophies of social science. They all (re)assert the importance of attending to the way epistemology, ontology, and ethics are intertwined in our analysis, with no one of these dimensions of philosophical analysis being able to claim a prior footing. More distinctively, they share a focus on what Barad (2007) has called *agential realism*—the idea that it makes sense to understand agency as a pervasive feature of the things of this world.

Agential realism is particularly well suited for understanding arts-based research (ABR). In the epistemology-centric discourse of contemporary education research, arts-based researchers have often felt compelled to defend their work as producing unique forms of knowledge. Art, however, has never been just about producing knowledge or even just about raising critical questions. Art is a means by which we sensitize ourselves to new possibilities of experience. In other words, art seeks to generate new modes of being in the world; it is simultaneously epistemological and ontological in its ambitions. Artists often speak about being receptive to the motive force of their materials. Likewise, we often speak of works of art taking on a life of their own in a community. Trying to explain the importance of ABR entirely in epistemic terms risks losing track of the ontological power and purpose of artistic endeavor. It is not surprising, therefore, that many arts-based researchers (e.g., Osgood et al., 2015; Rosiek, 2017; Springgay & Rotas, 2015; Springgay & Zaliwska, 2015) have been attracted to what Barad (2007) calls the "onto-epistemologies" of new materialist philosophy.[1]

There is work to be done, however, in working out the implications of new materialism for ABR. These new developments in the philosophy of science are not just sources of justification for affectively compelling descriptions. They also bring with them a call for increased ethical and political accountability in research. If inquiry contributes to the generation of new ontological relations, then inquirers of all sorts are responsible for attending to the consequences of those relations in their communities. Also, it raises the question: what are our ethical and political responsibilities in regard to nonhuman agents?

DOI: 10.4324/9781003412892-29

It turns out that the new materialists are not the only, nor the first, philosophical literature to develop agent ontologies.[2] Variations on the idea of nonhuman things being agentic, for example, appear in classic and contemporary pragmatism. The connection with pragmatism is especially important for the theme of this book, because so many in ABR are influenced by John Dewey's pragmatism. Therefore, in what follows, I review the similarities and divergences in the accounts of agential realism in these two literatures with an eye to their implications for our work as arts-based social science scholars.

## Roots of the New Materialisms

The phrase "new materialism" speaks to the conceptual tension from which this philosophical movement has arisen. Generally, the adjective "materialist" has been used to refer to social analysis that has its roots in Marxism. Marx famously turned German idealism on its head by arguing that ideas don't shape the material world nearly as much as the material world shapes our ideas. By "material," Marx was referring to the economic necessities that constrain our individual and communal activities, and thus shape our ideas, identity, and consciousness. He observed that views of everything from god and truth to national character and individual morality had evolved to support and perpetuate the given economic order. For example, he argued that religion, specifically the idea that we would be rewarded in an afterlife for our suffering in this life, functioned as "an opiate" that distracted people from doing something about the causes of their oppression in this world (Marx, 2014, p. 54).

This was a tectonic philosophical move. Prior to Marx, the prevailing assumption had been that ideas work an influence on the material world, by guiding human action and providing increased mastery of material things through the advance of science and social thought. The idea that economic materiality could conversely co-opt our minds and distract us from the questions that need to be asked shook the emerging confidence in scientific rationality in the West. Marxists argued, however, that the ideal of a rational society could be rescued by means of careful critical analysis that parsed sound evidence and argumentation from the distortions of capitalist and nationalist ideologies.

Poststructuralists took this Marxist hermeneutics of suspicion (Gadamer, 1984) a step further. They rejected the Marxist effort to rehabilitate authoritative rationality through critical ideological analysis, because this critical analysis left the individual Western rational subject unquestioned and unanalyzed. As Spivak (1996) observed,

> ... the will to explain is a symptom of a desire to have a self and a world. In other words, on the general level, the possibility of explanation carries the supposition of an explainable (even if not fully) universe and an explaining (even if imperfectly) subject ... every explanation must secure and assure a certain kind of being-in-the-world, which might as well be called our politics.
>
> (p. 32)

The form of subjectivity produced by the enlightenment ideal of rational explanation was that of a spectator subject, whose allegedly objective, dispassionate authority underwrites the authority of the technocratic colonialist state.

Poststructuralists critiqued this authority, not by claiming it was mistaken about its particular claims regarding social reality, but by questioning the very idea of grounding social analysis on claims about reality at all. Drawing upon Saussurian linguistic theory, they treated all knowledge claims as linguistically mediated phenomena (Derrida, 1998; Rorty, 1989).

By abandoning Marxism's economic reductionism, poststructuralism brought into focus the myriad ways that knowledge claims are an effect of power relations. No longer was critique focused solely on the way economics influenced our conceptions of knowledge. Critical analysis was also brought to bear on the way heteronormative discourses influence how and what we know about gender (Butler, 1993; Foucault, 1990), the way Eurocentric and white supremacist discourses influence our understanding of citizenship and humanity (Gilroy, 2001; Hall, 2005; McKittrick, 2015), and the way settler colonial discourses influence our conception of history, knowledge, and relationship to land (Said, 1979; Vizenor, 2008; Warrior, 1999).

Poststructuralism's most significant analytic weakness is located in the source of its strength. Its anti-foundationalism enabled it to leverage effective critiques of race and gender essentialism. This same anti-foundationalism, however, left it almost entirely reliant on a politics of critique. It lacked the means to affirm specific new forms of political solidarity—work that proletariat solidarity and various forms of gender and racial essentialism, despite their problems, had previously done. As a consequence, poststructuralism produced its own somewhat undifferentiated form of political subjectivity—the cosmopolitan ironic subject that in many practical ways resembled the individual liberal Cartesian subject (Jameson, 1991; Rosiek, 2013a, 2013b). According to some interpretations, this limitation left poststructuralism without the ability to respond to the material consequences of institutionalized oppression (Latour, 2007; Moya, 2000; West, 1993).

Enter the "new materialists." Frustrated with the well-worn debates between Marxist critical theorists and poststructuralist social theorists, new materialists have sought a social theory that preserves aspects of both. Like poststructuralists, these scholars seek to avoid a foundationalist metaphysics that assumes the purpose of inquiry is to identify the one exclusively correct representation of reality. On the other hand, they want to avoid a relativist nominalism that locates all meaning in the human activity of representation. Instead, new materialists assert that the material obduracy of things is protean, that matter does not sit passively awaiting our portraits of it. It moves, responds, and pushes back, sometimes violently, against our totalizing representational practices. In this way, nonhuman things are understood both as real and also as exceeding the logic of inquiry that seeks to refine a single best representation of social phenomena (Powell, 2015).

## Onto-Epistemologies and Agential Realism

As a comprehensive review of the new materialist literature is beyond the scope of this chapter, I focus on the work of one of the most influential and widely cited new materialist scholars, physicist and philosopher Karen Barad. Barad (2007) draws from the field of quantum mechanics—specifically the philosophical questions raised by diffraction grating experiments that revealed the wave-particle duality of light—to make profound points about the metaphysics of inquiry.

These relatively simple experiment turns out to have had extremely complicated—or at least counterintuitive—results. When a coherent beam of light was shown through two diffraction slits, alternating light and dark bands appeared on a far screen, indicating that light emerged from the slits in waves, expanding in concentric circles, like those created by a stone thrown into a pond. The two sets of concentric waves canceled or reinforced one another, creating the light and dark bands on the screen and confirming the wave nature of light. However, later experiments that measured the light as it came through the slits registered discrete packets of energy—in other words, as particles. Remarkably, when this measurement at the slits was conducted, the diffraction pattern shifted to that which would be expected of particles. It appeared that light changed its nature depending on how we measured it. Or, at the very least, part of its nature manifested to the exclusion of its other qualities in response to the way we set up our measuring apparatus. Forty years of increasingly sophisticated experiments have confirmed that light, when scrutinized closely, will perform as a wave or as a particle, but not as both, in response to our inquiries.

Physicists call the logic of this form of ontological interdependency between experimental apparatus and the manifestation of a physical phenomenon "entanglement." Barad holds our attention to the metaphysical implications of this entanglement. Among these implications is the idea that the inquiring subject and phenomena being studied do not preexist the experiment. Instead, the outcome of the experiment—the entanglement—is the ontological process that produces and defines the inquiring apparatus (including the subject of the inquirer) and the thing(s) being examined.

The most provocative implication, however, is that the object of inquiry cannot be considered inert in this process—simply awaiting discovery—nor as a simple projection of the agency of the inquirer. The inquirer and the object of inquiry are mutually formed in relation to one another. Barad refers to this as an *intra-action* (which emphasizes how both are constituted within the inquiry) as opposed to an *interaction* (which refers to an encounter between two previously existing and defined entities). Additionally, the ontological entanglement formed in the inquiry does not have one predetermined outcome; reality is pluralist. Light, for example, can manifest as both a wave or as a particle. Barad offers that, given the protean nature of both the inquirer and the inquired, it makes sense to consider both to be agential. The world, in other words, is not sitting still for our portraits of it. It moves in response to our efforts to capture it in a representation and, in so moving, shapes us as inquiring subjects.

Notice here that agency does not imply consciously laid out plans or even consciousness at all. It implies substantive existence that is not passive, but that actively forms relations in a process of inquiry—relations that could be otherwise. Understood in this way, we can begin to see the reason new materialist philosophies are compelling to contemporary social science scholars. It permits a form of social constructivism—the idea that the way we conceptualize our object of inquiry in part constitutes the nature of that object—while retaining the idea that the object is more than just our construction of it. We can engage in inquiry about schools, curriculum, and learning and find out something real about them. However, this discovery of something real does not exhaust the reality of the phenomena in question. The inquiry could be conducted differently, requiring a different subject relation to schools or educational processes, a different unit of analysis, all of which imply a different political and ethical relation to the focus of inquiry. This alternative inquiry would establish a different but no less real relationship with the school or educational process—just like the diffraction grating experiment reveals something real about light, that it has a wave nature and yet a different experiment reveals light has a particle nature.

The dynamic two-way link between agents in an inquiry transforms notions of responsibility in educational research. It implies that the ethics of inquiry go far beyond the need to offer a faithful and true representation of a phenomenon. It goes beyond expectations that the research not harm the people involved in the inquiry. It requires a comparative analysis of the relational modes of being generated between human and nonhuman agents through particular ways of knowing. In educational research, our ways of understanding schools and students set in motion particular modes of being for educators and communities. For example, in efforts to ensure certain basic literacy skills are mastered, systems of assessment can be imposed to assist in that effort. These assessments reveal real things about the literacy learning of students. The high-stakes nature of those assessments, however, works a transformation on the reality of the learning process. They introduce an anxiety into the process for stakeholders that was not there before. They introduce a narrow instrumentality to the learning process—learning is directed toward test performance, not generation of divergent possibilities of thought. Compliance within an expansive bureaucracy becomes the pervasive hidden curriculum of the learning process. In addition to fostering particular student understandings of topics, such testing systems end up creating particular subjectivities and experiences for students, parents, teachers, policy-makers, and researchers.

These subject effects and habits of experience are not intended by the human designers of these assessments. They are the consequence of institutional, discursive, and affective processes not entirely in the control of test designers. In Baradian terms, the educational setting has its own agency. The ways of being generated by our curricular and pedagogical decisions have consequences beyond the often narrow measures and foci of our research, yet we are responsible for our part in bringing these broader social and cultural effects into being. An agential realist approach to education research and policy-making would require us to attend to the full scope of the experiential consequences with which our research is implicated and to imagine them alongside the worth of other ontological paths not taken. In this way, agential realism implies that inquiry is, ultimately, an ontological and ethical enterprise as much, if not more than, an epistemic one.

The idea of inquiry being ontologically generative is familiar to arts-based researchers. Art has always been about more than providing conceptual clarity. Artistic representations and performances invite people into new holistic relations—conceptual, affective, collective, tactile, material, etc.—with the world in which we live. They explore possible modes of being and/or destabilize existing modes of being. They are prospective, more than retrospective, in that their validity is located as much in the way the art can catalyze futures that have been previously unimagined as it does in their fidelity to the world as it is. New materialism is, in a way, suggesting that all inquiry functions like this—that all inquiry, scientific or otherwise, is about generating modes of being in the world.

The scope of the transformation of inquiry proposed by these ideas is hard to overestimate. Detailed application to the social sciences, however, remains at an exploratory stage. I turn to furthering that exploration now.

## Intra-Action and Transaction, Agency and Purpose: Connections with Pragmatism

A significant proportion of the ABR community has been influenced by the work of pragmatist philosophers, most notably John Dewey and Richard Rorty (e.g., Barone, 2001; Barone & Eisner, 2010; Clandinin & Rosiek, 2006; Knowles & Cole, 2008; Siegesmund, 2012). Pragmatic philosophy has been useful to arts-based researchers for many of the reasons new materialist philosophy has recently proven compelling to this community of scholars. Whereas Barad writes about reality as *intra-active*, Dewey wrote about reality as *transactional*, both emphasizing the co-constituting character of inquiry. In *Art as Experience*,

Dewey (2005) wrote about how the medium in which we work shapes us as much as we shape it. Pragmatism sees human agency as limited, though significant, and bounded by the material, environmental conditions we face.

Pragmatism also treats inquiry as ontologically generative. As Dewey (1981) explains:

> Pragmatism thus has a *metaphysical implication*. The doctrine of the value of consequences leads us to take the future into consideration. And this taking into consideration of the future takes us to the conception of a universe whose evolution is not finished, or a universe which is still, in James' term "in the making," "in the process of becoming," of a universe up to a certain point still plastic.
>
> (LW 2:13)

The most widely circulated understandings of pragmatism, however, have lacked some compelling features of the new materialisms. First, classical pragmatism's emphasis on ethics has not frequently risen to the level of structural political critique. The constant refrains about democratic process in the abstract do not suffice for responding to specific global systems of oppression, such as worldwide white supremacy, patriarchal cultural and economic systems, intensifying global stratification of wealth, and access to life-sustaining resources. In the effort to valorize the epistemic authority and transformative potential of individual lived experience, pragmatists have been slower than Marxists and poststructuralists to identify and confront the way liberal democratic institutions can be complicit in processes of exploitation, avarice, and oppression.

It is this politically constrained version of pragmatism that still gets circulated most frequently in educational research circles, and it has cost the philosophical tradition the interest of some of the most ambitious curriculum theorists and educational justice activists of an emerging generation of scholars. This lack, however, is neither a necessary feature of pragmatic philosophy nor is it an actual feature of the tradition's history. In departments of philosophy, the last two decades have seen the rise of a more politicized version of pragmatic philosophy (McKenna, 2001; McKenna & Pratt, 2015; Pratt, 2002; Seigfried, 1996; West, 1989). These more contemporary interpretations of the pragmatic philosophical tradition locate it in a broader tradition of political and cultural activism seeking various forms of social transformation. In this new literature, the pragmatist aversion to totalizing epistemic and political projects remains. The distinctive merging of ontological and epistemological theory in pragmatism, however, is traced to a dialogic relationship with organized efforts at social change and resistance to systemic oppression.

The second compelling feature of new materialism that pragmatism apparently lacks is a developed conception of nonhuman agency. Although most of the classic and contemporary pragmatist philosophy literature adopts some version of Dewey's transactional realism (Garrison, 1994), it rarely suggests that agency is a pervasive feature of nonhuman reality—rarely, but not never. The primary exception to this pattern is a significant one—Charles Sanders Peirce, the widely acknowledged founder of the modern pragmatist philosophical tradition. Late in his career, his attention to the implications of ontologically generative conceptions of inquiry led him to the conclusion that a form of agency was a general characteristic of all things.

From the earliest stages of Peirce's scholarly career, he was focused on how inquiry could not be explained simply by an intention to represent things or events accurately. There were too many judgments involved and too much vagueness in analyses, despite the most heroic efforts to mathematize every phenomenon, for this common sense notion of scientific research to hold up to close scrutiny. Such a view could not explain, for example, how certain kinds of questions came to be asked in the first place, how elements of our fields of experience come to be considered salient data while others are ignored. These aspects of inquiry involve a speculative form of reasoning, intuitive risk-taking.

Peirce concluded that the validity of our inquiries could not lie simply in their correspondence to some preexisting objects to which we never have unmediated access. Instead, validity had to reflect a reliance on speculative forms of inference. Peirce encapsulated this idea in what he called *the pragmatic maxim*, which he modified many times over the years. In his essay entitled "Issues in Pragmatism," he expressed it as follows:

> The entire intellectual purport of any symbol consists in the total of all general modes of rational conduct which, conditionally upon all the possible different circumstances and desires, would ensue upon the acceptance of the symbol.
>
> (Peirce, 1905, p. 481)

In other words, it was the future consequences of adopting a representation that ultimately gave it meaning, not simply its match to present or past conditions.

What does the pragmatic maxim have to do with the concept of nonhuman agency? In working out the implications of this maxim, Peirce developed a theory of materialist semiotics. Signs, for Peirce, were embodied habits of interpretation and response that evolved in response to an entity's material environment. Without getting into the weeds of Peirce's semiotic theory, suffice it to say here that such habits were always formed in reference to possible future states of affairs.

The realm of future possibility is real, according to Peirce, no less real than those things that actually exist, though possessed of a different form of being than actually existing objects. These possibilities work an influence on the present Peirce offered that human and nonhuman processes are drawn toward possible ordered arrangements and activity in a way that is more than merely mechanical. There is, according to Peirce, an affinity between things of the present and being that exists *in futuro*. In humans, this manifests in the success of our guesses and inspired lines of inquiry—success that is more than random. These speculative and creative leaps are the necessary beginning of all inquiries and constitute a third branch of logic that Peirce called abduction. In nonhuman phenomena, it manifests as the stable and self-organizing features of matter and life—patterns whose existence requires not only causal mechanism, but also the possibility of particular forms of ordered existence for their manifestation. For Peirce, possibility precedes mechanism.

Peirce likened the influence of being *in futuro* to Aristotle's notion of final causes, which is contrasted to efficient or mechanical causes. Aristotle's concept of final cause is often interpreted as "purpose," which can sound anthropocentric because we presume only humans have purposes. Aristotle, Peirce, and others, however, are not referring to consciously laid plans when they refer to final causes. They are referring to activity being organized in reference to a future state of affairs (see Short, 2007, p. 54).

Peirce offers that all things, not just humans, participate in response, transaction, intra-action—call it what we will—that involve some degree of indeterminacy, and within that indeterminacy, the influence of being *in futuro* can be seen. It is visible as an ordering activity that includes mechanical causal mechanisms, but creates regularities not entirely determined by these mechanical processes. For example, oak seeds transact with their environment and produce not a completely predetermined form of tree with every branch and root in a specific place, but a general form of a tree. Light transacts with the experimental apparatus of the diffraction grating, producing ordered, but not determined, patterns. Humans have habits, organized around conscious and unconscious desires.

It is the possibility of these future ordered states that gives regular form to the phenomena in question. In fact, without the existence of possibilities around which activity can be organized, present materiality would be without form.

> ... utter nothingness ... would befall matter if it were to be deprived of the governance of ideas, and thus were to have no regularity in its action, so that throughout no fraction of a second could it steadily act in any general way. For matter would thus not only not actually exist, but it would not have even a potential existence; since potentiality is an affair of ideas. It would be just downright nothing.
>
> (Peirce, 1998, pp. 122–123)

These animist aspects of Charles Sanders Peirce's ontology were not adopted and developed by other well-known pragmatists such as William James or John Dewey. However, given the rise in interest in agent ontologies, this portion of Peirce's work is being given renewed attention across a number of fields (e.g., Deacon, 2012; Kohn, 2013; Rosiek & Kinslow, 2016). I turn now to their application to education research.

## Methodological Applications of Pragmatic Agent Ontology

One of the aforementioned challenges to working out the implications of agential realism for education research is the effort to distinguish between agents and non-agents. There is the danger that new materialist social science research could become a rewarmed form of phenomenology, where the material obduracy of things is described in great detail, just using a new vocabulary. The words would be new, but the project would still be one of description—ultimately positioning the researcher and reader as spectator subjects, in this case bearing witness to the activity of nonhuman agents. The subject-transforming and ontologically generative aspects of ABR would remain marginal in this appropriation of new materialism.

Peirce's conception of nonhuman agency provides a way to empirically distinguish between mere mechanism and agential activity. If agential activity is organized around some general forms of being *in futuro*, then it will be resilient to disruptions in a way that mere mechanical processes are not (Short, 2007). If a merely mechanical process has its immediate causal pathways disrupted, the activity will dissipate, will lose its form. Consider, for example, a car engine. Once a key element breaks, the engine will not reorganize to begin running again. An agentic phenomenon, however, will be temporarily dissipated, but will reorganize to seek the being *in futuro* that defines it. This kind of agency can be seen in the way electromagnetic phenomena reorganize in response to our measuring apparatuses to manifest as waves or particles. It can be seen in the way seeds unfold in response to their environment, adapting to resource availability, changing but always producing something in the form of a particular plant. It can be seen in people seeking to fulfill their own conscious and unconscious desires, despite any obstructions to this pursuit. It can be seen in stories taking on a life of their own, moving through the world, being appropriated, heard, and interpreted in different contexts, but nonetheless organizing emotions, thoughts, and community relations in some generally consistent ways. It can be seen in social systems, like racism, which adapts to every educational, legal, and political gesture that we devise to eliminate it and finds ever new ways to reproduce some version of racialized hierarchy.

This understanding of many varieties of entities having purposes also helps us to think about our ethical relation to nonhuman agents. Ethics, in such circumstances, would involve the negotiation of shared purposes. This sounds familiar in the context of human-to-human relations; we negotiate shared purposes with other people all the time. It involves listening, compromise, and imaginative reconstruction of our desires and identity in relation to the needs of others. The most ready image of such negotiation is one that occurs through language and thus would seem limited only to humans. However, even with human agents, this intra-action is far more than linguistic; it is tactile, tacit, enabled and constrained by the material traces of past history, and dependent on a network of relations with others.

With nonhuman agents, the imaginative work is, perhaps, more demanding. We have to think beyond conscious purposes, to contemplate our relationship with the ongoing activity of nonhuman phenomena organized in relation to some future possible general state of affairs. We then have to reimagine our own purposes and possibilities in relation to these other agents. This is not simply a voluntary process. In some cases, the materiality of this world coerces, compels, or seduces us into compliance with its ordering activity.

In a certain fashion, Western settler colonial cultures already do this; we are already deeply entangled with the nonhuman world. That entanglement is most often characterized by an instrumental relation. We study geology, plants, social systems, etc. in great detail, so as to predict their patterns and regularities. Those regularities, however, are assumed to be the product of efficient mechanistic causes and therefore available for manipulation without risk of losing possibilities on which those efficient causes depend for their organization. The activity of nonhuman phenomena is not understood in terms of the *final causes* that give them form, and thus the only final causes, the only ordering activities, that matter are presumed to be human ones.

Understanding nonhuman agents in terms of their relation to being *in futuro* provides a specific analytical approach to enacting an expanded ethical responsibility in our inquiries. This practice lies in the speculative interpretation of the future possibilities that give various nonhuman agents their general form. It is in the effort to negotiate divergent ontological ends that we become ethically entangled with nonhuman agents and that human subjectivities become something other than enlightenment spectators and capitalist consumers; we become cocreators of possible worlds.

## Implications for ABR

So, what are the implications for ABR of this diffractive reading of new materialist and pragmatist theorizations of nonhuman agency? In general, agential realism is a bold effort to extricate us from wearisome debates between realist and social constructivist conceptions of social science. It simultaneously offers an expanded understanding of our responsibility as researchers for the ontologically generative aspects of our work while also walking us back from a humanist hubris that attributes all meaning to human interpretive activity. The version of agential realism just sketched offers specific implications for how that ethical responsibility might be discussed and put into practice. It would involve making an effort to understand the ordering activity—purposes—of nonhuman agents. It would then require reenvisioning ourselves in relation to those purposes, not just understanding objects in relation to our own conscious purposes.

Finally, it would call for evocative affect-laden scholarship that invites audiences into particular subject- and object-transforming entanglements with various phenomena. This would ask more of us than research grounded in a politics of recognition (Coulthard, 2014; Fraser, 2003)—a practice of revealing previously hidden suffering or oppression. The goal of revelation is, of course, a reversion to an epistemic framing of research. It fails to address the unique ethical and political issues that arise when considering the way ABR is ontologically generative of both the object of the study and the subject of the reader/viewer/inquirer. An agentially realist ABR would require imaginative reaches beyond our taken-for-granted understandings of our objects of study and ourselves.

We would expect such a scholarly practice to look different than agonistic struggles over what constitutes the best possible description of educational phenomena. We would also expect that it will entail more than compulsive problematization of totalizing descriptions. The kind of scholarship described will require imaginative portrayals and performances that invite us to appreciate multiple formations of ourselves as subjects and agents, multiple relations with other human and nonhuman agents, and a variety of individual and collective futurities. It will require what one of the founders of contemporary arts-based education research, Tom Barone (2001, 2009), spent a career trying to press upon our attention—the need for an imaginative invitation into a heteroglossic future. Only now, the cast in those heteroglossic narratives will include nonhuman characters. It will require some degree of what Cornel West (1989, 1993) calls prophetic analysis—thinking and feeling our way through multiple conflicting ethical demands and a variety of available personal and collective identities with an eye to an ameliorated post-Anthropocene future.

## Postscript

Since the original publication of this article 7 years ago it is gratifying to observe that ABR in the social sciences has, perhaps more vigorously than I expected, grown in the directions described. Although art as a means of revealing hidden or suppressed truth continues to be well represented in arts-based social inquiry, we also see more future facing generative practices of research growing in prevalence and theoretical development. For example, Fikile Nxumalo (2021) drawing on both Black studies literature and posthumanist literature has used speculative narrations inspired by photographs of Black children in outdoor education settings to create representations, not of the truth of children's experience, but of the possibilities of that experience. The purpose of these stories, she says is "materializing Black futurities … I am interested in possibilities for imagining and noticing Black relational subjectivities in affirmative ways" (p. 1196).

Similarly, Afro-futurist scholar Stephanie Toliver (2021) published a book on qualitative methodology featuring a novel length science fiction story about the experiences of a young black female protagonist making her way through 2085 in a world where dreams are commodities to be controlled and extracted. The power of this work lies in the explicitly political nature of this art and the explicitly artistic means of enacting anti-racist politics. "Black authors create speculative texts that center Black characters in an effort to reclaim and recover the past, counter negative and elevate positive realities that exist in the present and create new possibilities for the future" (p. 4).

This work is being driven by scholars influenced by a variety of area studies including Black studies, decolonial studies, queer studies, and posthumanist studies. This is where the most promising futures for ABR, and social research generally, currently lie in my opinion.

## Notes

1 For examples of artists and art-based researchers self-consciously exploring these boundaries (see Garoian, 1999; Gómez-Peña, 2000; Springgay, 2016).

2 It is important to note whenever talking about agent ontologies that Indigenous philosophers and Indigenous studies scholars have developed and worked out the ethical implications of agent ontologies long before Western philosophers became interested in such things (see Rosiek & Snyder, 2017).

## References

Alaimo, S., & Hekman, S. J. (Eds.). (2008). *Material feminisms*. Indiana University Press.

Barad, K. (2007). *Meeting the universe halfway: Quantum physics and the entanglement of matter and meaning*. Duke University Press.

Barad, K. (2010). Quantum entanglements and hauntological relations of inheritance: Dis/continuities, spacetime enfoldings, and justice-to-come. *Derrida Today*, *3*(2), 240–268. https://doi.org/10.3366/drt.2010.0206

Barad, K. (2011). Nature's queer performativity. *Qui Parle: Critical Humanities and Social Sciences*, *19*(2), 121–158. https://doi.org/10.5250/quiparle.19.2.0121

Barone, T. (2001). *Touching eternity*. Teachers College Press.

Barone, T. (2009). Commonalities and variegations: Notes on the maturation of the field of narrative research. *The Journal of Educational Research*, *103*(2), 149–153. https://doi.org/10.1080/00220670903333189

Barone, T., & Eisner, E. (2010). *Arts-based research*. Sage.

Braidotti, R. (2013). *The posthuman*. Polity Press.

Butler, J. (1993). *Bodies that matter*. Routledge.

Clandinin, D. J., & Rosiek, J. (2006). Mapping a landscape of narrative inquiry: Borderland spaces and tensions. In D. J. Clandinin (Ed.), *Handbook of narrative inquiry: Mapping a methodology* (pp. 35–76). Sage.

Clough, P. T. (2009). The new empiricism: Affect and sociological method. *European Journal of Social Theory*, *12*, 43–61. https://doi.org/10.1177/1368431008099643

Coole, D. H., & Frost, S. (Eds.). (2010). *New materialisms: Ontology, agency, and politics*. Duke University Press.

Coulthard, G. S. (2014). *Red skin, white masks: Rejecting the colonial politics of recognition* (p. 256). University of Minnesota Press.

Deacon, T. W. (2012). *Incomplete nature: How mind emerged from matter*. W.W. Norton.

Derrida, J. (1998). *Of grammatology*. Johns Hopkins University Press.

Dewey, J. (1981). The development of American pragmatism. In J. A. Boydston (Ed.), *The later works, 1925–1927: Vol. 2. Essays, the public and its problems* (pp. 3–21). Southern Illinois University Press (Original work published 1931).

Dewey, J. (2005). *Art as experience*. Penguin (Original work published 1934).

Foucault, M. (1990). *The history of sexuality*. Vintage Books.

Fraser, N. (2003). Rethinking recognition: Overcoming displacement and reification in cultural politics. *Recognition struggles and social movements: Contested identities, agency and power* (pp. 21–32). Cambridge University Press.

Gadamer, H. G. (1984). The hermeneutics of suspicion. *Man and World*, *17*(3–4), 313–323. https://doi.org/10.1007/BF01250456

Garoian, C. R. (1999). *Performing pedagogy: Toward an art of politics*. State University of New York Press.

Garrison, J. (1994). Realism, Deweyan pragmatism, and educational research. *Educational Researcher*, *23*(1), 5–14. https://doi.org/10.3102/0013189X023001005
Gilroy, P. (2001). *Against race: Imagining political culture beyond the color line*. The Belknap Press of Harvard University Press.
Gómez-Peña, G. (2000). *Dangerous border crossers: The artist talks back*. Routledge.
Hall, S. (2005). Old and new identities. In P. S. Rothenburg (Ed.), *Beyond borders: In thinking critically about global issues* (pp. 220–223). Worth.
Jameson, F. (1991). *Postmodernism, or, the cultural logic of late capitalism*. Duke University Press.
Knowles, J. G., & Cole, A. L. (2008). *Handbook of the arts in qualitative research: Perspectives, methodologies, examples, and issues*. Sage.
Kohn, E. (2013). *How forests think: Toward an anthropology beyond the human*. University of California Press.
Lather, P., & St. Pierre, E. A. (2013). Post-qualitative research. *International Journal of Qualitative Studies in Education*, *26*(6), 629–633. https://doi.org/10.1080/09518398.2013.788752
Latour, B. (2007). Can we get our materialism back, please? *Isis*, *98*(1), 138–142. https://doi.org/10.1086/512837
MacLure, M. (2013). Researching without representation? Language and materiality in post-qualitative methodology. *International Journal of Qualitative Studies in Education*, *26*(6), 658–667. https://doi.org/10.1080/09518398.2013.788755
Marx, K. (2014). A contribution to the critique of Hegel's philosophy of right. Introduction. *Marx-Engels Reader*. W. W. Norton.
McKenna, E. (2001). *The task of utopia: A pragmatist and feminist perspective*. Rowman and Littlefield.
McKenna, E., & Pratt, S. L. (2015). *American Philosophy: From wounded knee to the present*. Bloomsbury Publishing.
McKittrick, K. (Ed.). (2015). *Sylvia Wynter: On being human as praxis*. Duke University Press.
Moya, P. (2000). *Reclaiming identity*. In P. Moya & M. Hames-Garcia (Eds.), *Reclaiming identity* (pp. 1–23). University of California Press.
Nxumalo, F. (2021). Disrupting anti-Blackness in early childhood qualitative inquiry: Thinking with black refusal and black futurity. *Qualitative Inquiry*, *27*(10), 1191–1199. https://doi.org/10.1177/10778004211021810
Osgood, J., Scarlet, R. R., & Giugni, M. (2015). Putting posthumanist theory to work to reconfigure gender in early childhood: When theory becomes method becomes art. *Global Studies of Childhood*, *5*(3), 346–360. https://doi.org/10.1177/2043610615597160
Peirce, C. S. (1905). Issues of pragmaticism. *The Monist*, *15*(4), 481–499. https://www.jstor.org/stable/27899620
Peirce, C. S. (1998). *The essential Peirce: Selected philosophical writings* (Vol. 2). Indiana University Press.
Powell, K. (2015). Breathing photography: Prosthetic encounters in research-creation. *Qualitative Inquiry*, *21*(6), 529–538. https://doi.org/10.1177/1077800415581889
Pratt, S. L. (2002). *Native pragmatism: Rethinking the roots of American philosophy*. Indiana University Press.
Rorty, R. (1989). *Contingency, irony, and solidarity*. Cambridge University Press.
Rosiek, J. (2013a). Beyond the autoethnography vs. ironist debates: Using Charles Sanders Peirce and Cornel West to envision an alternative inquiry practice. In N. Denzin & M. Giardina (Eds.), *Global dimensions in qualitative inquiry* (pp. 157–180). Left Coast Press.
Rosiek, J. (2013b). Pragmatism and post-qualitative futures. *International Journal of Qualitative Studies in Education*, *26*(6), 692–705. https://doi.org/10.1080/09518398.2013.788758
Rosiek, J. (2017). Art, agency, and ethics: How the new materialisms will require and transform arts-based research. In P. Leavey (Ed.), *The international handbook of arts-based research*. Routledge.
Rosiek, J., & Gleason, T. (2017). The philosophy of teacher education research: An onto-ethical turn. In J. Clandinin & J. Husu (Eds.), *The international handbook of research on teacher education* (pp. 29–48). Sage.

Rosiek, J., & Kinslow, K. (2016). *Resegregation as curriculum: The meaning of the new segregation in U.S. public schools*. Routledge.
Rosiek, J., & Snyder, J. (2017). Indigenous studies and the new materialisms: exploring the similarities and differences in their application of agential realism to methodological practices. *Workshop Presented at the 2107 International Congress of Qualitative Inquiry*.
Said, E. W. (1979). *Orientalism*. Vintage Books.
Seigfried, C. H. (1996). *Pragmatism and feminism: Reweaving the social fabric*. University of Chicago Press.
Short, T. L. (2007). *Peirce's theory of signs*. Cambridge University Press.
Siegesmund, R. (2012). Dewey through a/r/tography. *Visual Arts Research*, *38*(2), 99–109. https://doi.org/10.5406/visuartsrese.38.2.0099
Spivak, G. (1996). Explanation and culture: Marginalia. In D. Landry & G. MacLean (Eds.), *The Spivak reader* (pp. 29–52). Routledge (Original work published 1979).
Springgay, S. (2016). Learning to be affected in contemporary art. *PORTAL: Journal of Multidisciplinary International Studies*, *13*(1), 1–6. https://search.informit.org/doi/10.3316/informit.895182281917638
Springgay, S., & Rotas, N. (2015). How do you make a classroom operate like a work of art? Deleuzeguattarian methodologies of research-creation. *International Journal of Qualitative Studies in Education*, *28*(5), 552–572. https://doi.org/10.1080/09518398.2014.933913
Springgay, S., & Zaliwska, Z. (2015). Diagrams and cuts: A materialist approach to research-creation. *Cultural Studies? Critical Methodologies*, *15*(2), 136–144. https://doi.org/10.1177/1532708614562881
Toliver, S. R. (2021). *Recovering Black storytelling in qualitative research: Endarkened storywork*. Routledge.
Vizenor, G. (Ed.). (2008). *Survivance: Narratives of native presence*. University of Nebraska Press.
Warrior, R. (1999). The Native American scholar: Toward a new intellectual agenda. *Wicazo Sa Review*, *14*(2), 46–54. https://doi.org/10.2307/1409550
West, C. (1989). *The American evasion of philosophy*. University of Wisconsin Press.
West, C. (1993). *Beyond eurocentrism and multiculturalism. Vol. I: Prophetic thought in postmodern time*. Common Courage Press.

Chapter 30

# Troubling Certainty

## Readers' Theater in Music Education Research

*Kathryn Roulston, Roy Legette, Monica Taylor, and Celeste Buckhalter*

Originating in drama and theater studies, readers' theater involves interpreters reading scripts aloud in order to involve audience members in a "living experience" in which "the readers share the attitudes, viewpoints, and actions of a literary piece with an audience, causing the audience to experience the literature" (Coger & White, 1982, p. 5, 7). Taking up the notion of having speakers reading aloud from scripts, readers' theater has served in various educational settings to introduce participants—frequently, but not always students—to literature, language arts, history, and issues in medical practice (see, for example, Coger & White, 1982; Fredericks, 2002; Maher, 2006; Savitt, 2002).

Inquirers have used readers' theater as a method of representation to display qualitative data and findings to a variety of audiences (Quinn et al., 2021; Schneider, 2012), often in conference venues (e.g., Blair et al., 2011; Donmoyer & Yennie-Donmoyer, 1995). This form of creative analytic practice (Richardson, 1999) calls for audience participants to perform scripts supplied by the researchers and presenters (see, for example, Adams et al., 1998). By inviting audience members to become part of the presentation through reading texts aloud, or performing a musical interlude, researchers and presenters utilize two aspects considered key to readers' theater (Coger & White, 1982, pp. 12–13); *interaction* of audience members with the topic presented; and stimulation of audience members and readers' *imaginations* through vocal and embodied interpretations of texts.

Researchers in music education, however, are generally unfamiliar with the use of artistic modes of representation of research data, or other forms of arts-based inquiry that generate artistic products in the process of research (Vaughan, 2005, p. 3), even as other fields such as education, communication studies, and sociology have moved in these directions. In our reading, we have found only one published readers' theater related to issues in music education (Lamb, 1991). By involving audience members in the presentation of a script that drew on findings from our research project, and in the performance of a musical interlude composed for percussion instruments, we wanted to purposefully upset the usual passivity involved in listening to research papers at academic conferences. By inviting audience members to play tuned and untuned percussion instruments in a repeated musical interlude, participants and listeners stepped into the world of music education—albeit briefly—adding embodied musical experience to the spoken texts, which dealt with music teaching, research, and the everyday work of music teachers. Taking up Finley's (2003) challenge to "fully explore the potential uses of media other than verbal, linear texts for performing and (re)presenting inquiry" (p. 290), in this chapter we examine the following: How can educational researchers use readers' theater to engage audiences' imaginations through

DOI: 10.4324/9781003412892-30

interaction and performance of a script that involves nonverbal media such as instrumental performance?

We began by crafting a script using qualitative data we had collected during a one-year project that investigated how a teacher-research community that involved university educators and practicing music teachers might provide mentoring for beginning teachers (Roulston et al., 2005b). For our conference presentation, the script was organized into sections that represented the preliminary findings of our analysis of transcripts of meeting talks and interviews. By participating in reading the script aloud, our audience of educators, music teachers, pre-service teacher educators, and researchers were called upon to reflect on the opportunities and challenges of teacher-research collaborations, and the session concluded with a focused discussion led by one member of the group, Celeste. The excerpt from our original readers' theater that follows is framed by the repeated musical interlude that was composed, orchestrated, and taught to audience participants by Roy Legette (see Figure 30.1). Given that the readers' theater deals with issues in music education, the interlude is integral to the performance of the script, and the audience members were invited to both read text and make music. This excerpt was first performed in its entirety at the annual conference of Interdisciplinary Qualitative Studies facilitated by the Qualitative Interest Group (QUIG), in Athens, Georgia in January 2005. Readers—including those who counted themselves as "non"-musicians—were invited into the communal world of music making that was everyday to the music teachers who participated in the teacher-research project. This unsettling of audience members, who were expected to participate in the collaborative music making, in some ways mirrored the disorientation experienced and described by the two elementary music teachers who took part in a collaborative teacher-research project. That is, the audience came to know and experience, if even somewhat artificially, the challenges and rewards presented to the group members as a result of participating in the research project.

Below, we include "The Challenges of Teacher-research," which was the third section of the original four-part script—conceived as a "rondo"[1] in which the recurring section was that of the musical interlude. The challenges of teacher-research are many—lack of time for research, lack of support for the concept in schools, the difficulties involved in learning how to conduct research and, in Monica's case mentioned below, negotiating county approval procedures to conduct research (see Roulston et al., 2005a for further details). In this section, the dialogue is crafted from conversations that occurred during our monthly research group meetings. Here, Monica and Celeste discuss some of the challenges that they faced in formulating research questions, and designing independent studies that could be conducted in their classroom settings. We then reflect on our use of readers' theater, offering points for consideration by other researchers, educators, and music educators.

### A Readers' Rondo: The Challenges of Teacher-Research

The cast:

*C:* Celeste (an elementary music teacher)
*M:* Monica (an elementary music teacher)
*K:* Kathy (a faculty member in the College of Education)
*R:* Roy (a faculty member in the School of Music)
*N:* Narrator

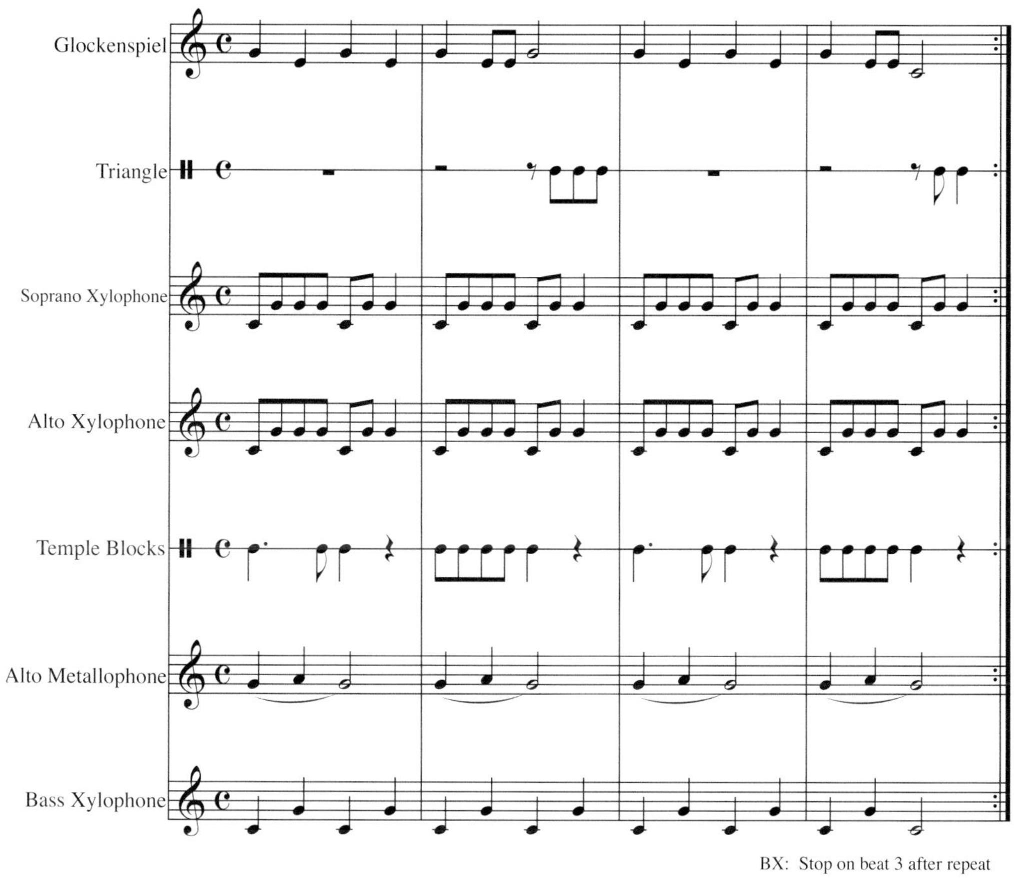


*Figure 30.1* Musical Interlude

– Musical Interlude

*N:* In our meetings, we discussed the problems we encountered in conducting research. Sometimes these discussions emerged from a question we used regularly in meetings, "What stood out for you in the readings?" As a group, we listened to one another's difficulties, gave advice where possible, and encouragement when there appeared to be no solutions to offer.

*C:* How to refine a research question. I spent hours with this page. We had a nice long relationship there for a while. The one thing on the page I have a huge star by was "avoid value laden words or phrases." I guess I knew that. Somewhere in the recesses of my mind I knew to avoid those, but they seem to creep up anyway, especially when you're so close to the situation. That's been a tough thing for me—getting rid of those value laden words and just stepping back from the situation removing myself ... a little bit.

*R:* That's hard

*K:* I think that's an ongoing struggle for all researchers.

*C:* Really?
*K:* Yeah, that's not unique to you.
*C:* Oh okay.
*M:* Another question I have is, given the time period that we have to do this research ... do you think ... I'm just worried about will it really be dramatic results ... that I will get?
*K:* That's what the question is.
*ALL:* (laughter)
*M:* Yeah.
*R:* You may come up with nothing.
*M:* Right.
*R:* I mean that's just the nature of the beast. Monica, do you think you could send us a draft of your proposal before our next meeting? We can kind of hammer it out at the next meeting and maybe solidify it?
*K:* I think that would be really good.
*R:* Because I'm concerned that we're going to run out of time. Once it goes to the County for approval, you can count on about six weeks before you get it back.
*K:* And if yours goes in on the next date that they have the meeting ... you won't get approval until the beginning of March.
*R:* You seem troubled by all of this.
*M:* Yes.
*R:* What's eating at you?
*M:* I guess where I wanted to go at the beginning and then with getting approval for the project. I just really didn't even think about having to write the proposal to fit with the school improvement plan and it kind of narrows everything now. Meeting the guidelines for the proposal has been very difficult. I would have rather stuck to a topic related solely to music. I have to now relate the project to literacy within the school improvement plan. It really controls your whole research process, I think, instead of it being a way to improve your teaching.
*R:* Threw a monkey wrench.
*K:* Though part of the school improvement plan calls for you to talk to teachers, because that improves your knowledge of the students. I'm wondering whether you could write that in as part of a project. Do you get scheduled time with the special needs teachers?
*M:* No.
*K:* So I was wondering ... whether you could have a consultation and talk to them about these ... particular 3rd grade students. Talk to them about the skills and the activities that they already do with the special needs teacher ... and then maybe that'll help direct what you could do in your classroom. Do you see that would work?
*M:* Um hmm.
*R:* What about you Celeste, how are you thinking about your study?
*C:* If I do a survey ... that one was really tough. I started to think about it and I teach 600 out of the 1200 students, so at first I was like it'd be great to get all 600 then I started thinking, let's be realistic.
*R:* If you created your survey, there are other issues. You'd want to pilot that survey, and you'd want to determine reliability, whether or not it measures what it's supposed to measure and does it do it consistently.
*M:* I was going to say, what would happen if you got all these surveys back and these parents said they want more musicals?

*C:* I know! I know! That's true.
*R:* As a teacher ... that informs your teaching right there.
*C:* Right.
*R:* That fact alone.
*C:* It also confuses my teaching. I'd like just a straight, clear shot. To know exactly what these parents want over here is going to be what we teachers are pushing for over here; and what the curriculum is pushing for over there is also what the administrators want. It's not all lining up.
*K:* No. It's really messy.
*C:* So, I think that's a big problem for me right now.
*M:* And classroom teachers really have a lot of responsibilities. It's hard, I think, to engage in research outside of those responsibilities. There are so many things that we have to be held accountable for. I think it's just hard right now, especially with all the legislation, to find time to engage in teacher research. It's the time issue. I just really don't see a lot of teachers saying, "I want to research, write this, and submit it, and get it published." I don't see that happening because of the everyday situations that they have to deal with. Especially now, coming up in April we have our state tests—that is a big thing that outweighs other things.
*K:* I think I've got the same issue that Monica said, finding the time to wrap your head around all of this is just really difficult and I recognize it's even more difficult for you ... because you have classes every half hour.
*C:* One of the frustrating things for me has been that my school is pretty large. You get lost in the shuffle if you don't make your presence known all the time. So the administrators don't remember that I'm there, and that I'm working on a research project. My administration has said, "We would like to read the end result," but it feels like they're not interested. I think for me, whenever I think of a teacher doing research within a school, I think if I were an administrator, I would want to know more about what is going on.
*R:* So it is don't ask, don't tell around there?
*C:* Pretty much.

– Musical Interlude –

## Reflecting on Readers' Theater

For members of our teacher-research group, using readers' theater was a new experience. To prepare the script for our conference presentation was both interesting and challenging as we revisited the hundreds of transcript pages containing our year-long discussions, and reflected on how our views and roles within the group had changed over time. One challenge involved deciding which excerpts to use from the voluminous data set. This was resolved by group discussion, while recognizing the fragmentary and partial nature of the completed script.

We structured the readers' theater in four parts: (1) our group's developing sense of community; (2) working with our differences; (3) the challenges of doing teacher research; and (4) group members' perspectives concerning the professional outcomes of involvement in the project. These sections were organized to mirror the journey that we had taken together as members of a collaborative research group. First, we started out by getting to know one another, and developing a sense of community in which we could work together productively. Over the year-long project, we began to recognize and work with the multiple perspectives we each brought to the project that were products of differences in cultural and racial background, teaching experience, theoretical perspectives to music education, and research background and training. The third section of the readers' theater dealt with the challenges faced by a group of educators coming together to work collaboratively on a teacher-research project. The final section dealt with participants' perspectives on the outcomes of the project (see Roulston et al., 2005b for further details). The musical interludes unified the actual performance and brought a sense of variety to the presentation that was not possible through words. For audience members involved in the playing of musical instruments, "parts" were learned and rehearsed quickly—and performers experienced a sense of pressure to "get things right." This dual sense of pressure—both in terms of being required to learn how to do things quickly and wanting to "do things the right way" mirrored the anxiety sometimes expressed at our monthly meetings by Monica and Celeste as novice teacher-researchers involved in the study.

Most of our audience members were involved in either reading the script or playing pitched or unpitched percussion instruments—and were highly engaged in the presentation. Through performing, our representations of our research experience were personalized for the audience participants, enabling them to grasp some of our thoughts and feelings in the process of the teacher-research collaboration. This engagement flowed over into the discussion that followed the presentation of the readers' theater, as participants teased apart issues raised in their reading, and reflected on their own experiences concerning theory and practice, teacher-research groups, and university-K-12 collaborations. For example, one of the audience members discussed his experience as a teacher-researcher in Wisconsin, and shared resources with others.

Performance of this readers' theater demonstrated to us that research does not have to be a collection of dry facts written on a page, but can be interesting, exciting, and speak to multiple audiences in a meaningful way. However, because readers' theater is so different to the usual presentations to which conference participants are more attuned, one challenge for researchers is to keep the audience's attention focused on the *content* of the presentation, rather than on the *process* of delivery. This point was underscored for us after our presentation when one of our audience members asked of our group: "What were the findings of the study?" And we had thought that the final section of the readers' theater had explicitly addressed that question! Contrary to what we had anticipated, this participant had been so engrossed in performing; it seemed that the substance of the text had been missed. Either that or the text we had chosen needed to be clarified. We have discussed this issue on a number of occasions since, and we as group members have mixed opinions on the value of using readers' theater for the presentation of "findings." We do agree, however, that readers' theater does achieve a level of interaction and audience engagement that does not occur when findings are read, as is common at academic conferences. One method that researchers might employ to prepare participants prior to the performance would be to outline the subject matter of the presentation and reiterate the main points through focused discussion at the conclusion of the performance.

Both students in university and college classrooms and conference participants are frequently faced with teachers and presenters who do all of the talking. Readers' theater provides an interactive and participatory means for students and listeners to claim ownership of instruction and knowledge through active involvement in its presentation. The ultimate success of this approach, as with any method of presenting or teaching, may well hinge on how interesting and engaging the researcher and teacher can make the subject matter. As we learned, great care must be taken in the construction, selection, and preparation of the text/s for performance. Yet, it is only through exploring the unknown, by opening doors, and troubling the certainties of the ways in which we conduct and re-present our research to others that we might learn; perhaps even stumble upon what we still have to learn.

## Postscript

### *Kathy's Reflection*

I have vivid memories of the audience members' eager and joyful participation in music-making as they performed the musical interlude composed and directed by my colleague Roy. *We were having fun!* Integrated with readers' theater, music-making centers music educators' work. Twenty years on, the concerns I had about the audience's reception of content have diminished. While content is important, I now see process as equally important. My recollections of our collective 2005 presentation are of process—not content; or being—not knowing. This speaks to the value of recognizing embodiment in qualitative inquiry. Ellingson (2017) calls on researchers to attend to the body-selves of participants and researchers. Readers' theater—with or without the musical performances depicted in this chapter—provides a way of attending to the body-selves of researchers, participants and the audiences to whom we address our research. Try it. Ask yourself: what happened? how does this feel?

### *Roy's Reflection*

Contextually, much has changed since 2005. I remember one of the public-school music teachers in our research group commenting on the difficulty of conducting research in the schools while faced with the pressures of accountability and legislation. An intimidating political environment and changing educational priorities, partially precipitated by divisive concept laws in some states, poses impediments to conducting research in the schools that did not exist almost 20 years ago. In addition, social media and other online platforms have become an integral part of everyday life. They provide teachers with a convenient and easier way to collect data. Platforms such as Facebook, Twitter (now X), Instagram, and Zoom provide possible tools for conducting research that were nonexistent or in their infancy when our research group was initially formed.

## Note

1 A rondo is a musical form characterized by different sections, interspersed with a repeated section (A): ABACA.

## References

Adams, N., Causey, T., Jacobs, M.-E., Munro, P., Quinn, M., & Trousdale, A. (1998). Womentalkin': A reader's theater performance of teachers' stories. *International Journal of Qualitative Studies in Education*, *11*(3), 383–395. https://doi.org/10.1080/095183998236548

Blair, H., Filipek, J., Lovell, M., McKay, M., Nixon, R., & Sun, M. (2011). Our journey to becoming ethnographers: An exploration of rhetorical structures as lived experience. *International Journal of Qualitative Methods*, *10*(2), 140–150. https://doi.org/10.1177/160940691101000203

Coger, L. I., & White, M. R. (1982). *Readers theater handbook: A dramatic approach to literature*. Foresman and Company.
Donmoyer, R., & Yennie-Donmoyer, J. (1995). Data as drama: Reflections on the use of readers' theater as a mode of qualitative data display. *Qualitative Inquiry*, *1*(4), 402–428. https://doi.org/10.1177/107780049500100403
Ellingson, L. L. (2017). *Embodiment in qualitative research*. Routledge.
Finley, S. (2003). Arts-based inquiry in QI: Seven years from crisis to guerrilla warfare. *Qualitative Inquiry*, *9*(2), 281–296. https://doi.org/10.1177/1077800402250965
Fredericks, A. D. (2002). *Science fiction readers' theater*. Teacher Ideas Press.
Lamb, R. (1991). Medusa's aria: Feminist theories and music education, a curriculum theory paper designed as readers' theater. In J. Gaskell & A. McLaren (Eds.), *Women and education* (2nd ed., pp. 299–319). Detselig.
Maher, J. (2006). *Most dangerous women: Bringing history to life through readers' theater*. Heinemann.
Quinn, M., Linville, D., & Christodoulou, N. (2021). Living histories, local stories, of race, place, and education: A qualitative study from the CSRA Oral History Project in readers theater. *Qualitative Inquiry*, *27*(3–4), 334–345. https://doi.org/10.1177/1077800420917417
Richardson, L. (1999). Feathers in our CAP. *Journal of Contemporary Ethnography*, *28*(6), 660–668. https://doi.org/10.1177/089124199129023767
Roulston, K., Legette, R., DeLoach, M., & Pittman, C. (2005a). What is "research" for teacher-researchers? *Educational Action Research*, *13*(2), 169–189. https://doi.org/10.1080/09650790500200283
Roulston, K., Legette, R., DeLoach, M., Buckhalter Pittman, C., Cory, L., & Grenier, R. (2005b). Developing a teacher-research group in music education: Mentoring and community through research. *Research Studies in Music Education*, *25*, 14–35. https://doi.org/10.1177/1321103X050250010501
Savitt, T. L. (Ed.). (2002). *Medical readers' theater: A guide and scripts*. University of Iowa Press.
Schneider, B. (2012). Participatory action research, mental health service user research, and The Hearing (our) Voices Projects. *International Journal of Qualitative Methods*, *11*(2), 152–165. https://doi.org/10.1177/160940691201100203
Vaughan, K. (2005). Pieced together: Collage as an artists' method for interdisciplining research. *International Journal of Qualitative Methods*, *4*(1), 27–52. https://doi.org/10.1177/160940690500400103

Chapter 31

# The Drama and Poetry of Qualitative Method

*Johnny Saldaña*

As a theatre artist, I have been trained to find the drama of everyday life so that it may be faithfully reproduced on stage for realistic plays. As a playwright, I have also been trained to find the poetry in everyday language so that it may inspire the creation of evocative monologue and dialogue. This conditioning preceded my study of qualitative inquiry by almost 25 years and greatly influenced my introduction to the literature.

When I first read selections from the canon of educational research and ethnography, I encountered everything from sterile reports to emotion-laden narratives. Just as there are some storytellers who are more theatrical than others, there are a few writers who are more dramatic than others. Contemporary works in narrative inquiry, qualitative research, auto/ethnography, and investigative journalism have provided riveting and sometimes haunting stories (e.g., Barbara Ehrenreich's (2002) *Nickel and Dimed: On (Not) Getting By in America*; Stephanie Land's (2019) *Maid: Hard Work, Low Pay, and a Mother's Will to Survive*). Yet, for some reason, I found myself initially drawn to and engaged with the methods literature most of all. There was something about the "how to" that kept me enthralled. I was evolving into a "research geek" (my term), and I was literally fascinated with fieldnote protocol, coding schemes, and analytic procedures. Depending on the author, even seemingly mundane research methods books contained inspired writing.

Wolcott (1995), in *The Art of Fieldwork*, reflects on the parallels between art and ethnography:

> My purpose in this book is to examine how fieldwork not only invites but also requires something of an artistic approach. [A]rt plays a significant role in my life, not merely in terms of what I enjoy and appreciate aesthetically, but as well in what I have been able to create, in spite of the absence of any recognizable talent. I like to think that there is something of the artist in me, some capacity not only for appreciating but for creating, just as I assume there is something of the artist in you, and in everyone.
>
> (p. 13)

When I read the works of Harry F. Wolcott during my qualitative research courses with Tom Barone and Mary Lee Smith at Arizona State University, it was in his articles and methods books that I found the drama and poetry of qualitative research. Wolcott's gift with language—even at the technical level—engaged me. And the series of articles dubbed "The Brad Trilogy"—an anthropological case study profiling Wolcott's relationship with a young man who eventually descended into paranoid schizophrenia—kept me in awe. "This is theatre," I thought to myself, and it would eventually influence my ventures into arts-based research (see Saldaña, 2005, 2011).

DOI: 10.4324/9781003412892-31

Some writers in the social sciences have a flair for evocative writing, even if their works are academic in reportage. Their prose is vivid or conversational and feels like monologue or dialogue that can be directly transferred—even from a methods textbook—onto the stage. Wolcott is one of those writers. Sentences from his texts found their way into our theatrical adaptation of *Finding My Place: The Brad Trilogy* (Saldaña, 2002). When appropriate, insightful and even humorous passages from *Writing Up Qualitative Research* (1990), *Transforming Qualitative Data: Description, Analysis and Interpretation* (1994), *The Art of Fieldwork* (1995), and *Ethnography: A Way of Seeing* (1999) became part of his monologues.

*The Art of Fieldwork* was particularly rich with "one-liners." For example, in the Prologue of the play, Wolcott addresses the audience on his love for ethnography: "In fieldwork, you immerse yourself personally—with passion, without apology—for the purposes of research. Fieldwork beckons, even dares you, to become part of what you study" (Saldaña, 2002, p. 171; Wolcott, 1995, pp. 239–240). Later, Harry notes that Brad can make a valuable contribution to a commissioned report on education if he consents to be interviewed: "Like Blanche DuBois in *A Streetcar Named Desire*, fieldworkers must rely on the kindness of strangers to help get where they want to go" (Saldaña, 2002, p. 177; Wolcott, 1995, p. 148). And when Brad catches Wolcott covertly writing field notes about his behavior, Harry notes to the audience in a tone reminiscent of Oscar Wilde, "We humans are not above making surreptitious observations, but we most certainly hate to get caught making them" (Saldaña, 2002, p. 185; Wolcott, 1995, p. 152).

Wolcott's (2002) *Sneaky Kid and Its Aftermath: Ethics and Intimacy in Fieldwork* includes the original Brad Trilogy articles, additional information and reflections on the case, and the ethnodramatic adaptation of the story, *Finding My Place: The Brad Trilogy*. The title character is a young drifter whom Harry befriends, but whose unforeseen mental illness and destructive behavior wreaks havoc on Wolcott's professional and personal life. I have included excerpts below from the dramatization as a sample of ethnodramatic dialogue and monologue: the beginning of Scene One, and the Epilogue. The former was Harry's choice for inclusion in this chapter to introduce the work, and the selection demonstrates the dramatization of qualitative data (Saldaña, 2003, 2011). The latter was my choice to showcase the poetic cadences of method. As for what happens in-between, read Wolcott's *Sneaky Kid* to find out.

## A Selection from *Finding My Place: The Brad Trilogy*

### *Scene One: Description*

*(SLIDE: Serendipity)*

HARRY

I first came to know Brad through what ethnographers sometime refer to as serendipity.

*(music up: "Heart of Glass" by Blondie)*

*(HARRY finds a bow saw on the ground, picks it up, looks at it curiously)*

Literally as well as figuratively, I discovered Brad in my own back yard, unannounced and uninvited.

*(SLIDE: BRAD's cabin)*

*(BRAD enters, carrying a sapling, stops when he and HARRY see each other; BRAD sets the sapling down, shuts radio music off; they look at each other warily)*

A 19 year-old had managed to construct a crude but sturdy 10-by-12-foot cabin at a remote corner of my densely wooded, 20-acre home-site, which my partner Norman has shared with me since 1968. He didn't know on whose property he had built his cabin, perhaps hoping he had chosen public land next to mine.

*(hands BRAD the saw, which he grabs)*

BRAD

*(defensively, to HARRY)*

Can I stay?

*(SLIDE: Early Encounters)*

HARRY

*(beat, as HARRY looks BRAD over; to audience)*

I attach great importance to first impressions.

*(HARRY stares at BRAD; BRAD starts packing up his tools)*

At the moment of our first and unexpected meeting, I felt hesitant about allowing him to remain on my land; yet I felt an even greater reluctance in insisting that he leave.

BRAD

*(to HARRY)*

I needed some place to get out of the wind and keep dry. The rent ran out. I knew the rains would continue and I'd have to do something.

HARRY

*(to audience)*

He had no money, no job, and no place to go. I couldn't see how I could claim to be any kind of humanitarian and throw him off my property.

*(SLIDE: Courtesy and Common Sense)*

*(HARRY picks up the sapling and examines it; to BRAD)*

I guess if you're going to be here, I need to know something about you: Where you're from? What kind of trouble you're in?

BRAD

*(takes sapling, saws into it)*

I'm not in any trouble. I'm not that stupid. I used to live at this end of town; my father still lives here but I never see him. And I've lived in a lot of different places, like California, Portland, out in the country; different places in town, like The Mission—you had to sing for Jesus before they'd feed you there—a halfway house,

*(slightly mumbling)*

reform school.

HARRY

Reform school?

BRAD

*(defensively)*

Yeah, but it wasn't really my fault.

*(SLIDE: Survival)*

I picked up my sleeping bag and the stuff I had and headed for the hills. I didn't know exactly what to do. I saw this piece of level ground and I set up a tarp for shelter. There were plenty of trees around. I decided to build a place for myself, because I wasn't doing anything anyway.

*(SLIDE: BRAD's cabin)*

*(HARRY looks at the cabin as BRAD describes it)*

I put up four posts and started dragging logs around till the walls were built. As I went along I just figured out what I would need. I got the stuff I needed—tools and nails—from new houses being built nearby. The roof's made of paneling that I carried up from some kid's tree fort. I knew about plaster because I had worked with it before, so I smeared some on the walls. So now, I've got this cabin. This is better than any apartment I've ever had, that's for sure. It really works good for me. Here I am.

*(beat; BRAD shrugs his shoulders)*

That's it.

*(SLIDE: Getting a Start and Building on Later)*

HARRY

It wasn't much of an introduction, but it marked the beginning of a dialogue that lasted almost two full years from that moment.

*(returns to his desk; BRAD turns on his radio to a loud volume and returns to fixing his bike; HARRY glares at him, goes to the radio and lowers the volume; HARRY sits on the lawn chair and watches BRAD work)*

*(music: "Jump" by the Pointer Sisters)*

I didn't expect him to stay. Norman has an aversion to people he identifies as "losers," and from the outset had as little to do with Brad as possible. But as time went on and Brad continued to make improvements, he gradually became as much a fixture about the place as was his cabin. We saw rather little of him at first, but I became *fascinated* with him and intrigued with his—

*(BRAD removes his shirt; HARRY stares at his muscled torso)*

chosen lifestyle.

(Saldaña, 2002, pp. 173–176)

* * *

***Epilogue***

*(SLIDE: Epilogue)*

*(HARRY picks up some of the index cards, sets the stage aright as best he can, puts away things in his desk)*

HARRY

In a professional lifetime devoted to teaching, research, and writing, I know little and understand even less about this case, the one that's affected me the most, and the one that continues to haunt me for answers I doubt I'll ever find.

*(SLIDE: Getting It Right)*

I felt I knew Brad so well, so intimately, that I would get a straight story—and get the story straight. I was reeling then, and continue to do so to this day, from realizing how little we ever know, heightened in this instance by the feeling that this time, in my own cultural milieu, my own language, and even in my own backyard, I had finally *gotten it right.*

*(getting angry, he slams the desk drawer shut)*

I just wish that it all might have turned out differently.

*(SLIDE: Meaning)*

What is this *really* a study of? The meaning of the story isn't precisely clear because meanings themselves aren't all that apparent or clear. We don't have neat findings, tidy hypotheses, conclusions that can be summarized or reduced to tables and charts. There are no guarantees, no umbrellas or safety nets, no foolproof scientific method to follow.

*(SLIDE: Validity)*
Fieldwork consists of more than collecting data, something that catapults it beyond simply being there. And whatever constitutes that elusive "more" makes all the difference. Regardless of outcome, I think the critical test is how deeply you've felt involved and affected personally. *Provocative*, not *persuasive*.
*(SLIDE: Understanding)*
*(HARRY is close to tears)*
After years of attending so singularly to the sanctity of methods, I finally realize that only *understanding* matters. We must not only transform our data but also *transcend* them. *Insight* is our forte! The whole purpose of the enterprise is *revelation*! When you emphasize description, you want your audience to see what you saw. When you emphasize analysis, you want your audience to know what you know. When you emphasize interpretation, you want your audience to ... understand what you think you yourself have understood.
*(pause)*
*(SLIDE: Last Words)*
*(he walks to the projection screen)*
In the end, we only abandon our studies; we never really complete them. The human condition doesn't remain static long enough for the work to be completed, even for an instant. You need to recognize when to keep reaching, when to focus, and when to stop.
*(SLIDE: face shot of BRAD)*
So. How *do* you "conclude" a qualitative study?
*(music up: "Father Figure" by George Michael; HARRY looks at slide of BRAD)*
You don't.
*(lights fade to black; SLIDE of BRAD fades to black as music rises)*

(Saldaña, 2002, pp. 209–210)

## Postscript

In my qualitative data analysis workshops, I address coding, categorizing, thematic analysis, assertion, and theory development, plus other conventional methods from the canon of qualitative inquiry. But I also include two arts-based units: found poetry composition with in vivo codes, and monologue writing inspired by dramaturgical coding. Most of my workshop participants are novices to qualitative research with a traditional background in quantitative, experimental research methods. When they learn that poetic and dramatic adaptations of data are possible as analytic outcomes, a few exhibit skepticism from what they perceive as a lack of rigor in the renderings. But most express surprise, if not joy, in the creative freedom generated by these two artistic approaches. I reassure the doubtful that such explorations can be for the researcher's eyes only as a heuristic to discover new meanings and insights from the data. But I also inform them that several prestigious academic journals such as *Qualitative Inquiry* regularly publish these genres of artistic works as legitimate scholarship.

My four decades of published research projects in theatre, education, and research methodologies range from factor analysis to narrative inquiry; from grounded theory to writing in role; from action research to autoethnography; and a variety of other qualitative research genres (Saldaña, 2018). I advocate that:

> Eclecticism is an essential skill for documenting social inquiry. The more diverse our expressive repertoire, the more each mode informs the others and the more credible, vivid,

and persuasive our accounts. I truly believe that being an artist has made me a better researcher, and being a researcher has made me a better artist.

(Saldaña, 2018, p. 25)

## References

Ehrenreich, B. (2002). *Nickel and dimed: On (not) getting by in America*. Owl Books.

Land, S. (2019). *Maid: Hard work, low pay, and a mother's will to survive*. Hachette Books.

Saldaña, J. (2002). *Finding my place: The Brad Trilogy*. In H. F. Wolcott (Ed.), *Sneaky kid and its aftermath: Ethics and intimacy in fieldwork* (pp. 167–210). AltaMira Press.

Saldaña, J. (2003). Dramatizing data: A primer. *Qualitative Inquiry*, 9(2), 218–236. https://doi.org/10.1177/1077800402250932

Saldaña, J. (2005). *Ethnodrama: An anthology of reality theatre*. AltaMira Press.

Saldaña, J. (2011). *Ethnotheatre: Research from page to stage*. Left Coast Press.

Saldaña, J. (2018). *Writing qualitatively: The selected works of Johnny Saldaña*. Routledge.

Wolcott, H. F. (1990). *Writing up qualitative research*. Sage.

Wolcott, H. F. (1994). *Transforming qualitative data: Description, analysis and interpretation*. Sage.

Wolcott, H. F. (1995). *The art of fieldwork*. AltaMira Press.

Wolcott, H. F. (1999). *Ethnography: A way of seeing*. AltaMira Press.

Wolcott, H. F. (2002). *Sneaky kid and its aftermath: Ethics and intimacy in fieldwork*. AltaMira Press.

Chapter 32

# Learning to Perceive

## Teaching Scholartistry

*Richard Siegesmund*

Over the last three decades, arts-based research in education has evolved in multiple directions from within both the social sciences and the humanities, as well as externally through the fine arts. These forces have expanded the tool kit for social science qualitative inquiry and brought a reconceptualizing of fine arts research practice. Scholartistry exists at a liminal point, a whirlpool, where these waves converge.

From the social sciences, scholartistry accepts a logical discipline of inquiry built upon inferential and abductive reasoning. The world beyond us is active, changing, reforming; it is not passively waiting for discovery. While it will never fully be knowable, it does reveal itself to us through the research apparatuses that we construct. These apparatuses make cuts into this external world (Barad, 2007), and cuts cause pain. Therefore, an ethical dimension of inquiry is the practice of epistemological humility (see Tom Barone, this volume). Our research is interactive; with this comes a burden of responsibility. What we leave behind from social science is a seemingly easy escape to "data driven decisions" that will identify the critical independent variable that controls an increase in desired commodities. Instead, apparatuses provide us with a new appreciation for the entanglements of matter (Barad, 2007) and an ever-increasing circumspection for the costs of unintended consequences.

From the arts, we take seriously that matter matters (Bennett, 2010). Matter is our embodied movement through space and in time, the metaphorical repositioning of language through poetry, the sensual response from audial musical perception of rhythm and tone, and the visual repurposing of materiality guided through touch and reflective light. Artists do not control these materials; they are in dialogue with them. Art is the inscribed record of these encounters between the nonhuman and the human. What we leave behind from art is a romantic claim to art's autonomy. Just as with the social and physical sciences, the arts make cuts that reveal our entanglement with the world—they do not create isolated disinterested aesthetic refuges.

Thus, scholartistry asks us to rethink our comfortable accepted binary definitions of research and aesthetics that keep these concepts bounded in their own separate categorical systems. It asks that we imagine these terms anew or that we reconsider what these terms once meant and how we came to drift so far from their original intentions (Siegesmund, 2013). John Dewey (1934/1989) maintained that to separate scientific research from artistry was a misunderstanding of both science and art. Such a bifurcation jeopardized both.

Dewey (1934/1989) also famously observed, "recognition is perception arrested" (p. 58). Cognitive vision science informs us that our eye is not a small still camera or video-capture device. Cameras will capture far more information than the eye records, because the brain's schematic frameworks cause the eye to constantly filtrate what appears to be

DOI: 10.4324/9781003412892-32

nonessential information. There is simply too much data in the world for the brain to process; together, the eye and brain take shortcuts. They develop schematic understandings of situations that avoid the messy problem of actually having to pay attention to all of it. People will collide with furniture that has been rearranged in a familiar room, because we move through space guided by expected, recognized schematic patterns. We are not actually looking where we are going. Perception takes too much effort; it is easier to move through a world we believe to recognize.

For Dewey, perception allowed for mindful navigating through the unanticipated. Perception was a means to heighten our awareness of space as encountered through time. I summarize Dewey's (1934/1989) discussion of this criterion in Chapter 8 of *Art as Experience* as follows: does the research reconfigure our sense of time and space in a way that allows us to place ourselves into different futures? As an example, in this book we see arts-based educational research (ABER) scholars such as Donald Blumenfeld Jones and Natalie LeBlanc map their experiences of a perceptive attentiveness of space unfolding in the passage of time to evoke a changing awareness of where we are and what we might be.

## A Lesson to Introduce Scholartistry

To create an opportunity for students to engage with this idea, I turn to a ubiquitous everyday tool: the lens-based camera that is now integrated into smartphones. A camera, whether used for still images or video motion capture, does not give us a passive recording of an external reality. Instead, to use the language of Karen Barad (2007) and New Materialisms, a camera is an apparatus that makes cuts and probes into the world. An apparatus is not a neutral device controlled by its operator. An apparatus opens a dialogic relationship between the machine and manipulator, the nonhuman with the human. With each cut an apparatus makes, new unforeseen opportunities emerge. Thus, the apparatus is not recording, but providing new information to the operator for possible future action. The qualities of the cuts the machine makes allow the world to be experienced and thought in new ways. The apparatus enables its operator to move through a physical world in new ways.

Here, scholartistry is in the reflexive knowledge of how an apparatus makes cuts into a vibrant materiality and how the scholar is in a dynamic interaction between the inhuman and human, which together engage with the empirical world. In this volume, Brooke Hofsess suggests the scholar who sets forth a selection of apparatuses for provoking new forms of audience-driven discovery is a new conception of art curation. Donal O'Donoghue (2015) makes a similar observation of the experiential turn in contemporary art.

To introduce Dewey's criterion to a classroom, I assign the following homework and give my students at least three days to complete this task:

1 Think of the place where you feel most yourself. Is it a special place in your home? A favorite place in the library? A café where you like to relax? Then go there and take a first picture of this place.
2 Then, move in closer and take a second picture of the same place (actually move closer, do not just zoom in) that still says something about the place.
3 Finally, take a third picture from really, really close up (!) that still suggests something about the place.

I have students post their pictures to a social media platform where the entire class can see the finished assignments. Comparing responses and looking for similarities as well as for differences is an important part of the task. To begin discussions, I do not allow students to talk about their own individual work, as this would introduce the specter of authorial intent that could discourage others from forming their own interpretation. They comment on the work of others. I begin with two questions: *What do you see?* and *What makes you say that?* The students are looking for visual evidence in the picture to back up their own interpretive claims.

### Searching Rather than Finding

What becomes evident in this exercise is the camera as a probing device. The visual evidence indicates that the person taking the picture usually has some plan when they begin to take the pictures. However, once the sequence begins and the photographer begins to move, new opportunities often appear to emerge. Eisner (2002) attributes to Dewey the phrase of *flexible purposing*, our ability to realize more profitable opportunities that appear during the midcourse of a project. In these situations, we make conscious decisions to change direction and seek different, possibly more rewarding shores than first intended.

### Images Reforming

A second outcome of this exercise relates to shifting scale relationships. Even if one stays true to course in focusing on one particular outcome, by moving closer and closer, the scale of the context changes. As Nick Sousanis explains in his contribution to this book, changing visual relationships of qualities can change the meaning we might make from the images.

Understanding how a moving, probing camera can change inquiry is particularly important for participatory arts-based methodologies like photovoice or photo elicitation, where too often a visual image is merely read as symbolic or representational recording. For example, because a bicycle is important to a participant, the participant may take a full-frame picture of a bicycle. What is left unexplored are perhaps the telling details that could be revealed by moving closer—like rusty sprockets that might reflect both use and neglect—or the contextual information that a more distant shot could provide. For example, where is the bicycle being photographed? How does the object live in its environment? What other factors contribute to the shaping of meaning?

An individual who holds an apparatus can engage in active exploration of possibility and the way things might otherwise be. However, this same individual can also assume a more passive stance of seeking out a predetermined statement and recording what the individual intended to find. Both approaches create arts-based research (ABR), but an attitude informed by scholartistry would be more inquisitive and aware that through iterating images, new possibilities and new perspectives emerge.

### Disturbing Aesthetics

A third objective of this lesson is for students to get a visceral sense of what it means to disturb conventional aesthetic ideas around perfect form. There is a popular conception of the perfectly arranged picture. Everything is in its place and must remain just so. Dewey is often erroneously credited for arguing that through good form the aesthetic achieves a moment of perfection, satisfaction, and satiation that shuts down further inquiry. In this volume, Charles Garoian challenges this historical misconstrual. Dewey considered the aesthetic stance that art was autonomous and divorced from context to be dysfunctional.

## Troubling Perception

This classroom exercise helps students begin to touch on these three objectives just mentioned: (1) the camera as an interactive, probing apparatus; (2) image iteration that allows the research to actively change visual relationships; and (3) disruption of the belief in aesthetic resolution. In class, I encourage the students to discuss the work of their peers through these three lenses. I try to avoid stepping in with my own analysis. I want the students to discover what they do when "just taking a picture." I try to avoid telling them what they have done. However, I can facilitate their understanding of what they discovered visually and their production of data, completed before they had words to articulate what they were doing or what the data even might be.

Scholartistry emphasizes the role of the researcher as an active creator of data within cultural contexts, who plays with possible levels of interpretation. In an era of social media, this is not a foreign concept to students. They are familiar with crafting the image they wish to project through social media. They consider the composition of the images; they curate the ones they think will be most effective. The presentation of who they are and the events of their lives are carefully fabricated. This lesson pushes an implicit knowledge that students already have toward a camera to a more explicit, reflective, and ultimately reflexive level.

What we wish to see and what we may wish to remember is seldom transparently evident, either in our language or in the image-worlds in which we live. Through scholartistry, researchers try to discover the emotional resonance that envelops language and symbols. Therefore, scholartistry challenges a digital, analytic interpretation of data: one or zero, seeing or not seeing. Scholartistry encourages an analogic process of layering: veneers, coatings, and glazes that are opaque, opalescent, translucent, and transparent. As Dewey and other postmodern educators have observed, education is a process of moving through layers. This often requires disruption and tension; it is not smooth and seamless. The unpacking of a vision is not a tranquil process of discovery of a passive world that has been elegantly recorded. Arts-based inquiry can frequently be painful and unpleasant (see the chapters in this volume by Madeleine Grumet or Monica Prendergast and George Belliveau). It is certainly always messy. It does not follow a clear order. It is frequently humbling. In this sense, it is dangerous, because it does not preserve the norm; it breaks the norm in order to achieve a new level of perception as we move through a changing, ever-reconstituting world.

## Postscript

Over the past decade, my colleague Kerry Freedman and I have adapted this lesson for workshops taught at the International Congress of Qualitative Inquiry (ICQI) and the European Congress of Qualitative Inquiry (ECQI). At these workshops, participants have 20–25 minutes to complete this assignment. Working in this condensed format, Kerry and I have been pleased that participants can realize the educational objectives for this lesson.

With continuing support of ICQI and ECQI organizers (we are grateful to Norman Denzin, Michael Giardina, and Karin Hannes), these workshops led to the publication of *Visual methods of inquiry: Images as research* (Freedman & Siegesmund, 2024). In this book,

Kerry and I argue that all forms of image generation are acts of data creation that can drive educational research in at least three ways:

1 As demonstrated in the lesson presented in this chapter, the creation of images literally and figuratively slows down the experience of a phenomenon so that it is possible to see into it more deeply. These images frequently convey complex, layered forms of information that exceed the image creator's immediate description. In short, *tacit knowledge* (Polanyi, 1967).
2 The ability to interpret a tacit dimension of sensed, somatic meaning through what Dewey calls thinking in "relations of qualities" (1934/1989, p. 52), is of equal importance to the ability to interpret symbols, signs, and other types of semiotic code.
3 Images frequently bring the previously unseen into visibility, thus opening new discussions about what has up until now been marginalized or underrepresented. This is particularly true through global iterations of visual culture.

These complex forms of seeing have long been taught in secondary school art classrooms. To see examples of such teaching, and the rubrics through which this learning is assessed, see *Authentic secondary art assessment* (Smilan & Siegesmund, 2024).

## References

Barad, K. (2007). *Meeting the universe halfway: Quantum physics and the entanglement of matter and meaning*. Duke University Press.
Bennett, J. (2010). *Vibrant matter: A political ecology of things*. Duke University Press.
Dewey, J. (1989). *Art as experience*. In J. Boydston (Ed.), *John Dewey: The later works, 1925–1953* (Vol. 10). Southern Illinois University Press. (Original work published 1934).
Eisner, E. W. (2002). *The arts and the creation of mind*. Yale University Press.
Freedman, K., & Siegesmund, R. (2024). *Visual methods of inquiry: Images as research*. Routledge.
O'Donoghue, D. (2015). The turn to experience in contemporary art: A potentiality for thinking art education differently. *Studies in Art Education*, *56*(2), 103–113. https://doi.org/10.1080/00393541.2015.11518954
Polanyi, M. (1967). *The tacit dimension*. Anchor Books.
Siegesmund, R. (2013). Dewey, a/r/tography, and ab-use of global dialogue. In N. Denzin & M. Giardina (Eds.), *Global dimensions of qualitative inquiry* (pp. 137–155). Left Coast Press.
Smilan, C., & Siegesmund, R. (Eds.). (2024). *Authentic secondary art assessment: Snapshots from art teacher practice*. Routledge.

Chapter 33

# Thinking in Comics

## An Emerging Process

*Nick Sousanis*

Let me dispense up front with any notion that I initially conceived of doing my dissertation in comics as a radical act. More simply: I'm a lifelong comics maker and I love making comics. As such, I knew well the sort of complex stories and ideas that could be addressed in comics. Given that comics authors have received the Pulitzer Prize and been finalists for the National Book Award, this seemed to me like an argument that had already been won and that what I was proposing was *no big deal*—simply an extension of what comics could do brought to a different audience. Of course I could do it. I never questioned, "why?" only charged ahead with, "why not?" Once I was more fully immersed in academia, I became acutely aware of the political implications of what I was proposing. This led me to embrace and actively advocate pushing the form of scholarship forward, and the work itself transformed into an argument for the importance of its own existence within this setting.

As someone who always felt at home with the discussion of ideas at university, I'd nevertheless shied away from taking up long-term residence because I felt that those discussions ended up staying within its walls. I wanted to see them leap out. Furthermore, I believed that the barrier to entry wasn't about intelligence, rather a matter of vocabulary. In comics, I saw a way to bridge the divide between scholarly and public dialogue. This didn't mean simplifying or dumbing the material down, rather leveraging the affordances of comics—their particular use of imagery and its interplay with text (McCloud, 1993)—as a way to make complex subject matter accessible and bring people into sophisticated conversations. As a comics maker from childhood, this way of working was second nature to me. Drawing and writing facilitated understandings that couldn't be attained otherwise. Playing in multiple modes is a return to what we all do naturally as children. Without asking if it's allowed, we draw, sing, dance, and write all at once. On that, I must note: when publicly reflecting on this experience, I've caught myself saying I feel fortunate that I was *allowed* to do this work. Hold on—"allowed"?! Why must we seek permission from someone else to work in ways that are best for us? As Ivan Illich (1972) critiqued schooling, "that one person's judgment should determine what and when another person must learn" (p. 42). Who decides what counts and what doesn't? The biases of the past become the unquestioned how it is. Can we imagine instead an education that encourages and cultivates the different ways in which each of us operates and finds meaning, recognizes these as fundamental to how we approach our learning, and brings them into the very core of our discourse? Arts-based methods offer us a vital play of discovery to lead us in surprising directions.

DOI: 10.4324/9781003412892-33

With that introduction, what follows is a discussion on my process and its evolution—from what I set out to do (and continue to do) to what the work became (and, I have come to realize, I was in fact doing all along).

## Removing Words; Removing Walls

The path toward my current approach to making comics was set in motion making short political comics around the 2004 US Presidential election. I wanted to discuss issues without simply rah-rahing for one team. That felt too easy and lacked the impact I sought. I couldn't see how it would broaden anyone's perspective. As an effort to reach both sides of the aisle, I stripped out labels and other sorts of divisive words, and instead used visual and metaphorical language that got at the core of what I was exploring without naming it. I felt that by removing the words that so quickly built up walls, I could give people a reason to stick around long enough to engage in difficult conversations and perhaps find common ground. The earliest of these formative pieces was about voting, or as I titled it, *A Show of Hands*—which featured hands as its central metaphor, and every single panel had to have something to do with a hand. Four years later, for the 2008 election, I made a comic called *Seeing Red/Feeling Blue*—that looked at the artificialness of our political divide by way of fictional red and blue animals—Elmo, Red Fish, Rudolph paired with Grover, blue fish, Babe the Blue Ox, and so on. It went on to incorporate such things as the red and blue lenses that enable 3D pictures to the red of our blood and blue of the sky we all share. I was using one thing in order to talk about another altogether.

As I started the doctoral program and transitioned into making scholarly comics, this approach of stripping away language became central to my process. In my work, I explore ideas around education, philosophical movements, scientific theory, and more in ways that remain true to the subject matter, but at the same time, deliberate attentiveness to word choice allows the work to be open to broader interpretation and accessible on a metaphorical level. You don't need to know what I'm talking about (in a specific sense) to know what I'm talking about (in terms of deeper meaning).

When I first arrived at school, I had the good fortune to have a class with the late philosopher of aesthetic education Maxine Greene. In that class, I made a comic about her (Sousanis, 2010), which led to an ongoing conversation between us that led to her becoming a member of my dissertation committee. Greene was 90 at the time and because of her frail health, class was held in her living room. While I could have drawn her likeness, to me that felt flat and wouldn't do justice to the vitality she exuded. I wanted to get at how she sees, the energy you experienced being in the room with her. I decided upon a metaphor of a top—something dormant until spun, when it comes alive and is unstoppable as it zips about. That was Maxine for me—darting from author to philosopher, connecting ideas across literature and history, spinning together a conversation that was our course. This project solidified an essential aspect of my development as artist-scholar: a steadfast determination to move far from the illustrational and use the comics form to do things I couldn't say in words (see Figure 33.1).

Shortly before I began the dissertation, my advisor, professor of English Education Ruth Vinz, invited me to create a comic for the closing chapter of her coauthored book *On Narrative Inquiry* (Vinz & Schaafsma, 2011) that in some way spoke to the future of research (Sousanis, 2011). Depending on who read it, the piece was either about the process of doing

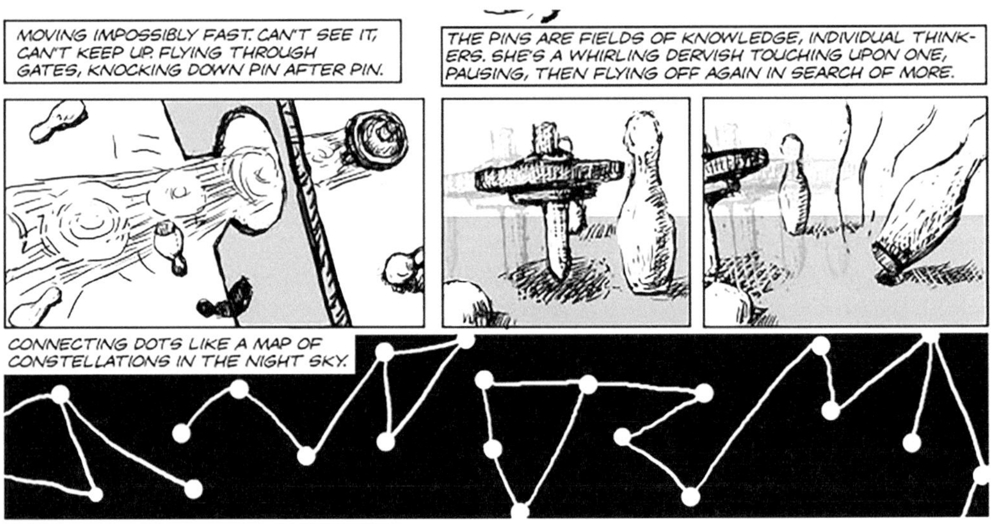


*Figure 33.1*

research, the activity of drawing, or the nature of seeing. Nothing in the comic ever stated what it was about, and in fact, it was equally about all of those things at the same time. I wanted readers to be able to enter with any background, but then to stick around and, upon reflection, start to wonder and make connections to things they hadn't thought of before. I took on the challenge of being knowledgeable to such a degree in all the different areas I was discussing so that someone who was versed in the specifics would appreciate it because I got it right (this extends to the drawing: it's crucial to me, that if I draw, say, a spider, it's not simply a generic recognizable spider, but a particular one, accurately drawn, used in this instance for a particular reason), but at the same time, the language I used stayed metaphorical so for the person not so well-versed, they read it in a different, but equally comprehensible way. I continued what I might describe as a sort of holographic approach with *Unflattening* (Sousanis, 2015)—depending on the angle you were looking at the work from, it reveals different aspects about itself, but they all come together to offer a deeper picture.

For *Unflattening* (as first conceived as a dissertation), I set myself some particular constraints from the start. I would name nothing. No field. No discipline. No philosophical movement. That didn't mean I wouldn't address them, but I would do so without using their language. This means a delicate negotiation of images and words—wherein my words are chosen so that they can both contain a multiplicity of meanings yet remain precise enough to mean exactly what I want, if you happen to know where I'm coming from. But again, it was okay with me if you didn't. This approach makes the work exceedingly difficult to categorize and shelve, but that's fine with me—so am I. So are we all. Respecting the complexity we all come with is one of the great challenges of education.

## Thinking as You Can't Do Otherwise

Somewhere around the midpoint of working on Unflattening (as a dissertation), I presented at the 2013 American Education Research Association conference (Ayers et al., 2013), in which arts-based researcher Donald Blumenfeld-Jones was in attendance and directed a question at me. In my slide-talk, I had gone into my process, and he said (I'm paraphrasing from memory), "What you are saying, is that in your work, your aesthetics equals your analysis." In other words, I was as concerned with making engaging artwork as I was with conducting serious research. They were on the same level of importance. And that felt exactly right to me. In Blumenfeld-Jones's articulation, he'd neatly captured the way I'd been going about my work that I wasn't completely aware of prior. The visual form is *never* a secondary pursuit—from the start, form and meaning are united and equally inform one another. And I feel that being beholden to these two forces, like holding onto two reins, in some way takes me out of the equation. That is, yes, of course, the idea and the work come from me, but my job is almost that of referee—to pay attention, to make sure both things are being observed equally, but not to be forcing the action. Rather to *let* the work emerge from this dance of discovery between the two. If the drawing is lovely, but it's not saying much of depth, I need to dig deeper into the research (my fieldwork takes place in texts) and see where that takes me. If I am saying a lot, but the drawings could be dispensed with, again, I have to rethink it on the drawing board. If you're going to do this work visually, the visual better do something for you *that you can't do otherwise*. Ultimately, if I hold on and keep paying attention to the interaction of form and content, I find that the work teaches me where *it* needs to go.

## Constraints and Play

It may seem here that something about my approach is at odds with itself. I've talked about letting the work happen, and I also stressed how much I set up numerous constraints for myself. To reconcile this, let me now address constraints. In his book *The Grasshopper*, Bernard Suits (1978) defines games as, "a voluntary attempt to overcome unnecessary obstacles" (p. 41). Whether playing a game or making artwork, constraints, these unnecessary obstacles, provide a space for *play*. The experimental poet Christian Bök—known for, among other things, his book *Eunoia* (2001), in which each chapter uses only a single vowel—pointed out (personal conversation, 2016) that simply following the obvious rules is not sufficient—a poem fails when the author doesn't observe enough constraints. It's in adhering to aesthetic rules of form (and other particular constraints) that we make work that sings.

## The Emergence of a Page

To better understand this process, I want to explore in greater detail a specific example, page 65 from *Unflattening*, which addresses the concept of multimodality (without, of course, calling it such). One of the primary difficulties in my work is always, what to draw? As I said before, I'd long since abandoned the illustrational. Working in a form almost exclusively known as a storytelling medium, I make comics that lack a narrative and have no ongoing characters populate my tales. Instead, with each page, I'm searching for ways to orchestrate the individual elements and the entire page composition to visually embody the ideas. I have to come up with imagery and plan out the overall arrangement of the reading experience.

My initial idea was an omelet—something made up of a variety of flavors that hold together while each one still remains distinct (contrast this with a smoothie, where everything is blended into a singular whole). This had the right sort of flavor (ha) for what I was going for, but didn't feel quite right. What I sketched out didn't move or move me in any engaging way. So, I tried again. I sketched out a typewriter keyboard—my thinking being that each key produces a unique symbol, and together they create greater meaning. Perhaps. On that same page, I sketched a very rough orchestra pit—thinking about the different instruments coming together to produce a symphony, yet still distinct and able to be distinguished from the rest. This was a resonant metaphor, but having drawn the keyboard in close visual proximity, I saw a connection between the way I had drawn each. The keyboard was, for some reason, curved like the orchestra, and you might imagine the conductor waving his baton from the location of the spacebar. And in fact, early typewriters were curved exactly in this way. This seemed promising. (I note here the importance in the discovery phase of making sketches that are, as Vinod Goel (1995) describes them, both dense and ambiguous—enough substance that you can see a lot into them, but not so tightly defined such that they are still open to multiple interpretations.) Many iterations later, I sketched a head with a network of varied signals as its brain that then all funneled down together into a single channel as they emanated from the mouth. This felt useful in getting at the idea of why we need multiple modes for our learning. As I quickly redrew this a few times to try out different ideas, I kept reducing the brain structure to more simplified shorthand, so that now it was little more than this curved grid—not unlike the keyboard-symphony sketch I'd already been working with. Aha—now I was getting somewhere! (see Figure 33.2).

I observed in Unflattening that "drawer and drawing journey into the unknown together" (p. 80), which follows from Suwa and Tversky's (1997) study of architects learning from their own sketches, in which they suggest that drawing provides a way of having a conversation with yourself. Working in comics is this powerful form of self-collaboration—my sketches are these wonderful partners that help me see in ways I couldn't without them. Our always active and incredibly powerful visual system perceives connections in our sketches invisible from our conscious intention. The sketches aren't a representation of my thinking—they extend my thinking beyond existing limitations.

Having formulated a rough idea of something to draw, I began working on laying out the page itself (see Figure 33.3). Working in comics means more than just attending to the linear sequence of individual images, for from the moment an author starts to plan out a page, the author must also contend with the spatial organizational structure of the whole page as well (Groensteen, 2007). Making comics requires thinking simultaneously about individual elements and the whole composition. And so, in addition to this keyboard-brain in a head with a music staff emanating from its mouth that would take up the majority of the page, I wanted an opening "paragraph" that introduced the meaning of multimodality. I came up with an idea to tell it in three short, horizontal boxes. I liked it—I could say what I wanted effectively in a rather efficient and neat way. But, this presented a new problem. If you read these three panels as I had laid them out, you would start at the top, read one horizontal panel, drop down and read the next, and drop down again to read the third panel. But then—I had stranded the reader midway down the left side of the page with no way to get back up to the top of the page to read the body of the page in the correct order. This presents a problem particular to comics—it is difficult to get people to move upward once you've sent them down. What to do? One solution is to use an arrow. Simple, it certainly works—people know how to follow arrows, and you can find examples of them in comics—particularly in earlier eras, but even occasionally still today. However, this practice tends to be frowned upon as inelegant—a literal sign that the creator didn't know how to get out of the corner he had boxed himself into. But, I was struggling, so just

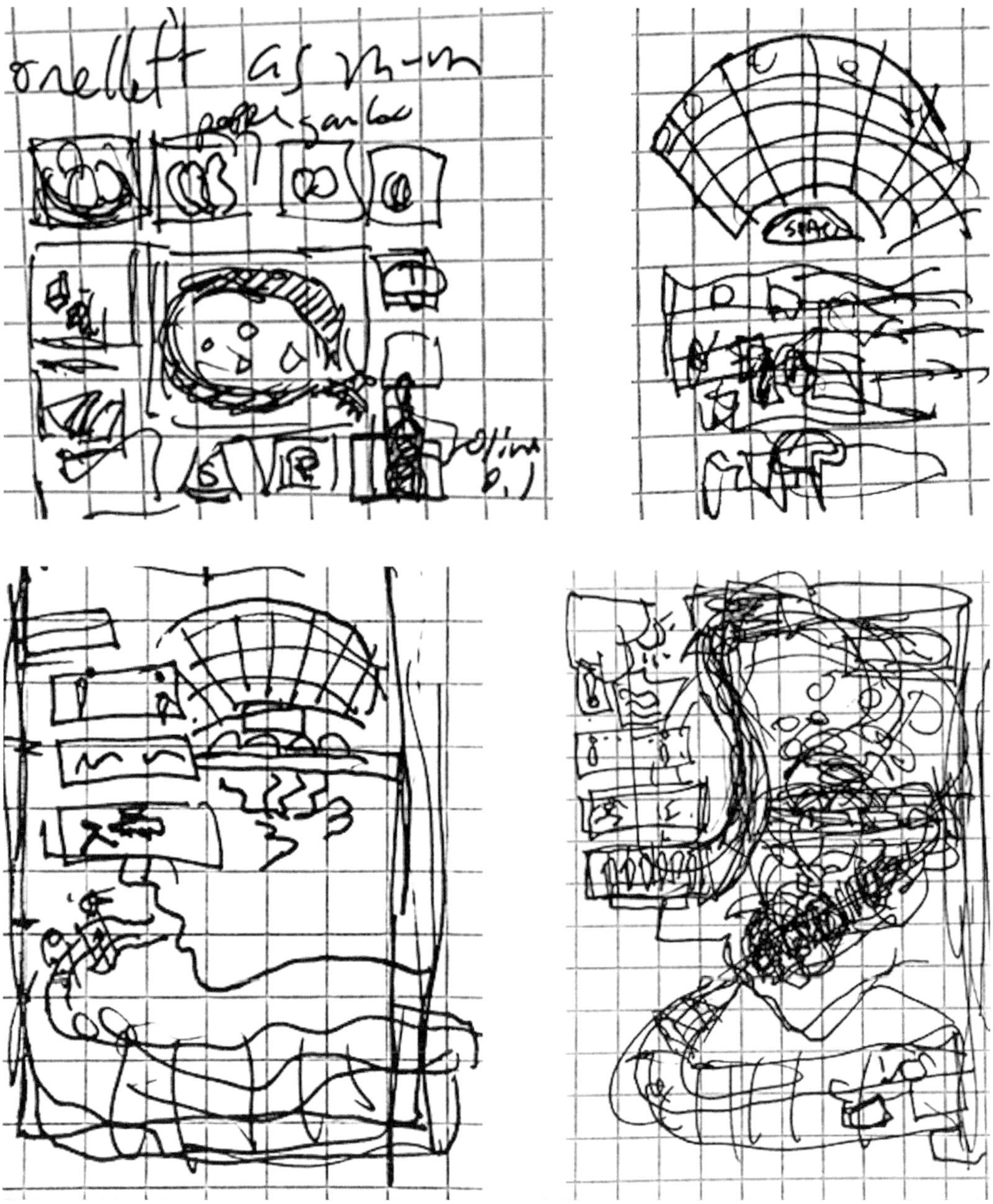

*Figure 33.2*

to try things out, I did sketch such an arrow, swooping up from the right side of the bottom horizontal box. And then, I noticed just how much this arrow I had drawn looked like a thumb. (Again, due to my sketches being both dense and ambiguous.) Of course! A thumb that was part of a hand that was typing on this crazy keyboard-brain thing I had drawn. In retrospect, the hands on the keyboard are completely obvious—someone needs to be

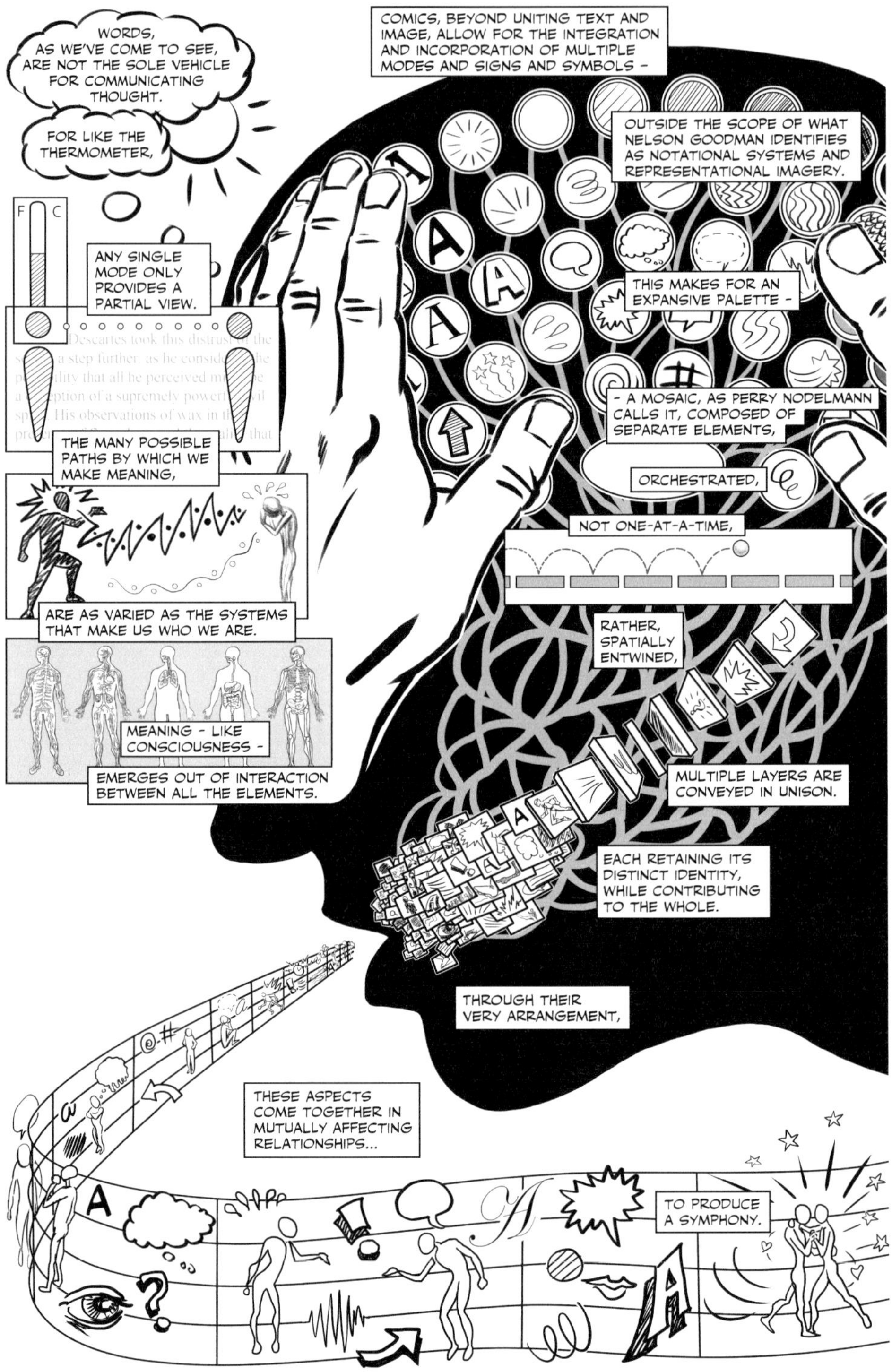
WORDS, AS WE'VE COME TO SEE, ARE NOT THE SOLE VEHICLE FOR COMMUNICATING THOUGHT.
FOR LIKE THE THERMOMETER,
F C
ANY SINGLE MODE ONLY PROVIDES A PARTIAL VIEW.
COMICS, BEYOND UNITING TEXT AND IMAGE, ALLOW FOR THE INTEGRATION AND INCORPORATION OF MULTIPLE MODES AND SIGNS AND SYMBOLS –
OUTSIDE THE SCOPE OF WHAT NELSON GOODMAN IDENTIFIES AS NOTATIONAL SYSTEMS AND REPRESENTATIONAL IMAGERY.
THIS MAKES FOR AN EXPANSIVE PALETTE –
THE MANY POSSIBLE PATHS BY WHICH WE MAKE MEANING,
ARE AS VARIED AS THE SYSTEMS THAT MAKE US WHO WE ARE.
MEANING – LIKE CONSCIOUSNESS –
EMERGES OUT OF INTERACTION BETWEEN ALL THE ELEMENTS.
– A MOSAIC, AS PERRY NODELMANN CALLS IT, COMPOSED OF SEPARATE ELEMENTS,
ORCHESTRATED,
NOT ONE-AT-A-TIME,
RATHER, SPATIALLY ENTWINED,
MULTIPLE LAYERS ARE CONVEYED IN UNISON.
EACH RETAINING ITS DISTINCT IDENTITY, WHILE CONTRIBUTING TO THE WHOLE.
THROUGH THEIR VERY ARRANGEMENT,
THESE ASPECTS COME TOGETHER IN MUTUALLY AFFECTING RELATIONSHIPS...
TO PRODUCE A SYMPHONY.

*Figure 33.3*

pressing those keys! But I hadn't thought of it. It was only the needs of the drawing, of getting the reader to move where I needed them to move (because of the constraints of the form) that forced my hand and got me to see something I wouldn't have otherwise. (There is much more that could be said here. The way I curved the lower right edge of the text box at the end of the horizontal panels as a way of blocking the reader from dropping down further and then gently nudging them upward through this open-ended box. The clouds in the upper-left corner double as thought balloons, their alignment and spacing such that one reads the text moving downwards and isn't tempted to slide off to the right, where I don't want you to go yet. All these almost imperceptible design choices in turn affect how ideas are articulated and where I go. (I'll leave other instances for the particularly curious reader to discover.))

## Art-Making as Investigation

Ultimately, I think it is these unanticipated discoveries that lie at the heart of working this way. What is discovered along the way wouldn't have happened, couldn't have happened, without the drawing being an equal partner with the investigation. When it's finished, it looks as if, of course, that's what I intended all along! But, the reality is it emerged from a process you're not fully in charge of. Incorporating art-making into your investigations requires embracing a certain amount of uncertainty—for, in the midst of it, you're not sure where it's headed or if you'll find safe shores. But, it's a journey rich in surprise—which is exactly what I feel research and learning should always be.

In setting out to do this work, I was concerned primarily with access—seeking to bring complex ideas to more people. But, in making the work, I found a real change in how I think and how I can understand things for myself. I see this in my students, too. In my classes, I watch as those without much drawing experience (and others with a fair amount as well) realize how much they already know about drawing—and how deeply this is connected to their thinking. And I see as they open to that possibility, that much like my own experience, they come to understand things differently, make connections they wouldn't otherwise do through the action of drawing. This is essential, and it points to arts-based ways of working not as separate activities reserved for artists, but fundamental literacies that everyone can bring to bear on their own thinking and ways of working.

## Postscript: On the Importance of Drawing Badly

In the original chapter, I wrote about how the dense and ambiguous nature of my sketches frequently leads me to make new discoveries and go in directions I hadn't anticipated through these conversations with my drawings. Sketching is how I understand my thinking. In jest, but quite truthfully, I have come to describe my process as, "I'm very good at drawing badly." This intentional indeterminacy is key to generating connections as the following example from my recent work attests. To set up, I'm retelling aspects of *The Odyssey* to talk about the creative process—drawing that story onto a tapestry that winds through a series of interconnected comics pages. Other narrative elements are depicted outside this tapestry, including several instances of a Minoan double-headed axe (which freed Athena from Zeus's brow) spinning through the pages. While making quick sketches of the axe—I noticed how much its twin heads resembled beams of light emanating from a lighthouse (Figure 33.4). Aha! I hadn't planned to include the fabled Lighthouse of Pharos, but it is significant in Odysseus's journey, and this accident of drawing led me to work the lighthouse into the narrative. It's these kinds of accidents that regularly surprise me. I make quite calculated, considered final drawings (Figure 33.5)—but the more I make this work, the more I understand that I need to keep drawing badly when I'm thinking—and trust that that will help me find unexpected destinations.

If you find yourself stuck—grab the biggest sheet of cheap paper you can find, and start making marks as quickly and loosely as you can. Put down ideas, sketch, scribble, and see what emerges to help you on your way. It will surprise you!

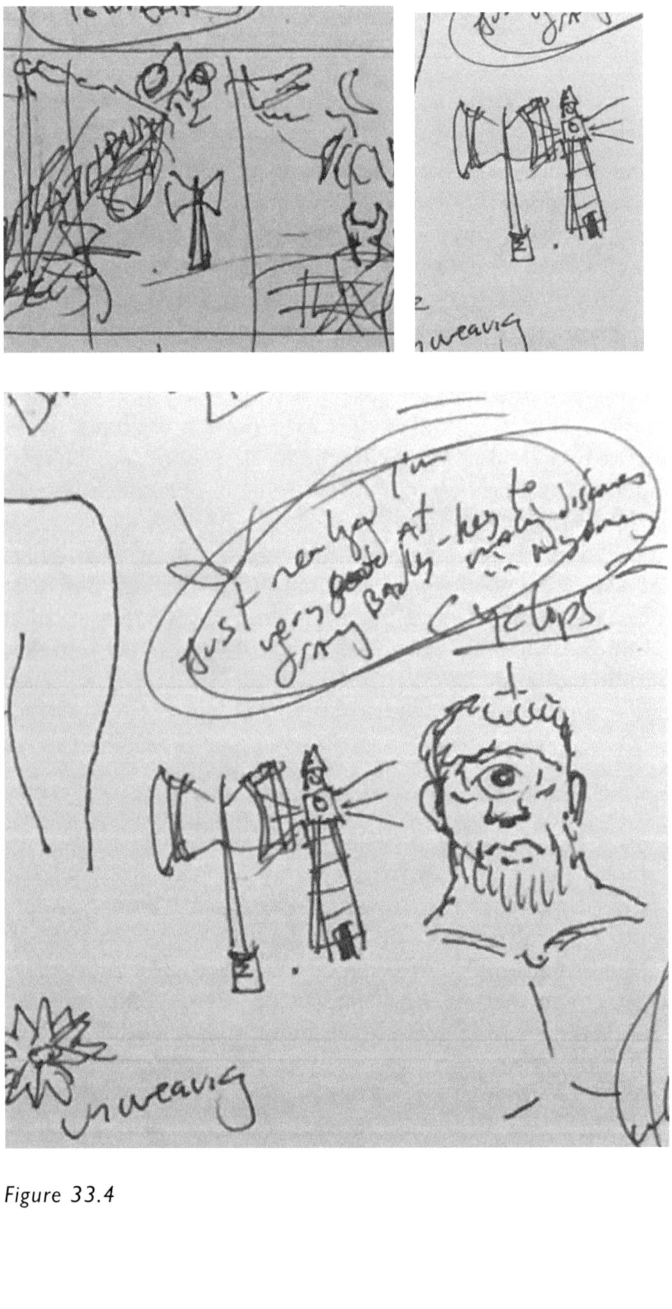


*Figure 33.4*

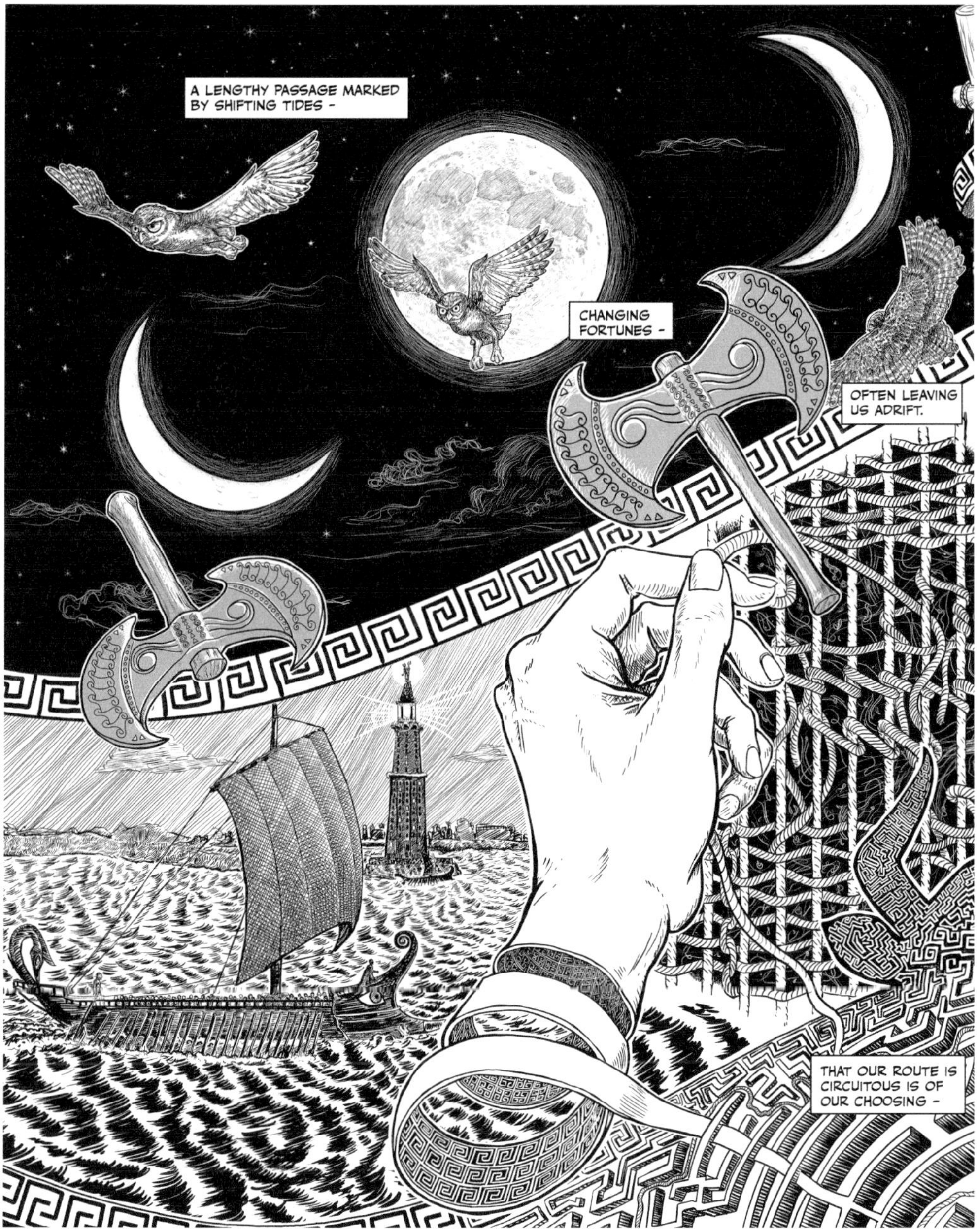


*Figure 33.5*

## References

Ayers, W., Sousanis, N., Weaver-Hightower, M., & Woglom, J. (2013, April). Making comics as educational research and theory. Session presented at the annual conference of the American Educational Research Association, San Francisco, CA.

Bök, C. (2001). *Eunoia*. Coach House Books.

Goel, V. (1995). *Sketches of thought*. MIT Press.
Groensteen, T. (2007). *The system of comics* (B. Beaty & N. Nguyen, Trans.). University Press of Mississippi.
Illich, I. (1972). *Deschooling society*. Marion Boyars.
McCloud, S. (1993). *Understanding comics*. Kitchen Sink Press.
Sousanis, N. (2010). Maxine says. In R. Lake (Ed.), *Dear Maxine: Letters from the unfinished conversation* (pp. 146–147). Teachers College Press.
Sousanis, N. (2011). Mind the gaps. In R. Vinz & D. Schaafsma (Eds.), *On narrative inquiry* (pp. 123–127). Teachers College Press.
Sousanis, N. (2015). *Unflattening*. Harvard University Press.
Suits, B. (1978). *The grasshopper*. University of Toronto Press.
Suwa, M., & Tversky, B. (1997). What architects and students perceive in their sketches: A protocol analysis. *Design Studies*, *18*, 385–403. https://doi.org/10.1016/S0142-694X(97)00008-2
Vinz, R., & Schaafsma, D. (2011). *On narrative inquiry*. Teachers College Press.

Chapter 34

# Nurse-in

## Breastfeeding and A/r/tographical Research

*Stephanie Springgay*

I'm sitting on an airplane *en route* to an academic conference. My laptop, diaper bag, breast pump, nursing pillow, stroller, and carseat have been stowed and I've managed to do up my seatbelt using my left hand, my right being otherwise occupied, holding my 11-week-old daughter to my breast. She nurses hungrily – looking up at my face occasionally to make sure that amid the chaos of traveling I'm still here. Other passengers are still boarding the plane. Some smile as they pass me, others avert their eyes, and a few try and steal a good peek at my breast. I personally couldn't care less as I settle into my seat and sigh. Boarding a plane is a lot of work these days. I don't travel light. But I'm sitting down now, everything in its proper place and my daughter is content, making noises of deep satisfaction. She'll drift off to sleep soon, waking up in yet another city. This is her third conference and long-haul flight. We're pros at making it work.

Two months later a *New York Times* article catches my attention. Outside the ABC studios in New York City 200 women have taken to the streets to nurse their babies protesting celebrity Barbara Walters, who on the talk show *The View*, remarked that the sight of a woman breastfeeding next to her on an airplane was "disgusting" and made her feel uncomfortable (Harmon, 2005). She applauded her co-host who was feeding her baby formula from a bottle.

At another conference, hosted in a large American city on the east coast, the conference facilities lack places to sit in the corridors, hallways, and common areas. I'm forced to hover on a cement floor in-between sessions.

The local and popular *Waffle Shop* asks my family to leave one Sunday morning over brunch. Another patron has complained about my nursing in public. It's a family restaurant after all.

On campus, while I'm surrounded by academic women, many of whom have had children during the course of their careers, it feels as if I'm the first woman to give birth and lactate. My office is not private, I share it with two grad students and the door has a large window. I'm offered an empty office space, cluttered with dusty books and empty boxes, where the only outlet for my *Medela pump 'n' style* is behind a bookshelf. For the remainder of term, I chose to invite grad students to my home or the local coffee shop; my daughter always joins us. What's more natural than coffee and milk? I'm asked by a colleague if I plan on holding office hours?

Completing my first year review, I find appropriate spaces on the standardized form to list two international art shows, more than a dozen published papers – many invited and a few peer reviewed, four successful conferences, and a busy service record. Mentoring undergrad and graduate students and committee work has its rightful place; as do the three research grants that I have been awarded. In the space between I write in "flesh and blood" (Dunlop, 1999) that I have also successfully managed to breastfeed my daughter exclusively. It was

DOI: 10.4324/9781003412892-34

a difficult beginning after a C-section, mastitis (twice), and the usual early stages of public discomfort. Maurya is growing steadily, she's ready to crawl, enjoys swimming classes and her favorite food is sweet potatoes. I found a great part-time babysitter affording me time to make use of my *Medela pump 'n' style* more often.

As I realized that mothering and my family life would not be recognized as relevant to my work, I felt that it was imperative to make art about my experiences in order to make my/breastfeeding/academic/working mother's reality known. While much of Western thought has celebrated the splitting of women's identity into "mother" or "other" – the perception that women cannot be both – re-thinking mothering from the perspective of "performativity" recognizes the relationality between mother and other (Springgay, 2007). As Emily Jeremiah (2006) writes, "To understand mothering as performative is to conceive of it as an active practice – a notion that is already progressive, given the traditional Western understanding of the mother as passive" (p. 21). In doing so, we shift our attention from motherhood as biological, selfless, and existing prior to culture, to a practice that is always incomplete, indeterminable, and vulnerable. A relational understanding of m/othering opens up the possibility of an ethical form of exchange between self and other and "allows us to understand the maternal subject as engaged in a relational process which is never complete and which demands reiteration" (p. 28). Mothering as performance "contain[s] the potential for a disruption of dominant discourses on maternity" (p. 25) and thereby makes room for maternal agency. Thus, it is not simply a matter of making oneself visible as a mother in the academe but about changing the way that mothering has been understood, conceived of, and practiced. This re-conceptualization of m/othering refuses to be split, while also remaining ambivalent.

In becoming a m/other I write/image/teach/research my lines between my daughter's, or as Renee Norman (2001) suggests, "I write on top of small scrawls and drawings, not to erase them, but so our writing is fused" (p. 1). This living in-between the lines reminds us that personal experiences are narratives that run alongside the dominant discourse in such a way as not to mirror it, but to disrupt it, and to render it malleable and in motion (Ellsworth, 2005).

Exposing aspects of life after birth I created a series of works titled *Nurse-in* and *Spillage* as a way to inquire into the visceral experience of m/othering; repulsion coupled with the necessity of nurture. Materialized out of felted human hair and glycerin soap, the breast pump and its parts – breast shield, milk storage containers, pads, and hoses – elicit dis/comfort and animate the uncertainty of meaning. Their functionality has been disrupted and made ambivalent, rupturing the commonality of domestic warmth with metaphors of the abject – the leaky, fleshy, and weighty body (Kristeva, 1982). Although the American Academy of Pediatrics recommends that mothers breastfeed exclusively for six months and if possible up to one year, citing that breastfed infants require less medical care in the long run, fewer than one-third of all new mothers in the United States continue breastfeeding beyond the first few weeks (Harmon, 2005; Sears & Sears, 2000). Self-consciousness about exposing themselves and the difficulties of finding spaces where nursing seems acceptable (and possible) are cited as primary reasons. The visual culture of the breast in Western society is one of sexuality, not maternity (Bartlett, 2006). The visual symbols we associate with breasts are of the Pamela Anderson variety, plump with silicone, not milk, smooth, hard, and perky. The abject leaky breast, blue-veined, with dark areola and a large protruding nipple is absent from our visual culture. Moreover, breastfeeding in public exposes one's mothering skills to public scrutiny in a culture that celebrates the disciplining of the body.

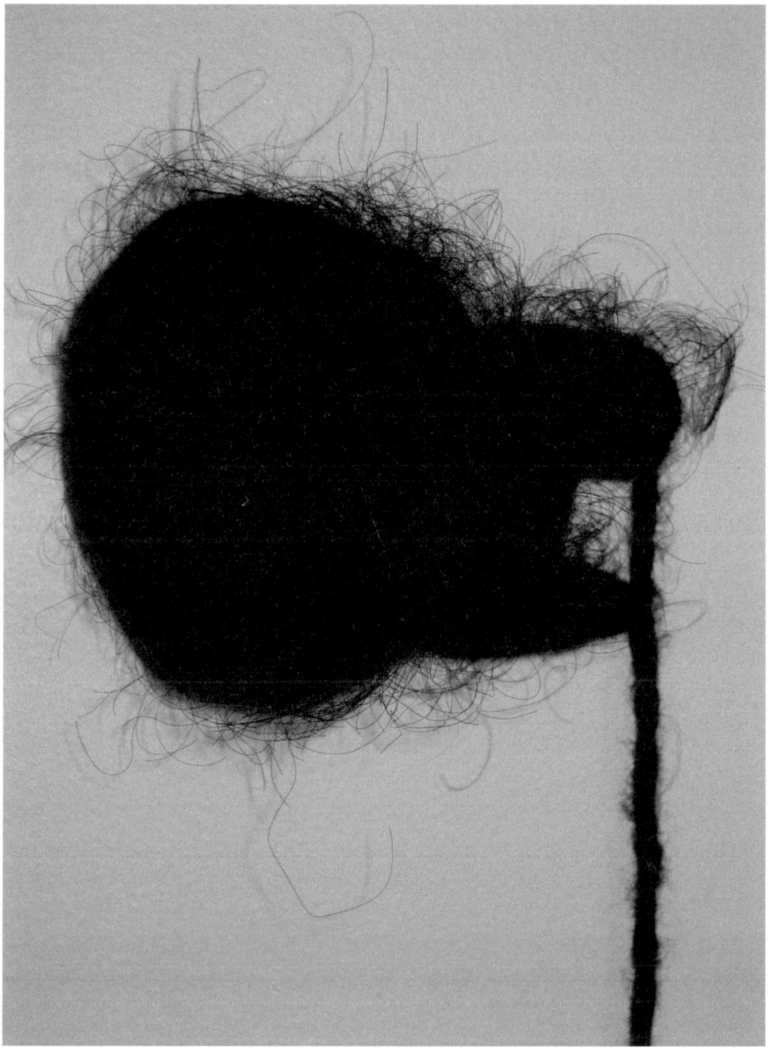

*Figure 34.1*

The installations, *Nurse-in* and *Spillage* (Figure 34.1), negotiate breastfeeding and mothering as personal experiences, disrupting their social and cultural constructions. The artworks represent the tensions between nurturing and productivity, discipline and intimacy, and family and work. Human hair and soap attest to the vulnerability and uncertainty of the maternal body and the fragility of the terms that define and shape mothering. Similarly, a/r/tography as a practice of living inquiry engages in the interstitial spaces between knowing and being. As a methodology of embodiment, never isolated in its activity but always engaged with the world, a/r/tography requires that one live a life open to inquiry that is redolent – engorged, leaking, spilling forth, and becoming something else altogether. It is a way of living, knowing, and being in the world through touch, where encounters with others are not defined by distance and objectivity, but through intimacy, proximity, and intercorporeality (Springgay, 2005). Like breastfeeding, a/r/tography is about intimacy and relationality, where passions govern knowing and understanding rather than discipline and reason.

## References

Bartlett, A. (2006). *Breastwork: Rethinking breastfeeding*. New South Wales University Press.

Dunlop, R. (1999) *Boundary Bay: A novel as educational research*. Doctoral dissertation. University of British Columbia.

Ellsworth, E. (2005). *Places of learning: Media, architecture, pedagogy*. Routledge.

Harmon, A. (2005). Lactivists taking their cause, and their babies, to the streets. *New York Times, June 7*, pg. B. 3. https://www.nytimes.com/2005/06/07/nyregion/lactivists-taking-their-cause-and-their-babies-to-the-streets.html

Jeremiah, E. (2006). Motherhood to mothering and beyond: Maternity in recent feminist thought. *Journal of the Association for Research on Mothering*, *8*(1/2), 21–33. https://jarm.journals.yorku.ca/index.php/jarm/article/view/5011/4205

Kristeva, J. (1982). *Powers of horror: Essays on abjection*. Columbia University Press.

Norman, R. (2001). *House of mirrors: Performing autobiograph(icall)y in language/education*. Peter Lang.

Sears, M., & Sears, W. (2000). *The breastfeeding book: Everything you need to know about nursing your child from birth through weaning*. Little Brown.

Springgay, S. (2005). Thinking through bodies: Bodied encounters and the process of meaning making in an email generated art project. *Studies in Art Education*, *47*(1), 34–50. https://doi.org/10.1080/00393541.2005.11652812

Springgay, S. (2007). Intimacy in the curriculum of Janine Antoni. In S. Springgay & D. Freedman (Eds.), *Curriculum and the cultural body*. Peter Lang.

Chapter 35

# Ethnographic Activist Middle Grades Fiction

## Reflections on Researching and Writing *Dear Mrs. Naidu*

*Mathangi Subramanian*

In the winter of 2013, soon after I arrived in Bangalore on a research fellowship, my husband and I attended an exhibition at an art gallery featuring photographs of a nearby slum that had recently been demolished. The images depicted children scavenging among rubble for their belongings, bereft women leaning on silent bulldozers, and piles of tin roofs and stolen power lines scattered among the detritus of the lives of hundreds of people.

Moved by the photos, my husband and I decided to go to the slum to see if we could help. We got in touch with a volunteer organization and, a few days later, found ourselves wandering behind a young woman with close cropped hair and a bag full of notebooks, carefully documenting the experiences of the slum dwellers scrambling to recover from the disaster.

My husband and I soon ran into a pair of girls who said they were in seventh standard, which means they were probably about thirteen years old. One attended private school and another went to the local government school. The one who was enrolled in the fee-paying school told us she hadn't attended classes in a week, making the other young woman roll her eyes.

"I don't know why you go to that place when the government school is so much better," Pratibha, the government school girl, told us. "At my school, the teachers understand. They care about us. They help us keep up with our work." Pratibha described teachers who went out of their way to help students maintain attendance, keep up in classes, and stay healthy. Clearly, the staff of her government school had witnessed trauma before and were well equipped to handle it.

When Pratibha's private school friend asked her about the quality of the teaching, Pratibha said, "Every year one or two students top the statewide exams. Just come see—the headmaster always puts a banner in front with their names."[1] She then declared that she fully intended to be on the banner during her tenth-grade year.

Pratibha's words crystallized a realization that had long been forming at the corners of my mind: that practically all my assumptions about gender, agency, and education in India were wrong. The literature on public education in India almost universally declared the current system an ineffective mess, blaming the confusion squarely on teachers, mothers, and students who were poorly trained and educated and cared little about their futures (Rao, 2010; Sharma et al., 2008). Hearing Pratibha, it was clear to me that this research was deeply rooted in problematic dominant narratives perpetuated by those in power.

My interaction with Pratibha made me wonder how I, the American-educated wealthy English speaker, could use my own power to counteract the deficit-laden claims so commonly found in academia and the mainstream media. What did it mean to privilege the

DOI: 10.4324/9781003412892-35

voices of those who believed in the system? How could I play a role without continuing to eclipse the stories of those who mattered? The answer, I felt, was not to work on behalf of girls like Pratibha, but in solidarity with them.

## Storytelling in Solidarity

Educational anthropologists have long viewed stories as powerful tools for change. Personal narratives of oppression build solidarity and community by providing platforms for discussion, healing, and action and making visible commonalities between the experiences of marginalized groups (Dixson & Rousseau, 2006; Solinger et al., 2008; Yosso, 2006). Critical race scholars use fictional counterstories to disrupt dominant narratives that reinforce dangerous and damaging power structures and to collectively envision a just world (Bell, 2003; Dixson & Rousseau, 2006; Solinger et al., 2008; Yosso, 2006). Beyond collective action, a key strand of participant action research views storytelling as a tool to empower individuals to take stock of their own lives and narratives in order to create change (Chowdhury, 2011; Dyrness, 2008; Sangtin & Nagar, 2006). Stories are particularly useful in these contexts because of their accessibility; everyone has a story to tell, and telling a good story does not require an extensive education.

As an anthropologist and novelist, I am particularly interested in the practice of using stories to "mak[e] the invisible visible" by bringing to light lived experiences erased by mainstream forces of oppression (Solinger et al., 2008, p. 5). Numerous feminist scholars based in South Asia, where I live and work, have both supported and critiqued the practice of telling the stories of low-income South Asian women in the interest of combatting the intersecting social norms that contribute to their continued marginalization. South Asian feminist Mohanty (2003), considered one of the founding voices of the movement, argues that using one's privilege to amplify the voices and stories of female laborers in particular is an effective act of solidarity, privileging women's lived experiences while avoiding exploitation. More recently, scholars like Chowdhury (2011) have criticized focusing on the individual empowerment of women through practices like storytelling workshops, saying that doing so makes the false assumption that training individuals will automatically lead to collective action. Instead, these authors argue, scholars should use their privilege to challenge social structures themselves and that marginalized women ought to tell their stories in their own way for their own purposes, rather than be under pressure to do so for the collective good.

In Bangalore, I received a Fulbright Fellowship to conduct an ethnographic study of teacher quality in publicly funded early childhood education. But, during my thirteen months of official research and an additional year of informal interactions, I found myself surrounded by the stories of women and girls who, though not directly related to preschool pedagogy, profoundly impacted my views on gender and education. Publishing academic papers about my findings felt both too clinical and too narrow of an audience. What, I wondered, could I do to amplify what I was witnessing, without standing in the way of women's voices?

I undertook several projects in solidarity with the participants in my study, including a writing workshop for girls focused on combatting slum demolition and a participatory photography exhibit in which preschool teachers documented their work. The primary output of my research, though, was created in my own voice: a middle grades novel entitled *Dear Mrs. Naidu*, published by the feminist press Zubaan books, in which I attempted to use my ethnographic research to craft a nuanced counterstory to the dominant narrative about submissive women and girls and a failed public education system in India (Subramanian, 2015).

## *Dear Mrs. Naidu*: Activist Ethnographic Storytelling

*Dear Mrs. Naidu* is the story of a twelve-year-old girl named Sarojini, whose best friend, Amir, moves out of the slum where they live and starts attending a private school. Fearing that this drastic change of economic status could be the end of their friendship, Sarojini tries to use a new law, the Right to Compulsory and Free Education Act of 2009, abbreviated as RTE, to secure a "seat" at Amir's school among those now allotted for "economically backward" students. When she is unable to do so, she teams up with a gang of local women and girls to improve her government school in hopes that Amir can be convinced to return.

Sarojini's allies include Deepti, a feisty, foul-mouthed twelve-year-old migrant worker determined to keep her education on track; Sujata Aunty, Sarojini's mother, a domestic worker who fights for individuals, but hesitates to pursue systemic change; Vimala Madam, a privileged human-rights lawyer whose interactions with Sarojini make her question her approach; and the Aunties, a band of slum women who both protect Sarojini and drive her crazy with their gossip. Her most trusted ally is another strong woman who, unfortunately, is long dead: the book is told through letters Sarojini writes to her namesake, poet Sarojini Naidu, who was one of the most famous female freedom fighters in the Indian struggle against British colonial rule. By reaching back through history, Sarojini compares her own struggle to that of Mrs. Naidu and often candidly seeks advice from her that she will never receive.

Sarojini's community, though faced with at times life-threatening poverty, is vibrant and loving, a reality I saw in my research but did not see in the academic or popular literature. This solidarity, loyalty, and affection among women and girls was something I wanted to capture in my story. On page 14, Sarojini writes to Mrs. Naidu,

> If I become rich, I'll probably move away, just like Amir did, and just like everyone does the second they make enough money.
>
> But sometimes I think I'd rather stay here and fix all the problems. I'd put cement down so we had real roads. I'd put pipes in so we could have water all the time. I'd get us a generator that we could all share, so we could stay warm in the rain. I'd ask the garbage collectors to come take the trash and I'd make sure every house had a roof.
>
> … most of the time, I love where I live. Like when we run out of cooking gas, and Mary Aunty lends us some to get through the month. Or when Amina Aunty's house floods, and Amma makes hot bhaji and invites her and her children over to warm up. Or when Hema Aunty's husband disappears and everyone knows he's going to come back home with blurry eyes and hot, nasty breath, and Kamala Aunty starts singing bhajans in her sweet, clear mynah-bird voice to help us all think about something else.
>
> (Subramanian, 2015, pp. 14–15)

This passage sets the foundation for Sarojini's approach to her life and her education. Although initially she looks for answers in rich, prestigious private schools, eventually her love for her community motivates her to change the place where she herself lives. Ultimately, Sarojini does not want to leave her world: she just wants her world to be a bit more hospitable.

Although I began the book intending to write about how girls from different walks of life experience education, the story soon transformed into a chronicle of an individual's place in a collective struggle for educational justice. The fact that the protagonist was a twelve-year-old girl left room to explore the oftentimes overwhelming journey of a young person finding her feet as an activist. Toward the end of the book, when her mission is looking especially hopeless, Sarojini writes,

> ... Today, I read about how in the 1930s, you wrote and then passed out all these pamphlets trying to educate Indians about the Britishers and to get people to support the freedom movement. You weren't the only one – it seems like lots of other Freedom Fighters wrote them too – but since you were a poetess, I'm pretty sure yours were the best.
>
> There's one you wrote that's addressed to girls. I'm not sure if you remember this exact leaflet, but it's kind of like a poem.
>
> My favorite lines go like this:
>
> "Do not think of yourself as small girls. You are the powerful Durgas in disguise. You shall sing the Nationalist songs wherever you go. You shall cut the chain of bondage. And free your country. Forget about the earth. You shall move the skies."
>
> What did you mean by that, Mrs. Naidu?
>
> Here's what I think you meant: I think you meant that even if you're small, like me and Deepti and Amir (even though Amir's not a girl), you shouldn't be afraid to try and make big changes.
>
> But here's the thing Mrs. Naidu. We are trying.
>
> But no one believes in us ...
>
> (Subramanian, 2015, p. 191)

Sarojini then lists "the people who don't think" that she and her friends can reform their school. The list includes her mother, all of the Aunties, and the headmaster of her school. The list of people who believe she can includes only Sarojini's teacher and Vimala Mam, but Sarojini admits that even these two are dubious, since their privilege blinds them with optimism.

In this letter, Sarojini pauses on Independence Day to take stock of how little progress she and her friends have made. This half of the letter reflects the tension I often witnessed in the slums where I did my research. Most, if not all, of the educators and mothers I met fiercely advocated for their students and children on an individual level. However, when it came to asking for structural changes such as salary hikes, better access to public services, and safety—all of which would have addressed underlying issues contributing to the perpetuation of poverty—most felt hopeless about the outcome. Sarojini's persistence in the face of the doubt of seasoned activists whom she loves and respects is, perhaps, the greatest change in her character—and a product of my own radical reimagining of my ethnographic data. It was also a reflection of my own personal struggle to analyze the disconnect between the women's facility in bending bureaucracy to serve their students' families and their complete lack of faith in the same systems to ever substantially change.

In the same letter, Sarojini continues,

> What if doing this ruins my reputation? What if Amma sacrifices and sacrifices and then I lose the seat because of what I've done?
>
> Or what if I end up staying at Ambedkar School and no matter how much we fix it, it doesn't get better and Amma has to spend her whole life washing dishes because I never get a good education and then never get a good job? What if Rohini Reporter starts writing about Ambedkar School and the government ends up closing it down, like the HM's old school? Then instead of helping the school, I would've made things much worse.
>
> (Subramanian, 2015, p. 192)

In this passage, I attempted to document another trend I often witnessed: that women and girls stood up to authorities often at great personal risk. Women who cared deeply about each other often advised their friends and daughters to "leave it," believing that the potential reward would not outweigh the personal risk. More privileged activists and scholars, like myself, often encouraged activism within these communities without having to worry about such dire consequences. Indeed, I often witnessed supervisors and local leaders lecturing poor women to stop worrying so much about what other people thought. To me, these words felt hollow, not to mention tone deaf to the realities faced by poor, low-caste, minority women who had to carefully weigh even the most basic requests against the interest of themselves and their families.

Sarojini concludes,

> I think you know what I mean, Mrs. Naidu, because the first Independence Day should've been one of the happiest days in Indian history, but ended up being one of the saddest. That's because India got broken up into two countries, and everyone forgot about Hindu-Muslim Unity and started hurting each other …
>
> So when you moved the sky, and people became free, they also became sad and scared and angry, even though that's not what you or Gandhiji or any of the other freedom fighters wanted.
>
> When there's so many people and possibilities dragging you down, Mrs. Naidu, it's hard to feel like a Durga in disguise.
>
> How do you forget the earth when it's always beneath your feet?
>
> And when no one wants to help you, how do you move the skies?
>
> (Subramanian, 2015, pp. 192–193)

By the end of the book, Sarojini does not accomplish everything she sets out to do. Amir stays enrolled at the posh Green Hill school, and Ambedkar Government School only receives a fraction of the support needed to make the substantial changes Sarojini initially envisioned.

However, Sarojini herself has undergone a substantial change, transforming into the type of woman that I witnessed throughout the course of my study: fearless, motivated, loyal, and deeply committed to her community. My intention in writing the book was to create a cast of characters unlike what I had seen previously in children's literature about India. The women in my book are flawed, but they are fierce. They may have complex and, at times, contradictory feelings about poverty and patriarchy, but they are never complacent. Most importantly to me, they are crafted with love and respect, and, although the book has its share of humor, I strove to ensure that their trajectories were never condescending.

*Dear Mrs. Naidu* has had both commercial and critical success, entering its second print run in India. In 2016, it was shortlisted for the Hindu-Goodbooks award in India and won the 2016 South Asia book award in the United States. Reviewers have recommended it for parents, students, and politicians, and it routinely finds its way onto lists for librarians and educators looking for powerful feminist reads.

It is particularly gratifying to visit schools and literature festivals where children who have read the book are excited to engage in discussion about activism, poverty, and equity. These students would not have been able to access my academic papers, and their teachers would not have been able to use my journal articles to anchor classroom discussions. It wasn't until I began engaging with the general public that I realized how personally gratifying it was to share my work outside of academia: my intention, as a researcher, was always to create change. Writing ethnographic fiction has given me that opportunity more genuinely than any other avenue I have used thus far.

Although I did my best to write in solidarity, I am sure that I have made mistakes. My fondest wish is that one day a girl like Pratibha will pick up this book (or, presumably, a translation) and tell me so. In the ideal world that I envision through Sarojini, that same girl will be inspired to write a new story and to make her world visible in a way that I never could imagine. The more I learn about solidarity, the more I believe that it is not about telling our participants' stories; it is about making space for our participants to tell their own.

## Editors' Postscript

Mathangi Subramanian published this chapter just after completing her doctorate in communications and education in 2010 when she was publishing her first book *Dear Mrs. Naidu* in 2014, a novel that would win the South Asia Book Award in 2016. This work showcased the intersections of ethnographic training and creative writing as well as a skillful ways to incorporate photography with participants in her creative research. What has followed has been an accomplished career as a widely read creative writer and scholar.

From her early experiences as a high school chemistry teacher in a border town in Texas to experiences in Bangalore documented in this chapter and among queer and neuro-atypical communities, she has begun a career as a professional thinker and storyteller. Her most recent novel, *A People's History of Heaven,* was recognized as a finalist for both the LAMBDA Literary Awards and the PFC-Valley of Words Awards and longlisted for the Center for Fiction First Novel Prize and the PEN/Faulkner Award, and was named a Skipping Stones Honor Book. Appearing in a wide variety of widely read periodicals including *The Washington Post.com*, and *Ms. Magazine Digital*, Subramanian showcases ways in which scholars in education can apply their training to reach wide public audiences through engaging creative and scholarly content.

## Note

1 Paraphrased and translated from a mix of Kannada and Tamil.

## References

Bell, L. (2003). Telling tales: What stories can teach us about racism. *Race and Ethnicity Education*, *6*(1), 3–8. https://doi.org/10.1080/1361332032000044567

Chowdhury, E. (2011). *Transnationalism reversed: Women organizing against gendered violence in Bangladesh*. SUNY University Press.

Dixson, A., & Rousseau, C. (2006). And we are still not saved: Critical race theory in education ten years later. In A. Dixson & C. Rousseau (Eds.), *Critical race theory in education: All God's children got a song* (pp. 11–30). Routledge.

Dyrness, A. (2008). Research for change versus research as change: Lessons from a *mujerista* participatory research team. *Anthropology and Education Quarterly*, *39*(1), 23–44. https://doi.org/10.1111/j.1548-1492.2008.00003.x

Mohanty, C. T. (2003). *Feminism without borders: Decolonizing theory, practicing solidarity*. Duke University Press.

Rao, N. (2010). Preschool quality and the development of children from economically disadvantaged families in India. *Early Education & Development*, *21*(2), 167–185. https://doi.org/10.1080/10409281003635770

Sangtin, W., & Nagar, R. (2006). *Playing with fire: Feminist thought and activism through seven Indian lives*. University of Minnesota Press.

Sharma, A., Sen, R., & Gulati, R. (2008). Early childhood development policy and programming in India: Critical issues. *International Journal of Early Childhood*, *40*(20), 65–83. https://doi.org/10.1007/BF03165840

Solinger, R., Fox, M., & Irani, K. (2008). Introduction. In R. Solinger, M. Fox, & K. Irani (Eds.), *Telling stories to change the world: Global voices on the power of narrative to build community and make social justice claims* (pp. 1–14). Routledge.

Subramanian, M. (2015). *Dear Mrs. Naidu*. Zubaan.

Yosso, T. (2006). *Critical race counterstories along the Chicana/Chicano educational pipeline*. Routledge.

Chapter 36

# The End Run

## Art and the Heart of the Matter

*Dana Walrath*

We have a joke in anthropology that whenever you don't know the answer to some question, the answer is always both, or malaria. The story of malaria reveals the absolute interconnectedness of every level of experience, from the molecular to the behavioral to the political. Early farming practices created the environment for mosquito vectors to thrive just as today's global political economy determines the lack of resources for the brown-skinned peoples of the tropics most impacted by this disease. Likewise, persistent racism and a history of medical experimentation on slaves and their descendants shape the experience of sickle cell disease, nature's biological solution to malaria. Medical anthropology, my academic home, demands that I think about biological mechanisms as well as the beliefs, practices, and power structures that impact us biologically. It is never a matter of either/or, but always of both. The same is true for the scholartist. We live in a land of interconnectedness. Art is personal, tender, and felt. It requires baring one's soul. Academic work trends toward the opposite: objective stances and data that reveal replicable truths. When we blend such different ways of thinking, of being, of educating, of revealing truths, we engage hearts and minds simultaneously, in doing so making change in this world.

I didn't set out to be a scholartist. Getting a doctorate in anthropology was my attempt at a practical response to the challenges of making a living through creative work. In my twenties, I was starting to show my work—large, colorful, abstract paintings and intaglio prints—in Manhattan's East Village and in Los Angeles. With funding from the New York Foundation for the Arts, I was an artist-in-residence for a public-school system. I was paying my bills, indeed my young family's bills, through art, teaching General Biology lab to undergraduates, waiting tables, and running a nursery school. But, as my other creations, three beautiful sons, demanded the time and attention all young ones require to thrive, I felt the pain of imbalance between my risky art career and that of my husband at the time. He was in medical school and residency as my art career was developing. In the eyes of society, his respectable work always took precedence over an uncertain career choice like mine. I began graduate school in anthropology with the ache of compromise, never imagining life as a scholartist.

How did I choose the supremely impractical discipline of anthropology? I was always a voracious reader. After I was put to bed at night, as a child, I would stand up by my window to catch the streetlight to keep on reading. But, I never imagined myself a writer. I never journaled, never wrote anything that wasn't required, except for occasional letters to friends or family. But, I never stopped loving books. Along the way, juicy ethnographies like Shostak's (1982) *Nisa* planted the seeds for a doctorate in medical anthropology. This respectable job, I hoped, would require me to read fascinating books.

In college, I had avoided academic writing with its abstractions and formalism by majoring in fine arts and biology. My first and only anthropology course was deadly esoteric,

DOI: 10.4324/9781003412892-36

academic, and I had stopped attending. When I met with the professor to explain my absence and my focus on art, he got teary and spoke of the regrets he had about not pursuing an art career. This echoed as I did my graduate work. But, writing a dissertation, a book, let me imagine myself as a writer, a teller of stories.

My dissertation on the evolution of human childbirth was as steeped in storytelling as it was in science. I challenged the narrative of the inevitable human "obstetric dilemma" (Krogman, 1951; Washburn, 1960) by tracing the collaboration between biological anthropologists and physicians to medicalize human birth. To me, this mid-20th century narrative seemed more biblical than scientific, claiming that the human habit of walking upright and our large brains left women with painful, difficult childbirth beyond what any other mammal experiences. Using Martin's (1987, 1991) insight that social process shapes scientific discourse, I showed how this depiction of female biology drew more upon contemporary gender norms than upon biological data (Walrath, 2003).

My work inspired younger feminist scholars but aggravated the old guard. I was especially dismayed at how some venerable female biological anthropologists, who had challenged the status quo in so many ways, still clung to the notion of inevitable and disproportionate human birthing difficulty, particularly in their works for popular audiences (Blaffer Hrdy, 1999; Rosenberg & Trevathan, 2001; Small, 1998). It seemed to me that personal experiences with the pain of childbirth, Cesarean sections, the humiliation of stirrups, hospital gowns, and the fear of a bad outcome left these scientists little room for other ways of understanding this normal biological process. These accounts lost track of the anthropological notion that culture shapes science, the objective, the factual, and that medicine functions as a system of beliefs and practices so beautifully demonstrated with respect to women's reproductive biology (e.g., Davis-Floyd, 1992; Ginsburg & Rapp, 1995; Jordan, 1978).

When I joined the academic workforce, I still didn't know I was a scholartist. I was writing stories and making art in snippets during stolen hours. I was also swimming upstream every day, the lone medical anthropologist in a College of Medicine, the professor responsible for bringing culture, diversity, death, dying, teamwork—the easy soft stuff—into the required curriculum. Exhausted and frustrated, I questioned my decision to have left creative work to get a PhD in anthropology.

Taking a leave of absence to care for my mother through dementia provided the alchemy I needed to become a scholartist. I balanced caring for her with creative work, discovering the power of graphic narratives, of comics, along the way. When I put the story of caring for my mother down on paper in the form of images and words that ultimately became my graphic memoir *Aliceheimer's* (Walrath, 2016), I realized that it was anthropological, that I was anthropological, that my academic training influenced how I cared for her and who I was. Comfort with alternate realities; a communications tool kit; a fondness for ritual and magic; a critical stance toward authority; the knowledge that medical systems are cultural systems; that rules are both arbitrary and central to social interaction; and that birth and death are not just biological happenings—all these eased our daily lives. When *Aliceheimer's* was embraced by other scholars as anthropology, the disparate pieces of my identity—medical anthropologist, artist, writer—integrated. I became whole. A scholartist.

From the vantage of this new integrated identity, I could see the presence of anthropology in all my creative work. For example, my dissertation on human childbirth had become a happy home birth scene in a novel set in New York City in the 1930s about eugenics, refugees, and intergenerational effects of trauma. With this non-medicalized childbirth scene, I wanted to empower young women to see an alternate reality, so that their babies might experience a more peaceful entry into life. Countering the prevailing scientific discourse on childbirth and drawing on birth practices from a lost homeland, this scene embodies the essence of medical anthropology.

Of course, all academic discourse challenges ideas, adds to them, and refines them. But, academics generally speak largely to one another in a specialized language. Art, on the other hand, makes the conversation public. It makes obscure theory accessible. As a scholartist, I get to challenge accepted dogma, taken-for-granted truths, facts denied for political reasons, and the pernicious beliefs and structural violence that maintain injustice. As a scholartist, I can make the social and political processes that shape sickness and health as visible as the biological.

My graphic memoir *Aliceheimer's* has an activist core. Written first as a short comic, then amplified by essays written in response to each drawing, it deactivates some of the stigma and fear surrounding mental illness within biomedicine, the dominant healing system of North American society. Based on the notion that the body can be repaired like a machine, biomedicine flounders with permanent hurts, troubles of the mind, states present from birth, or that are incurable, messy, or incapacitating and eventually lead to death. These conditions, lying outside of the preferred temporary sick role, scare us. To cope, society strips those living with these conditions of their personhood.

My graphic memoir (Figure 36.1), *Aliceheimer's*, shows how we treated Alice's hallucinations and disorientation as a special power. Instead of fighting about what was really there

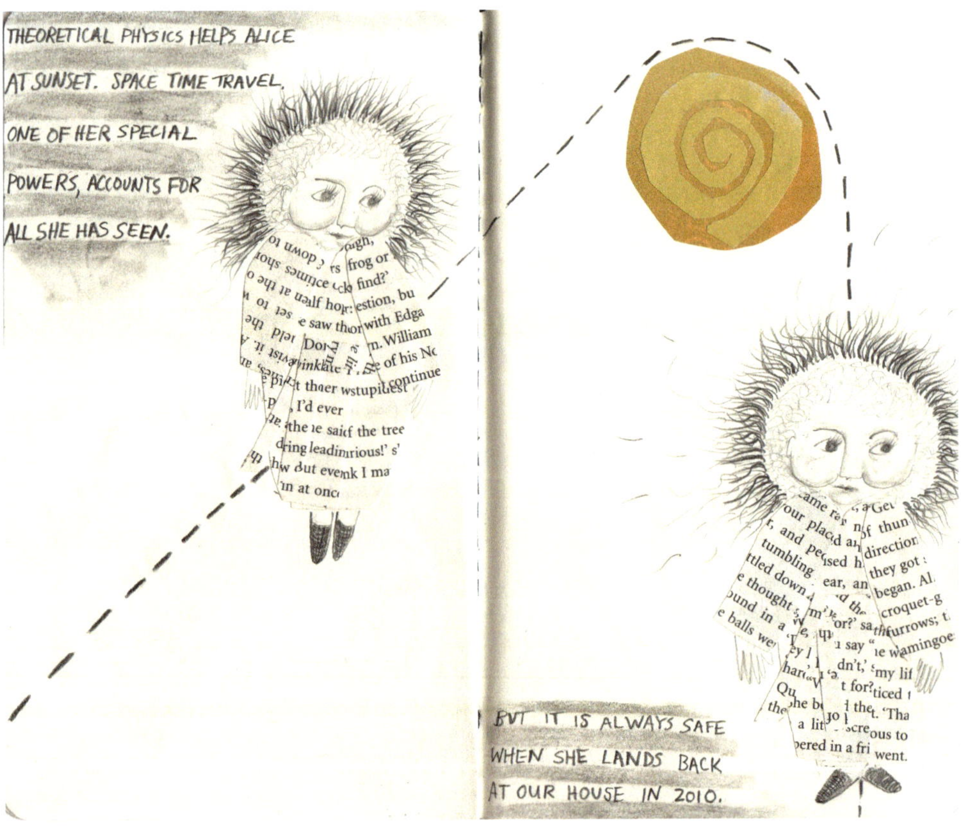


*Figure 36.1* Walrath, D., graphic memoir.

or where each of us was, we let her ability to travel through space and time peaceably account for our distinct realities. This made it possible for me to read the symbols buried in her travels. As I created the art, I used symbols such as cut text from Lewis Carroll's *Alice in Wonderland* to make Alice's bathrobe, her favorite garment, to convey our magical approach to living with dementia.

Consider the dominant story of dementia: a zombie story of bodies living without minds who must be removed from the rest of society into memory care. This zombie story rests upon a socially constructed notion of mind-body dualism so integral to science and biomedicine that it disappears. We forget that this dualism was an idea that French philosopher Descartes came up with back in the 17th century to persuade the church of the legitimacy of studying the body scientifically. We forget that cultures construct personhood, not biological processes.

*Aliceheimer's* makes Alice and dementia visible, restoring her personhood and her humanity in the process. An academic paper such as this one makes the statement that through stories, both visual and verbal, Alice becomes a complete person who retains insight, humor, compassion, and libido even as she has lost her memory. Minds engage with this statement. But when my 70-something mother Alice tells me, "You know, you must have been a cute little kid, I wish I had known you then," hearts engage. At that moment, I responded with, "you too." Witnessing this strange and tender conversation lets you feel me now and trust me when I say that through this journey I've come to know that dementia has given me the privilege of knowing my mother as a child, of knowing her core as well as my own. Through dementia, we've come to share a love and respect that eluded us before. In other words, we healed.

In a paper defining Critical Medical Anthropology (Figure 36.2), Scheper-Hughes and Lock (1987) laid out their notion of three interrelated bodies—the physical, the social, and the political—that together shape the experience of sickness and health. Because biomedicine, the dominant medical system in North America, is based on manipulation of the physical body, the social and political aspects of sickness and health can remain hidden. The social body determines the meanings given to distinct physical states and the boundaries of suffering. Other medical systems locate sickness not in individuals but in families and communities. The political body determines the global distribution of sickness and health. Globally the political body accounts for the fact that wealth means health.

We meet and understand others through story and it is healing for all of us—for the reader, the witness, and for the writer. Healing is not the same as curing a disease. It doesn't involve surgery or taking a pill. Healing involves sharing stories with one another, seeing the world through the eyes of others, knowing them, loving them, and in the process actively changing the quality of all our lives.

Love and healing have remained at the heart of my work as a scholartist even as I've moved from very personal subjects to the more abstract, fictional, and global. With academic roots in medical anthropology, I engage with the broadest definition of health as "a state of complete physical, mental, and social well-being and not merely the absence of disease or infirmity" (World Health Organization, 1946). This encompassing definition recognizes the terrible impact of genocide, war, and social injustice on human lives. This definition, like so much of what I learned in graduate school, gave me the confidence and language to make these "mega" health questions central to my creative work. Here again, art serves as a form of activism.

My verse novel, *Like Water on Stone*, loosely based on my grandmother's childhood, contains the truth of the Armenian genocide, the systematic killing of 1.5 million Armenians by the Ottoman government a century ago (Walrath, 2014). Scholarship unequivocally

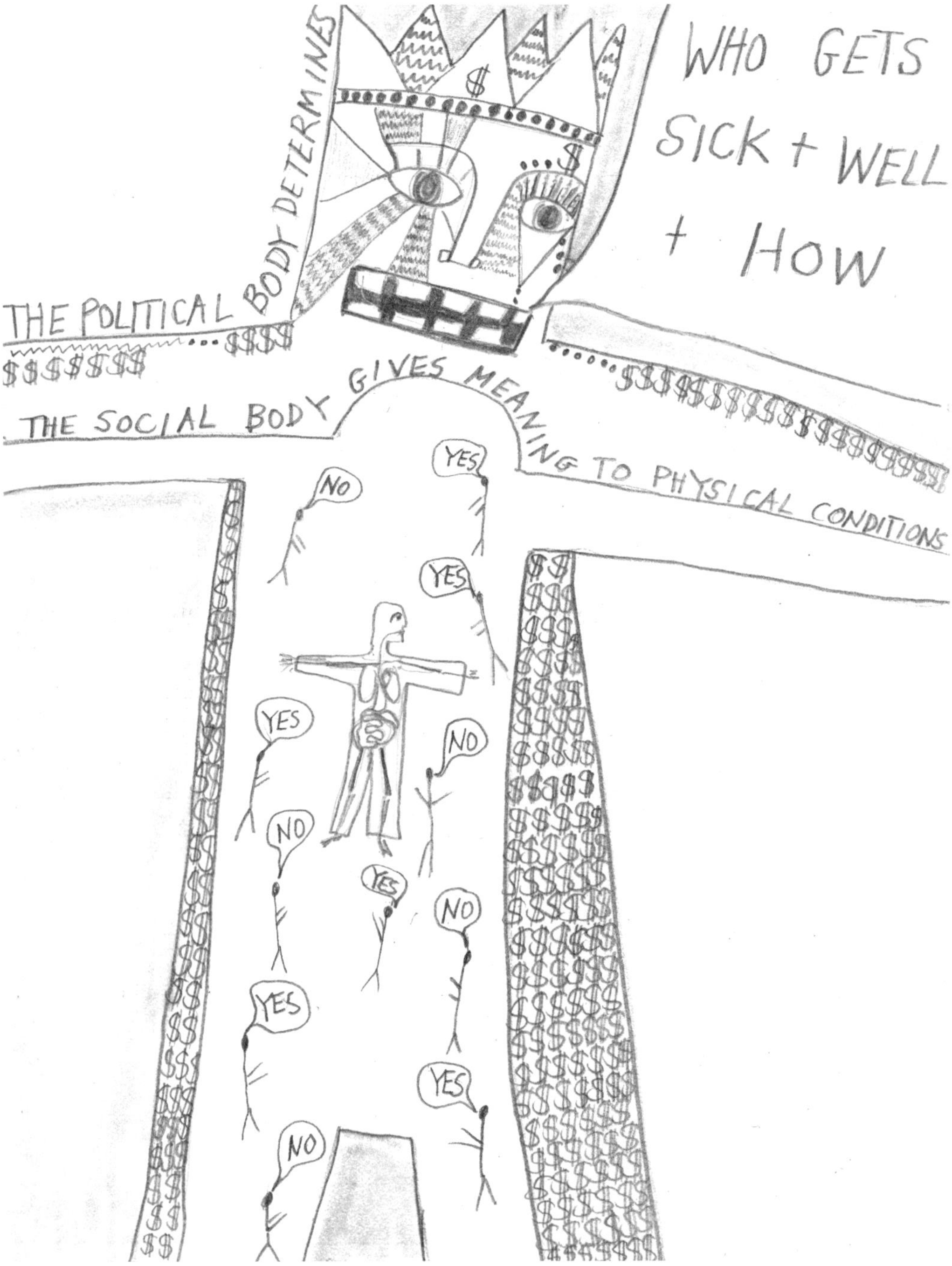


*Figure 36.2* Walrath, D., *The 3 Bodies.*

documents that this genocide took place. Yet, it is officially denied by the Turkish government, the successor state of the Ottoman perpetrators. On top of that, the strategic importance of Turkey has led some Western governments to tolerate this denial. As a scholartist, I made this history visible, by telling the story of three siblings who, like my young grandmother, hid during the day and ran at night hundreds of miles from their home to the safety of an orphanage in Aleppo.

As we say in America, this novel worked like a classic end run—a football play in which the ball carrier, instead of breaking through the defensive line, attempts to run around one end of it. If we think of politically motivated denial as the defensive line, then stories bypass these socially constructed lines and go straight to the hearts of individual citizens. As a scholartist, I can access an even greater truth: the simultaneous shared humanity and cultural/historical specificity, the very foundation of anthropology. This, too, flows in imperceptibly as readers' hearts open. As we disseminate the stories and realize that they are touching others, healing expands geometrically. I hear from American readers daily who spent hours on the internet learning about the Armenian genocide after they finished reading *Like Water on Stone*. Spreading our stories to the world counters denial politics.

Our stories can counter dangerous stereotypes, as the characters we create emerge as individuals within the readers' consciousness. With *Like Water on Stone*, I was determined to help refute the demonization of Muslims that has become all too common since 9/11. The story's brave Muslim characters who defied the genocidal policies of their governments to help their Christian neighbors, friends, and even family do this. They let us stand with greater humanity for justice. They let us resist the trap of bigotry-rooted vengeance. They neutralize the specious public rhetoric regarding the inherent violence of Islam. Teachers and librarians praise the book for its ability to open readers' hearts and minds to the millions of Syrian refugees today.

The healing from writing this book was also personal. Denial of history, of memories, impacts descendants of genocide. We have holes in the form of a disconnect from our homeland, from our language, from the people taken so brutally, from the stories that were never shared. In my case, my grandmother died before I was born. I never knew the details of how she survived, because in my family, as in so many families shaped by genocide, we never spoke about it. Writing a novel that imagines the journey of my young grandmother from the only sentence I had let my anger at the denial of this history diminish, making me a better advocate for global social justice, healing in its most ultimate sense.

My most recent art installation, "View from the High Ground," returns to genocide, to dehumanization, to the removal of personhood, and to my wish for a world healed from such forces. The installation transforms the stages of the genocide model (Stanton, 1996) originally formulated within academia and presented to the State Department by anthropologist Gregory Stanton in 1996 into something interactive, visible, and accessible. Academics might point out the ways that the stages of genocide model oversimplifies. As a scholartist, I focus instead on broad strokes, using the model to engage a wide audience into a conversation about dehumanization (stage 4 of 10)—the cognitive shift that permits atrocities such as genocide to take place.

Focusing on atrocities of the past 500 years (those committed against the first peoples of the Americas, slavery, Australian aborigines, the Armenians, the Holocaust, Cambodia, Bosnia, the Tutsi of Rwanda, and the Rohingya), the interactive portion of the piece consists of nine handmade books. Each book opens with a portrait of a person from that time and place drawn into the surface of an old zoology textbook, one that belonged to my mother, Alice, when she was a graduate student in zoology at Duke in the 1950s. I cut the portrait into thirds, separating the head, the torso, and the legs, allowing the viewer/reader to transform the human into the beasts, parasites, and vermin that appear on successive pages as well as various chimera.

The animals chosen for each book draw upon hate rhetoric and mythology, as well as the geographical and historical specifics of this dehumanization. The human figure reappears in the middle and the end of each book, showing the trajectory of that genocide. The interactive process of turning the pages embodies the fact that dehumanization is under human control. For the original installation, each book was embedded in a piece of slate and displayed on a long, tall table at an angle, as though it were a religious text at a lectern. The tabletop, made from a single 12-foot-long by 20-inch-wide piece of whitewashed poplar, was supported by pipes and furnace parts to engage with the natural vs. cultural bases of human violence. The interactive book portion of this piece will eventually become a freestanding element, a book that readers can hold in their hands.

The interactive portion of "View from the High Ground" shows the process of dehumanization in action during nine of the genocides of the past 500 years (Figure 36.3). The

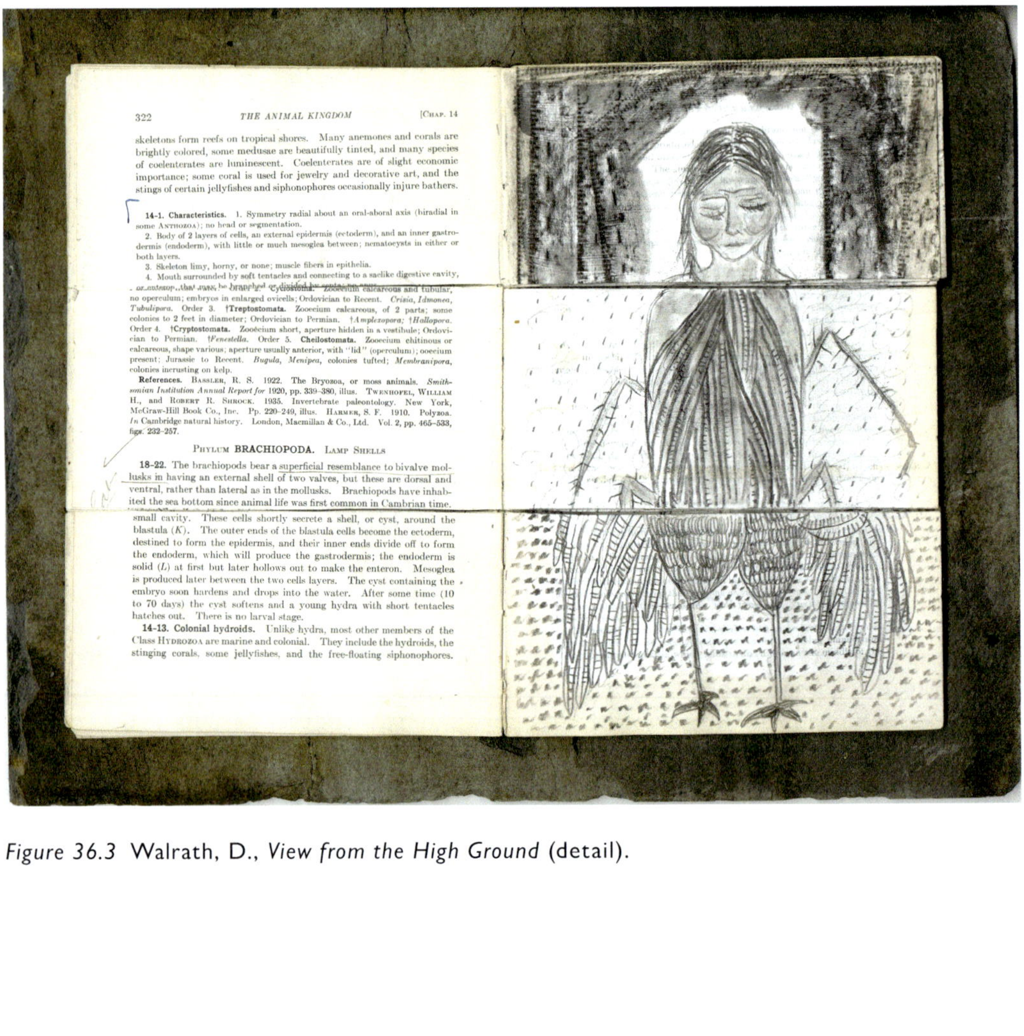


*Figure 36.3* Walrath, D., *View from the High Ground* (detail).

chimera on this page shows a woman, an American cockroach, and an eagle linked both meaningfully and stereotypically with many of the first peoples of the Americas as well as with the colonizers who destroyed them. In each handmade book, I chose specific animals that reflected the hate rhetoric and the mythology as well as the historical and geographical specificity of this dehumanization.

Open access, a shiny new part of the digital age, has long been the way of the arts. As poet and scholar Hyde (1979) explored in *The Gift*—a book I read as I was finding my identity as a scholartist—art takes place in a gift economy. Made to be shared, art withers and dies unless it gets it into circulation. Drawing on French anthropologist Mauss's (1954) work on reciprocity in gift exchange to explain his own drive to write poetry, Hyde describes the inherent challenges of making art in a market economy. With anthropology under my belt, in it I recognized both Mauss and my own creative drive.

Provided that they can wade through the hierarchies of practicality and value that pervade academia, scholartists can be somewhat protected from the market economy. Yes, my PhD has paid my bills. Ultimately, it gave me the freedom to earn my keep today through creative work. Academia, more structurally like capitalism than a gift economy, with its competition and scarcity, also has its own hidden rewards. It contains intangible gifts given in the form of knowledge. Through art, this knowledge transforms into wisdom, the kind of gray, complicated healing wisdom found in stories. Stories let us find common meaning and our shared deep roots without which nothing can flourish.

## Postscript

Seven years later, the creative works mentioned above continue to grow, while remaining anthropologically informed. I've transformed the interactive installation *View from the High Ground* into a book-length disaster comic titled *The Book of Genocides*, now under contract with Harvard University Press who will be releasing it as a trade book. This new iteration also contains blackout poetry redacted from the original zoology text, along with a series of graphic essays that provide a processual model of genocide, the history of each genocide and of the global legal mechanisms to end it, and personal memoir. I've also added the Palestinian Nakba in the spirit of hope for peace for the peoples of Palestine and Israel. In collaboration with a team in South Africa, I've codirected, cowritten, and created the art for two animations birthed by *The Book of Genocides*: *Between the Wall and the Sides* and a Virtual Reality animation *Girl Earth Fire Time*. The animations open users to feeling that genocidal violence derives from specific cultural forces that stem from the rise of civilizations—an extractive, hierarchical, and dominating social form—instead of our purportedly violent natures.

Compared to genocide, dementia remains my happy work. *Aliceheimer's* is now a chamber opera in which Alice tells her own story as a soprano no less. Writing the libretto was pure joy and gave me the chance to sketch out the *Aliceheimer's* sequel in progress titled *Between Alice and the Eagle*. They both get a host of other social justice issues on to the table from racial disparities in life expectancy, to who does the essential care work across the globe, to what are the health consequences of trauma. Now a days when I am asked to contribute to academic edited volumes I reply only if it can be in comics form. My op-comics such as "Dreaming of Never Again" (*The Nation* February 2024) aim to spark the discussions we need to end cycles of violence and to heal.

## References

Blaffer Hrdy, S. (1999). *Mother nature: The history of mothers, infants, and natural selection*. Pantheon Books/Random House.
Davis-Floyd, R. (1992). *Birth as an American rite of passage*. University of California Press.
Ginsburg, F., & Rapp, R. (1995). *Conceiving the new world order: The global politics of reproduction*. University of California Press.
Hyde, L. H. (1979). *The gift: Creativity and the artist in the modern world*. Vintage Books/Random House.
Jordan, B. (1978/1993). *Birth in four cultures*. Eden Press Women's Publications.
Krogman, W. M. (1951). The scars of human evolution. *Scientific American*, *185*(6), 54–57. https://www.jstor.org/stable/24950554
Martin, E. (1987). *The woman in the body*. Beacon Press Books.
Martin, E. (1991). The egg and the sperm: How science has constructed a romance based on stereotypical male-female roles. *Signs: Journal of Women in Culture and Society*, *16*(31), 485–501. https://doi.org/10.1086/494680
Mauss, M. (1954). *The gift: The form and reason for exchange in archaic societies*. W.W. Norton.
Rosenberg, K., & Trevathan, W. (2001). The evolution of human birth. *Scientific American*, *285*(5), 72–78. https://www.jstor.org/stable/26059423
Scheper-Hughes, N., & Lock, M. (1987). The mindful body: A prolegomenon to future work in medical anthropology. *MAQ*, *1*(1), 6–41. https://doi.org/10.1525/maq.1987.1.1.02a00020
Shostak, M. (1982). *Nisa: The life and words of a! kung woman*. Vintage Books/Random House.
Small, M. F. (1998). *Our babies, ourselves: How biology and culture shape the way we parent*. Anchor Books/Random House.
Stanton, G. (1996). The ten stages of genocide. *Genocide Watch*. https://www.genocidewatch.com/tenstages
Walrath, D. (2003). Pelvic typology and the human birth mechanism. *Current Anthropology*, *44*(1), 3–35. https://doi.org/10.1086/344489
Walrath, D. (2014). *Like water on stone*. Delacorte/Random House.
Walrath, D. (2016). *Aliceheimer's: Alzheimer's through the looking glass*. Penn State Press.
Washburn, S. (1960). Tools and human evolution. *Scientific American*, *203*(3), 3–15. https://www.jstor.org/stable/24940615
World Health Organization Preamble to the Constitution of WHO as adopted by the International Health Conference, New York, 19 June–22 July 1946; signed on 22 July 1946 by the representatives of 61 States (Official Records of WHO, no. 2, p. 100) and entered into force on 7 April 1948.

Chapter 37

# Putting Critical Public Pedagogy into Practice

## Reorienting the Career Path of the Teacher-Artist-Scholar

*Yen Yen Woo*

For the past few years, I've been plagued by self-doubt and frustration. My work as a faculty member in a university is supposed to create knowledge, teach, and increase the likelihood that my students (and with any luck, the broader world) will be able to process information logically, reasonably, and thoughtfully. Yet, at this point, just after the election of President Trump, we seem to have entered a "post-truth" era, where willful lies, sensationalism, and "alternative facts" are placed on equal footing with research and data, and internet trolls have more influence than hardworking scholars. In such a climate, how are we to speak, respond, and convince?

Disheartened, I sought consolation in various creative projects—a move that, I was pleased to discover, enriched my academic work and widened the impact of the work. To reinforce one's scholarly work with one's creative practices should seem uncontroversial, especially now, when people maintain multiple identities and everyone acknowledges that learning happens in a multitude of ways. Yet, we, as scholars in higher education, are often surprisingly restricted in the ways our careers can develop. For many institutions, the performance of scholarship continues to be tethered—to a disproportionate extent—to publication in academic journals. By fluke, I've managed to carve out a career integrating my positions as a university professor, teaching and conducting research, and as a practicing artist, albeit not without struggle. In this chapter, I argue why academic institutions should embrace this more holistic approach and share my journey, along with suggestions for those considering a similar career path.

### Learning Beyond the Boundaries of School

Graduate school was a heady time of expansive (and, needless to say, expensive) learning for me. It was New York City in the late 1990s, and I was newly arrived from my home country of Singapore, where I had been a high school teacher. I found myself learning a lot, not just from professors and texts, but also from my new surroundings. I remember being intrigued that the waitress at the cafe I frequented was also a doctoral student in philosophy. Meanwhile, I was intrigued by a short clip in *Time Out New York* magazine about a young man spending the year learning anything he could, including writing with his left hand. New York City made me feel that I didn't have to think about my own career and growth in a linear way and that I could—even should—take some risks.

Taking a leaf from improvisational comedy, I decided to say yes to interesting projects that came my way, even if they weren't entirely within my realm of expertise or comfort zone. This led me down some very unexpected paths. While pursuing my doctorate in

DOI: 10.4324/9781003412892-37

education, I wound up co-founding a very popular satirical humor website on Singaporean current affairs; publishing a best-selling lexicon of vernacular Singapore English (Goh & Woo, 2002); and making a feature film that played at numerous festivals (Woo & Goh, 2001). When I went on to become a professor in an education faculty with a full teaching and publishing load, I also wrote, directed, and produced a second feature film, which picked up several awards and was acquired for distribution in multiple territories (Woo & Goh, 2006); published two volumes of a children's graphic novel series (Goh & Woo, 2013, 2014); and designed a bilingual iPad app that was featured by Public Radio International, the British Broadcasting Corporation (Cox & Werman, 2013), and Fast Company (Salkowitz, 2012), among others. I have also written the book for a stage musical that opened in Shanghai and toured 25 cities in China.

While it seems that my artistic life runs parallel to my academic profession, the truth is that my scholarship informs my art, while my art has brought my scholarship to audiences outside the contemplation of peer-reviewed journals and conferences. My art and my academic work in the field of curriculum studies and the foundations of education aren't separate; they're part of the same continuum. I identify as a teacher, a scholar, and an artist—simultaneously.

## Finding the Thread

In my case, I recognized a common thread that enabled me to frame the commingling of my teaching, scholarship, and art—pedagogy.

Like cultural studies scholars such as Giroux (2000), Hall (1997), and Grossberg (2010), I see popular spheres as important pedagogical sites. They provide us with language to describe who we are and possibilities that we see for ourselves and "our kind" in this world. Learning doesn't just happen in classes and libraries, but also in spaces where "people actually live their lives" (Giroux, 2000, p. 355) and that aren't typically regarded as "educational" sites. This is precisely how a seemingly unrelated *Time Out* magazine interview article gave me a fresh perspective on the possibilities for my career. Images and narratives in movies, TV, and other forms of popular culture can easily generate notions of possibility and impossibility. Giroux (2000), for example, talks about culture as a site where "identities are continually being transformed and power enacted" (p. 354). No doubt, this is why there is so much contestation over representations of race, class, and gender in popular culture.

My artistic work, for instance, hews very much to what Freire (1993) calls "critical pedagogy," where familiar images are invoked to create the occasion for critical dialogue, unveil how categories of self and others are constructed, and reframe those seemingly natural perspectives.

I only came to see the critical pedagogy inherent in my cultural work, however, during my first year in New York City, when in a fit of homesickness, I co-founded a satirical website on Singaporean current affairs called "TalkingCock.com". Although rude-sounding, in Singaporean-vernacular English (or "Singlish"), the term "talking cock" means to engage in idle banter or talk nonsense and is descended from the English idiom "cock and bull story." The site, similar in its irreverent spirit to *The Onion* or *MAD Magazine* in the United States, was immediately popular and controversial, leading the Singaporean parliament to debate whether they could regulate the site, despite its being hosted outside Singapore's territorial boundaries.

A cornerstone of the site was our heavy use of Singlish, as our founding team felt it was a unique part of Singapore's polyglot culture. This was a deliberate riposte to the government's censorship of Singlish in radio and television broadcasts, which we saw as an unnecessary restriction on citizenship performance and very much an instance of the "cultural invasion" that Freire (1993) talks about (p. 133). In fact, a key feature of TalkingCock.com was the Coxford Singlish Dictionary, a crowd-sourced lexicon of Singlish terms. Like Spanglish or Chinglish, Singlish is a Creole-like mix of words from Malay, Tamil, and various Chinese dialects such as Hokkien and Cantonese, but with English as its lexifier.

In 2001, our Dictionary was published in print. Although we used traditional lexicographical methods in compiling the terms, we deliberately chose humorous examples of their use. Doing so highlighted the significant wit and creative wordplay inherent in many of the terms, which undermined the state's repeated efforts to paint Singlish as merely broken English as opposed to "good" English. Rather, we had shown it to be a source of pleasure and, because of its organic, homegrown origins, even something to be proud of. This made the dictionary extremely popular, and sales of the book remain brisk for many years. The dictionary also altered people's frame of reference. While many experienced what Mattar (2009) refers to as "popular cultural cringe" (p. 180) with Singlish, others defended it vigorously (Cavallaro et al., 2014). In perhaps the most tacit sign of concession to popular will by the government, a copy appeared in a newspaper photo of the United States and Singapore Free Trade Agreement negotiating teams (Low, 2003).

Today, Singlish is celebrated as a beloved part of our heritage. Its symbolic meaning continues to shift. Academics have studied it as an expression of the cultural politics of Singapore, while Singlish words have made their way into the actual Oxford English Dictionary (Lee, 2016). There are now novelists, poets, playwrights, and filmmakers who work unabashedly in Singlish. The meaning of Singlish has again shifted from "low culture" to "beloved culture" and has been redefined, with cultural producers and politicians sometimes even employing it to manufacture "authenticity" (Chong, 2011) for a young nation-state.

To me, this work was pedagogical, albeit not in the usual classroom or academic setting. We had reframed the familiar in a new context, let the audience experience the pleasure of the language rather than being didactic about its merits, and imbued a "low-class" vernacular language with legitimacy through the simple act of lexicography, without any need to label our actions as "political" or "playing cultural politics." Scholars began recognizing our work (see Lee, 2005; Poon, 2013; Tan, 2003; Wong, 2005), bringing my cultural work back into the academic realm, not just within education, but also across fields and disciplines such as language, politics, cultural studies, and journalism. I also began documenting my experiences in academic publications (Woo & Goh, 2007). Theory had helped me frame my cultural intervention, which then produced new knowledge and data, and everything circled back to transdisciplinary scholarship. This isn't to say, however, that the mere production of art necessarily begets this virtuous circle. Integrating art, scholarship, and teaching also often requires more work, not less, usually outside of one's comfort zone.

## Multiple Adaptations for Multiple Audiences

When I obtained my doctorate, I felt in some ways that it was a pyrrhic victory because I had spent so many years and so much effort on producing a document that few would read.

My dissertation was about how young people had been led by overarching national narratives to rationalize their past, present, and eventual future (Woo, 2004, 2008a). I had interviewed youths in New York City and Singapore and found that the often arbitrary and shortsighted ways the establishment defined success led kids to engage in intellectual contortions whenever it seemed they would deviate from the preferred path. I knew my findings would—should—be of interest to the general public, but there was no way in hell that a layperson would pick up my 300-page treatise. I don't see myself as contributing to scholarly knowledge if no one reads or sees my work, or is encouraged by it to engage in critical dialogue.

So, I decided to engage in an experiment: to turn my dissertation into the most accessible, mass-appeal product I could think of—a movie.

I adapted the Singapore findings of my dissertation into a screenplay, then ventured into many areas far outside my comfort zone—fund-raising, incorporation, production, payroll, scheduling, location scouting, cinematography, postproduction, festival strategy, and so forth. The resulting product was a 105-minute feature film titled *Singapore Dreaming*. As with my previous work, the movie used familiar images of everyday life in Singapore to place parentheses around what it means to be "successful," a "man," and a "woman" in the Singaporean context (Woo, 2008a, 2008b).

Beyond my wildest expectations, it was picked up by a major distributor who decided to premiere it at Singapore's largest cinema, followed by a general theatrical release on 20 screens. It then went on the international festival circuit, picking up several major awards in Europe, the United States, and Asia.

I wasn't content with just getting it on screens, however. I also worked with the department managing national education to design curricular materials that schools could use to discuss the issues in the movie. The film also allowed the data and the story to be a part of various conversations through screenings, articles, talks, and conferences. In 2016, for example, there was a conference and resulting book using the name of the film—*Singapore Dreaming: Managing Utopia* (Wee & Chia, 2016)—that got scholars and creators from different walks of life to imagine Singapore differently.

So again, my art, scholarship, and teaching had dovetailed. As you can see, though, I had brought my scholarship to new audiences not in one simple, neat product, but rather, in multiple pieces coalescing around central themes and objectives.

I feel that this multipronged approach has paid off, since even over a decade after its premiere, *Singapore Dreaming* continues to be revived in screenings in cinematheques, festivals, retrospectives, communities, and, crucially for me, schools.

I'm now employing a similar strategy with my current project, *Dim Sum Warriors*, a graphic novel ostensibly about kung fu-fighting dumplings that uses familiar tropes to place parentheses around what is considered "Chinese," and who is the "self" and the mysterious, threatening, or primitive cultural "other." It's been featured by the popular press, including *Time* and *Fast Company*, and received an honorable mention in *Publishers Weekly's* "Best Graphic Novels of 2012" (PW Staff, 2013). In 2017, the graphic novels have also been adapted for a stage musical at The Theatre Above in Shanghai.

While I enjoy classroom discussions and conference presentations, I also relish the moments when the author disappears and audiences feel the right to talk and discuss the subject in their own languages, without "authorization" from the "teacher." I get a special thrill being able to connect with, hear from, and think through the discussions of multiple publics—whether fellow academics, cultural critics, or different lay audiences—as I feel that this gives me a more complete and nuanced picture of my work. That, to me, is creating space for critical dialogue and a form of critical public pedagogy.

This "hub-and-spoke" strategy is based on a few controlling ideas, that are the same questions I ask in my teacher-education classrooms:

- Who are the different audiences we must engage?
- What are the most engaging modalities for working with these different audiences?

Just like we chafe against reductive assessments, we must also recognize that there are no one-size-fits-all ways of engaging readers, students, and audiences.

I also wish to emphasize that we have a responsibility to make our work as good as possible. By that, I don't mean a paralyzing standard of quality, but continuous thinking about our purposes, audiences, resources and how we can balance the demands of each to produce meaningful work. While I disagree with Pariser (2009) that there exists an artificial red line between scientific research and the creative arts, I do agree with the question that he poses: "Whom should an ill-researched and artless presentation impress?" (p. 16). I don't judge a piece of public pedagogy in terms of artfulness or artlessness, but I do ask whether it's good enough to create space for critical dialogue. Working through scholartistry isn't an indulgence in creative whim. For me, it must serve the purpose of critical public pedagogy.

## Three Practical Considerations

I've found three practical considerations that guide my current work.

### *Start Small*

Don't be afraid to start small and cheap. Once I've gained a certain level of understanding of my chosen form (usually after a deeply immersive period of research and consultation with experienced practitioners), I then commence modest "pilot" projects to help me assess the potential and pitfalls of the actual project ahead. It also helps me to identify potential collaborators who can bridge my weaknesses.

When I co-founded TalkingCock.com back in 2000, our team used a copy of Microsoft FrontPage (bought with my student discount), because that was the cheapest and easiest way we knew to start a website without having to learn HTML. The simple act of starting the site, primitive as it was, created something to which others could react and contribute. Similarly, in film, I first shot short films with borrowed lights and cameras, with a cast and crew composed of friends and family. It's now easier than ever to produce content, thanks to technological improvements and innovations such as crowdfunding (I ran a Kickstarter campaign to raise funds to print my graphic novels). A small beginning can thus have exponential consequences. In fact, many of the seed investors for *Singapore Dreaming* were fans of TalkingCock.com, so each project builds on the previous ones as we develop knowledge, networks of collaborators, and partners for future work.

### *Find Good Partners*

A recurring question I get from fellow scholars is, "How do you manage to do all this?" My answer is I have help—a lot of it. For some reason, the stereotype of the scholar toiling away alone or the savant whipping genius out of thin air in a studio does not hold. When you're integrating scholarship, art, and pedagogy, you will need collaborators.

My work has reached wide audiences thanks to the professionalism and expertise of my collaborators—the actors, directors of photography, composers, producers, programmers, artists, illustrators, publishers, etc.—who mitigate my various shortcomings and give me the courage to articulate ideas fully. I've found it important to make the work cheaply first, so there is a concept that is tangible, and make it worthwhile enough to attract a team who can make the work much more effective than I ever imagined it. Needless to say, it's also much more fun to play with others.

#### *Plan for Distribution*

Whatever you make, plan for distribution. That means getting a sense of how people will access and see what you have to offer. In fact, distribution has been my biggest challenge and will be yours as well.

Bookstores and newspapers are closing down; cinemas won't run your film unless it looks like the next superhero blockbuster; nobody buys DVDs anymore; streaming pays pennies on the dollar; and does anyone watch broadcast TV anymore? Like every independent filmmaker out there, I've had to bite my nails as I watch cinemas decide whether to axe one of my screens to make way for an additional screening of Spider-Man. With piracy, corporate consolidation, and shrinking aftermarkets, even the economics of filmmaking is at grave risk (Lang, 2017). While the Internet has the ability to make things available to millions with a click, getting people to see your stuff hasn't necessarily become easier. Despite the old gatekeepers of knowledge (those few TV channels, newspapers, and the academy—things that once dictated what is important) losing their stranglehold, getting content to audiences means you must now compete with social media, the 24/7 news cycle, fake news, cat videos, memes, video games, and all the other dings and pings from our multiple devices.

The result of the sudden tsunami of information sources isn't just wider and faster dissemination of content, but also a growing fragmentation of attention in society (Carr, 2011; Webster, 2016). Without attention, knowledge dies. If a tree falls in the forest of ideas and no one is around to hear it, it's dead. Jenkins et al. (2013) talk about how knowledge and media have to be "spreadable," but information overload gives everyone a much shorter time to spread their content, even with highly publicized and viral content; Pokémon Go was the rage one year, now it's pretty much passé. So, we must now work feverishly to spread our knowledge to our ever-decreasing slices of attention, as fast as we can.

For so many of us, the day we mail our manuscript to the editor is when we think the work is completed, and we can breathe a sigh of relief. And then, a little bit of us dies after it gets published and we realize that no one is really reading the work to which we had dedicated so many hours of our lives. In my experience, sending off the manuscript or completing production is the beginning of the next, possibly harder, mission of getting the work out. Planning for distribution means asking questions: How can audiences with whom I am trying to connect best access this knowledge? What different forms should this take? How can I build the audience with each piece of work? What are the different communities with whom I can work to spread the word? Should my book be supported by a podcast series? A complementary spoken word event? A supplementary website?

## Our Responsibility

Although the harsh new reality of ever-thinning attention seems demoralizing, we're also at a moment when we can experiment with multiple forms that can reach audiences much more easily than before. I would also argue we have no choice but to try, because it's never been so important for us as educators to participate in the public sphere. Besides, we know that influence comes only with time and effort, and we are used to playing the long game anyway.

By way of example, the single most common question the students in my classes on educational foundations ask me is, "Why didn't I know all this before?" This is in relation to a wide range of issues, from research on school reform to the interconnectedness of race, socioeconomic status, and the achievement gap; second-language learners; and on international comparisons of education. Their surprise is largely because the data often flies in the face of the impressions received from non-scholarly sources such as social and traditional media, exchanges with friends and family, and specific personal schooling experiences.

I believe this disconnect is because as educators and researchers, we've done a terrible job of shaping the dominant images, ideas, and narratives about education in the public sphere. We've done the studies, yes, but they sit in repositories that never reach the people, while special interests rush in to occupy the vacuum that we, in our negligence, have allowed to form. We need to step up.

This is especially crucial now, when the meaning of "facts" and "truth" also seems to be changing. In his recent documentary *HyperNormalisation* (2016), Curtis mentions Vladislav Surkov, one of President Putin's advisers, who has imported ideas from avant-garde conceptual art into Russian politics, specifically by undermining people's perceptions so that no one is sure whether something is real or fake. This deliberate sowing of confusion creates a constant state of destabilized perception in order to manage and control the public. We can see some of this happening in the aftermath of America's own recent 2017 election cycle, where people who lie openly can simultaneously complain that others are peddling fake news. Being an internet troll and spreading untruths is now a job, and trolls now get invited to the White House as part of the press corps (Marantz, 2017). This intentional riling of sentiments has caused people to retreat even further into their own political silos, while labels like "multiculturalism," "race," "diversity," "patriotism," and "nationalism" are now imbued with such partisan associations that sensible dialogue is shut down.

There is a growing sense of the irrelevance of higher education and a resentment toward intellectuals and academics (Donoghue, 2008). This toxic mood doesn't just affect the field of education; we are seeing it in other fields, as well. As educators, however, we have a particular responsibility to put things right because we have the knowledge and the tools. Integrating art and popular cultural work into our scholarly and pedagogic practices is one way of reviving our relevance with the public.

## Conclusion

At the time of this writing, the university where I currently work sends faculty the message that publication in peer-reviewed journals is the paramount yardstick of academic achievement. Creative work is tolerated, as long as faculty also fulfill their basic quota of peer-reviewed articles. On the face of it, this seems reasonable, as journals are supposed to reach highly specialized audiences, employ reliable evaluation practices, and have the requisite "impact factor" (the common practice of according a score to denote the number of citations a journal or article receives over a set period) that universities can use in determining promotion and tenure. There is, however, great controversy over the reliability of using citation indexes as a genuine measure of the impact of a journal and the validity of peer review (Cope & Kalantzis, 2014, p. 106). This focus also completely omits the necessity to engage wider audiences. With higher education needing to restore its relevance to the public (Jay, 2010; Willinsky, 2001), restricting scholarly knowledge to venues that require privileged access seems perverse.

In the meantime, the debate over whether art can be considered legitimate work for scholars continues—specifically, whether the arts can make for legitimate scholarship and what the boundaries should be for arts-based research (Pariser, 2009). These are quaint arguments. We don't have to be either; we can be "both-and" (Ellis, 2008, p. 114). The rest of society seamlessly manages multiple, border-crossing identities—why is the academy insisting on erecting artificial walls?

The good news is that significant pockets in academia are now moving toward valuing the roles of faculty as not just teachers and scholars, but also citizens and advocates. This can be traced to Boyer's (1990) treatise, where he talks about how "work of the professoriate" should expand to include "the scholarship of discovery; the scholarship of integration; the scholarship of application; and the scholarship of teaching" (p. 16). We see this expansive thinking about scholarship play out in various locations, too. For example, Imagining America is a consortium of 86 colleges and universities led by the University of Michigan and Syracuse University, to promote public scholarship that integrates the arts and scholarly work. Meanwhile, Ellison and Eatman (2008) outline a useful evaluative framework for acknowledging and rewarding scholarly art. There are a growing number of programs that take on the challenge of public scholarship to make "knowledge about, for, and with diverse publics and communities .... (which) contributes to the public good and yields artifacts of public and intellectual value" (Ellison & Eatman, 2008, p. 6), such as the University of Washington's Certificate in Public Critical Race Scholarship (https://ccde.com.washington.edu/certificate-in-public-critical-race-scholarship/), and the Rackham Program in Public Scholarship at the University of Michigan (http://www.rackham.umich.edu/publicscholarship/).

With the tools available today, integrating all our skills and knowledge isn't only possible, it's overdue. Our students and communities need hope, passion, resourcefulness, and inspiration; folding artistic practice into our scholarship and teaching does far more in that regard than trying to conform to specious assessment criteria (see Mitchell, 2008). It also enables us to reach more people than ever before and restore the legitimacy we've allowed to slip away. The current state of flux affecting all forms of media is also a boon, rather than a bane. The fact that rules have yet to ossify about genres and forms provides us with great opportunities to learn and lead. As educators, do we dare to step outside our comfort zones, to work in deeply collaborative ways with others, to speak in languages that our audiences find accessible, and to have them speak back in their own languages? In our scholarly work, we've been engaged in the banking model of education for far too long. Do we dare to engage, as Freire (1993) says, "with" and not "for" (p. 30)?

## Postscript

Since writing this chapter, we have seen Donald Trump elected to the U.S. Presidency for the second time. I have become increasingly concerned about the rise of exclusionary sentiments and rise of exclusionary sentiments and how social media encourages strong angry rants. In response, I've shifted my personal and pedagogical focus away from satirical work that may alienate as much as it engages. Instead, I prioritize work that fosters dialogue and common ground. This involves leveraging shared experiences and pleasurable encounters to create a foundation upon which to introduce unfamiliar ideas. Inspired by Freire's (1993) pedagogy, I continue to work with my students and collaborators to bridge divides and seed transformative conversations.

In addition, I have moved to lead the MA Arts Pedagogy and Practice Programme at a specialist arts institution, LASALLE College of the Arts in Singapore. My artistic practice is now an important part of the evaluation of my work, giving full expression to my identity as a teacher-artist-scholar. I am fortunate to work alongside talented postgraduate students who are not only accomplished artists but also dedicated educators. These students are pioneering innovative approaches to arts education and harnessing the transformative power of the arts to drive cultural change. They, too, identify as teachers-artists-scholars.

## References


Boyer, E. L. (1990). *Scholarship reconsidered: Priorities of the professoriate*. The Carnegie Foundation for the Advancement of Teaching.

Carr, N. (2011). *The shallows: What the internet is doing to our brains*. W.W. Norton.

Cavallaro, F., Ng, B. C., & Seilhamer, M. F. (2014). Singapore colloquial English: Issues of prestige and identity. *World Englishes*, *33*(3), 378–397. https://doi.org/10.1111/weng.12096

Chong, T. (2011). Manufacturing authenticity: The cultural production of national identities in Singapore. *Modern Asian Studies*, *45*(4), 877–897. https://doi.org/10.1017/S0026749X09000158

Cope, B., & Kalantzis, M. (2014). Changing knowledge ecologies and the transformation of the scholarly journal. In B. Cope & A. Phillips (Eds.), *The future of the academic journal* (2nd ed., pp. 9–83). Chandos Publishing.

Cox, P., & Werman, M. (Host). (2013). Comic book snacks that talk back in two languages [Radio broadcast]. In P. Cox (Producer), *PRI's the world in words*.

Curtis, A. (2016). *HyperNormalisation* [Motion picture]. British Broadcasting Corporation.

Donoghue, F. (2008). *The last professors: The corporate university and the fate of the humanities*. Fordham University Press.

Ellis, J. (2008). The humanities and the public soul. In K. Mitchell (Ed.), *Practising public scholarship: Experiences and possibilities beyond the academy* (pp. 113–121). Wiley.

Ellison, J., & Eatman, T. K. (2008). *Scholarship in public: Knowledge creation and tenure policy in the engaged university*. Imagining America.

Freire, P. (1993). *Pedagogy of the oppressed* (M. B. Ramos, Trans.). Continuum (Original work published 1970).

Giroux, H. A. (2000). Public pedagogy as cultural politics: Stuart Hall and the 'crisis' of culture. *Cultural Studies*, *14*(2), 34–360. https://doi.org/10.1080/095023800334913

Goh, C., & Woo, Y. Y. (2002). *The Coxford Singlish Dictionary*. Angsana Books.

Goh, C., & Woo, Y. Y. (2013). *Dim sum warriors volume 1: Enter the dumpling*. Yumcha Studios.

Goh, C., & Woo, Y. Y. (2014). *Dim sum warriors volume 2: Feast of fury*. Yumcha Studios.

Grossberg, L. (2010). *Cultural studies in the future tense*. Duke University Press.

Hall, S. (1997). The centrality of culture: Notes on the cultural revolutions of our times. In K. Thompson (Ed.), *Media and cultural regulation* (pp. 208–238). Sage.

Jay, G. (2010). The engaged humanities: Principles and practices for public scholarship and teaching. *Journal of Community Engagement and Scholarship*, *3*(1), 51–63. https://doi.org/10.54656/ROWM8434

Jenkins, H., Ford, S., & Green, J. (2013). *Spreadable media: Creating value and meaning in a networked culture*. NYU Press.

Lang, B. (2017, March 27). The reckoning: Why the movie business is in big trouble. *Variety*. http://variety.com/2017/film/features/movie-business-changing-consumer-demand-studios-exhibitors-1202016699/

Lee, M. K. (2016, May 12). Shiok! 19 Singlish items added to the Oxford English Dictionary. *Straits Times*. http://www.straitstimes.com/singapore/shiok-19-singlish-items-added-to-the-oxford-english-dictionary

Lee, T. (2005). Journalism and civil society in Singapore. In A. Romano & M. Bromley (Eds.), *Journalism and democracy in Asia* (pp. 15–27). Routledge.

Low, C. L. (2003, May 7). We took US team to eat prata. *The New Paper*.

Marantz, A. (2017, March 20). Trolling the press corps: The Trump administration disrupts the daily briefings. *The New Yorker*, 52–61.

Mattar, Y. (2009). Popular cultural cringe: Language as signifier of authenticity and quality in the Singaporean popular music market. *Popular Music*, *28*(2), 179–195. https://doi.org/10.1017/S0261143009001779

Mitchell, K. (2008). *Practising public scholarship: Experiences and possibilities beyond the academy*. Wiley.

Pariser, D. (2009). Arts-based research: Trojan horses and shibboleths. *Canadian Review of Art Education*, *36*, 118.

Poon, A. (2013). Common ground, multiple claims: Representing and constructing Singapore's "heartland". *Asian Studies Review*, *37*(4), 559–576. https://doi.org/10.1080/10357823.2013.844768

PW Staff. (2013, January 9). Ware's 'Building Stories' tops PW Comics World's 2012 graphic novel critics' poll. *Publishers Weekly*. https://www.publishersweekly.com/pw/by-topic/industry-news/comics/article/55420–ware-s-building-stories-tops-pw-comics-world-s-2012-graphic-novel-critics-poll.html

Salkowitz, R. (2012, December 12). The 10 coolest original digital comics of 2012. *Fast Company*. https://www.fastcompany.com/1682082/the-10-coolest-original-digital-comics-of-2012

Tan, K. P. (2003). Sexing up Singapore. *International Journal of Cultural Studies*, *6*(4), 403–423. https://doi.org/10.1177/136787790364002

Webster, J. (2016). *The marketplace of attention: How audiences take shape in a digital age*. MIT Press.

Wee, H. K., & Chia, J. (Eds.). (2016). *Singapore dreaming: Managing utopia*. Asian Urban Lab.

Willinsky, J. (2001). The strategic education research program and the public value of research. *Educational Researcher*, *30*(1), 5–14. https://doi.org/10.3102/0013189X030001005

Wong, J. (2005). "Why you so Singlish one?" A semantic and cultural interpretation of the Singapore English particle one. *Language in Society*, *34*(2), 239–275. https://doi.org/10.1017/S0047404505050104

Woo, Y. Y. (2004). *Citizen 2.0: Youth temporalities and citizenship across Singapore and New York City*. Unpublished doctoral dissertation. Teachers College, Columbia University.

Woo, Y. Y. (2008a). Youth temporalities and the cost of Singapore's educational success. *Discourse: Studies in the Cultural Politics of Education*, *29*(2), 159–178. https://doi.org/10.1080/01596300801966781

Woo, Y. Y. (2008b). Engaging new audiences: Translating research into popular media. *Educational Researcher*, *37*(6), 321–329. https://doi.org/10.3102/0013189X08324229

Woo, Y. Y., & Goh, C. (2001). *Talking Cock the movie* [Motion picture]. Wu Liao Media.

Woo, Y. Y., & Goh, C. (2006). *Singapore dreaming* [Motion picture]. 5C Films Pte Ltd.

Woo, Y. Y. J., & Goh, C. (2007). Caging the bird: TalkingCock.com and the pigeonholing of Singaporean citizenship. In K. P. Tan (Ed.), *Renaissance Singapore? Economy, culture and politics* (pp. 95–113). NUS Press.

Chapter 38

# Being Pregnant as an International PhD Student

## A Poetic Autoethnography

*Kuo Zhang*

As a kind of grotesque image of the physical, pregnancy can be viewed as an example of the unfinished and open body, which challenges perceptions that the body is "a strictly completed, finished product" that remains "isolated, alone, fenced off from all other bodies" (Bakhtin, 1984, p. 29). Such unfinished and open characteristics of pregnancy and birth stories create more space for the carnival spirit, "the chance to have a new outlook on the world, to realize the relative nature of all that exists, and to enter a completely new order of things" (Bakhtin, 1984, p. 34). During pregnancy process, we have numerous opportunities to reflect on the relationship between the "self" and "others" and to explore Bakhtin's (1981) concept of "heteroglossia" in relationship to the different voices and discourses behind the experience of pregnancy.

Given the fact that babies can be born anywhere in the world, pregnancy and birth stories across cultures add multiple layers to the carnival discourse and embody diverse cultural beliefs, power dynamics, and social enthymeme—"a 'password' known only to those who belong to the same social purview" (Volosinov, 1976, p. 101). The social enthymeme related to pregnancy and birth includes numerous maternal subjects, such as "reproductive technologies, genetic engineering, abortion rights, welfare reform, and custody law" (Pollock, 1999). To some extent, they tend to deepen the marginalization and disempowerment of immigrant mothers, who are isolated in the new culture and usually get stuck in the middle, a third space, which does not belong to their home culture or host culture. For example, the "scares" during antenatal care, that U.S. mothers come to learn are somewhat "normal," are even more frightening and unclear to immigrant mothers.

It is even more challenging for women to be pregnant while pursuing a PhD degree. Doctoral studies require students to mainly focus on academic research, while the dramatic change of becoming a new mom tends to involve full dedication to motherhood and family. *Mama PhD* (Evans & Grant, 2008) is an anthology of first-person narrative accounts of balancing motherhood and academic work, edited by Evans, a mother and PhD student unsure if she will complete her degree, and Grant, a mother with a PhD who resigned from teaching after child birth (Kuperberg, 2009). It includes 41 essays by women with PhDs that explore the possibility of "blending family life with life in the ivory tower" (Evans & Grant, 2008, p. xxiii), especially in the humanities and social sciences. Another anthology edited by Monosson (2008), a mother and PhD toxicologist, includes essays written by 34 mother-scientists in the natural sciences and highlights the "accomplishments, challenges and choices made by women scientists as they combine motherhood and career" (Monosson, 2008, p. 5). The stories of success and failure in these books contain several common themes, such as the importance of female mentors, the timing of planning pregnancies, and

DOI: 10.4324/9781003412892-38

challenges to academic research and careers. Challenges for PhD mothers are multiplied by immigrant status, making their lives more complex and vulnerable. In a recent study, Vega (2016) addresses the pregnancy stories of mothers of color who are graduate students as "hyper visible, yet invisible" (p. 3), and points out that PhD student mothers must battle stereotypes of "inability" and commitment to academics, as well as racial and gendered microaggressions. Due to these challenges, doctoral years are usually not regarded as the best or even an appropriate time for pregnancy and birth stories. In some cultures, it is still an implicit taboo for students (at any level) to get married and/or become pregnant. However, it seems that the perfect time never comes in life. Babies can be born not only anywhere but also anytime within a woman's childbearing age.

As a second-year PhD student from China who studies Language and Literacy Education in a southeastern American university, I chose the road not taken by most of my peers to conceive a new life and academic research at the same time. Through autoethnographic poetic inquiry, I go further afield by doing the following taboo work in the academy: (1) work with a focus on self to evoke emotional resonance with audience; (2) work with an explicit subjectivity—not trying to be objective, but still providing insights to explore the larger world; and (3) social science that includes the arts as part of the empirical process and representation of "findings" for both "self" and "other" discovery.

This chapter will address my pregnancy story in the following way. First, it will provide a brief literature review of the qualitative work on pregnancy and birth stories in recent decades, with a special focus on immigrant mothers. Second, it will explore the use of poetic autoethnography as a powerful tool for social research. Third, the methods and contexts of this study are described. Then, nine poems are presented to help capture the most powerful and heteroglossic moments and scenes and the key themes in my personal pregnancy stories. Finally, borrowed from Hanauer's (2012, 2014, 2015) poetic inquiry approach, I end with a short postscript to reflect on the process and meanings of my poetry writing and poetic autoethnographic research.

## Qualitative Studies on Pregnancy and Birth Stories

As a natural process of human life, pregnancy can have different meanings for different people. According to Simonds et al. (2007):

> Pregnancy is sometimes a contraceptive failure, a side effect of a not very reliable method of birth control. Pregnancy is also the effect of a successful treatment for infertility. Pregnancy is a condition of a woman's body, to be distinguished from ovulation, menstruation, and menopause. Pregnancy is the presence of a man's baby in a woman, as when a man wants a woman to bear him a son to carry on his name.
>
> (p. 4)

Building on research in multiple areas, such as health science, midwifery, feminism, and education, numerous in-depth studies have been done to explore the meaning and experience of pregnancy and birth from diverse approaches. Based on informal interviews with 39 men and women who gave birth from the mid-1980s to the mid-1990s in the United States, Pollock (1999) illustrated the importance of birth stories in her ethnographic masterpiece, *Telling Bodies Performing Birth*: "birth stories put the maternal body—in all its carnal, social, and political plenitude—center stage" (p. 8). Pollock's (1999) book aims to give women a platform to voice topics typically left to the margins of birth discourse, such as "the mother's body, prenatal deaths, sex, conception, genetic counseling" (p. 7), and, therefore, challenge "the discourses that encourage us to think about and practice birth in isolation and so, however unwittingly, to serve prevailing body polities" (p. 19). Two emerging themes resonate across Pollock's (1999) book, as well as throughout pregnancy and birth qualitative studies.

The first theme is to challenge the linear "comic-heroic norm of birth storytelling" (Pollock, 1999, p. 7), which tends to follow a "progressive structure inculcated in prenatal classes and pregnancy handbooks by which planning becomes conception becomes pregnancy becomes a ten-fingers-and-toes birth—the 'nine months and counting' model of birth storytelling" (Pollock, 1999, p. 4). Seftel (2006) further explores nonlinear/nonmainstream birth stories, demonstrating how the arts can serve as a vital tool to help heal pregnancy loss. She articulates that, "rather than seeking out simplified and sanitized points of view, the arts offers a range of experiences—as messy, contrary, and unpredictable as they need to be in order to capture authentic reactions to these emotional complex losses" (p. 30). Here, art is viewed as a kind of therapy in healing pregnancy loss. Hawkins (2015), taking a different approach, uses arts-based research (ABR) through poetic transcription of case-study interview data as a research method to capture the essence of one woman's early pregnancy loss experience. These studies not only investigate the marginal discourse in pregnancy and birth stories but also demonstrate how the arts offer a unique lens to influence emotions and speak to larger audiences.

The second theme in Pollock's (1999) book warns of the powerful trend of medicalization,

> the process by which medical and technical expertise overtook not only both ends of life, birth and death, but changed the way we understand our bodies, making them objects of abstract, anatomical knowledge systems, largely unintelligible except by clinical translation.
>
> (p. 11)

Simonds et al.'s (2007) study further compares the binaries between the medical and midwifery models. Their findings suggest that while the medical model organizes itself around a search for pathology in which the doctor shoulders most responsibility, the midwifery model regards pregnancy as a normal and healthy situation and returns the responsibility to the birthmother herself.

As global immigrant populations continue to grow in recent decades, qualitative researchers have shown a dramatically increasing interest in the lived experiences of pregnancy, birth, and motherhood among immigrant women (e.g., Benza & Liamputtong, 2014; Cross-Sudworth et al., 2015). Benza and Liamputtong (2014) conducted a meta-synthesis of 15 qualitative studies published between 2003 and 2013 related to pregnancy, childbirth, and motherhood experiences for immigrant women, concluding that their many challenges included isolation and loneliness coping with a newborn at home, financial needs associated with pregnancy, social oppression, racial discrimination, disempowerment and negative interactions with health-care givers, lack of recognition of antenatal and postpartum care, lack of familiarity with multiple health providers, and not knowing what to expect during childbirth. While these challenges are quite common in the immigrant pregnancy and birth studies mentioned previously, the theoretical approaches, research methods, and ways of presenting findings that different researchers employed were highly diverse. In a recent study, Vega (2016) employed Coyolxauhqui's silencing pregnancy story as an image to reflect on her own pregnancy experiences as a Chicana mother PhD. According to Vega (2016), Coyolxauhqui's story reminds us of the fragmentation of misogyny we experience physically, spiritually, and intellectually in the ivory tower:

> Physically, women's bodies are policed to not have children during their academic careers. Spiritually, women's emotional and creative pathways for creating knowledge are not validated. And intellectually, their academic knowledge is "required" to produce "good" knowledge, negligent of emotion, creativity and feeling.
>
> (p. 2)

Vega's (2016) self-study provides a unique perspective to explore pregnancy and birth stories in the context of the academic world and delves into the hidden injustice that people already take for granted and, therefore, ignore. As a recent newcomer to the United States pursuing a doctoral degree in education, my goal is to add to these voices, complicating birth story narratives and informing existing health-care practices with pregnant, international women giving birth in the United States.

## Methodological Approach: Poetic Autoethnography

According to Cahnmann-Taylor (Chapter 8)

> the literary, visual, and performing arts offer ways to stretch a researcher's capacities for creativity and knowing, creating a healthy synthesis of approaches to collect, analyze, and represent data in ways that paint a full picture of a heterogeneous movement to improve education.
>
> (p. 84)

As a part of art-based inquiries, poetic inquiry has gained growing interest among qualitative researchers in recent decades. According to McCulliss (2013), using poetic inquiry in research is to:

> incorporate poetry in some way as an analytical device, whether in data collection, as a tool to view data in unique ways that can help yield new insight, or as a way of representing findings to peers and the general public.
>
> (p. 88)

McCulliss (2013) further points out that poetry perhaps gets closer to the essence of qualitative methodology than any other approach in retelling lived experience and allowing for a more in-depth and holistic understanding of a particular group or population. Prendergast (2009) explores the essence of poetic inquiry in a more artful way, stating that "creating poetic inquiry is a performative act, revealing researcher/participants as both masked and unmasked, costumed and bared, liars and truth-tellers, actors and audience, offstage and onstage in the creation of research" (p. xxiii).

Unlike traditional scientific inquiry, which seeks generalizability, in the statistical sense, of the world beyond the research, poetic inquiry seeks "metaphoric generalizability" (Furman, 2007) to connect author and audience. In other words, "while a poem usually starts out with one person's experience, it attempts to move beyond the study of one person to the study of many" and helps "stimulate an empathetic understanding in the reader" (McCulliss, 2013, p. 89). As a result, the clear-cut borderline between "self" and "others" has been blurred and transformed to a contact zone where the "'I' is an 'other,' then; [which] becomes a world of others ... It is 'I' & 'not-I' ... I is infinite. I contains multitudes" (Rothenberg, 1994, p. 524).

With regard to the role of poetry in ethnographic study, Richardson (1998), an anthropologist and poet, elaborates that:

> Poetry, as a special language, is particularly suited for those special, strange, even mysterious moments when bits and pieces suddenly coalesce. These moments arrive with a sharp poignancy in the field, when the ethnographer, away from home and in a strange culture, has a heightened sense of the frailty of being human. In such a sense, poetry appears to be a way of communicating instances when we feel truth has shown its face. Finally, poetry, although a special manner of speaking, may in fact be closer to what it is to be human than more ordinary talk—given that we humans, that is, you and I, are not ordinary facts stored away in nature's warehouse.
>
> (p. 451)

As poetic inquiry gradually gained its legitimacy in ethnography, many researchers adopted autoethnographic poetry to explore personal and sociocultural issues, such as the journey of writing as a healing modality (Blinne, 2010), explorations of researching older expatriate men (Furman, 2015), experiences of living and growing up as a second generation Kindertransport survivor (Hanauer, 2012), transformative effects of poetry and narrative on the person writing it (Maurino, 2016), the trail of forming researcher identity and legitimacy of voice (Naidu, 2014), and the exploration of one's own and others' second-language acquisition (Cahnmann-Taylor, 2016). As a relatively new approach in ethnography, autoethnography is a research method that is "highly personalized, revealing texts in which authors tell stories about their own lived experiences, relating the personal to the culture" (Richardson, 2000, p. 935). The self or "I" in autoethnography can be regarded as a vehicle of research to explore sociocultural phenomena (Furman, 2015). According to Naidu (2014), poetic autoethnography tends to merge "conceptual, cognitive and emotive aspects of human experience. It allows for audiences to concurrently participate in the researcher's experience and make subjectively meaningful interpretations by appealing to the audience as hermeneutic beings" (p. 2).

The current study employs a series of autoethnographic poems in exploring my pregnancy stories as a Chinese PhD student in the United States. The poems are autoethnographic, in that they "explore the researchers (*sic*) connections to broader socio-cultural issues" (Furman, 2015, p. 104). As a poetry lover, I started composing ancient-style Chinese poems in elementary school, translated and published my own bilingual book of poetry during my college years in Beijing, and further connected the dots through taking graduate-level poetry writing courses for creative educators in the United States. Since 2014, I've served as one of the board moderators in the Chinese Ancient-style Poetry Forum, the largest online poetry-writing forum with more than 220,000 registered members. In this way, I keep reading, providing feedback to other poetry writers, and composing and posting my own poems to exchange ideas. Since Chinese is my mother tongue, I can tell the subtle difference between each word and the inexpressible poetic taste behind each line. While my Chinese poems tend to catch every nuance of emotions in life, my English poems follow a completely different path to tell stories and present events.

When I first started writing English poems, I felt my Chinese and English poetry-writing were highly divergent in two different worlds. However, as I went further, I gradually found there was always a poetic heart that could transfer freely across languages and cultures. Although I might not have the "right" word to put in my English poem due to language barriers, my poetic heart helps me capture the "right" moments for poems. In addition, second-language poetry-writing provides additional opportunities for "self-expression and hybridized identity, for cultivating a critical, post-colonial voice, and for reflecting on one's home language and culture in newly critical and complex ways" (Cahnmann-Taylor et al., 2015, p. 22).

This poetic heart also plays a unique role in my academic research through presenting both a "small t" truth—an accurate description of my perspective and experience in reality—and the large "T" truth—seeing the hidden themes and meanings behind the surface, "the depth of feeling and music in the original situation" (Cahnmann-Taylor, 2003, p. 33) "with the eyes of the spirit" (Glesne, 1997, p. 213), which blurs the borderline between the "self" and "others" and provides implications to larger audiences in research and society. During the process of my poetic inquiry in this project, I have used poems to track the chronological "weeks" of my pregnancy, starting from April 2016, and present the stories in different social contexts, such as hospitals in China and the United States, airport customs, and the university classroom. These stories are indeed *my* stories as I experienced them in reality. However, I cannot isolate myself from the voices of "others," as I consistently absorb nutrients from informal chatting with my Chinese and American friends on child-related topics; the talk with female mentors who have balanced academic research and childcare well; reading literature on pregnancy and birth; listening to other mothers' stories who have/don't have similar experiences; and joining online mothers groups in China and the United States to hear mothers' concerns, complaints, different prenatal and postpartum care practices, etc. All these different voices, refracted by diverse historical, sociocultural beliefs, present a highly heteroglossic texture of harsh conflicts and human nature common across cultures, creating a carnival moment for poems. That's the reason why I chose poetic autoethnography to present the findings of this study.

The purpose of this chapter is to speak to a larger audience and contribute to the understanding of immigrant mothers' experiences as a social, cultural, and educational phenomenon, with the hope that by sharing my story, my poems will draw implications for international students and immigrant mothers as well as people working with international students and immigrants in medical-care situations. The poems are presented to explore key themes related to birth and pregnancy stories of immigrant mothers in an academic world. They are not accompanied by interpretive or explanatory texts, "in the spirit of the poetic tradition's call to 'show don't tell.' The poems should speak for themselves" (Furman, 2015, p. 104).

## Pregnancy Stories of a Chinese PhD Student in the United States

*Genesis*
In the second semester of my PhD,
my mom started sending me

cute babies' photos.
It became an eternal topic
for our weekly Skype meetings
across the Pacific Ocean.
"Hurry up! You are almost 30!"

My father-in-law formally talked
with my husband:
"When do you plan to have a baby?"
"顺其自然 (Shunqiziran)."—Let nature take its course.
(S-I-L-E-N-C-E)
"Don't take any contraception."
"Um."

"Do you have any kids?"
The seventh time
I heard this question
from my Chinese & American friends,
I knew a due date
truly existed
not just for final papers.

*Week 5: The First Prenatal Visit*
The baby is 100% Made in USA.
But when I got the sweet news,
I was in my hometown—
Shenyang, a big city in northeast China.

"Patient Zhang Kuo, please go to No. 5 consulting room."
called by an electronic voice
from the queuing machine.

The doctor glanced at my test result.
"You are pregnant.

Keep it or have an abortion?"
My big smile became awkward.
Hastily I said, "I want it! I want it!"
"Then you can go home now."

As the machine called the next patient,
I complained to my mom,
"She is so rude and cold!!!"

"Why did you say that?
Isn't it the normal way
a doctor should be?"

*Week 9: Back to America*
I didn't tell the Chicago custom official
how my Great Grandpa ploughed
in Shandong Province
with his foot-bound wife.

Nor that
Grandpa braved his journey to the Northeast,[1]
served as a coal miner, then
a local official in the Communist Party.

And that my parents,
like the phoenixes rising from a chicken coop,
became first generation college students after the Culture
Revolution,
that they settled down in the capital of Liaoning Province.

Though the official claimed to know all my stories:
Lagos for 8 months in 2010, 4 entries to Beijing,
US state of Georgia 5 times since 2011 …,
and how many more years, months and days I can legally stay.

*Welcome back!.*
He smiled,
returned
a smuggler's passport.

He didn't know I was carrying
a tiny undocumented immigrant
& US citizen
in my secret garden.

One who'll speak a language that
belongs to.
*evil capitalists.*
in my grandpa's eyes.

*Week 11: The First Prenatal Visit in the US*

The front office lady gave me
a small white paper package
and a transparent urine bottle.

"Be sure to wipe before you do it,
then put it in the box on the wall."
"Uh, do you mean I should wipe … my hands?"
"Oh, no." The lady laughed.
She put her hand around her privates.

"Wipe here."

"Ohhh! I see." I laughed, too.
But still, I missed the latter part of her words.
Holding the bottle full of urine,
I searched around the passage.
"It is just there, on the wall, inside the restroom."
Another lady helped me out.
Later, I told my husband,
"I really feel I'm stupid here."
"Don't worry!
It is just the first time."

*Week 20: Boy or Girl?*
It is against the law for a doctor
to reveal the gender
of a baby in China.
But if you bribe
or know someone who knows the doctor,
it's no longer a big deal.

My parents didn't know what I was
until the day I was born.
After hearing the "bad" news,
my grandma stayed in hospital.
A lifelong cold war broke out
between my mom and her in-laws.

断子绝孙 (duan zi jue sun)—
die without sons and grandsons
the most venomous curse to Chinese people.
I am the terminator

who denied my father's right
to be buried in the ancestral grave.

"Would you like to know the baby's gender?"
asked by my sonographer.
"Yes, please."
The proud sign of a male
towered on the screen.
"You see! It's a boy!"

My parents-in-law got the "good" news
in a Skype call.
"Oh! A BIG Grandson!!!"
They grinned from ear to ear.
"如你所愿吧? (Ru ni suo yuan ba?)"—Is it as you wish?

"没有啦。(Mei you la.) Nono, boys and girls are the same."

*2 Days after Week 20: A Phone Call*
"Hello, this is Athens Regional Midwifery.
You need to make an appointment with Dr. Godwin
—a maternal-fetal specialist."
"??? Okay … I need to see Dr. Godwin?
But, but for what?"
"Our doctor rechecked your ultrasound
and found some problems."
"Problem??? What problem?!!
They said everything was normal!"
"Well, it might turn out to be normal.
But … the doctor found
intracardiac foci, multiple choroid nexus cysts and prominent kidneys
. … So, you need to see Dr. Godwin."
(??????????????????????????)
"… kidney …?"
"Yes."
"O … Okay … So … what is the time and address?"
"It's at 10 am on Sep. 27th.
The address is 700 Sunset Drive, Suite 301."
"Sweet? What is sweet?"
"That is the doctor's room number."
"How do you spell that?"
"S-U-I-T-E. Suite."
"Ah … Oh … Okay. Thank you."
"Do you have any other questions?"
(Yes!!! But is it ridiculous to ask her
to repeat every word slowly?)
"No … I don't have questions."
"Bye."

*Week 23: Dr. Godwin*
Not all pregnancy stories
have a happy ending.
But when the sun started glowing,
inside a half-ripen fluffy melon,
you can hardly connect it
to something abnormal.

For three weeks,
I touched the gentle but strong kicking
and teared at night

I hated hearing "Congratulations",
felt so hurt to see my Korean friend
holding his little girl's hand downstairs

I dig into the Internet for all the worst.
*Edwards syndrome, stillborn ....*
and presented a fake smile in the Skype meetings

I must be ice-cold and ghost-like
when I lay on Dr. Godwin's table
"You see this big white area in his head?"

"Yes." I looked at the screen.
and my heart sank to somewhere *abysmal.*
Isn't funny I suddenly remember this GRE word?

"I didn't see anything significant.
All the cysts have disappeared.
IT'S A HAPPY BOY!!!"

*Week 30: Antenatal Education*

No music.
No story.
You use Bakhtinian dialogism
to babble with Vygotsky.

You make me feel less guilty
to sleep too much.
We catch up on the papers,
and celebrate co-authorship.

You kick a rhythm in class discussion,
and draw a hill inside my belly.
I know you love the professor's voice
and art-based inquires.

## Postscript for the Second Edition

When I finished the first draft of this chapter, I was 32 weeks pregnant. I plan to continue my poem writing during the whole process of pregnancy and birth. This autoethnographic poetic investigation helps capture unspoken but inerasable moments and offers a "liberating and transformative effect" (Maurino, 2016, p. 208) on me as I have struggled hard as a pregnant international PhD student in the huge sociocultural gaps of pregnancy-related practices and beliefs between China and the United States. The poems can also be a treasure for my incoming son, who will inevitably become "a banana person"—the stereotyped

Asian American who appears "yellow" on the outside, but inside "white"—at least, to some extent. I have felt the need to help my son understand the cultural and family origins and experiences, aspects of gender, language, and culture that occurred during his gestation. In addition, the exploration of my personal story and the insights conveyed by the poems serve as a means of speaking to the larger world, raising questions to the marginalized and often-overlooked discourses that immigrant moms in the academy must face, such as the explicit and implicit pressure of baby plans, barriers in cross-cultural communication, differences and isolation in medical practices, the inheriting and fracturing of cultural origins, and gender discrimination.

My hope is that the empirical process of writing these poems reflexively as a form of inquiry can contribute to the understanding of the immigrant mothers' experience as a social, cultural, and educational phenomenon, one which requires the language of poetry to express into new futures.

## Postscript for the Third Edition

Re-reading the chapter I wrote six years ago feels like revisiting a different chapter of my life. In the past six years, my life has undergone dramatic changes: from being a pregnant woman to becoming a mother of three, from a PhD student to a tenure-track Assistant Professor, and from a student-visa holder to a U.S. permanent resident. My family has moved across the country, from Georgia to Colorado, then Vermont, and now to upstate New York.

Since writing this chapter, I continued my research on the lived experiences of international graduate student mothers, culminating in my dissertation, *Learning the 'Language' of Motherhood as International Graduate Student Mothers* (e.g., Zhang, 2020, 2021). This study involved 11 international graduate student mothers who gave birth to their first children during their studies in the United States. I employed a Bakhtinian theoretical framework, discourse studies, and poetry writing to explore the diverse voices in these mothers' stories of pregnancy, birth, and motherhood, and how they developed their ongoing, dynamic, multifaceted, and embodied "language" of motherhood.

Continuing my poetic inquiry, I have made my voice heard through published poems that focus on cross-cultural motherhood, motherhood in academia, immigration, and linguistic microaggressions. As a teacher educator, I integrate the arts and ABR into teacher education programs, and explore how arts-based learning creates vibrant intercultural exchanges of intellectual thought and supports culturally sustaining education.

The experience of pregnancy and motherhood has profoundly transformed me, revealing the intersectionality of identities and the complexities of disadvantage. It has led me to research areas I had never previously considered, deepened my understanding of new cultures and languages, and allowed me to re-experience childhood in another country. This growth has enriched my ability to connect with and better understand my students. The role of motherhood exhausts but also fuels me in my life, research, and teaching.

Finally, I'd like to share a recently published poem as a poetic postscript to my chapter.

*When My Kids Start to Speak English (Zhang, 2025)*

It begins.
I gently remind them:
"Speak Chinese at home."

They reply, "Hao ba (okay)."

But as they race their cars,
laughter spills through their room—
strings of English pearl again.

A letter from school arrives:
my second grader has met
the criteria to exit ELL services.

I fold the good news,
tuck it quietly
into a drawer.

## Note

1 Brave journey to the Northeast: 闯关东 (Chuang Guandong), literally "Crashing into Guandong," is descriptive of the rush into Northeast of the Han Chinese population, especially from Shandong peninsular, during the hundred-year period starting at the last half of the 19th century. This region, the traditional homeland of the ruling Manchus, was previously closed to settlement by Han Chinese during the Manchu Qing Dynasty.

## References


Bakhtin, M. M. (1981). *The dialogic imagination: Four essays by M. M. Bakhtin* (M. Holquist, Ed. & C. Emerson & M. Holquist, Trans.). University of Texas Press.

Bakhtin, M. M. (1984). *Rabelais and his world* (H. Iswolsky, Trans.). Indiana University.

Benza, S., & Liamputtong, P. (2014). Pregnancy, childbirth and motherhood: A meta-synthesis of the lived experiences of immigrant women. *Midwifery*, *30*, 575–584. https://doi.org/10.1016/j.midw.2014.03.005

Blinne, K. C. (2010). Writing my life: A narrative and poetic-based autoethnography. *Journal of Poetry Therapy*, *23*(3), 183–190. https://doi.org/10.1080/08893675.2010.498214

Cahnmann-Taylor, M. (2003). The craft, practice, and possibility of poetry in educational research. *Educational Researcher*, *32*(3), 29–36. https://doi.org/10.3102/0013189X032003029

Cahnmann-Taylor, M. (2016). *Imperfect tense*. Whitepoint Press.

Cahnmann-Taylor, M., Zhang, K., Bleyle, S. J., & Hwang, Y. (2015). "Searching for an entrance" and finding a two-way door: Using poetry to create East-West contact zones in TESOL teacher education. *International Journal of Education & the Arts*, *16*(21), 1–29. Retrieved from http://www.ijea.org/v16n21/

Cross-Sudworth, F., Williams, M., & Gardosi, J. (2015). Perinatal deaths of migrant mothers: Adverse outcomes from unrecognized risks and substandard care factors. *British Journal of Midwifery*, *23*(19), 734–740. https://doi.org/10.12968/bjom.2015.23.10.734

Evans, E., & Grant, C. (2008). Introduction. In E. Evans, &. C. Grant (Eds.), *Mama, PhD: Women write about motherhood and academic life* (pp. xvii–xxv). Rutgers University Press.

Furman, R. (2007). Poetry and narrative as qualitative data: Explorations into existential theory. *The Indo-Pacific Journal of Phenomenology*, *71*(1), 1–9.

Furman, R. (2015). Autoethnographic exploration of researching older expatriate men: Magnifying emotion using the research pantoum. *Creative Approaches to Research*, *8*(3), 102–114.

Glesne, C. (1997). That rare feeling: Re-presenting research through poetic transcription. *Qualitative Inquiry*, *3*(2), 202–221. https://doi.org/10.1177/107780049700300204

Hanauer, D. I. (2012). Growing up in the unseen shadow of the Kindertransport: A poetic narrative autoethnography. *Qualitative Inquiry*, *18*(10), 845–851. https://doi.org/10.1177/1077800412456960

Hanauer, D. I. (2014). Experiencing the Blitz: A poetic representation of a childhood in wartime London. *Qualitative Inquiry*, *20*(5), 584–599. https://doi.org/10.1177/1077800413489

Hanauer, D. I. (2015). Being in the Second Iraq War: A poetic ethnography. *Qualitative Inquiry*, *21*(1), 83–106. https://doi.org/10.1177/1077800414542697

Hawkins, J. M. (2015). Stunned: Ectopic pregnancy loss. *Health Communication*, *30*, 419–422. https://doi.org/10.1080/10410236.2014.891454

Kuperberg, A. (2009). Review: Women with PhDs speak out about motherhood. *Women's Studies Quarterly*, *37*(3/4), 311–316. https://dx.doi.org/10.1353/wsq.0.0187

Maurino, J. P. (2016). Transformations of the self: A narrative and poetic based autoethnography. *Journal of Poetry Therapy*, *29*(4), 207–221. https://doi.org/10.1080/08893675.2016.1215376

McCulliss, D. (2013). Poetic inquiry and multidisciplinary qualitative research. *Journal of Poetry Therapy*, *26*(2), 83–114. https://doi.org/10.1080/08893675.2013.794536

Monosson, E. (2008). Introduction. In. E. Monosson (Ed.), *Motherhood, the elephant in the laboratory: Women scientists speak out* (pp. 1–20). ILR Press/Cornell University Press.

Naidu, T. (2014). Autoethnographic realization of legitimacy of voice: A poetic trail of forming researcher identity. *Forum: Qualitative Social Research*, *15*(1), 1–19.

Pollock, D. (1999). *Telling bodies performing birth: Everyday narratives of childbirth*. Columbia University Press.

Prendergast, M. (2009). Introduction: The phenomena of poetry in research. In. M. Prendergast, C. Leggo, & P. Sameshima (Eds.), *Poetic inquiry: Vibrant voices in the social sciences* (pp. xxxv–xxxvii). Sense.

Richardson, L. (2000). Writing: A method of inquiry. In. N. K. Denzin. &. Y. S. Lincoln (Eds.), *Handbook of qualitative research* (2nd ed., pp. 923–948). Sage.

Richardson, M. (1998). Poetics in the field and on the page. *Qualitative Inquiry*, *4*(4), 451–462.

Rothenberg, J. (1994). "Je est un autre": Ethnopoetics and the poet as other. *American Anthropologist*, *96*(3), 523–524.

Seftel, L. (2006). *Grief unseen: Healing pregnancy loss through the arts*. Jessica Kingsley.

Simonds, W., Rothman, B. K., & Norman, B. M. (2007). *Laboring on: Birth in transition in the United States*. Routledge.

Vega, C. (2016). Coyolxauhqui: Challenging patriarchy by re-imagining her birth story. *InterActions: UCLA Journal of Education and Information Studies*, *12*(1), 1–7. https://doi.org/10.5070/D4121028567

Volosinov, V. N. (1976). Appendix I: Discourse in life and discourse in art (concerning sociological poetics). In N. Bruss (Ed.), *Freudianism: A Marxist critique* (I. R. Titunik., Trans., pp. 93–116). Academic Press.

Zhang, K. (2020). Learning the "language" of motherhood as international graduate student mothers: A poetic ethnography. *Art/Research International: A Transdisciplinary Journal*, *5*(2), 309–344. https://doi.org/10.18432/ari29539

Zhang, K. (2021). Embrace the uncontrolled nature of poetry writing: A poetic ethnographic study on international graduate student mothers' intercultural discourses. *Qualitative Inquiry*, 27(3–4), 429–443. https://doi.org/10.1177/1077800420920696

Zhang, K. (2025). When my kids start to speak English. *The MacGuffin*, *40*(3), 155.

Chapter 39

# Conclusion

## The Tensions of Arts-Based Research in Education Reconsidered

*Richard Siegesmund and Melisa Cahnmann*

A complex array of goals guides inquiry. The product of inquiry—which education scholars often call "research"—can be used for a diverse range of purposes. Different methods of inquiry, guided by different goals, produce different products, which serve different needs. A hammer is a very efficient tool that, when handled skillfully, produces remarkable results. However, it is a very poor tool—even an inappropriate choice—if the task is removing a countersunk screw. Therefore, the conduct of inquiry requires recognizing the most appropriate tool for the job the researcher seeks to accomplish.

As few real-life situations correspond to a multiple-choice question, choosing a method of inquiry is not as simple as correctly distinguishing between a nail and a screw. Education, for example, is a complex lived exchange involving human beings. Complexity exponentially increases with interactions between growing numbers of individuals. Thus, attempting to grasp the magnitude and character of complexity—be it a single individual or individuals in relationship to others (i.e., a classroom)—is an initial task in research.

Assessing the magnitude of complexity begins by naming questions. This is no small feat: to bring what has not been said into sound, image, language, and movement. The act of naming itself, may exclude critical aspects of the character of complexity and thus unintentionally diminish magnitude. Staking out the territory to be explored is risky business. Recognizing the character of complexity within these inquiry questions is the second task. Constructing a method for investigating the identified complexity is the third task. This investigation can take one of two forms: resolving a problem or challenging the imagination.

The first response frames complexity as a solvable problem. From this point of view, inquiry exacts clarity. However, in this second response, complexity is a challenge to imagine something new: to cast a wider net of what our mind might hold. From this perspective, inquiry seeks to conceive something that has been heretofore outside of comprehension. Both paths of inquiry produce research. Neither path demands a quantitative or qualitative approach. Either works. Both paths allow for hybrid forms that might include traditionally conceived scientific methods as well as arts-based methods. This collection of writings seeks to demonstrate how arts-based methods expand the researcher's toolkit, adding paintbrushes and line breaks to our box of hammers and nails, fieldnotes, interviews, graphs, charts, algorithms, and maps. In particular, we want to show how arts-based research (ABR) helps us see more of the world than what we had previously seen or considered.

It is important to think about what is the right tool for the job. Therefore, we take up the five tensions of ABR in education that Eisner outlines in Chapter 10 of this book which appeared in the first edition in 2008 and still remain relevant today: (1) The imaginative vs. the referentially clear; (2) The particular vs. the general; (3) Aesthetics of beauty vs.

DOI: 10.4324/9781003412892-39

verisimilitude of truth; (4) Better questions vs. definitive answers; and (5) Metaphoric novelty vs. literal utility. We reflect on each of these points and each chapter in this collection to illuminate how contributors to this volume have addressed them and how these questions have perhaps evolved since the first edition. In turn, this generates greater clarity regarding the construction of effective works of ABR.

## The Imaginative vs. the Referentially Clear

ABR offers the layered versus the linear, the cacophonous versus the discursive, and the ambiguous versus the aphoristic. What is the advantage of pursuing the direction of the imagination? First, it is an achievement of mind to recognize the fullness and complexity of the layered, the cacophonous, and the ambiguous. Comprehending complexity is not a given. In fact, the tendency, today it seems, is to favor simpler, less effortful ways of thinking and problem-solving, even when more creative and complex approaches might be more accurate. Our sensory systems are not recording devices that take a full and complete imprint of the world around us. We must learn to see. Perception itself—before analysis—is cognitive (Arnheim, 1969). Semiotic theory refers to the sensory bank of pre-analytic sensory impressions as the *experiential store* (Suhor, 1984). These impressions may be coded into meaning through language, numbers, images, music, or any other symbol system. However, inquiry is not limited to coding the experiential store into meaning. A goal of inquiry can be building and expanding the experiential store itself. For example, this expansion of experience is an explicit goal of a/r/tography and the field of research creation.

Attempting to comprehend complexity is effortful. Comprehension is not reduction: reducing entanglements to a linear string of reasoning and taming them through categorization. One dives into complexity. That pool is never fully mapped or known. You plunge into an immersive experience. You grapple to make sense of it, starting from where you are and making sense as you go. Natalie LeBlanc (Chapter 23) allows sense to guide her as she walks through abandoned schools. Her methods do not include a predetermined check-list of things to photograph. She strives to be attentive to what is neglected and derelict. She attempts to see what we haven't seen. Her questions address that to which we ceased paying attention. Her work is arts-based as she allows the beauty she finds in abandoned schools to guide her to recognize what has gone unnoticed. Barbara Bickel (Chapter 5), Rita Irwin and Stephanie Springgay (Chapter 18), and Nick Sousanis (Chapter 33) provide examples of building an experiential store—that they go on to analyze further through both language and image. Monica Prendergast and George Belliveau (Chapter 28) speak to the transgressive aspects of experience, and the abject activities from which one may choose to turn their eyes: the "noise" that seemingly distracts from our good works.

Carl Leggo (Chapter 24) and Mathu Subramanian (Chapter 35) refer to the attending to and nurturing of this experiential store as the ecology of personal and professional experience at home and away from home. Just as our natural environments can be denuded and impoverished, so too our experiential store can be desiccated and withered. This is not a problem of aesthetic appreciation; it is a problem of thinking. If the experiential store is shrunken, then there is a limited data bank from which to encode meaning.

However, it is important in education to avoid one's own cultural prejudice guiding a rush to judgment about the quality of another's experiential store. This may occur when dealing with children who come from different cultural or economic backgrounds than one's own, or who have a particular medical diagnosis. These children often have great skills or just different ways of problem solving. This may come from experiences associated with one's life being in constant precarity with limited access to resources for survival. ABR can help us open our hearts minds, so that in learning to listen, we might be changed. The ABR performances practices discussed by McGovern (Chapter 27) include methods that allow scholars not only "to write about others but also to embody and be changed by them" (p. 282). Consider Kristina Lyons's (Chapter 26) poem "Upon Traveling to Nosara" (p. 272). This poem records the experiential store of the researcher traveling by public bus in Costa Rica, yet this aspect of experience is normally stripped from our academic methods of reporting. What do we lose in understanding the complexity of field research, in a fuller understanding of another place, or even in our sensitivity for training new researchers for the challenges of inquiry when such evidence is silenced?

Nevertheless, the educational researcher is not deploying arts-based inquiry to portray complexity as a kind of Rorschach test on which the reader can decode meaning from inkblots. Here, John Dewey offers important insights regarding complexity and empiricism. Dewey too acknowledged this bank of experience. He claimed that in this mental realm of consciousness—before symbolic thought—we think in terms of the relations of qualities (Dewey, 1934/1989, p. 51) which possess felt intuitive meaning. Eisner (1994) observes that through numbers, language, images, music, and our body we express the felt meanings found in the relationships of qualities through forms of representation. Inscribing relationships of qualities in forms of representation such as poems, paintings, and dramatic performance demonstrates skill in qualitative reasoning (Eisner, 2002). Through inscription of forms of representation, qualitative reasoning becomes publicly accessible. We can then discuss these varieties of representations in language. Thus, imagination expands discourse. In turn, discourse holds the promise of improving the referentially clear by helping us to see the structure of qualitative reasoning (Eisner, 2002).

The philosopher Ludwig Wittgenstein (1953/1973) maintained that the poet (and by implication any artist), could build qualities of relationship into complex meanings. Language could not guarantee a concise, analytic, and definitive translation of aesthetic meanings. Different readers would have different words to interpret the intentions of the poet. However, Wittgenstein maintained that close readings, grounded in the work itself, and not the fantastical extrapolations of the reader, would share a family resemblance of meaning. Through these family resemblances, meaningful communication that expands understanding can occur. In any given artwork what is meaningful would not entail a linear analytic formula, but a constrained circle of communication. Elliot Eisner (1991) also saw such informed communities of agreement as a form of validation. Therefore, ABR is not open to any interpretation. The validation of interpretation requires informed judgment. The researcher perennially plays with the tension between an open and yet inscribed circle.

A distinguishing feature of arts-based inquiry is that the researchers seldom make an *art-for-art's-sake* (discussed by Cahnmann, Chapter 8) claim that their work is beyond analysis. More than conventional artists, arts-based researchers often explain their work and offer cues as to how to read their representations in relationships to social science. For example, consider the Talmudic-like use of endnotes in the work by Douglas Gosse (Chapter 13). In Johnny Saldaña's theatrical work (Chapter 31), slide projections supply important orienting cues to how the creative text is addressing a social-science concern. Adrie Kusserow furnishes an introduction that explains the sociological problem of Sudanese refugee resettlement that she addresses at the beginning of her poem "Lost Boy" (Chapter 22).

Traditionally, because the dramatist, poet, painter, or composer were not employing discursive, referentially clear language to communicate, they were considered incapable of doing so. Therefore, it was the task of the dramaturge to help the audience learn about the context of the playwright, the literary critic to help make the craft in a poem or piece of fiction more clear, or the art critic to interpret the visual to an uncomprehending public. Arts-based inquiry suggests, as Tom Barone (2001) claims, that the trained researcher is capable of playing "two games at once" (p. 171). The external critic is no longer necessary. The trained artist can assume this role. The arts-based researcher can both create and critique, challenge and explain. This is core to understanding of the term scholartistry.

Even as the researcher assumes the mantle of both artist and critic, ultimately, a question arises over the concept of clarity itself. The Polish–British sociologist and philosopher Zygmunt Bauman (1992) appealed to the aesthetic concept of *freischwebend*—which literally means, to float freely or hover above—as a critical step in the sequence of inquiry. Knowing requires moments of not knowing: a state of being lost in order to find. It also suggests that not everything is knowable, and that wisdom distinguishes between what we can positively affect and what is beyond our grasp. This is the aesthetic foundation of Barone's call (Chapter 2) for epistemological humility in research. *Freischwebend* suggests that clarity is the recognition of complexity, and not every aspect of complexity is solvable. To see complexity is a challenge for research as is distinguishing between what can and cannot be changed. We cannot and should not change Africa's roar in a young man (Kusserow, Chapter 22). We must struggle to hear and hold Jesusa's laugh (Jenoure, Chapter 20). In this sense, the tension between the imaginative and the referentially clear is inherent and critical to the conduct of ABR.

## The Particular vs. the General

The intellectual promise of arts-based methods is that they not only allow the researcher to work with the symbolic tools of words and numbers but also expand the researcher's palette to allow attention to the relationships of qualities (Dewey, 1934/1989) in data creation, collection, analysis, and reporting. A quality might be the solidity or transparency of a mass, the rhythmic intensity of meter and beat, or the shape of gesture made by the body in space and time. Our awareness of qualities comes from attending to the particular. We must pay attention to note a quality. Paying attention is the habit of a disciplined mind.

Mass, rhythm, and shape have no significance in themselves, but relationships of qualities of mass, rhythm, and shape have the power to communicate feeling and emotion (Damasio, 1999; Shusterman, 1999). They communicate nonverbally through the flesh. We feel them. Our capacity to think in relationships of qualities does not replace symbolic processing. It contextualizes it. We see deeper. Our understandings are more resonant. Damasio (1999) demonstrates how rationality is situated within felt reaction. If we cannot situate rationality within the proper qualitative relationships, then rationality is impaired. This is a problem for education that demands research. As Kristina Jacobsen demonstrates in Chapter 19, such research can take the form of being a singer and a lap steel guitar player in an otherwise all-male country band in the Navajo lands of Arizona and New Mexico.

By attending to qualities, such as Kristina Lyons's poem about a breakdown in the road (Chapter 26), the researcher bears witness to the complexity of a moment and its resonance in society. Human emotions and feelings are conveyed. Is this poetic rendering merely a reporting or is it illuminating? Answering this question points to a profound difference between how arts-based inquiry or traditional research methods conceptualize their respective audiences.

Traditional social science often conceives of the researcher as the intellectual authority. In this view, research offers prescribed treatments that the readers—the audience—are to explicitly follow in order to obtain the described benefits. The procedures for creating a sample from which to generalize allow the researcher to communicate to the reader the level of confidence the reader can anticipate for receiving the benefits described in the research if procedures are followed. Thus, generalizability views the audience as an essentially passive recipient of the researcher's found wisdom.

Aesthetic theory offers an alternative to generalizability. In his early twentieth-century criticism of cinema, the cultural critic Walter Benjamin (1939/2003) considered the shifting role of the audience from passive appreciator of a fixed knowable meaning in a work of art, to a dynamic interactant in which individuals and groups create their own meaning and response. Echoing Benjamin, Barone (Chapter 2) argues that a virtue of excellent ABR is its accessibility to a broad audience. Much like Benjamin's critique of cinema, Barone (Chapter 2) goes on to argue that qualitative ABR has the capacity to resonate in the public imagination and thus affect serious social and policy change. This change is not achieved by convincing the audience through a numeric confidence ratio that the research is correct, but by inviting members of the audience to apply the insights of arts-based inquiry to their own lives: to be engrossed. Instead of viewing the audience as a blank slate which receives and records the researchers' meaning, Barone envisions an audience that is an active participant in authoring meaning along with the researcher. Thus, the test for generalizability in ABR is its ability to both widen a circle of conversation and to ask better questions, what Barone (Chapter 2) calls *conspiratorial conversations*. Such an effort is seen in Omi Osun Joni Jones's work (Chapter 21) as her collaborative scholarship draws attention to experiences in the academy as an African American woman; in Douglas Gosse's (Chapter 13) narrative attention to layers of marginal identity among gay and lesbian youth in Newfoundland; and in the performative work of Petula Sik-Ying Ho, Celia Hoi-Yan Chan, and Sui-Ting Kong (Chapter 15) as forms of political protest in Hong Kong. Communities form through such conversations. From these communities, social action may emerge. Thus, ABR might aspire to engaging social change. However, the methods of change are different from traditional research, which applies change top-down through the intellectual authority of the researcher. ABR seeks change from the bottom-up through grassroots circles of conversation. As Barone (2001) has noted, the person who did most to change the child labor laws in Great Britain in the nineteenth century was an author of fiction: Charles Dickens.

Qualitative research has traditionally challenged the terminology of social-science research. Alan Peshkin (1988) questioned objectivity as an undisputed standard in research. His research added subjectivity to the toolkit of inquiry. Similarly, generalizability may be a term that applies only to particular forms of research. In *The Enlightened Eye*, Eisner (1991) proposed the term *consensual validation* to replace mechanistic definitions of generalizability. A work of ABR will attain consensual validation if informed audiences carefully discuss and validate the work. Did a data-poem or ethnodrama initiate broadening dialogues? Do these dialogues improve upon conversations of the past? Had the ABR allowed people to understand complexity more fully, look more closely, and consider aspects of reality that had previously gone unnoticed? Tom Barone (Chapter 2) pushes this concept by asking ABR to achieve a standard of critical persuasiveness in which the work is compelling enough to begin a conversation. Omi Osun Joni Jones (Chapter 21) suggests a standard of collective autoethnography where the work engenders a deep empathetic understanding that generates dialogue. Irwin and Springgay (Chapter 18) remind us that a deep sense of responsibility must guide these standards.

For example, all of these arts-based standards are present in Douglas Gosse's story of queer youth in Newfoundland. The research opens up the landscape. It brings to our attention a story that needs to be told. It helps us to see a portion of lived experience that previously may have been invisible to us. It is persuasive and vulnerable. It is a story of the particular, yet Gosse's work resonates with stories of queer youth around North America, from Newfoundland, Canada to Columbus, Georgia in the United States and perhaps elsewhere around the world. From this story, readers in education and other related fields may be able to act with greater understanding. Our perception and sensitivity to the world is increased.

The task of ABR is, as the poet William Blake described it, "to see the world in a grain of sand." The particular becomes research when it advances understanding (Barone & Eisner, 1997); an investigation of the particular, whose sole goal is to produce aesthetic pleasure, is not research. Therefore, ABR negotiates the tension of finding the resonance that provokes widening and deeper conversations out of the particular. The aesthetic provokes new questions. It does not close down conversation by providing a summative conclusion. Great works will prove the point. Traditional generalizability is not an applicable issue.

## Aesthetics of Beauty vs. Verisimilitude of Truth

In the work of Joanne Elvy (Chapter 11), three women confront us. From a formal aesthetic perspective, these photographs are exceptional. They exploit the full value range of a gray scale, moving from stark white to the deepest black. The contrapposto of the women's bodies subtly connects these women to the traditions of antiquity as much as the framing also situates these individuals in the present. These images are the work of an artist who is skilled with the camera and the medium of black-and-white photography. A museum might exhibit these works without explanatory text. However, aesthetic beauty is not the sole purpose of the work. Aesthetic beauty is a tool that Elvy uses to draw the reader into looking closer at Cuban women's lives 40 years after the revolution. It is a tool for starting a conversation.

In Elvy's case, this is a conversation about dignity and the transformative power of education. These women are giving testimony. Elvy is employing her aesthetic powers to honor the stories of education that these women are telling. She does not intend the text to furnish a full discursive explanation. The text is only enough to orient the viewer and redirect attention back into the photography. To paraphrase Michael Polanyi (1967), the image tells more than words can say. Perhaps, too, in the case of ABR, words help say more than what is communicated through the images alone. Similarly, in the work of Natalie LeBlanc (Chapter 23), Jorge Lucero (Chapter 25), and Nick Sousanis (Chapter 33), the images stand alone without captions. One cannot not turn to a label to try to understand what one is looking at; these authors are asking the reader to perceive.

Eisner refers to the verisimilitude of truth because science too can only make its best guess as to what truth is. What is true today could change tomorrow (Kuhn, 1970). In statistics, we discard outliers because they muddy the picture. However, what do we lose when we discard a specific case in order to make the numbers work? What have we chosen not to see and dismiss as insignificant? Science can shift when a reorientation of vision discovers that what was once deemed as irrelevant suddenly becomes crucial. Multiple authors in this edition speak to how the outlier response can often shed critical insight into what we deem to be normal.

Arts-based researchers often look explicitly for outliers. What was the case that did not fit the data pattern? Why did we want all data to belong to the pattern in the first place? Barone (Chapter 2) reminds us that aesthetic rendering of truth often disrupts the master narratives in our midst and produces an alternative to consider. In this way, arts-based researchers, like many qualitative researchers, play with "truth" when they excerpt an interview text—only arts-based researchers might go further: breaking lines, creating composite characters, crafting a data-poem. Conventional scientific inquiry can and often does manipulate perceptions of data as well—changing the ways in which data are analyzed and presented. A great difference may be that ABR is more likely to claim its inventions, whereas more conventional inquiry designs may be more likely to hide them.

In the eighteenth century, Immanuel Kant (1790/1987) proposed that the purpose of the disruption caused by aesthetic beauty created a freefall of the imagination. In this freefall, old categories of thinking would be shattered. The mind would generate new categories that would encompass these new ideas. In this manner, rationality renews itself and does not stagnate or become ossified. For Kant, the aesthetic and imaginative were critical to rational inquiry. Over a century later, Einstein observed that a science that was limited by the scientific method was ultimately impoverished and sterile (Holton, 1996). ABR is a structured response to Kant's aesthetic theory and Einstein's challenge to the imagination. Thus, it is integral to the highest traditions of Western rationality.

## Better Questions vs. Definitive Answers

Ruth Behar (1996) speaks of making herself a vulnerable observer. This requires setting aside privilege and power and assuming a stance that Barone calls epistemological humility. As discussed earlier, this assumes a different kind of relationship with one's research participants and with readers of research. It is no longer a process of telling; it is a process of sharing and listening. The researcher is inviting questions and new voices into her "poetic anthropology" (Behar, Chapter 3).

How we listen can be complex. Kathy Roulston, Roy Legette, Monica DeLoach, and Celeste Buckhalter (Chapter 30) challenge our conventional ways of listening by juxtaposing how we listen while creating a piece of music in a performance, to how we listen in the conduct of qualitative research. By drawing us into the challenging experience of performing music, the authors seek to develop a greater empathetic understanding of the difficulty of conducting research and the challenge of preparing teachers who are critical, reflective practitioners in music education. By asking the audience to become performers—something they have not been trained to do—they duplicate the experience of how we ask teachers to conduct research into their own practice—which, similarly, up until this point in their education, they have not been trained to do. The anxiety that the audience shares in suddenly being asked to become musical performers replicates the anxiety that teachers have when suddenly asked to become researchers. Thus, the work seeks to engage the audience in a shared process of questioning and answering. This differs from traditional research where the researcher is the all-knowing vehicle of analysis.

Importantly, the questions raised in art do not require a rush to form. As Jorge Lucero observes (Chapter 26), there are "gestures, inquiries, and energies" that are in play before something coalesces into a definitive answer. By focusing attention on to what Dewey

(1934/1989) called a quest for the organization of energies, ABR eschews a rush to judgment that not only holds the promise of better questions but can also reveal the fault lines in our supposedly definitive answer.

## Metaphoric Novelty vs. Literal Utility

Good research tells a story. Stories differ in their emphases on the prosaic and poetic. Stories may be dry and technical, or they may be lively and imaginative. However, all stories have a narrative thread, and metaphors frequently furnish the framework that sustains the theme. Literal utility requires a good story. One cannot win the hearts and minds of audiences to implement research-driven change if you don't have a convincing narrative.

New metaphors allow our thoughts to shift and fold. New associations emerge (Lakoff & Johnson, 1980). Metaphors provide ways of understanding an issue by comparing it to a parallel image/expression from a different, already familiar reality. Metaphors help us conceptualize the conduct of research. Thus, metaphoric thinking of all kinds is critical to the utility of research.

But while all research that seeks utility requires narrative and metaphor, not all research requires utility. The concept that research has utility is based on a metaphor that associates education with industrial manufacturing (Tyack & Hansot, 1982). Through this view, research affords precisely calibrated equipment and tools that facilitate the highest level of production (i.e., learning) for the lowest cost. In the utilitarian concept of research, human beings are a random collection of gemstones: each properly categorized and efficiently tooled through the proper sequential treatment that produces the greatest value (i.e., societal worth) with the most efficient use of resources.

Breaking with the technocratic metaphor, Eisner (1997) describes research as publicly accessible transformations of consciousness. In his view, the task of preparing educational researchers is one of creating opportunities to engage in heightened states of awareness. Through deliberate, sequential activities that translate primary experience into communicable form, researchers can share their work with a wider constituency concerned with issues of learning. In this view, researchers are storytellers. We are metaphor makers. The value of our metaphors is in the degree they help us see the world in new and meaningful ways. Do these new metaphors help us integrate aspects of our lives that were previously minimized, denied, or left unseen? How do these new metaphors "make sense" of experience? Is the goal for a researcher's metaphors to transform consciousness feasible, or perhaps, egotistical?

Eisner shifts the metaphor for research from demonstrating cost-efficient practice to expanding a circle of communication. This metaphor allows us to value educational curricula that help students demonstrate processes through which they come to know—not merely demonstrate prowess of memorization—even if these practices are time-consuming and costly. The primary aim of research is not to produce knowledge with the least resources, but "to advance human understanding" (Eisner, 1997, p. 5).

However, metaphoric novelty in itself does not necessarily advance human understanding. Novelty may be aesthetically pleasing. It may even prompt lively conversation. However, conversation itself is not a measure of the aesthetic or practical worth of ABR. The conversation has to help us see more deeply. The conversation has to lead to better questions. A conversation that is an entertaining divertimento, which helps to pass the time, is not inquiry-driven.

Here we pause to consider the counter augment that Charles Garoian (Chapter 12) so forcefully raises by returning to the work of the artist Allan Kaprow and his performance-based visual art that he called Happenings. Many outside a small circle of cognoscenti were—and continue to be—derisive of Happenings as an art form. To them, it was—and still remains—the epitome of vacuous metaphoric novelty. However, as Garoian points out, Kaprow's work was not vapid escapism, it was a deliberate attempt to break preconceived structures of perception grounded in a close reading of the aesthetic philosophy of John Dewey. Through powerful, authentic experiences, built on relationships that had never before existed, Kaprow aspired to provoke new forms of thinking into emergence. How successful Kaprow was, and the legacy he left to the arts and ABR can be debated, but Kaprow was not pursuing novelty as an end in itself. Kaprow's purpose was deepening conversations.

Terry Jenoure (Chapter 20) also describes deepening conversations as an outcome in her encounter with South African youth. Her arts-based experience becomes authentically collaborative with her learning as much from the young men in her workshop as they from her. The research and work take on a shared responsibility. Omi Osun Joni L. Jones (Chapter 21) does not simply tell us what it means to be a female African American academic, but she brings us to a point where we can viscerally feel her struggle. She brings us to a point of collective scholarship. Kakali Bhattacharya (Chapter 4), Kuo Zhang (Chapter 38), and Stephanie Springgay (Chapter 34) also dare to address aspects of female identity that the academy suggests would be best unseen, or irrelevant to how we choose to pursue the advancement of understanding. These scholartists explore the boundaries of the restrictions imposed by a preemptive disembodied parsing of the definition of intelligence.

Hannah Arendt (1968) observed that aesthetics is a means of creating communities of caring by speaking to what is emotionally most dear to us. By confronting tensions in how we make meaning and synthesize the experiences of our lives in a visceral, embodied way, communication can lead to empathetic understanding that is the basis of community. This concern motivates the scholartistry of Dana Walrath (Chapter 36) as she seeks to communicate the complexity of caring for an aging parent suffering from dementia. What do education scholars learn from such stories? How do these stories build new communities for what is important to know and to be prepared to do? The communities that come out of circles of sharing are not rule-governed—where politically correct dictates control behavior—but are self-regulated through felt concern for others. Walrath's research demonstrates how ABR can contribute to building such communities.

We acknowledge that this view of aesthetics—as a philosophy of building deeply caring communities—is far from a conventional definition of a philosophy of beauty. Once again, we emphasize that, while art may pursue beauty as a goal, our interest in art is as a vehicle that propels research. If one is concerned about art for art's sake, reinterpreting a poem or painting in language that addresses praxis is not necessary for its appreciation. However, we argue that the poem, musical interlude, theatrical gesture, or visual representation of semiotic meaning or repetitive ritual may enable both researcher and reader to see into languages of theory and practice through what Donald Blumenfeld-Jones (Chapter 6) calls *wild imagination*.

Similarly, language also facilitates our understanding of qualitative relationships. In Chapter 7, John Borstel explicates how a language of critique allows the tacit dimensions of aesthetic performance to be revised, clarified, and made more resonant. The points of connection and communication swell. The promise of inquiry to affect change improves. Metaphors should generate new dimensions of understanding. They should augment—or trouble—our capacity for explanation.

## Assessing Validity

The five tensions inherent in ABR create criteria for judging its soundness and worth. From the tension of the imaginative vs. the referentially clear, we ask how effectively the work expands perception. Is the scholartist building a pre-symbolic, qualitative database from which to encode and inscribe meaning? Do these works of scholartistry exhibit qualitative reasoning? We can determine a work's value through close, critical examination. When we discuss the outcomes of our examinations, do our findings exhibit what Wittgenstein (1953/1973) called family resemblances—close similarities of interpretation that allow for comparative discussion? Does the work inspire dialogue? If our meanings are diffuse, scattered, and monologic, the claim of the artwork as a work of research is more problematic. Finally, do the conversations that emerge from arts-based educational study and analysis help us understand issues of teaching and learning in new ways? The hope is for the arts-based study in question to hold discussion open and resist closure.

The second tension is the particular vs. the general. Again, does the work help us to attend to qualities of a question or problem that heretofore might have gone unnoticed? How is the audience brought into this process of discovery? Does the audience become an active participant in the construction of meaning, or is the meaning imposed on the reader by the researcher? Does the experience of the particular bring the reader and the researcher together in a sense of shared conversation and responsibility?

The third tension is the aesthetics of beauty vs. verisimilitude of truth. Is beauty evoked to open or close a conversation? A successful work of ABR initiates, extends, and develops a conversation rather than a summative conclusion. As Immanuel Kant asked, does beauty help us to reconstruct reality—or does it only offer pabulum that lulls us into complacency?

The fourth tension is better questions vs. definitive answers. Lively and rich discussion is not an indicator of a successful work of arts-based inquiry. The discussion must be purposeful. It must be directed and lead to greater understanding. Not all discussion leads to positive growth. If a work of ABR generates misunderstanding, which closes discussion with audiences the work seeks to address, then there is a serious flaw. After reading a successful work of ABR, we should be able to frame better questions toward making our communities more caring, embracing, and inclusive. How has the inquiry advanced understanding?

The fifth tension is metaphoric novelty vs. literal utility. Do the metaphors employed in the work of scholartistry expand our understanding? Alternatively, are they simply novel, witty, or ingenious? Does the metaphor make felt qualitative meaning more accessible?

Together, these criteria can establish the validity of a work of ABR. These criteria also provide a basis for guiding the development and refinement of such a work. As Dewey (1934/1989) observed, criteria help the artist know what to do next. Criteria help the artist-researcher know how to make a work of scholartistry better.

## Arts-ased Research as a Hybrid Form

In this text, we have argued against art as a separate, isolated form of human experience that stands apart from how we understand and make sense of the world. We believe art to be a part of rationality. It has a role in structured inquiry. In this view, we are arguing for art for scholarship's sake as we discussed in this book's introduction (Chapter 1). We support the use of the term scholartistry (Neilsen, 1998) because it captures this integration of purpose.

We see the arts as woven into existing methods and methodologies for researching education. We seek to expand the palette of options available to researchers, not to restrict it.

Such an expansion raises questions regarding the training of educational researchers. There are a limited number of class hours in a program of study. What is the most effective use of those hours? What skills should we expect from those who wish to conduct ABR?

Most, but not all, of the scholartists represented in this text have had formal aesthetic training in their art form at either the undergraduate or the graduate level. From this background, they have purposively blended their training as artists and/or their engagement in the arts into their empiricism and theory building. They do this in an attempt to push the boundaries of what we can see within education. They manipulate perception in purposeful, hybrid ways that interweave the symbolic and non-symbolic in order to create personal meanings, interpretations, and hypotheses. In short, scholartists apply hybrid methods of research because of their own hybrid backgrounds and training in combining the arts and the social sciences. However, by demonstrating the structured intelligence in the hybrid methods of arts-based inquiry, scholartists not only broaden the field of research but also broaden our discussions of what needs to be considered in educational opportunities in K-12 schools, our pre-service teaching programs, and the graduate training of researchers. In this sense, the cognitive flexibility, adaptability, repurposing, and invention that characterize arts-based educational research (ABER) is a skill set that we may reasonably set as a goal for general education. Thus, the kind of hybrid training that up to now has been restricted to a relatively small number of arts-based educational researchers, might point the way for how the arts should be built into the curriculum at all levels of education. We believe, all researchers, regardless of prior artistic training, can develop artistic sensibilities in data analysis and draw on artistic craft to elicit data and share findings. Likewise, we believe all youth and adults should be encouraged to engage in the arts to the greatest extent possible regardless of whether or not they pursue years of specialized training to become "artists" in the traditionally elitist sense of the term. Contributors to this volume illuminate the varied ways the literary, visual, and performing arts engage collective dialogue and imagination. We hope selections from this volume inspire experienced artist-researchers and beginners alike.

## Expanding Understanding Through ABER

Perception is an unfolding of new insights, develop over time within an individual. Our sensory intake system is not digital; perception is not a faculty that operates in either on or off mode. Perception is not fixed. Two individuals standing side by side seldom have the same experience of perceiving an object. Perceptions are also influenced by where we were born in the world, the languages we learn to speak, the color of our skin, our gender, and many other qualities of human existence as discussed by so many of our international contributors including Hwang (Chapter 17), Woo (Chapter 37), and Zhang (Chapter 38) from Korea, Singapore, and China respectively. Dewey (1934/1989) claimed that developing faculties to discern nuance is a desired educational outcome. This is significant as perception improves with instruction. It takes training to see and hear delicacy of tone, to attend to subtlety in value, or recognize the qualities that contribute to a sense of intensity. Thus, one educational outcome of ABER is improving the objective, perceptual skills that produce qualitative reasoning.

Arts-based inquiry adds to the conversation regarding how researchers learn to perceive and report meaning. Yet as several contributors observe, tensions remain in opening our research to include the arts in methodology. As Madeleine Grumet (Chapter 14) observes, tensions remain in including the arts in education. Nevertheless, to continue to push at these tensions is timely work. Currently, throughout the entire educational system, facile definitions of intelligence drive our standardized tests. What is counted as intelligence is what our current paradigm of psychometrics can measure (Gardner, 1999). Even art curriculum and conceptions of learning in art can fall prey to simplification. It is all too easy to ignore deep structures of thinking (Stiggins et al., 2004).

An awareness of the structure of thinking requires knowing how we move between nonsymbolic realms of qualitative meaning to the inscription of symbolic meaning in a variety of forms of representation. These symbolic forms can be linguistic, numeric, visual, musical, and somatic. A demonstration of deep thinking is not a facile surface manipulation of symbols, but a demonstration of the process through which these symbols take significance.

Ultimately, ABER not only shifts the focus to how we inquire but also models a new vision of curriculum. ABR demonstrates strategies that might inform our thinking about how we allow students to exhibit their coming to know. These strategies encompass our sensory gathering systems and blend qualitative reasoning with semiotics. The qualities of mind that these scholartists explore lead to qualities of mind, and sensitivities to others, that we surely want instructors and students to demonstrate—beginning in early childhood instruction and through doctoral study. At any level, education should capture the fullness of experience.

ABER is capable of reflecting the resonance of lived experience by refocusing attention on the interplay between nonsymbolic and symbolic meaning to form understanding. We begin to create such understandings at birth. We do not outgrow qualitative thought with acquisition of language. The dialogue between non-symbolic and symbolic thinking continues throughout life. It is part of living. The precise perceptions of felt relationships and exquisite attention to nuance often define the highest levels of performance in many professions. Not the least of these is teaching: expert teachers know how to purposely navigate through felt reactions of students to foster learning. Thus, ABR holds the promise of improving our understandings of learning and how education in diverse communities occurs.

ABER is particularly well suited for understanding—and demystifying—the human relationships that enhance learning. Such research can provide evidence that helps us understand how excellent teaching engages students in the structures of deep learning. The outcome of such learning is personal agency: autonomous individuals who have the capacity to imaginatively shape their own lives by having the courage to write their own stories.

## Postscript

At the end of Chapter 10, Eisner states that his five tensions created by ABR stem from a conventional belief that education and research should be rooted in what is true and certain. The philosophy of what is true and certain is called epistemology. Since the first version of this chapter was published 2008, there has been a rising concern in both education and research with how we experience this world, and the meaningful truths we make from that experience. In philosophy, this is called ontology. In Chapter 29, Jerry Rosiek points out the major fissures that have risen in the wall that separates epistemology and ontology. Rosiek maintains we can draw from the discipline of physics and its new field of agential realism "that inquiry is, ultimately, an ontological and ethical enterprise as much, if not more than, an epistemic one" (Rosiek, Chapter 29). Physics tells us the world is not as true and certain as we might once have thought. In short, one cannot argue for purity of either side of the epistemology/ontology divide. Attempts to set artificial principles of scientific research in education (Shavelson & Towne, 2002) are as misbegotten a project as claims for an arts-for-arts-sake aesthetic justification guiding arts research. In this blended, interactive reality, scholartistry continues to deal with the enduring tensions that Eisner set forth in 2008.

The ontological turn in ABR research can be seen in the successful careers that scholartists have built over the past 20 years (Bickel et al., 2023). However, recently in the United States there has been a vituperative, anti-intellectual backlash against research in higher education, that suggests that leadership in the methodological future of ABR will come from outside of the United States either through continued strong national research leadership in countries like Canada, or through such relatively new organizations such as the European Network of Qualitative Inquiry (ENQI). These appear to be fruitful sites for intellectual engagement and the continuing evolution of scholartistry. ABR scholarship crosses geographic boundaries as much as it crosses ontological and epistemological boundaries. The contributors to this third edition are teaching and conducting work in the arts and social sciences around the globe. As editors, we have been welcomed ABR speakers in Canada, Europe, Latin America, the Middle East, and Asia. Our personal border crossing continues with Richard relocating from the United States to Switzerland and Melisa beginning to teach in a Munich study abroad program and move into collaborative literary translation of contemporary Chinese poet, Nianxi Chen (Cahnmann-Taylor & Zhang, 2023; 2024).

Looking back at those who have contributed to earlier editions of this compilation of ABR scholartists, we mourn some losses and celebrate many new beginnings. As editors, we are reminded of our own commitments to the empirical and aesthetic foundations of this work. The arts are grounded in direct experience of the tangible world and the intangible universe that envelops us. However, if education should be more than the feckless transfer of true and certain knowledge and instead embrace the experiential/ontological turn in education, this has profound implications for our conceptions of the arts themselves and how the arts should be taught alongside courses in research methods. If we seek to teach authentic inquiry in the practice of art, then a balanced approach between epistemology, ontology, and ethics is necessary. Embracing this balance (the synthesis of scholartistry), would alter art practice, conceptions of arts research, and criteria for judging finished artistic work (Bishop, 2012). In turn, this balance of epistemology, ontology, and ethics becomes pillars for the core criteria in ABR that leads us, as Maxine Greene might say, into a future that is—not yet.

## References


Arendt, H. (1968). *Between past and future: Eight exercises in political thought.* Viking Press.

Arnheim, R. (1969). *Visual thinking.* University of California Press.

Barone, T. (2001). *Aesthetics, politics, and educational inquiry.* Peter Lang.

Barone, T., & Eisner, E. W. (1997). Art-based educational research. In R. M. Jaeger (Ed.), *Complementary methods for research in education* (pp. 73–94). American Educational Research Association.

Bauman, Z. (1992). *Intimations of postmodernity.* Routledge.

Behar, R. (1996). *The vulnerable observer: Anthropology that breaks your heart.* Beacon Press.

Benjamin, W. (2003). The work of art in the age of its technological reproducibility. In H. Eiland & M. W. Jennings (Eds), *Walter Benjamin: Selected writings, volume 4, 1938–1940* (pp. 251–283). Harvard University Press (Original work published 1939).
Bickel, B., Irwin, R. L., & Siegesmund, R. (Eds.) (2023). *Arts-based educational research trajectories: Career reflections by authors of outstanding dissertations*. Springer Nature.
Bishop, C. (2012). *Artificial hells: Participatory art and the politics of spectatorship*. Verso Books.
Cahnmann-Taylor, M. & Zhang, Kuo (2023, Aug). "From Records of Explosion: Five Poems by Nianxi Chen." *Plume Magazine* (144). https://plumepoetry.com
Cahnmann-Taylor, M. & Zhang, Kuo (2024). "Three poems by Nianxi Chen: 'The Hibiscus is blooming', 'Village on the Xia River', and 'Slowing Rush Hour Down.'" *Terrain Magazine*. www.terrain.org
Damasio, A. R. (1999). *The feeling of what happens: Body and emotion in the making of consciousness*. Harcourt Brace.
Dewey, J. (1989). *Art as experience* (J. Boydston, Ed.). Southern Illinois University Press (Original work published 1934).
Eisner, E. W. (1991). *The enlightened eye: Qualitative inquiry and the enhancement of educational practice*. Macmillan.
Eisner, E. W. (1994). *Cognition and curriculum reconsidered* (2nd ed.). Teachers College Press.
Eisner, E. W. (1997). The promise and perils of alternative forms of data representation. *Educational Researcher*, *26*(6), 4–10. https://doi.org/10.3102/0013189X026006004
Eisner, E. W. (2002). *The arts and the creation of mind*. Yale University Press.
Gardner, H. (1999). *Intelligence reframed: Multiple intelligences for the 21st century*. Basic Books.
Holton, G. (1996). On the art of scientific imagination. *Daedalus*, *125*(2), 183–208. https://www.jstor.org/stable/20013446
Kant, I. (1987). *Critique of judgment* (W. Pluhar, Trans.). Hackett (Original work published 1790).
Kuhn, T. S. (1970). *The structure of scientific revolutions* (2nd ed.). University of Chicago Press.
Lakoff, G., & Johnson, M. (1980). *Metaphors we live by*. University of Chicago Press.
Neilsen, L. (1998). *Knowing her place: Research literacies and feminist occasions*. Caddo Gap Press.
Peshkin, A. (1988). In search of subjectivity – one's own. *Educational Researcher*, *17*(7), 17–21. https://doi.org/10.3102/0013189X017007017
Polanyi, M. (1967). *The tacit dimension*. Anchor Books.
Shavelson, R. J., & Towne, L. (Eds.). (2002). *Scientific research in education*. National Academy Press.
Shusterman, R. (1999). Somaesthetics: A disciplinary proposal. *Journal of Aesthetics & Art Criticism*, *57*(3), 299–314. https://doi.org/10.2307/432196
Stiggins, R., Arter, J., Chappuis, J., & Chappuis, S. (2004). *Classroom assessment for student learning: Doing it right – using it well*. Assessment Training Institute.
Suhor, C. (1984). Towards a semiotics-based curriculum. *Journal of Curriculum Studies*, *16*(3), 247–257. https://doi.org/10.1080/0022027840160304
Tyack, D. B., & Hansot, E. (1982). *Managers of virtue: Public school leadership in America, 1820–1980*. Basic Books.
Wittgenstein, L. (1973). *Philosophical investigations* (3rd ed., G. E.M. Anscombe, Trans.). Macmillan (Original work published 1953).

# Index

*Note*: Italic page numbers refer to figures.